KT-375-618

N 0097642 3

The Institute of British Geographers
Special Publications Series

25 Wetlands

EDITOR: Dr N. J. Thrift
University of Bristol

18 River Channels: Environment and Process
Edited by Keith Richards

19 Technical Change and Industrial Policy
Edited by Keith Chapman and Graham Humphrys

20 Sea-level Changes
Edited by Michael J. Tooley and Ian Shennan

21 The Changing Face of Cities: A Study of Development Cycles and Urban Form
J. W. R. Whitehand

22 Population and Disaster
Edited by John I. Clarke, Peter Curson, S. L. Kayasha and Prithvish Nag

23 Rural Change in Tropical Africa
David Siddle and Ken Swindell

25 Wetlands: A Threatened Landscape
Edited by Michael Williams

In preparation

Salt Marshes and Coastal Wetlands
Edited by D. R. Stoddart

Demographic Patterns in the Past
Edited by R. Smith

Teaching Geography in Higher Education (no. 24)
John R. Gold, Alan Jenkins, Roger Lee, Janice Monk, Judith Riley, Ifan Shephard and David Unwin

The Geography of the Retailing Industry
John A. Dawson and Leigh Sparks

The Making of the Urban Landscape
Jeremy Whitehand

The Impact of Sea-level Rise in Europe
Edited by M. J. Tooley and S. Gelgersma

Asian-Pacific Urbanization
Dean Forbes

For a complete list see p. 391

Wetlands

A Threatened Landscape

Edited by
Michael Williams

Basil Blackwell

First published 1990
First published in USA 1991

Basil Blackwell Ltd
108 Cowley Road, Oxford, OX4 1JF, UK

Basil Blackwell, Inc.
3 Cambridge Center
Cambridge, Massachusetts 02142, USA

British Library Cataloguing in Publication Data

A CIP catalogue record for this book is available from the British Library.

Library of Congress Cataloging in Publication Data

Wetlands: a threatened landscape/edited by Michael Williams.
p. cm. — (Special publications series/Institute of British Geographers; 25)
Includes bibliographical references.
ISBN 0-631-16614-9
1. Wetlands. 2. Wetland ecology. 3. Wetlands—Economic aspects. 4. Wetland conservation. I. Williams, Michael, 1935–
II. Series: Special publications series (Institute of British Geographers); 25.
QH87.3.W47 1990
333.91′8–dc20 90-30985

Typeset in 10½ on 12pt Plantin
by Hope Services (Abingdon) Ltd.
Printed in Great Britain by The Alden Press Ltd., Osney Mead, Oxford

Contents

Preface

Wetlands comprise about 6 per cent of the world's surface. In the past wetlands were considered to be wasteland and worthless, and change and transformation have been the predominant themes when considering them. In recent decades, however, wetlands have assumed a new attraction and value. On the one hand, they are still being reduced in size as modern draining techniques make them even more attractive as potential agricultural land, and their flatness, coastal location and perceived worthlessness make them obvious locations for large plants, harbours and waste disposal. Wetlands are truly 'a threatened landscape'. On the other hand, they have become more valued as their hydrological-physical, chemical, biological and socio-economic benefits are acknowledged. In addition, wetlands are increasingly perceived as an environment where air, water and land, and their fauna and flora, meet in an attractive and delicate way, and this has caught the scientific and popular imagination. Demands for their conservation and non-use are now widespread.

These shifts in the perception of wetland use and value are recent. In the late 1950s when I became fascinated by the story of the Somerset Levels, a floodable wetland of area some 650 km^2 in the southwest of England, the emphasis was wholly on the achievement of their transformation from swamp and bog to one of the most productive pastoral farming areas in the country over a span of nearly seven centuries. The focus of attention was on understanding the hydrological-physical basis of the flood problem, and the social, economic and technical processes which led to a change in the visual landscape and the geography of the region. None of the modern concerns were articulated overtly – except perhaps over-draining – although with hindsight one realizes that they were present. For example, the nineteenth-century pioneering archaeological work of Arthur Bulleid and H. St. George Grey on the Glastonbury and Meare Lake villages was a portent of the rich vein of wetlands archaeological research that was to come (chapter 5), as were Godwin's palaeobotanical studies on the raised bogs of Shapwick Heath during the 1940s. The enormous eel and fish catches during medieval times, and the value placed by the commoners during the seventeenth and eighteenth centuries on access to the fish, fowl and peat turfs which were threatened by draining schemes, were indications of the abundant biological yield of the wetland. The constant debates in engineering proposals over the containment and exclusion of flood waters versus periodic controlled flooding were forerunners of the arguments on flood hazard perception.

It was not until the early 1970s that the argument for the preservation of the peat moors as a unique biological assemblage and archaeological site gathered momentum; it was even suggested that there be purposeful re-flooding in order to preserve them. If *The Draining of the Somerset Levels* were to be written today it would include another chapter on wetland values and their conservation, and parts of the existing evidence would be interpreted differently.

In this book an attempt is made to bring the two views of wetlands together, so that what can be termed pride in achievement and concern at loss can be viewed side by side. To do this, in the first chapter a framework is set out in which the rise of knowledge about wetlands is traced, the definition of what wetlands are is considered, and their extent and location are outlined. The positive functions and benefits that have led to the shift in wetland perception are then discussed. Many of these themes are picked up in the succeeding chapters.

Successive chapters on the hydrodynamics, morphology, sedimentation, soils and ecology of wetlands provide a thorough foundation for an understanding of their dynamics and properties. These are followed by a fascinating glimpse of the cultural value of wetlands as a repository for archaeological artefacts. There then follow four chapters on impacts that have resulted in wetland losses – agriculture, industry, urbanization and recreation – which lead on to the penultimate chapter in which wetland gains and losses are assessed. In the final chapter measures taken in a number of localities to protect wetlands are surveyed, and some of the ideas expressed throughout the book on values, processes and impacts, are gathered together in a retrospective survey.

Throughout, the perspectives are global, the concepts generic and the viewpoints varied, coming as they do from many disciplines. The case studies and examples are drawn from throughout the world, and a distinctive feature is the emphasis on tropical as well as temperate wetlands. It is hoped, therefore, that this treatment of wetlands is different from anything attempted before, with an emphasis on commonalities rather than exceptions, on past as well as present and broad synthesis rather than detailed study. No attempt is made to be definitive: not all areas of the world or all themes are covered, but hopefully those who wish to pursue more detailed wetland studies can use these chapters to find their way into the extensive literature.

I wish to thank the Publications and Special Publications Committees of the Institute of British Geographers for their encouragement to embark on this volume, and for the willingness with which my fellow authors contributed to it. Angela Newman, Gillian Hardman and Brian Urbaszewski drew the maps for chapters 1, 3, 6, 7 and 11, and Alexandra Mendel assisted with the compilation of the bibliography and in many other ways. An invitation from Professor Michael Conzen to spend some time at the Department of Geography at Chicago University provided many incidental facilities and a congenial atmosphere in which to think, write, and complete the editing of this work, for which I am grateful.

Michael Williams,
Oriel College, Oxford

Acknowledgements

We are grateful for permission to reproduce the following figures:

Figures 1.2 and 1.3: Elsevier Science Publishers, Physical Sciences & Engineering Division; figure 2.10: Professor Gerald Friedman; figure 4.1: Harcourt, Brace and Jovanovich; figure 4.2: Elsevier Science Publishers, Physical Sciences and Engineering Division; figure 4.5: Kluwer Academic Publishers; figure 10.2: Springer-Verlag; figure 10.6: American Association for Advancement of Science, © 1975.

1

Understanding Wetlands

Michael Williams

1.0 INTRODUCTION

There are a number of distinctive major landscapes in the world that have caught the attention of many disciplines as being a focus for their studies. Arid lands, mountain lands, tundra lands, polar lands, Mediterranean lands, mid-latitude grasslands, tropical rainforests and savannas, for example, have all at some time been considered by botanists, biologists, ecologists, soil scientists, historians, archaeologists, geographers, economists and land managers, to name but a few, from their varying points of view. Wetlands are another such major landscape, but it is only since the late 1960s that they have engaged the attention of a range of scholars in an effort to understand their variety and complexity, yet essential unity.

The relative recency of this interest has much to do with the character of the wetlands themselves, and with the way that they have been perceived in the past. Although wetlands occupy about 6 per cent of the earth's surface, unlike other landscapes of comparable size they are not climatically based or induced and therefore do not occupy large contiguous stretches of land. Giving them their simplest definition, wetlands are lands with soils that are periodically flooded. Therefore they are ubiquitous and found in nearly every climatic zone from the tundra mires of the poles to the tropical mangroves of the equator, and in every continent except Antarctica. Plates 1.1 and 1.2 illustrate the extremes of variation in one continent – Australia.

With very few exceptions, such as the Everglades of Florida or the Fens of eastern England (with original areas of about 10 000 and 4000 km^2 respectively) they rarely cover large areas. More often than not they are found in scattered locations, and are intermittent and local in their occurrence. Consequently, the growth of knowledge about wetlands, which has revolved around the problem of defining, classifying and understanding their various

Plate 1.1 Wetland extremes. Alpine wetlands: Spencer Creek, Mount Guthrie, Tasmania (Courtesy D. Mercer)

Plate 1.2 Wetland extremes. Tropical wetland in the vast and largely unexplored mangroves of the lower Normanby River, far north peninsula of Queensland. (Courtesy D. Mercer)

functions, characteristics and values, has been delayed until research workers began to see the commonalities which bound them together.

In addition to the real problem of coming to grips with wetlands as a physical entity there has been the problem of their perception. Hitherto, wetlands have been considered wastelands and therefore worthless. Their transformation through draining, dredging and infilling seemed a fitting fate for them. In recent decades, however, wetlands have assumed a new attraction and value for a great variety of reasons, not least of which is the fact that they are being eliminated at an alarming rate and are rapidly assuming the status of an endangered species. At the same time there is a growing appreciation of their natural functions, and the values that humans attach to them. They are one of the most fruitful areas of archaeological research, and they are the ideal setting in which to study the interactions between physical processes and human actions that encapsulate and exemplify many of the themes of man's impact on his environment. Also, the new-found beneficial functions of wetlands seem in danger of being lost with draining and infilling.

2.0 KNOWLEDGE OF WETLANDS

2.1 *Attitudes to wetlands*

There has been an explosive growth of knowledge about and a radical change of attitude to wetlands during the last few decades. Before the early 1960s wetlands were largely neglected and unappreciated, and were probably the most poorly understood of landscapes and ecosystems, being neither sound land nor good water. In Europe, academic research on and knowledge about them broadly revolved around three foci of interest. First and earliest were botanists who explored the processes of bog and mire formation (Moore and Bellamy 1973, Gore 1983a, b, Moore 1984), and geomorphologists, hydrologists, and sedimentologists who looked at the dynamics of coastal marsh formation particularly since Late Quaternary times (Steers 1964, 1973). Both had a long history of serious scientific research since the mid-nineteenth century (chapter 2). A second, and later, focus of research which grew out of the previous work was the palaeobotanical analysis of peat bog structures, with its associated implications for understanding past climatic regimes and sea-level changes. the advent of related vegetation change, ^{14}C dating and palynology was crucial to this endeavour which was closely associated, in Britain at least, with the work of Godwin (Godwin 1956, 1981). A third focus of research had its origin in seventeenth-century antiquarian interests (Dugdale 1662), but came to serious academic fruition in more recent decades with the work of historians (Smith 1943, Thirsk 1953, Hallam 1965), and more particularly of historical geographers (Darby 1940a, b, 1983, Sheppard 1958, Lambert et al. 1960, Williams 1970). These workers were concerned with unravelling the long-drawn-out process of human adaptation and change to a hazardous environment, and the consequent modification and evolution of the cultural landscape.

In the United States, all the aforesaid foci of interest existed. Detailed botanical studies of individual wetlands were numerous (e.g. Chapman (1938, 1940) and Teal (1962) on coastal wetlands, and Transeau (1903) and Dachnowski-Stokes (1935) on inland wetlands), and some cultural geographers were interested in the evolution of wetland landscapes (e.g. Meyer 1935, Hewes 1951, Hewes and Frandson 1952, Kaatz 1955). However, in addition there were two distinctive strands of interest and support in wetland awareness in the United States that did not exist to the same degree elsewhere.

First, there was the rapid adoption after about 1950 of integrated ecological studies by workers like J. M. Teal, L. R. Pomeroy, and Eugene and H. T. Odum that simulated intellectual curiosity about wetlands. In addition, the setting up of research centres devoted to the study of wetlands (e.g. the Center for Wetland Resources at the State University of Louisiana, Baton Rouge, the Center for Wetlands at Florida University, and the Sapelo Island Marine Institute in Georgia (Mitsch and Gosselink 1986, p. 12) gave an added focus to enquiry.

Second, there was the active and practical interest in wetlands stimulated by the recreational, hunting and wildlife enthusiasts. Their interest in the wild and the primitive, perhaps best expressed as a concern or love of 'nature' and 'wilderness', was part of a deeply-held ethos that was, and still is, central to much of American history and culture (Nash 1973, Fritzell 1979). It had active support from the Fish and Wildlife Service (FWS) of the Department of the Interior (DOI) which, under the Migratory Birds Hunting and Conservation Act of 1934, had the right to sell 'duck stamps' which have to be purchased by all wildfowl hunters. Since 1934 over $250 million has been raised, and bulk of the funds has been used to purchase 970 000 ha of waterfowl habitats, most of which are wetland (Office of Technology Assessment (OTA) 1984, pp. 72–3). In addition the private duck hunting lobby Ducks Unlimited (600 000 members) has actively promoted its aims through fund-raising ($400 million since 1937), and has purchased, created or manages over 100 000 ha of wetlands and carried out a sustained campaign of lobbying and advertising (Hoffman 1988). The Audubon Society and the Nature Conservancy Council have also had a widespread and effective impact on public opinion.

During the immediate post-war period, the FWS – the guardian of the duck-breeding grounds – became concerned about the impact of continuing wetland losses on fish and wildlife populations. The loss was approaching 121 000 ha/yr (Shaw and Fredine 1956). This report was one of many strands that fed the increasing awareness of the general public and Federal agencies to environmental issues during the early 1960s and which gave wetland preservation a popular basis of support. The general public became aware of wetland losses by dredge and fill operations in estuarine and coastal locations, and, in addition, their newly discovered positive functions for flood protection and water quality maintenance were also stressed. By 1972, many coastal states had enacted legislation to protect their shores (chapter 11).

In England and Wales events did not proceed in the same way. There was no wildlife/wilderness lobby comparable with that of the United States, although the activities of the Royal Society for the Protection of Birds (RSPB), the Nature Conservancy Council (NCC) and the privately initiated venture of the Wildfowl and Wetlands Trust, founded by the late Sir Peter Scott at Slimbridge on the Severn Estuary, kept alive the idea of preserving breeding grounds, particularly for migratory birds. However, such concerns were peripheral to the aim of maximizing food production. The spectre of low agricultural production since the 1930s, food shortages and the need for greater self-sufficiency during the Second World War and the immediate post-war period put the emphasis on agricultural expansion and intensification. Government support came under the Land Drainage Acts of 1930 and 1976 which organized catchment boards to oversee drainage activity. Liberal grants were made available by the government to these boards and to individuals to drain and upgrade wetland. So overwhelming was this emphasis that it was not until the 1970s that the first murmurs were heard about the deleterious effects of land draining on wildlife and flora (Lucas and Walters 1971, Hill 1976). A very similar ethos and sequence of events prevailed in much of the rest of Europe, even more beset with problems of post-war reconstruction (chapter 11). The Common Agricultural Policy (CAP) of the European Economic Community (EEC) has encouraged even greater wetland conversion during recent years.

During the 1970s, events gathered momentum in the United States. The recognition of the importance of wetlands for water quality control and a growing appreciation of their recreational and aesthetic qualities led to the Federal government's taking a greater responsibility for their preservation.

Through Section 404 of the Federal Water Pollution Control Act (FWPCA) of 1972 (later amended and strengthened as the Clean Water Act of 1977) new standards were established for dredge and fill activities, and the objective and purpose of the activities of the powerful Corps of Engineers was redefined. The Corps is the major contractor of Federal programmes in waterways involved in 'interstate commerce' and has vast resources and expertise in reclamation works, river diversions and dam-building. From this time on permits were needed for dredge and fill operations, with permission to be given only after an examination of a project by, amongst others, the FWS and the Environmental Protection Agency (EPA), although most agricultural and silvacultural activities are excepted. Water quality concerns and the realization that wetlands had been lost at the rate of 121 000 ha/yr for the last two decades brought matters to a head. In 1977 President Carter issued Executive Orders 11988 and 11990 – Flood Plain Management and Wetland Protection – which made wetlands protection a matter of national policy. The Corps of Engineers now had to reinterpret its activities and responded to the wetland considerations contained in Section 404 of the 1972 Act (chapter 11). Thus the legal and administrative framework for protection was gradually put into place; it now remained to define what a wetland was.

2.2 *Wetland literature*

This account of the late onset of administrative interest in wetlands is paralleled in the scientific and academic literature. Two recent authoritative and wide-ranging works on wetlands have been analysed for their citation count. The 986 pages of *Ecology and Management of Wetlands* (Hook et al. 1988) and the 680 pages of *Wetland Functions and Values: The State of our Understanding* (Greeson et al. 1979) offer an interesting and informative insight into wetlands research. First is the explosive growth in research as evidenced by the citations. Of the approximately 2051 citations in Hook et al., almost 48 per cent are from the 1980s, 37 per cent from the1970s (the major shift coming after 1975), 8 per cent from the 1960s and 5 per cent from before 1960. In Greeson, published ten years earlier, the concentration in the 1970s was more striking: over 84 per cent of the citations were published during that decade, 14 per cent during the 1960s and a mere 2 per cent before 1960. There are, of course, other possible reasons for this distribution, but whatever they are the net result is an impressive concentration of work in the last few decades that coincides with the new legislative and administrative concerns. From a state of relative ignorance about wetlands before 1960 we have moved into an era characterized by a vast expansion of knowledge and a thriving 'wetlands industry', often located in specialized wetland research centres.

Since 1977 there have been at least a score of major publications on wetlands, only one, that of the International Institute of Land Reclamation (1983), dealing with the older concerns of reclamation, all the others being concerned with wetland functions and/or dealing with wetland management (table 1.1).

The emphasis of much of this recent work is on the commonalities of

Table 1.1 Major symposia, conferences and books on wetlands, 1977–1988

1977	Chapman, *Wet Coastal Ecosystems* (428 pp.)
1978	Good et al., *Freshwater Wetlands: Ecological Processes and Management Potential* (378 pp.)
1978	Kusler and Montanari, *Proceedings, National Wetlands Protection Symposium* (255 pp.)
1979	Greeson et al., *Wetland Functions and Values: The State of our Understanding* (674 pp.)
1979	Johnson and McCormick, *Strategies for the Protection and Management of Flood-plain Wetlands and other Riparian Ecosystems* (410 pp.)
1981	Clark and Benforado, *Wetlands of Bottomland Hardwood Forests* (401 pp.)
1982	Zinn and Copeland, *Wetland Management* (149 pp.)
1982	Gopal et al., *Wetlands – Ecology and Management* (514 pp.)
1983	Gore, *Mires: Swamp, Bog, Fen and Moor: General Studies* (440 pp.) and *Regional Studies* (479 pp.)
1983	Patten et al., *Ecosystem Dynamics in Freshwater Wetlands* (340 pp.)
1983	International Institute for Land Reclamation and Improvement, *International Symposium: Polders of the World* (730, 443, 730 pp.)
1983	Wapora Inc., *The Effects of Wastewater Treatment Facilities on the Wetlands of the Midwest* (342 pp.)
1983	US Environmental Protection Agency, *Freshwater Wetlands for Wastewater Management. Environmental Impact Statement* (380 pp.)
1984	Ong Jin-Eong and Gong Wooi-Khoon, *Productivity of the Mangrove Systems: Management Implications* (190 pp.)
1984	OTA, *Wetlands: Their Use and Regulation* (208 pp.)
1984	Teas, *Physiology and Management of Mangroves* (106 pp.)
1986	Mitsch and Gosselink, *Wetlands* (485 pp.)
1988	Zelazny and Feierabend, *Increasing Our Wetland Resources* (370 pp.)
1988	Hook et al., *The Ecology and Management of Wetlands* (1090 pp.)

wetlands, while earlier studies were concerned with unique entities, with processes rather than with empirical description and, above all, with cross-disciplinary links so that, for example, ecologists were examining the relationship between plant distributions and hydrology (chapter 2). In some ways, it could be argued that the specialization has gone too far and that in the detail of the minutiae of research the larger picture and the synthesis have been lost, as has the world picture because so much of the work is focused on the United States. These are some deficiencies which it is hoped to rectify in this book.

3.0 DEFINITION

The term 'wetlands' is a relatively new one to describe the landscape that many people knew before under different names. Because wetlands occur in many different climatic zones, in many different locations and have many different soil and sediment characteristics, they have become an integral part of the landscape since earliest times, and sometimes of the economy as well. Consequently they have been given various names which add considerably to our confusion. In England, for example, wetlands have been large enough to acquire regional names, such as the Fens of eastern England, the Broads of Norfolk, the Carrs of Humberside, the Levels of Somerset and the Mosses of Lancashire. However, these names say little about their composition or origin: the Somerset Levels and Fens consist of organic peat soils, marine clays and river alluviums, Romney Marsh is almost entirely composed of marine sands and shingle, and the Carrs are composed of peat. Further confusion arises with the use of yet other names, such as mires, bogs, sloughs, swamps and marshes. For example, in Somerset the individual low-lying peat and alluvial levels are called 'moors', a term common in the Netherlands and Germany for high peat lands.

Waksman (1942) has found 90 English terms to describe peat lands, peats and peat-like qualities, and undoubtedly the list has grown since then. In the United States, few terms occur uniformly throughout the country in either scientific or vernacular usage. Unlike Europe, little distinction is made between peat and non-peaty wetlands, perhaps because peatlands comprise a smaller proportion of wetlands in the 48 lower states. The term 'marsh' is generally reserved for wetland dominated by graminoids, grasses or herbs, and 'swamp' for wetland dominated by woody plants, as in the cypress swamps and river bottom hardwood swamps of the South. 'Bog' is used to denote ombrogenous mires, but the distinctions between all these three are not always clear. Fen is rarely used, but there are some distinctive additional terms, such as wet meadow, wet prairie, glade and pothole in the northern Plains, and pocosin in the Carolinas (Gore 1983a, pp. 26–8; Hofstetter 1983, pp. 201–2). A thorough discussion of terminology is given in chapter 2.

Whatever the name given to them (and Gore (1983a) has suggested the term mire to cover all types), the distinguishing feature about all these types of wetland is the interplay between the land and the water, and consequently they partake of the characteristics of both (OTA 1984, pp. 28–32). The invasion of water can be caused by a variety of factors such as the periodic overflowing of rivers in valley bottoms or flood plains, the rise and fall of tides along the coast, impeded surface flow due to tilting, uplift or landslip, occasional tidal inundation caused by land subsidence or by unusual climatic events, deposition of sediments in estuaries or deltas, the impediment of subsoil draining by impervious lower strata or horizons, and particularly by permafrost, or the rising of the water-table above the surface level. All these contribute to standing water, or to saturated or waterlogged soils. The causes are infinite and often work in combination; for example, storm surges can block river outfalls at high tide causing the overflow of already bank-full river discharges many kilometres inland.

If hydrology is the key to the formation of wetlands it is not necessarily the total explanation of their distinctiveness. We all know wetlands when we see them, with their characteristic vegetation of, for example, swamp grasses, sedge or cypress trees and intermittent patches of water, but it is difficult to describe the common features of that vegetation which makes the wetlands stand apart from other landscapes. Part of that distinctiveness lies in their ecological composition and character which arises from the fact that they are situated at the junction between dry-land terrestrial ecosystems and permanently wet aquatic ecosystems. They differ from both, but at the same time partake of the characteristics of either. This is one of the reasons why wetlands have been so neglected and their distinctive features and commonalities have not been appreciated until recently.

At the simplest level we can say that their soils are formed and conditioned by standing water or waterlogging and are adapted to anoxic biochemical processes. Their vegetation is adapted to wet conditions (hydrophytes) because it is water-covered for at least a part of the growing season and is thus deficient in oxygen. It also decomposes slowly and contributes to the process of wetland formation by either trapping silt or forming, in time, actual soil (peat). Much of the fauna is adapted to dwelling in either deep water (fish and shellfish) or dry land (waterfowl) but moves seasonally into the wetland. To these three obvious and crude distinguishing ecological features of soils, vegetation and fauna (but note some qualifications about these in desert interior wetlands (chapter 2), we must add a number of other ecological functions that are less obvious and more subtle. Wetland soils are physically volatile and are in constant flux with the decomposition and erosion of sediments with river flow, flood and tidal shift. Additionally, different vegetation flourishes or dies with changes in predominant water sources, e.g. rushes die if water becomes too rich in nutrients. The interaction between water level, sedimentation and decomposition is finely balanaced, and within the soil there are biochemical processes at work as energy flows through the ecosystem leading to the transformation and trapping of nutrients. All these factors lead to the creation of a highly diverse ecosystem, partaking of aquatic and terrestrial sources, which means that wetland ecosystems are amongst the most productive in the world so that they and their products have been a constant lure to humankind (Shaw and Fredine 1956; OTA 1984, pp. 21–30; Tiner 1984, pp. 2–3; Mitsch and Gosselink 1986, pp. 10–14).

Some of these characteristics and relationships are developed more fully in section 6.0 of this chapter and in chapters 2, 3 and 4 which deal with the hydrodynamics, sedimentation and erosion of wetlands, and with the ecological relationships in the wetlands in both the temperate and tropical regions. Suffice it to say, the physiological and behavioural similarity of plants and animals and the physical conditions found in the wetlands of the world have much in common, although they vary enormously in detail.

4.0 CLASSIFICATION

The definition and classification of wetlands has gone through many stages (Mitsch and Gosselink 1986, pp. 450–69). The most elaborate categorization is that formulated by the FWS of the United States in 1979 as a response to the new protective legislation of two years before, and to facilitate the making of an inventory of the natural wetlands in the country. Cowardin and his associates acknowledged the difficulty, if not outright impossibility, of arriving at a 'single, correct, indisputable, ecologically sound definition' because of the diversity of wetland types and because of 'the demarcation between wetland and dry land lay along a continuum' (Cowardin et al. 1979, p. 4). Therefore they incorporated the three criteria of hydrographic vegetation, hydric soils, and the degree and frequency of flooding and/or soil saturation into their classification.

Five major divisions or systems, each of which share similar locational-geomorphological, hydrological and biological characteristics, were recognized. There are the coastal wetlands which include (a) marine and (b) estuarine wetlands, and the interior wetlands which include (c) riverine, (d) lacustrine and (e) palustrine wetlands. In this classification the first four systems include wetland and deep-water habitats, but the palustrine includes only wetland habitats. The presence or absence of organic soils does not play a significant role in the classification and is only one of many additional 'modifiers' to all systems and their classes. Figure 1.1. shows the distribution of the five systems diagrammatically. The classification is set out with its diagnostic characteristics in chapter 2, table 2.1, although slightly modified from the original with its North American bias so as to be applicable to wetlands throughout the world.

Undoubtedly, it is the estuarine and palustrine systems that account for the bulk of the world's wetlands, and these two give the most familiar and popularly known types of marshes and fens/bogs/swamps.

5.0 EXTENT AND LOCATION

Without a commonly accepted and agreed terminology and definition there cannot be accurate mapping of wetlands nor can their area be calculated. Therefore the determination of definition, location and extent are interrelated problems. Wetlands have probably been more surveyed and assessed in the United States than in any other part of the world, but 14 estimates between 1907 and 1987 have produced little agreement. All that can be said is that, while estimates of the 'original' wetland hover around 50×10^6 km^2, 12 estimates of current wetland vary between 21×10^6 and 37×10^6 km^2, and average out at 28.35×10^6 km^2 (Hofstetter 1983). If there is this uncertainty in the minutely and thoroughly surveyed territory of the United States with its topographical, soil and geological agencies, now much more uncertain will it be in the relatively unsurveyed portions of the less developed world?

Of course, the problem lies in the scattered nature of wetlands, the definition of what depth of organic soil constitutes wetland and the sheer lack of exploration and survey. For our purposes perhaps the best we can do is to obtain a generalized view of wetland distribution. Figures 1.2 and 1.3 are taken from the most authoritative works on organic wetlands (mires) (Gore 1983a, b) and coastal wetlands (salt marshes and mangal) (Chapman 1977), and they are perhaps as far as we can go without engaging in detailed and minute study of

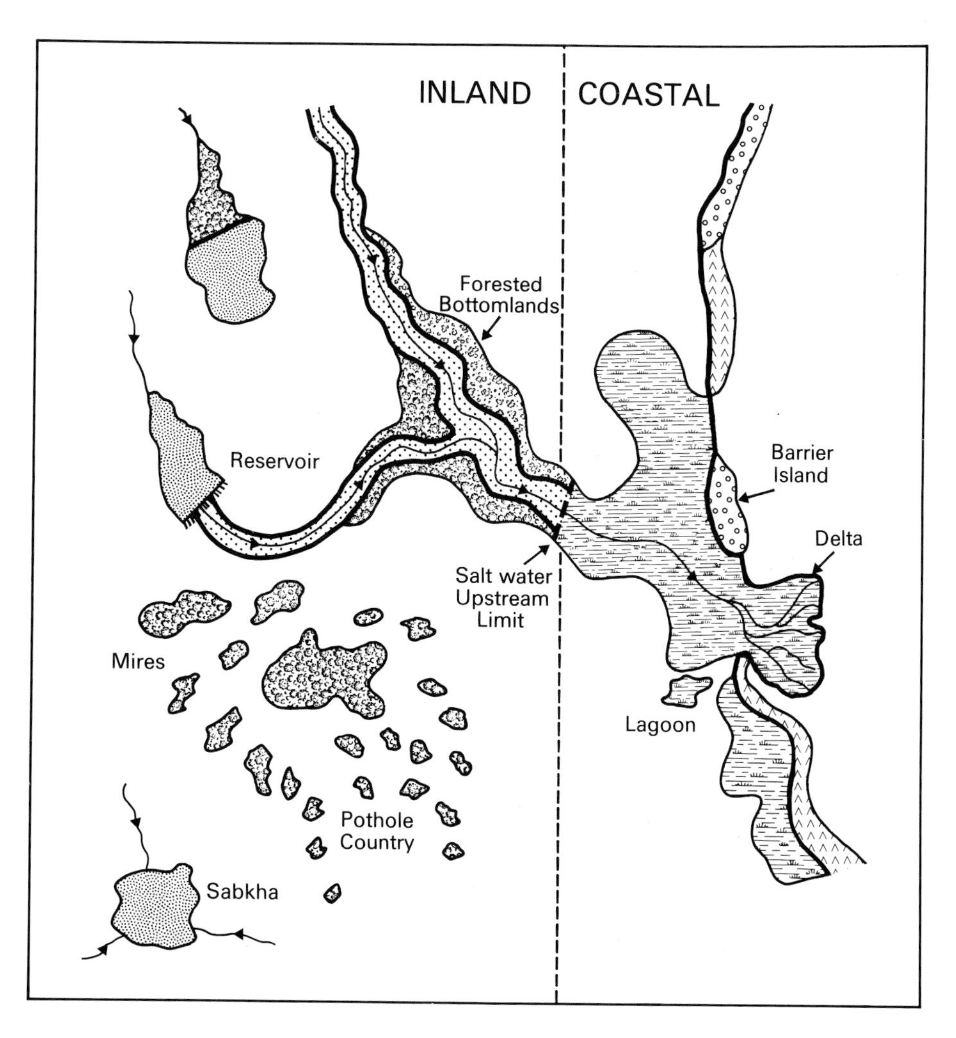

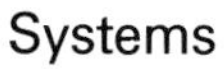

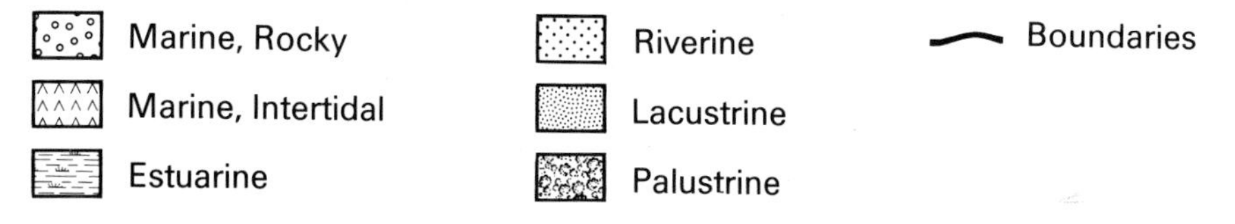

Figure 1.1 Diagrammatic sketch of wetland types
(after Tiner 1984, p. 5)

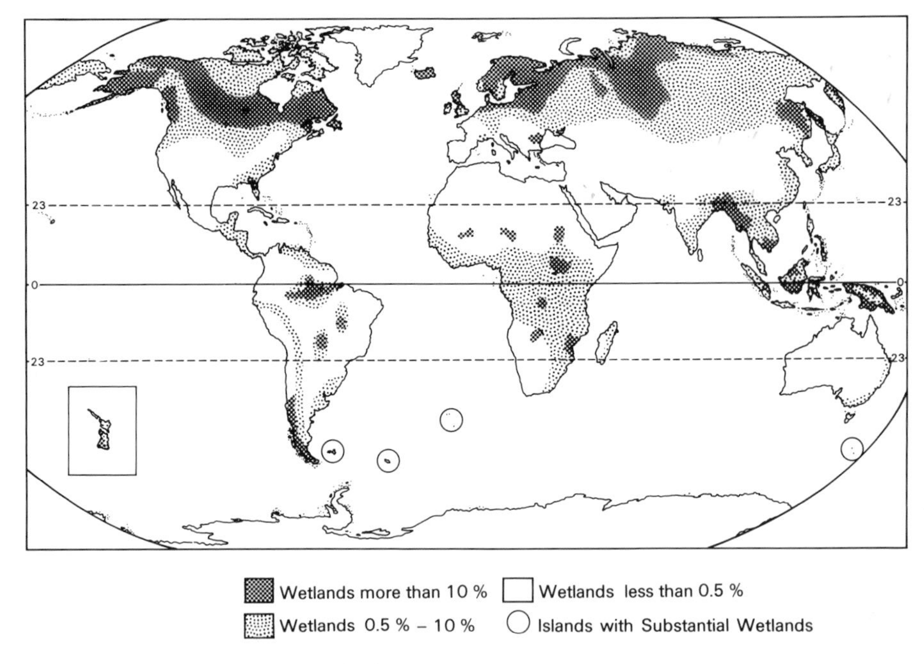

Figure 1.2 Global distribution of mires
(after Gore 1983a, end-covers)

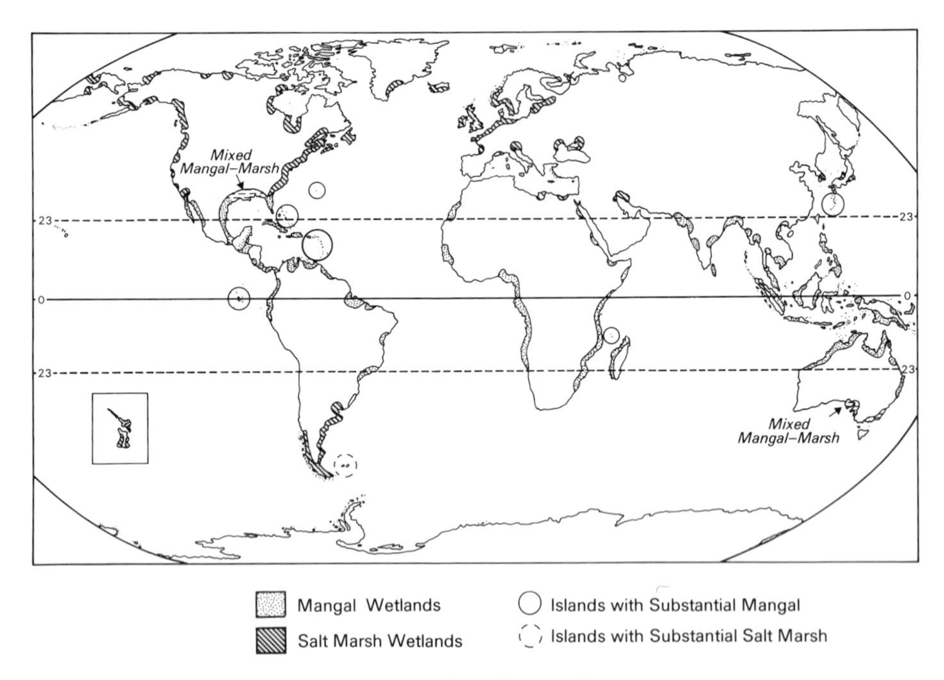

Figure 1.3 Global distribution of salt marsh and mangal
(after Chapman 1977, end-covers)

Table 1.2 Estimated area of wetlands and their primary production by climatic zone

		Area		*Production*		
Zone	*Climate*	*(km² × 10³)*	*(% total of zone)*	*(t/ha)*	*(× 10⁶t)*	*(% total for zone)*
Polar	Humid-semi-humid	200	2.5	4	43	3.2
Boreal	Humid-semi-humid	2558	11.0	13.5	1086	7.2
Sub-	Humid	539	7.3	37	278	3.0
borial	Semi-arid	342	4.2	19	382	5.7
	Arid	136	1.9	13	177	8.9
Sub-	Humid	1077	17.2	192	6502	40.8
tropical	Semi-arid	629	7.6	40	2511	21.9
	Arid	439	4.5	90	3951	55.3
Tropical	Humid	2317	8.7	255	24273	31.4
	Semi-arid	221	1.4	60	1326	5.9
	Arid	100	0.8	40	400	15.2
World total		8558	6.4	–	40929	24.0

Figures have been rounded off.
Source: Rodin et al. 1975, Mitsch and Gosselink 1986, p. 4.

each country or region. The figure of 8558 × 10^6 km² (table 1.2) is probably the most exact possible for their extent, with about a quarter of the total being coastal wetlands and the remainder being inland wetlands (see also chapter 2).

6.0 FUNCTIONS, VALUES AND BENEFITS

The recent rise in awareness of the importance of wetlands has much to do with an enhanced appreciation of their many positive, ecological and environmental *functions* and the *values* that society puts on those functions. Needless to say, it is difficult to say where a function becomes a value and there is much imprecision about these terms; however, an attempt will be made here to distinguish between the two, and the word *benefit* will be used where we cannot clearly separate a function from a value.

There are many ways of categorizing these functions and values. Tiner (1984) gives three categories: fish and wildlife 'values', environmental quality 'values' and socio-economic 'values'. The OTA report (OTA 1984) gives two categories: intrinsic 'values' and ecological services and resource 'values'. The possibilities of combining these values and functions under different heads is endless.

Here, four broad categories of functions are employed, i.e. physical/hydrological, chemical, biological and socio-economic, as these best fit the basic processes at work in wetland environments and are also more directly applicable to the chapters in this book. Of course, none of these categories is exclusive and each can have a profound effect on the other. For example, chemical pollution will affect biological processes and thus wildlife habitats.

Secondly, no one benefit is exclusive to any one category, so that flood control, for example, could be thought of as a hydrological benefit (a natural function) as well as a socio-economic benefit (have a value).

In a review of over 400 publications on wetland benefits, Sather and Smith (1984) concluded that shoreline protection, water quality, primary production, nutrient utilization, bird habitats and consumptive uses were well authenticated, but that other benefits, particularly the non-consumptive (aesthetic) benefits, were not (table 1.3). However we know that it is largely the non-quantifiable and non-authenticated benefits that are increasingly the driving force behind the rising awareness of wetland consciousness in the western developed world. The developing world, however, can rarely afford the luxury of these non-financial benefits in the face of constant pressure to increase food production, although paradoxically it is the increased pace and volume of the investigations on wetland functions that is showing that sometimes greater financial rewards result in developing countries and in distressed regions of

Table 1.3 Wetland functions: authentication in the literature

Function	*Authentication*			*Assessment methods*	*Total studies examined*
	Good	*Fairly good*	*Poor*		
Hydrology					
Flood control	–	6	–		
Ground-water recharge/discharge	–	1	4	11	33
Shoreline anchorage and dissipation of erosive forces	4	1	2		
Water quality					
Waste water treatment	6	–	–		
Toxic substances	6	–	–	10	37
Nutrients	2	–	–		
Food-chain support/cycling					
Primary production	8	1	–		
Decomposition	–	–	–	5	139
Nutrient export	–	3	4		
Nutrient utilization	6	2	–		
Habitat					
Invertebrates	–	–	5		
Fisheries	–	9	–		
Mammals	–	7	–	16	130
Non-game birds	8	1	1		
Game birds	3	–	–		
Socio-economic					
Consumptive use value	9	3	–		
Non-consumptive use value	–	–	8	14	63
					402

Source: Sather and Smith 1984

developed countries from leaving wetlands intact, or at least managing them carefully, than would result from converting them to dry land. For example, safaris to African swamps to see wildlife bring in much hard currency, as in the Okavango Delta in Botswana, and the extension and wildlife management of the Land Between the Lakes in western Kentucky and Tennessee has led to a modest increase in regional prosperity (Thach et al. 1986).

7.0 PHYSICAL/HYDROLOGICAL FUNCTIONS

7.1 *Flood mitigation*

Floods are the main hazard to human occupation in lowland areas (plate 1.3), and wetlands that have been assiduously reclaimed and drained often hold the key to flood mitigation. Wetlands temporarily store run-off water and thereby protect downstream localities which are often former wetlands now reclaimed.

Plate 1.3 Because of their very nature all wetlands are prone to flooding, and therefore all settlements near wetlands are equally subject to this natural hazard. Floods cause damage and disrupt communications in all lowland environments, as in this instance when the River Parrett inundated the main streets of Taunton, Somerset, during the early 1960s. (Courtesy Photoprints)

In this way, the flood bank-full height is reduced and the velocity of the moving water lessened (Novitzki 1979). The slow release of water from a number of tributaries is thus 'desynchronized' (Tiner 1984), and not all flood waters reach the main channel at the same time.

The essential truth of this has long been recognized in land drainage engineering and river regulation works, where temporary spill-over areas in water meadows and pastures are provided to relieve the pressure of high flood levels on areas further downstream, protect levees and embankments from being breached, and generally to mitigate the flood crest as in the Washlands in the Fens and in many other lowland areas (plate 1.4). If this function is important in agricultural areas, then it is even more important in urban areas where loss of life and property will almost certainly be greater.

Very rarely has the importance and value of these natural mitigation strategies been quantified, and techniques for assessing the effectiveness and exact nature of their role have not been developed. Nevertheless, in the United States it is thought that an area of 500 000 km^2 has a flood problem in the 48 continguous states (Tiner 1984, p. 21) and that the flood damage in 1975 was $3.4 billion, a figure that must undoubtedly have risen to more than that by now.

A more exact calcuation was made in the case of the flood works on the lower Charles River near Boston, Massachusetts, where the Corps of Engineers considered a number of alternative flood alleviation schemes, namely (a) a large storage reservoir, (b) extensive embankments and walls alongside the river, (c) major flood protection works and (d) the purchase of 17 natural wetlands with an area of 3408 ha. On the basis of an analysis of a major downpour equivalent to 5 inches of rain it was concluded that run-off from the 477 km^2 of the Charles River (with extensive adjacent wetlands) peaked at only 91.2 m^3/s and took about a month to dissipate, whereas in the 360 km^2 of the adjacent Blackstone catchment, which had no wetland, it peaked at 478.7 m^3/s and took about a week to run off. Wetlands were the key to the different flood performances, and it was calculated that flood damage costs on the Charles River would rise in proportion to the loss of wetland through embankment, with a 40 per cent loss increasing damage by about $3.2 million annually, a total loss equalling damage averaging out at $17.6 million annually. Thus the wetland purchase and preservation alternative was chosen as the least expensive and most effective solution (US Corps of Engineers 1972; Carter et al. 1979, p. 349; Sather and Smith 1984).

Many other studies show that wetlands reduce stream flow and hence floods; for example, potholes in the North Dakota prairies store nearly 75 per cent of total water run-off (Novitzki 1979, Ludden et al. 1983) and peak floods would be 60–65 per cent less if a watershed had at least 15 per cent of its area in wetlands or lakes compared with a situation where no lakes or wetlands were present (Zinn and Copeland 1982).

The implications of this work for the less developed world are enormous. Instead of costly dam-building and dredging, the retention of fringes of wetland with the continuation of land uses sympathetic to them might yield

Plate 1.4 The natural tendency of rivers to overflow their banks and inundate lowland areas has been built into this scheme of spillways in the banks of the mid-section of the River Parrett in the Somerset Levels. The Aller Moor Spillways release the peak flood waters onto the surrounding lowland pastures, thus relieving pressure on riverbanks downstream and helping to 'desynchronize' the flood peak. Provided that the flood water passes off within a couple of weeks no permanent harm is done to grassland
(Courtesy Douglas Allen)

major dividends in flood control. Centuries of embanking and reclamation on the Ganges-Brahmaputra delta have reduced wetland by many hundreds of square kilometres and this is part of the cause of the severity of the downstream flooding that has occurred there with heavy loss of life in 1975 and almost annually since.

7.2 *Coastal protection*

It is clear that coastal marshes absorb wave energy and reduce erosion on estuarine shorelines, and so buffer the land from storms. More than 50 per cent of wave energy is dissipated within the first 2.5 m of the marsh, a figure which rises to 80 per cent at 10 m and is virtually eliminated at 30 m (Knutson 1978). Similarly, erosive tidal flows can be dissipated by plant stems growing in marshes and near dunes (Dean 1979). As potential wave damage to the shore line is decreased, so there is an increase in sediment deposition with a further decreased potential for erosion, a process that can be accelerated by deliberate marsh planting, particularly *Spartina* species (Woodhouse et al. 1976). The process is self-reinforcing; under conditions of abundant sediment load deposition, marshes are prograded seaward, reducing the energy of tidal waters flowing across the marsh which releases their sediment burden. Coastal marshes are sinks for the suspended sediment which can accumulate at rates of between 8 and 37 mm/yr.

The implications of this natural process are manifold.

1 In the developed world the effects of storm surges, hurricanes and similar natural disasters could be lessened by marshland accretion and growth, and not through reclamation and more protection, which merely pushes the hazard further out to sea. Costly protection works, which often exceed £1 million per kilometre, could then be avoided. In addition coastal accretion is affected by many other activities, such as flood control, freshwater diversions and coastal dredging. When it is realized that in the United States 300×10^6 m^3 of sediment are removed annually from navigable channels, then this alone must cause enormous alterations to the sedimentation regime, to say nothing of what happens where it is disposed.
2 In the less developed world of the tropics, there is an urgent need to encourage mangrove propagation and discourage reclamation in flood-plain delta areas, such as Bangladesh, where storm surges may be as high as 4 m. However, new islands of mud are quickly embanked and drained in an effort to create new land, mangroves cannot gain a hold and facilitate more accretion, and existing mangrove forests are cut for increasingly scarce fuel wood. Now the government of Bangladesh is encouraging the replanting of mangroves to protect embankments in over 65 000 ha (Wijkman and Timberlake 1984, Maltby 1985).
3 Globally, sea levels are thought to be rising by possibly as much as 3.0 mm/yr as a result of melting polar ice and the thermal expansion of ocean waters due to increases in atmospheric temperatures associated with the greenhouse effect. Locally the rise may be greater because of coastal subsidence (e.g. Eastern England, Galveston Bay). If this is so, then the encouragement of coastal accretion would seem to be a crucial survival strategy (chapter 2).

7.3 *Recharging aquifers*

Whereas the benefits of wetlands in dissipating floods and coastal erosion are reasonably well understood and authenticated, their role in ground water recharge is more debatable. The variety of wetland types, soils and geological settings, local and regional ground-water flows, and the ratio of vertical to horizontal hydraulic conductivity of a basin are some of the many factors that cause considerable variations from place to place (Carter and Novitzki 1988). Negative feedbacks are easier to prove. It is probable that if local wetlands are drained in areas of moisture stress, then the stock and domestic drinking-water supplies will suffer, as for example, in the Prairie pothole region (Leitch 1981), and that interference with ground-water withdrawals will cause salt-water seepages into freshwater aquifers. However, the difficulty is to designate a particular wetland as being either an area of discharge or recharge, and to analyse its influence on ground-water supplies. Whichever it is does not, perhaps, matter that much, as both are valuable functions. (Siegel 1988, pp. 59–67).

7.4 *Sediment trapping*

It is evident that wetlands are sinks for sediments; therefore they can clear the suspended matter in both marine and fresh water, thereby improving water quality. Rates of deposition range between 2 and 45 mm/yr, although extremes of many metres have been known to occur in sheltered estuaries and river outfalls. Sedimentation is greatest where the water moves slowest, and entrapment is enhanced by vegetation taking hold either naturally or after having been deliberately planted, as has been done with various types of *Spartina* grasses. In addition, flocculation of suspended clay particles can occur at the interface between fresh and salt water (Boto and Patrick 1979). The benefits of the process are manifold. Excessive downstream sedimentation hinders the working of drainage sluices, storage reservoirs and dams for hydroelectricity schemes, and in the case of reservoirs ultimately reduces their capacity and shortens their life (plate 1.5). Even the dredging of choked channels is eased by disposing the slurry back into adjacent wetlands and allowing it literally to filter slowly through the vegetation and back into the main channel, often completely clear of sediment and with less contaminants. Secondly, the decreased turbidity of water increases the sunlight reaching phytoplankton and other minute organisms, which then multiply and are a source for food for fish, shellfish and wildfowl, as well as being aesthetically and recreationally more appealing.

While the presence of suspended sediments is detrimental to water quality, they have a strong tendency to absorb nutrients, pesticides, heavy metals and other toxins such as chlorinated and petroleum hydrocarbons. Once deposited and ‘trapped’ in the wetland these substances can be either removed by the wetland plants or undergo slow decomposition.

7.5 *Atmospheric and climatic fluctuations*

Although little research has been done on the topic, there are indications that wetlands may play an important part in global biogeochemical fluxes. Armentano and Menges (1986) suggest that temperate organic soil wetlands act as a net carbon sink, and absorbed between 57×10^6 and 83×10^6 tons/yr before widespread draining reduced their ability to do this. Since the end of the

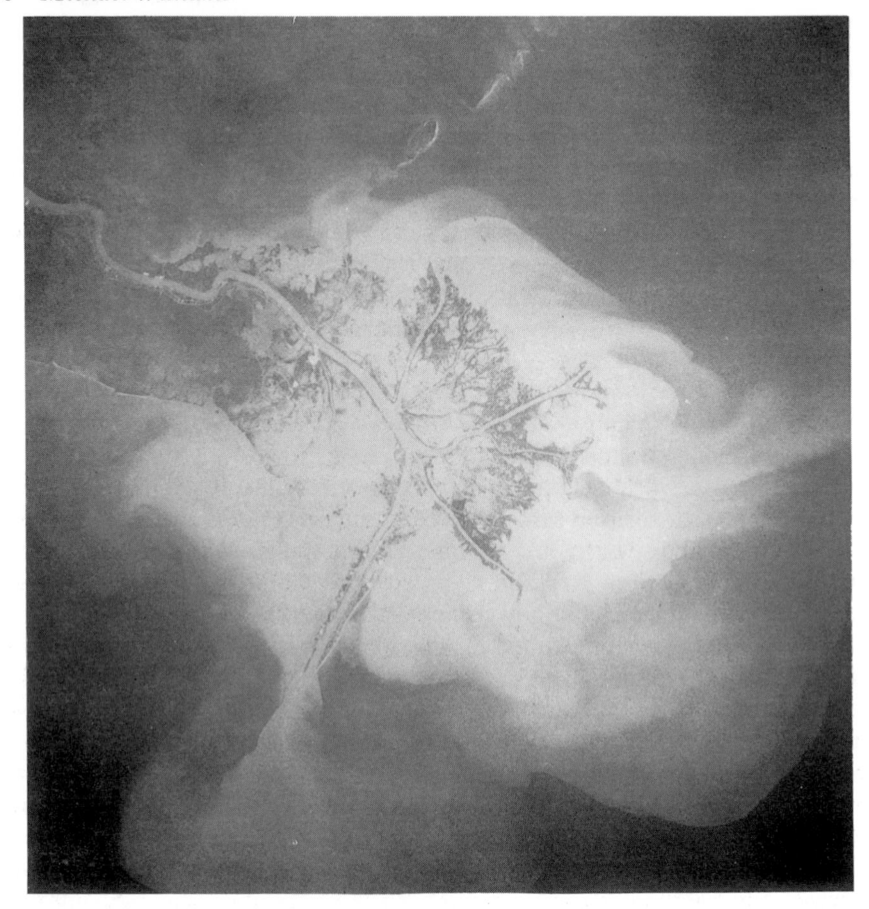

Plate 1.5 The enormous sediment load of major rivers is illustrated in this view of the Mississippi delta showing the discoloration of the water many kilometres out to sea. None the less, the deposition would be even greater were it not for the many dams and reservoirs constructed upstream that trap the sediment, a function formerly performed by natural unreclaimed wetlands. The area covered by this Space Shuttle shot is roughly 75 km from east to west.
(NASA SI3–39200–9)

eighteenth century peat burning alone might have added (590–700) $\times$ 10^6 tons of carbon to the atmosphere, and draining might have added another (4140–5600) $\times$ 10^6 tons, which are signficant amounts in the total global carbon budget.

The knock-on effects of these changes on global warming and increases in sea level (chapters 2 and 10) are difficult to calibrate, but if the rise by 2100 is anywhere between the 1.40 and 3.45 m suggested then it will be crucially important for wetland survival.

8.0 CHEMICAL FUNCTIONS

8.1 *Pollution trapping*

Because wetlands intercept the run-off from uplands before it reaches channels, they trap water and filter out pollutants, thus improving its quality (Kadlec and Kadlec 1979). Foremost is their role in removing the nitrogen and phosphorus that comes from the use of ever-increasing quantities of nitrogenous and superphosphate fertilizers on farmland (Van der Valk et al. 1979, Gilliam et al. 1988). The over-nutrient-rich water causes rapid plant and algal growth (eutrophication), and the rapid spread of undesirable aquatic plants that absorb oxygen in lakes, ponds and slow-moving waters reduces the ability of the water to support marine life and, of course, affects the quality of drinking water and recreational activities.

The removal of the pollutants is accomplished by a number of means. In the case of phosphorus, there is some uptake by the plants and it is also reduced by being absorbed and settling in anaerobic sediments, but there are finite limits to the amount of phosphorus removed. In contrast, wetlands are very efficient at removing nitrogen, again by plants but more particularly by bacterial metabolism at the water-sediment interface which promotes nitrification-denitrification. Nitrification is the transformation of nitrogen into molecular nitrogen and gaseous oxide. Between 40 and 90 per cent of nitrogen can be removed in this way. Denitrification is caused by anaerobic bacteria found in the wetland sediment that convert nitrate nitrogen into atmospheric nitrogen (Sloey et al. 1978, Bastian and Benforado 1988). However, Snyder and Snyder (1982, pp. 107–9) concluded that the primary role of plants in the water treatment process is physical rather than metabolic because they supply the substrate for bacterial growth and the medium for physical filtration and absorption, and restrict algal growth and wave action.

8.2 *Removal of toxic residues*

In much the same way, toxic residues from waste products, such as heavy metals, pesticides and herbicides, can be removed from the water by ion exchange and absorption in the organic and clay sediments (in effect they become buried in the sediments) and by uptake by plants, particularly the bullrush (*Schoenoplectus lacustrus*), the common reed (*Phragmites australis*) and the water hyacinth (*Eichhornia crassipes*), which is an aggressive colonizer of warm still waters. The effectiveness and efficiency of these processes varies between 20 and 100 per cent, depending on the pollutant and the type of wetland, and can be enhanced by deliberate planting of absorptive vegetation.

8.3 *Waste processing*

A third and very practical chemical function of wetlands is their ability to process human and animal waste material in an extremely efficient way (Valiela et al. 1976, Kadlec 1979). Their ability to do this revolves around three factors: their very high primary productivity, which means that their prolific growth takes up pollutants from the water and substrate, the absorption of pollutants by the high rate of sediment deposition and the bacterial action in the sediments.

The evidence for this function is based on a number of celebrated case studies. For example, domestic sewage has been emptied into Brillion Marsh, Wisconsin, in the catchment of the Manitowoc River, Wisconsin, since 1923. The marsh removes an average of 86.2 per cent of the coliform bacteria from faeces, 80.1 per cent of the biological oxygen demand, 43.7 per cent of the chemical oxygen demand, 29.1 per cent of the suspended solids and 13.4 per cent of the total phosphorus, and reduces the turbidity by 43.5 per cent (Boto and Patrick 1979). Similarly, the 207 ha of the Tinicum Marsh, just south of Philadelphia, handles partially treated sewage, and on a daily basis removes 7.7 tons of biological oxygen demand, 4.9 tons of phosphorus, 4.3 tons of ammonia and 138 lb of nitrate. It also adds 20 tons of oxygen to the water daily (Grant and Patrick 1970). Studies from a wide range of wetland types in North America are reviewed by Whigham (1982), and he concludes that peatland systems are most capable of long-term processing. However, the example of processing for over 50 years in the mangroves and salt marshes around Calcutta (Furedy 1983, Ghosh and Sen 1987) shows that one cannot be dogmatic. Much needs to be done before this function is comprehensively quantified.

9.0 BIOLOGICAL FUNCTIONS

9.1 *Productivity*

The biological yield of wetlands is enormous. They are amongst the most productive ecosystems in the world, rivalled only by some tropical rainforests and the most intensively cultivated areas of land, such as prime corn fields in the Midwest of the United States. Table 1.4 lists the net primary productivity ranges and means for major global ecosystems (Leith 1975); the production by climatic zones can be found in table 1.2. The disproportionate contribution of wetlands to the global total is emphasized: 24 per cent from 6.4 per cent of the earth's surface. Variations of net primary productivity within different wetland types are not known globally, but Richardson (1979) has calculated the relative productivity of some North American wetlands on the basis of tonnes per hectare per year, all of which exceed grassland say by a factor of between 2 and 5 (table 1.5).

Many wetland plants (autotrophs) are perennials and are nearly all leaf with little or no woody or thickened tissues. Therefore they are constant and efficient converters of solar energy (photosynthesis) to fix carbon and create biomass. In addition, their root systems are specially adapted to take up inorganic nutrients and incorporate them into inorganic forms. Moreover, repeated flooding and/or tidal flux provides constant new supplies of nutrients and circulates others. There is no lack of moisture for plant growth.

Table 1.4 Net primary product by main vegetation units

Unit	Net primary productivity Range (g/m²/yr)	Approximate mean
Forest		1290
Tropical rain forest	1000-3500	2000
Raingreen forest	600-3500	1500
Summergreen forest	400-2500	1000
Chaparral	250-1500	800
Warm temperate mixed forest	600-2500	1000
Boreal forest	200-1500	500
Woodland	200-1000	600
Dwarf and open scrub		90
Tundra	100-400	140
Desert scrub	10-250	70
Grassland		600
Tropical grassland	200-2000	700
Temperate grassland	100-1500	500
Desert (extreme)		1
Dry desert	0-10	3
Ice desert	0-1	0
Cultivated land	100-4000	650
Fresh water		1250
Swamp and marsh	800-4000	2000
Lake and stream	100-1500	500
Total for continents		669

Source: Leith 1975, p. 205

Not much of the natural production is eaten directly, except perhaps for wild rice, cranberries and the like, although cattle, sheep and wild game graze on the herbaceous growth at low tide or in non-flooded periods. The greatest food value of wetland comes from the death of the plants to form detritus on which heterotrophic organisms such a larvae, fungi, bacteria and protozoa thrive.

Table 1.5 Productivity of some North American wetlands

	Productivity (t/ha/yr)
Cat-tail marshes	27.4
Reed marshes	21.0
Freshwater tidal	16.2
Swamp forests	10.5
Sedge-dominated marshes	10.4
Bogs, fens, muskegs	9.1
Grassland	5.1

Source: Richardson 1979

This forms the basis for the aquatic food web of high-yielding animals and fish such as salmon, crabs, shrimps and worms (Crow and MacDonald 1979, de la Cruz 1979, Murkin and Wrubleski 1988). Thus, the wetlands can be regarded as 'the farmlands of the aquatic environment' (Tiner 1984, p. 19) where large volumes of food are produced. Of course, there are other products, such as timber in river bottom lands, reeds for thatching and, above all, the peat itself which is a valuable fuel in some economies.

Although the relationship between wetlands, net primary productivity and abundant invertebrate life, and hence fish and animal life, is beyond doubt, the mechanisms of the food chain are imperfectly understood. First, the process of decomposition on which the productivity depends, and how it relates to the food chain, is not fully known, and rates of decomposition will vary with a host of local physical factors including salinity, flow and, above all, temperature. Secondly, the efficiency of the wider food chain depends on the export or flushing of the nutrients from the wetlands to other areas (e.g. estuaries or further out to sea) on the assumption that detritus is the main source of nutrients. However, the role of marshes in supporting fish and shellfish production is not convincing (OTA 1984, p. 60). Finally, the pathways whereby the nutrients are incorporated into food chains is not well established. It is done either by the grazing of living plants or by the consumption of dead material by lower-level heterotrophs, which in turn become the indirect source of wetland-derived nutrients to higher-level consumers. The grazing pathway is well authenticated; the detritus pathway is not (Sather and Smith 1984, pp. 24–8). Despite these uncertainties, however, the fact remains that wetlands have an abundant natural production that is most likely going to be lost if they are drained, although it could be replaced by higher-yielding crops like corn or sugar cane.

9.2 *Habitats*

Perhaps the most widely known and generally most appreciated function of wetlands is that they provide habitats for a variety of plants and animals, particularly wildfowl. The literature on this is highly localized, and therefore it is difficult to specify habitats for particular animals and plants without recourse to detailed accounts and inventories of the fauna of individual countries which is beyond the scope of this chapter. Nevertheless, because of the strength of the fishing and wildlife interest in the United States, its wetland habitats and their populations are known in more detail than are those for anywhere else, and this information is drawn on in order to illustrate general themes where there is a lack of evidence elsewhere.

Wetlands are the habitat of invertebrates and cold-blooded vertebrates which contribute to the support of the wetland faunal community as a whole through both trophic and non-trophic roles (Clark 1979). Consequently, wetlands also figure largely in the cycle of many freshwater and coastal fish which feed on wetland-dependent food, use the wetlands as nursery grounds and often spawn in the aquatic parts of wetlands (Peters et al. 1979). The greater the extent of wetland the greater is the yield of fish (Turner and Boesch 1988), and the nature and abundance of vegetation also affect numbers.

The bulk (i.e. nearly two-thirds) of the United States commercial and salt-water fish catch is probably dependent on the coastal estuaries and their wetlands. Between 66 and 90 per cent of the commercially important fish and shellfish species on the Atlantic and Gulf coasts depend on their coastal marshes or estuaries for at least part of their life cycle (McHugh 1976). On the Pacific coast wetlands are essential for the spawning of salmon species. The evidence is that in other continents something approaching the same proportions of fish and shellfish are dependent on wetlands, a factor of even greater importance in countries of the developing world because fish are often about the only source of protein available.

Some animals are entirely wetland dependent while others are only partially so. For example, in North America the muskrat, nutria, beaver and marsh rat fall into the dependent group, and the otter, mink, racoon and species of deer fall into the non-dependent group (Weller 1981). Each animal has its own particular territorial range, with the muskrat and beaver having the broadest range from the Arctic to the warm southeast of the continent in both salt and fresh water, while the nutria are restricted to Louisiana and surrounding states with warm and fresh water. Larger mammals, such as the alligator and crocodile, inhabit the coastal wetlands of Florida, North Carolina and west to Texas, as well as the Northern Territory in Australia.

The importance of wetlands as year-round habitats, breeding grounds and areas of wintering for migratory birds is the most well-known and well-researched function of all. Indeed, it is the function that was responsible for the heightening of awareness of wetland values and gave the initial impetus to the conservation of wetlands in many parts of the world (plate 1.6). The great bulk (perhaps as much as three-quarters) of all birds that use wetlands in one way or another are probably non-game birds (Kroodsma 1979), but other than the facts that they tend to follow riparian wetlands for food, water and cover, and use north-south more than east–west river channels, the ecological relationships and patterns are not well understood (Wauer 1977).

The situation for game birds or waterfowl such as duck, geese and swans is different, however. They have been analysed from every conceivable angle and their relationship with wetlands is well authenticated and clear. In North America, nesting and breeding grounds for ducks and geese are primarily in the northern freshwater wetlands, particularly in the prairie-pothole region of the United States and adjacent areas of Canada, and in the tundra wetlands of Alaska (figure 1.4). The relationship between breeding and these wetlands is borne out by the diminution of numbers consequent on the reduction of wetlands with draining. The wintering areas are in the greatest concentrations of wetlands – on the Gulf coast, in the Mississippi valley, in the Chesapeake Bay area and in the Central Valley of California. Also important are the smaller areas of coastal salt-water and freshwater marshes and bottomland hardwood forests (Flake 1979).

These breeding and wintering areas are linked by four major flyways, the

Plate 1.6 The sight of migrating wildfowl landing or taking off from wetland habitats was the first and probably most powerful cause for positive action of wetland preservation. Here Bewick swans are taking off from a wetland in the north of England
(Courtesy Joe Blossom, Wildfowl and Wetlands Trust, Slimbridge)

Atlantic, the Mississippi, the Central and the Pacific, which are followed in the biannual migrations. The presence of small stop-over wetlands along these flyways is crucial for the survival of the birds, although geese and several species of duck meet part of their autumn and spring food demand from farm grains. An FWS inventory of waterfowl moving by flyways during the period 1976–85 suggests that an average of some 23.3 million birds are on the move, 3.3 million (14 per cent) on the Atlantic flyway, 7.4 million (32.0 per cent) on the Mississippi flyway, 5.6 million (24 per cent) on the Central flyway and 7.0 million (30 per cent) on the Pacific flyway (table 1.6). Of this total, the dabblers or surface ducks (mallards and pintails) tended to be evenly distributed over all flyways except the Atlantic, bay divers and sea ducks were concentrated in the Atlantic, but geese were much more evenly spread over all four flyways (Bellrose and Trudeau 1988).

In the eastern hemisphere, the location and migration of game and non-game birds appears to be more complex, and the research, being international, is probably less well coordinated. Nevertheless, it is known for wildfowl, at least, that breeding grounds exist in tundra wetlands in eastern Canada, Greenland, Iceland and northern Scandinavia and Russia, and the main wintering grounds are widely distributed in wetlands over three continents. Of major significance

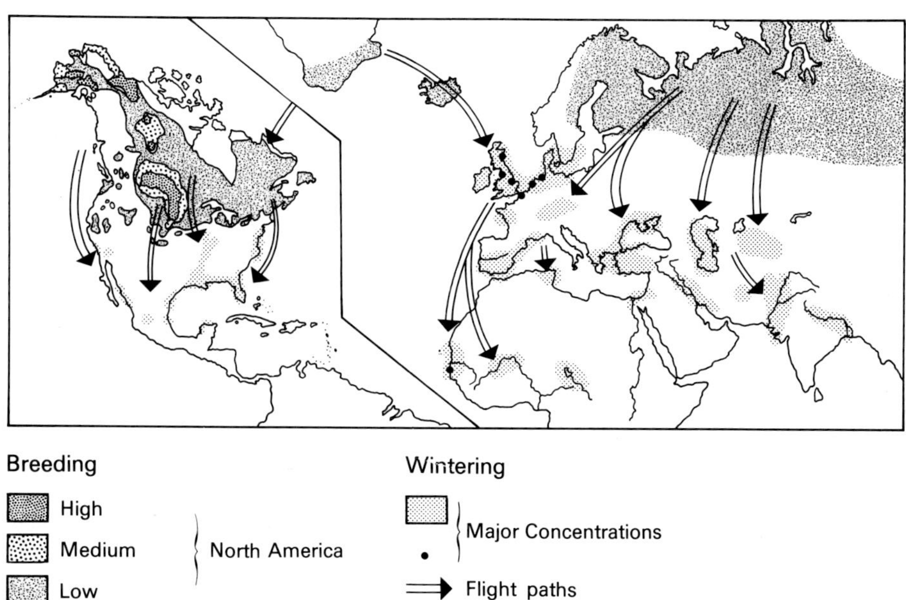

Figure 1.4 Wildfowl breeding and wintering grounds, and flight pathways
(after OTA 1984, p. 53; Atkinson-Willes 1976, p. 200)

Table 1.6 Distribution of winter waterfowl by flyway, United States 1976—1985

Waterfowl	*Number of birds (×1000 (%))*				
	Atlantic flyway	*Mississippi flyway*	*Central flyway*	*Pacific flyway*	*Total*
Dabblers	684	5131	3546	5665	15026
	(4.6)	(34.1)	(23.6)	(37.7)	(100.0)
Bay divers	1421	725	419	413	2978
	(47.7)	(24.3)	(14.1)	(13.9)	(100.0)
Sea ducks	196	3	0	92	291
	(67.4)	(1.0)	(0)	(31.6)	(100.0)
Geese	1036	1554	1641	804	5035
	(20.6)	(30.8)	(32.6)	(16.0)	(100.0)
Total	3337	7413	5606	6974	23300
	(14.3)	(31.8)	(24.0)	(29.9)	(100.0)

Source: Bellrose and Trudeau 1988, based on FWS data

are the shallow tidal estuaries and mudflats of the numerous inlets on the mild ice-free shores of northwest Europe, around Ireland, Britain, the Netherlands, Denmark and northwestern Germany. However, there are other wintering grounds further south in the Mediterranean, the Middle East and northern Africa, which are fewer in number but individually larger than those in northwest Europe and are often the outcome of the wide spreading of water as interior drainage systems debouch into dry lands. In the Mediterranean, there are the coastal marshes of southern Spain and France (the Camargue and its associated lagoons) and the important wintering grounds of Tunisia, Algeria and Morocco, particularly Lake Ischkeul and the Sebka Sedjoumi and Sebka Kelbia in Tunisia. The Danube delta and other bodies of water around the Black Sea, particularly in Turkey, form another wintering area, as do wetlands in the general region between the Caspian Sea and the Persian Gulf, and from Turkestan to Pakistan. A sixth major area lies in sub-Saharan Africa in the Senegal river in Mauritania, the internal delta of the Niger and the swamps that result from the interior drainage of Lade Chad on the Chari-Logone flood plain.

Migration paths are complex and often cross for different species, and there is no clear or consistent relationship between breeding and wintering wetlands. Counts taken each January from 1967 to 1974 showed that over 5 million ducks, swans and coots were present on average, and 7 million at the maximum, which must be taken as a good sample of the wider bird population on these wintering grounds (Atkinson-Willes 1976). Individual estuaries are outstanding in the distribution. Of overwhelming significance is the Banc d'Arguin in Mauritania, one of the largest intertidal flats in the world, which in 1973 supported 750 000 wading birds. At the other end of the flyway path is the Wadden Sea, the area of intertidal mudflats and sandbanks between the Netherlands, Denmark and the Federal Republic of Germany, where nearly 450 000 waders are present with an average density of 216 birds/km^2, compared with 11 birds/km^2 on the Dutch coast, and between 2.8 and 3.4 birds/km^2 over the open sea. Following these in importance are the deltaic region of the Netherlands (185 000), Morecambe Bay (179 000), the Baie du Mont St Michel (140 000) and so on. It is probable that these figures could be doubled in order to include all wetland wintering birds (Prater 1976).

10.0 SOCIO-ECONOMIC BENEFITS AND VALUES

In many cases, the foregoing functions can be translated into tangible benefits or values. Flood and storm-water drainage protection in particular but also erosion control, water quality and the harvest of natural products are all amenable to numerical cost-benefit analysis. However, the list is not exhaustive and can be supplemented by a whole range of directly economic consumptive values that flow naturally from wetland composition and processes, such as food, fish, fibre and fuel – the harvest of the wetlands (Palmisano 1979). All these are removed physically from the wetlands and may lead to their modification and transformation, and hence are far from positive reasons for leaving them undrained and undisturbed.

In addition, there are many social non-consumptive benefits that usually defy quantification, but none the less are becoming increasingly important. There are the active non-consumptive benefits, such as the use of wetlands for recreation and leisure activities, and the passive non-consumptive benefits – wetlands as aesthetically satisfying and beautiful environments, as sites for scientific and archaeological research and as sites of heritage and educational value. How one places a 'value' on a wildlife habitat, a place where one sees birds land and take off in their biannual migratory journey or the knowledge that archaeological remains lie buried (or *may* be buried) in the peat defies rational analysis. Sometimes, it is true, the aesthetic can be translated into the numerical; a wetland habitat may produce a value x of fish, generate y licence fees or generate a value z of local trade, and this sort of calculation is often used to justify non-use. Even so, the equation is rarely complete and is assuredly difficult to solve (chapter 11). The active and passive elements are also difficult to disentangle at times. However, the recent work of Pearce and his associates (Pearce et al. 1988, 1989) on the resource accounting of the so-called 'free' environmental goods, in an effort to curb waste and pollution, opens up new vistas for investigation.

10.1 *Consumptive values: food*

Reclaimed wetlands produce new soils which are the basis of an enlarged food production. This has been the fundamental reason for wetland transformation and diminution throughout the centuries, and will continue to be so in future as increased food production is a national goal of every developing country in order to feed its rapidly growing population (chapters 6 and 7).

There is much uncertainty about the total area of land already drained. L'Vovich and White (1990) suggest that it may be as much as 1.6×10^6 km^2 by 1985, some of which is drained land connected with the 2.65×10^6 km^2 of irrigated land (Zonn and Nesenko 1982). Segeren (1983) suggests that as much as 8.65×10^6 km^2 of land is hampered in some way by poor drainage, of which 4.5×10^6 km^2 is already in polders or drained, and an additional 800 000 km^2 needs to be reclaimed by the year 2000 in order to provide for world food needs (table 1.7).

Whatever the truth of these figures, and there is clearly much disagreement, the actual value of the reclaimed land is immense, but this is of less significance than the annual yield of crops from the land. Because of the high organic content of the soil, the large stored supplies of nutrients, the relatively low susceptibility to erosion, the low energy and labour requirements and the ease of application of modern farm technology, wetland soils always contribute an amount to the farm economy of any nation that is disproportionate to their area. Dideriksen et al (1979) estimates that in the United States, 42.1×10^6 ha of wetland soils (not the same as wetlands, but certainly land that requires drainage) are in cropland. The greatest amount is in the highly productive Corn Belt states (14.6×10^6 ha), the Lake states (6.67×10^6 ha) and the three Delta states (6.43×10^6 ha). Together, all the wetland soils produce crops to a

Table 1.7 Estimates of drained land, and potential and future needs

	Drained (1985)[a] *(× 1000 km³)*	*Potential for polderization*[b] *(× 1000 km²)*	*Area needed by 2000*[b] *(× 1000 km²)*
South America	78	1193	229
Africa	24	1384	266
Asia	320	853	164
North America	676	359	69
Europe	377 }	368	70
USSR	122 }		
Oceania	9	–	–
Total	1606	4157	798

Sources: (a) L'Vovich and White 1990, table 7; (b) Segeren 1983

value of $9 billion, or about a quarter of the estimated $37 billion value of major crops throughout the country in 1977, and this does not include the value added for livestock raised or grazed on the wetland crops. In almost all cases, the erstwhile wetland soils are amongst the highest yielding of all soil types, producing prime yields in corn, soybeans, grain feeds and cotton. Crop yields in the Fens of England are the highest in the country and those of the Netherlands are probably amongst the highest in Europe.

10.2 *Consumptive values: fish, fowl and fauna*

The total world catch of fish and shellfish, and its breakdown into estuarine-dependent and non-estuarine-dependent components is probably impossible to calculate globally, but again, if the example of the United States is anything to go by, perhaps as much as 60–65 per cent of the world's catch might be attributable to wetlands. In 1980, 63 per cent of the 2.945 billion kg catch was of wetland-dependent fish, and it was valued at $1.15 billion, some 51.5 per cent of the $2.23 billion total catch (Leitch and Scott 1977, Peters et al. 1979, OTA 1984, pp. 54–5).

In addition to fish and shellfish, a number of valuable mammals live in wetlands (Chabreck 1979). By 1980, 8.6 million muskrat, 1.3 million nutria, 394 000 mink and 16 000 alligators were 'harvested' in the United States at an estimated value of $0.95 billion in furs and skins. Closely related to the yield of animal life from the wetlands are the activities of hunters and part-time sportsmen. This, of course, has overlapping links with non-consumptive functions, as some engage in these activities less for the yield and more for the experience. What value one can put on that is difficult to arrive at, except as follows: it is claimed that recreational fishermen in the United States spent $13.1 billion on wetland-dependent fishing in licences, travel and equipment (Peters et al. 1979). Similarly, in 1980–1, 5.3 million people spent $638 million hunting migratory birds, and 1.9 million people killed 12.9 million ducks and 1.7 million geese (FWS 1982).

Similar data for other countries are not available, but there is more than a hint of the vast natural harvest of the wetland from some detailed examples of the mangal in Thailand. When converted to rice paddies they produce $168/ha/yr, but they produce $206/ha/yr in shrimp fishing and slightly over ten times that amount when carefully managed (Christensen 1983, p. 5). Even when untouched, the mangal-dependent open-water fisheries produce $100/ha/yr (table 1.8). More than 176 000 ha of tidal mangal lands in the Philippines and 41 000 ha in Thailand have been converted into brackish water aquaculture ponds and produce abundant milkfish and shrimps (de la Cruz 1984, Librero 1984). Also most of the (3–4) $\times 10^6$ of mangal could be utilized for open-water aquaculture in which artificial nesting areas are provided. These yield between 90 and 180 tons/ha/yr. More recent estimates put mangal losses in Indonesia, the Philippines, Malaysia and Thailand at between 411 000 and 487 000 ha/yr, overwhelmingly concentrated in the first two countries, with some 425 000 ha being proposed for aquaculture development in the future (McVey 1988).

Table 1.8 The value of present and potential uses of mangroves, Thailand

	Present ($/ha/yr)	*Potential ($/ha/yr)*
Wood gathering	160	590
Charcoal	30	400
Estuary fishery	30	30
Mangrove-dependent fishery	100	100
Oyster culture	?	60
Shrimp farming	206	2106
Rice farming	165	–

Source: Christensen 1983, p. 5

10.3 *Consumptive values: fuel*

For centuries, rural communities in northern Europe have laboriously cut peat for fuel, and the practice still continues in remote areas of Ireland, the Highlands and Islands of Scotland, and northern Scandinavia and Russia (plate 1.7). In more recent decades, however, hand-digging has given way to industrial production on a large scale. At first, massive bucket-type dredges or scoops known as baggers were used to cut peat into sods which were easily transported and utilized in a variety of industrial and domestic situations (plate 1.8). Since the early 1950s, however, the trend has been to use more versatile light machines that produce a crumbed or powdered peat (milled peat) which is usually either fed directly into electrical power stations or processed further by densification to produce pellets or briquettes for both industrial and domestic space and water heating. These provide a clean uniform fuel with a calorific

Plate 1.7 Peat cutting for fuel has been carried out for centuries if not millennia in the countries of northwest Europe. In many places it is still cut in the traditional way with two-sided spades that slice out the wet peat, which is then stacked and dried before use (Courtesy Irish Tourist Board)

Plate 1.8 Modern peat extraction in Ireland. Large peat bogs are stripped and their surface is exposed to facilitate drying. The peat is then shaved off by machines, such as the one above, and stacked ready for use. The loose crumbly peat can be used in furnaces and industrial plant, but peat for domestic use is often compacted into briquettes
(Courtesy Bord na Móna)

value of 18 MJ/kg, which can be raised significantly by carbonization processes. Where extensive deposits are present, power generation is an attractive financial proposition, particularly where it substitutes for imported energy and reduces foreign exchange requirements (Bjork and Graneli 1978, Bord na Móna 1985).

Worldwide production of peat and fuel has risen from 46.7×10^6 tons in 1950 to about 90×10^6 tons in 1980, although Kivinen and Pakarinen (1981) believe that it may hve been as much as 108×10^6 tons by the late 1970s. There is a massive concentration of production in three countries in the northern hemisphere: USSR (89 per cent of the world total), Ireland (6.2 per cent) and Finland (3.4 per cent) (see table 1.9) which accounts for 1.5 per cent, 15 per cent and 2.0 per cent respectively of the total energy consumption of those countries. Other countries with vast deposits pursuing plans for production are Canada, Sweden and the United States (figure 1.5) particularly Minnesota where it is calculated that 400 000 ha of peat 3.3 m thick would be capable of supplying the state's energy needs for 32 years.

The value of peat production is difficult to estimate accurately because of the variable quality of peat, initial capital costs and the volatile price of alternative energy sources, but at 1984 prices its delivery cost per gigajoule was \$3.20 (or \$3.61 for briquettes) compared with \$2.10–\$2.90 for industrial coal, \$5.40–\$6.10 for anthracite coal, \$6.30 for medium-weight oil and \$9.00 for kerosene. Although the overall value of peat production is uncertain, its profitability is without doubt, and this together with the fact that it is easy to harvest, that it may be the only source of fuel in an area which lacks fossil fuels and that the land can ultimately be used again for other productive purposes makes these advantages difficult to weigh against the detrimental impacts of deteriorating water quality, excessive run-off, subsidence and destruction of natural habitats and wildlife that sustained extraction implies, and the pollution of residues from toxic chemicals from fuel conversion plants (Moore and Bellamy 1973, Farnham 1979, Winkler and De Witt 1985). The Norfolk Broads in eastern England and the Rijk den Duizend Eilandtjes – the Realm of a Thousand Islands – in north Holland (see chapter 6, plate 6.1) are the ultimate examples of what sustained extraction can do over many hundreds of years (Lambert et al. 1960). Another potential use of wetlands for energy purposes is to grow crops yielding high biomass on them (e.g. willow) and harvest them on a regular basis (Pratt and Andrews 1981).

Although not a fuel, the production of horticultural peat often accompanies the production of fuel peat as it uses the waste and less pure peat. Its production in 1980 was over 130×10^6 tons, and is leading to the destruction of many peat wetlands such as Thorne Waste near Hatfield Chase and many parts of the Brue Valley in the northern Somerset Levels.

10.4 *Consumptive values: fibre*

Whereas peat reserves 30 cm thick or more may occupy 421×10^6 ha (Kivinen and Pakarinen 1981), and might even be as extensive as 500×10^6 ha, wetlands

Table 1.9 World fuel peat and horticultural peat production, 1980

Country	*Fuel (× 1000 tons)*	*Horticultural (× 1000 tons)*	*Total (× 1000 tons)*
USSR	80000	120000	200000
Ireland	5570	380	5950
Finland	3100	500	3600
FRG	250	2000	2250
China	800	1300	2100
USA	0	800	800
Canada	0	490	490
Poland	0	280	280
Sweden	0	270	270
Czechoslovakia	0	270	270
GDR	0	170	170
UK	No data	170	170
France	50	100	150
Denmark	0	110	110
Norway	1	83	84
New Zealand	0	10	10
Others	100	2900	3000
Total	*c.*90000	*c.*130000	*c.*220000

Source: Bord Na Móna 1985, p. 8

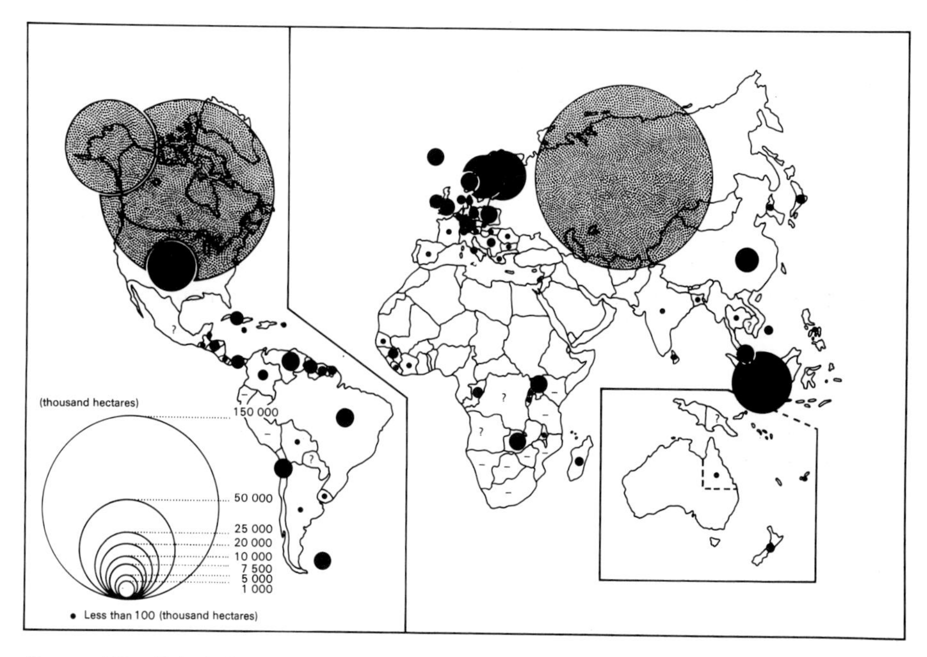

Figure 1.5 Global distribution of major commercially potential peat deposits. Values over 25×10^6 ha are stipple shaded for clarity
(after Bord na Móna 1985)

that carry commercially valuable forest are probably only a quarter as extensive. Two types of forest are considered here, the hardwood bottomland forests of the United States and the mangal of south and southeast Asia.

Bottomland hardwood forests occupy flood plains that consist of saturated soils which are inundated during a portion or on several occasions through the year. In total they may occupy between 22.2×10^6 ha (Johnson 1979) and 23.5×10^6 ha (Turner et al. 1981). Taking the Johnson figure of 22.2×10^6 ha, some 12.9×10^6 ha are in the south and are composed of oak-gum-cypress forest (plate 1.9), and the remainder are in the north and are composed of elm-ash-cottonwood forests. The management of these forests is through the manipulation of the natural stands rather than through reforestation. The stands have a prolific growth in these moist environments so that an average hectare has 112 m^3 of merchantable timber on it and some cypress swamps have as much as 420 m^3. Thus Johnson estimates that an average timber value is $617/ha, which means that the standing tree value of the southern hardwoods is about $8 billion. Much less is known about the north, but the 850 000 ha of black spruce alone have an average value of $536/ha, which totals $455 million. However, these are largely once-and-for-all yields and cannot compete with the year-in year-out yields of the forest lands converted to agriculture (chapter 6). So compelling has this argument been that between 1960 and 1975 the bottomland hardwoods in the south have been felled at a rate of 175 000 ha/yr

Plate 1.9 Between about 1880 and 1920 the extensive cypress swamps of the southern and central United States were extensively exploited for their highly prized water-resistant timbers. The scars of this activity can still be seen in the landscape. The radial tracks were made by dragging logs across the swamp by winches, usually mounted on floating 'pull-boats', to a common loading point or 'set' in the dredged canal, as in the foreground. Then the logs were loaded onto barges and moved via the canal to the mill
(Courtesy US Army Corps of Engineers, 1981)

and the land converted to soybean fields (Sternitzke 1976, Turner et al. 1981, p. 17).

The area of mangal in south and southeast Asia is thought to be about 3.4×10^6 ha. It contains a large variety of different forest types from mature *Rhozophera* that can exceed 40 or 60 m in height, to younger stands of secondary forest a few metres high that result from frequent harvesting and pruning, to areas completely altered and converted into fishponds and paddies. With the exception of *Heritiera fomes* in the Sundrabans, mangal forest does not make good millable timber; rather, its constructional use is confined to poles for urban scaffolding and the manufacture of small wooden objects, tanbark and even pulp. The trunkless nipa palm produces good thatch, shingles and sap for alcohol. The overwhelming use of mangal is for charcoal and fuel wood.

The wood produces an even heat and little smoke, and is ideal for domestic purposes.

With so many uses the mangrove swamps are under great pressure, and although theoretically a renewable resource they are fast becoming non-renewable. In Thailand, with 307 715 ha of mangal, between 167 000 and 179 000 ha have been leased on concessions to timber companies with untold effects, and another 40 800 ha have been converted into shrimp ponds (de la Cruz 1984). In the Philippines the record is even clearer. Mangroves have been reduced overall from 418 990 ha in 1967 to 249 138 ha in 1976. Constant cutting for domestic uses and export pulp to Japan (Walsh 1977) has depleted the volume and growth potential so that old growth constitutes only 4.8 per cent of the area remaining but contributes 63.8 per cent of the volume of timber (table 1.10). Although mangrove timber constitutes only less than 0.5 per cent of the overall timber of the country by volume, it is so highly prized that it consistently contributes between a quarter and a third of the fuel wood and charcoal. Therefore there is a disproportionate impact on the mangrove forests, which is made all the worse by a doubling of fishpond areas from 88 681 ha in 1952 to 176 231 ha in 1977 (Librero 1984) (see also chapter 10). Clearly the indiscriminate harvesting of the fibre from the mangal forest will cause depletion in time. Yields of 1.9 m^3 ha/yr in unmanaged mangroves in Bangladesh have been pushed up to 8 or even 10 m^3 ha/yr with careful management in Thailand (Christensen 1983, p. 6), but this presupposes a 20-30 year rotation of cutting which seems increasingly unlikely in many countries as their area of mangal decreases.

Table 1.10 Mangrove timber in the Philippines: area and volume, 1976

	Area	*Volume*
Total	246 699 ha	7 468 000 m^3
Reproductive bush	50.2%	16.0%
Young growth	45.0%	20.2%
Old growth	4.8%	63.8%

Source: Librero 1984, p. 81

11.0 NON-CONSUMPTIVE BENEFITS

The non-consumptive benefits of wetlands include scenic, recreational, educational, aesthetic, archaeological, scientific, heritage and historical benefits that are difficult to define, let alone quantify. These overlap and intertwine, and consequently a precise definition is not possible or, perhaps, even desirable (Sather and Smith 1984).

As pointed out before, these non-consumptive values have usually been considered of secondary importance compared with the direct consumptive and economic products of wetlands and the physical, chemical and biological services that they provide. Perhaps this is not surprising as non-consumptive values are intangible and can be highly personal and subjective (Niering and Palmisaro 1979, Reimold and Hardinsky 1979). Often the topic is entered through the media of literature and art (Fritzell 1979, Niering 1979) or through scenic or visual-cultural assessments (Haslam 1973, Smardon 1983, 1988). Additionally, because there is no way of measuring these values objectively, it is difficult to compare non-consumptive with consumptive benefits, or one type of non-consumptive type with another non-consumptive type in the same wetland. The one non-consumptive benefit that can sometimes be quantified is that of recreation, as the number of people participating, and what they are prepared to pay for the privilege of that participation in the form of licence fees, equipment or travel, is a measure of sorts. Thus it is estimated that 83.2 million Americans spent $14.8 billion on observing and photographing fish and wildlife in 1980–1 (FWS 1982), but of course there is a fine dividing line between this passive appreciative activity and the more active hunting and fishing activities, which move one over firmly into the consumptive-yield type of calculation. Some of these issues are tackled in chapter 9 on the recreational impacts on wetlands, and some of the archaeological-historical values are treated further in chapter 5.

12.0 ASSESSMENT OF VALUES

So far, an attempt has been made to outline some of the beneficial intrinsic functions of wetlands and the imputed or computed values placed on them, all of which have been instrumental in changing attitudes towards wetlands. However, in the everyday world of wetland management there is a point where any function/value will be pitted against another, either through ignorance or entrenched attitude (e.g. draining land for food production and destroying its function of biologically enhancing water quality) or through deliberate policy in a management plan that attempts to resolve conflicts and pressures in land use, such as residential development versus coastal protection functions. Immediately, the question moves from what the uses of wetlands are in their natural state to how they should be used. Inevitably, attempts are made to quantify benefits in order to resolve conflicts, and a vast literature has been generated on this topic (Greeson et al. 1979, Reppert et al. 1979, Adamus 1983, Larson 1985). Yet despite the fact that there are over 5600 abstracts in the US FWS Value Data Base there is little unanimity as to how to resolve these questions, as most research is done by wetland scientists who, by and large, have non-cultural and non-economic perspectives (Leitch and Shabman 1988).

12.1 *Assessment problems*

Any assessment is beset by a number of generic problems (Queen 1977, Mitsch and Gosselink 1986, pp. 406–11) which can be listed as follows.

1 The sheer diversity of wetland types and their functions and products makes the weighting of their functions and values difficult. In short, wetlands are multivalue systems.
2 Wetland values increase as wetland areas decrease, particularly as wetlands are often interspersed between and interrelated with other wetland areas and even with the totality of the landscape.
3 Cost-benefit analysis is not applicable to non-consumptive functions or, indeed, to common property rights.
4 Commercial values are finite but wetlands may provide benefits that will last for ever.
5 Benefits from natural functions and characteristics do not necessarily accrue to wetland owners, but are public amenity rights.
6 Information on functions and processes, and even on the precise nature of impacts, is limited despite a massive research effort during the last few decades.
7 Even where functions are well authenticated there may be significant differences of opinion as to their value to humankind, i.e. there are conflicts of value perceptions.

Several attempts have been made to assess consumptive and non-consumptive benefits in monetary terms such as coastal erosion (Wass and Wright 1969), fisheries and water quality (Gosselink et al. 1974) and timber (MacDonald et al. 1978), and then dividing the market value of the products by the area of the wetland concerned to arrive at an average value in dollars or pounds sterling per hectare. However, objections to this approach are numerous. It is based on artificial marketplace values that do not recognize the ecological interdependence of wetland functions, the use of wetland size as the denominator in the value equation assumes that size is a limiting factor, which may not be true, the cost of harvesting the product is not deducted from the final value, as has been pointed out in the examples of consumptive studies given already (Shabman and Batie 1980), and it is assumed that wetlands have the same level of productivity or benefit throughout their extent, which is patently not true (Foster 1979).

Over and above all these specific criticisms there exist two flaws common to all assessment studies: firstly, wetlands have several harvestable products and not just one, and no methodology exists for evaluating all products simultaneously; secondly, the value of non-consumptive benefits is still not capable of being calibrated unless some sort of 'shadow' value is placed on them, which suffers from the fact that they are not established by the interaction of supply and demand forces in the market. Perfect markets do not exist in nature (Leitch and Shabman 1988). In every case, the value attached to one small piece of wetland may be minute, but as it is usually a part of some larger system its value may be magnified and therefore become significant. The evaluation of natural resources has been neglected.

12.2 *Other approaches*

In the light of the near impossibility of assigning monetary values, other methods and approaches have been suggested. Odum (1979) has suggested a hierarchical conceptualization of assessment approaches (table 1.11) which at least gives priorities to values and incorporates temporal and spatial diversity and their levels of complexity, so that over time the shift from local to global concerns and from individual owner to society at large are recognized, as is the ability to place 100 per cent market values on the lower levels of the hierarchy but almost zero values on the upper levels which are concerned with the whole of humanity. As we have seen in the previous discussion, the fish and wildlife categories were the first to be recognized and generally accepted by the public, and so this table is, in a sense, chronological as well. However, Odum voices the timely warning that their market values and adjunct services may well be inflated by conservationists and sportsmen 'eager to justify preservation' (Odum 1979, p. 18). As pressures for change (impacts) increase with time and the more complex ecosystemic functions, such as flood protection, recharge, water quality and biological productivity for food and fuel, have to be emphasized. The last mentioned is particularly problematic as studies suggest that moderate water flows and normal seasonal flooding enhance productivity, although prolonged flooding supresses it. Somewhere between this ecosystem level and the global level is the chemical function of assimilation and moderation of human and farming wastes (fertilizers). Finally, wetlands may have an ultimate and unquantifiable function – that of atmospheric stability and global life support.

Table 1.11 A hierarchical schema of wetland values ranked chronologically and by scale

		Economic value (% of total)	
Hierarchy	*Functions/values*	*Market*	*Extended (internalized)*
Population level	1 Fish and wildlife	100%	5%
Ecosystem level	2 Hydrological		
	3 Productivity		
Global level	4 Waste assimilation	0%	100%
	5 Atmospheric		
	6 Life support		

Source: Odum 1979, p. 17

The problem of summing these benefits is not easily solved unless possibly (a) energy and water flows between the component parts are analysed and quantified, (b) a scaling and weighting approach is adopted and arbitrary values are assigned to maximum functions, e.g. perfect control of water quality would qualify for 100 per cent, or (c) a replacement value approach is adopted in which the loss of a 'free' service is costed (for example, how much would it cost to replace the tertiary treatment function of a large river or wetland?)

(Westman 1977). As before, in all these three alternatives there is a problem in looking at one isolated wetland and evaluating its functions and values without realizing that it is part of a larger whole. Odum's schema mobilizes knowledge and approximates to the realities of the situation as perceived by those engaged in wetland studies, but it does not solve the problem of comparative assessment.

Finally, in the light of the absence of the success of quantified schemes of comparative assessment two practical and fairly rapidly applied assessment methods have been suggested and tested, the Ontario and the FWHA/Adamus schemes. The Ontario method was begun in 1981 as a response to the need to evaluate and make an inventory of provincial wetlands which were experiencing heavy loss. In this on-site assessment scheme values are grouped into biological, social, hydrological and special features components and each is given a theoretical maximum of 250 points. The four major components have 17 major subcomponents and 48 minor subcomponents. The wetlands are then divided into seven classes on the basis of the total scores assigned and thus given preservation priorities. Inevitably the scoring has a heavy subjective element within it and varies according to the observer. Nevertheless it does give a *relative* value for each wetland that is claimed is 'both highly objective and reproducible' (Glooschenko et al. 1988).

The Adamus method is another rapid assessment method designed for professional engineers, botanists etc. who have to make rapid decisions 'within a few hours' on comparative functions, and therefore values, with an eye to preservation or allowing development. It is not based on weights and scores like the Ontario method but on 'logical word sequences' in which a series of questions are asked about the wetland's watershed, topography, vegetation and other features, and the answers are ranked on a three-point scale of high, moderate and low. There are five levels of enquiry (Adamus 1988); (a) a rapid assessment based on topographical maps, (b) a deeper assessment based on topographical maps and air photographs and (c) a more accurate assessment based on a one-hour visit to the site; (d) and (e) have not yet been developed.

Both methods have the virtues of simplicity, speed and the establishment of values in one wetland *vis-à-vis* another. Both methods have the disadvantages of subjectivity, and the problem of distinguishing precisely the wetland to be studied and/or the interrelationship of any one wetland with neighbouring wetlands.

Until these problems can be solved satisfactory wetland assessment will be an imprecise tool. Therefore it is clear that the investigation of the functions of wetlands, and consequently the placing of values on those functions so as to be better able to assess the likely result of impacts and make informed decisions about protection and preservation versus development, still has a long way to go.

2

Wetland Morphology, Hydrodynamics and Sedimentation

Antony R. Orme

1.0 INTRODUCTION

Wetlands are transitional environments. In a spatial context, they lie between dry land and open water – at the coast, around inland lakes and rivers or as mires draped across the landscape. In an ecological context, wetlands are intermediate between terrestrial and aquatic ecosystems. In a temporal context, most are destined either to evolve into dry land as a result of lowered water tables, sedimentation and plant succession, or to be submerged by rising water-tables associated with relative sea-level rise or climatic change. Geologically, individual wetlands are ephemeral features of the earth's surface, subject to change, although the stratigraphic record is replete with examples of past wetlands such as the Carboniferous coal swamps of Laurasia. Scale is important, however. Large wetlands change relatively slowly and may be perceived as permanent by the human eye, whereas small marshes may be erased by flooding or sedimentation during a single storm. Of particular significance in human terms, especially in this technological age, are the rates of change and the extent to which wetland change may be accentuated by human activity.

Wetlands are defined as biophysical flatlands or slopes with perennial water tables at or near the surface. Their foundations may lie upon poorly consolidated debris or on rocky substrate but, because their usually low energy environment favours accumulation, they soon acquire a cover of sand, mud or organic matter. In the following discussion, a broad distinction is made between coastal wetlands found in estuaries, lagoons, deltas and some open coasts, and interior wetlands found in riverine, lacustrine and palustrine environments whose only common denominator is a high water-table (table 2.1). In most respects this is also a distinction between salt-water and freshwater wetlands, except that in arid lands interior marshes are commonly saline, whereas estuarine wetlands respond to fresh, brackish and salt-water influences. The above definition may pose problems for some scientists. Many ecologists, for example, identify wetlands with the presence of distinctive hydrophytic vegetation and hydric soils. In deserts, however, coastal or interior wetlands may exist as sabkhas whose hypersaline waters wholly or largely inhibit plant life. On the coast, tidal and storm forces may inhibit plant

Table 2.1 Classification of wetlands by system, location, water properties and vegetation

System	*Location*	*Water regime*	*Water chemistry*[a]	*Vegetation type*
Coastal wetlands				
Marine	Open coast	Supratidal	Euhaline-mixohaline	Shrub wetland
		Intertidal	Euhaline	Salt marsh, mangrove
		Subtidal	Euhaline	Sea grass, algae
Estuarine	Coastal sabkha	Supratidal	Hyperhaline-mixohaline	Algae, barren sabkha
	Estuaries deltas lagoons	Supratidal	Mixohaline-fresh	Brackish-freshwater marsh, shrub wetland
		Intertidal	Euhaline-mixohaline	Salt marsh, mangrove
		Subtidal	Euhaline	Sea grass, algae
Interior wetlands				
Riverine	River channels	Perennial	Fresh	Aquatics, algae
		Intermittent		Aquatics, emergent wetland
		Ephemeral		Aquatics, emergent wetland
	Flood plains	Ephemeral or stagnant	Fresh	Emergent wetland, shrub and forest wetland
Lacustrine	Lakes lake deltas	Perennial >2 m deep	Fresh limnetic	Aquatics, algae
		Perennial-intermittent <2 m deep	Fresh littoral	Aquatics, emergent wetland, shrub/forest wetland
	Sabkhas	Ephemeral	Hypersaline-mixosaline	Algae, barren sabkha, some phreatophytes
Palustrine	Ponds	Perennial	Fresh littoral	Aquatics, algae
	Turloughs	Intermittent	Fresh	Aquatics, emergent wetland
	Lowland mires	High water tables	Fresh	Aquatics, *Sphagnum* moss, bog plants, emergent wetland, shrub wetland, forest wetland
	Upland mires	Perennial to ephemeral surface water		

[a]Halinity refers to ocean-derived salts and salinity to land-derived salts. The prefixes are defined in terms of parts per thousand salts as follows: hyper, >40‰; eu, 30–40‰; mixo, 0.5–30‰ (brackish); fresh, <0.5‰.

growth on tidal flats which might support extensive vegetation under more protected conditions elsewhere. Thus a simple physical definition is preferred. Therefore it follows that the limits of wetlands are found where saturated or periodically flooded terrain gives way to drier conditions. In vegetated wetlands, this limit will more or less coincide with the transition from hydrophytes and hydric soils to mesophytes or xerophytes and non-hydric soils.

2.0 SCIENTIFIC BACKGROUND

Wetlands have long been known to fishing, hunting and farming folk. The global rise of sea level after the last glacial maximum, the Flandrian transgression, undoubtedly imprinted itself on the minds of primitive coastal peoples and became embodied in their folklore. Likewise, the Holocene climatic changes which transformed lakes and shallow marshes into intractable bogs must have affected inland peoples, notably in northern Europe around 2500 years ago when climatic deterioration in the early Iron Age caused fresh peats to blanket Bronze Age landscapes. Wetlands were largely shunned by most people (though see chapter 5), at least until peat-cutters and then drainage engineers began to reclaim and thereby eliminate these environments, especially from the seventeenth century onwards.

The physical character of wetlands began to attract serious scientific attention in the seventeenth century. Gerard Boate (1652) classified Irish bogs in the seventeenth century, Dutch engineers were devising increasingly ambitious reclamation schemes and Russian scientists began seriously discussing the industrial uses of peat in the eighteenth century. By the early nineteenth century, the need for more agricultural land to feed the growing urban and industrial areas of Europe accentuated interest in wetland reclamation. In Scotland, Rennie (1807–10) and Aiton (1811) recognized the roles of water chemistry, plant succession and terrain in bog growth. Meanwhile, observations on the relationship between fresh and salt water in river mouths began paving the way towards an understanding of estuarine hydrodynamics. Major advances began after the middle of the century with the emergence of geomorphology, hydrology and sedimentology as discrete disciplines. Thereafter three phases of scientific enquiry are recognized: before 1950, between 1950 and 1970, and since 1970.

Before 1950 emphasis was on descriptive disciplinary studies rather than comprehensive approaches. This was a formative period during which many discoveries were made, classifications attempted and some misleading notions emerged. On the coast, formal studies of tidal flats were launched by Dutch and German scientists in the nineteenth century (Hagen 1863), with significant English language research coming later, for example in Kindle's (1917) analysis of ripple marks in the Bay of Fundy. The concept of the turbidity maximum was measured as early as 1893 in the Gironde estuary (Glangeaud 1939). Modern delta studies began with research on the Fraser River delta (Johnston 1921) and the Mississippi River delta (Trowbridge 1930, Russell 1936, Fisk 1944). Cross-disciplinary studies were at first rare, a notable exception being the combination of morphology and hydrodynamics in the delta studies of the Mississippi River survey of 1857–60 (Humphreys and Abbot 1861).

The late nineteenth and earlier twentieth centuries also witnessed major advances in the study of interior wetlands, first in northern Europe and then in North America. From the presence of tree stumps in peat bogs, Blytt (1876) divided Holocene time into climatic phases, thereby triggering a fascination between climate and wetland dynamics that still continues. Weber (1900) coined the term *Grenzhorizont* for the sharp boundary below the fresh *Sphagnum* peats initiated by climatic deterioration around 2500 BP. He was also among the first to use quantitative pollen analyses. Following European leads, Ganong (1897) studied the physical controls over bog growth in Canada, Clements (1916) examined plant succession in wetlands and the cyclic regeneration theory of peat bogs was developed. The complex relationship between location, hydrology, stratigraphy and flora of the Canadian muskeg was investigated (Lewis and Dowding 1926). Meanwhile, in eastern Europe the continuing interest in the industrial uses of peat led to the creation of several experimental peat stations in the early 1900s and to the opening of the first peat-fired power station in Russia, near Moscow, in 1915. Sukachev's (1914) classic work on mires provided the foundation for extensive work on wetlands in the 1920s and 1930s.

Following the Second World War, the second phase saw improved instrumentation lead to the accumulation of much empirical data. Two regions dominated research on coastal wetlands: the Gulf coast of the United States and the southern shores of the North Sea. Supported by improved coring and dating techniques, understanding of the Mississippi delta and the barrier-lagoon systems along the Gulf coast was refined, particularly regarding late Quaternary changes (Fisk and McFarlan 1955, Shepard 1956). In the Netherlands, wetland studies were stimulated by reclamations in the Ijsselmeer and by the Delta Plan in Zeeland. In the Wadden Sea, Van Veen (1950) was among the first to describe correctly the morphology of ebb and flood channels, while Van Straaten and Kuenen (1957) and others evaluated the role of lateral and vertical sedimentation in tidal flat morphology. The structure and development of tidal flats and salt marshes were described along the German and Danish coasts (Gierloff-Emden 1961, Reineck 1967), on Scolt Head Island (Steers 1960) and in the Wash (Evans 1965). In France, wetland studies focused on the upward growth of salt marshes (Guilcher and Berthois 1957), the evolution of the Rhone delta (Duboul-Razavet 1956) and the hydrodynamics and sedimentation of the Loire estuary (Berthois 1960). Following the leads of Godwin (1940, 1978) in the English fens and Jessen (1949) on Irish bogs, this phase also saw much attention given to wetland evolution using palynology, now aided by ^{14}C dating. Wetland ecology, especially water chemistry, also received much attention, but cross-disciplinary research was relatively rare.

The present phase of wetland research since about 1970 has seen the growth of specialization and cross-disciplinary studies in which morphology, hydrodynamics and sedimentation are interwoven. In the mid-1960s sedimentologists began relating sedimentary structures to flow dynamics (Middleton 1965,

Simons and Richardson 1966), just as geomorphologists began seriously examining the relationship between form and process (Leopold et al. 1964), and ecologists were examining more closely the relations between hydrology and plant distribution in wetlands (Ingram 1967, Romanov 1968). Two other changes also occurred. First, knowledge about wetlands distant from traditional research centres began to be widely disseminated, for example from the sabkhas of the arid tropics, the arctic regions of Canada and the USSR and the coastal wetlands of China. Secondly, resulting from this wider understanding, misleading notions began to be challenged or corrected. For example, owing to the plethora of early work, the Mississippi came to be regarded as having the typical delta. New studies elsewhere, as in the Orinoco (Van Andel 1967) and Niger (Oomkens 1974), now led to recognition of the wide variability of delta form and structure (Coleman and Wright 1975). Inland, the cyclic regeneration theory of bogs, the widely disseminated orthodoxy of the earlier twentieth century, has been discredited, the hummock-hollow morphology of bogs recognized as a chance occurrence and a phasic theory of bog growth based on wet and dry climatic phases postulated (Barber 1981).

Despite these advances, much remains to be discovered. For example, little is known about the functioning of wetland systems in tropical Africa, or in the Amazon basin where about 1×10^6 km^2 of mostly wet terrain lies within 100 m of sea level. Furthermore, problems of definition and classification continue to plague wetland studies. Thus, whereas wetlands may cover as much as 170×10^6 ha or 18 per cent of Canada, recent estimates of peatland have varied from 5.9×10^6 ha to 130×10^6 ha (Zoltai and Pollett 1983). Human interference with wetlands compounds the problem and creates a sense of urgency for further research. It is estimated that the United States had 51.4×10^6 ha of wetland in the mid-nineteenth century but has only 26.3×10^6 ha today (Goodwin and Niering 1975). Peat originally covered 1.3×10^6 ha or 16 per cent of Ireland but is now being removed at an accelerated rate.

The following discussion presents a cross-disciplinary perspective on the wetland as a physical system which seeks to emphasize commonalities rather than exceptions, while recognizing the distinction between coastal and interior wetlands and the wide variability inherent in these systems.

3.0 COASTAL WETLANDS

Coastal wetlands are unified as a system by low gradients, low wave energy, fine-grained sediments and pervasive salt-water influences. Such conditions are found in estuaries, lagoons, deltas and other inlets, and along open coasts protected by offshore barriers, coral reefs or wide tidal ramps. Tides are the most significant hydrodynamic influence because they determine the changing level of salt-water impact on water tables, freshwater outflows, erosion and sedimentation. The greater the tidal range along low gradient coasts, the wider are the intertidal wetlands, as seen around the British Isles, the Bay of Fundy and the Yellow Sea. Even along microtidal coasts, however, low gradients and high sedimentation rates may combine to produce extensive wetlands, for example in the deltas of the Mediterranean and around the Gulf of Mexico. Wave and current energy above critical threshold levels will inhibit wetland development, notably by restricting the stabilizing role of vegetation, while occasional storm surges may have a devastating impact on established wetlands.

3.1 *The Flandrian transgression and later sea-level changes*

The world's present coastal wetlands mostly originated with the culmination of the main Flandrian transgression some 5000 years ago. This transgression, caused by the melting of the ice sheets of the last glacial stage, was not spatially uniform because of the variable response of the earth's crust to loading by ice, water and sediment. Nevertheless, in general terms it began slowly around 18 000 BP, accelerated to an average rise in sea level of 10 m/1000 yr between 15 000 and 7000 BP, and then slowed. During the maximum transgression open coasts remained unstable and such wetlands as did develop were submerged or destroyed by subsequent high-energy conditions. Many bays and estuaries also remained open water because submergence rates far exceeded sedimentation rates. In more protected areas, however, the sedimentary record shows that wetlands formed during the transgression pass vertically upwards into modern wetlands at the present shoreline. The waning stages of the Flandrian transgression after 7000 BP and the relative sea-level changes of the past few thousand years are particularly relevant to an understanding of modern wetland dimensions.

Wetland deposits in the stratigraphic record have long been used to infer changing sea levels, as shown by Blytt's (1876) pioneering work on coastal peat bogs and Godwin's (1940) masterly studies of the English Fenlands. Recognizing that fen peats start to form on land as water-tables rise to the surface in response to rising sea-level, a large body of empirical data backed by ^{14}C dates now exists for the waning stages of the Flandrian transgression (plate 2.1) (e.g. Tooley 1978, Shennan 1983). In the English Fenlands such evidence indicates five phases of positive sea-level tendencies and four phases of negative tendencies before 2500 BP.

On broad continental shelves off modern barrier-island coasts, tidal flats and vegetated wetlands of late Pleistocene and early Holocene age are found buried beneath the transgressive deposits of the very barriers behind which they had formed (Leatherman 1983). On the Delmarva Peninsula, eastern United States, the Holocene barrier-lagoon sequence shows basal freshwater marsh, followed by salt marsh peats and lagoonal muds, and finally by sediments of the transgressing barrier beach (Kraft et al. 1973). This vertical transgressive sequence is identical with the horizontal sequence in the direction of the transgression (figure 2.1). Similarly, along the New England coast, freshwater peats occur along the inner margins of the modern tidal marsh but farther seaward lie at depths of 10–15 m and are overlain successively by estuarine muds, mid-tide salt-marsh peats and high-tide salt-grass peats.

Plate 2.1 Peat of Holocene 'submerged forest' in the intertidal zone, Hartlepool, northeast England
(Courtesy A. R. Orme)

As the main transgression waned after 7000 BP, sedimentation rates began to exceed the sea's ability to submerge or remove these deposits, and the open water of estuaries and lagoons began to constrict (plate 2.2). In Connecticut, where the average submergence rate from 7000 to 3000 BP was 1.2 m/1000 yr but has declined to 0.85 m/1000 yr over the past 3000 years, the decrease in the submergence rate coincided with a change from open muddy estuaries to tidal wetlands (Bloom 1964). Similar changes in the submergence-to-sedimentation

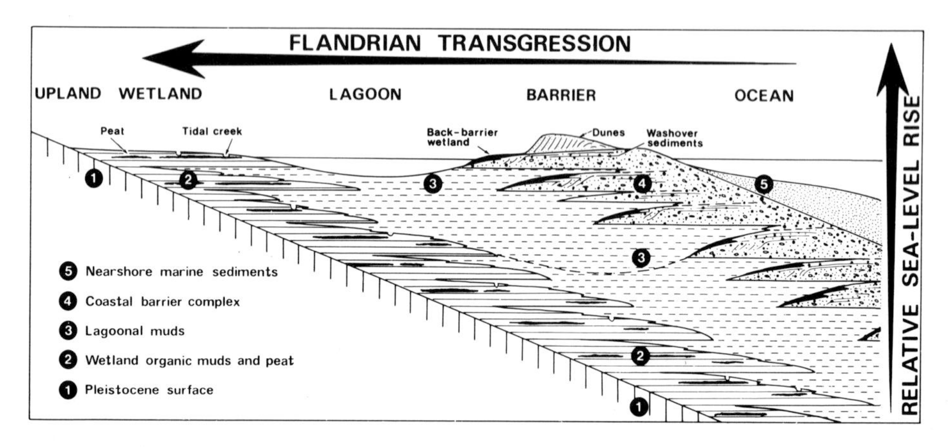

Figure 2.1 Schematic diagram showing how a relative rise of sea level against a sloping surface produces a vertical barrier-lagoon-wetland sequence that is identical with the horizontal sequence in the direction of the transgression

ratio are documented throughout the Atlantic coast of the United States during later Holocene times (Belknap and Kraft 1977).

Lake St Lucia along the southeast coast of Africa is a good example of an open lagoon created by the Flandrian transgression which has since been largely transformed into wetland. Immediately after the main transgression, this lagoon covered 912 km^2 and continued south into the 253 km^2 Mfolozi lagoon (Orme 1975). These lagoons together formed a water body measuring 1165 km^2 in area, 112 km long and up to 40 m deep. Today, after at least 5000 years of sedimentation, segmentation and reed swamp encroachment, aided by recent human activity, Mfolozi lagoon no longer exists and Lake St Lucia has been reduced to a shallow lagoon averaging 312 km^2 in area, 40 km long and less than 2 m deep (figure 2.2).

Whereas coastal wetlands have been favoured by approaching sea-level stability over the past 7000 years, they have continued to be modified by modest sea-level changes attributable to isostatic forces, subsidence and continued or renewed eustatic influences. Certainly hydro-isostatic loading of continental shelves continued after the main transgression and may explain, in part, the modest continuing rise of sea level at the coast over the past 7000 years.

Plate 2.2 Slapton Sands, Devon, England: a Flandrian barrier-lagoon-wetland system formed across the submerged mouths of several small streams
(Courtesy A. R. Orme)

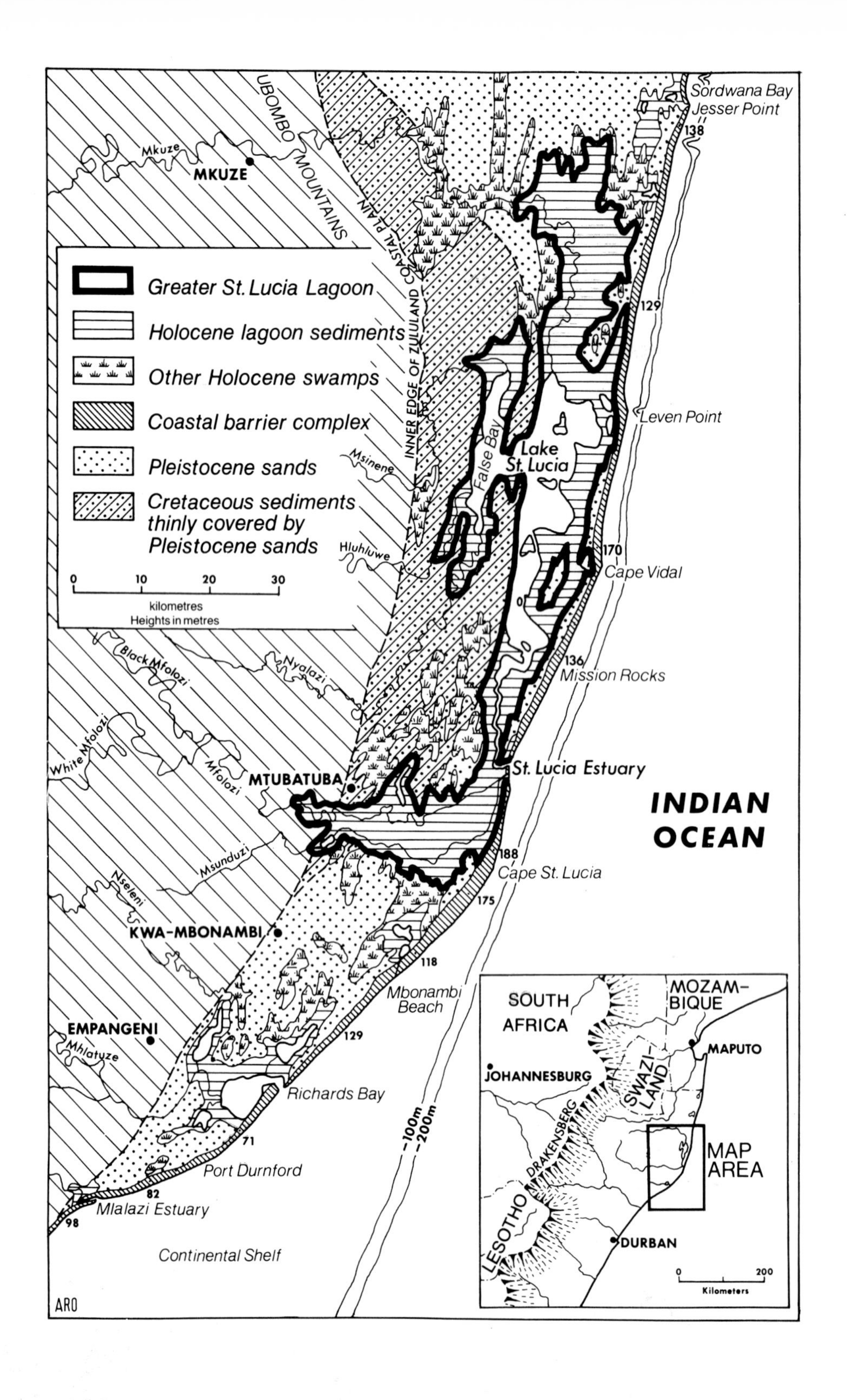
Greater St. Lucia Lagoon
Holocene lagoon sediments
Other Holocene swamps
Coastal barrier complex
Pleistocene sands
Cretaceous sediments thinly covered by Pleistocene sands
0 10 20 30
kilometres
Heights in metres
UBOMBO MOUNTAINS
INNER EDGE OF ZULULAND COASTAL PLAIN
Mkuze
MKUZE
Sordwana Bay
Jesser Point
138
129
Leven Point
False Bay
Lake St. Lucia
Msinene
Hluhluwe
170
Cape Vidal
0
136
Mission Rocks
Black Mfolozi
Nyalazi
White Mfolozi
Mfolozi
MTUBATUBA
St. Lucia Estuary
INDIAN OCEAN
Msunduzi
188
Cape St. Lucia
175
Nseleni
KWA-MBONAMBI
118
Mbonambi Beach
EMPANGENI
Mhlatuze
129
Richards Bay
-100m
-200m
71
Port Durnford
82
Mlalazi Estuary
98
Continental Shelf
ARO
SOUTH AFRICA
MOZAMBIQUE
MAPUTO
JOHANNESBURG
SWAZILAND
DRAKENSBERG
MAP AREA
LESOTHO
DURBAN
0 200
Kilometers

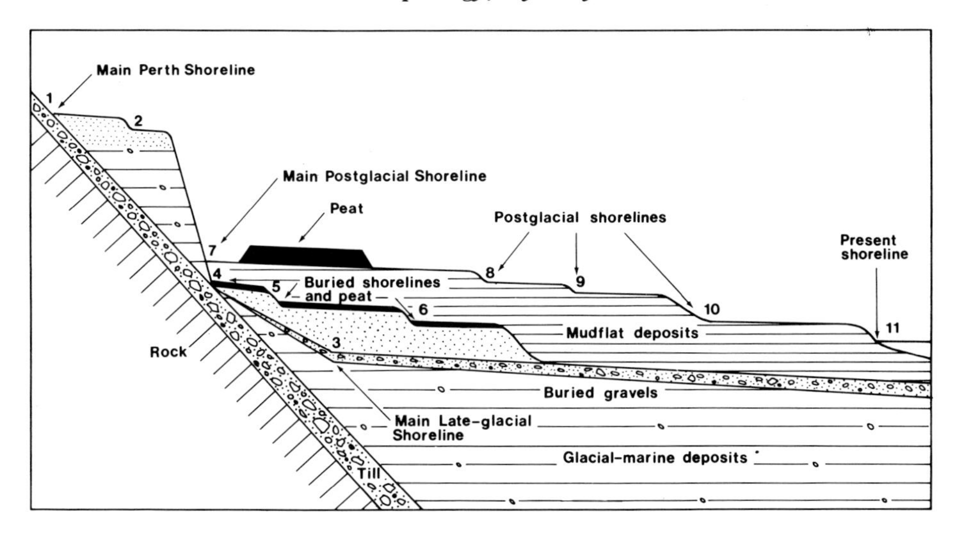

Figure 2.3 Schematic diagram showing emplacement and subsequent isostatic uplift of Holocene mudflats into carselands, Firth of Forth, Scotland. The numbers refer to the shoreline sequence. Shorelines 1, 2 and 3 formed along the isostatically emerging coast as Pleistocene glaciers fluctuated farther west. Shorelines 4, 5 and 6, formed between 10 300 and 8600 BP, were buried by mudflats during the Flandrian transgression to shoreline 7 around 6800 BP. As the transgression waned, isostatic uplift raised the mudflats which were then trimmed by regressive postglacial shorelines 8, 9 and 10
(after Sissons 1983)

In formerly glaciated areas such as northern Europe and Canada, isostatic rebound has had a significant impact on wetland development. In these areas the complex relationship between eustasy and isostasy during the Flandrian trangression produced an interfingering of terrestrial, wetland and marine environments. In areas, such as southwest Norway where the trangression continued after or was faster than isostatic rebound, freshwater wetlands were transformed into salt marsh or reed swamp before complete inundation (Hafsten 1983). In other areas, where isostatic rebound continued after the main transgression, wetlands were raised above sea level to form interior bogs or dry land. In this way wetlands around Hudson Bay and the Gulf of Bothnia were raised as steps behind emergent beach ridges, and relict mud flats in southeast Scotland were transformed into broad carselands. Radiometric dating of emergent wetlands gives a useful measure of the timing of both the transgression and isostatic uplift which, for example, indicates that the Scottish carselands were above sea level by 6600 BP (figure 2.3) (Sissons 1983).

Subsidence occurs in many coastal areas in response to regional tectonism or sediment loading and compaction. Around the Mississippi delta these forces

Figure 2.2 Lake St Lucia, South Africa: a 1165 km^2 Flandrian lagoon reduced by sedimentation, segmentation and reed swamp encroachment to 312 km^2
(Orme 1975)

combine to aggravate wetland loss (Walker et al. 1987). Geosynclinal subsidence of Mississippi depocentres is linked to active fault systems that parallel the Gulf coast and to flowage of thick salt deposits at depth beneath the delta. The problem is compounded by dewatering under sustained loads, particle rearrangement under compression and decomposition of organic matter. Because high depositional rates may yield sediments more than 100 m thick in the 1000–1500 years it takes for delta-lobe progradation, compaction processes and wetland subsidence may continue after the location of delta deposition has changed. If we ignore global sea-level rise for the moment, compaction and subsidence on the Louisiana coast presently amount to 1.49 cm/yr, significantly larger than the vertical accretion rate of marsh deposits of 0.60–0.75 cm/yr (DeLaune et al. 1978).

Crustal subsidence caused by sediment loading is found in most large deltas while compaction occurs wherever soft sediments are deposited rapidly. However, whereas such forces cause wetlands to be lost to the sea, they may also create new wetlands farther inland as shown by the later Holocene evolution of the Dutch coast where subsidence is now only 0.015–0.025 cm/yr (Jelgersma 1979). In contrast, regional tectonic uplift may form extensive intertidal areas on former subtidal deposits, as appears to have happened in the northern Spencer Gulf, South Australia, since 1700 BP.

Over the past 5000 years, periodic marine transgressions have continued to occur but, owing to regional variations and a lack of reliable baselines, it is not clear whether these are pulses in a lingering Flandrian rise or independent events. Some historic transgressions have had a dramatic impact on wetlands, mainly because quite small changes of sea level are influential along low coasts. For example, a transgression in the southern North Sea between AD 500 and AD 1350, possibly related to both subsidence and global warming, eventually breached a more or less continuous coastal barrier from Denmark to the Netherlands, isolating the Frisian Islands and creating extensive wetlands around the Wadden Sea. Deposition of the youngest intertidal deposits in The Wash also began around this time (Evans 1965). After a late medieval pause, transgression recommenced in north Germany in the sixteenth century (Rohde 1978), but was deferred to the early nineteenth century in Sweden where between 1850 and 1970 the eustatic rise averaged 1 mm/yr (Morner 1973). Along the Atlantic and Gulf coasts of the United States, wetland areas have been halved over the past century, partly as a result of human activity which makes it difficult to discern the effects of sea-level rise. However, ^{210}Pb dating suggests that in Chesapeake Bay net accretion rates of 1.7–3.6 mm/yr have not kept pace with a sea-level rise of 3.9 mm/yr since 1940, thus explaining widespread recent wetland losses (Stevenson et al. 1985).

It is this most recent rise of sea level that most concerns modern wetland studies. Estimates of the eustatic rise over the past century obtained using tide-gauge data and compensating for local earth movements vary from 1 to 4 mm/yr (Gornitz et al. 1982). Projections for future sea-level rise are tied to evaluations of the greenhouse effect, i.e. the impact of increased CO_2 and other gases and particulates on atmospheric temperature and thereby on glacier melting and ocean level. One estimate suggests a global rise of sea level of 1.44–2.17 m by AD 2100, with a possible rise as high as 3.45 m with major regional variations (Hoffman et al. 1983). The probable effect is that while lower wetlands will be lost to the sea, their inner margins will be extended by transgressive tidal influences and rising water-tables. More dramatically where protective barrier islands are breached by rising seas, the wetlands behind them will be eroded or smothered with washover sands.

The combined influences of eustatic, isostatic and tectonic forces on wetland growth are well illustrated in central California. The sea entered San Francisco Bay through the Golden Gate about 11 000–10 000 years ago, and the relative sea level rose at a rate of 2 cm/yr (20 m/1000 yr) and spread laterally inland as rapidly as 30 m/yr until 8000 BP (Atwater et al. 1977). Freshwater marshes were replaced by marine sediments, and tidal marshes were confined to the margins of the open bay. The rate of rise then declined tenfold from 8000 to 6000 BP, and has averaged 0.1–0.2 cm/yr (1–2 m/1000 yr) from 6000 BP to the present. The earlier rate greatly exceeded the sedimentation rate but, as the submergence rate declined, tidal flats and salt marshes prograded into the bay (figure 2.4). Holocene salt marsh deposits have undergone about 5 m of tectonic and possible isostatic subsidence over the past 6000 years – a rate of about 0.08 mm/yr superimposed onto the eustatic effect. Subsidence is even more pronounced along the San Andreas fault zone as it passes through the wetlands of nearby Bolinas Lagoon (Berquist 1978) (figure 2.4).

3.2 *Zonation and morphology*

Coastal wetlands occur typically in the intertidal zone, but reach into the supratidal zone in storm-wave and very low gradient environments while their sedimentary foundations lie in the subtidal zone. Mean high water (MHW) is often used to distinguish between upper and lower wetlands. Coastal wetlands are also defined in terms of salt marsh or mangrove swamp zonation, notably where these emergent communities cover the tidal range (plate 2.3). However, the presence or absence of vegetation is not a good basis for zonation because many wetlands are partly or wholly typified by tidal flats, barren except for algae, which may never acquire a vegetation cover. Further, along arid and semi-arid coasts tidal flats often merge inland with supratidal sabkhas whose hypersaline ground-waters discourage plant growth.

Wetland dimensions reflect both tidal range and coastal gradient. Along macrotidal coasts, where the spring tidal range varies from 4 to 20 m, wetlands are often extensive. The Yellow Sea, where spring tides range over 5 m, is flanked by tidal flats up to 25 km wide. The mesotidal North Sea, with spring tidal ranges of 2–4 m, has extensive marginal wetlands which cover 60 per cent of the Wadden Sea in tidal flats and salt marshes from 3 to 35 km wide and, except for subtidal creeks, channels and estuaries, some 500 km long (figure 2.5). In microtidal areas, with spring tidal ranges of less than 2 m, wetlands are usually less extensive except where coastal gradients are low, as in various Mediterranean deltas and along the Gulf coast of the United States. In these

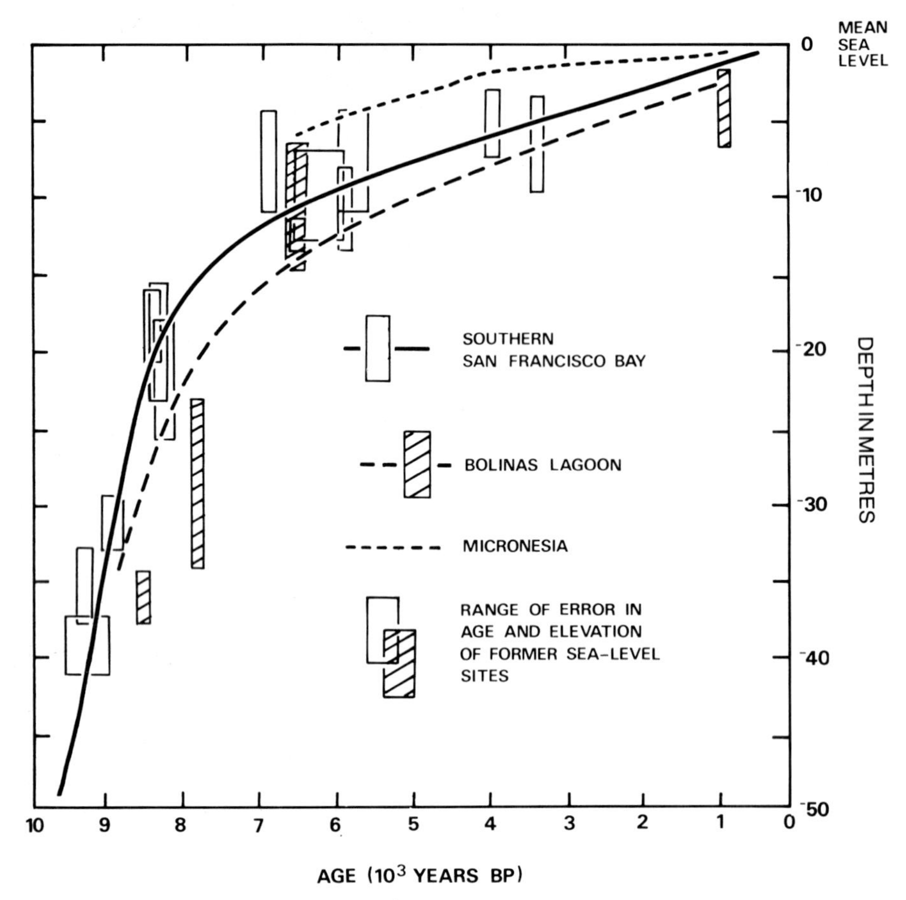

Figure 2.4 Holocene sea-level changes in southern San Francisco Bay and Bolinas Lagoon, California. Based on radiocarbon-dated wetland vegetation, the curves demonstrate tectonic and possible isostatic subsidence when measured against eustatic sea-level change in Micronesia
(after Atwater et al. 1977, Berquist 1978)

areas sea-level fluctuations caused by wind-forcing or storm surges are more important than tidal range, but wetland responses are similar. Coastal gradient also explains why extensive wetlands occur along the low-lying Atlantic coast of the United States whereas there are few large wetlands along the steep Pacific coast.

In terms of morphology, tidal flats and vegetated wetlands share certain similarities, such as low average slopes between 0.05° and 1°, but show many differences. Tidal flats extend with little relief from supratidal flats, characterized by dessication cracks and wrinkled algal mats, across low intertidal slopes, typified by various bedforms both parallel and perpendicular to the shore, to the steeper subtidal zone (figure 2.6). Bedforms are a distinguishing feature of tidal flats; their development in vegetated wetlands is inhibited by plant baffling. In the sand-dominated tidal flats of the Bay of Fundy, where the

Plate 2.3 Mugu Lagoon, Ventura County, California, November 1946. The wetlands lie behind a sandy barrier beach breached by a tidal inlet seen here discharging into the ocean at low tide. The spring tidal range is 3 m. The sandy subtidal channels contain *Zostera marina* and *Ruppia maritima*. They are flanked by bare low flats and low marsh dominated by *Spartina foliosa* and *Salicornia virginica*. The high marsh is floristically more varied and contains salt pans
(Courtesy Fairchild Collection, University of California, Los Angeles)

spring tidal range is 16 m and current velocities are correspondingly swift, tidal currents generate extensive megaripples and sand waves (Knight and Dalrymple 1975). Low-amplitude permanent sand ridges have been observed on tidal flats on Vancouver Island (Hale and McCann 1982), while persistent mud ridges parallel to the tidal currents are known elsewhere.

In cold regions such as the Canadian Arctic, ice gouging, ice rafting and ice melt processes play an important role in determining the morphological, sedimentological and biological zonation of tidal flats (McCann and Dale 1986). Fractured sediment-laden ice on tidal flats breaks up in late spring and ablates rapidly at a time when offshore ice is still in place. This produces a short dynamic phase of sediment transport and redistribution within the intertidal

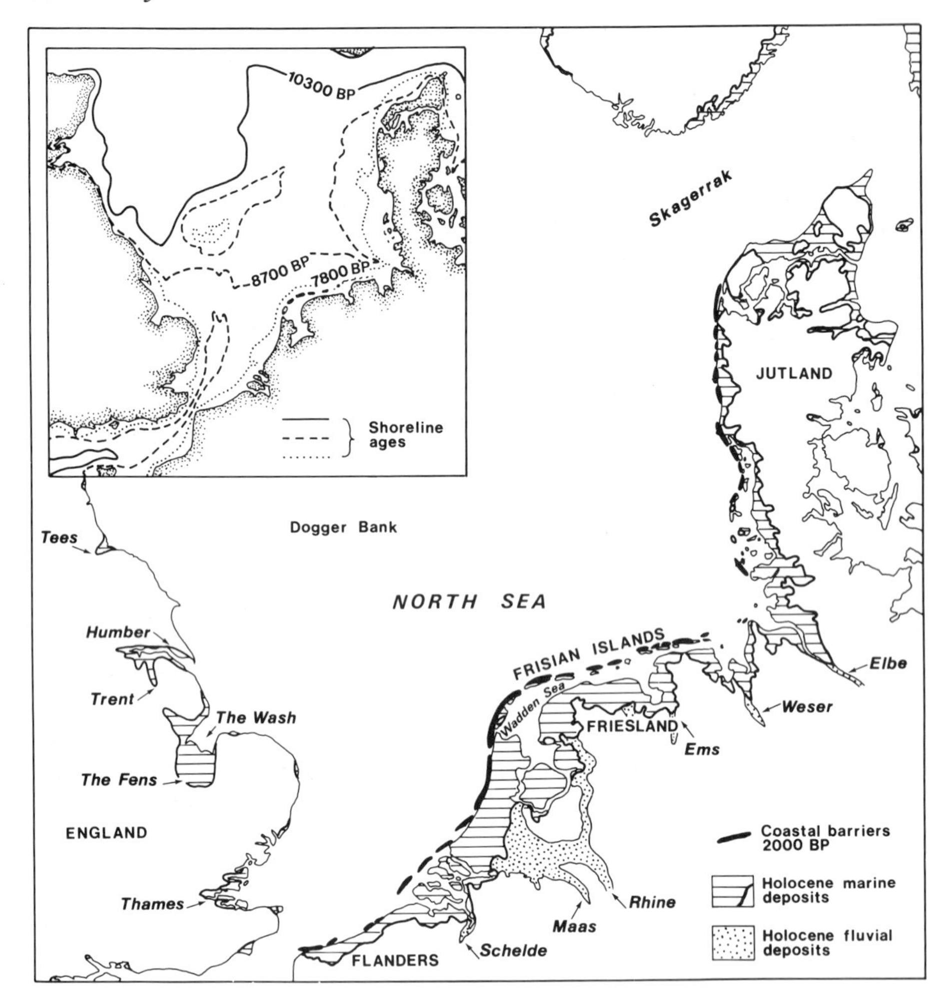

Figure 2.5 Maximum (non-synchronous) extent of the North Sea during later Holocene time and (inset) the earlier Holocene progress of the Flandrian transgression. By 5000 BP, with sea level only 5 m below present, coastal barriers near the present coast combined with decelerating sea-level rise to promote extensive wetland development, with intertidal and fluvial deposits and peat accumulating on shallow marine sediments behind the barriers (after Jelgersma 1979, and others)

zone, with sediment loading measured at over 63 000 t/km^2 in one study on Baffin Island. In the St Lawrence Estuary, drift ice has been observed to gouge furrows 20–40 cm deep and up to 2 km long, and basins up to 40 cm deep and 2 m wide, during the spring thaw (Dionne 1969). Mud-boils up to 20 cm high and 25 cm across are formed by the upward expulsion of fluidized mud under pressure from overlying sediments and accumulating ice. Flowslides are probably important tidal-flat modifiers in most climatic regimes, having been observed on slopes as low as 0.03°–0.08° along the northeast coast of South America (Wells et al. 1980).

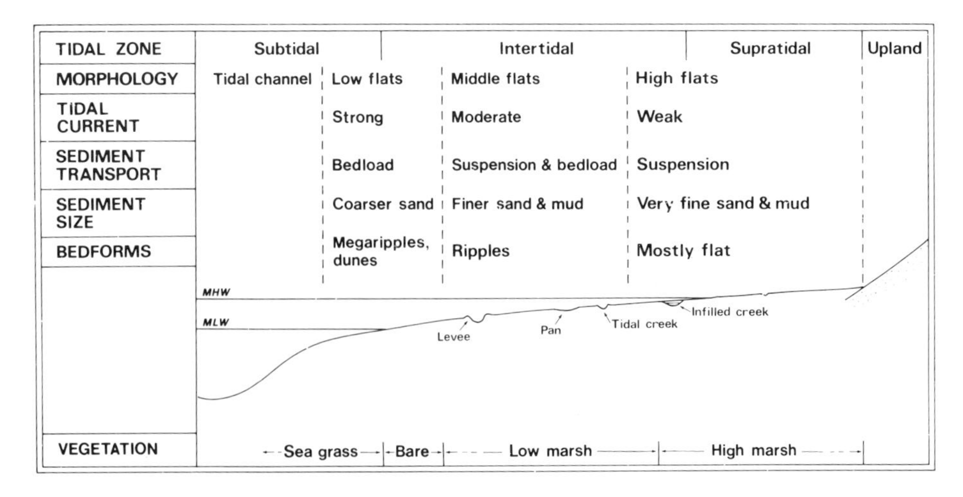

Figure 2.6 Zonation of a coastal wetland

Tidal flats are amenable to zonation based on the duration of tidal influence and its effect on current velocities, sediment characteristics, bedforms and surface morphology. High flats are inundated for the shortest time, more or less coincident with slack water, and are dominated by muds that settle from suspension and generate little reflief. Middle flats experience longer inundation, thereby ensuring both bedload and suspension deposition, the interfingering of mud and sand, and modest bedforms. Low flats are inundated longest during a tidal cycle, experience the swiftest bottom currents and thus dominant bedload sedimentation, causing sandy sediment to be fashioned into megaripples, dunes and sand waves. Thus tidal flats can be zoned as mud flats, mixed flats and sand flats, with relief and bedform size increasing seaward as tidal current velocities increase and sediments coarsen.

The development of salt marshes and mangrove swamps is favoured by the more passive hydrodynamic and net depositional conditions of the higher intertidal zone and nearby supratidal flats. Relatively long quiescence and subaerial exposure between tidal cycles favours plant growth and restricts surface relief. Under sheltered conditions, these communities may extend throughout the intertidal zone. Many factors are involved in the development of vegetated wetlands, including climate, sediment composition, relief, hydrodynamics and overall coastal stability, so that the following generalizations should be treated with care.

Salt marshes can be divided into low marsh and high marsh (plate 2.4). The low marsh, usually the younger more active sedimentary environment below MHW, is flooded more or less daily and is usually dominated by one genus, such as *Spartina* which is particularly characteristic of low marshes around the Atlantic rim. *Spartina* may extend throughout the intertidal zone, to be replaced in the subtidal zone by sea grasses such as the ubiquitous *Zostera* and the warmer-water *Thalassia*, *Posidonia* and *Syringodium*, all of which help to

Plate 2.4 Tidal creeks and channels in the *Salicornia*-dominated high salt marsh, Morro Bay, California
(Courtesy A. R. Orme)

trap sediments. The high marsh, straddling the intertidal-supratidal boundary above MHW, is floristically more varied, in part because longer exposure allows fresh ground-water and precipitation to dilute salt water. Halophytes such as *Salicornia*, *Distichlis* and, more poleward, *Puccinellia* are common, with *Phragmites* along the landward margins. The transition towards brackish and freshwater marsh is associated with *Juncus*, *Typha*, *Scirpus* and *Cyperus*. The above plant zonation may imply succession or marsh maturation in a prograding environment, or it may simply be environmental adaptation. In Baja California, for example, *Spartina foliosa* extends farthest seaward but is more or less coextensive with *Salicornia virginica* and *Salicornia subterminalis* (figure 2.7).

In tropical and subtropical areas, mangrove swamps show similar zonation and the higher intertidal zone is again favoured because seeds are more readily established in muddy substrates of sheltered low energy areas (plate 2.5). In general, plants with breathing roots, such as *Avicennia* and *Sonneratia*, which have vertical respiratory roots or pneumatophores, and the stilt-rooted *Rhizophora*, *Bruguiera*, *Ceriops* and *Lumnitzera*, grow in the intertidal zone, occasionally to mean low water (MLW). Mangroves without breathing roots, such as *Conocarpus*, grow to landward. Mangroves are killed when temperatures

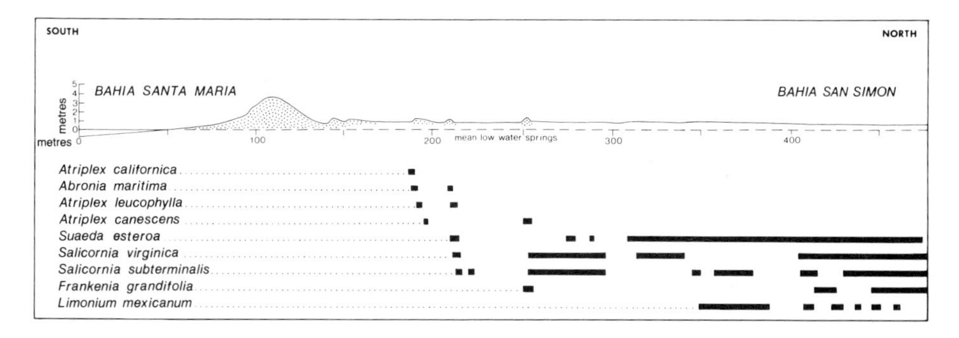

Figure 2.7 Transect across a coastal salt marsh, Baja California, Mexico. *Salicornia* and *Suaeda* dominate the marsh behind a bare sandy barrier but hummocks of blown sand are being colonized by other plants
(after Orme 1973)

below −3°C persist during the reproductive cycle and are best developed where mean temperatures for the coldest month exceed 16°C and the seasonal range does not exceed 5°C. Because stilt-rooted mangroves are less tolerant to cold than pneumatophore plants, *Avicennia* is a common pioneer in sandy substrates towards the poleward limits of mangrove growth, for example, in the northern Red Sea. In warmer areas such as the southern Red Sea, *Rhizophora* normally precedes *Avicennia* as a pioneer of organic muds. In Malaysia, *Avicennia* and *Sonneratia* pioneer mid-tidal aras, followed inland by extensive *Rhizophora*, with *Bruguiera* occurring only in areas flooded by spring tides. Mangrove swamps tend to be most extensive in the humid tropics and become progressively restricted through subhumid and semi-arid zones, until they form only narrow fringes along most arid coasts. Salt marshes and mangrove swamps are not mutually exclusive. In the Red Sea, for example, representatives of both communities live together. However, as the mangrove canopy closes over, salt marsh plants decline.

The morphology of salt marshes and mangrove swamps is subtle, measurable in decimetres, but even small changes in elevation are important to plants. The highest areas are levees formed by overbank deposition alongside tidal creeks. Levees may rise 30 cm or more above the surrounding marsh. In contrast, low areas are often characterized by salt pans – bare areas inherited from tidal flats or abandoned channels (Yapp et al. 1917) or possibly attributable to marsh collapse caused by subsurface piping (Kesel and Smith 1978). Salt marshes also experience episodic wave erosion that forms low cliffs, 0.5–2.0 m high, whose form is maintained by the intricate roots of marsh plants. Marsh cliffs have been attributed to the effects of sea-level change, but they are more likely to be intrinsic features of vegetated wetlands.

In vegetated and bare wetlands alike, tidal creeks interrupt surface continuity, providing access for the flood tide and a drainage network for the ebb. On tidal flats of macrotidal coasts, the creek system is often composed of numerous relatively straight steep channels perpendicular to the shoreline. With lower tidal ranges and more vegetation, complex dendritic networks

Plate 2.5 *Avicennia marina* dominates these mangrove wetlands along the Saudi Arabian coast of the Red Sea, south of Jedda, lying both on the landward side of the emergent coral reefs and along the distant mainland shore
(Courtesy A. R. Orme)

develop with small finger-tip tributaries forming in the high flats where tidal velocities are least, and progressively higher-order channels forming downslope until the largest creeks erode well below mean sea level (MSL). The main tidal channel near Den Helder at the west end of the Wadden Sea is entrenched 40 m below MLW and has mean surface tidal velocities of 1.9 m/s. Network growth is most rapid on bare tidal flats and slows as plant stems and roots of a developing vegetation cover retard lateral and vertical migration. Nevertheless, the drainage network of tidal marsh networks may reach 10 km/km^2, significantly higher than fine-grained terrestrial drainage densities of around 1 km/km^2. This greater density must reflect both the larger and more frequent water cover found on wetlands and the bidirectional flow regime.

Tidal creeks change through time by lateral migration in much the same way as do rivers, with erosion and bank collapse along outside meander bends and point-bar progradation. In tidal creeks in salt marshes on Sapelo Island, Georgia, erosion accomplished by tidal current scour, slumping and decapod bio-erosion caused lateral migration that ranged from 0.68 to 4.44 m/yr (Letzsch and Frey 1980). In another study, however, tidal creeks have revealed higher meander amplitudes but lower lateral migration rates (0.21 m/yr from 1940 to 1972) than freshwater channels (0.32 m/yr), which may be due either to compositional and vegetational variables (Garofalo 1980) or to the peculiarities of reversing tidal currents. Creek dimensions tend to reflect tidal range and tidal current velocities, with channels several metres deep common to macrotidal coasts. Channel form also reflects sediment size, with impermeable muds conducive to surface flow more likely than permeable sands to preserve well-defined channels. Plants with extensive root networks, like *Salicornia*, are also more likely to preserve steep banks against scour, although such banks are more prone to slumping. Water flowing into creeks from the higher flats during the ebb also promotes rapid headward erosion, which in turn encourages creek piracy.

The relative importance of different morphological components varies greatly with local conditions. In southern California, for example, the 476 ha intertidal area of Mugu Lagoon comprises 80.3 per cent salt marsh, 6.5 per cent salt pans, 10.9 per cent tidal flats and 2.3 per cent tidal creeks. In the 365 ha of wetlands in the Tijuana estuary, 250 km to the southeast, salt marsh comprises 58.4 per cent, salt pans 6.8 per cent and tidal flats and creeks 34.8 per cent.

3.3 *Hydrodynamics of wetland initiation*

Since coastal wetlands are situated at the interface between terrestrial and marine environments, their hydrodynamics are understandably complex. The most important influences are tides, waves, currents, river discharge and ground-water seepage, all of which vary considerably in space and time. Seasonal variations in river discharge, for example, affect stratification, circulation, sedimentation, nutrient levels, dissolved oxygen and other important properties of wetlands. Because of low gradients, surface wind stress and meteorological forcing of coastal waters also have a major impact on water levels. During Hurricane Camille in August 1969, low barometric pressure and winds of over 200 km/h drove water levels to 5.2 m above MSL in the normally microtidal Mississippi delta, causing extensive damage to salt marshes although regrowth was rapid and returned to pre-hurricane levels within a year. The effects of Hurricane Gilbert in September 1988, when barometric pressure plunged to 861 mbar and winds gusted to 282 km/h in the Caribbean and Gulf of Mexico, were similarly dramatic. Cyclones in the Indian Ocean and typhoons along the coasts of eastern Asia may be likewise disastrous to coastal wetlands, but the latter often show great resilience. The interdependence of ground-water and vegetation is also important: water uptake by roots lowers water-tables, causing aeration of sediments which in turn influences plant vigour. Above all, implicit in these influences on wetland development is the relationship between fresh water and salt water, for this affects both the physical character of wetlands, notably through hydrodynamics and sedimentation, and the relative importance of salt-water and freshwater organisms.

Because of the density contrast between fresh water ($\rho \approx 1.00$ g/cm^3), and salt water ($\rho \approx 1.025$ g/cm^3), these two fluids tend to maintain separate identities with the denser salt water overlain by fresh water. In the absence of currents, mixing of these two water masses is limited to the upward flux of salt water by diffusion processes and the vertical advection of salt water by upward-breaking internal waves at the sharp interface. With currents present, mixing becomes more efficient and the interface is broken up by advection. Pritchard (1955, 1967) classified estuarine hydrodynamics based on density contrasts and the relative importance of diffusion and advection. He recognized three types of estuary – highly stratified, partially stratified and vertically homogeneous. A highly stratified estuary has its river discharge separated from a landward-thinning wedge of salt water by a sharp boundary layer along which vertical advection of salt water dominates (figure 2.8). In a partially stratified estuary, tidal influences encourage turbulence and the mixing of river discharge and salt water across a less distinct boundary layer. In a vertically homogeneous estuary, tidal currents are sufficiently swift to erase density contrasts and water halinity is vertically constant as it diminishes upstream. The landward limit of

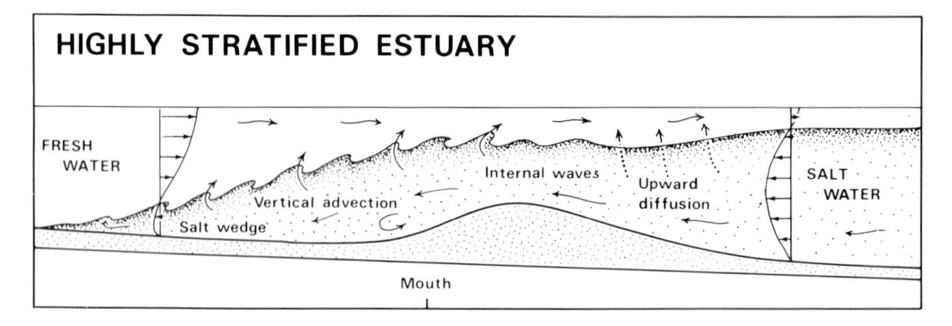

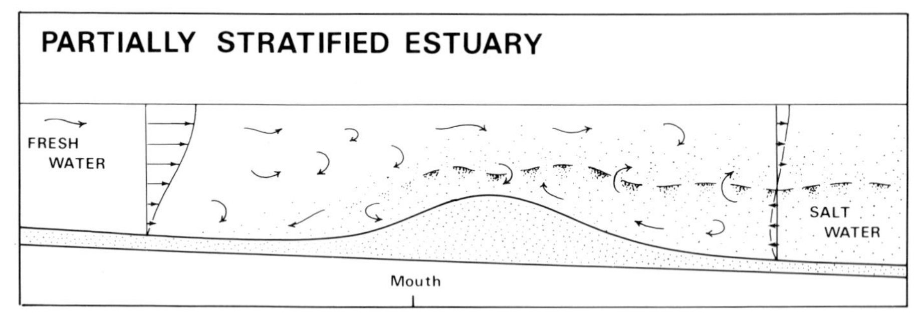

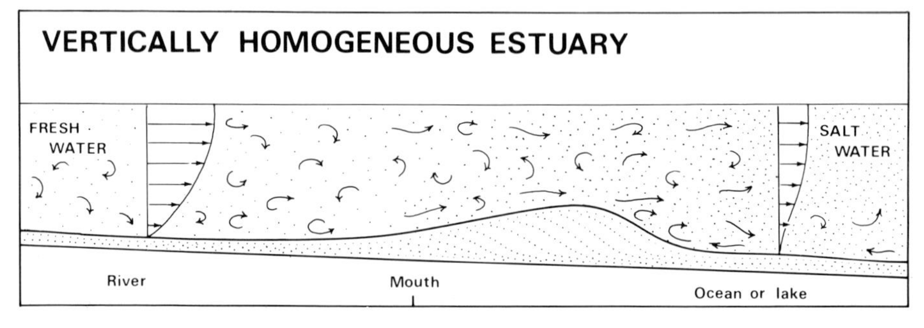

Figure 2.8 Hydrodynamics of river-dominated estuaries, reflecting the spectrum of interactions between salt water and fresh water. Relative velocity profiles and loci of maximum deposition (bars) are also shown

estuaries can be defined as where total halinity falls below 0.5 parts per thousand. The above scheme is really a continuum whose end members – highly stratified and vertically homogeneous estuaries – are comparatively rare. Furthermore, some partially mixed estuaries actually oscillate between stratified and homogeneous conditions on a fortnightly cycle that correlates with neap and spring tides respectively, for example, several Virginia estuaries (Haas 1977) and the Aune and Gironde estuaries (Allen et al. 1980). The three-dimensional circulations of wetlands also suggests that a two-dimensional perspective is oversimplified.

Estuarine circulations thus reflect the relative magnitudes of river discharge and tidal flux as influenced by the geometry of the system. Where tidal range and wave power are relatively small, river-dominated systems develop, typified by buoyant outflows and salt-wedge intrusion, or friction-dominated partially mixed outflows, or intertia-dominated vertically homogeneous outflows with fully turbulent jets (Wright 1977). Such conditions are found primarily along low-energy microtidal coasts, including many deltas. Where marine processes are significant, water and sediment discharged by rivers are soon redistributed by tides, waves, currents and, in Arctic waters, sea ice. Estuaries in arid lands may behave very differently because they lack freshwater flows for most of the year. In the Salum and Casamance estuaries in Senegal, tidal flows dominate and there is a net discharge upstream owing to massive evapotranspiration from mangrove swamps and tidal flats. Halinity thus increases inland, and ponded hyperhaline waters then produce a salt wedge directed downstream towards inflowing less haline sea water. This reverses normal geomorphic and sedimentary patterns (Barusseau et al. 1985).

The above considerations are relevant to wetlands because the hydro-dynamics involved affect both the location and rate of the sedimentation processes which construct wetlands, and the distribution of dissolved oxygen and inorganic nutrients so important to wetlands. Some examples will clarify this statement.

Highly stratified estuaries with buoyant outflows and salt-wedge intrusions are found at the mouths of many deltas, such as the Mississippi, Po and Danube, in most fjords like Hardanger Fjord, Norway, and at many other river mouths, at least for part of the year. Such estuaries occur where the ratio of width to depth is small and the ratio of river flow to tidal flow is large. Initially, with strong two-directional flow, suspended sediments are concentrated at the halocline, i.e. the interface between outflowing fresh water and intruding salt water. When the lower flow weakens or retreats seawards, sediment settles toward the bottom, to be entrained and carried landward as the salt wedge re-enters the estuary (Meade 1972). Net sediment flux is slowly upstream with deposition taking place around the nose of the salt wedge, and eventually accreting upwards into wetlands.

Where tidal flow increases relative to river flow, the added turbulence erases the sharp halocline of the salt-wedge estuary. In this partially stratified system, suspended sediment and resuspended bottom sediments are carried landwards by tidal flows to the limits of salt water. Shoaling associated with turbidity maxima paves the way for eventual wetland emergence. Most estuaries fall into this category: the Savanna River, upper Chesapeake Bay, the Sacramento-San Joaquin system as it enters San Francisco Bay, the Demerera River of Guyana and many European estuaries like the Gironde, the Mersey and Southampton Water (Dyer 1973).

Along macrotidal coasts where tidal flux is large compared with river flow, vertically homogeneous or well-mixed estuaries predominate. In the Thames estuary the slight downward increase in density is sufficient to promote net landward movements of sediments near the bottom for distances of 25 km (Inglis and Allen 1957). Other tide-dominated estuaries include the Colorado, Changjiang (Yangtze), Ganges-Brahmaputra, Shatt-al-Arab and Ord river mouths. In the Ord river mouth, northern Australia, the tidal prism exceeds the mean river discharge by a factor of nearly 3000, and mutually evasive, bidirectional ebb and flow currents exceed 3 m/s (Wright 1977). Tidal currents thus account for more sediment transport than rivers, and sediments brought into river mouths during floods are soon remoulded into elongate tidal shoals or removed upstream and shoreward by flood tides, to be deposited where hydrodynamic forces are negligible. Some of the world's most extensive coastal wetlands have developed in this way.

3.4 *Hydrodynamics on the wetland surface*

Once estuarine deposits accrete upwards into the intertidal zone, subsequent morphological and sedimentological changes depend largely on hydrodynamic forces working on and around the wetland surface. Because wetland hydrodynamics function in a three-dimensional water body whose depth is very small compared with its length and breadth, wave energy is muted and wetlands respond most readily to the relative strength and duration of ebb and flood tides. Some wetlands are dominated by flood-tidal currents, notably during storms, and others by ebb-tidal currents (figure 2.9). This affects patterns of erosion and deposition, as reflected in unidirectional or bidirectional bedforms and structures. The ebb-dominated tidal dynamics of the salt marshes landward of Sapelo Island, Georgia, produce bedforms that maintain an ebb-oriented geometry throughout both ebb and flood (Zarillo 1985).

In tidal creeks, currents usually reach maximum velocities and erosive competence during later ebb or earlier flood stages when water is being funelled through small channel cross-sections, commonly at velocities over 1 m/s. Tidal-creek sediments are thus relatively coarse and variable, with many erosional discordances. As the flood rises, water spills onto broad wetland surfaces above the creeks, velocities decrease to 0.2 m/s or less, sheet flow replaces channel flow and entrained sediments begin to settle, the coarsest as levees and crevasse splays alongside creeks. Most suspended sediment probably settles out during slack water as the flood turns towards the ebb and flow competency is minimal. During the earlier ebb, deposition continues as gentle slopes and shallow channels of the high flats inhibit swift currents. For these reasons, coarser sediments commonly occur towards low-tide levels

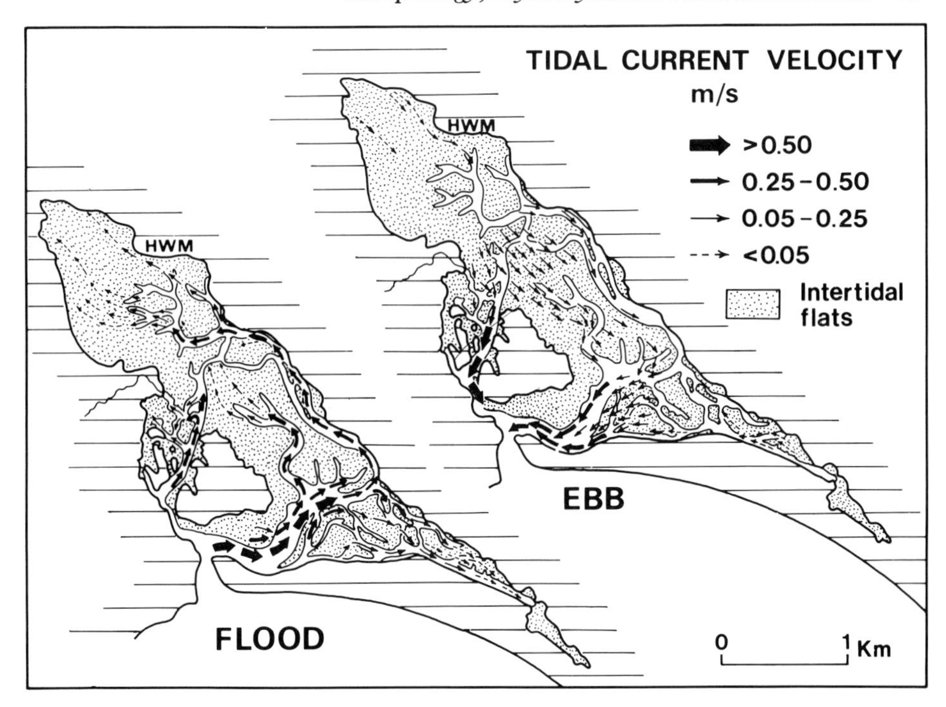

Figure 2.9 Tidal circulation in 4.45 km^2 Bolinas Lagoon, California. Some 70 per cent of the lagoon is floored by intertidal sands and muds derived from the 43 km^2 drainage basin and eroding cliffs west of the inlet. Kent Island, a supratidal wetland just inside the lagoon, separates the maximum flood and ebb currents which often exceed 1 m/s.
(after Ritter 1970)

whereas finer sediments concentrate towards the higher inner margins of wetlands. The relatively short duration of tidal slack water inhibits deposition of all suspended sediments, in contrast with river-dominated wetlands where the longer slack between stream floods favours deposition. Wind also influences tidal currents by enhancing floods and depressing ebbs.

Hydrodynamic processes are affected by the presence or absence of vegetation. Salt marsh grasses like *Spartina* increase bed friction, reduce current velocities, dampen wind waves, inhibit bedforms, discourage erosion and promote deposition. The stems of mangroves and reeds impede currents and disrupt turbulence patterns. In Westernport Bay, Australia, *Avicennia marina* helps to create depositional terraces around high spring tide levels, but where the mangroves have died the terraces have been degraded (Bird 1986). Roots, algae and bacteria all help to fix sediments, while clay flocculation may be assisted by salts extruded from plants seeking to maintain osmotic balance.

In contrast, the absence of vegetation on tidal flats and creeks allows waves and currents much freedom, generating greater sediment mobility and distinctive bedforms. Ripples of various types are readily generated by waves and tidal currents on bare tidal flats, especially those composed mostly of sand.

With velocities rising well above 1 m/s, tidal creeks develop megaripples and dunes with wavelengths up to 10 m.

Water-tables within wetlands reflect a complex response to the frequency and duration of tidal submersion and freshwater seepages, as influenced also by surface morphology and sediment infiltration capacity. In permeable sediments the water-table may rise to the surface during high tide, whereas in impermeable sediments it is slow to respond. The position of the water-table is important to the salinity of wetland sediments, the potential for brine evaporation from interstitial salts, and plant selection and growth.

3.5 *Sediment sources*

Sediments forming wetlands can be derived from allochthonous (external) or autochthonous (internal) sources, or both. Allochthonous sediments are mostly fine-grained clastic materials delivered in suspension by rivers, tidal and wave-induced currents and wind. Autochthonous sediments are of biogenic or chemical origin, derived either by the accumulation of plant and animal detritus or by the *in situ* precipitation of evaporite deposits from brines. Much recycling of wetland deposits also occurs through resuspension by tidal currents and waves, migration of tidal creeks and erosion of marsh cliffs.

The rate and volume of river sediment delivered to wetlands depend partly on the erodibility of the upland basin and in part on the magnitude and frequency of precipitation and stream flow. Erosion indices relating rainfall energy and sediment loss generally show direct correlation with suspended sediments reaching the coast. In general terms, high-magnitude floods in erodible basins deliver large volumes of sediment to estuaries, where that portion that is not flushed seawards will settle. Subsequent resuspension by turbulence generated by wind waves and various currents then allows these sediments to be redistributed by tidal and other currents towards estuarine margins. Thus 40 per cent of the fluvial sediment load reaching the Changjiang estuary, China, is deposited there, probably because the high organic content in the suspended particulate matter favours organo-aggregate deposition (Milliman et al. 1985). Conversely, estuaries at the mouths of low-gradient basins dominated by chemical weathering receive relatively low quantities of suspended sediments, as shown by the Zaire estuary. Suspended sediments in estuaries of the southwest United States range from 10 to 50 000 mg/l, whereas estuaries of pristine rivers in the northeast United States have concentrations of only 1–25 mg/l.

The contribution of coastal sediments to wetland accretion is more complex. Suspended sediment concentrations in ocean surface waters are small compared with river concentrations, varying from 0.1 to 1 mg/l at the Atlantic Ocean off North America (Manheim et al. 1970). Their contribution to coastal wetlands is correspondingly small. However, where waves and currents can sweep and entrain unconsolidated sediments on shallow continental shelves, the contribution may be significant. For example, mineralogical analyses indicate that much of the sediment in the Wadden Sea is derived from the

North Sea (Faverjee 1951). In the Severn estuary, dead foraminiferal assemblages from intertidal and subtidal deposits reveal a net landward transport of fine material over the past 9000 years (Murray and Hawkins 1976). Powerful littoral drift delivers twice as much sediment from the Amazon to the Orinoco delta than is provided by the Orinoco River itself (Van Andel 1967). Extreme events such as hurricanes may shift large volumes of sediment across barrier islands and into lagoons and estuaries.

Cliff erosion of incompetent materials is another coastal source. Thus poorly consolidated Quaternary deposits forming the Holderness cliffs, eastern England, are the major source of sediments in the Humber estuary and its southern margins (Al-Bakri 1986). About 1.6×10^6 t of sediment, 25 per cent of it silt and clay, is supplied annually by local shore erosion to northern Chesapeake Bay (Biggs 1970). Cliffing of Quaternary deposits may also account for most sediments transported on the flood into The Wash (Shaw 1973). Conversely, the growth of a healthy salt marsh may inhibit local cliff erosion, as observed in the Severn estuary.

Wind-blown sand and silt may also contribute to wetlands lying downwind. Thus wind-blown sand contributes 93–98 per cent of all sediment found to depths of 0.6 m in wetlands behind the barrier-dune complex at Morro Bay, California (Orme 1990). In cold regions, ice-rafted sands and gravels may be introduced to coastal wetlands during spring break-up, at which time turbulence resuspends fine sediments that had settled beneath winter ice cover (Dionne 1984).

In reality, wetlands are often composed of materials from several sources, with their eventual deposition determined by the net circulation pattern which in turn reflects the relative magnitude of river and tidal flows and basin geometry. Thus wetlands of the Dutch delta region annually receive about 4.5×10^6 t of river muds from the Rhine (0.6×10^6 t), Waal (2.5×10^6 t), Maas (0.7×10^6 t) and Scheldt (0.7×10^6 t), about 3.5×10^6 t of sediment from the sea and about 1×10^6 t of material from *in situ* biological activity, reworking of older deposits and dredging (Terwindt 1977). Wetland sediments in Alsea Bay, Oregon, comprise both coastal sands carried in by tidal currents mainly in summer and river sediments introduced mainly in winter (Peterson et al. 1982). In Sandyhaven Pill, a drowned valley in south Wales, tide-dominated deposits occupy 65 per cent of the area, wave-dominated deposits 22 per cent, cliff-derived sediments 12 per cent and river deposits 1 per cent (King 1980). In the Teign estuary, southwest England, it has been shown using trace element techniques that barium derived from past mining activity characterizes river input, that strontium from carbonate skeletal debris indicates landward transport of marine sediments and that caesium is a good geochemical indicator of local Permian red-bed contributions (Merefield 1981).

Biogenic materials may contribute significantly to wetlands, especially where the supply of inorganic sediments is low, such as along formerly glaciated coasts. Detritus of intertidal *Spartina* and subtidal *Thalassia* is often found interbedded with mineral sediment after these plants have been sheared off above their roots by storms, ice or hypersalinity. In the anaerobic conditions common to wetlands, peat forms from the degradation of plant remains in association with mineral sediments. Because of its high water content and thus compressibility, peat readily autocompacts, thereby allowing for continued organic productivity and decay at the surface until a considerable thickness accumulates. However, where inorganic sedimentation is high or plant detritus is consumed by intense biological activity or removed by tidal flushing, as along the southeast and west coasts of the United States, continuous peat beds are rare and peat lenses are localized. Despite luxuriant marsh growth in Georgia, for example, about 90 per cent of the above-ground primary productivity enters the detritus food chain and is lost to wetland accretion (Reinhold et al. 1975). In the Mississippi delta, various marsh mats adapted to different salinities float on or overlie black oozes and organic-rich clays which compact to peats several metres deep.

Other biogenic contributions to wetlands include skeletal and pelletal carbonates and shells. Small animals, notably suspension feeders and detritus feeders, extract organic and inorganic debris from the water column and process it into pellets which settle more readily than individual clay or silt particles. Tidal flats among warm-water coasts are often largely composed of such debris. On Andros Island in the Bahamas, intertidal and low supratidal lime muds are formed largely of faecal pellets produced by the gastropod *Batillaria* (Shinn et al. 1969). Around the Persian Gulf, tidal flats composed of skeletal and pelletal carbonates merge shoreward with evaporites such as gypsum and anhydrite precipitated supratidally from brines washing across coastal sabkhas. Shell beds 32 km long and up to 18 m thick underlie some Louisiana wetlands. In Georgia, the oyster *Crassostrea virginica* forms large colonies along marsh creeks but only small isolated clumps on marsh flats (Edwards and Frey 1977). In San Francisco Bay, colonies of the introduced mud-boring clam *Geukensia demissa* effectively riprap creek banks, although the once extensive native oyster *Ostrea lurida* has been decimated by pollution (Pestrong 1972). One measure of the latter's importance to wetland accretion is that, between 1924 and 1970, 30×10^6 t of oyster shells were dredged for use in the local cement industry.

3.6 *Sediment composition and structure*

In terms of composition, wetland sediments can be broadly classified as siliciclastics or carbonates, a reflection of climate and sediment sources. Siliciclastics are derived mostly from rivers and nearby shelf and shore erosion, and are thus common constituents of wetlands in rainy and stormy climates. Carbonates are common to warm tropical and subtropical climates where organisms thrive in the absence of sediment-laden floods or where arid and semi-arid conditions favour evaporites. Transitions between humid and arid climates have mixed siliciclastic-carbonate wetlands.

In siliciclastic wetlands, materials of sand, silt and clay size occur with quartz dominating the sand fraction and kaolinite, illite, chlorite and montmorillonite characterizing the clay fraction. Gravels are rare except as mud balls derived from the erosion of semi-consolidated muds. Sands introduced by higher-energy currents are often quite distinct from muds deposited under low-energy conditions. The muds of many wetlands are mostly silts (60 per cent of Wadden Sea tidal flats, 72 per cent of The Wash in terms of fine-grained sediment), with clays and organic particles in varying ratios. The organic fraction is usually composed of skeletal and pelletal material, often with large quantities of siliceous diatom frustules and shell fragments. Bacterial activity commonly alters organic matter into hydrogen sulphide which reacts with ferrous compounds in the water to produce sulphides. Table 2.2 shows some wetland properties.

Table 2.2 Physical properties of wetland sediments, San Francisco Bay

	Salt marsh		*Tidal flat*		
	Salicornia	*Spartina*	*Flat*	*Channel*	*Levee*
Median grain size diameter (∅)	9.1	9.4	9.5	7.8	8.1
Graphic standard deviation	3.4	3.2	2.9	3.2	2.8
Moisture content (%)	104.0	139.0	146.0	120.0	96.0
Dry density (g/cm^3)	0.64	0.57	0.42	0.54	0.77
Shear strength (kg/cm^2)	0.20	0.11	0.06	0.11	0.15
Organic content (%)	18.3	14.6	5.3	6.9	4.2

Median grain size values ($\varnothing = -\log_2$ mm) all fall within the very fine silt to clay fraction. Graphic standard deviations all show very poor sorting.
Source: modified after Pestrong 1972

Siliciclastic sediments and wetland morphology are interdependent, fining upward in the stratigraphic column and fining inward across the surface. Subtidal deposits range from muds to coarse sands, with ripple bedding, few living shells and weak bioturbation. Intertidal flats are typically formed in clayey silts alternating with sands and skeletal remains, all strongly bioturbated. Flaser, lenticular and cross-bedding reflect changing waves and tidal currents. Supratidal flats and marshes are commonly underlain by clayey sands and silts introduced on the flood tide and deposited during and after slack water.

Carbonate wetlands have been studied on oceanic platforms such as the Bahama Banks and along continental margins such as the Persian Gulf and Shark Bay, Western Australia. Ideally, carbonate wetlands are characterized by either a lime mud–algal mat sequence, as in the Bahamas and in the West Indies, or a lime mud–evaporite sequence as in the Persian Gulf (plate 2.6). On Andros Island in the Bahamas the supratidal zone is exposed for more than 75 per cent of the year and comprises laminated lime muds and algal tufa, with root structures of mangroves and marsh grass (Shinn et al. 1969). Intertidal flats, exposed for 54 to 75 per cent of the year, are dominated by bioturbated pelletal lime muds. The subtidal zone contains mostly soft pelletal aragonitic muds. In contrast, behind the barrier beaches of the Trucial Coast, supratidal sabkhas are characterized by precipitation of gypsum and anhydrite from brines, succeeded in lagoons by intertidal algal mud flats and stromatolites

Plate 2.6 (*The scene extends to the plate on page 71, with a slight overlap*) Salt ponds and adjacent mangroves, southeast peninsula, St. Kitts, West Indies. The salt ponds occupy the crater of a submerged volcano and are floored by lime muds and algal mats. They are

(laminated limestone structures formed in association with algae), and subtidal pelletal lime muds and sands probably produced by precipitation of aragonite from sea water (Evans 1970).

Distinct, more or less parallel or wavy laminations are the most common sedimentary structures of wetland deposits, readily observed in eroding tidal channels and artificial cuts. Such stratification usually occurs because the greater velocity of the flood-tidal current introduces suspended sediment that settles by gravity, perhaps aided by other processes (see below), which the weaker ebb-tidal current cannot wholly remove. Thus thin layers of coarser sediment survive from one tidal cycle to another, veneered with fines deposited on intertidal flats, but not in creeks, during and after slack water. Lenses of coarser rippled sediments and cross-bedded deposits often reflect storm conditions. Without a rise in sea level, there is an upper limit to deposition whereby the wetland surface approaches a dynamic equilibrium between thin laminated sedimentation and trimming by sheet-flow erosion.

Whereas the deposition of coarser sediments is reasonably well understood, the deposition of clay-size materials continues to evoke controversy. Electrolic flocculation has often been invoked to explain deposition of clays which are so small as to otherwise remain suspended indefinitely. This is a process whereby individual clay particles combine into clay aggregates when introduced to salt water. The aggregates are larger, denser and more prone to settle. Differential flocculation has been invoked to explain parallel laminations in some salt

periodically replenished by sea water penetrating the barrier on the right, yielding halinities ranging from 40 to 150‰ in water no more than 2 m deep. They have been the site of periodic salt extraction since the seventeenth century
(Courtesy A. R. Orme)

marshes (Pestrong 1972). However, whereas salt-clay flocs may develop where freshwater sediments enter saline environments, flocculation must lessen in importance as suspended clays reach chemical equilibrium with salt water. Accordingly, other processes have been recognized including the biogenic pelletization of clays by suspension-feeding animals and the formation of organoclay aggregates (Frey and Basan 1978). Indeed, biochemical processes leading to deposition may be more important than geochemical processes.

Parallel laminations of wetland sediments may be frequently disrupted or deformed by mud cracks, plant and animal bioturbation, ground ice and drift ice. Mud cracks may be produced by desiccation upon exposure to the air, or underwater by synaeresis, a rapid dewatering of sediments by colloid ageing after deposition. Wrinkled algal mats are also produced by desiccation.

Bioturbation may transform laminated sediments into unstructured homogeneous masses, as often happens in the Atlantic coastal marshes of the United States (Edwards and Frey 1977). Where the process is less complete, burrows and root traces may penetrate several decimetres below the surface, with relict bioturbation at greater depth. Biogenic reworking is commonly associated with burrows created by worms (*Arenicola, Nereis*), molluscs (*Cardium, Mytilus*), crabs (*Uca*) and ghost shrimp (*Callianassa*), and with the roots of *Juncus, Spartina* and other plants. Where rapid sedimentation or physical reworking of surface sediments by currents occurs, bioturbation is poorly developed or preserved.

3.7 *Sedimentation rates and wetland progradation*

Precise sedimentation rates are difficult to assess because wetlands grow episodically by both vertical and lateral accretion. Theoretically, in stable environments wetlands develop initially by vertical accretion on a flat or sloping subtidal surface, but once this surface is raised into the intertidal zone a dynamic equilibrium between sedimentation and erosion inhibits further significant upward growth. Thereafter lateral progradation becomes more important, both by deposition of new sediment and by lateral transfer of existing sediment. Where subsidence or rising sea level is important, however, vertical accretion and lateral progradation may continue together. The wetlands of most deltas and the subsiding shores of the southern North Sea are favoured in this way. Unusual events may sometimes rejuvenate wetlands. For example, faulting during the San Francisco earthquake in 1906 caused the floor of Bolinas Lagoon, California, to drop abruptly some 25–35 cm and to shift 4 m laterally, decreasing the intertidal wetland area but affording a larger basin for renewed sedimentation (Gilbert 1908).

Sedimentation rates in most wetlands amount to only a few millimetres a year (table 2.3). Although interesting, the data in table 2.3 should be treated with caution for several reasons. First, the values are for vertical accretion, although Le Fournier and Friedman (1974) found lateral progradation on the coast of France to be 10^6 times faster than deep-sea vertical accretion (figure 2.10). Second, vertical accretion rates vary widely across wetlands, from several centimetres a year in lower intertidal areas to less than 0.001 cm/yr on high marshes (Pethick 1981). Third, in the equilibrium state of a well-developed wetland, accretion areas may become erosion sites and vice versa. Fourth, rapid sedimentation often alternates with long periods of slower sedimentation, non-sedimentation or even erosion. Thus the rates presented are net values, although the range of rates may provide a better understanding of the dynamics of each system. Mobile Bay, Alabama, currently receives 4.3 $\times 10^6$ t of suspended sediment annually, producing an average accretion rate of 0.56 cm/yr, although this ranges from 0 to 3 cm/yr across the estuary (Ryan and

Table 2.3 Vertical accretion rates for selected wetlands

Environment	*Net vertical accretion rate (cm/yr)*	*Range of rates (cm/yr)*
Salt marsh ($n = 9$)	0.64	0.01–3.00
Tidal flats ($n = 4$)	1.09	0.22–2.00
Estuaries (subtidal, $n = 7$)	0.52	0.00–3.00
Bays and lagoons (subtidal, $n = 12$)	0.24	0.03–0.60
Deltas (subtidal, $n = 8$)	7.30	0.15–45.0
Natural lakes ($n = 8$)	0.38	0.05–1.40
Sabkha evaporites ($n = 2$)	0.85	0.40–2.00
Peat bogs ($n = 4$)	0.34	0.01–0.98

Source: values derived from references in text

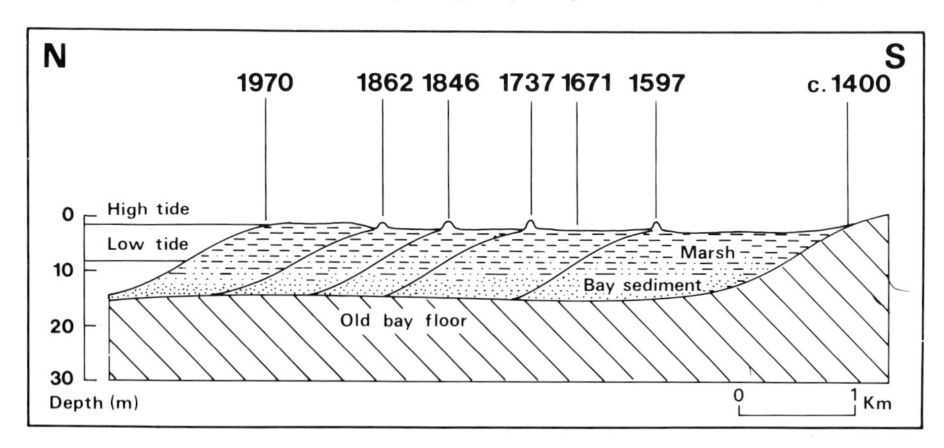

Figure 2.10 Schematic section across wetlands in Authie Bay, Picardy, France, showing lateral progradation of nearly 1 km/100 yr. Time lines dated by reclamation dykes cut obliquely through horizontal bay and marsh sediments.
(Modified from Le Fournier and Friedman 1974)

Goodell 1973). Although tidal-flat accretion in the Netherlands averages 1–2 cm/yr, several metres of sediment may accumulate in a few days, notably after storms and where tidal creeks shift course. Similarly, in West German tidal flats, where sedimentation rates have averaged 0.22 cm/yr over the past 1900 years, rates of 1.15 cm/yr have been measured over 4 years, 145 cm/yr over 8 days and 2.1×10^6 cm/yr over several seconds (Reineck 1960). Delta deposition is highly variable in time and space, with up to 40–45 cm of material accumulating annually in front of the Mississippi and Rhone deltas but much less on the delta surface farther inland. Despite some wide ranges, table 2.3 does distinguish between the relatively rapid vertical accretion of bare tidal flats and the slower sedimentation of higher salt marshes. Tidal flats also accrete more rapidly than the subtidal parts of estuaries and lagoons, which emphasizes the importance of the intertidal zone as a prime locus of deposition.

Lateral progradation of wetlands can be measured by reference to repeat surveys, remote sensing and old maps. On the central west coast of France, between the Loire and Gironde estuaries, wetlands have prograded up to 2 km over the past three centuries, but often at the expense of erosion elsewhere in the vicinity (Guilcher 1981). In southern England, rapid progradation of salt marshes followed the spread of *Spartina anglica*, an amphidiploid form of *Spartina townsendii*, after 1870, although this has since slowed and some areas have experienced erosion. Mangrove swamps are rapidly prograding along the northeast coast of South America, between the Amazon and Orinoco deltas, and along the Queensland coast of Australia, where the role of *Avicennia* pneumatophores in mud stabilization has been well documented (Spencerley 1977).

Progadation and accretion may sometimes occur under unusual natural circumstances. For example, some 70 per cent of the 24 km^2 Ohiwa Harbour in the Bay of Plenty, New Zealand, is now occupied by tidal flats and vegetated marshes whose development accelerated after the Taupo pumic eruption of AD 131 filled up-coast bays and caused Ohiwa's enclosing barrier spit to build rapidly eastward at 3 m/yr (Richmond et al. 1984).

In recent centuries, however, it is human activity in upland basins that has frequently affected sedimentation rates in downstream wetlands, notably by changing the relative importance of river and non-river sediment sources. Forest clearance and wasteful farming practices east of the Appalachian Mountains in the eighteenth and nineteenth centuries greatly increased fluvial sediment yields and caused wetlands to prograde rapidly into formerly open water, for instance around Chesapeake Bay. Augmented by land clearance for urban development, some $2 \times 10^6 m^3$ of sediment are now being deposited annually near the tidal limits of the Potomac estuary (Schubel and Meade 1977). Nutrient loading from municipal wastes is further stimulating plant growth in many estuarine wetlands. Elsewhere, mining waste has accelerated wetland development, notably in Cornish estuaries choked with china-clay debris.

Hydraulic gold mining in the Sierra Nevada foothills, California, after the 1849 gold rush greatly increased wetland accretion and progradation in San Francisco Bay, while also altering the tidal prism and the bay's flushing regime. Although hydraulic mining ceased in 1884, the impact of sediment moving through the system continued. Gilbert (1917) estimated that $1816 \times 10^6 m^3$ of debris were eroded by mining and natural forces between 1850 and 1914, of which only 2 per cent reached the ocean while 48 per cent was deposited within San Francisco Bay. He estimated that it would take a further 50 years for the debris remaining in the valleys to reach the bay, an estimate since confirmed.

In contrast, wetland reclamation may change the role of an estuary from a sediment sink to a source of sediment for the continental shelf. In the Seine estuary, 130 years of reclamation has replaced broad tidal flats and marshes with a narrow jettied channel which has concentrated ebb flows and river discharge, and thereby increased the flow competence and removal of intertidal and subtidal sediments (Avoine et al. 1981).

3.8 *Wetland erosion*

Whereas it may be argued that most coastal wetlands are in dynamic equilibrium with their present environments, with modest erosion and sedimentation as self-adjusting elements of the system, their low gradients render them susceptible to erosion should conditions change. Some erosion is natural, for example in the Mississippi delta where the wetlands of abandoned distributary lobes are being eroded while active distributaries create new tidal flats. In Poole Harbour, southern England, the spread of *Spartina anglica* between 1899 and 1924 was accompanied by 70 cm of marsh accretion (Bird and Ranwell 1964). Between 1924 and 1952, however, the *Spartina* area declined by 20 per cent and erosion set in, possibly attributable to biological changes in the plant but local sea-level change cannot be ignored. Erosion in many areas is attributable to human activity, either directly through interference with the coastal wetlands or indirectly through reductions in sediment yields owing to reservoir construction inland. For example, in the southeast United States sediment yields to estuaries are one-third of what they were in 1900.

4.0 INTERIOR WETLANDS

Interior and coastal wetlands usually share wetness, hydrophytes and hydric soils in common but little else. Interior wetlands occur across a wide range of environments – from rivers to lakes to mires, from arctic muskeg to equatorial swamp forest, from flats to hill slopes, from low-energy mires to relatively high-energy river channels, and from fresh water to hypersaline hydrologies. Their waters have great chemical diversity dominated by Ca, Mg, Na and K cations and CO_3, SO_4 and Cl anions. Interior wetlands exist independently of sea level, except near the coast where water-tables respond to tidal fluctuations and salt-wedge intrusions. Again, except near the coast, they were unaffected by the Flandrian transgression. However, their development has been much influenced by Holocene climatic changes, as demonstrated by the record preserved in the bogs.

Despite the considerable differences between interior and coastal wetlands, the physical principles relating hydrodynamics and sedimentation are not abrogated. Swift velocities increase flow competence and particle entrainment; slack waters encourage deposition. These principles apply whether the environment is a river channel, a lake or a mire, although flows are swifter, turbulence greater and entrainment easier in rivers than elsewhere. In contrast, because stream velocity and flow competence are soon reduced on entering relatively inert bodies of water, lakes favour net deposition and wetland progradation.

The relative importance of different water sources varies considerably in interior wetlands, and this in turn affects water chemistry and vegetal response (figure 2.11). Riverine wetlands gain and lose water mostly as stream flows, with ground-water seepage and evapotranspiration becoming more important on flood plains with distance from the river. The water budget of lacustrine and palustrine systems is more complex and reflects primarily the climate and to some extent the substrate conditions, both of which vary greatly in time and space. In tropical and temperate humid lands, lacustrine wetlands depend on a variable combination of stream flow and ground-water, with the latter becoming more important where permeable substrates occur. Such wetlands lose much water through evapotranspiration, the losses becoming less in colder regions. Lacking perennial stream flows, the water balance of ponds mostly reflects the ratio between precipitation, ground-water and evapotranspiration. Turloughs are created by seasonally high water-tables with ponds forming in the wet season and wetlands surviving through the dry season if ground-water remains within about 2 m of the surface. In more arid regions, wetlands receive

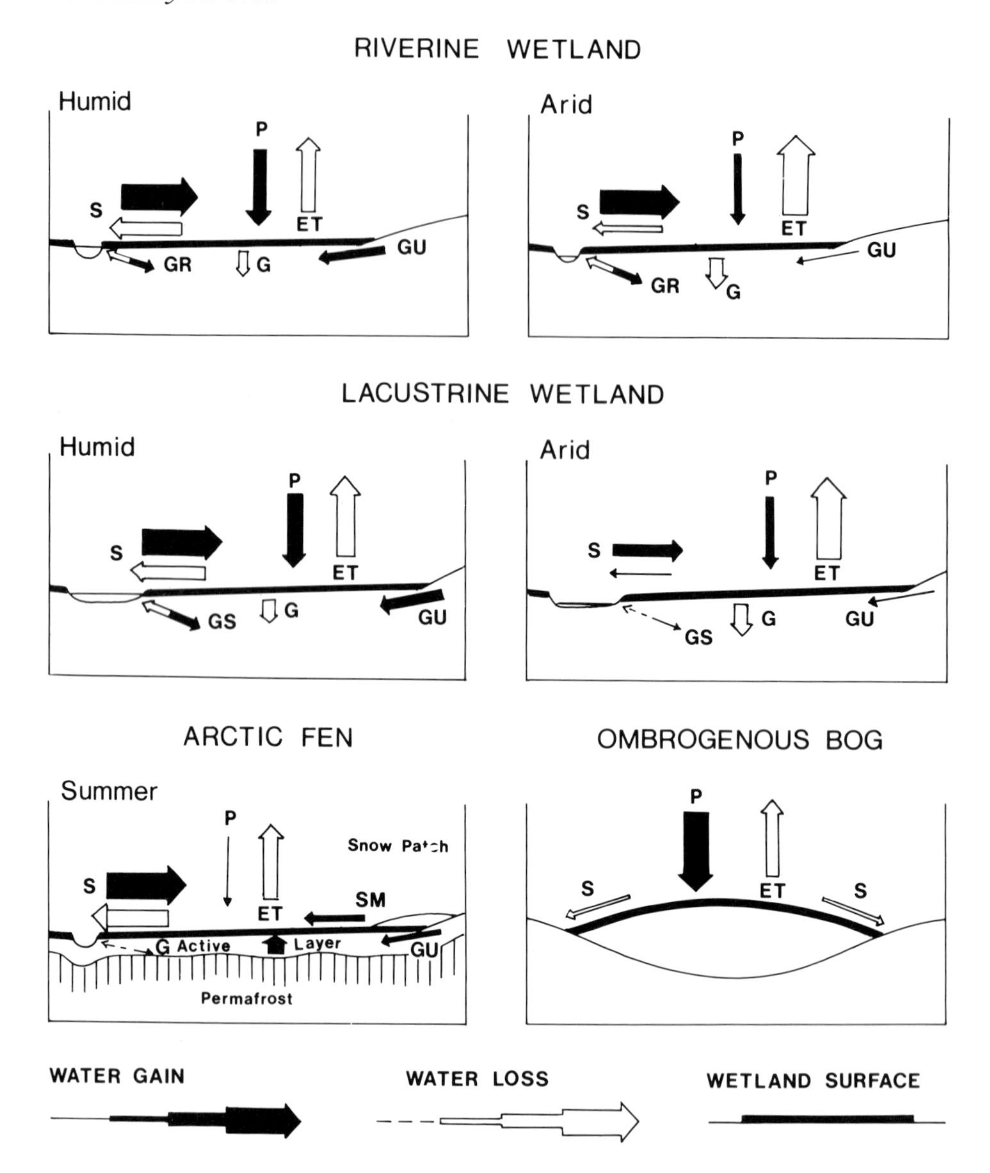

Figure 2.11 Relative water balance in different interior wetlands (arrows indicate magnitude and direction of flow): S, surface-water flow; G, ground-water flow; GU, ground-water flow from upland; GR, ground-water flow to or from river; P, precipitation; ET, evapotranspiration; SM, snowmelt

water mostly from ephemeral stream flows, often of high magnitude, but evaporation exceeds precipitation, often by a large margin, thereby creating sabkha evaporites. Riverine wetlands in arid lands are fed by allogenic waters draining from humid areas, for example in the Colorado and Nile valleys. In regions underlain by permafrost, wetlands are fed primarily by the lateral flow of water at or just below the surface and derived from lakes, streams and late-lying snow patches during the thaw season.

The complex interaction between ground-water and surface water is amenable to computer simulation but difficult to evaluate in the field. It appears to reflect substrate geometry, anisotropy of porous media and hydraulic head, and the last variable in turn is related to water-table configuration as influenced by water movement through the vadose zone (Winter 1983). Evaporation and transpiration, which are such important components of lacustrine and palustrine systems, are controlled by wind and vapour fluxes over the wetland. They are greatest where warm dry air and high winds occur, notably in hot deserts, and least where cool air at or near saturation point overlies the wetland, notably in cool temperate lands. In cold regions, evapotranspiration is further reduced by snow and ice covers which intercept energy fluxes (Winter and Woo 1988).

The following discussion will not repeat the principles presented earlier, but will focus on the morphology, water properties and vegetation relationships of the three interior wetland systems, and examine the evolution and physical character of mires in particular (table 2.1).

4.1 *Riverine wetlands*

Riverine wetlands are freshwater habitats found in and alongside stream channels and on adjacent annual flood plains (plate 2.7). Contrary to Cowardin et al (1985), this categorization considers annual flood plains to be part of the active fluvial system but places tidal riverine areas in the estuarine system (see table 2.1 and figure 1.1). Valley bogs and terrace wetlands not specifically related to contemporary flow conditions are considered palustrine. Wetland vegetation reflects flow velocity and stage, with velocity in turn being positively related to the morphological variables of slope and channel or flood-plain shape, and negatively related to boundary roughness.

With swift perennial flows, plant life in channels is mostly restricted to algae. With slack perennial flows, a wide variety of plants appear, mostly to disappear again during floods. These include aquatic mosses, vascular aquatics such as floating duckweeds (*Lemna, Spirodela*) and rooted pondweeds (*Potamogeton*), and emergent herbaceous genera like cattails (*Typha*), bulrushes (*Scirpus*) and the reed *Phragmites australis*. Where flows are intermittent or seasonal but ground-water levels remain high, emergent herbaceous plants may survive but shrubs and even trees may invade the wetland. In ephemeral flows and on annual flood plains, high ground-water tables are essential to wetland occurrence but under favourable conditions forest wetlands may develop. In the southern United States, such flood plains may be dominated by swamp white oak (*Quercus bicolor*) or bald cypress (*Taxodium distichum*). Farther north, flood-plain forests commonly carry cottonwoods (*Populus*) and willows (*Salix*).

The water balance of channel wetlands is controlled simply by inflows and outflows of river water (figure 2.11). The balance for adjacent flood plains is

Plate 2.7 Riverine wetland along the lower Colorado River valley near Blythe, California. Despite desert conditions, allogenic waters favour both wetlands alongside the river and agricultural reclamation, although flooding along the lower Colorado River is now controlled by dams
(Courtesy Spence Collection, University of California, Los Angeles)

more complex. Because flood-plain sediments are commonly permeable, a rise in stage causes some river water to pass laterally into bank storage through influent seepage. This in turn causes ground-water levels to rise in adjacent flood plains, a feature well illustrated from flood-plain wetlands along the Platte River, Nebraska (Hurr 1983). Flood plains also receive water through seepage from neighbouring uplands. Water losses from flood-plain wetlands occur by infiltration to ground-water and from there by effluent seepage to streams, and also by evapotranspiration. Transpiration from flood-plain locations is particularly efficient because the wet surface and shallow ground-water allow plants to transpire at maximum potential (Winter and Woo 1988). Finally, the water balance of riverine wetlands differs from that of lacustrine and palustrine wetlands in that the former reflects conditions across the entire drainage basin, whereas the latter is more local. Thus surface flows in such large rivers as the Amazon and the Mississippi reflect in part precipitation and snowmelt in distant high mountains.

4.2 *Lacustrine wetlands*

Lakes, and therefore lacustrine wetlands, occur in two physical situations, namely topographic lows and areas underlain by impermeable materials. Topographic lows are created by a wide variety of erosional and depositional processes. For example, glacial erosion may excavate bedrock hollows, as seen in the Canadian and Fennoscandian shields, while glacial deposition may cause postglacial waters to be imponded behind terminal and recessional moraines, between drumlins or in kettle holes on dead-ice moraines (plate 2.8). Such lakes and wetlands most commonly occur inside the limits of the last glaciation where drainage patterns are still deranged. Beyond those limits, sufficient time has elapsed for drainage systems to become better integrated and for lakes to be filled, although some extensive wetlands may remain. Lakes also form where drainage has been dammed by fluvial deposits, encroaching sand dunes, landslides or tectonism. Large and small hollows are created by tectonic subsidence, as in the east African rift valleys and in sag ponds along California's San Andreas Fault, and by solutional subsidence in limestone areas, notably in Florida, the Yucatan peninsula and central Ireland. Impermeable materials favouring wetlands include the clay-rich beds of former glacial or proglacial lakes, such as the glacial Lake Agassiz in central North

Plate 2.8 Lacustrine fen between drumlins, near Clew Bay, County Mayo, Ireland (Courtesy A. R. Orme)

America. Permafrost, namely earth material that has remained frozen through at least two successive winters and the intervening summer, is essentially impervious and, where it is continuous, supports some of the world's most extensive wetlands in northern Canada and northern Siberia. Where partial melting of the permafrost has occurred, thermokarst depressions also support lakes and lacustrine wetlands.

Lacustrine wetlands occur in and around two chemically distinct areas: perennial freshwater lakes in humid lands, and salt lakes and sabkhas in semi-arid and arid lands. Lakes are distinguished from ponds by size and depth, the former covering more than 8 ha and being more than 2 m deep (table 2.1).

Freshwater lakes have two habitats: a limnetic zone, more than 2 m below low water, which is floored by rock, gravels and sand but mostly mud, and a littoral zone extending from the shore to 2 m below low water. The limnetic zone will harbour a variable fauna depending on substrate, and towards the margins aquatic plants such as the stonewort algae *Chara*, *Nitella* and *Tolypella*, the moss *Fontinalis*, and floating vascular plants such as *Lemna* and *Spirodela*, the water nut (*Trapa natans*) and water ferns (*Salvinia*). In the shallow littoral zone, rooted vascular aquatics such as *Potamogeton* pondweeds, ditch grasses (*Ruppia*), water weed (*Elodea*) and water lilies (*Nymphaea*, *Nuphar*) occur. These are often joined by erect rooted hydrophytes such as wild rice (*Zizanea aquatica*) which forms dense stands in central North America during summer and autumn by dies back or is destroyed by ice in winter. Grasses such as *Phragmites australis* and grass-like emergents like *Typha*, *Scirpus* and *Carex* sedges also occur. In arctic wetlands, peats commonly form in the littoral zone from the decay of *Carex*, *Salix* and other plants.

The hypersaline surface and near-surface waters found in salt lakes and sabkhas tend to inhibit all but the best-adapted algae and higher plants. The west side of the Death Valley sabkha, California, is characterized by an orderly sequence of phreatophytes arranged according to their salinity tolerance. Next to the bare salt pan, pickleweed (*Allenrolfea occidentalis*) tolerates up to 60‰ salinity (Hunt 1966). Farther from the pan, rush (*Juncus cooperi*) and salt grass (*Distichlis stricta*) tolerate 30‰–40‰ salinity, and these are succeeded inland by inkweed (*Suaeda*), tamarisk (*Tamarix gallica*, *Tamarix aphylla*), alkali sacaton grass (*Sporobolus airoides*) and others until the honey mesquite (*Prosopis juliflora*), which tolerates no more than 5‰ salinity, marks the transition to xerophytes on nearby alluvial fans (figure 2.12). Brine evaporation in the 520 km^2 pan is similarly zoned in terms of solubility: the first to precipitate are the least soluble carbonates ($CaCO_3$, $MgCO_3$) around the pan margins and at the base of the sequence, followed by sulphates ($CaSO_4$, Na_2SO_4) and finally by extensive chlorides, mostly halite ($NaCl$), in the pan's centre.

Similar plant successions and evaporate sequences are found in other sabkhas of the world. In Egypt, for example, interior wetlands at the Siwa and Moghra oases are associated with shallow ground-water and brackish to salt lakes. The vegetation is dominated by *Oressa cretica*, *Juncus rigidus*, *Alhagi maurorum*, *Imperator cylindrica* and *Typha elephantina*, associated with soluble salts totalling 44‰–66‰ in the top 25 cm of soil, but dropping quickly to 1.8‰–4.8‰ around 50 cm in depth (Zahran 1982).

Direct precipitation onto and evaporation from the surface are more important in lacustrine wetlands than in riverine systems (see figure 2.11). Furthermore, although stream flow continues to be part of the water balance, many scientists argue that lacustrine wetlands store water and release it more slowly over an extended period. Storage, which is reflected in the contrast between inflow and outflow hydrographs, is commonly attributed to small hydraulic gradients and the low hydraulic conductivities of peats and related wetland deposits. Storage capacity is thought to be greater in temperate regions where peat is thickest than in arctic areas where peat is thin and permafrost limits subsurface storage, or in tropical swamps where evapotranspiration losses are great. However, it can be argued that peat, despite high porosity, has a large specific retention that holds water against gravity within the unsaturated zone. With pore spaces partly occupied by water in retention, there is little additional capacity for new water. This, added to peat's low hydraulic conductivity, maintains high water-tables and even wet ground surfaces, thereby facilitating surface outflows. Soviet scientists have shown that even capillary rise is sufficient to keep bog surfaces moist if the water-table in the peat is no deeper than 0.2 m (Romanov 1968).

Arctic and subarctic wetlands have their storage capacity limited by the presence at shallow depth of continuous or discontinuous permafrost. In an arctic fen in Keewatin, Canada, the summer water balance revealed inputs of 430 mm of water from an adjacent lake, 146 mm from snowmelt on the surface,

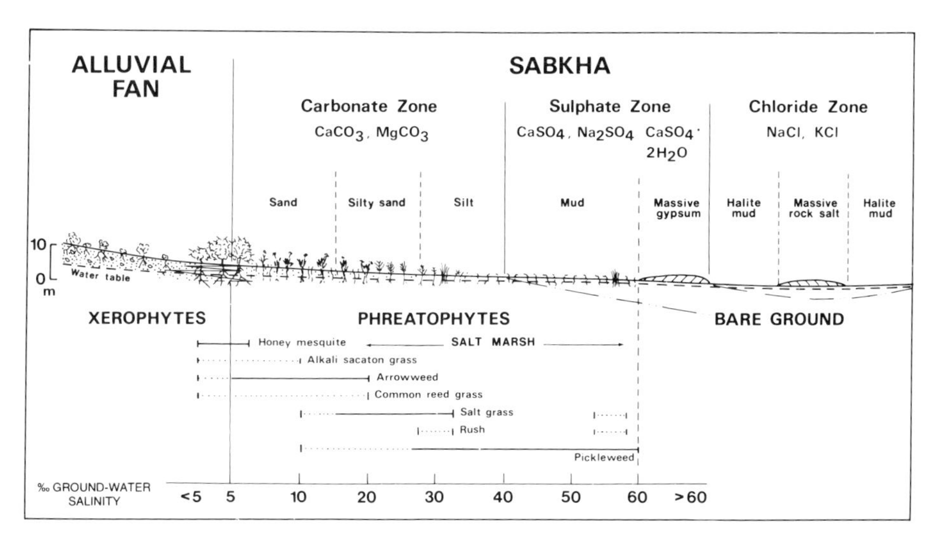

Figure 2.12 Idealized transect of a vegetation and evaporite sequence, Death Valley sabkha, California. Although carbonates are commonly first and chlorides last to precipitate in a sabkha, many salt minerals occur in various amounts throughout, and the relationship between ground-water salinity, soil salinity and vegetation is complex
(Vegetation after Hunt 1966)

34 mm from rainfall and 251 mm from the melting of ground ice in the underlying peat to give a total of 861 mm (Roulet and Woo 1986). Outputs during the period comprised 331 mm of surface discharge, 1 mm of ground-water flow limited by the low gradient and low hydraulic conductivity of the peat and 223 mm of evaporation to give a total of 555 mm. Thus water storage increased by 306 mm during the summer, largely because evaporation was replaced by melting ground ice, but most of this reverted to ice or was drained from the wetland as winter arrived. Wetlands overlying discontinuous permafrost in valleys behave in a similar way. In central Alaska, for example, valley wetlands dominated by black spruce (*Picea mariana*), Labrador tea (*Ledum groenlandicum*) and blueberry (*Vaccinium*) generated rapid surface flows during storms because high water-tables limited storage capacity (Dingman 1973). In contrast, in the prairie wetlands that overlie clay-rich tills, end moraines and outwash deposits from Alberta southeastward to Iowa, the water balance is dominated by gains and losses directly from the atmosphere; surface water flows are insignificant except during snowmelt, but modest ground-water interaction affects the chemistry of the wetlands. As seasonal hydrological fluctuations diminish and microclimates become less severe south towards the Gulf coast of the United States, lacustrine wetlands become floristically more complex and swamp forests are often well developed, for example from Wisconsin at intervals southwards along the Mississippi valley.

Lacustrine wetlands are widespread in the humid tropics, for example in the remarkable floating papyrus swamps of Lake Victoria. The response of such wetlands to changing hydrologies and water chemistry is well illustrated from Lake St Lucia in South Africa, which originated as a coastal lagoon but whose middle and inner parts now behave as a lacustrine wetland. The main plant communities within the wetland are reed swamp dominated by *Phragmites australis* and *Cyperus papyrus*, evergreen swamp forest dominated by *Ficus hippopotamus, Ficus sycamorus, Syzygium coratum, Barringtonia racemosa* and others, small patches of mangrove swamp with *Bruguiera gymnorhiza* and *Avicennia marina*, and marsh grassland occupied by hygrophilous grasses, sedges and rushes (Orme 1975). Because these communities offer valuable food and shelter to a rich and varied fauna, including the world's southernmost large breeding populations of *Hippopotamus amphibius* and *Crocodylus niloticus*, changes in hydrology and water chemistry which affect the vegetation in turn disrupt animal life and related food chains.

As discussed earlier, Lake St Lucia now averages only 312 km^2 in area and less than 2 m in depth. It exchanges water readily with the atmosphere but, owing to intermittent barrier growth across its mouth, less readily with the sea. Mean annual rainfall over the lake averages 1000 mm, 60 per cent of which falls from October to March. Mean annual evaporation is about 1320 mm. Thus, to survive, the system must depend on erratic freshwater inflows from its 8900 km^2 drainage basin, or on incursions of sea water up The Narrows (figure 2.2). The relative contributions of these two sources strongly influence the lake's salinity and ecosystem vitality. During floods, the lake may rise to 1 m above MSL and cover 417 km^2; negligible salinity is recorded at river mouths but the horizontal salinity gradient rises southward to reach seawater values of 35‰ in the estuary. Most of the lake behaves as a freshwater lacustrine system with aquatics such as *Potamogeton* flourishing. During normal dry seasons, stream flow is much reduced, small streams stop flowing and effluent seepage from swamps diminishes. Lake levels drop and salt water penetrates farther up The Narrows. Freshwater vegetation begins to suffer stress as salinities rise above 10‰. During prolonged drought, stream flow ceases, lake levels drop below MSL and, provided that the estuary remains open, high tides push salt water through The Narrows. When Lake St Lucia falls to 1 m below MSL, sea water floods into the estuary at about 7 m^3/s. Much of this reaches the main lake and evaporates, raising salinity above normal seawater values and reversing the normal salinity gradient (figure 2.13). During extreme drought, salinities of 80‰–120‰ may occur in the lake, and *Phragmites* swamps in particular die back and come to resemble the burned-over stubble of harvested grain fields (plate 2.9). *Potamogeton* disappears and even the sea grass *Zostera marina* comes under stress. Thereafter, a chain reaction spreads as plankton, fish, birds and larger animals all suffer. Recent attempts have been made to alleviate the more extreme problems, but the situation in Lake St Lucia remains as an example of the changes that can beset such wetlands.

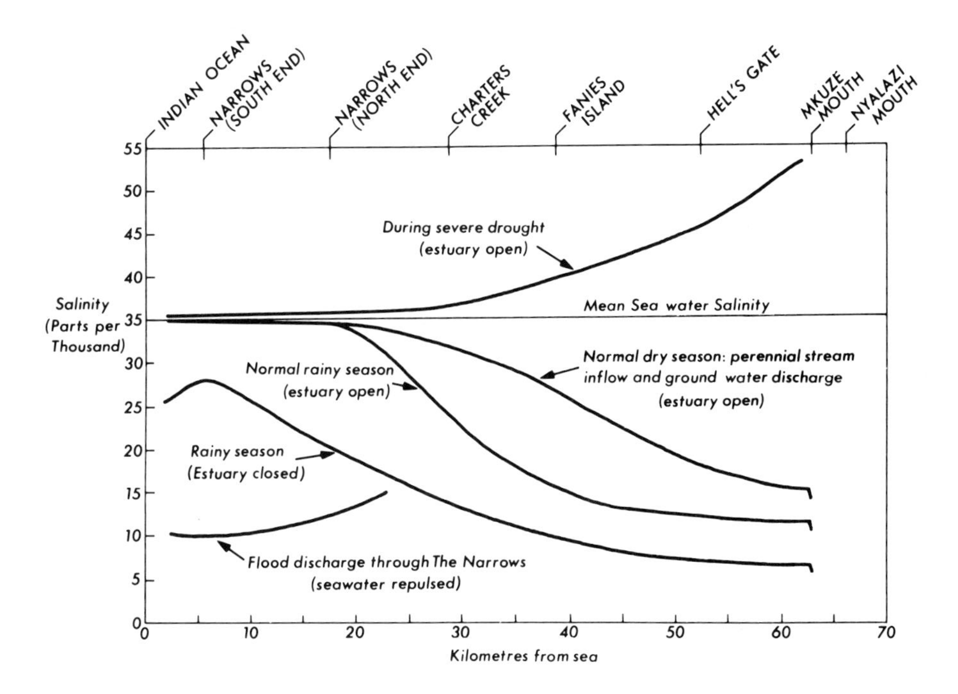

Figure 2.13 Lake St Lucia, South Africa, showing how horizontal salinity gradients change under different conditions
(Orme 1975; data courtesy of Natal Parks, Game and Fish Preservation Board)

Plate 2.9 (a) Flourishing *Phragmites australis* reedswamp, with hippopotamus for scale, Lake St Lucia, South Africa, October 1971. (b) *Phragmites australis* reduced to low stubble by hypersaline conditions, Lake St Lucia, South Africa, November 1971
(Courtesy A. R. Orme)

4.3 *Palustrine wetlands*

These wetlands comprise a wide range of physical situations, water regimes, chemistries and vegetation types. They include wetlands traditionally called by such English names as mire, marsh, swamp, bog, fen and carr, by such American Indian terms as muskeg and pocosin, and by a multitude of names elsewhere. The term *mire* has recently been advocated to cover all variants (Gore 1983a), but semantic problems continue to plague wetland categorization worldwide.

The distinction between palustrine and other interior wetlands is arbitrary because these systems often merge laterally with one another while, in a temporal sense, palustrine bogs commonly develop from lacustrine fens. Palustrine wetlands usually originate in similar physical situations to lacustrine wetlands, namely topographic lows and areas underlain by impermeable materials. Later, however, with the development of ombrogenous bogs, the underlying surface becomes much less important than climatic controls. Oligotrophic mires develop in regions where annual precipitation far exceeds evaporation, namely in cool temperate to arctic regions. These are normally areas vacated by Pleistocene ice sheets which have left a legacy of deranged drainage and isostatic response to former ice loading. Paludification often followed isostatic emergence so that former coastal wetlands were transformed into interior mires and became mantled with peat. In the Hudson Bay lowlands and around the Gulf of Bothnia peat thickness increases from a few centimetres near the present coast to several metres inland in direct relation to the duration of isostatic emergence.

The world's most extensive interior wetlands are mostly palustrine systems. In cool temperate to arctic regions such mires may cover vast tracts of land, interspersed only with bare rock and lakes. About 30 per cent of Finland, some 10.4×10^6 ha, came to be occupied by mires following deglaciation, although this area has since been halved by drainage and reclamation. Similarly, peatlands, once covered about 16 per cent of Ireland, or 1.3×10^6 ha. The USSR has 83×10^6 ha of peatland alone, of which 39×10^6 ha occur in western Siberia, plus a large area of marshes and swamps farther south where peat formation is less important (Botch and Masing 1983). Canada's muskeg and other interior wetlands cover perhaps 170×10^6 ha or 16 per cent of the country (Zoltai and Pollett 1983). In the southern hemisphere, wetlands occur in the Magellanic tundra complex of southernmost South America where, despite the absence of permafrost, impermeable soil horizons caused by gleying or iron pans combine with high precipitation and low evaporation to form bogs dominated by *Sphagnum* mosses and liverworts. Similar conditions favour bog growth in Tasmania and New Zealand.

In mid-latitudes, oligotrophic bogs become less significant and the relative importance of mesotrophic swamps and eutrophic fens increases. In relatively flat areas of North America and Eurasia, vast wetlands may develop. In the coterminous United States, for example, oligotrophic bogs and related peats are less significant than in Canada and mostly occur in cool temperate regions near the Canadian border, notably in Maine and the western Great Lakes area. Mesotrophic to eutrophic wetlands occur as wet prairies from Wisconsin westward to Montana, and at frequent intervals throughout the Atlantic and Gulf coastal plain from New Jersey to Texas and inland through the Mississippi basin. Prairie wetlands include palustrine areas covering up to 4000 ha with Manna grasses (*Glyceria*) and sedges (*Carex*), and the lacustrine and riverine systems previously noted. *Spartina pectinata* and *Tripsacum dactyloides* dominate mesic wetlands over several hundred square kilometres along the Missouri and other major rivers.

Wetlands in the southeast United States vary considerably in size, sediment type and vegetation, but include some of the country's largest peat areas, most notably in the Dismal Swamp of Virginia and North Carolina, the Okefenokee Swamp in Georgia and the Florida Everglades. The Dismal Swamp once covered 5000 km^2 but now has an area of about 84 km^2, Okefenokee Swamp still covers around 1600 km^2 and the Florida Everglades originally occupied more than 10 000 km^2 from Lake Okeechobee to the coastal wetlands around Florida's southern tip (Hofstetter 1983). Vegetation throughout most of the coastal plain reflects water depth, water chemistry and substrate conditions. Deep swamps in the Mississippi basin are dominated by bald cypress (*Taxodium distichum*) and tupelo gum (*Nyssa aquatica*), but on better drained swamps along the Gulf coastal plain these are largely replaced by *Taxodium ascendens* and *Nyssa sylvatica*. Shallow swamps are usually dominated by *Salix*. Peaty swamps overlying the acid soils of poorly drained coastal terrain are dominated by Atlantic white cedar (*Chamaecyparis thyoides*), often in association with various pines and swamp hardwoods, but these species have declined significantly in recent decades, often at the expense of red maple (*Acer rubrum*). Pocosins, or evergreen shrub bogs which are often partly ombrotrophic, occur on poorly drained interfluves and terraces along the Atlantic coastal plain, notably in the 'Carolina bays'. The Florida Everglades were historically a vast graminoid wetland containing scattered tree islands, much modified since by drainage impoundments and canals. The Everglades have an average southward slope of 2.8 cm/km. The graminoid wetland was dominated by a wide variety of submerged, floating and emergent aquatics, with the saw grass (*Cladium jamaicense*) accounting for up to 70 per cent of the cover. Owing to a near-tropical climate, the tree islands contain both warm temperate plants like sweet bay (*Magnolia virginiana*) and tropical species like the fig *Ficus aurea*.

In Eurasia, the USSR has vast expanses of temperate wetlands. Notable among these are the Pripyat Marshes (Poles'ye) of Byelorussia which occupy a broad tectonic basin mantled by glacial and fluvioglacial deposits. These marshes contain alder swamps dominated by *Alnus glutinosa*, pine bogs with *Pinus sylvestris* and fens characterized by *Pragmites australis*, *Carex* and *Equisetum*. Peat deposits have accumulated under mostly eutrophic conditions. To the south, reed and sedge ferns are interspersed with the forest steppe from the Ukraine to central Asia.

In the tropics, palustrine wetlands often merge laterally with lacustrine and riverine swamps, as around Lake Victoria and the Sudd of Sudan respectively, but because evaporation consistently exceeds precipitation, bogs are not found below 2000 m. At lower elevations, wetlands are either graminoid swamps, characterized by the dominance of one species such as *Cyperus papyrus*, *Cladium mariscus*, *Phragmites australis* or *Typha domingensis*, or swamp forests dominated by *Ficus*, *Syzygium* and other genera already noted in Lake St Lucia. At middle elevations, fens may be associated with the major peat-former *Pycreus* or with *Phragmites australis* or with a mix of *Syzygium* and various heath plants (Thompson and Hamilton 1983). In areas of heavy rainfall above 2000 m, valley bogs may develop in association with *Carex* and locally *Sphagnum* notably in east Africa's higher mountains, but blanket and raised bogs are very rare in the tropics.

4.4 *The character and evolution of fens and bogs*

Mires favouring peat formation are commonly divided into fens and bogs, each with relatively distinct physical and vegetal properties that reflect their environment and evolution (table 2.4). However, there is a broad transition between true fen and true bog while, in a temporal scenario, fens may evolve into bogs.

Fens are typically minerotrophic in that they are mostly fed by telluric water derived by lateral drainage or ground-water inflows from sources beyond the fen margins, with some atmospheric precipitation directly onto the fen surface (table 2.4). Well supplied with minerals from soils and rock weathering, the water chemistry of fens is eutrophic or alkaline, grading to mesotrophic or neutral as precipitation increases or nutrient supplies diminish. At the surface,

Table 2.4 Classification of bog and fen characteristics

	Bog	*Fen*
Shape or character	Raised bog Blanket bog	Treeless fen Tree fen, carr, swamp forest
Water source	Ombrotrophic (atmospheric precipitation directly onto bog surface)	Minerotrophic (mostly telluric water from lateral drainage or ground-water inflow)
Water chemistry	Oligotrophic Acid, mineral poor	Eutrophic-mesotrophic Neutral-alkaline, mineral-rich
Peat genesis	Ombrogenous Mostly topogenous	Geogenous Topogenous or soligenous
Typical plants in middle to high latitudes	*Sphagnum* *Eriophorum* *Rhynchospora* *Carex* *Scirpus* *Pinus* *Picea* *Larix* *Thuja*	*Carex* *Scirpus* *Phragmites* *Cladium* *Equisetum* *Sphagnum* *Pinus* *Alnus* *Betula*

a distinction can be made between treeless fens characterized by *Carex, Scirpus, Cladium, Cyperus, Heleocharis* and other sedges and grasses, and tree fens or carrs characterized in colder regions by *Alnus, Betula, Salix* and a field vegetation of sedges and grasses. Fens are floristically rich and varied, especially in warmer regions. Fen peat forms under geogenous conditions in which surface and subsurface geochemistry is a dominant control, with water being either soligenous (flowing) or topogenous (stagnant). Most valley 'bogs' are really soligenous fens. The distinction between treeless fens and tree fens is reflected in the difference between marsh peats composed of sedges and grasses, and wood peats containing much woody debris. Most mires form as soligenous riverine and lacustrine fens or as topogenous palustrine fens and, with a continuing throughflow of minerotrophic waters, remain so. Where minerotrophic inputs decline, however, waters become increasingly acid and fens are transformed into 'poor fens' and eventually into bogs.

Bogs are typically ombrotrophic in that their water comes directly from atmospheric precipitation onto the bog surface as rain, snow, hail, dew or frost (table 2.4). As such, mineral supplies are very limited and water chemistry is oligotrophic or acid. At the surface, typical fen plants yield to other sedges and grasses like *Eriophorum, Rhynchospora* and *Molinia*, to dwarf shrubs like *Myrica gale* (bog myrtle) and ultimately to *Sphagnum* mosses. Better drained bog margins may favour some tree growth, notably *Alnus, Pinus, Picea* and *Larix*. In terms of morphology, it is common to distinguish between raised bogs and blanket bogs. Raised bogs usually form in topographic lows in pervasively wet climates, initially as lacustrine or palustrine fens whose accumulating plant debris raises the surface until minerotrophic waters diminish and further mire growth is ombrotrophic. Thereafter, provided that the rate of accumulation of vegetal matter exceeds the rate of decay, bog growth will continue until a characteristic domed or raised bog is created whose centre may be several metres above its outward-sloping margins. Minerotrophic conditions and thus fens may persist beyond the bog margins. Blanket bogs develop in regions of persistent precipitation, low evaporation and poor drainage. They overlie both topographic lows and hill slopes underlain by impermeable clay or iron pans. Their disregard for modest slope changes and their dependence on atmospheric precipitation has sometimes led blanket bogs to be termed 'climatic bogs' (plate 2.10). Blanket bogs evolve in much the same way as raised bogs, with fen peats on hillsides accumulating until minerotrophic conditions are replaced by ombrotrophic conditions and *Sphagnum* mosses become dominant. Ultimately, raised and blanket bogs grow through the accumulation of ombrogenous peats which, because of poor drainage, are typically topogenous (see plate 1.5).

Sphagnum mosses play an important role in the growth of bogs, although their precise significance and the role of *Sphagnum* hummocks in the cyclic regeneration of bogs has occasioned much controversy. *Sphagnum*'s myriad cells trap precipitation and the small quantity of nutrients contained therein, and use these as needed for growth. This activity is concentrated in the acrotelm, the active permeable and thus aerobic upper zone at and just beneath

Plate 2.10 Blanket bog south of the Twelve Bens, Connemara, Ireland. Rainfall in the area ranges from 1500 to 2500 mm annually and measurable rain falls on over 250 days a year (Courtesy J. K. St Joseph, 10/86426)

the bog surface. Hummock-building species such as *Sphagnum fuscum* will form mounds to the limits of available water as long as accumulation rates exceed decay rates. These conditions normally prevail only in the top 20–30 cm of the bog. Below that level, in the catotelm, high water-tables promote anaerobic conditions and partially decayed plants accumulate as peat.

Some of the world's most extensive mires are represented by fens of middle and low latitudes, such as the prairie wetlands of central North America, the swamps of the southeast United States, central Africa and southeast Asia, and the Pripyat Marshes of eastern Europe. Even in low evaporative environments, such as the Canadian muskeg and Siberian mires, fens are common because available precipitation is relatively low. However, where available precipitation is high and evaporation remains low, notably on the west side of continents in cool temperate regions, true bogs may develop.

The biostratigraphic record preserved in fen and bog peats tells us much about the climates and environmental changes under which they formed. This record has been well revealed in Ireland by the pioneering work of Jessen (1949) and later Mitchell (1965), and both the growth and destruction of Irish bogs have been documented (Orme 1970). This record helps to illustrate the global pattern of wetland change in Holocene times.

In Ireland, as elsewhere, pollen analysis, microfaunal studies and radiometric dating have provided a good record of environmental change over the past 15 000 years. Ireland's present wetlands began forming during the waning stages of the last glaciation as the main ice sheet retreated from its lowland margins (figure 2.14). Thereafter wetland development can be related to traditional pollen zones and assemblages. Around 13 000 BP, in the cold oceanic conditions of Zone I, open tundra spread across a vacated glaciated landscape whose many lakes and deranged streams favoured wetlands although the accumulation of muddy substrates and arrival of suitable plants were initially slow. During Zone II, around 12 400 to 10 900 BP, warmer conditions encouraged streams to carry partly organic muds (gyttja) into lakes and fen development was associated with such plants as *Eleocharis, Ranunculus* and *Littorella*, while a *Betula-Juniperus* parkland developed elsewhere. Zone III, from 10 900 to 10 000 BP, was a relatively short cold snap which saw the redevelopment of cirque glaciers in the mountains and a reversion to herbaceous tundra elsewhere, but lake fens probably survived at reduced rates of productivity.

The Holocene Epoch began with a brief transition phase, Zone IV from 10 000 to 9500 BP, during which *Betula-Juniperus* parkland prepared the way for the *Corylus-Pinus* assemblage of Zone V from 9500 to 8000 BP and the *Corylus-Pinus-Quercus-Ulmus* woodlands of Zone VI from 8000 to 7000 BP (Mitchell 1976). In the lakes and rivers among these woodlands, both treeless and tree fens flourished. The pollen record from Zone V in particular reveals the arrival and spread of many temperate fen plants such as the submerged aquatics *Utricularia* and *Ceratophyllum*, the pondweed *Potamogeton*, the water lilies *Nuphar* and *Nymphaea*, and sedges and grasses such as *Carex, Cladium mariscus, Schoenoplectus lacustris* and *Phragmites australis*. If ground-water levels remained steady, the fen margins were invaded by *Salix, Betula* and perhaps *Pinus*, and the fen was extinguished. If water-tables rose, fen plants expanded their range and herbaceous fen peats began to mantle wood peats. The continued growth of fen peats during the Boreal climatic phase (Zones V and VI) suggests that Ireland did not experience the relatively dry climate of contemporary Europe, although the spread of woodlands to the west coast indicates that conditions were less stormy than later.

Around 7000 BP, a dramatic change appears in the pollen record heralding Zone VII which lasted to around 2500 BP. Moisture-loving *Alnus* rises rapidly in the pollen rain, while raised bogs associated with highly humified *Sphagnum* become signfiicant. These events indicate greater wetness and have led to the designation of a warm wet Atlantic phase of climate under which the postglacial woodlands reached their greatest extent. However, bearing in mind

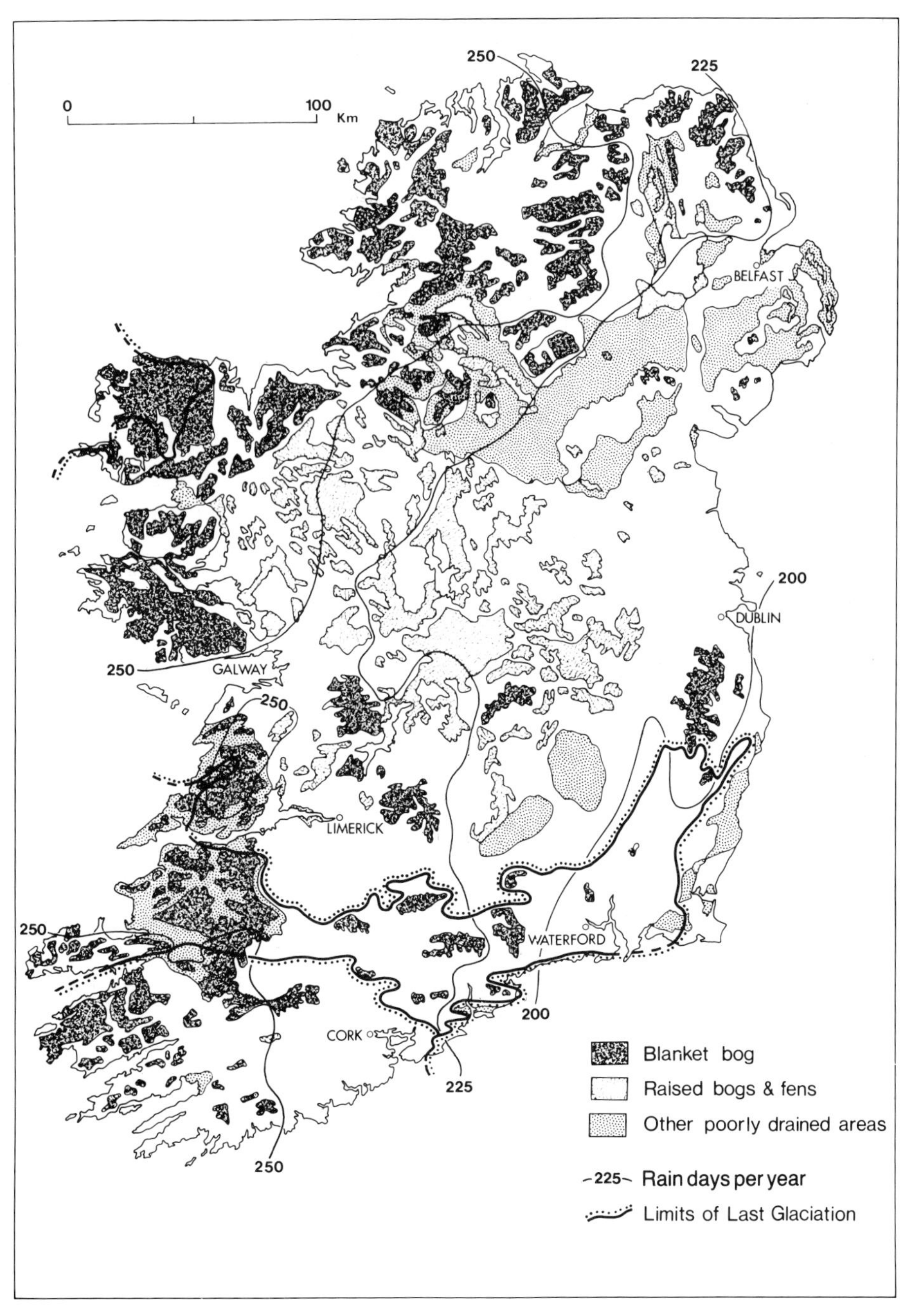

Figure 2.14 Wetlands of Ireland relative to glaciation limits and rain days. Raised bogs lie within areas of low relief and deranged drainage inherited from the Last (Midlandian) Glaciation. Although blanket bogs lie within areas exceeding 1000 mm of annual precipitation, it is the persistence rather than the total quantity of precipitation that favours bog growth. The number of rain days annually is a useful measure of this persistence

(Orme 1970; bogs generalized from a map prepared by the Geological Survey of Ireland in 1907 before significant reclamation began)

the earlier discussion, it may be argued that the transition from fen to bog, or from minerotrophic to ombrotrophic conditions, can also be accomplished by the accumulation of fen peat to a threshold wherein fen plants can no longer draw upon nutrient-rich ground-waters and thus yield to plants like *Sphagnum* that can flourish under ombrotrophic conditions. Thus, 7000 years ago, raised-bog growth may have been favoured without climatic change. However, it seems unlikely that so many fens would reach a critical threshold more or less simultaneously, or that *Alnus* would spread so rapidly without some climatic change. However, fens did survive, both as distinct features around lakes and rivers, and as rims around expanding raised bogs.

Neolithic farmers arrived in Ireland sometime before 5500 BP, adding a new and complex dimension to interpretations of the pollen record and wetland growth. By the ensuing Bronze Age, which began around 4000 BP, the bogs were a sufficient hindrance to movement that wooden trackways were built across them, in Ireland, in the Somerset Levels of southwest England and elswhere (chapter 5). Furthermore, it has been argued that the shifting cultivation practised by these early farmers increased leaching, podsolization and iron-pan formation in forest clearings, and that these iron pans impeded drainage which in turn favoured fen plants and ultimately bog growth. Certainly in several parts of Ireland, field banks, dwellings and burial sites of Neolithic and Bronze Age origins have been observed beneath blanket bogs. However, it seems more likely that the growth of blanket bogs was climatically induced, aided locally by human activity. In Ireland, blanket bog began forming before 4000 BP and is still forming today, but there have been significant changes in bog growth during this time. Initially bog growth was relatively slow, perhaps 1 cm in 140 years (A. Smith, in Mitchell 1976), leaving sufficient time for humification or decomposition.

Around 2500 BP, during Ireland's late Bronze Age and heralding pollen Zone VIII (2500–1500 BP), well-humified peats in both the raised and blanket bogs were overlain with fresh to moderately humified peats, an indication of accelerated bog growth. This boundary is the *Grenzhorizont* of Weber (1900) which, throughout northern Europe, has been linked traditionally to a climatic deterioration around the beginnings of the Iron Age. After possibly warmer drier conditions between 5000 and 2500 BP (the sub-Boreal phase?), the sub-Atlantic climate after 2500 BP became wetter and more windy and the summers perhaps 2.5 °C cooler than before. During this period, which continues today, raised and blanket bogs reached their maximum extent, at least until attacked by human activities.

Blanket bogs spread indiscriminately across western Ireland and also occur in the Antrim Plateau and the Wicklow Mountains. They vary from a few decimetres to more than 6 m in depth but, although they may occur on slopes of up to 20°, bogs more than 2 m deep often become unstable when heavy rains reduce their shear strength, causing dramatic bog bursts. Although they occur in areas with between 1000 and 2500 mm of annual rainfall, it is the persistence rather than the total quantity of precipitation that is important. The blanket bog around Glenamoy in northwest Ireland experiences 1500 mm of rainfall over 270 days annually. Over an 11-month period, a natural bog near Glenamoy received 1098 mm of precipitation and lost 485 mm to evaporation and 519 mm to surface run-off, for a net gain of 94 mm. The peat was observed to remain saturated for long periods and even during summer dry spells the water-table seldom fell more than 25 cm below the surface (Burke 1975). The hydraulic conductivity of the peat was also low, ranging from 18 to 130 mm/day. In contrast, measurements from a nearby plot provided with drains 3.5 m apart and 0.8 m deep indicated a run-off of 870 mm for a net loss of 257 mm, or 351 mm more than the undrained bog. This experiment shows how drains can produce a negative water balance for a bog, an effect that is cumulative and will cause shrinkage of the peat mass and a redirection of drainage from undrained towards drained areas. In many areas, peat cutting and rill erosion have exposed blanket bog to wind deflation until isolated peat haggs are left standing on bare rock. Everywhere, persistent rains and low evaporation maintain downward and lateral flows in the bog system so that organic acids forming in the peat are never neutralized by mineral bases from underlying sources. Thus acid peats may even be found on limestone.

The raised bogs of central Ireland average around 6 m in depth but may locally exceed 10 m. They developed mainly from fens occupying lakes and poorly drained hollows in the early postglacial landscape, and with the development of ombrotrophic conditions expanded and coalesced across low water-partings. Fens survive in favourable locations, notably around Lough Neagh and Lower Lough Erne, and alongside the Shannon, Barrow and Suir rivers farther south, but large areas of fen have been drained and reclaimed, just as some of the most extensive raised bogs have been stripped to fuel the peat-fired power stations and then converted to forestry and agriculture.

5.0 CONCLUSION

Wetlands are transitional between dry land and open water, and between terrestrial and aquatic ecosystems. Their normally low gradients render them susceptible to change should there be an adjustment in the external forces operating on nearby land and water. Change may also be produced by forces internal to wetlands, notably in the relationship between hydrodynamics and vegetation growth. Thus, although many wetlands may appear to be in equilibrium with their environment, that equilibrium is neither static nor can it sustain close investigation. Complicating any generalizations is the recognition that the internal dynamics of coastal and interior wetlands tend to be different. Coastal wetlands tend to achieve a steady-state of equilibrium whereby change occurs within a reasonably constant condition. This is because their morphodynamics are determined by sea level, or more precisely by the trimming effects of tides which condition the range of elevations over which tidal currents, wave action, river flows and saturation can function. Interior wetlands may initially be constrained by stream flows and ground-water levels, but under ombrotrophic conditions they may continue to raise their surface independently of these water sources, such that a steady-state equilibrium is less readily achieved.

The theme of wetlands threatened by human activity calls for a concluding perspective from the physical sciences. The world's present wetlands came into existence in response to prolonged changes in the environment. This chapter began by showing how coastal wetlands responded to the Flandrian transgression by migrating up the continental shelf until, after sea-level rise diminished, some form of steady-state was achieved between morphology, hydrodynamics and sedimentation. The chapter closed by discussing how fens and bogs responded to changing postglacial climates until distinctive forms became established. In both scenarios, it is often assumed that the present condition of wetlands represents a steady state equilibrium, with surface form responding to changes that are compensating over time. This is not necessarily so. Coastal wetlands are now responding to a modest rise of sea level whose effects are likely to be cumulative, causing further landward migration of salt marshes and mangrove swamps as their seaward margins are progressively submerged or eroded. Interior wetlands may well be responding to global climatic changes whose true magnitude is as yet difficult to define, but which could lead to either desiccation or inundation depending on the area. Sea-level rise and global climatic change are presumably related and represent vast forces that are probably beyond human control, although the extent to which society has caused or can control the 'greenhouse effect' is hotly debated.

Human impacts on wetlands are undeniably impressive. In middle latitudes in particular vast areas of wetland have been drained and reclaimed. However, in the longer term, are these changes more significant than the modifications induced by global climatic change and rising seal level? Are wetlands being destroyed by human activity in some localities, while being created elsewhere by the vast forces of nature?

3

Soils and Ecology: Temperate Wetlands

Peter D. Moore

1.0 INTRODUCTION

Wetland ecosystems have one main feature in common, namely their subjection to temporary or permanent waterlogging. This common experience has led to a number of other ecological similarities in the physiological and behavioural peculiarities of their inhabitant plants and animals, and in the physical and chemical conditions found in their soils. However, despite these basic similarities, there exists a very considerable range of wetland habitat types depending upon such factors as salinity, hydrology, climate and successional stage (see figure 1.2).

The underlying ecological unity of wetlands is best appreciated when they are viewed as ecosystems, using the approach pioneered and developed by Odum (1969) for successional systems, in which the flow of energy through and the cycling of chemical elements within the system form the basis for understanding its ecological structure and function. In this review of temperate wetland ecology and soils, this approach will be adopted to provide an overview of the dynamics of ecological processes. The variation in habitat types and the consequent modifications in energy flow and nutrient cycling patterns will also be considered. After this, it will be possible to examine the sensitivities of temperate wetland ecosystems to disturbance of various kinds.

2.0 THE WETLAND ECOSYSTEM

The one characteristic of wetland ecosystems which determines the nature of their ecological processes is their subjection to high ground-water-tables and the influence this may have upon the inhibition of decomposition and the transport of materials (both organic and inorganic) into the system from outside (allochthonous material). Any suppression of decomposition and input of allochthonous organic matter modifies the flow of energy through the ecosystem, while the supply of nutrient materials is also influenced by the input of dissolved and suspended inorganic matter in the flow of water. These two influences will be considered in turn.

2.1 *Wetland energetics*

A basic scheme to illustrate the flow of energy through the wetland ecosystem is shown in figure 3.1. The input of energy into the system comes via sunlight and the photosynthetic activity of the plants, the primary producers, and also in allochthonous organic matter washed from other ecosystems. The relative importance of these two sources will vary considerably between different types of wetland ecosystem. In estuarine mud flats, for example, the bulk of the energy input is from allochthonous organic matter, with only a small supply of local (autochthonous) energy production from such organisms as diatoms and pioneer mud-inhabiting higher plants such as *Salicornia* and *Zostera*. In freshwater swamps, in contrast, the local energy input from *in situ* vegetation usually exceeds the energy importation in water flow, and in raised bogs, where the water supply comes only from rainfall, almost all energy supply is autochthonous.

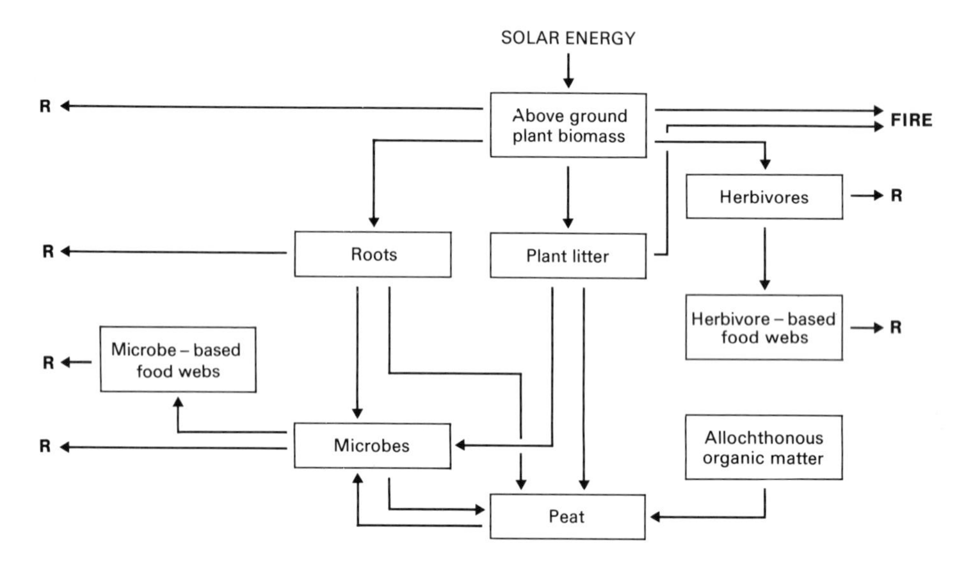

Figure 3.1 Model of energy flow within a mire ecosystem. The arrows indicate the direction of energy and R represents the energy lost in the process of respiration

The energy fixed in photosynthesis (gross primary production) is partly used for the metabolic maintenance of the plants and partly for the growth of tissues such as stem, leaves and roots and in reproduction (together constituting net primary production). The living tissues of photosynthetic plants may be consumed by grazing animals, whether microscopic plankton that feed upon diatoms or higher animals that graze upon larger plants. Much of the energy they consume is used in respiration and is lost to the ecosystem as heat. Those plant tissues which survive the impact of grazing die and join the accumulating allochthonous organic matter in the substrate as litter.

Soil organic matter in the wetland ecosystem forms an energy resource for many heterotrophic organisms (those living organisms which cannot fix their own energy). These include detritivores (mobile animals that scavenge for dead materials) and decomposers (microbes-bacteria and fungi). These also use the energy-rich foods they consume to satisfy their own energetic requirements with a loss of respiratory heat.

In all these general respects, the wetland ecosystem is similar to most others. It differs, however, in the imbalance found in the overall energy budget. In a steady state ecosystem the rate of energy input is equalled by the rate of energy output; hence reservoirs of energy, such as the biomass of living organisms and the organic matter in the soil, remain reasonably constant despite the flow of energy through them. In an imbalanced system the size of these reservoirs changes in response to a difference between energy inputs and the sum of energy outputs. Such an imbalance can come about in a variety of ways. If an ecological system is in the course of succession, the biomass will normally be increasing, and so outputs of energy fall below the inputs. If an ecosystem is being harvested by human activity at a rate that is in excess of its productivity, then the biomass reservoir will shrink. If the consumption is low and decomposition of organic material is inhibited, as in the case of wetland ecosystems where waterlogging restricts microbial activity, then soil organic matter accumulates within the system. The accretion of muds in coastal wetlands and of peat mainly in freshwater wetlands is a consequence of this incomplete decomposition and is a characteristic of this type of habitat.

The energetics of a mire can be summarized in the following equation:

$$\mathrm{GPP} + \mathrm{IMP} = \mathrm{B} + \mathrm{ER} + \mathrm{EXP} + \mathrm{P}$$

where GPP is the gross primary productivity, IMP is the imported organic material, B is the change in ecosystem biomass, ER is the respiration of the entire ecosystem (including plants, animals and microbes), EXP is the exported organic material and P is the growth in soil organic matter. This formula applies to any wetland ecosystem, but the precise pattern of energy movement and storage varies according to such factors as hydrology, productivity and successional stage. This can be illustrated by reference to a range of wetland types.

2.2 *Energy patterns: mudflats, salt marshes, swamps and fens*

In order to examine the variation of energy balance in different mires, a variety of types will be considered individually. In the case of peatland habitats there are many confusions in the literature concerning the terminology used. The terms used here (as in Moore 1987a) are those considered to be most widely accepted among peatland ecologists; some of the terms, however, are used in different ways by American ecologists.

Mud flats are saline wetlands, often developed in estuarine conditions, in which the major source of energy is allochthonous organic matter. Detritivore activity is high and forms the basis of complex food webs at the top of which are many wading birds. Some of the higher plants of such habitats, although of lesser importance in terms of energy input, are also an important resource, such as *Zostera* as the main food of brent geese (*Branta bernicla*).

Salt marshes are successful vegetation types often developed from mud flats and differ in their higher green plant biomass. Hence they have higher input of autochthonous primary production and, at their higher levels, a reduced flooding frequency resulting in lower rates of organic and inorganic sedimentation.

Net primary productivity in salt marshes is very variable both geographically and from one season to another (Morris 1988). Published values vary from 0.25 kg/m/yr to over 3 kg/m/yr (Stout 1988). These figures apply to above-ground net production only and the indications are that below-ground production is in excess of this. Herbivore consumption is generally low; Parsons and de la Cruz (1980) estimate grasshopper grazing in *Juncus* marshes at only 0.03 per cent of the net production. Effectively, such levels of grazing can be neglected in the overall energy budget of the system.

In many temperate salt marshes the highest biomass achieved within the succession is the high marsh vegetation consisting of monocotyledonous herbs, often rushes such as *Juncus maritimus* and *Juncus gerardi* in Europe and *Juncus roemerianus* in North America. As marine flooding becomes less frequent, allochthonous organic matter input is reduced, apart from tide-line detritus. Decomposition rates depend upon the nature of the plant detritus (*Juncus* tissues decay less rapidly than *Spartina* (Stout 1988)) and the degree to which soil water levels fall between tides and allow the entry of atmospheric oxygen into the soils. Above the soil surface the litter is exposed to alternate wetting and drying, and the decomposition rate is at its greatest. Stout (1988) has collated information on litter loss rates and finds an average loss of 47 per cent dry matter each year. Once incorporated into the soil, decomposition rates will become slower, both because of the poorer availability of oxygen and because the more palatable materials will already have been exploited by the first wave of microbes. Some anaerobic bacteria continue to operate using sulphate ions rather than oxygen as an oxidizing agent.

Swamps are freshwater wetland ecosystems most characteristic of lake margins and the upper reaches of estuaries, in which both allochthonous (mainly inorganic) and autochthonous organic matter contribute to the accretion of the sediment (figure 3.2, A). All freshwater, peat-forming ecosystems can be referred to by the general term *mire*. Swamps are usually dominated by herbaceous monocotyledonous plant communities, often attaining heights of 2–3 m above the water surface. By definition, a swamp has a water-table permanently above the sediment surface. Spence (1982) has reviewed records of water depth in different types of temperate swamp and has shown that the growing-season water-table may be as much as 1.5 m above the sediment surface in swamps of bulrush (*Schoenoplectus lacustris*) and horsetail (*Equisetum fluviatile*), although average figures are about 0.9 m. It is possible for swamps to maintain themselves in deeper water by forming a floating carpet of vegetation, often extending from marginal swamps around the edge of a lake. This is often found in swamps dominated by cattails (*Typha*) and bottle sedge (*Carex rostrata*) in temperate areas, but is more characteristic of tropical swamps dominated by papyrus (*Cyperus papyrus*), as described by Gaudet (1979).

One distinctive feature of swamps is their low diversity of species and the degree of dominance exhibited by just one species, such as bulrush, reed or cattail (reedmace). The high water-table offers little opportunity for smaller species to form an understorey vegetation. This simplicity of structure does not diminish productivity (see below), but it has profound effects on the vertebrate inhabitants of swamps, demanding, for instance, high levels of sophistication in nesting techniques for birds.

The input of organic matter by water transport is not usually great unless the wetland is fed by eroding peat in the uplands or lies in an estuary. The local vegetation is often highly productive, frequently exceeding 1 kg/m/yr (Bradbury and Grace 1983). There are records of some sedge (*Carex*) swamps in New Jersey (Jervis 1969) and some cattail (*Typha*) swamps in Czechoslovakia (Kvet 1971) reaching net production values in excess of 2 kg/m/yr; these values relate to above ground production only. The below-ground production, in the form of rhizomes and roots, may well equal that seen above ground, and this contributes directly to the organic fraction in the soil. Figures showing the comparability of above- and below-ground production in swamps are recorded in the work of Klopatek and Stearns (1978) for example. Bradbury and Grace (1983) have assembled data on the productivity of a range of swamp types and they do not feel that the total net primary production in swamps often exceeds 3 kg/m/yr. Such figures place swamps and certain types of salt marshes among the most productive of wetland ecosystems, and possibly among the most productive ecosystems in the world.

The soils accumulated in this type of habitat, however, are not exceptionally rich in organic matter, despite the high organic input from primary productivity. This implies that rates of decomposition must be very rapid. Mason and Bryant (1975) have studied decomposition in swamps and have recorded complete degradation of the leaf tissues of such swamp plants as reed (*Phragmites*) and cattail or reedmace (*Typha*) in less than 2 years. This rate of tissue breakdown is evidently adequate to remove most of the energy-rich material from the system, and so very little becomes incorporated into the sediment.

The main supply of oxygen to the submerged rhizomes of swamp plants is by diffusion through the plant tissues themselves. This diffusion, through lacunae in the tissues, may be so efficient that it supplies the oxygen demands of surrounding soil (Stepniewski and Glinski 1988) and may contribute to the

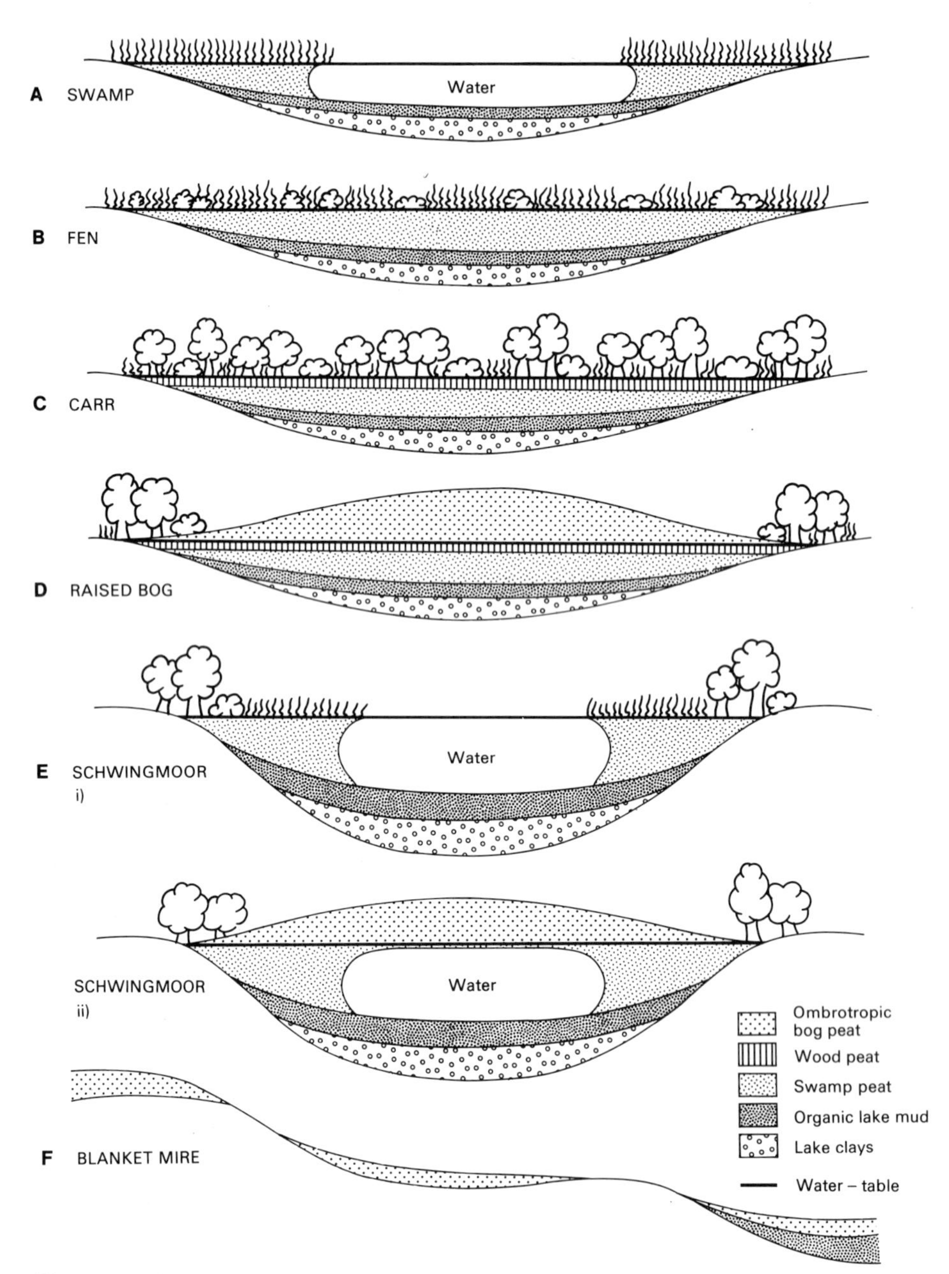

Figure 3.2 Idealized sections of various types of mire, showing the sediment profiles and the arrangement of vegetation. Cross-sections A-D describe a hydroseral succession in which open water becomes invaded by swamp, fen and carr vegetation, finally giving way to bog following the invasion of *Sphagnum* moss. Cross-sections E show the progressive development of a schwingmoor, where floating mats of vegetation colonize the lake surface and form a platform upon which bog vegetation can develop. Cross-section F represents a blanket mire developing over plateaux and slopes in response to wet conditions due to high precipitation and low temperature, often exacerbated by the removal of a former forest

maintenance of decomposition. The movement of oxygen into the below-ground plant tissues is matched by a reverse diffusion of carbon dioxide. Even so, concentrations of this gas can reach levels of 20 per cent.

The sediments that accumulate beneath swamp ecosystems are usually rich in allochthonous inorganic matter brought to the site of deposition by ground-water flow. This is partly due to the strong flow of water through such lacustrine and deltaic ecosystems and to the year-round flooding they experience. A wetland system in which such movement of ground-water takes place, bringing with it not only energy-rich but also nutrient materials, can be termed *rheotrophic* (Moore and Bellamy 1973). The rhizomes of the major swamp plants survive very much better than other tissues; having been developed in the anaerobic sediments beneath the water, they have not had to spend time as litter, either in the air or in the oxygenated surface layers of water, where decomposition can be expected to occur more rapidly.

Fen is a wetland type often following swamp in the development of hydroseral succession (figure 3.2, B). It differs from swamp mainly in its hydrology, having a summer water-table at or below the sediment surface but being flooded in winter. Spence (1982), for example, records the depth of the growing-season water-table in meadowsweet (*Filipendula*) fen as 0.14 m below the soil surface, and 0.25 m below in the case of sweetgrass (*Glyceria maxima*) fen. The wetness of fens, particularly in winter, may be maintained by topographic features of the site (topogenous fens) or by the lateral flow of water (soligenous fens).

The species diversity of fens is invariably higher than that of swamps, as is shown by the work of Wheeler (1984, 1988) in Britain. Often the dominant species of the swamp stage survive as important members of the fen community and contribute very substantially to their productivity, but the lower growing-season water-table allows other less flood tolerant species to join the community. Unmanaged fen, however, develops a high biomass and this is often associated with a reduction in species richness (Wheeler 1988).

The net primary productivity of fens is generally lower than that of swamps and varies with such factors as climate and nutrient supply. Bradbury and Grace (1983) have collated values, most of which lie in the region 0.5–1 kg/m/yr for above-ground production. The input of allochthonous material is likely to be smaller than in the case of swamps because of the reduced flow of water through the system.

The soils accumulating beneath fens experience a higher degree of aeration, especially in summer, and so their decomposition process is seasonally active, though the waterlogged conditions of winter can permit the survival of even some delicate tissues such as bryophyte remains. As a consequence of the lower inorganic input to fens in comparison with swamps, the organic content of fen peats is relatively higher.

2.3 *Energy patterns: swamp forests and carrs*

In North America some authors restrict the term 'swamp' to wetlands dominated by woody vegetation and use the term 'marsh' for the herbaceous vegetation here called 'swamp'. This terminology is not applied by all American authorities (e.g. Gleason and Cronquist 1964) and it is considered here that the European system has more precise definitions and is easier to operate for purposes of mire classification (Moore and Bellamy 1973, Moore 1984).

Rheotrophic mires with high water-tables may bear forest vegetation, which often invades swamp and fen if the process of succession is not interrupted (plate 3.1). In the management of such wetlands, the swamp and fen stages can be maintained either by removal of biomass in the form of harvested above-ground tissues or by continually raising the water-table. The former management technique operates both by reducing the energy (in the form of litter) available for the build-up of sediment and by restricting the invasion of woody species. It is the basis of ancient forms of fenland management when reeds were harvested for thatch.

Clearly, the biomass present in this kind of ecosystem is very much greater than that in the non-forested types of swamp, but the species richness (number of plant species per unit area) is generally lower than in fens. Above-ground net primary productivity is usually less than in swamps. Values range from about 0.6 kg/m/yr for *Alnus-Fraxinus* (alder and ash) swamps in Michigan (Parker and Schneider 1975) through about 0.7 kg/m/yr for *Taxodium distichum* (swamp cypress) communities in Georgia (Schlesinger 1978) to over 1 kg/m/yr for *Thuja-Betula* swamp in Minnesota (Reiners 1972). Thus the highest levels of above-ground productivity achieved by swamp forests begin to overlap with

Plate 3.1 Alder carr (*Alnus glutinosa*) with trees becoming established on tussock sedge (*Carex paniculata*) in Sutton Park, West Midlands
(Courtesy P. D. Moore)

those of herbaceous swamps, but figures are generally lower. Lower-latitude swamp forests have higher productivities, such as the swamp forests of Florida with net above-ground values of 2–3 kg/m/yr (Gower et al. 1985).

The higher overall net primary productivities achieved by herbaceous swamps is a consequence of the patterns of resource allocation in herbs and trees. In the herbaceous perennial that dominates most swamps, the energy fixed by photosynthesis is devoted partly to the growth of above-ground organs and partly to the growth of below-ground organs. The latter are an unfortunate necessity as far as the plant is concerned since it needs to take up nutrient elements in solution, it needs anchorage and it requires a water supply to compensate for the inevitable water losses sustained during the gaseous exchanges involved in photosynthesis. This means that about half the net fixed energy is directed underground and cannot be employed more gainfully in the development of more photosynthetic tissues. However, most of the above-ground structures of these swamp plants are photosynthetic, and hence investment in such tissues increases the productive potential of the plant.

In the case of trees the same constraints apply as far as the development of below-ground tissues are concerned, although even more support and anchorage is necessary for these more bulky plants. Above ground, however, a considerable proportion of the newly fixed photosynthetic materials becomes invested in non-productive support systems in the form of woody trunk and branches. To use an economic analogy, the plant can be considered to invest its energy gains either in the form of productive tissues, in which case it will gain even higher levels of interest in the next growing season, or in non-productive tissues, which yield no interest. More energy being allocated to support tissues in the high biomass sytems means less return on capital. In this way the photosynthetic efficiency of a herbaceous system is maintained above that of the higher biomass forested system.

The peat developed in forested swamp communities consists of the remains of woody tissue, together with a variable amount of inorganic sediment, depending on the pattern of flow of water through the ecosystem. Woods are naturally rich in anti-microbial agents, such as resins and tannins, normally functioning to protect the living tree from pathogens and grazing animals. It therefore decays relatively slowly. Godshalk and Wetzel (1978) showed that fibre content is also important in restricting decay rates. The rate of decomposition of plant tissues is closely, and inversely, related to the total fibre content of the tissue. However, lower overall productivity, fluctuating water-table and irregular input of inorganic sediment mean that peat accretion in forested swamps is often slow. Fluctuations in the water-table leads to periods of oxygenated conditions, especially during the summer, and this enhances peat and litter decomposition. Rapid sedimentation is occasionally recorded in the sediment stratigraphy of wooded swamps, often as a result of high inputs of allochthonous, usually inorganic, material brought by catchment erosion. This is well illustrated by a valley carr in southern Spain (Moore 1987b, Stevenson and Moore 1988) in which human deforestation of the catchment by Bronze Age agriculturalists resulted in increased water flow from the catchment and consequent soil instability, leading to rapid inorganic sedimentation within the carr. When this happens, the preservation state of plant material, especially wood, is greatly enhanced.

Events of this kind, however, may create such energetic floods that erosion of sediments takes place within the carr, leaving a hiatus in the sediment stratigraphy. This example illustrates the manner in which wetland ecosystems, as a result of their unusual energetic patterns and accumulating organic reserves, leave a record of their own history in their sediments. Such a record means that more information is available concerning the sequence of vegetation in wetland succession than in any other type of ecosystem. Rather surprisingly, however, few attempts have been made to collate such information to produce models of wetland succession (Walker 1970, Tallis 1983).

2.4 *Energy patterns: bogs*

Bog is a term that should be reserved for those acid nutrient-poor peat-forming ecosystems that are dependent entirely on rainfall for their water and their nutrient supply (*ombrotrophic* systems). The term bog includes elevated raised bogs that may or may not be forested, blanket bogs and certain parts of schwingmoor and valley mire complexes (figure 3.2, E and F). Stratigraphic studies of sediments, such as those described above, indicate that bogs often succeed forest in their development, and they represent an unusual type of succession in that the later stages are often lower in living biomass than preceding stages. Bogs are often dominated by plants of relatively small stature, such as mosses, especially the true bog mosses (*Sphagnum*). These are the plants mainly responsible for the successional process from forest to bog, for their growth creates local micro-habitats in which nutrients are depleted and acidity is increased, thus rendering the regeneration of the swamp woodland trees more difficult. Different species of *Sphagnum* have different tolerance limits with respect to nutrient supply and they replace one another during the course of the mire succession, eventually leading to domination of the bog vegetation by acidophilous species. Other plants present in bog ecosystems include herbaceous monocotyledons, such as the cotton sedges (*Eriophorum*) and various dwarf shrubs, often belonging to the family Ericaceae (such as *Calluna*, *Erica*, *Ledum*, *Chamaedaphne* etc.). Many bogs, such as the raised or domed bogs of both oceanic and continental temperate regions (plate 3.2), develop in isolated peat masses over former lake basins or estuarine swamps (figure 3.2 D). Others, such as the blanket mires (plate 3.3) that are found in only the most oceanic regions, form an extensive peat cover over plateaux, hill slopes and valleys, but only where the rainfall is adequate to maintain waterlogging even in sites which are by nature water-shedding.

The productivity of bog systems is generally lower than that of the preceding successional stages. Typical figures from British bogs, dominated by *Calluna*, *Eriophorum* and *Sphagnum* fall in the region of 0.3 to 0.8 kg/m/yr (Forrest and Smith 1975). Similar sites in Canada (Reader and Stewart 1972, Reader 1978) also yield figures of 0.1–1.0 kg/m/yr, although some of the sites they quote may

Plate 3.2 Raised mire surface with pools and hummocks, Clara Bog, central Ireland
(Courtesy P. D. Moore)

Plate 3.3 Blanket mire dominated by cotton sedges (*Eriophorum vaginatum*) and heather (*Calluna vulgaris*) on the hills of eastern Wales
(Courtesy P. D. Moore)

not be bogs in the sense used here, but poor fens (they use the hybrid term 'bog marsh' to describe some of their sites). Some bogs are forested, such as the continental boreal bogs of Canada, Scandinavia and the USSR as well as the tropical bog forests of the southeastern Asiatic region, particularly Sarawak. Boreal forested bogs bear mainly coniferous trees, often pine (*Pinus*), spruce (*Picea*) or tamarak (*Larix*). Although they have a higher biomass than non-forested bogs, their productivity is often of the same order. Reader and Stewart (1972), for example, give a figure of about 0.4–0.5 kg/m/yr for forested bog vegetation in Manitoba. Peat formation in such bogs still proceeds rapidly, however, providing excellent conditions for the preservation of plant tissues, including the lignified tissues of the former trees.

Despite the low productivity of true bogs, their rate of peat accumulation is surprisingly rapid. Aaby and Tauber (1974) estimated rates on the basis of radiocarbon-dated peat profiles and quote values varying from 0.16 to 0.8 mm/yr for raised bog peat in Denmark. They also found that the higher growth rates were accompanied by lower degrees of humification, i.e. the degree to which plant tissues had been broken down by the activity of microbial decomposers. The rapid peat accretion must therefore be due to low decomposition rates rather than high productivity.

Water arrives at the surface of a raised bog almost entirely in the form of atmospheric precipitation; therefore particulate inorganic matter arriving at the surface of such mires will mainly be in the form of rain-washed dust. There are records of such dust contributing a significant proportion of the accumulating peat, particularly where the bog is situated close to prairie vegetation when blown soils and the silica phytoliths from decaying grass tissues may be deposited onto the bog surface in some quantity. More often, however, peats from bog systems have a very low inorganic component. The ash content of pure *Sphagnum* peat is usually less than 5 per cent and often less than 1 per cent (Clymo 1983).

Decomposition processes are greater in the surface layers of peat, where air penetration occurs during relatively dry periods. Clymo (1965) placed samples of *Sphagnum* in muslin bags and buried them at various depths in a bog peat profile. He showed that the loss in dry weight of *Sphagnum* tissues was about six times as great at the surface of bog peat than at a depth of 50 cm. The higher rates of decomposition in Clymo's experiment are confined to a relatively narrow zone of surface peat, only about 20 cm in depth, although the precise depth varies from one bog to another. This loosely compacted surface layer of peat (termed the *acrotelm*, as distinguished from the more compacted waterlogged anaerobic *catotelm* below (Ingram 1978, 1983)) is also of considerable hydrological significance, for most of the lateral movement of mire water takes place through it as a consequence of its greater hydrological conductivity. Even within the acrotelm Bragg (1982) has demonstrated that the hydraulic conductivity in the upper part is three times as great as in the layers where it abutts on to the catotelm.

As a result of the poor levels of microbial activity in bog peats, the state of preservation of plant and animal material within the peat is often extremely good. Even the delicate tissues of bryophyte leaves may be preserved intact and allow precise identification of fossils. Many factors contribute to the exceptionally low rates of decomposition in such sites, including efficient waterlogging (the mosses themselves retain up to 20 times their own weight of water) and the rapid rise of organic matter build-up which soon results in an object dropped upon the mire surface becoming engulfed and taken below the critical level into the anaerobic catotelm. Low pH is maintained in part by the ion exchange properties of the *Sphagnum* plants which release hydrogen ions into their surroundings, and this keeps decomposition down. Also, it is possible that the production of anti-microbial toxins by the plant tissues may be a factor in determining the low decomposition rates in *Sphagnum* peats. The traditional use of *Sphagnum* as a wound dressing may well be related to this property.

2.5 *Energy patterns: floating bogs*

Just as some swamps can develop as floating rafts and colonize deep aquatic basins, so floating or 'quaking' bogs can develop on top of the rafts of floating swamp vegetation (Figure 3.2, E). The German word for this mire type, *Schwingmoor*, is often also used in English (plate 3.4). Such mires are found in the eastern United States (Conway 1949) and also in Europe (Tallis 1973). As in the case of bogs developed over stable swamps, fens and carrs, the

Plate 3.4 Schwingmoor (quaking bog) with *Pinus sylvestris* invading the floating carpet of *Sphagnum* moss
(Courtesy P. D. Moore)

development of a schwingmoor is dependent on the invasion and establishment of *Sphagnum* and its associated species. This process has been demonstrated stratigraphically in one schwingmoor site in Wales (French and Moore 1986). Forested schwingmoors may display a concentric zonation pattern in which trees become increasingly stunted towards the centre of the mire. This appears to be due to the tendency of central trees to sink through the peat raft and thus suppress their own root development by waterlogging. The outer trees are usually established in firmer peats.

The energy flow patterns of schwingmoors are similar to those in other ombrotrophic bog systems.

3.0 HYDROLOGY AND NUTRIENT CYCLING

Unlike most terrestrial ecosystems in which a major contributor to the nutrient supply is the weathering of the soil parent material, wetlands do not in general rely directly upon this source within the ecosystem but may receive the products of weathering from other ecosystems within the catchment. The basal parent material of the wetland itself is often insulated from the roots of the plants by a thickness of sediment. That sediment itself may supply nutrient material as the organic matter decomposes or ions are released by exchange, but the supply of water to the system through drainage and rainfall also form major sources of chemical elements for the vegetation.

The hydrology of a mire, especially the question of whether its water supply is mainly from ground-water drainage or from rainfall, is therefore critical in determining its supply of nutrients. Figure 3.3 shows a general scheme for water movement through a mire.

The nutrient richness and hence the floristic richness of rheotrophic mires is dependent on the concentration of plant nutrient elements in the ground-water flow and also on the rate of that flow through the system. In the case of

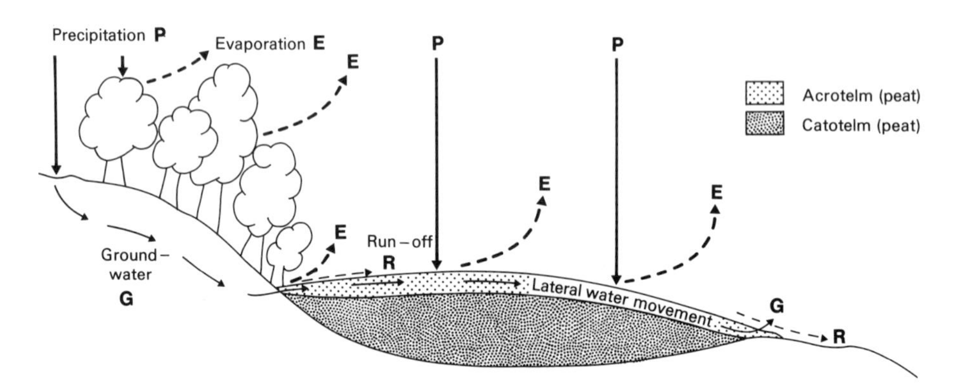

Figure 3.3 Diagrammatic representation of a mire showing the main features of its hydrology. The course of water movement to a large extent determines the supply of nutrients to the vegetation on the mire surface

Plate 3.5 Extensive reedswamp (*Phragmites australis*) developed around the perimeter of Cors Fochno, a raised bog in western Wales
(Courtesy P. D. Moore)

swamps and some fens, the supply of water and the rate of water flow is usually adequate. If the concentration of nutrients is low, then the productivity and population density of certain species, such as reeds (*Phragmites australis*), may be affected and more demanding species, such as *Typha latifolia*, may be excluded (plate 3.5). Even if the concentration of elements in the ground-water is adequate but the flow rate is slow, species with high demands may be unable to survive. On the basis of nutrient supply it is possible to distinguish a range of rheotrophic mire types, from rich to poor (see the account of mire variation in Eurola et al. (1984)).

A range of mire types also exists in which the nutrient supply varies even within the peatland system, being richer in some parts than others, depending largely on patterns of water flow. In valley mires (figure 3.4), for example, the course of a stream through the sytem provides the best supply of nutrients, and here the most demanding types of vegetation are found. Lateral parts of the system, with slow water movement, bear poorer less demanding vegetation types and some regions may develop true bog systems (Rose 1953). These mires are perhaps best termed 'mire complexes', since they have some elements of rheotrophic fen character and some of ombrotrophic bog.

Complications in hydrology can be quite unexpected and produce results in the vegetation that are difficult to explain. For example, Wilcox et al. (1986) describe a bog site in the Lake Michigan area of North America where an artesian hydrology has produced an upwelling of nutrient-rich waters in the

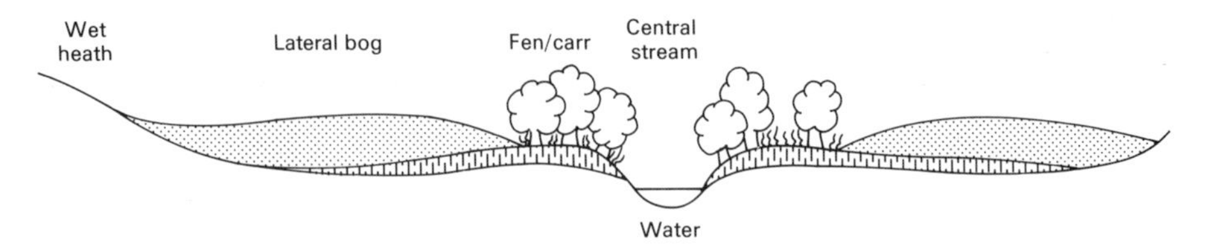

Figure 3.4 Ideal section of a valley mire complex. The fastest water flow occurs in the central area, so that this region receives the greatest supply of nutrients and therefore bears more demanding vegetation such as fen and carr. Lateral areas receive a slow percolation of acid water and develop from poor fen into bog

centre of an acid bog. This illustrates very well the importance of hydrological patterns of flow in determining the structure and vegetation of a mire.

Many other mire types, especially in boreal regions, exhibit a complex microtopography with ridges or hummocks alternating with pools or extensive runnels. There are many theories to account for their surface patterns, including the original ground-form, frost action, the hydraulic properties of peat, regeneration cycles, lateral peat movement etc. (e.g. Foster et al. 1983). From the point of view of hydrology and nutrient cycling, the important consequence of surface pattern is the effect that it has on the water movements over the surface of such a mire. In the high-latitude continental *aapa mires* or 'string bogs', for example, ridges and elongate pools are arranged at right angles to the direction of slope, and drainage water meanders through the complex system of waterways, bringing a supply of nutrients. The ridges, although only elevated by a metre or less, do not receive this flush input and bear a less nutrient demanding vegetation (Eurola et al. 1984). Therefore some peatlands cannot be categorized simply as rheotrophic or ombrotrophic, but contain a complex assemblage of both elements.

In the case of the rain-fed ombrotrophic raised mires that form domed peat masses, especially in the oceanic areas of western Europe, the nutrient supply is largely determined by the chemistry of the rainfall. In a study of the raised mires of western Ireland, Bellamy and Bellamy (1967) showed that hydrogen ions and sulphate ions in particular increase as one moves from the areas most influenced by sea spray into more continental locations, while sodium and chloride decrease.

Nitrogen cycling in mire systems, as in terrestrial systems, is more complex since it can be fixed from the atmosphere by various microbes. Several plant species found in mires have symbiotic associations with bacteria, including *Alnus glutinosa* (Bond 1974), *Myrica gale* (Dickinson 1983) and various Leguminosae (such as *Lotus pedunculatus* and *Genista tinctoria*). Free-living cyanobacteria (especially in rheotrophic mires) and those involved in lichen symbioses may also contribute; Granhall and Sernander (1973) were able to detect nitrogenase activity in a subarctic mire using the acetylene reduction technique. Moore and Bellamy (1973) quote a number of assays from various mires also using this technique and the indications are very clearly in the direction of rheotrophic mires having higher rates of nitrogen fixation. Free-living nitrogen-fixing bacteria are unlikely to be important components of peatland microbial communities, especially not in the acid bog peats (Dickinson 1983).

It may well be that the low availability of nitrogen and phosphorus has resulted in the evolution of insectivory among some ombrotrophic mire species.

4.0 ECOSYSTEM STUDIES AND WETLAND CONSERVATION

The ecosystem approach provides a view of wetlands that can be helpful in the determination of management programmes for their conservation. The key to many aspects of conservation is in the control of successional development and, in the case of wetland ecosystems, this often entails the management of energy flow, hydrology and nutrient supply.

The retention of swamp and fen ecosystems involves arresting the succession by preventing further build-up of biomass within the system and, if possible, preventing further sediment accretion. Harvesting the biomass periodically can assist in this process by reducing litter production, but it may also place a strain upon the course of energy storage in rhizomes if it is practised too frequently, as in the case of *Cladium mariscus* at Wicken Fen (Conway 1936). The alternative approach is to manage the water-table directly by raising it artificially (using dams or pumps) or by lowering the sediment surface (excavation).

Rheotrophic mires are, by their very nature, more sensitive to pollution than ombrotrophic mires. This results from their hydrology, for they receive drainage water from their surrounding catchments, whereas the surface of an ombrotrophic mire is usually relatively well insulated from ground-water. Farming or afforestation in the mire catchment can lead to eutrophication, particularly to an input of leached fertilizers, especially nitrates. This can result in increased productivity in swamps, but usually leads to dominance by robust species and a decrease in diversity. The ability of fast-growing swamp species like *Typha latifolia* to absorb nutrients from drainage water has led to proposals that they could be used as agents for water improvement, but this is most likely to be of value in tropical swamps (Gaudet 1979). Particularly vulnerable to nutrient enrichment are the highly calcerous fens and marshes which may lose sensitive species as a consequence of eutrophication. Valley bogs are also easily damaged by eutrophication, for they normally receive an influx of acid nutrient-poor water from their catchments.

Pesticides may also accumulate in rheotrophic mires and cause damage to invertebrate communities and sometimes to the vertebrates that feed upon them. In the Coto Doñana wetlands of southern Spain, substantial inwash of pesticides from surrounding farmland has resulted in disastrous mortality among resident and migrating wildfowl.

The ombrotrophic mires are less sensitive to water pollution because of their direct dependence on rainfall as their main source of water. However, they may receive pollutant material via dust input and from dissolved and suspended material in rainfall. Some mires receive a substantial aerial input of calcium from soil erosion and agricultural liming, and this may play an important part in the nutrient cycling of a calcium-poor ecosystem. Acid rain is also affecting the pH of many mires. A survey of Scottish mires by Skiba et al. (1989) has shown that there is a close correlation between the pH of the surface peat and the deposition of acid rain.

Nutrient cycling in mires can be disrupted by human activity in the form of frequent firing. Fire causes a loss of certain nutrients from the ecosystem in smoke (mainly nitrogen, sulphur and, to some extent, potassium) and releases other elements into the soil. Here it may be leached out of the system or become attached to exchange sites on the peat. The two consequences of these events are short-term flushing and enriching of the ecosystem, which may encourage more demanding species such as *Molinia caerulea* on acid bog surfaces, and long-term depletion of the nutrient reservoirs. On heathland sites, Chapman (1967) has shown that most elements, with the exception of phosphorus, are replaced by dissolved chemicals in rainfall over a 12 year period, and the same probably applies to bog sites. Frequent or high-intensity fires can be very harmful, however, especially in ombrotrophic mires.

It must be noted that some types of mire vegetation seem to need periodic burning in order to control the build-up of biomass and the resultant competition from trees. Most notable in this respect are the pitcher plant bogs of the southern states of North America. Folkerts (1982) considers that fire also maintains a low nitrogen status in these communities and thus favours insectivorous plants in the competition for this element.

The relative isolation of mires from other ecosystems of the same type can present problems for re-invasion following a catastrophe such as fire. This is particularly the case with raised mires, which are effectively island ecosystems isolated from one another by often extensive areas of alien habitats. The rheotrophic systems are less isolated in that water flow can prove an appropriate means for recolonization. One outcome of this is reflected in the seed sizes of plant species from the two types of habitat (Moore 1982). Figure 3.5 shows the seed sizes of plants from British mires arranged according to the type of mire system within which they are found: rheotrophic, mesotrophic and ombrotrophic. Not only is the greater diversity of species in rheotrophic systems apparent from this diagram, but it is also clear that only small-seeded species are able to maintain populations on ombrotrophic mires. Most of these are wind dispersed, and hence are able to travel over wide areas from one isolated raised mire to another. One of the few exceptions to this is the cloudberry (*Rubus chamaemorus*) which bears a collection of drupes in a conspicuous pink mass and is eaten and dispersed by birds. In Britain this plant is usually associated with upland blanket mires that are wide in extent and not isolated in the manner of raised mires.

Herbaceous plants play an important part in the vegetation of most mire types, and the species occurring have a range of adaptations enabling them to cope with waterlogged conditions. Among these is the structural development

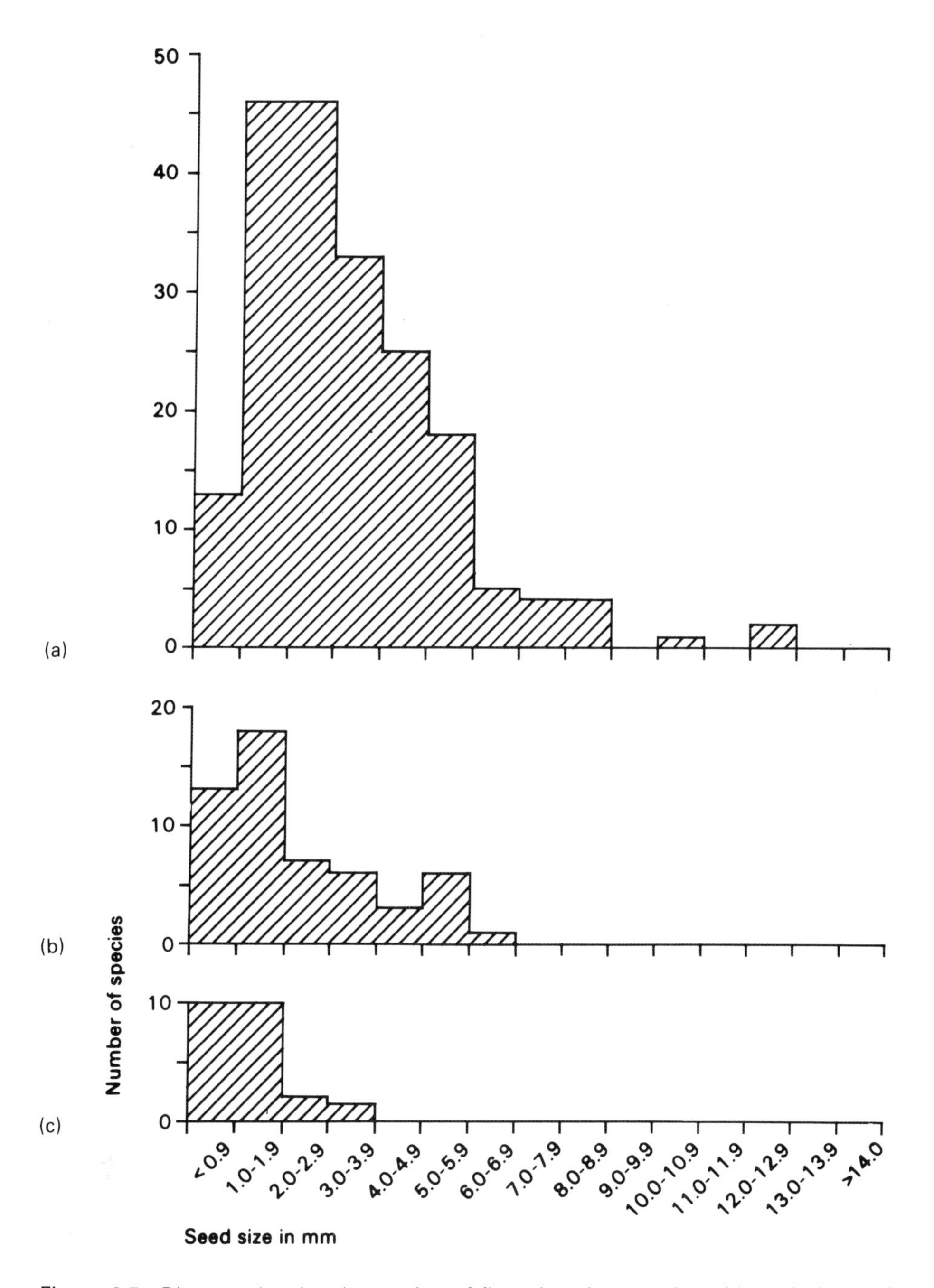

Figure 3.5 Diagram showing the number of flowering plant species with particular seed sizes (mm) in three mire types: (a) rich fen (rheotrophic); (b) poor fen (mesotrophic); (c) bog (ombrotrophic). In bog sites there are fewer species and most have small seeds – an adaptation to the problems of isolation encountered in dispersal

of air channels by which an oxygen-containing atmosphere can be made available to roots, thus enabling them to respire aerobically. A consequence of this type of adaptation, however, is sensitivity to physical damage such as that caused by trampling. Hummocks and lawns of bog mosses are similarly sensitive to such damage, and so all mires need to be protected from excessive trampling.

Slater and Agnew (1977) examined the rate of recovery of a *Sphagnum* lawn following trampling by recording the volume of individual footprints. They found that a footprint often lasted 2 years and even then recovery was largely cosmetic, for certain changes in species composition, such as an increase in the abundance of *Rhynchospora alba*, persisted. This susceptibility to trampling is now widely recognized, and the maintenance of public access to wetland sites may require the laying of wooden walkways. A recently observed complication of this solution, however, is the toxicity to *Sphagnum* mosses of copper-based wood preservatives that are often used on these structures (A. D. Q. Agnew, personal communication).

These examples illustrate the value of ecosystem studies of energy flow, nutrient cycling and hydrological relationships in the development of management plans for temperate wetland ecosystems.

4

Soils and Ecology: Tropical Wetlands

Thomas V. Armentano

1.0 TROPICAL WETLANDS

Throughout much of the tropics water regularly accumulates over portions of the landscape to levels near or above the soil surface. In freely draining soils, the accumulation is brief, but in some places the soil becomes waterlogged thereby initiating physical and chemical transformations that collectively characterize wetland soils. Hydromorphic properties such as anaerobiosis, build-up of chemically reduced salts and organic compounds and reduced microbial activity develop, creating unfavourable conditions for most plants. Specially adapted species, however, tolerate or even require wetland soil conditions, thus giving rise to the types of ecosystems characteristic of flooded soils.

In the tropics, wetland ecosystem types differ depending on the length of time the soil is saturated each year, the depth of water, the climatic regime, the soil parent material and other factors. Many wetland areas, at least until recent decades, have escaped the impact of human occupancy because of their remoteness or unsuitability for agriculture, but others such as the valley swamps of the Irrawaddy River in Burma (chapter 7), the Chao Phraya in Thailand and the Mekong in Vietnam have long supported lowland rice cultures. In recent decades, however, population pressures accompanied by technological advancements have extended human influence into previously unused wetland areas. For example, the peat formed in papyrus swamps of East Africa has been found suitable after drainage for cultivation of several crop varieties. In Indonesia, emigrants from crowded Java have, with mixed success, converted coastal swamps of adjacent islands to cropland (chapter 11). Despite these inroads and the likelihood that further losses will occur, the major tropical wetland types are still represented among the natural ecosystems of the tropics. What follows is an overview of the natural features and ecological properties of some of the more important types.

2.0 MANGROVE WETLANDS

Wherever sheltered tropical shores are flooded by tidal waters, mangrove swamps develop (see figure 1.3). A taxonomically diverse group of woody plants, mangroves are adapted in various ways to flooded saline environments. Plants sharing these adaptations are mostly trees belonging to five plant families. Because mangroves are restricted to coastal saline swamps and because few other species tolerate such environments, mangroves form easily recognized forest formations throughout the tropics.

The number of mangrove tree species found in a given coastal swamp varies widely. In the western hemisphere and in western Africa the number of species may range up to 20, but more commonly is no more than four, particularly in the subtropics. In the Caribbean region, for example, many sites are dominated by red (*Rhizophora*) and black (*Avicennia*) mangroves with a narrow zone of white mangroves (*Laguncularia*) near the upper tidal line and a scattering of button mangroves (*Conocarpus*) where the coast is only occasionally flushed by tidal waters.

In the eastern hemisphere, the number of species may range up to 50, resulting in complex communities (figure 4.1) although not all species occur on the same sites. Most locations include *Rhizophora* and *Avicennia* and also numerous other taxa. For example, in a mangrove forest on the west coast of southern Thailand, Komiyama et al (1987) found 22 species in a plot of a little over 1 ha. Bunt and Williams (1980) observed 35 species along the east coast of Queensland, Australia. Perhaps because of their greater diversity, Asian and Australian mangrove systems appear to be generally more productive, with up to twice the productivity of their subtropical western counterparts (Boto and

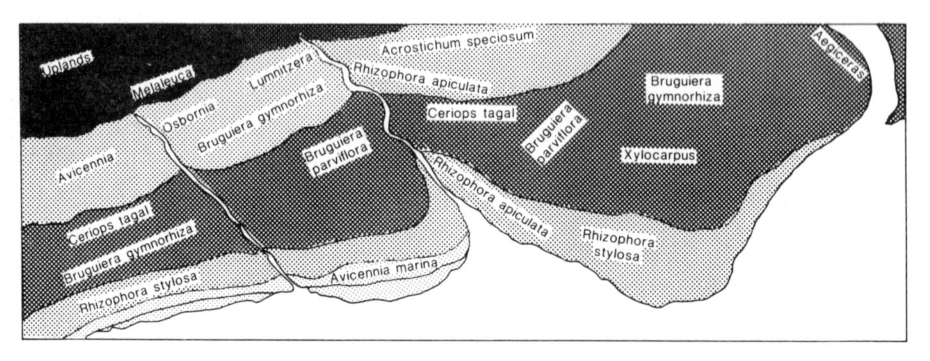

Figure 4.1 Mangrove zonation on part of the Queensland coast of Australia. *Acrostichum* is a genus of tall ferns found in the landward fringes of mangrove swamps in the neotropics and the palaeotropics. *Ceriops tagal* is a shrub or small tree that often forms dense thickets in mangrove swamps from the east African coast to Taiwan and Australia. Except for *Acrostichum* and *Melaleuca*, all named taxa are considered mangroves, although *Aegiceras* usually only occurs where there is a nearby freshwater source
(Modified from McNae 1968)

Wellington 1984). Moving westward through Asia into drier climates, mangroves become more local in distribution or disappear altogether. Human disturbance has been most severe along the Indian peninsula and many mangrove areas there are badly degraded. Yet in this same region, along the Bay of Bengal at the mouth of the Ganges-Brahmaputra Rivers, lies the Sunderbans, the largest mangrove forest of the world, originally some 800 000 ha but now reduced to about half that area (chapter 7). In Africa, diversity and productivity are relatively low compared with the mangrove forests of Asia. The scarcity of large embayments and estuaries and the generally semi-arid climate limits mangroves to mostly short-statured forests (generally less than 10 m in height) having relatively few species.

Although mangrove swamps, like all forests, are dominated by the tree stratum, mangrove ecosystems consists of a wide range of producer, consumer and decomposer organisms (McNae 1968). For example, in the seaward zones subjected to regular tides, complex communities are found attached to the aerial roots of *Rhizophora* and other mangroves. The organisms include bacteria, rotifers, shellfish, barnacles, tunicates and algae of many kinds. Many fish and crustaceans, some of commercial importance, are commonly associated with these communities and the species present may change seasonally (plate

Plate 4.1 Mudskippers, air-breathing fish unique to tropical mangrove swamps, among the aerial roots of *Sonneratia* sp., in a West Malaysia mangrove
(Courtesy T. V. Armentano)

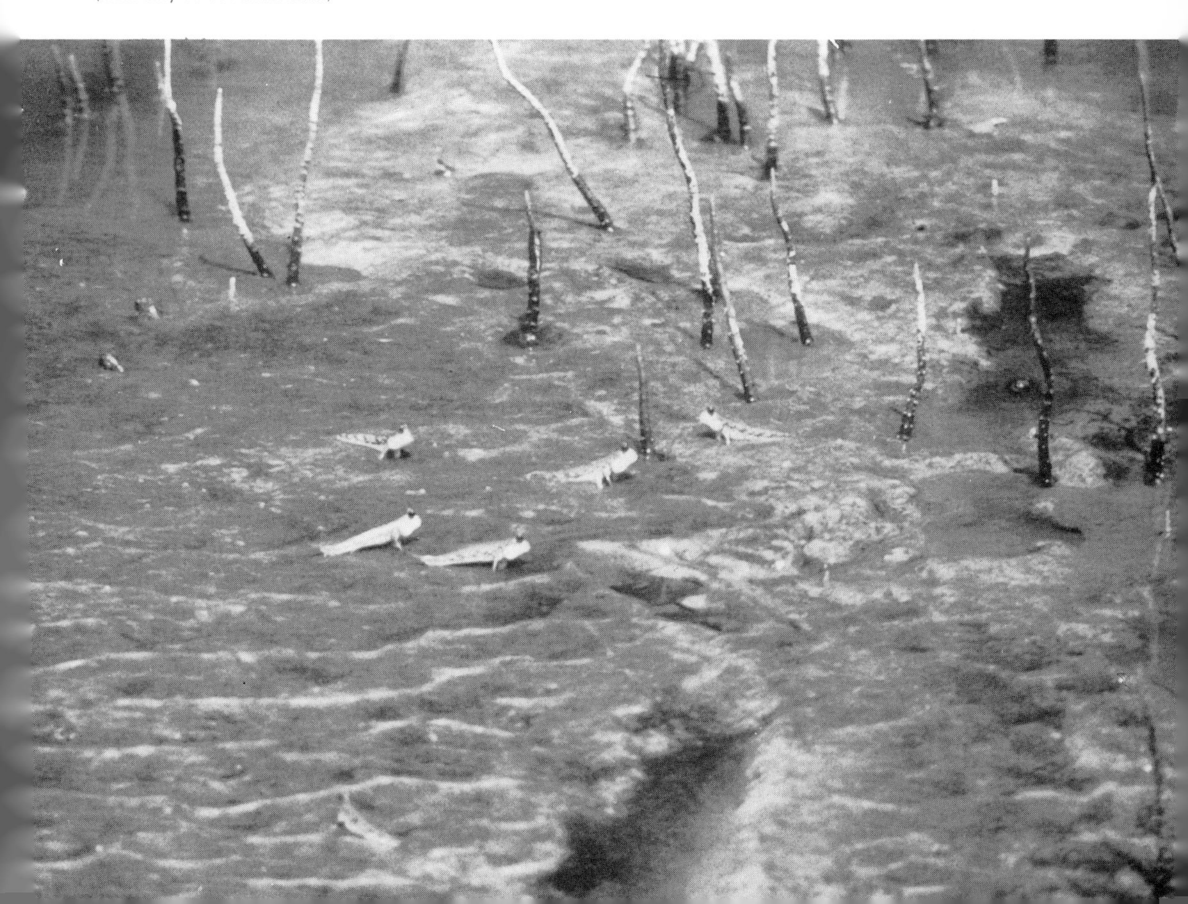

4.1). Mangroves also support a variety of terrestrial organisms such as insects, birds and even tree crabs, which consume mangrove leaves or fruits.

2.1 *Mangrove productivity and nutrient relations*

Odum et al. (1982) have summarized the diverse energy sources available to consumers within mangrove ecosystems. They range from microscopic phytoplankton to sea grasses and from decomposing mangrove leaves to bacterial chemosynthetics. The relative importance of the various sources varies from swamp to swamp, depending on local conditions. For example, where mangroves are associated with clear relatively deep water, phytoplankton (such as diatoms) can be important carbon sources for consumers spending part of their life cycle within mangrove swamps. In these circumstances, rooted sea grasses and benthic algae of the adjacent waters also supply energy to swamp consumers. Organic matter originating from phytoplankton and algae attached to mangrove prop roots may also contribute significantly under clear water conditions to food chains within mangrove ecosystems and adjacent water bodies. In other swamps, particularly where waters are not frequently flushed, the organic matter derived from leaves and other parts shed by mangroves may serve as important energy sources for aquatic food chains.

Limited study suggests that the muddy sediments in which mangroves thrive provide energy for certain kinds of bacteria which are capable of metabolizing the chemically reduced compounds that accumulate under anaerobic conditions. Most important are the sulphur bacteria which convert the abundant sulphates in seawater to reduced sulphur forms (such as hydrogen sulphide). Consumers such as rotifers or tiny arthropods ingest the bacteria, thus secondarily utilizing the energy released by sulphate reduction. In some salt marshes, and perhaps also in some mangrove swamps, bacterial metabolism of sulphur compounds is the beginning of a major energy pathway.

The rate of organic matter synthesis (productivity) of an ecosystem sets limits to the amount of energy available to support communities and food chains. Although mangrove productivity varies widely in response to soil quality, the age of the stand and species present, an overriding factor in any one region appears to be accessibility to tidal flushing and freshwater inflow. Thus Day et al. (1987) found that in Campeche, Mexico, a mangrove forest located at a river mouth where rainy season flooding augmented river waters, produced 2458 $g/m^2/yr$ of dry organic matter, a value that places mangroves among the most productive of the earth's ecosystems. In contrast, a nearby stand along a channel where tidal exchange was reduced produced only 1606 $g/m^2/yr$, underscoring the importance of hydrological conditions in determining growth potential. A similar pattern holds for other Caribbean sites (Lugo and Snedaker 1974) and in Australia and New Guinea (Boto et al. 1984). Abundant fresh water supply may also alleviate soil deficiencies such as in Cape York, Australia, where productivity is higher than expected judging from the soil phosphorus deficiency there (Boto et al. 1984). Under the extreme conditions observed by McNae (1968) in Africa and Lugo and Snedaker (1974) in Florida, mangroves may be limited to dwarfed forests (less than 3 m) where growth is very slow. Here, environmental stress such as high soil salinity appears to divert most fixed energy from storage or new tissue formation to maintenance respiration or some other physiological mechanism that allows the mangrove to cope with the stress.

Lugo and Snedaker (1974) report that, in Florida, nutrient cycling between sediments, tidal water and trees proceeds at different rates depending on tidal exchange. In riverine forests, usually dominated by *Rhizophora*, cycling is rapid and forests are better developed and more productive than in basin forests. Where tidal exchange and freshwater access are low, *Rhizophora* stands are replaced by monospecific forests of smaller slower-growing *Avicennia germinans*. The reduced tidal activity in basin forests allows a higher fraction of the deposited litter to accumulate within the ecosystem as sediment organic matter, often in the form of peat (Twilley et al. 1986). Peat sometimes also forms in red mangrove stands. If accumulated over extended periods, the peat may, in conjunction with sediments, maintain the land elevation against the rising level of the sea.

The mechanisms explaining the productivity differences between basin and riverine forests lies in the chemistry of tidal waters. Slowed tidal exchange lowers sediment oxygen levels, allowing reduced toxic chemicals such as sulphides to accumulate, and limits the transport of inorganic sediments and associated nutrients to the ecosystem. Particularly where there are extended dry periods, basins cut off from freshwater distributaries develop high water and soil salinity, exerting osmotic limits to growth even in salt-adapted mangroves (Lugo and Snedaker 1974). Although these relationships have been established empirically primarily for Caribbean sites, they probably apply generally for most mangrove areas.

2.2 *Linkages to offshore waters*

The coastal location of mangrove swamps suggests that energy and nutrient linkages to offshore waters are important. Consequently, mangroves often have been described as sources of sustenance for fish and other marine organisms. However, whether the litter (leaves, twigs, leaf scales, propagules, bracts, flowers and even insect frass) exported from mangrove swamps to estuaries and other tidal waters contributes significantly to aquatic food chains cannot be verified in every swamp studied. In fact, under some circumstances mangroves represent accumulation points for organic material imported from surrounding waters, or act as sinks rather than sources for many elements including nitrogen and phosphorus.

Energy relationships between mangroves and adjacent waters appear to vary with spatial factors and hydrological conditions. At one extreme, in frequently flooded mangrove forests such as those along tidal rivers, litter decomposition and nutrient export occur rapidly, releasing large quantities of organic matter that become available for support of food chains. Quite different are forests in backwater areas that are restricted by limited tidal exchange. Production is lower here and much organic matter remains in the sediments. Seven studies summarized by Odum et al. (1982) suggest the range of annual organic matter released to adjacent waters from mangrove forests. The mean export of particulate carbon ranged from 0.7 to 6.6 t/ha/yr. The importance of these forests for food chain support clearly would vary widely. However, because only one of the seven studies included the dissolved carbon fraction, which is difficult to measure, organic matter export values are somewhat, perhaps significantly, under-estimated. Much of the carbon in the organic matter of litter fall and root exudations may, in fact, be exported in dissolved form during irregular but intense storm events, but few sites have been analysed in this regard.

Where mangroves fringe large water bodies or line freshwater distributaries that open into large bays or estuaries, evidence indicates that mangrove-derived carbon is less important to the offshore aquatic food chain than where the receiving waters are relatively small relative to the mangrove area (de la Cruz 1985). However, mangroves adjacent to small bays and inlets can serve as important energy sources for offshore consumers and function similarly for mangrove-dwelling consumers (Rodelli et al. 1984).

2.3 *Mangrove adaptations*

In addition to having to tolerate oxygen-depleted soils that accumulate chemically reduced compounds such as organic acids, ferrous iron and hydrogen sulphide, mangroves must adapt to salt concentrations in soils far exceeding the tolerance of most land plants. The salinity levels of mangrove soils vary with location and regularity of tidal exchange. In basin or back swamp areas subject to limited tidal exchange and limited freshwater inputs, evaporation often drives salinities several times higher than seawater salt concentrations (about 30‰).

To meet the chemical and salinity stresses imposed by the intertidal environment, mangroves have developed a unique set of adaptations, some of which they share with other wetland plants and with halophytes of arid saline environments. Evidence indicates that mangroves are fully capable of growing in freshwater habitats but cannot compete with other species. Consequently, mangroves thrive only in the intertidal environment where competitive stress from non-mangrove species that lack adaptation to saline conditions is minimal.

Most conspicuously, mangroves display aerial roots that absorb atmospheric oxygen through longitudinal pores, enabling the trees to avoid the stresses of anoxic sediments (plate 4.2). Compared with other tropical trees, mangroves allocate a relatively large fraction of production to roots (Komiyama et al. 1987). Inside the aerial roots are large air spaces within loosely packed thin-walled cells (aerenchyma) which facilitate transfer of oxygen to the subterranean roots. The latter systems tend to be relatively poorly developed, restricted to the thin upper sediments and involved only secondarily in nutrient absorption and support.

Plate 4.2 Aerial pneumatophores of *Avicennia marina* and arching roots of *Rhizophora* sp. in a New Guinean mangrove
(Courtesy Armando de la Cruz)

In *Rhizophora*, long arching woody prop roots form a dense, often interwoven layer a few feet above the sediments. In addition to absorbing and translocating atmospheric gases, the prop roots anchor the red mangroves against the strong tides and frequent storms that characterize the most seaward habitat where *Rhizophora* is usually found. The pantropical *Avicennia* (black mangrove) and three Asian genera, *Lumnitzera, Carapa* and *Sonneratia*, the latter a tropical Asian genus of five species, form cylindrical erect tube-like roots extending several inches above the sediments. They also possess lenticels and aerenchyma. In these species, long horizontal cable roots just beneath the sediment surface anchor the trees and help translocate oxygen. Trees of the Old World genera *Bruguiera* and *Ceriops* have 'knee roots', small aerial roots that curl in and out of the sediment surface, which are another morphological adaptation facilitating oxygen transfer. In keeping with its preferred niche on higher ground further from the sea than the black and red mangroves, the white mangrove of tropical America and West Africa seldom develops aerial roots. Instead, a dense array of lenticels on the lower trunk meets its oxygen needs.

Salinity stress in mangroves is withstood either by excluding salt from internal tissues or by tolerating the high salinity. All true mangroves possess one or both of these traits. Red mangrove and other salt-excluding species filter out the salt in sea water at the root cell surface by 'reverse osmosis'. Although most plants absorb fresh water through the roots by taking advantage of the lower dissolved chemical content of soil water than in internal tissues (osmosis), the red mangrove reverses this gradient by preventing tissue water loss and 'pulling' water into the roots against the normal gradient. According to Scholander et al. (1962), reverse osmosis is made possible by the high negative pressure generated in the water-conducting system of the trees (xylem) by the removal of water at the leaf surface by transpiration. Even with reverse osmosis, however, salt concentration in red mangrove sap far exceeds that found in terrestrial plants (Scholander et al. 1962). Thus the red mangrove must also tolerate high salinities.

In contrast, the black and white mangroves and trees of the Asian genus *Aegiceras* secrete salt crystals from leaf glands after concentrating the salt from tissue water. Such an adaptation is shared with many plants of saline habitats such as salt deserts. These trees tolerate higher sap salt concentration than do the salt excluders. Where hypersaline conditions occur, as in poorly drained areas subject to limited tidal exchange and extended rain-free periods, *Avicennia* survives by both excluding and secreting salt. Leaf and fruit abscission also releases salt, as does the development of tissue succulence which packs large quantities of water into the tissues, thereby reducing the salt concentration (McNae 1968).

Persistence in intertidal environments requires that all stages of a plant be adapted to flooding and salinity stresses. Thus mangrove seedlings, at least for short periods, must tolerate salinities that may reach 90 parts per thousand. However, in red, white and black mangroves the youngest and perhaps most sensitive stages of the embryonic plant avoid contact with the saline environment by remaining attached to the adult plant. These trees produce reproductive structures called propagules. Within the propagule, the zygote develops uninterruptedly through to the seedling stage without a period of arrested development, thus distinguishing it from seeds. Few other higher plants exhibit this adaptive pecularity. The propagules, after dispersal, have the advantage of being able to respond immediately to favourable conditions by extending an already developed root into the sediment. However, because mangrove seedlings generally remain viable for extended periods of time and float freely, the tides may distribute them great distances until a favourable substrate is encountered. These adaptations help explain the distribution of *Avicennia, Rhizophora* and *Laguncularia* throughout the neotropics and palaeotropics.

Because black and white mangrove seedlings seem to require 5 days or more free from tidal waters to become established (Rabinowitz 1978), the two species, at least in the neotropics, are restricted to higher portions of the mangrove system. In contrast, the very large red mangrove propagules that exceed 15 g weight and 20 cm in length can establish themselves in shallow tidal waters in a shorter time.

2.4 *Distribution of mangrove species*

The distribution of the various mangrove species along shorelines varies with the interplay of physical, chemical and biological forces active in the intertidal area. Along some coastlines, mangroves are distributed in distinct species-specific zones. In many areas of the Caribbean, *Rhizophora* usually occupies the lowest portion of the intertidal zone, *Laguncularia* occupies the landward stretch and *Avicennia* is located in between. According to Davis (1942), the pattern recapitulates the successional sequence that begins with colonization of mud flats by *Rhizophora*. Thus, in Davis's view, vegetation modifies the habitat, rendering it more favourable for a succeeding vegetation stage. Newly stabilized sediments are colonized by *Rhizophora*, but continued sediment trapping by its roots on older sites creates conditions more suitable for *Avicennia*. As the vegetation develops, shading of the soil surface and ripening of the sediments tend to inhibit red mangrove regeneration. *Laguncularia* succeeds on former *Avicennia* sites after continued land-building distances the sites from most tides, or after sediment accumulation raises the land surface above tidal waters.

Studies of the more complex Asian mangrove forests also suggest that, in some locations, plant succession explains species distributions over time. In one of the few long-term studies of mangroves, Putz and Chan (1986) report on a mangrove stand that may represent the sole remaining patch of mature mangrove forest on the Malaysian peninsula. Sample plots established by the Malaysian Forestry Department in 1920 and annually inventoried through 1950 were resurveyed by Putz and Chan in 1980. Changing growth and survival rates over the 60 year period reflected gradual shifts in the favourability of site conditions.

Between 1920 and 1930, trees of *Rhizophora apiculata*, for example, grew rapidly but in 10 years became crowded. Growth rates of this species declined over the longer period from 1920 to 1950. The long-term study clarified that dynamic changes characterized the seemingly stable swamp forest. Although large trees were quite long lived over the census period, tree death and invasion by young trees, particularly beneath the canopy gaps formed by tree falls, clearly were important processes. A general tendency towards increasing species diversity and increased abundance of shade-tolerant trees was also observed. The somewhat shade-tolerant and long-lived *Bruguiera gymnorrhiza* gradually increased in importance, as did *Bruguiera parviflora*. The latter persists under shade as a seedling or small tree, enabling it to respond opportunistically to canopy gaps which allow light to penetrate to the forest floor. Overall the increasing tendency for shade-tolerant species to increase under the canopy of the more tolerant *Rhizophora* of more seaward zones creates a species replacement pattern resembling classical plant succession. Putz and Chan suggest that similar processes characterize the long-term dynamics of much of the prograding coastline on both sides of the Straits of Malacca.

In contrast with the conclusions of Putz and Chan (1986) and Davis (1942), some investigators have deduced that in other areas physical factors dominate biotic processes, forcing mangroves to distribute themselves according to their adaptations to these features. Thus, along the shores of the Gulf of Mexico in Tabasco, Mexico, coastal deltas change rapidly in relation to sedimentation patterns, freshwater discharge, subsidence, compaction and sea-level rise (Thom 1967). Here, mangrove forest succession appears to respond to these factors rather than influencing them in a major way. New freshwater distributaries discharging into delta areas gradually form levees that emerge above water level, providing suitable habitat for grasses and sedges. These plants increase sediment accumulation, gradually creating conditions suitable for levee building and channel deepening which allow woody shrubs such as *Avicennia germinans* to colonize. Eventually, according to them, *Rhizophora* encroaches on the *Avicennia* stands and often replaces them. However, eventually the distributary is abandoned by upstream diversion of freshwater sources. Sediment sources are slowly cut off, ending the land-building phase. Subsidence or sea-level rise may then inundate these sites, forming ponds or lagoons and thus breaking up the mangrove forest. The geomorphic cycle is completed when a stream distributary opens the submerged areas again after it achieves an elevational gradient advantage over the current distributary. Thus, rather than unidirectional succession involving a pattern of vegetation zonation, a repeated cycle of mangrove development, degradation and re-establishment responds to geomorphological changes driven largely by the competition between freshwater-derived sedimentation, subsidence and sea-level rise.

In the Tabasco site studied by Thom (1967), mangroves appear to play at most only a secondary role in trapping sediments. In many areas, however, evidence that individual mangrove trees do facilitate sediment accumulation is incontrovertible. Bird (1986) measured sediment surfaces under and around *Avicennia* mangroves in Victoria, Australia, to evaluate the trees' geomorphological role (figure 4.2). He found increased mud stabilization within the pneumatophere network and confirmed that *Avicennia* promotes intertidal surface accretion. Sediment sulphur content also can influence species distribution. In Bermuda, Nickerson and Thibodeau (1985) observed that red and black mangroves grow intermixed in a pattern linked to soil sulphide levels. Sulphides, especially as hydrogen sulphide or pyrite, form under anoxic conditions, and sometimes accumulate to toxic levels. The sulphur originates from sea water, but the energy needed by bacteria to reduce the sulphate salt to sulphide comes from organic matter found in mangrove peat. *Rhizophora* cannot tolerate high sulphide levels as can *Avicennia*, but decomposing *Rhizophora* roots provide the primary organic matter substrate for sulphate reduction. Thus, the authors hypothesize, *Rhizophora* colonizes raw sediments low in sulphide, but gradually root residues allow the sulphide to reach levels no longer tolerated by *Rhizophora*. At these places, *Avicennia* replaces *Rhizophora*. The hypothesis is strengthened by the alternating distribution of the two species over a cross-section of the upper intertidal zone parallelling soil sulphide levels.

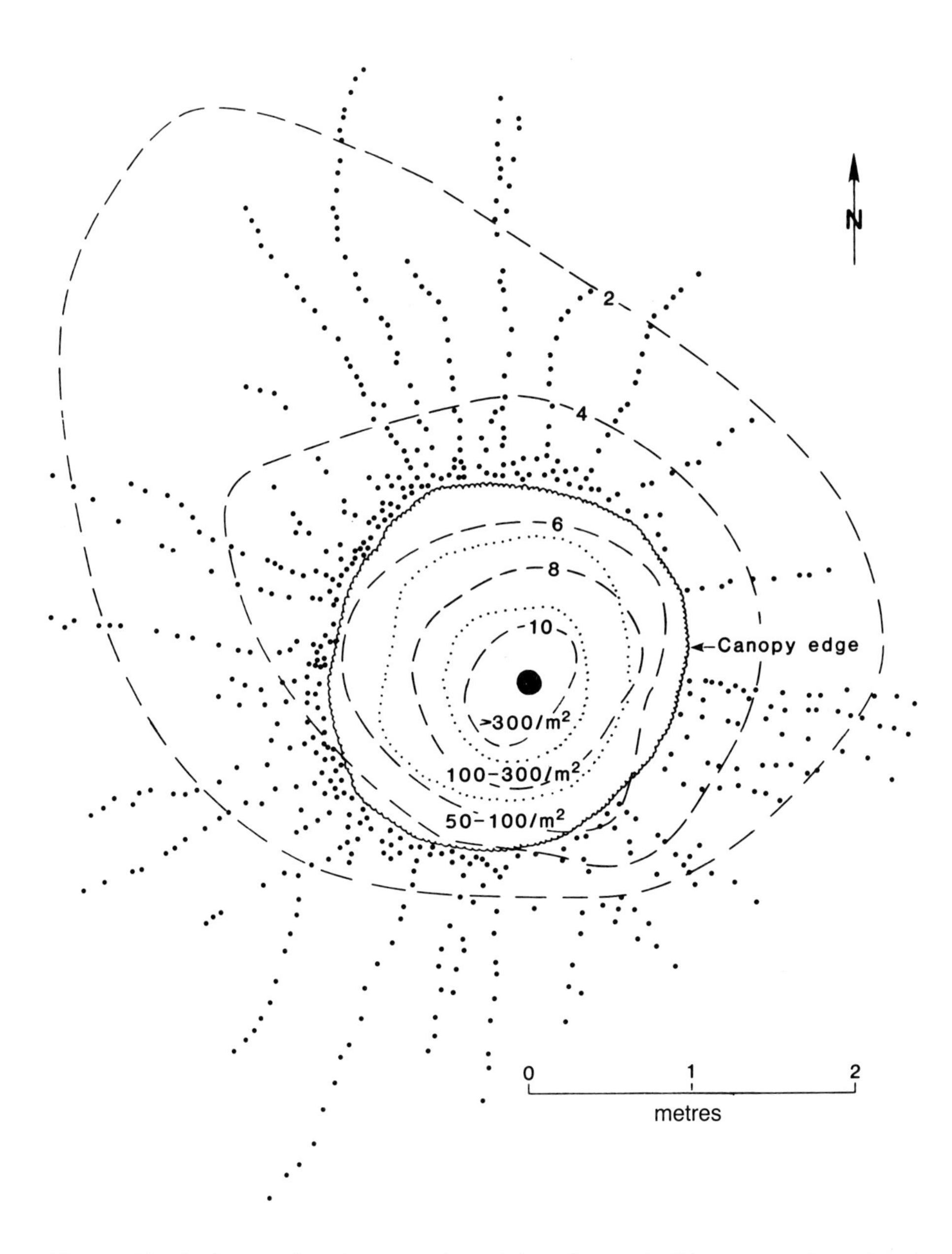

Figure 4.2 Sediment elevation around an *Avicennia* tree in Westernport Bay, Victoria, Australia. The dots represnt pneumatophores and the broken lines are contours in centimetres. The skew of the contours to the northwest is a response to prevalent southeasterly wave action
(after Bird 1986)

These and other studies clearly indicate that coastal swamps are not simple homogeneous ecosystems but complex systems whose dynamics are determined by the particular characteristics of each site. Hence, where sea levels are rising relatively rapidly, mangrove zones might actually migrate inland (Lugo and Snedaker 1974) rather than extending the terrestrial fringe. However, as Davis observed, where relative sea level is static or falling, mangroves can advance seaward as a function of sediment accumulation. In tropical deltas, such as the Irrawaddy in Burma, where rates of deposition of eroded materials are high, mangrove expansion probably follows sediment deposition but may help stabilize it. However, careful observation is needed to ascertain whether the trees are promoting or just responding to the sediment accumulation.

Nowhere is mangrove advancement more evident than in western Indonesia. Sea level has stabilized over the past 4000–5000 years, and land-building has been occurring here at rapid rates (Chambers 1980). Aerial photographs clearly show the formation of new offshore mud banks in eastern Sumatra, and parts of the coastline are advancing into the Straits of Malacca at rates averaging 20 m/yr. Colonization begins with *Sonneratia* species along the seaward edge of the mainland and nearby islands. The pneumatophores of *Sonneratia* dampen wave impact, retain detritus and sediment and indirectly provide habitat for burrowing crabs. Soil mounding above tide levels by crabs enhances soil aeration which improves sites for seed germination by other mangroves. During swamp development, the soil undergoes compaction while marine influences decline. *Sonneratia* is eventually succeeded by several other mangroves, including *Bruguiera* species and *Rhizophora* species and by the nipa palm along rivers (Samingan 1980). The interplaying factors that promote the rapid coastline extension in the Malaysian region include a large volume of sedimentary material supplied by erosion of inland highlands, rapid plant growth, heavy year-round rainfall and a stabilized sea level. Perhaps nowhere else in the world are the processes necessary for mangrove swamp expansion present in such an optimum blend.

3.0 FRESHWATER WETLANDS

In contrast with the relatively predictable intertidal wetland communities found along shorelines of tropical continents, freshwater wetland habitats vary greatly, causing corresponding diversity of vegetation types. On each continent distinctive wetland types seem to prevail like the 'floating meadows' of the Paraña, Magdalena and Amazon Rivers in South America, the papyrus marshes of highland East Africa and the peat swamp forests of Malesia. The three continents also have wetland types in common, like high montane bogs, riparian swamps and grass marshes. A brief overview of various wetland types developing in non-saline tropical areas is given below, with discussion of selected major types in some detail.

3.1 *Some wetlands of tropical South America*

Throughout tropical South America, including Amazonia, the world's largest block of tropical forest, wetlands are confined chiefly to the flood plains of the major rivers and to coastal lowlands. Although the Amazon drains the great Andean mountain chain, by the time the river reaches central Amazonia it slopes no more than 1.5 cm/km. These gentle slopes cause the river and its tributaries to meander, braid and branch, creating islands, oxbows and internal deltas of great complexity. Because of the large volumes of water transported by the Amazon and its tributaries and the dynamic migratory nature of the rivers themselves, relatively large areas have been influenced by the flood-plain environment. Salo et al. (1986), using satellite imagery, estimated that 27 per cent of the Amazonian lowland had been subject to riverborne sediment deposition or erosion during the past several thousand years, and that at present 12 per cent of the forest is in a successional stage responding to earlier disturbance by riverine processes.

Much of the current flood-plain area in tropical South America is subject to extended dry periods of 6 months or more, an unfavourable condition for wetland development. However, large areas are inundated by 5–10 m or more of overflow waters in the wet season. Close to the river channel, flooding is increasingly prolonged. Forests occurring here show increasing tolerance of the saturated soil condition characteristic of wetlands. Extensive 'floating meadows' composed mostly of herbaceous aquatic plants are found within the river channels and associated backwater pools and overflow lakes, and forests tolerant of prolonged soil inundation are present on less deeply flooded areas.

The great diversity of aquatic communities and inundation types of Amazonia has been relatively little studied. Sparse information is available on productivity, for example, although it is clearly related to the nutrient content of flood waters. A confusing terminology is still in use by various authors seeking to categorize the lowland communities. Prance (1979) has attempted to standardize the terminology of climax inundation forest types. Her system is used below to summarize briefly the major flooded habitat types of the Amazonian forests.

Forests seasonally flooded by annual river cycles, the commonest inundation type, are divisible into two subtypes according to the sediment content of the drainage waters. Whitewater swamp (*varzea*) forest is flooded by relatively sediment-rich waters that drain the Andean or pre-Andean highlands and can be found several kilometres from the riverbanks. Trees are tall and the species composition is diverse; buttress roots and pneumatophores are common. Among the interesting species are the native rubber tree (*Hevea brasiliensis*), the poisonous spiny sand box tree (*Hura crepitans*), which reaches a height of 200 ft, and the massive buttressed kapok (*Ceiba pentandra*). The understorey is rich and characterized by tall members of the banana and ginger families.

Near the coast, where seaward rivers are blocked by regular high tides, the rivers overspill, flooding surrounding areas largely with fresh water. This tidal *varzea* forest resembles the seasonal *varzea* in species composition and high biomass. Palm swamps are often found here, exhibiting nearly total dominance by *Mauritia flexuosa* or *Euterpe oleracea*. Elsewhere *Virola surinamensis* and many other hardwoods occur, mixed in varying degrees with palms.

Rivers draining the bleached white sands and acid podzolic soils of central Amazonia carry clear or black waters stained by organic acids. The waters are extremely infertile. The *igapó* forest flooded by these waters is relatively poor in species and much less productive than the *varzea* forests. Trees are small and their leaves are small, dense and fibrous, features associated with nutrient-limited environments, wet or dry. Many of the species found here are restricted to this habitat. As flooding duration declines in the *igapó*, the diversity of the vegetation increases as species less tolerant of prolonged flooding occur.

In the *igapó* forest areas and associated overflow lakes, decomposition proceeds more slowly than in adjacent terra firma forests because the infertile waters limit decomposer activity. During the water draw-down in the dry season, much of the *igapó* litter is exported and the nutrients are lost to the forest system (Irmler 1979). In contrast, in the *varzea* areas the heavy sediment loads of the white water bring in large quantities of nutrients that support decomposers and enable the vegetation to act as a net sink for the transported nutrients, retaining them within the ecosystem.

Although no true lakes occur in Amazonia (all standing waters are created by the river system), the previously mentioned areas of standing water can be classified as black water, white water or clear water lakes, each type differing in chemistry and composition of plankton, algae and other organisms (Rai and Hill 1980).

Much less extensive than seasonally flooded forests are the permanent swamp forests. These tend to be relatively local, associated with seasonal swamps but forming only where soil remains waterlogged. In the back-swamps water is commonly held behind a natural levee or other barrier that impedes horizontal drainage, while the clay soils impede vertical drainage. Species diversity is low, and is restricted to forms that tolerate the anoxic reducing conditions of the soil. Roots growing out of the above-ground stem are a common adaptation that bypasses the lack of soil oxygen. Peat formation is quite rare in Amazonia but may occur in permanent swamps.

Many of the backwaters and overflow lakes contain extensive floating vegetation mats that develop centripetally from the water's edge. The framework of these 'floating meadows' is an interlocking mat of aquatic grasses. At times the floating meadows detach and are transported downstream. Junk (1970) describes how, near Manaus, Brazil, *Paspalum repens* grows rapidly during the rising water stage. *Paspalum* and other grasses originate as small rooted plants, but as the waters rise these produce elongated stems, breaking their ground connection with deepening water. Stems may extent up to 14 m horizontally. Hollow internodes in the stem favour floating, and long entangled root systems help bind the mat together. As water levels drop, the mats may drift out of the lakes into the Amazon. Along the river's edge, some attach to dry ground and develop as typically terrestrial grass.

Many other species combine with the mat-forming grasses, including the water cabbage (*Eichhornia crassipes*), floating ferns (*Azolla* and *Marsilea* species) and the water lettuce (*Pistia stratiotes*). Some floating mats contain the tree-like *Montrichardia arborescens* of the skunk cabbage family *Araceae*. *Montrichardia* often develops a root system exceeding 6 m, which stabilizes the floating vegetation mass. Where this mass is sufficiently long lived, trees reaching 6–8 m or more may become established. Junk (1970) describes a floating mass 200 m wide, 3 km long and more than 4 m thick in a white water *varzea* lake near Manaus. In black water areas aquatic macrophyte growth is much reduced compared with that in white water zones.

The growth rate of the mat-forming grasses is quite high during the rising water season, sometimes reaching about 30 t/ha biomass during the 8 month vegetative stage. This high proportion rate might be expected to lead to accumulation of large quantities of organic material. However, because of the high temperatures and the water draw-down during the dry season, the ageing and dead plant material decomposes rapidly (Junk 1983). The Amazonian floating meadows share several features with the African fringing papyrus marsh described below.

3.2 *Freshwater wetlands of northern South America*

In contrast with southeast Asia, true organic or peat soils are relatively rare in South America. Within all of Brazil, there is only about 100 000 ha, well under 1 per cent of the total for southeast Asia. The largest peat swamps, covering over 10^6 ha, occur in the Guianas (Surinam, Guyana and French Guiana) within a larger wetland forest type that in Surinam covers 4 per cent of the total forest area of the country (Bubberman and Vink 1965). The large coastal region is characterized by hydromorphic soils (Beek and Bramao 1968) and it is here that nearly all the wetland forest is found. Most of the peat occurs as a shallow layer over young hydromorphic soils. During periodic droughts fire can sweep through the peat, destroying the forest and the peat layer. Both commercial forestry and agriculture are practiced in peat swamps, the latter on artificially drained sites. The Guianan peat forests developed on old marine clays of low permeability formerly formed under mangroves. The coastline is still expanding here and along adjacent Brazil, building on sediments transported by tidal currents from the mouth of the Amazon.

Swamp forests of the Guianas include a shifting mosaic of wetland types that vary according to inundation period. For example, seasonal swamp forests consisting of palm or hardwood-dominated stands develop on sites subject to periodic drying out on gley or alluvial soils (FAO 1981a). Shallow peat may form in the flats where drainage is poor. Guianan swamps share some species in common with Amazonian seasonal swamp forests: *Hura crepitans*, the palm *Euterpe oleracea*, the kapok tree and *Carapa guianensis*, which is an important tree in both locations.

Many tidal rivers in the region from Venezuela through the Guineas are lined with mangroves for 30–40 miles or more inland, indicating the extent of saline waters. Behind the river levels, however, swamp forests extend over the alluvial flats and continue beyond the influence of salinity (Myers 1935), merging with lowland tropical forest. The leguminous tree *Mora excelsa* dominates wet riverine areas in the Guianas as it does in Trinidad and nearby islands. Its canopy may exceed 40 m in height. Dutch foresters, who are responsible for nearly all the research emanating from Surinam, also distinguish a tall swamp forest, with soils which are wet year-round, that may form on alluvial silt or peat. Characteristic large trees such as *Virola surinamensis, Tabebuia insignis* and *Symphonia globulifera* are of commercial interest. As inundation and waterlogging increase, productivity and diversity decline and the forest may form only one stratum. The peat forests on the young coastal plain, with *Virola* and *Symphonia*, are included here.

Other types of wetlands in Latin America are often associated with major tropical rivers, where they form deltaic plains at the river mouth. For example, a large deltaic wetland covering over 10^6 ha is found in Tabasco, Mexico, where the Grijalva and Usumacinta rivers and adjacent riverways converge (West et al. 1969). Here, behind the mangroves, are dense herbaceous marshes dominated by the large banana relative *Thalia*, sedges (*Cyperus*), cattails (*Typha*) and other genera. Brackish shrub swamps are found between the mangrove forests and freshwater marshes.

A large area of the Venezuelan Orinoco delta consists of a fluvial-marine sedimentary plain (Pannier 1979) covering 22.5×10^6 ha. Although not entirely flooded, the area contains many wetland types. Large freshwater palm swamps and herbaceous marshes replace old mangrove swamp sites as shoreline aggradation diminishes tidal influences while shifting the mangrove zone seaward. Swamps include the same species of *Symphonia*, *Carapa*, *Pterocarpus* and others found in the Guianas. These species extend into Central American wetlands while *Symphonia* appears again in West African swamps. *Euterpe* and *Manicaria* palms are also characteristic (Pannier 1979). Herbaceous marshes in the Orinoco plain share species and communities with Amazonian floating meadows – *Montrichardia*, *Paspalum repens* and other floating and aquatic plants. At the sea's edge, mangroves (*Rhizophora*, *Avicennia* and *Laguncularia*) colonize estuaries, nearby islands and flat intertidal plains. Substrates range from coral rubble to sand, peat and clay. Peat from the remains of sedges, ferns and grass marshes forms layers to 4 m in depth on the seaward plains and in large troughs which originate in zones of contact between fluvial and marine waters.

Inland of the delta formed by the Atrato River in northern Colombia and between the two mountain ranges is another large lowland that floods yearly. Palm swamps occupy basins and the sides of levees (Vann 1959). Large shallow lakes not unlike those around the Orinoco and Amazon flood plains are choked with herbaceous marsh plants – the large *Cyperus giganteus* which resembles the African papyrus, other sedges, *Paspalum* and *Montricardia*. The lake depressions are filled to varying degrees by organic muck – the residue of incompletely decomposed marsh plants. Colonization by emergent plants ordinarily follows lake infilling, leading to swamp forest development.

On the Pacific coast of Colombia, behind the 400 mile stretch of mangrove forests that fringe the sea from the Ecuadorian border northward, extensive freshwater tidal forests form a zone of 0.3–1.2 km wide (West 1956). Twice daily tides back up the fresh streams which overflow, creating conditions favourable for growth of tall swamp forests, including *Mora, Campnosperma panamensis* and species described for the Orinoco region. These forests extend inland, blending into non-flooded rain forest in a pattern similar to the coastal environment of the Guianas.

4.0 COASTAL SWAMPS OF MALESIA

The most extensive coastal freshwater swamp forests in the tropics occur in southeast Asia, particularly in Malesia, from Sumatra to western New Guinea (figure 4.3). Throughout much of this area, rainfall is evenly distributed year-round or is markedly less seasonal than in most of the tropics. Consequently, protracted waterlogging characterizes relatively large areas of the fine-textured soils originating from erosion of interior uplands.

The Malesian coastal plain, aided by swamp formation, has been aggrading in relation to the sea level in much of the region over the past 5000 years. Before then, during the late Pleistocene and Holocene epochs, sea level had undergone large shifts in elevation in response to global climate changes. Based on radiocarbon analysis of peat cores from the Straits of Malacca, Geyh et al. (1979) established that the sea level 8000–4000 years ago rose 5 m above current heights and then receded to present levels as wet tropical conditions replaced the drier savannah conditions believed to have prevailed at the end of the Pleistocene. Until the rapid sea-level rise, a land bridge spanned the southern Malacca Strait and swamp forests formed peat now deeply submerged in the Straits. Although details differ, a similar trend in sea level was observed off the coasts of New Guinea, Java, Mauritania, Mozambique and the Ivory Coast (Bird and Soegiarto 1985). Currently in parts of Malesia, heavy fluvial deposition of sediments proceeds at rates high enough to offset land subsidence, resulting in formation of large deltas near rivers and in aggrading shorelines. As described earlier, mangroves colonize the mud flats and delta sediments, but behind them fresh and brackish swamps develop on the older poorly draining mangrove clays and peats.

4.1 *Peat swamps*

Large peat swamps are a distinctive feature of the Malesian coastal plains (figure 4.3). Their aggregate area exceeds 20×10^6 ha, more than half in eastern Sumatra and northern Borneo; they are also extensive in western New Guinea, southern Borneo and the Malayan Peninsula. In west Malesia nearly all such swamps are in coastal plains, although Furtado and Mori (1982) describe Tasek Bera, an alluvial peat swamp lake ecosystem located 80–100 km from the coast within the southern Malayan peninsula. Peat swamps are conspicuously absent in the Philippines, Java and the Moluccas, except for one

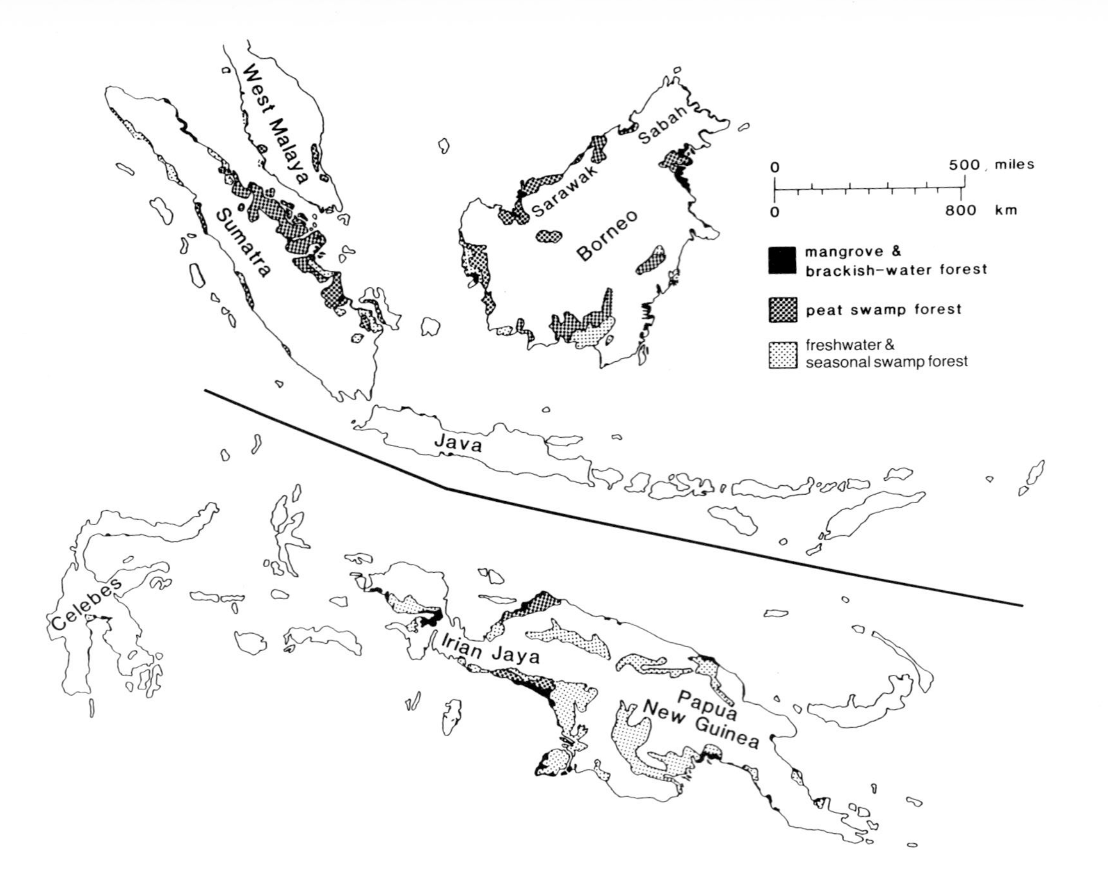

Figure 4.3 Location of major wetlands in western and eastern Malesia. Perimeter boundaries are approximate and include within them substantial areas of non-wetland habitat. Many small wetlands could not be depicted. The herbaceous swamps of Papua New Guinea are included within the freshwater category
(after Whitmore 1984)

area in Sulawesi and two peat deposits near the Gulf of Thailand in Indochina. In Malesia they are associated with large non-peat-forming swamps on gley or alluvial soils and share some tree species in common, including many dipterocarps. Peat with basal ages of 4000 years or more (Anderson 1964a) commonly rest upon marine clays marking the former location of mangrove swamps that colonized intertidal mud flats. The high salt and sulphate content of the marine clays may inhibit microbial activity, thus allowing roots, leaves and woody debris to be converted to peat rather than to decompose (Anderson 1983).

Over the past 4000–5000 years many peat forests have continued to accumulate peat, sometimes to more than 15 m. Large peat swamps of interdistributary basins initially accumulated peat rapidly in response to the availability of mineral-laden (eutrophic) river water and ground-water. As time passed, the deepening peat mass isolated the peat forest from mineral waters and partial decomposition acidified the peat, leading to an acidic (pH 3.0–4.5) infertile (oligotrophic) stage which, at the extreme, receives nutrients only from the atmosphere (Anderson 1964a, Morley 1981). A central dome of deep peat or a flattened bog plain forms in the interior. The developmental sequence resembles that of boreal bogs. Most of the interior mass here consists of coarse largely undecomposed fibric peat (figure 4.4). The high-acidity low-base status and scarcity of certain trace minerals assures slow microbial activity.

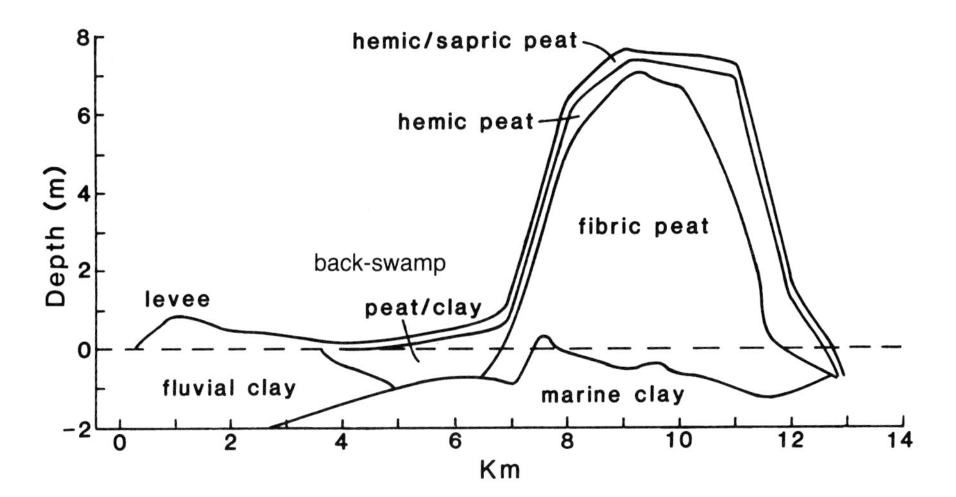

Figure 4.4 Cross-section of a Bornean freshwater peat swamp that developed along an accreting shoreline. The swamp developed in a depression between coastal river levees. The underlying marine clay was deposited under mangroves during a period of higher sea level. The fluvial clay was deposited by the river and supports a more diverse and productive forest (after Driessen 1978)

Driessen and Rochimah (1976) describe how progressive soil nutrient loss and consequent forest depauperization lead to dense less-productive systems in large peatland interiors consisting of relatively few species with low-nutrient requirements. Over this period, ash content, pH, bulk density of peat and rates of peat accumulation also decline (Driessen 1978). These peats are unsuitable for agriculture. Few plants, other than those so adapted, could thrive on these soils without intensive management.

Close to rivers where swamps are more fertile, peat layers are shallower, less acidic and higher in mineral content, while vegetation is more diverse and productive. Peripheral and riverine swamps continue to benefit somewhat from surface run-off from the interior peat dome, but are primarily enriched by contact with ground-water and nutrient inputs from adjacent ecosystems. In much of western Malesia, many shallow peat swamps have been artificially drained for agriculture.

Anderson (1983) describes a sequence of six forest types that form concentric zones in the large coastal swamps of Sarawak. Outer zones are diverse, tall (to 60 m) and similar to mineral soil forests in the area. An understorey of rattans and stemless palms is typical. Where peat is relatively shallow, tree roots may have access to underlying mineral soil, thus bypassing the problems of deep peat substrates. In deep peat areas, however, species diversity drops. In some areas, only a few species join *Shorea albida*, or *Shorea albida* occurs alone, a pattern strikingly different from other tropical forests. This gregariousness appeals to the logging industry because *Shorea albida* is a commercially valuable species. In the bog plains, trees may be pole like with narrow crowns and slender boles, susceptible to wind and lightning damage (Anderson 1964b). Spacing between trees is broad and tree heights are below 15 m. As in stressed mangroves, stunting reflects the adverse growing conditions.

As in most of the Malesian and adjacent southest Asian non-wetland forests, members of the *Dipterocarpaceae*, a large family of tall (to 60 m) high-quality lumber-yielding trees, are conspicuous. Besides dipterocarps (e.g. of the genera *Shorea, Hopea, Anisoptera*), trees such as *Combretocarpus rotundatus* (one of the few freshwater mangroves), *Durio carinatus, Calophyllum* species, *Campnosperma macrophyllum* and many others occur. *Pandanus* (screw pine), a tree-like monocotyledon, sometimes occurs here. Most peat forest species are restricted to swamp environments. Only a few, such as the leguminous *Koompassia mallacensis*, are also important in well-drained forests.

On peninsular Malaysia, tree composition is more mixed, but two *Shorea* species and *Koompassia* are relatively frequent under specific conditions (Symington 1943, Wyatt-Smith 1959). Many of the Bornean peat species are absent, and dome and bog-plain swamps seldom develop. Sumatran swamps are structually similar to their Bornean counterparts.

4.2 *Ecological aspects of tropical peat soils*

Oligotrophic peat swamps differ strikingly from many other wetland types, but in some ways resemble oligotrophic forests on well-drained soils. In the moist Amazonian caatinga forest, for example, soils are sandy infertile podzols with thin humus layers. These small-statured forests are drained by 'black water' rivers that favour *igapó* forest development downstream in Amazonia. Trees develop a surficial root mat closely associated with the humus (about 40 cm deep) where most nutrients are found (Jordan and Herrera 1981). Driessen (1978) observed a similar nutrient concentration in the top 25 cm of tropical peat forest. Caatinga forests, somewhat like domed peatlands, depend principally upon meterological nutrient inputs (Jordan 1982). In both caatinga and interior peat forests, vegetation biomass and species diversity are lower than in tropical forests on more fertile sites.

Oligotrophic forests possess adaptations producing efficient nutrient retention and internal recycling which reduce leaching losses to rates below meterological inputs. On more fertile forest sites, leaching rates usually exceed atmospheric inputs. The acidic nature of peatland and caatinga forests inhibits nitrification, thus reducing leaching of soluble nitrate, and may inhibit ammonia volatization. The surface distribution of the stored nutrients and the roots, and the oligotrophic condition, suggest that tropical peatland nutrients are conservatively cycled. In Malesia, peat swamp forests and tropical heath forests formed on infertile soils also have similarities in structure and species composition (Bruenig 1987) apparently related to similar water and nutrient limitations.

Two important ecological properties of peat swamps that result from the tendency to accumulate large quantities of organic matter can be briefly mentioned. Many peat swamps have been accumulating organic matter uninterruptedly for 4000 or 5000 years. Consequently, undisturbed peatlands, whether in tropical or boreal climates, function as long-term repositories (sinks) for organic matter unless fires burn them so deeply as to reduce previous accumulations (Armentano and Menges 1986). In humid Malesia, however, a long-term net sink is characteristic. Chan (1982) estimated that productive (non-swamp) dipterocarp forests in Malaysia averaged 8 kg/m^2 in soils, whereas in peat forests the value just to 1 m depth was 76 kg/m^2. Associated with the carbon are large quantities of nitrogen, sulphur and other elements. Because of these high element densities, peatlands must be viewed as important contributors to global biogeochemical cycles (Armentano and Verhoeven 1990).

The accumulation of a large mass of soil organic matter in peat swamps influences the quality of drainage waters through sorption or chelation of cations in incoming water or precipitation. Partly decomposed peat retains many times its weight of water and has a high cation exchange capacity (Driessen 1978). Consequently, water draining undisturbed tropical peat swamps is often very low in mineral content (Viner 1975) and tends to be dominated by hydrogen, chloride, sulphate and dissolved organics rather than by calcium, magnesium and bicarbonate as in minerotrophic wetlands and many upland ecosystems (Malmer 1975, Kirby-Smith and Barber 1979). In this sense, drainage waters resemble the black waters of Amazonian rivers. As long as inputs do not overload the organic matter increment, the peat mass efficiently removes many incoming materials such as nitrogen and phosphorus in association with carbon accumulation. However, most of the nitrogen and phosphorus thus fixed is ordinarily unavailable for plant uptake.

4.3 *Other Asian wetland types*

Associated with the oligotrophic peat swamps in Malaysia and Indonesia are several kinds of swamp forests that form on alluvial soils near the coast and near rivers. Such areas also occur in Thailand, Burma, southern India and elsewhere, but for the most part they are generally small and extensively disturbed.

Non-peat swamp forest soils are hydromorphic, either gleys or alluvial, with the latter often cultivated for centuries. Inundation is usually more protracted than in lowland forest on well-drained soils, but somewhat less than in peat forests. Peat formation is absent or restricted to shallow layers. Consequently, in many places tree roots are never separated from mineral-rich river or ground-water, resulting in productive diverse forests, although exceptions occur. Franken and Roos (1983), for example, found 70 species in a 2000 m^2 plot in freshwater swamp forest in central Sumatra – as many as or more than in adjacent non-swamp forests.

In Burma and the Sunderbans, the outer mangrove forests yield immediately inland to other tidal forests in deltas. The delta habitat provides some dilution of salinity by river water and monsoonal rains. An intermixing of mangroves and other swamp species occurs, creating forests of high diversity. The genus *Heritiera* is important here, with two species reaching 30 m in height. The genus is highly prized commercially in Bangladesh and Burma, and in the latter country often occurs in dense stands. However, in India, owing to the eastward shift of the mouth of the Ganges River, decreased freshening is diminishing forests such as those of *Heritiera* which depend on brackish conditions for their best development.

In peninsular Malaysia logging of freshwater swamps has been extensive, often leaving behind small-statured stands characterized by *Melaleuca leucadendron*, a disturbance-tolerant tree (Wyatt-Smith 1964). In Borneo and Sumatra, however, large swamp tracts remain although they are of increasing interest to the forestry industry, particularly in Sarawak and Sabah where the valued ramin (*Gonostylus bancanus*), now largely logged out of more accessible areas, and alan (*Shorea albida*) sometimes occur in virtually pure stands, often on shallow peats.

4.4 *Swamps of eastern Malesia*

On the large island of New Guinea extensive fresh and saline wetlands occur along the coastal fringe and in major river basins. These ecosystems have been little studied and the full typology of vegetation may not yet be known. It was not until 1983, for example, that a substantial portion of the extensive forested wetlands in Irian Jaya (the west half of New Guinea) were recognized as peat swamp forest (Whitmore 1984).

Freshwater swamp forest is extensive in the plains of the Fly-Strickland and the Sepik-Ramu river systems in Papua New Guinea (PNG), south and north respectively of the great central massif. Many of the forests are flooded by minerotrophic water carrying alluvium from the relatively young central highlands, leading to formation of less acidic eutrophic peat than found in many western Malesian peat swamps. Elsewhere, however, acid histosols are found in the most poorly drained flood-plain and mangrove areas. In the Gogol Valley east of the Sepik River lowlands, progressively poorer drainage in the lowlands coincides with the following sequence: poorly drained terrace forest, swamp forest, sago palm-fern swamp and nipa palm swamp (Davidson 1979) (plate 4.3). Close to the coast, the nipa stands intergrade with mangroves that face the sea. Paijmans (1976) describes several kinds of herbaceous marshes that cover extensive areas in PNG. Where flooding regimes fluctuate widely, tall *Saccharum* grass marsh develops. In relatively deep water, diverse communities are formed by sedges, herbs and ferns reaching a height of 2.5 m and often rooted in partly floating peat and debris mats. Grass marsh on river plains may also form mats that detach and float downstream. Grass genera familiar from other tropical or even temperate lands (*Phragmites, Leersia, Echinochloa, Coix* and others) join *Saccharum* on seasonally and permanently flooded plains.

In Irian Jaya swamp forests cover huge areas in the flat river basins south of the central massif and in the intermontane depression in the north. Many tree genera are shared with Borneo but some important swamp species such as members of the genera *Couthovia, Parkia* and *Serianthus* attain prominence only in Irian Jaya (FAO 1981b). As in PNG, sago palm swamps are common. Oligotrophic peat swamps are extensive, often forming the central dome configuration, as in Borneo. Species diversity is high with elements common to the Indo-Malayan flora at generic and higher taxonomic levels, but many species differ. Dipterocarps occur among the dominants but are less important than in western Malesia. As in Sumatra, species of *Campnosperma* are tall dominants in freshwater swamp forest (Paijmans 1976). Other dominant genera such as *Dillenia* are also important elsewhere in Malesia or Asia, while *Syzygium* and *Alstonea* extend to Africa and *Terminalia* to South America.

As they do further west in Malesia, spongy-wooded papery-barked trees of the genus *Melaleuca* occupy swamp areas subject to disturbances in Irian Jaya and PNG. Fires sweep through tropical swamp areas most often in monsoonal climates such as southwest PNG, but also in ever-wet peat swamp areas (a 1983 fire burned about half a million hectares of peat swamp in western Borneo). Fire may kill many swamp trees but *Melaleuca* resists all but the most intense fires. Where fires are relatively frequent and flooding is seasonal, *Melaleuca* may form monospecific tree stands over substantial areas (Paijmans 1976). Destructive forestry and partial artificial drainage also favour *Melaleuca*, which also acts as a troublesome weed in the Florida Everglades where dense stands are encroaching on native vegetation.

Although swamps throughout the tropics often contain palms, either as secondary species or local dominants, in Malesia and to a lesser extent elsewhere in southeast Asia swamp palms play a central role in the life of local peoples. Over large areas of swampy lowlands, especially coastal areas, the sago palm (*Metroxylon sagu* and *Metroxylon rumphii*) may form continuous stands

Plate 4.3 Edge of brackish water nipa swamp in West Malaysia. Palm fronds are harvested by local inhabitants for building material (especially for roofing) leaving a somewhat open canopy in the swamp
(Courtesy T. V. Armentano)

ranging above 20 m in height. Most commonly it dominates peat soils rather than wet mineral soils where competition from hardwoods is greater. In non-peat wetlands, sago occurs in the understorey beneath tall trees such as *Campnosperma*, a characteristic tree of freshwater swamp forests. Sago, found extensively in PNG where natural stands cover about 10^4 km^2 (Kainuma 1982), extends to Borneo and more sparingly to nearby islands. Starch derived from the sago trunk forms a staple food source for indigenous people and a feedstock for the food industry. Cultivation as far back as the fourteenth century has extended the range of the sago. In addition, within its original range, some sago swamps are apparently not of natural origin (Tan 1980).

In the brackish swamps found behind mangrove forests in Malesia and Southeast Asia is a zone composed almost entirely of the nipa palm (*Nypa fruticans*), a short-stemmed long-leaved tree with a pith containing sugary starch. Nipa also lines tidal channels and often intergrades with mangrove in the landward fringe of the saline zone where it is exposed to the highest spring tides. Except perhaps for the coconut, the nipa supplies the most diverse array of useful human products among the palms and perhaps all tropical plants. Leaves are used for thatching roofs, mats, blankets and other products. The juice is fermented to make a drink and is extracted for sugar. Leaf bases form fishnet floats and several tree parts are burned for fuel (Fong 1985). Because of its value, nipa has been established outside its native range. Other swamp palms such as the climbing rattans (*Calamus* species) and *Raphia* species, which occur widely in the tropics, are used for furniture and basket-weaving, especially in southeast Asia.

5.0 SOME WETLAND TYPES OF AFRICA

Although wetlands of many types are found in tropical Africa, the most distinctive is perhaps the papyrus marsh. Papyrus (*Cyperus papyrus*) is a large sedge, usually 3—5 m in height but sometimes reaching 10 m, making it, after bamboos, one of the world's tallest non-woody plants. Papyrus grows in dense stands along lake edges and in waterlogged drained river valleys, most commonly in the vicinity of Lake Victoria and Lake Kioga in Uganda and in the highlands on either side of the great Rift Valley that extends from southernmost Sudan to Lake Malawi (plate 4.4). Extensive papyrus wetlands are also found along the lower White Nile in southern Sudan and more sparingly in the Ethiopian highland lakes (e.g. Lake Tana), in Madagascar and southward into South Africa. They are absent from West Africa and the great riverine swamps of the Congo Basin.

In the southern Sudan where the White Nile leaves the highland lake district, about 10^5 km^2 of permanent marsh, named the Sudd, shares a great flat basin wth rivers and flood-plain grasslands (Rzoska 1974). Islets of papyrus and rafts of aquatic plants sometimes detach and drift downstream during high water, obstructing boat traffic. The rivers meander in the flat terrain and in the wet season flood lands far beyond the swamps. During the long dry season, however, these flooded lands become parched, leaving only the marshes to

Plate 4.4 Papyrus swamp near Nairobi, Kenya
(Courtesy Armendo de la Cruz)

green the landscape. The marshes form on fine poorly draining clay soils deposited by the river, in places forming surface peat layers. *Phragmites kharka*, a cosmopolitan plant of tropical zones, commonly replaces papyrus at the marsh's landward edge and where draw-down affects the entire wetland habitat. *Typha angustifolium*, the familiar cattail of the temperate zone, is another cosmopolitan form that competes successfully with papyrus under certain conditions. *Typha* flourishes in eutrophic waters, and not the low-solute infertile waters to which papyrus is best adapted.

In many places in the Nile River system, communities of floating aquatics extend from the marsh proper into deep waters. These floating meadows share species in common with the neotropics, but unfortunately species such as the water lettuce (*Eichhornia crassipes*) are not native to Africa. The water lettuce has run rampant, as alien species often do, upsetting ecological relationships and causing difficulties for local inhabitants. Papyrus occurs just landward of the floating aquatics, in some places as a narrow fringe, but elsewhere as a broad nearly monospecific zone, dense and tall, which is a visual and physical barrier to penetration (figure 4.5). Behind the tall papyrus in shallower water, a far broader grass marsh may extend nearly to the edge of the temporarily flooded zone. Such a pattern is repeated elsewhere in Africa, although species may differ. However, papyrus usually occupies sites where water depths vary

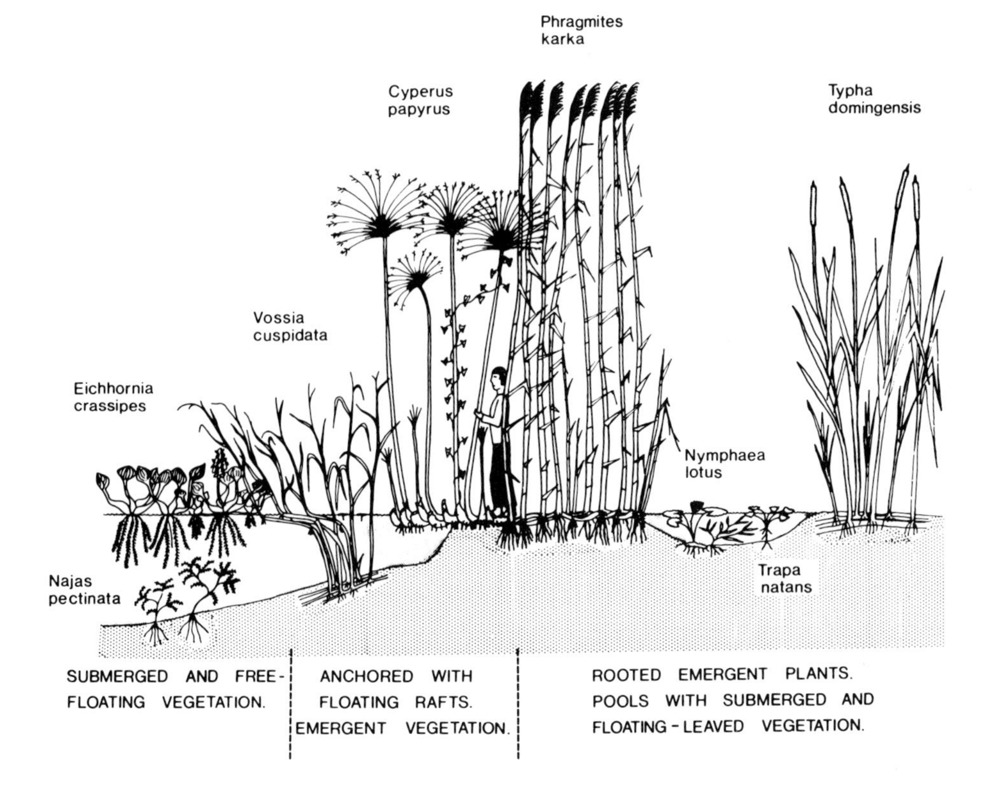

Figure 4.5 Cross-section of the permanent swamp vegetation along the Upper Nile River in southern Sudan. The diagram is a simplified representation of some of the major species found in this wetland type, but other species in various combinations also occur (from Denny 1984)

relatively little over an annual cycle – a preference that keeps it away from more landward zones of wetlands where dry season draw-down is often substantial.

The most productive papyrus marshes are found in the highlands (up to 2000 m) where temperature and evapotranspiration are lower than in the hot tropical lowlands. Highland papyrus can attain a standing dry weight biomass of 3 kg/m^2, exceptional for a herbaceous community, perhaps because dark respiration, slowed by the cool mountain nights, increases retention of photosynthetic products, thus leaving more to accumulate as biomass (Thompson et al. 1979). The same workers observed that standing biomass increases with elevation at least up to 1890 m above sea level. Other factors such as nutrient limitations in lower elevations, however, cannot be ruled out as part of the explanation for the altitudinal trend (Jones and Muthuri 1985). Annual productivities reaching 120 tons/ha of carbon are sometimes achieved in highland papyrus, a rate equivalent to productive maize yield (Thompson 1976) and five times that of the productive Mexican mangrove site studied by Day et al. (1987). These high rates are due at least in part to papyrus having a

C4 photosynthetic pathway, an efficient mechanism found most commonly in tropical grasses for fixing derivatives of atmospheric carbon dioxide.

Concentrations of nitrogen, phosphorus and other minerals are low in papyrus tissues as they are in other emergent macrophytes (Gaudet 1975). However, papyrus concentrations are low even within the macrophyte group, suggesting great efficiency in achieving growth under low-nutrient conditions. Papyrus also shares with other macrophytes the ability to extract minerals from infertile waters or sediments, and to release through decay and exudation organic compounds that serve as energy sources for a very diverse consumer food chain, which in many places includes humans. Along Lake Victoria well-developed papyrus marshes effectively remove sediments from water flowing in from adjacent savannahs, releasing higher-quality water to the lake (Thompson 1976). From his studies of papyrus marshes around Lake Naivsha, Kenya, Gaudet (1980) has for the same reasons described the marshes as ecological buffer zones.

Papyrus stands occur in dense aggregations that preclude the presence of most other marsh plants (Thompson et al. 1979). Light intensity within the lower levels of the marsh is quite low, attesting to the efficiency of light capture by papyrus. Most of the light absorption and, consequently, the photosynthetic activity is carried out by the dense crown of ray-like bracts that make up the inflorescence. Leaves are poorly developed and physiologically insignificant. About 25 per cent of the papyrus mass is found below the sediment surface as roots and rhizomes. The peat that frequently develops beneath papyrus where it contacts the sediment surface sometimes accumulates to over 1 m in depth. Peat accumulation is less obvious along lake edges where papyrus forms a floating mat similar to the grass-dominated 'floating meadows' of South America. Here roots are found primarily in floating rafts of papyrus roots, rhizomes and their decay products. In valley sites, papyrus peat soil is attractive for agriculture and as fuel. Marshes in Uganda, Kenya, Rwanda and Burundi have been 'reclaimed' through permanent drainage, destroying the marsh.

Outside the White Nile and Rift Valley lake region, papyrus occurs in several large overflow marshes associated with large interior rivers. Some, like the Okavango Swamp in northern Botswana and the Lake Bangweulu swamps in southern Zaire, retain permanent papyrus marsh with organic soils. As elsewhere, papyrus marsh fringes deeper waters with floating aquatics arrayed in masses where sunlight penetrates (Werger 1978). *Phragmites-Vossia* grass marsh also occurs. Landward, grasses tolerant of soil moisture fluctuations replace marsh. In other interior wetlands, papyrus is highly restricted or absent because of soil salinity (e.g. Lake Chilwa) or the paucity of waters of suitable year-round depth. *Typha* and *Phragmites* are often dominant under such conditions.

Space allows only brief mention of other African wetlands. Some of the largest undisturbed tropical swamps, such as the flood-plain swamps of the Congo River and its tributaries, estimated by Balek (1977) to occupy over 6.5 $\times 10^6$ ha in Zaire alone, occur in central Africa. Although viewed as a great untapped timber resource, even to this day the swamps are largely un-utilized because they are located in largely inaccessible and thinly populated areas. Consequently, they have been relatively little studied and are little altered from their primaeval condition. Elsewhere in Africa, swamp forest occurs either as narrow strips along the smaller rivers in drier climates, or is absent. However, some extensive tracts remain along large rivers found south of the semi-arid zone from Guinea to Angola and Kenya to Mozambique (plate 4.5).

In coastal West Africa (e.g. Liberia, Sierra Leone and Nigeria), fresh and brackish swamps develop behind mangroves and near river deltas, and on the flat plains behind the levees of large rivers in locations comparable to Colombia, the Guianas, Borneo and elsewhere. Because of human disturbance, unfavourable topography and the generally semi-arid climate of some areas, both the mangrove and non-saline swamps cover smaller areas than in Asia and Latin America. A rich flora differing from Asia and South America is involved. *Symphonia globulifera*, *Raphia* palms, *Nauclea* and *Mitragyna* are some of the taxa common to at least one of the other continents. Adaptations to flooding - pneumatophores, buttresses, adventitious roots – are, as elsewhere, found in African swamps (Richards 1953).

Plate 4.5 *Phoenix reclinata*, a common freshwater palm in seasonal and shallow-water swamps, in riparian zones and many flood plains throughout much of central Africa from Uganda to Mozambique, Angola and Nigeria
(Courtesy Armando de la Cruz)

Peat swamps form locally where drainage is most impeded. Lassoudiere (1976) describes a 1200 ha peat swamp in the Ivory Coast where the Agneby River empties into the Gulf of Guinea. A third of the swamp was already drained for banana cultivation when the report was written, but some forest remained. *Raphia* and *Mitragygna ciliata* were among the dominants.

6.0 CONCLUSION

The foregoing survey of tropical wetlands makes it clear that a great diversity of ecosystem types has developed in response to the varied conditions shaping the wetlands environment. The major factors determining wetland vegetation composition and productivity appear to be the hydrological regime, including the depth and duration of inundation, the chemical composition of the water, and the chemical and physical nature of the substrate available for soil formation. Interactions of species are also important but less well understood. At the general level, none of these relationships are unique to tropical wetlands, but the tight linkages between controls and community responses are remarkable.

Clearly small changes in the hydrological regime of tropical wetlands are enough to cause degradation or total destruction of wetland ecosystems. For example, drainage of mangroves, brackish marshes or even freshwater marshes which developed upon marine clays often leads to formation of highly acidic sulphide-rich soils which become so highly acidic as to be toxic to plants. As a result, thousands of hectares in the Mekong River lowlands and elsewhere in Asia and to a lesser degree in Africa lie barren, devoid of native plant cover.

Little is known of the capacity of many tropical wetland types to tolerate disturbance, but the ability of native vegetation to recover from drainage and intensive logging appears limited because of the narrow requirements of the species and the fragility of the wetland habitat. The more nutrient-poor wetlands, like oligotrophic systems everywhere, are particularly susceptible to degradation or delayed recovery when developed for commercial resource extraction. In fact, uness resource extraction is practised with minimization of disturbance in mind, degradation often follows. In many areas it is evident that, left undisturbed, wetlands can perform valuable services like flood limitation, water quality maintenance and wildlife sustenance indefinitely, while yielding commodity resources only over the short term.

5

Wetland Archaeology: A Wealth of Evidence

Bryony Coles

1.0 INTRODUCTION: THE SIGNIFICANCE OF WETLAND ARCHAEOLOGY

'The archaeology record consists all too often of battered pieces of stone, lumps of corroded metal, fragments of indestructible pottery, shapeless banks of earth and amorphous hollows in the ground – axe-heads without handles, whorls without spindles, hinges without doors and unfurnished rooms.' So wrote Gordon Childe (1956, p. 12) as a prelude to discussing the importance of ethnography for the archaeologist, but he could as well have been introducing the subject of wetland archaeology where axe-hafts and spindles abound, doors and rooms are identifiable and even furniture may survive. Whereas the loss of organic material is common on dryland sites, in wetlands where waterlogging followed close on decomposition, even quite fragile materials can survive for thousand of years. From structural timbers through composite artefacts such as arrows or sickles to string, nets and fishing lines, the wetland archaeologist is blessed with an abundance of evidence paralleled only on sites at the other extreme, in desiccated desert conditions.

The quality of the evidence for past human activity is also enhanced from wetlands by the relatively frequent preservation of undisturbed contexts. On a dryland settlement people trample their rubbish, dogs and pigs scavenge, and weathering can be severe. Subsequent peoples may plough or dig new foundations, while burrowing animals contribute to stratigraphic confusion. All these processes and the many others which reduce the archaeological record can take place in settlements on wetland margins, but there are times and contexts where water ensures immediate and undisturbed preservation. In the Somerset Levels, a wooden trackway built through dense reed swamp about 6000 years ago lay in the wet from the first, and the chips of wood axed off planks and pegs survived amidst the *Phragmites* rhizomes, along with diverse

My thanks go to Jennifer Warren for typing, Mike Rouillard for drawing many of the illustrations and above all to John Coles without whose work this paper would not have been possible.

artefacts dropped by the track-builders and users. Rapid peat accumulation ensured that the structure was waterlogged and blanketed from an early date. In the circum-Alpine region, prehistoric settlers on the lake margins dropped their rubbish into the waters, and abandoned their dwellings when lake levels rose or when fire swept through the settlement and structures collapsed into the water. Continued sedimentation sealed structures and artefacts together, and although storm erosion and fluctuating water levels would affect some sites subsequently, others have survived untouched until the present day. In Florida, near the present Cape Canaveral, the Indians of 8000–7000 years ago wrapped their dead in matting bundles and laid them in a shallow pool, to be exposed again only in the last decade through drainage and housing development. These instances, which will be examined further below, illustrate the quality of evidence which wetlands can yield to the archaeologist, a record of the past which is both more complete and less disturbed than is the dryland norm.

Wetland archaeology also benefits from the close correlation of environmental evidence with that for human activity. A lakeside settlement may survive as several occupation layers, each of which contains pollen and plant macrofossils and perhaps beetle exoskeletons alongside the human debris, allowing the palaeo-environmentalist to fit the sequence of environmental change in the vicinity with episodes of occupation and abandonment of the settlement. Often, much of the evidence is both artefactual and environmental, and this is particularly true of structural timbers. An oak plank or post gives information about woodworking technology, about the nature of local woodlands and about the chronology of the structure or site it came from. Most of this information comes from tree-ring analyses, in particular from dendrochronology. The significance of recent developments in this field is explored further below, for its implications for our understanding of prehistory are enormous and barely recognized as yet.

It is curious that wetland archaeology, which figured so prominently during the formative decades of the study of prehistory in the mid-nineteenth century, was subsequently underestimated and poorly integrated into the discipline. There are exceptions, of course, most notably in Switzerland, but even here there have been times when there was little contact between wetland and dryland studies. One reason may be the sheer wealth and complexity of the evidence. In the 1850s and 1860s, when Keller published the extraordinary discoveries from around the Swiss lakes (e.g. Keller 1878), they formed the basis for continental chronologies, and all archaeology was so new that nothing was exceptional (Coles and Coles 1989). However, by the end of the nineteenth century, Keller's followers were not part of the archaeological establishment. This is not to say that they were outcasts, but neither Frank Cushing in Florida nor Arthur Bulleid in England found their work integrated into the growing body of knowledge about the past. This was particularly true of Cushing's results from Key Marco (see below) and happened even with Bulleid's excavation of Glastonbury in the Somerset Levels, which is regularly included in syntheses on the Iron Age but always as an exceptional site and with little bearing on dryland interpretation, whereas what was exceptional was the state of preservation of the settlement and not its initial existence.

In the middle decades of the twentieth century, there have been important wetland excavations, most notably from the circum-Alpine region with continuing Swiss work on large bodies of water such as Zürichsee and Lake Neuchâtel, and in the smaller peat-filled relic lakes such as Wauwilermoos. In southern Germany settlements on Bodensee and in the Federsee peats were likewise investigated, with large-scale operations at sites like Wasserburg-Buchau. There was work beyond the Alps as well, at Biskupin in Poland, for example, in the Fens of eastern England, and at Star Carr in Yorkshire. Thus, by the 1960s, a considerable body of expertise had been developed in allied palaeo-environmental studies and in the interpretation of the often complex evidence retrieved from waterlogged deposits.

In the last couple of decades, there appears to have been an expansion of wetland archaeology for several reasons. Foremost amongst these must be the acceleration of drainage and associated development (chapters 6 and 7) which has occurred on a global scale and which has prompted an archaeological response in all continents. Fortunately, technical developments have facilitated the response, from polythene, plastics and pumps to keep wet evidence wet, through the use of computers to cope with the quantities of data, to the advent of underwater archaeology which has enabled the investigation of hitherto inaccessible but threatened sites (e.g. Cortaillod-Est or Tybrind Vig (see below). Unfortunately, legislation and finance have not on the whole kept pace with either the need for wetland excavation or with the increasingly time-consuming and sophisticated techniques of investigation required. However, today the potential of wetland archaeology is increasingly recognized (J. Coles 1986) and a wider archaeological interest catered for (Coles and Lawson 1987, Purdy 1988), and so it is to be hoped that the time and the money will be forthcoming for the full investigation of sites under threat. Equally important is the preservation of sites in their waterlogged undisturbed state, a subject that is returned to at the end of this chapter, once the nature of wetland archaeology has been further explored.

2.0 'FIRST' SITES

Wetland archaeology has no special claim on Palaeolithic studies, and frequently ignores events earlier than the end of the last glaciation. However, a number of key Palaeolithic sites are from wetland contexts, disguised by their present dryness, and several later sites from around the world, significant because they hold the first known evidence for particular human activities, are also from wetlands.

One of the earliest and most famous examples, Olduvai Gorge, was not a gorge, but a lakeside at the time of its occupation by ancestral hominids. In one episode, people would seem to have set up a windbreak, and the surviving bone indicates the exploitation of diverse environments including the lake. We do not know whether people hunted and fished or scavenged at this stage, two million years ago, but the presence of bones from crocodile and fish amongst others suggests that these animals were being eaten (Leakey 1971). The Olduvai sites are known chiefly because of the publicity given to the hominid remains such as *Zinjanthropus*, and for the association of these remains with worked artefacts. The information about early hominid behaviour is extended by the survival of relatively undisturbed activity areas or camp sites and of some evidence for diet in the form of animal bones.

Early European evidence, although much later than that from Africa, is also to be found from waterside contexts. Many thousands of stone tools have been exposed at Bilzingsleben in the German Democratic Republic (GDR), along with organic remains such as fragments of wood, all preserved in shallow-water sediments dated at least 400 000 years ago. At Hoxne in eastern England, Early Palaeolithic peoples camped around a lakeshore, and dropped or discarded their hand-axes and other tools. These, protected from subsequent glacial or peri-glacial action and, in due course, from ploughing, survived with undamaged edges so that, upon excavation, use-wear analysis has enabled their original functions to be determined. The hand-axes included meat choppers and cutters, and woodworking tools (Keeley 1980). Pollen has also survived at Hoxne, and indicates an opening-up of the dryland forest canopy and an increase in hazel, probably contemporary with people's use of the lake edge.

Outside Europe, wetlands offer some interesting insights into the human colonization of other continents. In America, for example, there has been, and still is, some controversy over the antiquity of human settlement. Several North American sites are now sufficiently well dated to argue that people moved across the Beringian land bridge before the end of the last glaciation, but a presence earlier than 20 000 years ago is hard to prove and some would put the arrival several millennia later. Recent work at the wetland site of Monte Verde in southern Chile (Dillehay, 1987, 1988) has revealed a small settlement of people who lived off wild plant and animal foods, and made diverse stone tools and wooden artefacts. Radiocarbon dates from well-stratified samples place the activity around 13 000 years ago. Southern Chile is a long way from Beringia, perhaps 15 000 km, and the presence of people here at the end of the last glaciation must argue for their arrival in the north of the continent many generations earlier. Monte Verde may yet demonstrate a much earlier human presence in the continent, for lower levels of the site, dated about 34 000 years ago, contained inconclusive evidence for human activity: possible hearths, charcoal and fractured pebbles. The excavators' definitive report has just been published (Dillehay, 1989).

The early use of wetlands is also known from Australia and New Guinea. In Australia wooden tools of 9000–10 000 years ago were discovered at Wyrie swamp in southeast of South Australia (chapter 6). This was a swampside camp where both stone and wooden tools were manufactured during a period of relatively low water; the whole site was later sealed by rising waters. The wooden artefacts include a spear, digging sticks, a javelin point and what seem to be boomerangs made of the Drooping Shevak which still grows in the swamp. An earlier site on Lake Bolac in Victoria is an encampment on a soil now forming a lunette in the lake. The site may have been a lake-edge kill or butchery camp where red kangaroo, now to be found only 300 km to the north, were captured. Levee sites in Australia, as elsewhere, were favoured places for settlement, industry and burial, and it is believed that some of these contain well-preserved evidence for early activity, perhaps dating back to more than 10 000 years ago (Luebbers 1975). The initial occupation of Australia is of course now known to have been much earlier than this.

Kuk swamp in Papua New Guinea is a valley-floor wetland where plant domestication and swamp cultivation is attested from 9000 years ago, evidence for some of the earliest such horticulture in the world. The site also revealed successive phases of more elaborate systems of agriculture, and these involved the first efforts at wetland drainage. Other work in the region has concentrated on fringe grasslands at Ruti where prehistoric stone tools provided a hint of ancient activity. Excavation revealed a complex of low mounds, basins and ditches which probably date to 5000–6000 years ago; the swamp was partly drained by primitive channels in order to introduce a cultivation system for banana and taro. This and other sites in the Ruti swamp preserve environmental indicators that suggest upland settlement and cultivation of yam, sugar cane and greens, and thus the swamp-margin occupations reflect a combination of both dryland and wetland interests that provided harvests from three sources: the cultivated upland, the drained wetland and the untamed swamp with its myriad wildlife (Gillieson et al. 1985, Gorecki and Gillieson 1985).

3.0 POSTGLACIAL EUROPE

The many lakes left in the wake of retreating ice-sheets have often provided good conditions for the preservation of archaeological and environmental evidence. They were widespread in prehistoric northern Europe, surviving now as peat-filled basins with perhaps a much reduced central body of water. The people who settled their shores between 10 000 and 5000 years ago did so as foragers, living off wild plants and animals and moving to exploit different seasons of the year. The evidence suggests that lakesides may have provided a focus to settlement, a place to return to and to inhabit for longer than elsewhere, a place where a range of activities took place, leaving a varied archaeological record.

Star Carr was one such settlement. Excavated by Grahame Clark, with environmental work carried out by Harry Godwin, the evidence from Star Carr was soon established and has since undergone many re-interpretations by scholars around the world (Clark 1954, 1972, Legge and Rowley-Conwy, 1988). The site was on the shore of a freshwater lake in what is now the Vale of Pickering in northern England, and it was occupied early in the Mesolithic, at least 10 000 years ago. The lake was fringed with reeds, and birch and pine grew on the surrounding dry land. As with Tybrind Vig (see below), what was preserved at Star Carr was not the centre of a settlement but its waterside edge, along with the occupation debris which spilled over from the activities carried out there. The shoreline was consolidated with wood, mostly brushwood and small birch trees. Some of the trees were no doubt felled by people using the small flint axe and adze blades found on the site, but recent research has shown that other trees bore beaver tooth marks and had been felled by those industrious animals (Coles and Orme 1983). It is quite likely that the Star Carr humans took advantage of the wood from a beaver lodge or dam when organizing their own settlement. They may have deliberately chosen a beaver clearing because such places are often full of chopped-up dead wood handy for fuel and are attractive to game such as elk and deer because of the quantity of young shoots which spring up from the stumps of beaver-felled trees. The remains of a birchwood paddle suggest that people ventured onto the lake, but otherwise no recognizable wooden objects were recovered from Star Carr.

We have to turn to sites from continental northern Europe for a quantity of wooden finds from the earlier Mesolithic. About 300 km north of Moscow, in the Lacha lake basin, lies the site of Nizhneye Veretye. Recent work by Oshibkina (1982) has established a boreal date (roughly 10 000–9 000 years ago) and retrieved a number of interesting wooden artefacts. Most were made of pine, either Scots pine (*Pinus sylvestris*) or Siberian pine (*Pinus sibirica*), and some birch, aspen and fir was used. The species reflect the composition of the boreal forest which colonized northern regions soon after the retreat of the ice. The Nizhneye Veretye artefacts (figure 5.1) include the remains of several bows, notched at the ends to hold the bowstring. One possible fragment of a bow is wrapped around with bark as if for a handgrip. Various different types of wooden arrows and arrowhead were found, some blunt-ended to stun birds or fur-bearing animals, some pointed to pierce the quarry and one slotted for the insertion of small stone barbs. In some cases arrowhead and shaft were made from a single piece of wood; in others a relatively short wooden arrowhead (e.g. 15 cm long) was designed for attachment to a separate shaft, in a manner analogous to the bone and antler points of contemporary and earlier peoples. Axe or adze handles were carved out of a single piece of wood, usually cut from the base of a tree-trunk where the roots splayed out or where there was a burr, so that the bulge of the root or burr provided a solid but resilient lump of wood to hold the blade. A similar choice of material for axe handles was to be made by circum-Alpine peoples several thousand years later. Two decorated pieces of wood were found, lightly incised with fairly simple geometric patterns. The artefacts are either domestic or for hunting and, as with Star Carr, there is little to suggest the use of water resources despite the lakeshore location of the site.

Further evidence comes from Friesack in the GDR (Gramsch 1987). Friesack was a favoured location, occupied off and on for at least 3000 years until about 8000 years ago. Many finds of flint, bone, antler, wood and fibre (figure 5.2) have been made from well-stratified contexts, making it possible to attribute them to particular phases of occupation. Microliths and other worked flint and bone points occurred in all levels. One bone point from early levels still had some of its wooden shaft, stuck on with pitch. Amongst the earlier finds were fragments of Scots pine spears, arrowshafts and a blunt arrow-head,

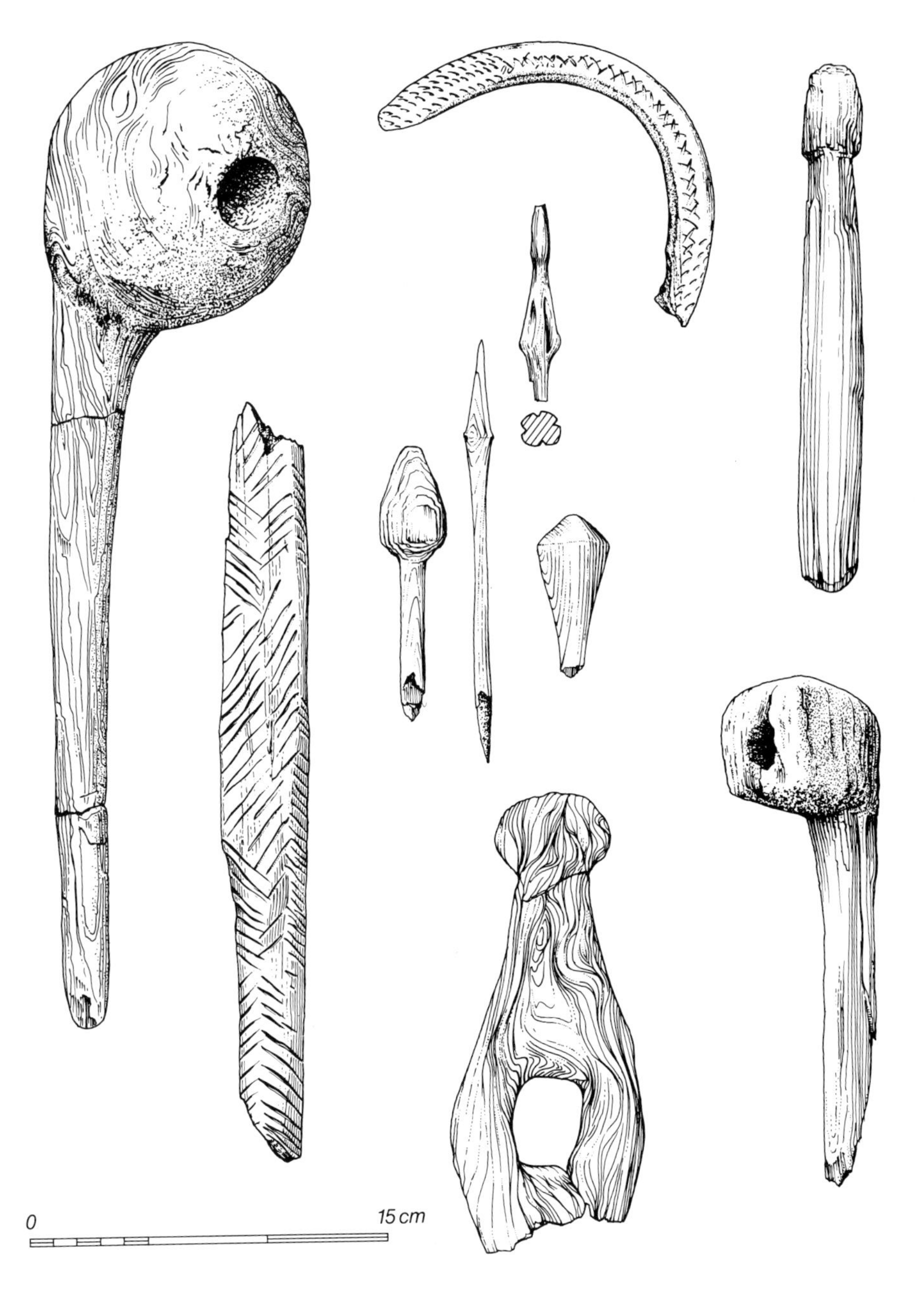

Figure 5.1 Wooden artefacts from Nizhneye Veretye, USSR: top left and bottom right, hafts for axes and smaller blades; top centre and lower left, decorated pieces; top right, end of a bow; centre, various arrowheads; lower centre, handle for a small chopper
(after Oshibkina 1982)

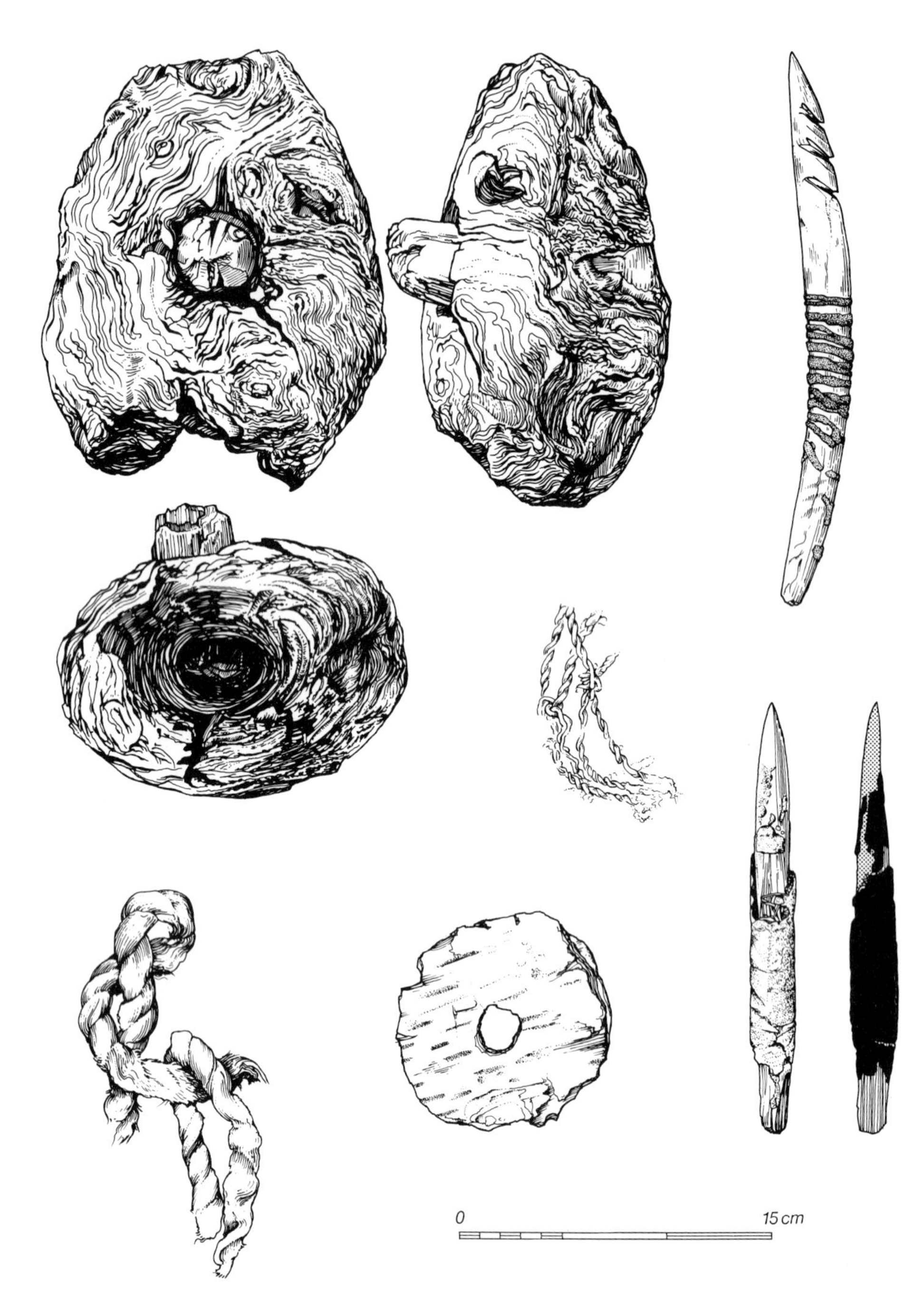

Figure 5.2 Wooden, bone and fibre artefacts from Friesack, GDR: top left, three views of an axe or adze haft made from an alder root; top right, barbed bone point with binding; lower right, bone point stuck with pitch to wooden shaft; centre, net fragment; lower left, rope; lower centre, birch bark float
(after Gramsch 1987)

all suggestive of hunting. Fishing is better represented than at Nizhneye Veretye or Star Carr, probably because the location had enabled earlier colonization by freshwater fish. The exacavators recovered a mountain-ash paddle, a birch bark net float and pieces of rope, perhaps belonging to nets, from early levels. Another paddle and several fragments and pieces of net date a few centuries later. From this period there was also an antler axe with a wooden shaft, and an axe handle made from an alder root designed for the blade to be held in a large burr or knot of wood, as with the Nizhneye Veretye handles of similar date. A wooden tray and a birch bark container survived in remarkably good condition, along with a possible digging stick and various wooden rods tied up with string. Late finds, dating from about 9000 to 8000 years ago, are more enigmatic: a Scots pine stick pointed at both ends, a small rod of alder pierced down the centre.

A millennium after Friesack was abandoned (or, more strictly, after evidence for human activity ceased to be preserved) conditions around the shores of Denmark led to the survival of similar but greatly increased evidence for human exploitation of water resources, and for the equipment which people used in their daily lives and perhaps on special occasions also. In the north of Denmark land has risen *vis-à-vis* the late Mesolithic sea levels, and the classic site of Ertebolle, along with many contemporary middens, has been stranded inland and dry. In southern Denmark, by contrast, land has sunk and the coastal marshes and lagoons of 7500–6000 years ago are now submerged, along with the evidence for human settlement in these environments. It was not until subaqua clubs began to flourish, after the Second World War, that the full archaeological potential of submerged sites was realized. Amateur divers have been responsible for many discoveries, epecially off the south coast of the island of Fyn, and since the mid–1970s they have worked with archaeologists to build up a more systematic picture of ancient coastlines and the density of prehistoric settlement. As knowledge increases, it becomes possible to predict the locations favoured by Ertebolle fishermen, and to direct underwater surveys to likely areas. One such was the bay of Tybrind Vig, on the west coast of Fyn, where in 1978 Hans Dahl found the site of Tybrind Vig, subsequently excavated by himself and fellow divers under the direction of Soren Andersen. Several preliminary publications have appeared (e.g. Andersen 1987), and the location, economy and artefacts of this late Mesolithic settlement are known in some detail.

At the time of occupation there was a protected lagoon of calm water about 1.5 × 3 km across and sheltered from the sea by a sandbar or a spit of land. Fed by two freshwater streams, the lagoon waters were brackish, the shores fringed with reeds backed by shrubby growth of hazel, birch and elder with mixed oak woodland behind. The settlement was just above the reeds on the north side of the opening to the sea. Here, people fished in the shallow waters or set off by boat for other places, and they threw out the rubbish from house and hearth. The debris of all this activity accumulated underwater amongst the reeds. When the sea level rose and the inhabitants moved away, material which had accumulated in the reed bed was protected by sediments although the settlement itself, on slightly higher ground, appears to have been eroded away. The excellent preservation of wood and other fragile plant materials indicates that Tybrind Vig has been continuously waterlogged since the time of occupation, which was from about 5500 BC to about 4000 BC.

The excavated evidence included many artefacts related to fishing. There were two long canoes hollowed out of lime trunks, and several ashwood paddles with heart-shaped blades. Three of the blades were decorated with a pattern cut into the light ashwood and filled with a brown colour. Enough survives on one blade to show a bold curvilinear pattern, infilled with lines of dots (figure 5.3). Another blade has a light linear pattern. Other forms of art and decoration are not unknown but are scarce at this time, and the Tybrind Vig wooden paddles show us something quite new in the inventory of Ertebolle material culture. Fine basketry, netting, coarse textiles, rope and string have also been recovered and conserved; much use was made of willow bast and twigs for these, and their condition of preservation is good enough for details of the plaited ropes and not quite knitted textiles to be examined (figure 5.4).

Tybrind Vig has much else to offer, but there is space here to note only two further items, both relating to the consumption of fish. Pottery encrusted with burnt food was retrieved from the site, and fish scales and bones, probably from cod, were identifiable among the charred remains (figure 5.4). The bones of herring, mackerel, salmon, eel, plaice or flounder and dab have also been identified from the site. Secondly, analysis of the skeleton of a young woman, found buried with a baby, showed a relatively high level of ^{13}C which would indicate that she ate mostly seafood, some of it no doubt in the form of fish, but also perhaps sea mammals, birds and molluscs.

The theme of fishing can be followed through in the material culture of farmers who in due course settled many of the wetland areas of prehistoric Europe. Aspects of farming economy in the wetlands will be touched on below. Here, the focus is on fishing equipment, and on the exceptional preservation of organic evidence from waterlogged settlements which allows the recognition of artefacts and activities invisible in most other contexts. Circum-Alpine settlements of the Neolithic, dating from shortly beore 4000 BC, have yielded much relevant material (figure 5.5). There are barbed antler harpoon heads, possibly used for spearing fish or the larger aquatic mammals. There are bone fish hooks, in varying sizes, and nets with different gauge of mesh, both of which suggest that more than one species of fish was sought, although fish bones recovered from these contexts are primarily from pike. Nets were controlled in the water with weights, usually of stone or fired clay and likely to survive in a wide range of conditions, and also with floats, frequently cut from bark and unknown except from wetland contexts. The Alpine evidence is diverse, wide ranging and well preserved, but it is interesting to note that in essence all the technology was already known at Friesack, four millennia or more earlier.

One fishing artefact peculiar to the circum-Alpine Neolithic is a variant on the net weight and is an embodiment, in itself, of the virtues of wetland archaeology. It was made by wrapping four or five rounded pebbles in a bark

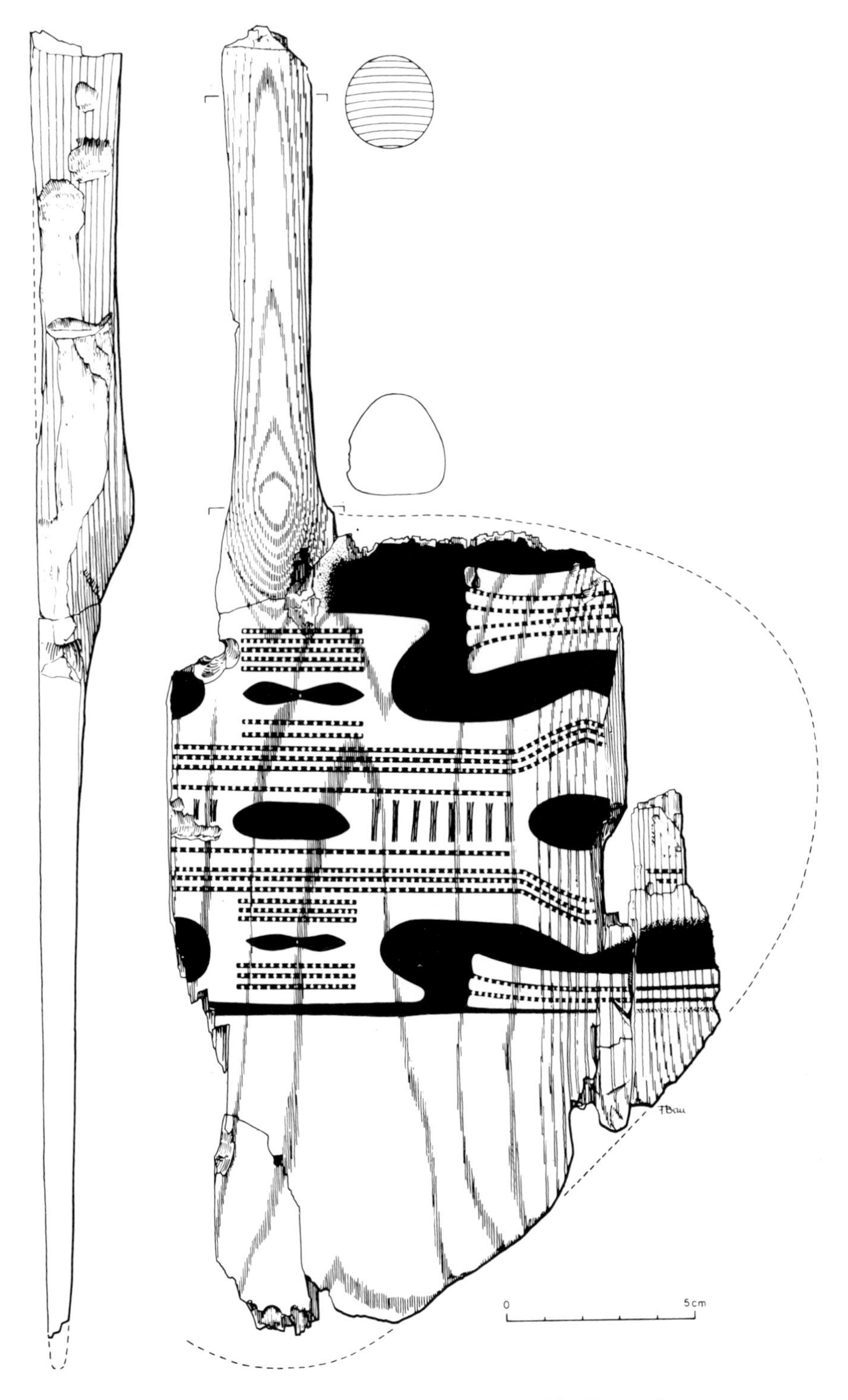

Figure 5.3 Decorated ashwood paddle from Tybrind Vig, Denmark (from Andersen 1987)

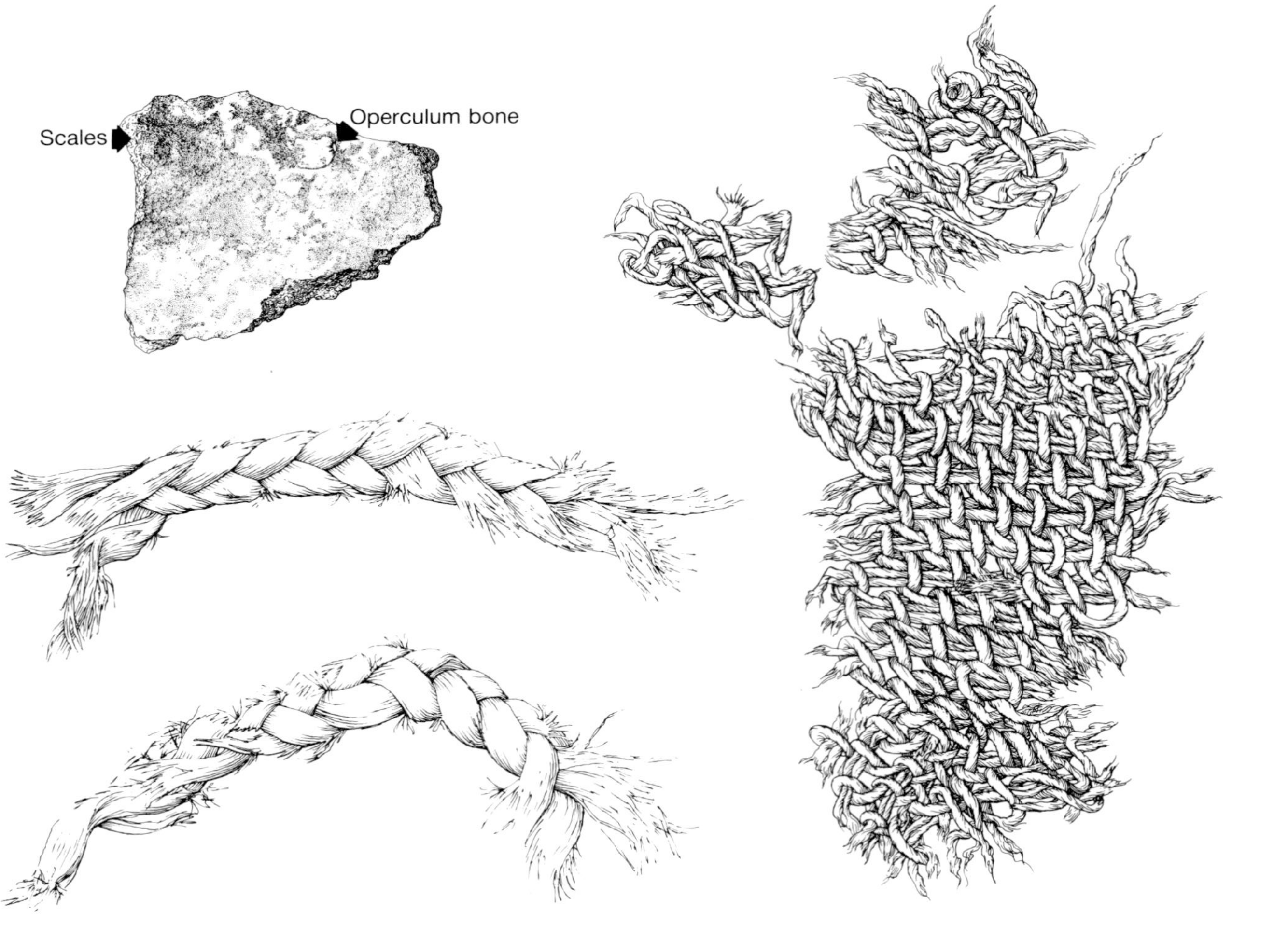

Figure 5.4 Textiles and potsherd from Tybrind Vig. The textiles are plant fibre, probably willow bast; the upper plaited rope is 8 cm long. The potsherd has encrusted fish remains

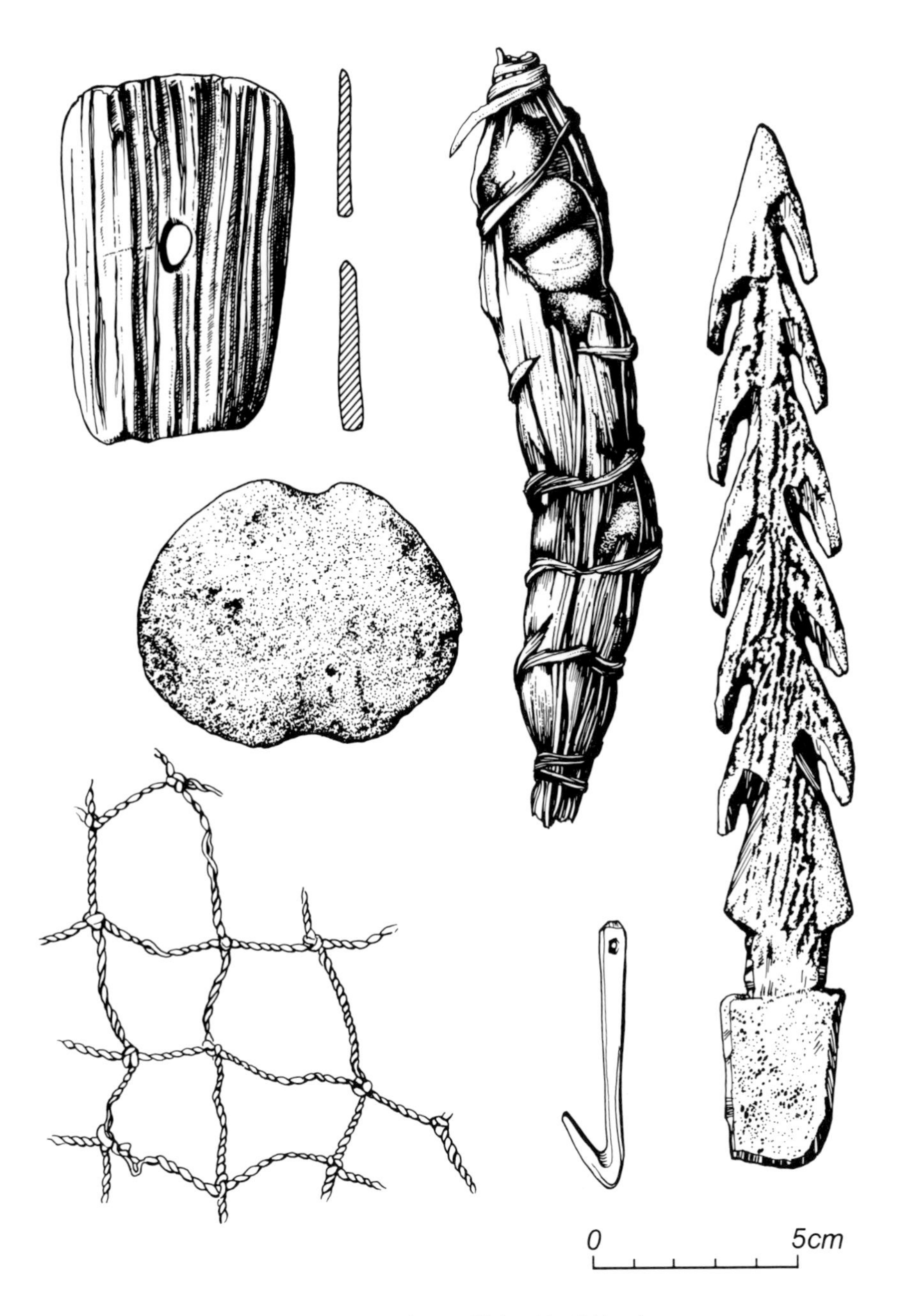

Figure 5.5 Fishing equipment from circum-Alpine Neolithic sites

roll and tying up the ends like a sausage or a cracker (figure 5.5). Without the preservation of the bark, all that would remain of this simple, basic object would be a row of pebbles, and on a site disturbed in antiquity, or subsequently, not even the ordered arrangement of the stones would survive. There is no way in which a few pebbles could be shown to be a net weight, even with the knowledge that such artefacts had existed. It is only from waterlogged contexts, with complete survival of a composite organic and inorganic object, that recognition of an artefact and interpretation of its function is possible.

One last example will underline the significance of wetland sites for studying past material culture. It is the site of Fiavé, near Trento in northern Italy. Here, on the shores and islands of Lake Carera, people settled from the Late Neolithic and throughout the Bronze Age. They built their houses on the shores of the lake and its islands, and out over the water as well. Day-to-day debris accumulated below the houses over the water, and when fire ravaged the settlement, house and contents were liable to collapse into the lake, their remains surviving because of carbonization, waterlogging or a combination of the two. In addition to the structural evidence, Fiavé has yielded an extraordinary inventory of material culture, which has been published with commendable speed and detail by Perini and his colleagues (Perini 1984, 1987a, b). Small-handled drinking cups were quite common, generally carved out of a block of maplewood, with a few examples made from other species such as silver fir, beech and lime. One of the maplewood cups had been broken at the rim in antiquity and repaired by sewing it up with a flexible length of spruce (plate 5.1). Other vessels were both made and repaired by sewing together thin pieces of wood.

Amongst other household artefacts, beaters were common. These ingenious objects were made from the top of a conifer, usually *Abies alba*, using the lead shoot as handle and the five radiating top branches, cut to a few centimetres in length, as the blades. Wood was used, as one might expect, for spoons and ladles, and a great range of pins, needles, awls and toggles. In addition to the spindles (made from various species, not *Euonymus*) to be expected from waterlogged settlements, spindle whorls of wood were recovered, prompting reflection on Childe's description of the archaeological record and suggesting that even he may have under-estimated the loss from so many dryland but not desiccated sites.

The Fiavé inventory continues with outdoor tools such as sickles, complete composite objects with beechwood handle and flint blade secured with pitch or gum. A yoke and an ard indicate cultivation of the fields from which crops were harvested with the sickles. Wood working is attested with axe hafts, wedges and beechwood mallets, not to mention the abundant surviving structural and artefactual evidence. However, if one object is to illustrate the wealth of Fiavé, and the eye-opener which it provides on the range of Bronze Age material culture, it must be a personal possession. A hat or helmet made of tightly woven basketry was recovered (figure 5.6). The framework was of split spruce and reed, probably *Phragmites*, around which were woven flexible *Viburnum* shoots to build up a close-fitting conical helmet with a small rim. Whether

Plate 5.1 Maplewood cup with repaired rim from wetlands at Fiave, Italy (diameter, 19.5cm) (from Perini 1987b)

cloche hat or warrior's casque we do not know, but its very presence challenges thought about all that is normally missing from the prehistoric record.

4.0 PRECISE CHRONOLOGIES

Prehistory for long dealt in relative chronologies, and still does so in many cases. It is possible, through stratigraphy and typology, to establish the sequence of events – what followed what – and to correlate these with some confidence from one place to another, but to establish duration is another matter. Without knowledge of duration, the interpretation of process, of the nature and impetus to change, will always be hampered. It was not surprising, therefore, that the general availability of radiocarbon dating in the 1960s was hailed as a revolutionary agent in prehistoric studies. However, radiocarbon dating was, and is, no more than a greatly refined means of relative dating which allows a broad estimate of duration but never focuses on the human life span.

Dendrochronology, in contrast, allows events to be tied down to a particular year, perhaps even to the season of the year, and where chronologies are available, sequences of events can be set on an absolute time-scale. The information which has come from this precision dating is immediately enlightening, but the full potential of the technique has yet to be realized. Before long, the chronology of settlements built and occupied several thousand years ago will be better understood than that of deserted medieval villages, if the former were built of oak and the timber has survived through waterlogging.

The potential of dendrochronology has been ably demonstrated at a number of circum-Alpine sites, in addition to those described here, but some selection is required to allow space for the detail which will illustrate the significance of such a dating technique. The first to be considered is the site of Hornstaad-Hörnle I on the shores of Bodensee in southern Germany. Here, an initial farming settlement was established shortly before 4000 BC, but it does not

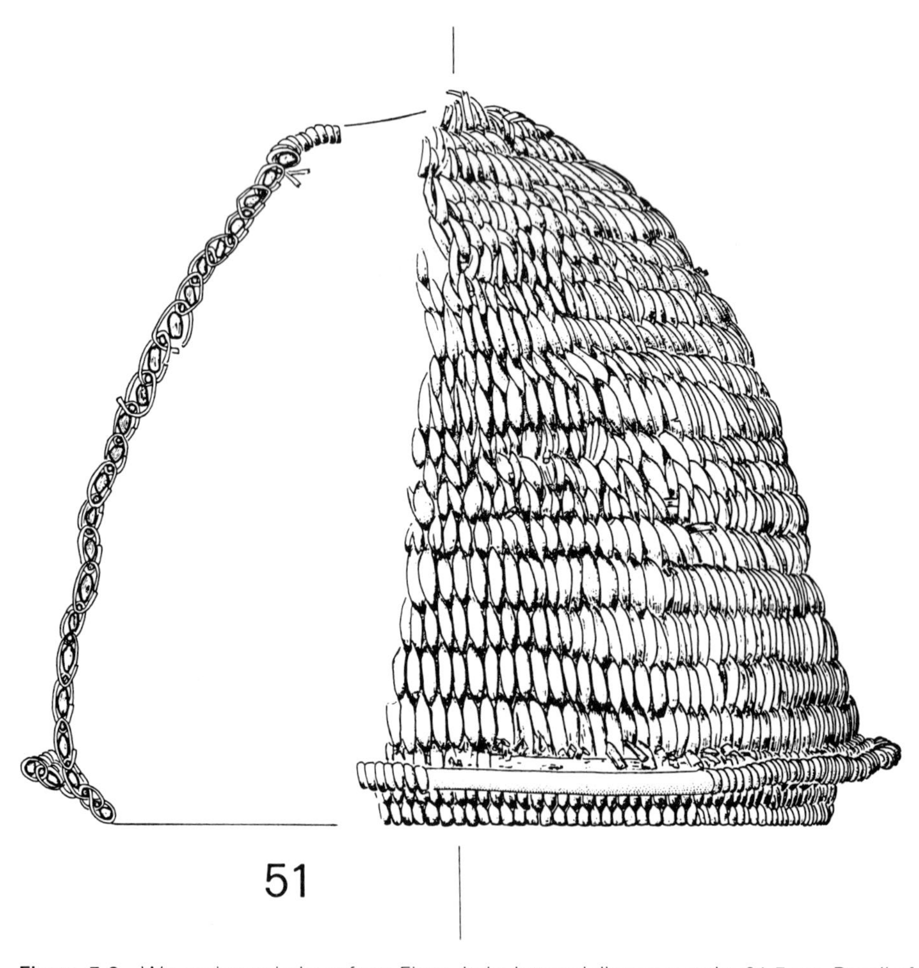

Figure 5.6 Woven hat or helmet from Fiave, Italy. Internal diameter at rim 21.5 cm. Detail of construction is also shown
(from Perini 1987b)

immediately concern us because its surviving timbers have not been matched to any dated long-term chronology. A few centuries after the first settlement was abandoned a new village was built using oak wood, which has provided a local tree-ring sequence that can be matched to dated regional chronologies. Detailed study of the size and the age of the wood has also enabled André Billamboz to reconstruct various aspects of the local forest and its exploitation (Billamboz 1985).

Broadly speaking, building of the second Neolithic village at Hornstaad-Hörnle I took place over a period of 80 years in five bursts of activity (figure 5.7). In 3586 BC the first trees were felled and two houses were built within the excavated area. The oaks used were 80–90 years old and 30–35 cm in diameter; the trunks were split longitudinally into quarters or more, and used to make a house framework about 10 m × 5 m. The next main phase of building was from 3570 to 3562 BC, when the first houses were repaired and one or two new buildings were put up. The oaks used were 50–60 years old and generally under 30 cm in diameter; the smaller trunks were split only in half and the larger ones as before. Bit by bit during these years, one of the first houses had most of its uprights replaced.

After a gap of 21 years, there was a great burst of activity from 3541 to 3531 BC, and new structures can be traced within the excavated area. From the evidence available, the settlement was not so much expanding as filling in. The trunks used were generally 40 years old and 20 cm or less in diameter, and they had begun to grow after the first building phase. In their early years they had grown vigorously, but then the rate slowed, a pattern typical of coppiced growth; it is very likely that the wood used had sprung from the stumps of the oak trees felled in 3586 BC or soon after. Most of the trunks were simply halved, and the houses were slightly smaller than before, a reflection of the size of the wood used. Within this phase some structures were rebuilt or extensively repaired, such as the house built in 3540 BC, and were given a new set of uprights only 4 years later.

From 3522 to 3518, house builders were active again and setting up larger-sized houses once more. Their source of wood was probably the same coppiced oak as that used in the previous phase. In the interval and with reduced competition, the trunks had reached diameters of 35 cm or so. Finally, in the years 3508–3507 BC, trees over a century old were felled. These trees were of an age and size that one might have thought no longer existed in the vicinity, given the use of coppiced wood in the preceding decades. Around 3530 BC, however, the trees that were to be felled in 3508–3507 BC were already older and larger than the trunks used then.

This pattern of forest exploitation is fascinating, as it emerges from the detailed tree-ring analyses still undergoing refinement. A progression can perhaps be traced from initial settlement in an area of closed mature forest where large trees were felled as much to make fields as to build houses. Regeneration from the stumps was soon allowed or encouraged, whilst further mature trees were felled. Once the coppiced growth had reached building size, effectively four decades after the first felling, it was used exclusively despite

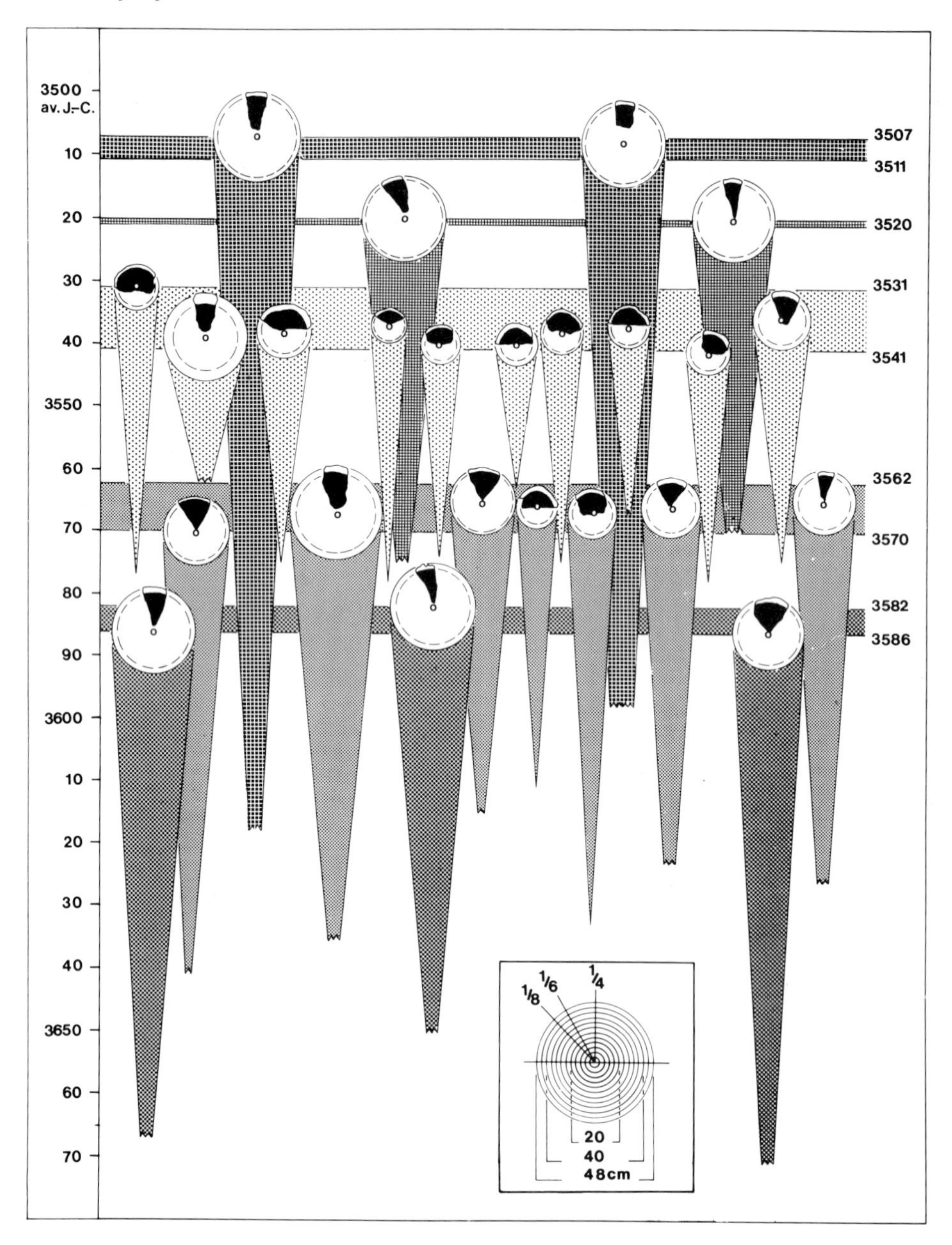

Figure 5.7 Dendro-diagram from Hornstaad-Hörnle I. See text for explanation (from Billamboz 1985)

larger wood being available. This suggests that it was preferred, which is understandable given that it is easier to fell a small tree than a large tree with a stone axe, and less splitting was needed to prepare the wood for use in a building and that the coppiced pole was effectively a ready-made house post.

The return to mature trees might suggest that supplies of well-grown coppiced wood had run out, although the stumps should have regenerated anew. Whatever the case, the Hornstaad-Hörnle piles tell not only of dwellings, but also of eight decades of settlement in a forested landscape and something of the interaction of people and forest. It is doubtful if such precision could be obtained from settlements where only post-holes survive, whatever their age.

Moving on 2497 years from Hornstaad-Hörnle I, and south to Lake Neuchâtel, we come to the later Bronze Age settlements at Cortaillod which are also dated by dendrochronology. The spreads of surviving posts from these sites have long been known and recorded aerial photographs taken by Vouga between the wars (plate 5.2). Recent excavation and sampling for dendrochronology has allowed the posts to be disentangled into the houses, streets and palisades of successive villages, shifting along and up the lakeshore in response to changing water levels (Arnold 1986). First came Cortaillod-Est, consisting of eight rows of houses and a fence or palisade on the shoreside. The plan of the village suggested a single building episode following an ordained pattern. Dendrochronology indicates otherwise (figure 5.8). Starting in 1010 BC, six rows of two to four buildings each were set up by 1001 BC, and variously repaired between 996 and 991 BC. The settlement was enlarged between 996

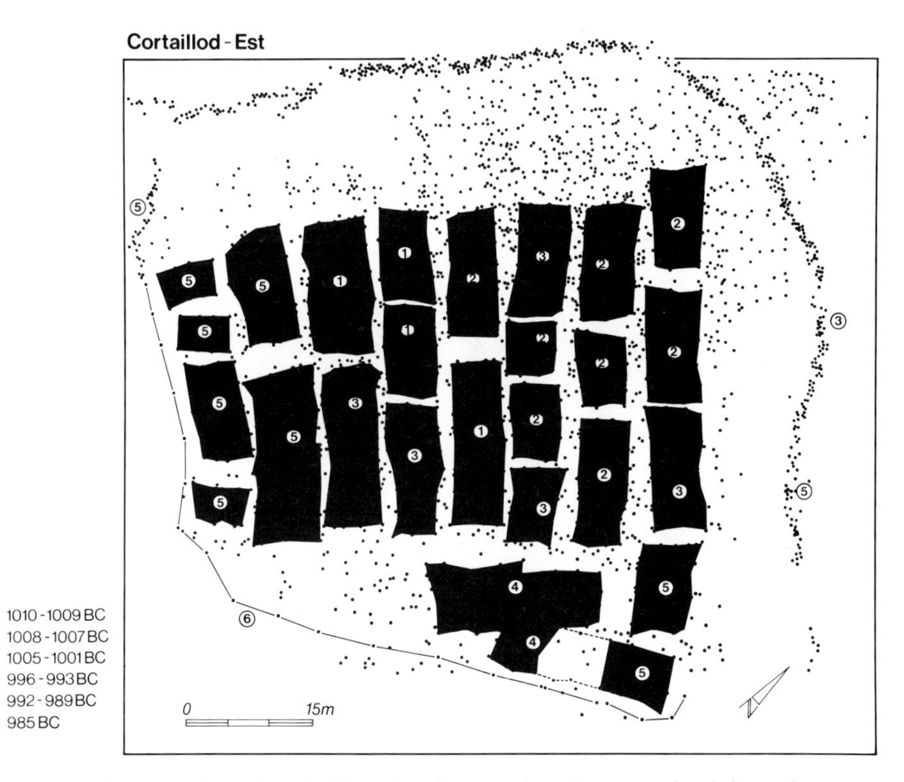

Figure 5.8 Cortaillod-Est: plan of village development based on tree-ring information (after Arnold 1986)

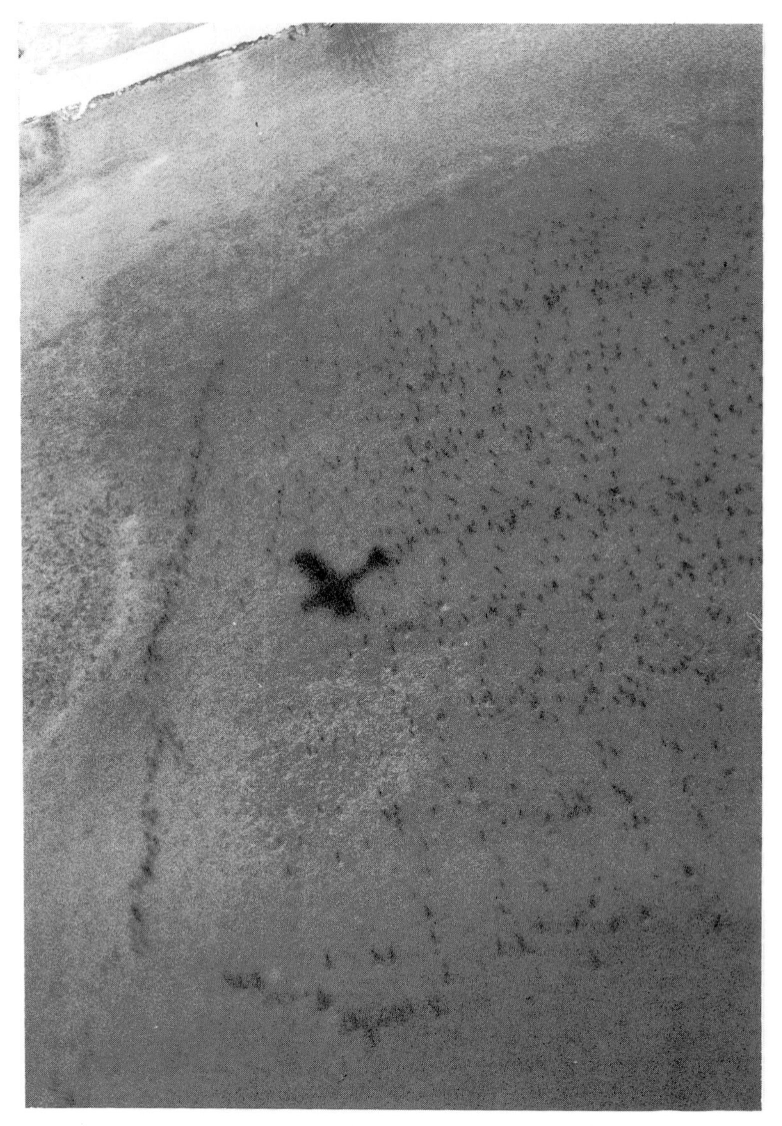

Plate 5.2 Cortaillod-Est showing the pattern of post-holes in the wetlands (taken about 1925–7)
(Courtesy Vouga)

and 989 BC and in 985 BC a fence line was set up on the lakeside. Further repairs can be identified, continuing until 969 BC, with some more recent wood (955 BC) coming from the side of the village closest to the shore. It is possible that the whole village was shifting shorewards to the poorly preserved and uninvestigated site of Cortaillod-Plage. Limited study of the immediately adjacent site of Cortaillod-les-Esserts has revealed a triple lakeside palisade and building activity between 870 and 850 BC, which suggests that this settlement may result from another minor shift within the bay of Cortaillod in response to fluctuating water levels. It is interesting to find that the regimented layout of dense parallel rows of houses within a fence could develop over several decades, as was the case at Cortaillod-Est. If there were only the plans to go by, and no dendrochronology, interpretation in terms of a single short building episode would be very likely.

As suggested above, the full impact of dendrochronology has yet to be felt, and the transference of results to traditional typological and radiocarbon-assisted chronologies has barely begun.

5.0 NORTH AMERICAN WETLANDS: A NEGLECTED ARCHAEOLOGICAL RESOURCE?

The extensive wetlands of North America were visited, inhabited and exploited in antiquity no less than those of the Old World. There is evidence for heavy use in some cases, occasional frequenting in others and sometimes little or no trace of a human presence. The focus of North American archaeology, however, has never been on the wetlands but, if anything, on desiccated dryland remains. Individuals have nevertheless grasped the potential of waterlogged sites and, often working in difficult swamp conditions without much support, either technical or financial, they have retrieved evidence of considerable importance for the study of American prehistory, its sigificance by no means confined to the wetland environment.

A pioneer in this field was Frank Cushing, a man inspired by Keller's *Lake Dwellings of Europe*. At the very end of the nineteenth century he undertook excavations at the coastal site of Key Marco, on the west coast of Florida (figure 5.9). The story of his adventurous expedition is told elsewhere (Gilliland 1975, Coles and Coles 1989), and the results are briefly outlined here. The prehistoric Indians of Key Marco occupied the tip of a low flat island on the Gulf of Mexico and seem to have created a system of canals and lagoons protected behind a sea wall. At the Court of the Pile-Dwellers, the scene of Cushing's excavations, a canal led from sheltered inland waters into a lagoon or harbour roughtly 27 m × 33 m, Cushing's 'Court'. This was surrounded by a shell bank, and shell jetties or extensions of the bank reached into the harbour. The Indians' buildings were on the dry banks, and little was preserved. Their debris fell into the waters of the Court which gradually silted up and always remained waterlogged. Here, a wealth of material was recovered, almost all of it now dated to AD 750–1513, before any contact with European explorers.

Figure 5.9 Map of Florida, showing the sites mentioned in the text

Subsistence was water based, and canoes were probably the means of access to the varied wetland environments in the vicinity of the site. There were plentiful fish, waterfowl and shellfish to be had for food. Shell, sharks' teeth and coral supplemented wood and other plants for making artefacts.

Cushing found over 3000 artefacts, of which 1000 were taken away in reasonable condition, many having been recorded by photograph and watercolour. There were fish nets with floats, pounders and wooden vessels, and many other everyday items. Less domestic in nature were the extraordinary pieces of painted and carved wood. These included a wooden board with a kingfisher-like bird painted on it, another incised with a leaping dolphin and the side of a box decorated with a dragon-like creature. A number of carved and painted masks have human or animal features (plate 5.3). The human masks were sometimes painted with geometric designs and sometimes given exaggerated noses or shell-inlay eyes, and one had a twisted asymmetry reminiscent of Indian masks from further north. Animal masks and figureheads include a wolf-like creature, a painted deer's head with separate flaring ears and a pelican. One human figurine was found, and a delicate small carving of a

Plate 5.3 Human and animal masks from Key Marco, Florida
(Courtesy Smithsonian Institution, Washington, DC)

kneeling feline which Cushing described as a 'man-like being in the guise of a panther'.

Many of the representations, whether painted, incised or three-dimensional carvings, show a mixture of human and animal traits, and it is likely that they pertain to the myths and ceremonies of the Key Marco inhabitants. The great number of such objects recovered from the Court are suggestive of a ceremonial centre rather than an ordinary village. However, a similar wealth of wooden representations has been recovered from other North American wetland sites, most notably the later coastal site of Ozette (see below). Thus it may be that many villages had such wealth, which has only been preserved in waterlogged conditions. Alternatively, or in addition, the wealth of wetland subsistence resources may have favoured the development of art, as is evident on the North Pacific coast. Wetland sites with their abundance of evidence often present these two possibilities of interpretation.

An inland site in Florida, currently under excavation, offers a potential similar to that of Key Marco for establishing the nature of Indian economy and artefacts before Europeans arrived. With modern controlled excavation and environmental studies it is proving possible to trace developments across 1500 years up to the time of contact, and to determine the changes wrought by the arrival of Europeans. The site is Hontoon Island in northern Florida (figure 5.9), which is being investigated by Barbara Purdy (Purdy 1988). The large island, which lies in the middle of freshwater marshes and lakes drained by the

St John's River, has a number of shell middens, one of which lies adjacent to the water where waterlogged midden deposits are to be found. Preliminary trial excavations have yielded a vast amount of economic information showing the exploitation of wetland species of plant, fish, amphibian, bird and mammal, with very little from the dry land (not that much dry land was available in the immediate region). The animals included mussels and snails, seven species of turtle, water snakes and alligators, numerous species of fish, manatee or sea-cow and several waterfowl. Agriculture was relatively unimportant in the pre-contact period, whereas after AD 1500, although there was no direct European presence, the Indians seem to have farmed more and to have made greater use of land resources in general. The reasons for this somewhat enigmatic change, together with evidence for development in the material culture, which includes waterlogged wood, should emerge from future seasons of excavation.

The extensive wetlands of Florida have also yielded numerous dugout canoes, which Purdy has recorded and in a few cases attempted to conserve by immersion in protected natural pools or springs. The lack of conservation facilities, so evident in this case, has also affected the finds from Key Marco which, although in museum storage, are deteriorating through neglect. Neither canoes nor carvings excavated a century ago excite much interest. However, one recent discovery in Florida has attracted much public interest and support, the repercussions of which may benefit wetland archaeology throughout the state and beyond. The site in question is the burial pool at Windover, near Cape Canaveral.

The pool at Windover was originally a shallow depression in the calcareous bedrock, now filled by freshwater peats which have preserved both the environmental record and the human and cultural remains that came to rest in the waterlogged peats. Over 7000 years ago the pond was used by Indian hunter-gatherers as a burial ground; the bodies were wrapped in grass mats or other coverings, placed in the water and fastened to the pond bottom by stakes (figure 5.10). Peats gradually filled the pond and sealed the burials until recent drainage and excavations for a housing development exposed them. Work has now succeeded in recovering over 160 bodies, of which half are children. The waterlogged peats have preserved some of their clothing, their wooden and other grave-goods, and brain tissue of over 90 individuals; flesh, skin and hair have not survived the 7000 years of waterlogging. The peats and the water are nearly neutral. The twined and woven fabrics of plant fibres have perhaps been the most important discoveries, as they are by far the oldest surviving fabrics in eastern North America and demonstrate quite sophisticated tight weaving. The brain tissue, although exciting much public interest, has added little so far to our knowledge of prehistoric peoples in America.

Children at Windover seem to have been favoured, at least in death, as evidenced by the generous artefacts placed by them: they include wooden, bone and antler objects. One child had suffered in life from a degenerative spinal disorder, and probably would have required special care during the 12–15 years of life. Some of the adults were as much a 65–70 years old, a quite remarkable age to achieve at such a time and place, and with such a life-style as

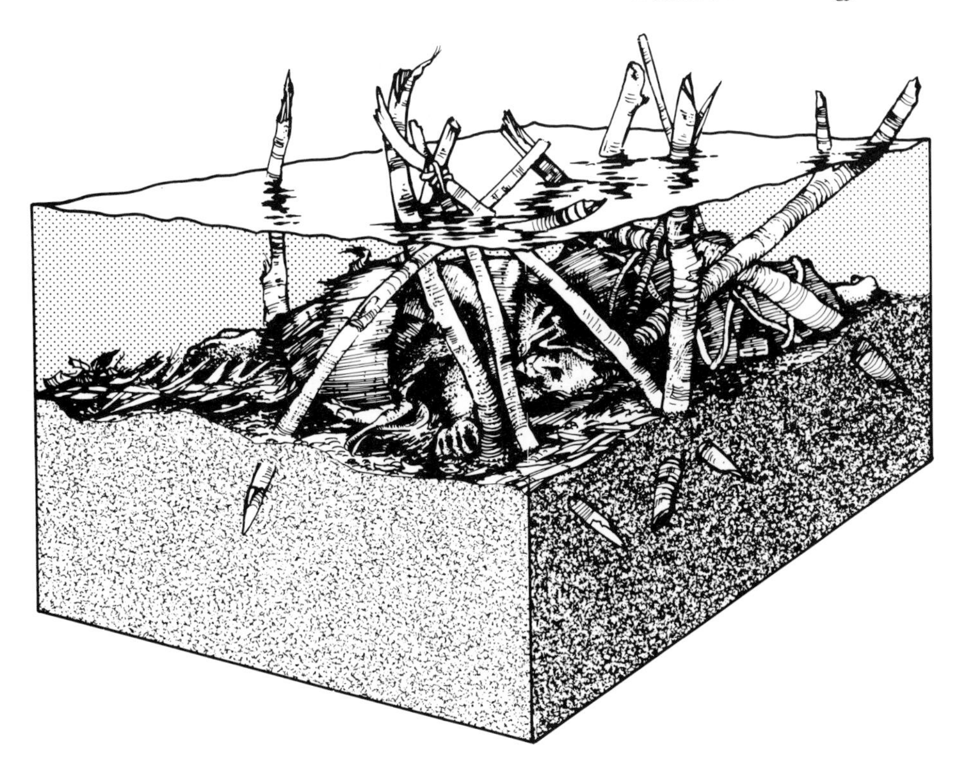

Figure 5.10 Reconstruction drawing of burial from Windover, Florida

we often assume hunter-gatherers to have had. The teeth of some of the humans show that plants such as cabbage palm were regularly chewed, but better evidence of diet has survived in the abdomens of some individuals. One body still retained thousands of seeds of edible fleshy fruits, particularly elderberry, with some grape and prickly pear cactus. There are also a few seeds of holly and black nightshade, both traditionally parts of other drinks, the holly featuring in the ritual Black Drink of the historical southeastern Indians and the nightshade a medicinal plant. The seeds suggest that this individual died in late spring or summer, and other bodies show similar seasonally distinct foods. Two other bodies, however show a different pattern. One adult male and a child of 2 had eaten little or no fruit but had large amounts of crushed fish bones in their abdomens. The Windover burial pond has only been partially examined: the remainder is now sealed again to await future refinements in recovery and analyses (Doran and Dickel 1988).

There are, or were, many other sites in the extensive wetlands of Florida where human remains and their accompanying grave-goods survived in exceptional condition. At Fort Center in the basin of Lake Okeechobee, communities of Indians contemporary with the later Bronze Age inhabitants of Europe practised maize horticulture on earthworks raised above flood-water levels. The settlement persisted and in time an elaborate burial ritual was developed. The bodies of the dead were wrapped in textiles and placed on a wooden platform erected over an artificial pond of dimensions 20 m × 12 m. The edges of the mortuary were embellished by carved pine totem poles sunk into the pond bottom and standing well above the 150 bundled bodies. The 30 totems bore the effigies of eagle, turkey, owl and duck, as well as otter, bobcat and other animals.

A further wet burial site is known from Little Salt Springs on the west coast of Florida (figure 5.9). About 12 000 years ago people camped here beside a deep natural well. Intermittent occupation took place over the following millennia against a background of rising water levels. About 7000 years ago, swampy shallow waters were extensive and the people who settled along their edge buried their dead in the shallows, in a manner reminiscent of the Windover burials. The bodies were partly wrapped in grass or leafy materials, or placed on leafy wax myrtle branches, and then pinned or held underwater on the soft peaty bottom by wooden stakes. As at Windover, the bodies decayed slowly, and at least one, buried 6000 years ago, still retained its brain when recovered in 1979. It is believed that over 1000 burials were put into the swamp.

North American wetland sites are by no means confined to Florida, and the northern Pacific coast is another region where evidence is being retrieved from wetland contexts for the economy, technology and arts of pre-contact Indians. One site currently under investigation lies near the mouth of the Hoko River, on the coast of Washington State (Croes 1988). Two phases of occupation on the shore led to accumulation of debris in the river, the first from about 3000 to 2500 years ago and the second from about 900 to 1000 years ago. People came here to fish, and the Hoko River is still known for a strong salmon run in late summer and autumn. Several species of fish were recovered, not just salmon. Bentwood fish hooks with spruce-root or cedar-root lines, made in several distinct types, were fairly common. Experimental fishing in Seattle aquarium has determined that the different types of hooks were effective for catching different species of fish. Fish blood has been identified on some of the stone blades from the site, and analysis of the skeletal elements represented by the fish bones suggests that the catch was being processed to preserve it for consumption elsewhere.

Ninety per cent of the artefacts from Hoko River were made of wood and plant fibre. Skirts of shredded cedar bark were preserved, and large baskets for collecting shellfish along with little baskets intended to hold a bentwood fish hook. Basketry hats sometimes had a topknot or knob, similar to the hats worn by nobles of the region in recent times. The wooden artefacts include a carved piece, a further instance of the preservation of prehistoric art through waterlogging.

Ozette, along the coast from Hoko River, is a more recent setlement. It came to an end about AD 1750 when the village was buried by a landslide. Erosion by heavy seas 350 years later exposed the remains to scavengers and other destructive agencies. The descendants of the Ozette people, whose oral tradition had kept alive memory of the disaster, requested a controlled excavation to save the site from looting and to protect the bones of their ancestors. The site was large and complex, and the conditions of preservation were excellent (Daugherty 1988). The many bones, shells and seeds indicated that subsistence had been based on water resources, as at Hoko River, and the village had been well placed for whale hunting.

Material culture was based on wood and plant fibres, and several hundred thousand items were recovered including many fragile baskets. Items relating to the water and fishing included paddles and fragments of canoes, nets and fish hooks, and harpoons and harpoon sheaths. Many of the wooden objects were decorated. Wooden bowls might have handles carved into human or animal heads, or a whole figure could form a container, with the head and legs as handles and the hollowed-out body as a dish. Box fronts and planks were decorated with incised animal motifs and perhaps inlaid with teeth. A three-dimensional cedarwood carving of the dorsal fin of a whale, standing about 1 m high, was inlaid with over 700 white sea-otter teeth and painted red and black, part of the design being a thunderbird. The art preserved at Ozette is an important demonstration of the Indian traditions and skills that existed shortly before European contact.

North along the Pacific coast, moving into British Columbia, many more wet sites are known. On the east coast of Vancouver island, 150 km north of Victoria, the Little Qualicum site lies at the mouth of the river of that name. As at Hoko River or at European sites such as Tybrind Vig, there is evidence of occupation on the shore and well-preserved midden material in the intertidal zone in front of the settlement area. Once again, much of the material culture is organic and much of it relates to fishing, including a heavy stone bound with cedar-branch rope and used as an anchor and a 1.5 m length of lattice-work from a fish weir. Many salmon and other fish bones testify to what was caught. Little Qualicum is dated to about 1000 years ago. Further north at Lachane, Prince Rupert Harbour, the waterlogged midden of a coastal settlement dating from 2500 to 1600 years ago has been investigated. This site has yielded little fishing evidence, and no bone, but a good range of domestic artefacts demonstrates the woodworking skills of the inhabitants and many wooden wedges, of the sort used to split wood, were found. There were baskets, wooden bowls, bentwood boxes and a cedarwood handle for a box lid carved in stylized animal form.

From Lachane in the northwest to Key Marco in the southeast, the wet sites of North America demonstrate a twofold value for the archaeologist. Waterlogging has preserved categories of evidence infrequently encountered on dryland sites, evidence which suggests a secure economic base founded on the exploitation of abundant coastal, estuarine or freshwater resources. Perhaps because of economic security, perhaps only because conditions are right for preservation, many of the sites have yielded decorated and carved wood. Comparisons with northern Europe suggest a similar abundance of wetland resources in the postglacial period, but only occasionally has carved or decorated wood been found, Tybrind Vig providing one of the most notable examples. Recent work in North America and, most importantly, the publication of that work, indicates a growing awareness of the richness and rewards of wetland archaeology in the continent. If the potential is now realized in any degree, it will be thanks to the efforts of a few determined people who have worked steadily and with little support against the grain of the rather dry archaeological trends of recent years.

6.0 TRACKWAYS IN CONTEXT

The once extensive peatlands of northern Europe which formed under conditions of reed swamp or raised bog, were visited, exploited and traversed by the peoples who lived around their margins and on the peninsulas and islands in the bogs (see chapter 2). Whereas people around a lake could travel by boat, there was not always sufficient clear open water for such an easy means of transport through a reed swamp,and certainly not across a raised bog. Yet the terrain was, by definition, wet, boggy and potentially treacherous. To cross, a firm footing was needed, and from about 6000 years ago to quite recent times this was provided by building wooden trackways. The weight of wood and the passing traffic ensured that the structures were soon embedded and then engulfed in waterlogged peats which preserved the wood for centuries or millennia. Their discovery depends on drainage and the exploitation of peat for fuel or horticulture, and so in most cases a structure is threatened as soon as it becomes known. Where peat-workings are extensive and archaeologists have been active, numerous examples of trackways are now known although few still exist. The regions where observation and investigation have been fullest are the German province of Lower Saxony, the Bourtanger Moor which spans the border between the Netherlands province of Drenthe and Lower Saxony, and the Somerset Levels in the southwest of England.

Recent work by Casparie on the Dutch side of Bourtanger Moor has led to the publication of Neolithic, Bronze Age and Iron Age trackways in a series of papers which pay detailed attention to the environmental as well as the archaeological evidence (Casparie 1982, 1984, 1986). As a result, Casparie has been able to argue that the trackways of the Bronze Age, one of which is dated by dendrochronology to 1350 BC, were built to exploit the bog-iron ore which had formed by that period. Confirmation came with the discovery of an iron punch securely associated with the Bronze Age structure, which incidentally demonstrated a probably local iron-working technology well before the archaeologists' conventional start of the Iron Age.

In Lower Saxony some 200 trackways are known, thanks to survey and excavation carried out by Hayen over recent decades (Hayen 1987). It is not possible here to do justice to the results of his often single-handed work, but an indication can be given by reference to just one structure. In about 300 BC a trackway was built across Wittemoor, striking northwards from dry land across the bog for over 3 km to a small but navigable stream which in turn flowed into the River Weser. The southern part of the trackway was built of oak timbers, presumably felled from the adjacent dry land. Further out into the bog, alder was used, felled perhaps from the stream edge. The logs were worn, as if by passing waggons and as if the loads moving north to the stream were heavier than those coming the other way. Elsewhere, Hayen has retrieved ample evidence for wheels and waggons, and even the hooves of draught animals.

At one point on the Wittemoor track a small watercourse was crossed, and here the structure soon broke up in use. The short unstable stretch of trackway was marked in antiquity by fires beside the track, and vertical oak posts and two tall carved wooden figures. One was set in a peat hummock, and the other in a perforated plank. When the track went out of use, soon after building, the figures were laid flat on the bog surface and covered with loose peat. The significance of these figures is not altogether clear, except that they marked a dangerous stretch of the route.

The trackways of the Somerset Levels come from a relatively small area of peat. This area was dominated by reeds with occasional fenwood when the first trackway was built around 6000 years ago, and largely raised bog by the end of the prehistoric period. Many different structures and diverse stray finds have been recorded (Coles and Coles 1986, Somerset Levels Project 1975–89), leading to a relatively detailed knowledge of environmental change and human activity from the Neolithic to the end of the Iron Age. One structure stands out from the others for its age, its design and the wealth of associated environmental and artefactual evidence. This is the Sweet Track, discovered in 1970 and excavated and analysed by members of the Somerset Levels Project in the following years. It has been named after the man who discovered it, Mr Ray Sweet.

The Sweet Track was a raised walkway, built about 3800 BC to cross nearly 2 km of reed swamp that lay between dry land and a mid-marsh island. Its single plank walkway was held about 40 cm above the soft ground surface by pairs and groups of obliquely crossed pegs retained by a ground-level rail (plate 5.4). Oak, ash and lime were used for planks, and almost all the common species of a mixed oak forest were exploited for the pegs and rails. The straight uniform growth of much of the roundwood used for these supporting timbers is indicative of coppiced growth, either fortuitously sprung from the stumps of felled trees and shrubs or perhaps already produced by some system of forest management akin to that practised by contemporaries at Hornstaad-Hörnle I. The external evidence for coppicing is supported by analysis of the tree-rings, which has been particularly fruitful for the Sweet Track (Morgan 1988). Oak, ash and hazel have all added to the understanding of the structure. Hazel and ash growth patterns, like those of the oak, indicate that the bulk of the wood was felled in one season and a few pieces were added as repair timbers in the next 11 years, but no evidence has been found for repairs at a later date. This suggests that the track was in use for a little over a decade, an interpretation supported by examination of fungal attack on the wood, which was not advanced.

The oak timbers used for planks came from mature trees at least four centuries old, except for a short stretch at the southern end of the trackway where younger trees were used. The older trees were of considerable girth, and

Plate 5.4 The Sweet Track, Somerset Levels. Note the long straight centre rail crossed by oblique pegs at right angles. The pegs originally supported planks, which in this stretch of the trackway hae been removed by flooding, and one has come to rest in the top left-hand corner of the excavation
(Courtesy Somerset Levels Project)

were split radially to provide planks wide enough for the walkway (30–50 cm). The younger trees had to be split across the centre to give planks of a similar width, and it is noteworthy that this could be achieved with the technology of the time when timber-working depended on stone axes and wooden wedges and mallets. The evidence for two stands of timber of different ages implies mature primary forest on the central island and younger woodlands at the southern end, with perhaps an early episode of forest clearance followed by regeneration 120 years before renewed clearance took place to build the trackway. The earlier clearance is not evident in the pollen record, but the one associated with the track building can be identified. The indicators of cultivation are stronger near the southern terminal of the Sweet Track than near the northern end where it abuts the central island.

The reed swamp traversed by the trackway was not altogether uniform. Analyses of pollen, plant macrofossils and beetles from a central area (Caseldine 1984, Girling 1984) indicate particularly wet conditions, with an abundance of aquatic plants and insects. There was also the raft spider (*Dolomedes*) which hunts small fish and insects in permanent bodies of water. At this point the trackway substructure had been reinforced during initial building, and repair wood was subsequently added. All the signs are of a difficult area, although no evidence was found for special treatment along the lines noted for the Wittemoor trackway.

The Sweet Track was merely a footpath, barely 20–30 cm wide, stretching away through high reed beds which masked the ends once a traveller had begun his or her walk. Hazards of high water, obscuring reeds, slippery wet planks and projecting pegs all combined to make the walkway precarious. Passing places for chance encounters have not been found. Hence, along the line there is the debris of passing traffic. Flint flakes, unmoved since loss and cushioned by the peat, lie along the track sides. Some were used to cut wood, others for reeds and other plants, and a single flake was used to cut hide. Arrowheads of flint point to hunting expeditions: traces of glue or of arrowshafts or of binding string were preserved on several of them, and a number of bow fragments were also recovered. A fine flint axe and a jadeite axe-head were found beside the track timbers. These two unhafted unused axe-heads suggest either accidental losses or deliberate acts of deposition for a purpose unknown to us. Pottery found along the track included heaps of sherds making almost complete pots, accidentally broken by clumsy travellers; in one case, a pot had held hazelnuts, and in another a wooden spurtle or stirrer was being carried along with, perhaps, gruel. Other artefacts round along the track line represent other objects discarded during use in the swamp. Bows, digging sticks, spades or paddles, wedges, handles, pins, a spoon, a mattock, a comb, toggles and a carved bowl are in no way spectacular or even carefully fashioned; they are the common variety of artefacts that have perished on contemporary dryland sites. Everything found on, in or beside the track was contemporary. This is not archaeological contemporaneity, which may with luck be only a century, but more likely a quarter millennium in duration, but it is real time. Everything, artefacts of stone, flint, pottery, wooden planks and pegs, the swamp, and the forests, fields and coppices on the dry land around, was in existence and in operation, either passively or actively, at one moment in time. One group of unnamed people saw it all, and were a part of it all. They and their settlement have perished, leaving only the footpath as witness to their presence.

7.0 THE ADVANTAGES OF A WETLAND LIFE

Once the nature of wetland environments contemporary with past human settlements has been established, the question is often posed as to why people lived where their houses were liable to flood and where bog, marsh and swamp with attendant insects surrounded them. To ask such questions is to a certain extent ethnocentric, a reflection of our own views about damp surroundings which is increasingly negative as electric wiring and fitted carpets become the norm. The following brief survey of the possible positive aspects of a wetland life may also be ethnocentric, but it will redress the balance a little. It attempts to relate to the ever-increasing body of evidence available concerning prehistoric habitation in wetlands worldwide. Aspects to consider are resource abundance, climatic amelioration and defence.

Resource abundance is particularly well demonstrated at circum-Alpine sites of the Neolithic period and, in the case of Fiavé, during the Bronze Age. Nineteenth-century and recent excavations have yielded quantities of different species of wild foods and raw materials, both plant and animal. In the early Neolithic levels at Hornstaad-Hörnle I, for example, the following have been identified: perch and tench in addition to the pike already noted, many deer and a fair number of aurochs and wild pig, along with beaver, hedgehog and birds. Only a quarter of the animal bones identified came from domestic species, mainly cattle and the remainder pig, dog and goat (Kokabi 1985). The fauna is indicative of wet and forested environments, as is the flora. Fruits collected included strawberry, raspberry, blackberry, crab-apple, hazelnut, sloe and chinese lantern. Many other wild plants were consumed as foods, flavourings or medicines, even black bindweed, black nightshade and ground ivy. Crops were grown, the cereals mostly wheat with some barley. Opium poppy and flax were also cultivated (Rösch 1985). These are both crops that flourish in deep and moist soils in a temperate climate, and they could have been grown for the oil content of their seeds. They are, however, multi-purpose crops, flax yielding fibre for rope and textiles if retted and the poppy an opiate or sedative.

The cropping of woodlands around the settlement has already been discussed. In addition to timber, people had yet another use for the forest. Birch bark was collected and gum extracted which was used extensively to stick things together, arrowheads to arrowshafts and sickle blades to sickle hafts for instance. The gum served a further purpose: oblong lumps have been found with tooth-marks in them, highly reminiscent of modern discarded chewing-gum.

The growing of flax and opium poppies indicates relatively warm moist soils. Farmers who cultivated land immediately around lakes may have benefited from a slight amelioration of temperatures compared with the hinterland. The possibility has been examined in some detail for the circum-Alpine lakes (e.g. Sakellaridis 1979), and receives support from evidence coming from wetlands on the other side of the world in New Zealand.

On North Island, New Zealand, the Maori built *pa*, or defended settlements, in swamps as well as on the better-known dryland location. Excavation of three swamp *pa* around the small Lake Mangakaware (Bellwood 1971, 1978) has revealed well--preserved structural timbers and provided relatively good economic information (figure 5.11). Wild resources were exploited over a wide territory and crops were cultivated locally. What is interesting is that the latter were grown directly in the soils around the lake without any need to raise soil temperatures artificially as happened elsewhere. The Maori, arriving in New Zealand with crops from their warmer homelands in Polynesia, are known to have added gravel to their terraced fields to retain heat and to ensure crop yields in the relatively cool New Zealand soils. Around Lake Mangakaware such steps were not apparently necessary.

Maori *pa* were also sited for defence, and location in a swamp was recognized as a viable alternative to a defended hilltop or spur of land. Whether circum-Alpine settlements were defensive in nature or not is argued at length (e.g. Pétrequin 1984), and there are other categories of wetland settlement which are generally accepted, rightly or not, as primarily defensive. Amongst these are the crannogs of Ireland and Scotland (Morrison 1985), small artificial islands set in a lake with one or two houses on them. Many were first built in the first millennium BC and their use continued into recorded times when, in Ireland at least, defence was certainly one function. However, as with the Maori *pa*, there may have been more than one attraction in a watery setting, in particular in Scotland where any possible climatic amelioration was welcomed. Many other examples could be given of wetland settlements that have a defensive aspect but also benefited from the economic advantages of the locality, such as Biskupin in Poland and its several contemporaries of the later prehistoric period (Rajewski 1970).

8.0 THE NEED TO PRESERVE

Drainage of wetlands is a familiar phenomenon. Whether it precedes agriculture or peat extraction, it is likely to cause the irreversible decay of organic archaeological evidence contained in the formerly waterlogged deposits. Neolithic axe-hafts and Mesolithic textiles cannot be restored once they have dried, distorted and cracked or powdered, nor can the wood of a structure be reconstructed if worms and insects have begun to invade because of falling water-tables. In this respect, archaeological evidence does not differ from palaeo-environmental evidence, which is equally vulnerable and irreplaceable. But both differ from the living components of a wetland, the flora and fauna,

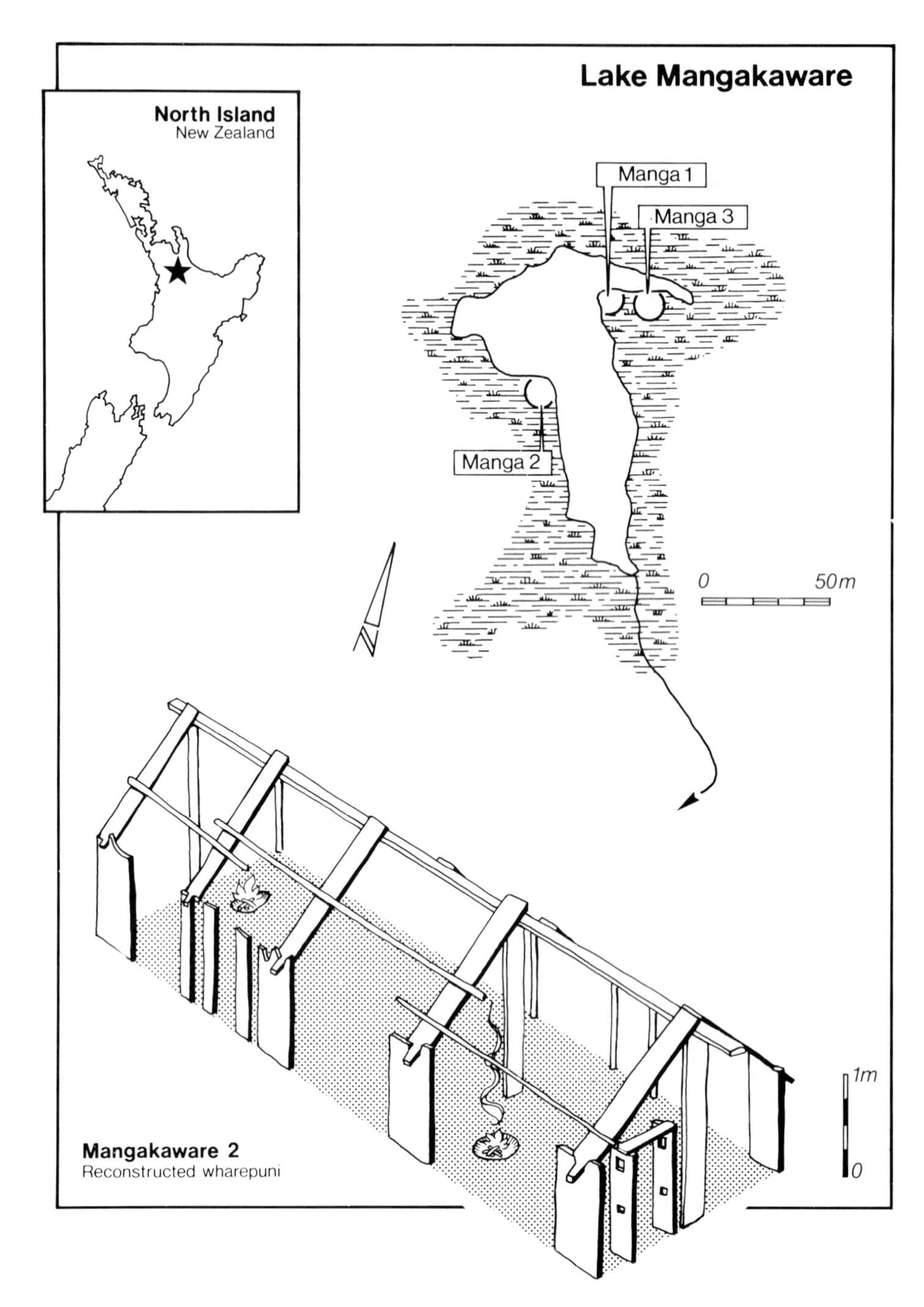

Figure 5.11 Location of a swamp *pa*, Lake Mangakaware, New Zealand, with reconstruction drawing of timber framework for a house
(after Bellwood 1971)

which can to a limited extent be restored to a dried-out wetland by the re-introduction of water and sympathetic management. The distinction is relevant, because it means that if a wetland with archaeological value can be kept wet, a wildlife value can probably be added or enhanced to give a twofold reason for active preservation of the area. Such was the case with a stretch of the Sweet Track in the Somerset Levels where heritage and nature conservation interests came together to set up a reserve (Coles 1987).

In 1980, ten years after its discovery, the Sweet Track had been excavated at various points along its line. Intervening areas were checked by small trenches which picked up the track line and ascertained the state of the wood. One 500 m stretch of the track ran through an area currently covered by fenwood vegetation and managed as a Nature Reserve by the Nature Conservancy Council, who held the land on lease from Fisons plc, a major peat extraction company. Over the next few years, the 16.8 ha block of land was purchased from Fison's for £95 000, a rate below its value as land with permission for peat extraction. A grant for the purchase came from the National Heritage Memorial Fund, after a joint request by the Nature Conservancy Council, English Heritage and the Somerset Levels Project, based on the combined archaeological, palaeo-environmental and wildlife value of the reserve.

Because the land around the reserve was being drained and lowered by peat-cutting, further action was necessary. A grant of £35 000 financed the building of a clay bund around the three exposed sides of the rectangular reserve to hold water in. A system of pumps, pipes, flood valves and ditches carries water from an outside reservoir into the reserve and along the known line of the trackway which lies undisturbed under about a metre of peat. Monitoring tubes at regular intervals make it quick and easy to check that the water level is being maintained above the level of the Neolithic wood. The system became fully operational in 1985 and appears to be entirely successful, although continued action at a minor level is required and not always for the expected reasons.

The water which is pumped into the reserve comes from a collecting pond on the edge of a wide peat-cutting area. If this runs dry, and it can do, the only water available is the nutrient-rich supply from an adjacent major drainage channel. This water is not ideal for the track wood, nor for the present-day wildlife, and it is avoided as far as possible. Secondly, left undisturbed, the fenwood flourishes, and intervention is necessary to maintain the required range of habitats. Thirdly, part of the reserve is under unimproved wetland pasture which needs to be mown late in the summer. For this operation, the water level has to be lowered briefly to allow a tractor to work, but only briefly or the buried trackway will suffer. If the grass is not mown, the pasture will soon be colonized by fenwood species. In other words, there is no respite from vigilance, although any threat from peat extraction has been averted.

The Sweet Track reserve is not a unique phenomenon in the wetland achaeology world. In the Netherlands, shipwrecks buried in the Ijsselmeer polders have been sealed and covered with clay to protect them from reclamation of the surrounding land. At Flag Fen near Peterborough in England, a Bronze Age timber platform and settlement has been sealed and flooded, except for the small area currently under investigation. Around the shores of Lake Neuchâtel in Switzerland various attempts have been made to protect prehistoric settlements from erosion, usually through some means of reinforcing the covering deposits before they are washed away. If the current trends of increased drainage and development continue, and if archaeological survey and excavations keep pace, the opportunity will be there to increase the number of actively preserved sites. If this is done wetland archaeologists will have awarded themselves a monitoring task well into the future. But if nothing is done now, there may soon be nothing left to do, such is the fragile nature of waterlogged remains. That would be a great loss.

6

Agricultural Impacts in Temperate Wetlands

Michael Williams

1.0 INTRODUCTION

Agriculture and the production of food have been the main reasons for the elimination of the bulk of the 1 606 000 km^2 of wetlands considered to have been drained by 1985, nearly three-quarters of which has occurred in the temperate world (chapter 1, table 1.8). Draining for agriculture has been one of the major transformation processes on the earth's surface, although it has rarely been examined in a systematic way (Wagret 1969).

The most obvious manifestation of this transformation is the total change in the hydrological system with the elimination of standing water and the reduction of waterlogging, the abandonment of old water courses and the construction of new ones. In addition, new landscapes of roads, fields and settlements emerge, soils are changed in composition and elevation, natural vegetation is largely eliminated and new crops introduced (Sheail and Wells 1983). Traditional and often sustainable systems of exploitation based on the natural ecosystem and its annual fluxes are replaced by high-energy sedentary agricultural systems. For draining to be successful, the transformation of the landscape must be complete so that all the original characteristic soils, hydrology and vegetation are replaced. In short, old geographies are swept away and replaced by new geographies.

What follows is an examination of some examples of agricultural transformation in the temperate world: the Netherlands and Fens that fringe the North Sea, the wet prairie and Mississippi bottomland hardwood forests of the United States and the swamps of the southeast of South Australia. These examples illustrate differences in causes of wetness, and the technical solutions employed to overcome that wetness. They range in size from the near continental to the regional, and in time from the beginning of the first millennium AD to the present. In conclusion, an attempt is made to bring together some of the commonalities of the different transformation experiences.

2.0 THE NORTH SEA FRINGES

For over 1000 years, the wetlands of Europe, particularly the intertidal marshes, marine deposits and accumulated silts and peats fringing the North Sea in England, Holland and adjacent countries (chapter 2, figure 2.5), and the glacially impeded drainage of the interior of the continent (French 1959; Skoropanov 1961, pp. 1–12; Wagret 1969, pp. 70–4, 85–9, 95–103) have been subject to a sustained attack in order to exploit their natural products, to protect existing reclaimed lands from inundation and eventually to convert the wetland into permanent grazing and agricultural land.

In both the Netherlands and England there is abundant evidence that settlement had occurred in and around the wetlands since prehistoric times (chapter 5), but evidence of purposeful change becomes clearer from post-Roman times (Hallam 1970, pp. 22–113), particularly from the tenth century onwards. From then until the fourteenth century, population growth, economic expansion and urban revival laid the foundations of European civilization. There was a move from self-sufficiency in agriculture during the early Middle Ages to the production of surplus food and fibre during the later Middle Ages. Growing numbers of non-agriculturalists could be fed and clothed, and in the process the European landscape was transformed, principally by woodland clearing, but also by wetland draining and heathland reclamation (Darby 1951, Glacken 1967, pp. 318–20, 330–41).

2.1 *The traditional wetland economy*

Because most settlement of wetlands during the pre-modern era tended to be located along the margins of the uplands and flood-free islands, there has been a tendency to think of the wetlands as an extensive negative morass. However, nothing could be further from the truth. Although the areas were under water sometimes for years on end, more often than not they were flooded for only a limited period during the late autumn to winter. The ground was technically part of the manorial 'waste' but it was also valuable land zealously guarded and rigorously managed by the surrounding settlements. Evidence abounds from about 1000 to the end of the fourteenth century of the natural productivity and wealth of the wetlands. There was a hierarchy of usefulness that depended on the degree of wetness of the particular part of the wetland, which was often a function of the seasonal flux of water. Nearly every watercourse had its fishing weirs and fisheries, and eel renders reached tens of thousands per annum in scores of places in the Somerset Levels (Williams 1970, pp. 26–9) and the Fenland (Darby 1983, pp. 22–4). Fish and eels fulfilled many of the uses of currency as debts, payments and rents were often paid in them. Wildfowl were also highly prized and were an important part of the diet, but although there are hints of their value, there is no one great body of evidence to show how important they were. Salt pans, and rush and sedge collection were important locally, and turbary (peat cutting) is mentioned increasingly from 1200 onwards when large areas of peat were removed for fuel because fuel-wood supplies were scarce in the vicinity of the European wetlands. The record of extraction is sketchy and erratic in places, but in the Norfolk Broads in eastern England, archaeology, palaeobotany and the evidence of documentary and sedimentary research shows conclusively that the area occupied by the open water of the Broads as we know them today is no more than drowned medieval peat diggings (Lambert et al. 1960). If the extraction equalled the volume of the present lakes then at least $250 \times 10^6 \, m^3$ of material must have been removed before the water/land levels changed relative to each other in the early fourteenth century and drowned the diggings, as indeed happened in many other instances in the Netherlands.

However, it was common grazing in the marsh and peat lands that were most valued activity in the wetlands. Pasture rights for cattle and sheep became an integral part of the medieval economy as groups of settlements agreed to demarcate parts of the emergent wetland for their own exclusive use. Often the land was held in common; the village cattle could graze in unlimited numbers on the wetland, only to be rounded up, branded and culled once a year. Some villages and landlords began to subdivide their lowland in order to establish and protect specific individual rights. These demarcations were often the cause of bitter disputes and 'range wars' as, for example, those between Wells and Glastonbury in Somerset, or Crowland and its surrounding villages in the Fenland, which are rich in detail about the usefulness of the wetlands and indicate the valued position of pasture rights in these wetland economies. The division had greater significance than that, however, for if taken further the establishment of ownership inevitably meant 'enclosure' of the land and its being taken out of common use, and was thus the first step in its permanent reclamation by embankments, dykes and ditches (Williams 1982).

Taken as a whole, the evidence suggests that the practice of unlimited shared commoning (intercommoning) was open to abuse and was unsatisfactory, and that the length of the grazing season and the value of natural pasture was uncertain because of flooding. Therefore, in order to ensure the pastures against human and natural depredations, reclamations were made in the common wetlands, a trend encouraged by the growing concern during the medieval period to obtain specific property rights in more limited areas and the universal push towards 'wasteland' reclamation, be it woodland, heathland or wetland, in the wake of expanding population numbers.

In the creation of new meadows for hay and in the extension of the grazing season lay the best means of enlarging the economy because winter fodder was the crucial deficiency in medieval stock farming and the provision of year-round protein intake. A hectare of periodically flooded pasture converted into meadow could equal, or more usually exceed, the value of a comparable hectare of cropland. Thus, wherever landward flooding was an assured annual event, as in the lowest portions of the Hull valley, the Somerset Levels, the Thames river valley and estuary, and the Fenland or the riverine and delta areas of the Netherlands, reclamation for meadowland was the norm and cropping was restricted to the uplands. Elsewhere in the wetlands, where there were superior silt soils and less regular flooding (other than sporadic marine inundations), as in the siltlands of the Fens and parts of northern Holland, reclamation aimed at creating new cropland. The building of walls and embankments, both out towards the sea on the intertidal marshes and inland into the lower peat fens and moors, meant that each successive intake widened the area of permanent settlement and reduced the area of wetlands.

2.2 *Early reclamation*

In both England and the Netherlands, the extent of wetland reclamation in the centuries before about 1350 was impressive. It was not a story of continuous success; there were many setbacks as storm surges breached seawalls, and over-extraction of peat for fuel and over-utilization of the peat soils lowered the surface and caused embankments to be undermined and/or water to seep into the hollows. But all in all, even small-scale piecemeal reclamations culminated in the transformation of large areas of wetland into dry land.

In the Fens the siltland, which lay about 2–3 m above the level of the inland peat, was occupied by the seventh century, but it was when population pressure built up from the early twelfth century onwards that the ordinary freehold farmers of the siltland cooperated in a massive feat of reclamation which won some 41 km^2 from the marshland bordering The Wash and over 233 km^2 of peaty fenland, all mainly for cropping. The chronology of this remarkable reclamation has been unravelled by Hallam (1965) from hundreds of medieval charters, rent rolls and grants, and its physical manifestation can be traced on the ground by a series of massive east-west-trending embankments, each marked by a major road today (figure 6.1). These walls were crossed by major north-south roads that allowed access to their new lands, and were also the alignment of parallel drains on either side. New offshoot settlements were created in the new lands. Similar but more small-scale fragmented reclamation occurred in the Somerset Levels (Williams 1970, pp. 40–74) and the Hull valley (Sheppard 1958).

Everywhere, religious houses played a major part in the reclamation of these wetlands, providing the organizational expertise and capital as they attempted to enlarge their estates and rent rolls. In the Levels and the Hull valley they were in the forefront of change, whereas in the Fens they tended to become involved later, aggrandizing the estates of the freeholders who had done the reclamation many years before. In the Netherlands it was a mixture of both. Either way, however, the mark of success of reclamation during this period is the fact that the value of drained land rose more rapidly than did that of surrounding areas, so that the Fenland silts and Somerset clays were amongst

Figure 6.1 Reclamation in the medieval Fenland. There was more reclamation further east in Cambridgeshire, which is not shown on this map
(after Hallam 1965)

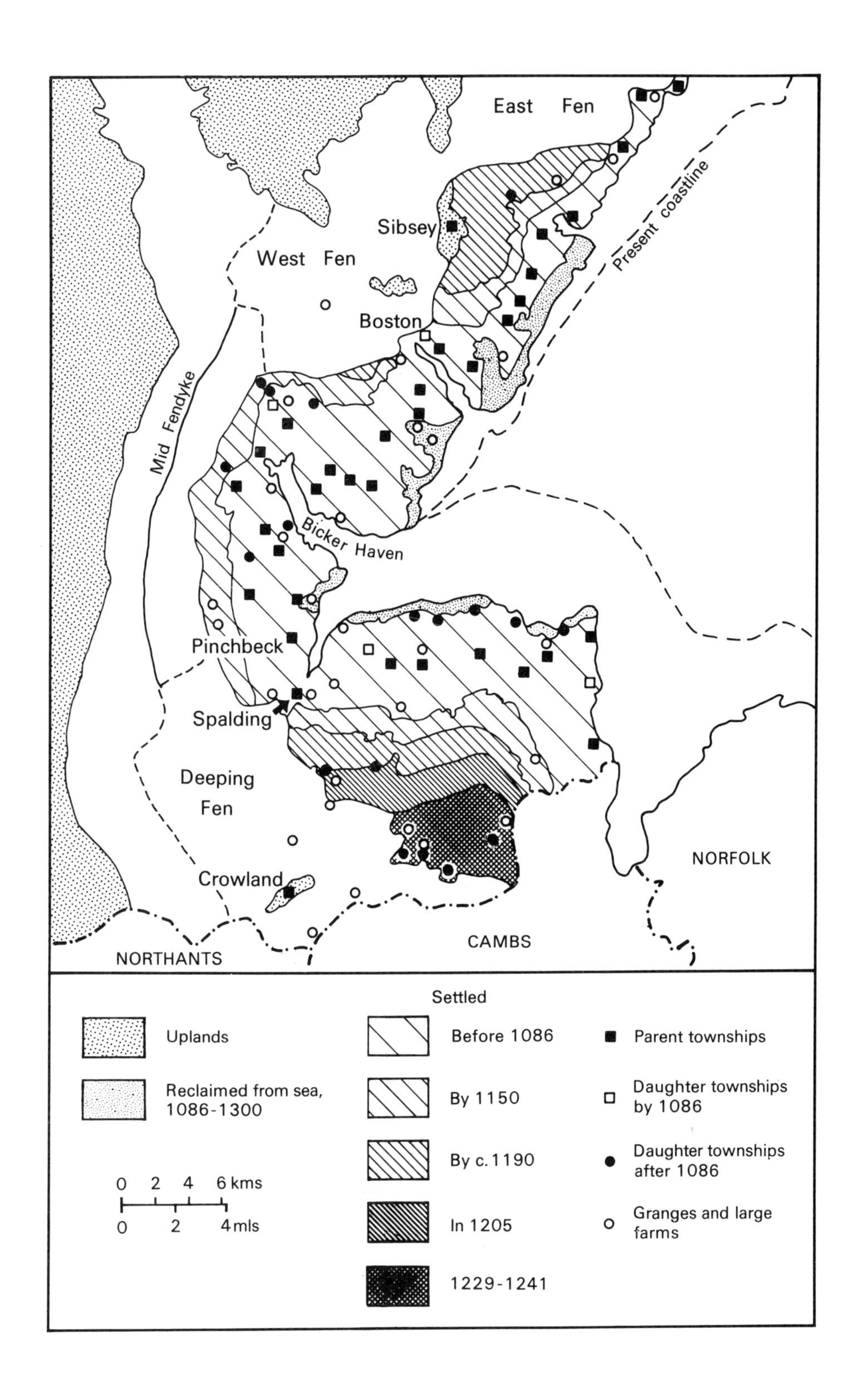
East Fen
Sibsey
West Fen
Boston
Present coastline
Mid Fendyke
Bicker Haven
Pinchbeck
Spalding
Deeping
Fen
Crowland
NORFOLK
CAMBS
NORTHANTS
Settled
Uplands
Reclaimed from sea, 1086-1300
Before 1086
By 1150
By c.1190
In 1205
1229-1241
Parent townships
Daughter townships by 1086
Daughter townships after 1086
Granges and large farms
0 2 4 6 kms
0 2 4 mls

the most prosperous areas in England during the mid-fourteenth century (Williams 1970, pp. 75–81; Darby et al. 1979; Darby 1983, pp. 20–8). The splendid medieval churches that grace these rural settlements today grew more on the profits of grass, supplemented by fish and fowl, and not, as might be supposed, wholly on crops.

In Holland, the evidence of extensive reclamation begins earlier and goes back to before the modern era (Besteman 1988). Within its confines, the country encapsulates nearly the whole experience of wetland transformation in the temperate world, and has strong regional peculiarities, which depend on the nature of the original wetland (de Jong and Wiggers 1983), be it coastal marsh, riparian silts, lake bottoms or peat bogs (figure 6.2). The story is highly complex and puctuated by setbacks of re-flooding and loss as much as of gain, so that only the most superficial outline can be given.

In the northern provinces of Gronigen and Friesland settlers had occupied the intertidal salt marshes from as early as 500 BC in some instances, adapting rather than modifying their watery environment by building thousands of artificial mounds or *terpen* on which dwellings were erected out of the reach of the flood waters. Today they still form distinctive islands of houses, orchards and trees that rise above an otherwise flat treeless landscape of former salt marshes. Gradually, however, dykes and embankments with simple sluices which opened and shut with the ebb and flow of the tide were constructed to protect the land and these enabled reclamation to be carried out in larger areas. During the twelfth century the word 'polder' appeared (Lambert 1985, p. 84) which indicated a more purposeful phase in land transformation rather than protection alone. Indeed, by the beginning of the fourteenth century over 1000 km^2 of coastal Gronigen was enpoldered, as was the former estuary of Middlezee. The inland peat bogs were now safe from seaward erosion. This polder building caused numerous problems such as higher tides and rivers that could not discharge their waters successfully, and extensive peat diggings inland left hollows that rapidly filled with water, formed lakes and generated waves which eroded surrounding dykes. Further east in Freisland, a further 800 km^2 was reclaimed, including the lower Lauwers, Fivek and Dollard estuaries, but great storm surges in 1287 claimed over 50 000 lives and the Dollard estuary, which had been progressively lowered by peat digging and over-draining, eventually reverted back to wetland. Many *terpen* were buried under marine deposits and not found again until re-reclaimed during the late sixteenth century (Lambert 1985, pp. 86–96).

In the western coastlands in what is today South Holland and West Utrecht, settlement was initially confined to a narrow 10 km wide strip of the coastal dunes (the Old Dunes) that stretched from the Texel Island in the north to the present Rhine Delta in the south. Behind these dunes there had developed large oligotrophic cushion peat bogs, up to 15 m thick in their centres, standing above the surrounding land, with the surplus water draining away naturally down their slopes. From the tenth century onwards, settlers moved inland, colonizing these previously uninhabited peat bogs, and encouraged in their venture by large-scale grants from lay and ecclesiastical lords who wished to expand their territory and rental income. The colonists made simple straight ditches in the peat, radiating out from the centre of the raised bog, which, because of its natural slope, allowed the excess water to drain away. When the peat dried out colonists burnt and cultivated it repeatedly, although later, when the bogs sank and the water-table approached the surface, they changed to pastures. These movements have been traced in minute detail in two case studies which resemble that of Hallam in the Fens: one of the Rijnland, an area of 625 km^2 around the channels of the Oude Rijn (Old Rhine) in south Holland

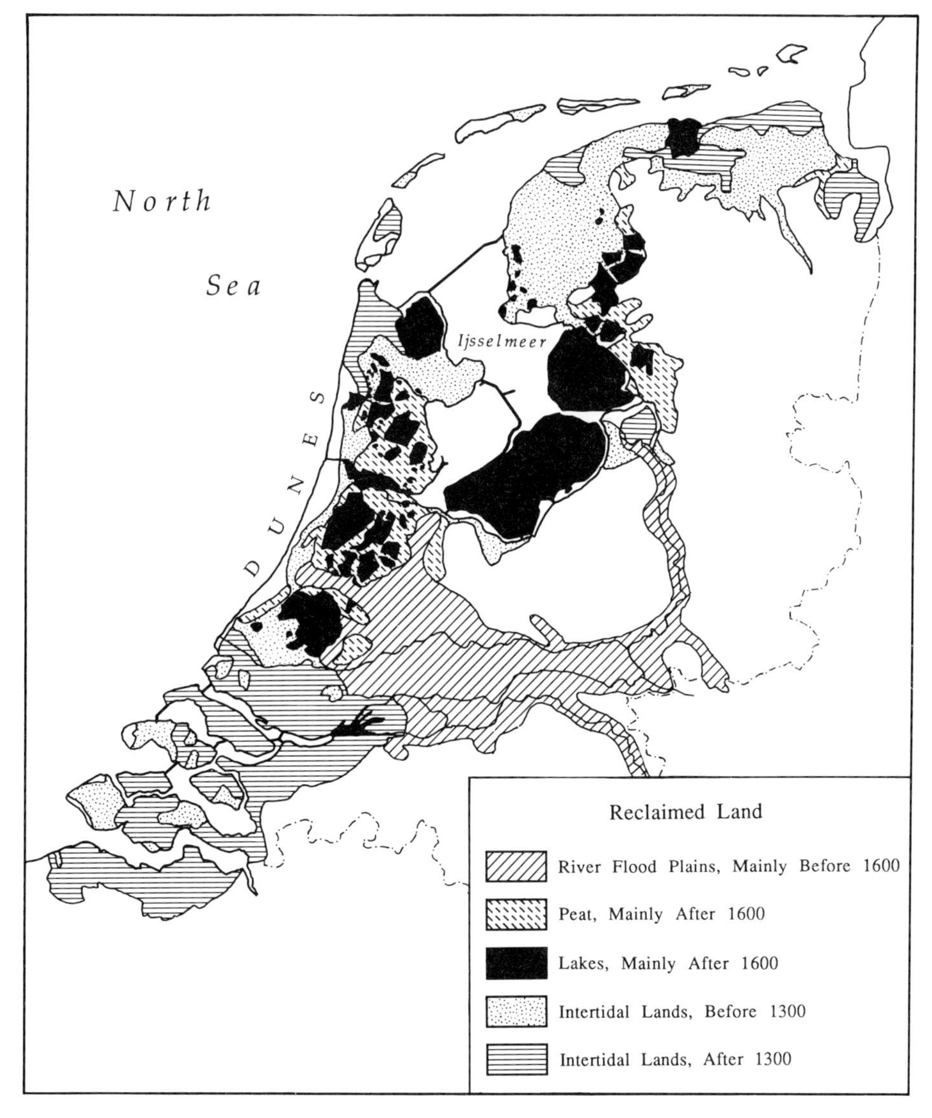

Figure 6.2 The reclamation of different types of wetland in the Netherlands (after de Jong and Wiggers 1983, p. 224)

(Tebrake 1985, pp. 190–210), and one in Kennermerland, an area of some 400 km^2 just east of the dunes in north Holland (Westenberg 1974).

Repeated draining, together with the burning of the peat in order to prepare an agricultural bed, caused major physical changes in the peat bogs. Initially, the low water-table caused compaction of the bogs owing to the weight of the dried-out upper layers, and draining caused their shrinkage through oxidization and subsequent erosion, mainly aeolian, all of which was accompanied by peat cutting for fuel for local farms and more distant towns. The result was the formation of the distinctive region known as the Rijk der Duizend Eilandtjes ; Realm of a Thousand Islands (plate 6.1). The surface of the peat was being lowered at a rate of at least 1 m per century at a time when it is thought that average sea levels were rising and storm activity was increasing in the warm climatic phase of 1150–1300 (Lamb 1982). Water broke through the coastal dunes frequently; there were six major tidal surges in both the twelfth and thirteenth centuries, 12 during the fourteenth and eight more during the next 50 years, each inundation leaving deposits of silt, eroding the peat, and leaving lakes in the depressed and eroded peat bog edges. Consequently, there was now a need for a comprehensive system of dykes, dams and sluices to be constructed in a polder-like manner to ensure protection from lake and sea erosion, which had been unecessary before but which was now essential in order to ensure the success of reclamation.

In the lowlands of the Rhine and its delta further south again, reclamation proceeded apace during the eleventh and twelfth centuries when large areas in the river back-swamps were reclaimed, and repeated attempts were made to aid natural deposition and encourage island growth in the delta. Space does not permit us to recount the details of the complex history of success and failure, prone as the reclamations were to repeated storm surges, inundation and the destruction of settlements and lives. In 1436 at least 20 villages were destroyed and over 10 000 people drowned in the flooding of Groote Waard island alone (Lambert 1985, pp. 110–24).

Lambert (1985, p. 122) suggests that, on balance, between 1250 and 1500 probably as much land was lost to the sea as was gained. On the positive side, however, we can say that the methods and procedures of an engineering, administrative and maintenance nature which had been developed were so successful that they were to change little during subsequent centuries. The knowledge, wisdom and self-assurance accumulated during these early centuries was compounded by considerable success as well as failures. When viewed in this light, the polder with windmill pumps that first appeared during the early fifteenth century was no dramatic breakthrough but 'rather the quiet application of available technologies' to the changing hydraulic conditions by a group of people 'who were well versed in diking and draining activities' (Tebrake 1985, p. 219), so that the great activity in draining that was to come was an inevitable progression and not a revolution in wetland management.

Plate 6.1 The Rijk der Duizend Eilandtjes (Realm of a Thousand Islands) looking west towards the settlement of Broke op Langedijk, north of Almaar, north Holland. Drainage channels were cut towards the centre of the raised peat bog to facilitate drainage from the thirteenth century onwards. However, centuries of burning, cultivation, and shrinkage and extraction of the peat have reduced the level of the land to the water-table and cultivation has had to be replaced by pasture. In more recent times, with closer control of the water levels, the islands have been ideally suited for early potatoes, cabbages and other vegetable crops as the surrounding water disperses frost and the fringing reeds protect them from cold winds. Increasingly the intervening stretches of water are being filled in so that access can be obtained by land rather than boat
(Courtesy KLM Aerocarto-Schipol)

2.3 *The 'Golden Age'*

Plague, economic recession and the accompanying run-down of the maintenance of drainage works, together with storm surges and the continued shrinkage of the peat, put a brake on reclamation activity for the next 150 years. However, after 1500, it was resumed, with the impetus coming primarily from Holland where a new wave of agricultural innovation and a general increase in trade engendered a new interest in long-term land improvement. It was the 'golden age' when Dutch merchants spanned the globe with their trade, and Holland became an urban and urbane society and achieved an artistic and commercial brilliance that neither Reformationary zeal nor rebellion against their Spanish overlords could diminish.

The land remaining to be reclaimed was either below sea level or actually sinking on already drowning peat bogs. The need was to go beyond gravity drainage and the simple animal- and human-operated scoop wheels of the earliest polders. Wind provided the answer. Windmills for grinding grain were mentioned as early as 1240, but windmills for draining did not become common until after 1500. The earliest known was at Alkmaar, in the middle of the vast complex of lakes that had accumulated in the old peat lands just east of the coastal dunes, north of Amsterdam/Haarlem. They were small inefficient post mills in which the whole body of the mill had to rotate in order for the sails to come into the wind. This limited their size and abiity to lift water between 1.5 and 2.0 m, which was done with scoop wheels. The great technological innovation came with the movable cap or *boverkruier*, some time before 1573. This required much less effort to move, mills could be taller, and sails longer, and therefore more powerful and responsive to even light breezes. Their water lift was increased to 3.5–4.0 m, and if gangs of mills were used this lift could be increased two or three times. In addition to these technological innovations, early experiments in draining organization whereby groups of agriculturalists taxed themselves to pay for permanent dyke masters, mill operators, and overseers brought a greater professionalism and efficiency to draining operations.

From the end of the sixteenth century onwards, a succession of windmill-drained polders (or *droogmakerijen*) were started, usually financed by wealthy merchants and townspeople seeking an outlet for their capital. Dozens of lakes north of the Ij, all probably remnants of the peat bogs flooded after the subsidence and cutting in the fourteenth century, were reclaimed between 1595 and 1635 (Lambert 1985, pp. 182–4), the seven largest accounting for 23 400 ha, at depths varying between 2 and 4 m (figure 6.3). The largest, Beemsteer (7174 ha), needed 49 windmills to maintain its new water-table 3.5 m below sea level.

While these spectacular transformations were in progress in western Holland, shallower peats were being stripped from bogs in the peat lands of the south and the Rhine delta in response to growing urban demands for fuel. Deeper cutting meant flooding and windmills as new lakes appeared, and the once separate Haarlemmermeer, Leidsemeer, Oudemeer and Speieringmermeer joined into one vast water body that had grown to 16 000 ha by 1700, so that probably as much land was lost by peat excavation as was won by enpoldering. In the delta area repeated storm surges resulted in more land losses, but some older smaller polders were joined together in Walcheren, Schouwen, Flakkee and Hoehne Waard, foreshadowing a contemporary policy of in effect shortening the length of wall to be maintained while strengthening it. In all, about 300 km^2 were reclaimed (Lambert 1985, pp. 190–1).

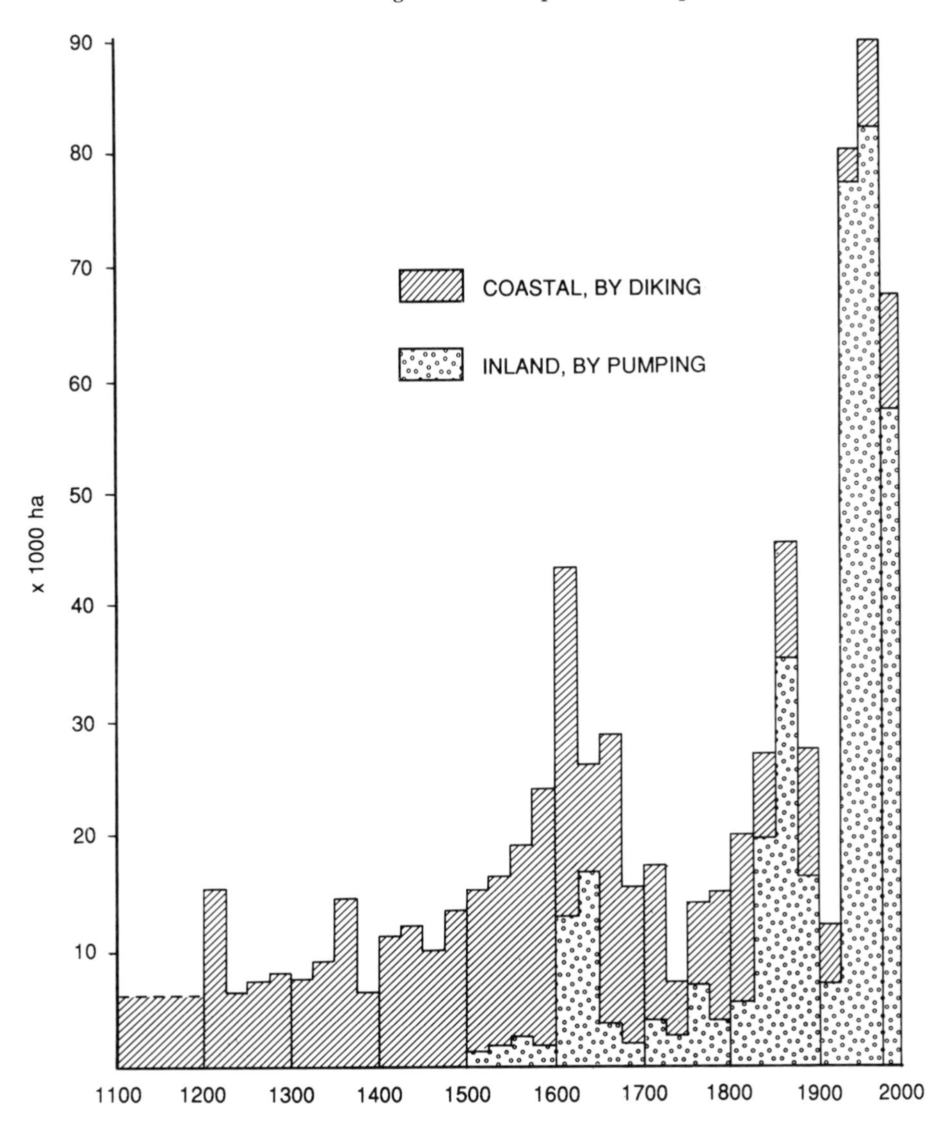

Figure 6.3 The chronology of reclamation and drainage in the Netherlands, *c.*1100–1990 (after Wagret 1969)

After the reclamation of the siltlands during the twelfth to thirteenth centuries, eastern England, like Holland, experienced the same economic downswing and stagnation in economic activity, with plague, recession and incessant storm damage, all compounded in the later sixteenth century by the break-up of the estates of the monasteries and religious houses which had played such a central part in the reclamation and maintenance of draining in the past.

Although a short distance from each other across the North Sea the draining problems of the Fens were very different from those of Holland. Basically the Fens was a large basin scooped out of the Jurassic clay, overlain on its seaward side by a belt of marine-deposited silts that extended between 10 and 20 km inland, and which stood at a slightly higher level than the accumulated mixture of peat and silts that overlay it on its landward side, thus impeding the seaward flow of water. The need was to clear the landward peats of the standing water by breaching the clay belt with straight maximum-fall river channels which took the upland fresh water to the sea by the shortest route possible. In addition, the outfalls needed to be secured with sluices to stop the inland movement of tidal water, which, in effect, dammed the outfalls and caused flooding inland, and brought large deposits of silt upstream, which could have a similar deleterious effect. Between the outfalls, sea-walls were needed to protect the coastal lands.

Although the draining problems were different from those of Holland, there is little doubt that there was much interplay of ideas and common influences. England was also entering a golden age of trade, commerce and global expansion, and many merchants were looking for ways of investing money in long-term agricultural projects, which were now becoming more profitable because of new farm arrangements, new crops, and experiments with fertilizer and husbandry, many introduced from Holland (Grove 1981). Thus, throughout the sixteenth and early seventeenth centuries, many schemes were put forward by people with draining and agricultural experience in the Netherlands (Darby 1983, pp. 46–64). Although these schemes came to nothing, the idea gradually emerged that the Fenland had to be treated as a whole and not in county pieces, that long straight channels giving maximum fall were desirable and that, at the very least, the elimination of summer flooding was both desirable and economic.

Many of the difficulties over agreeing to a scheme of draining were not technical but a result of the divided interests of the parties involved. It was a four-cornered fight: the Crown claimed ownership of all 'waste' and needed money, and therefore wanted it drained; the merchants wanted a solid long-term return on capital; the commoners who used the wetlands for summer grazing, fowling, fishing and fuel gathering wanted no change at all; the seafaring merchants of the busy ports of Boston on the Witham, Wisbech on the Nene and Lynn on the Ouse, all on the coast in early medieval times but now some 10–12 km inland because of continued coastal sedimentation and marsh reclamation, wanted no alteration in water levels or accessibility (i.e. no sluices) in the outfalls.

The breakthrough came in 1630 when the Earl of Bedford and 13 other 'adventurers' undertook to drain the south central portion of the peat fens (the Middle Level) on behalf of local landowners in exchange for 38 500 ha of the land. They engaged Cornelius Vermuyden, a Dutch hydraulic engineer who was already working on the draining of the wetlands in Axholme in Yorkshire. Vermuyden advocated a number of major straight cuts and sluices which were put into operation. After the hiatus of the Civil War and the problems caused by the destruction of some of the drainage works by the commoners, work was resumed in 1649.

It would be impossible to itemize the details of each drain cut and sluice built, and the manipulation of water levels across the Fenland in order to minimize flooding, but, suffice it to say, the major and outstanding works of these two phases were the Old Bedford River (1637) and the wider New Bedford River or Hundred Foot Drain (1651) cut parallel but separated by about a kilometre (figure 6.4). They ran for about 36 km between Earith and Denver, cutting off a long and circuitous course of the Ouse and increased the fall of the water. By operating sluices at each end of these new cuts freshwater floods were allowed to spill over into the intervening Washlands, thus holding them back until sea-water levels at the outfalls went down (Darby 1983, pp. 64–83) (plate 6.2). Many other works were carried out in other parts of the southern and northern (Lincolnshire) fens, each distinguishable by its straight lines which cut across the old natural drainage channels (figure 6.4).

The consequences of the combined draining works were threefold. First, the grazing season was extended, cropping spread, and land values rose. These were solid economic advantages. Flooding, however, was by no means eliminated and there were still plenty of fish and fowl, especially in the northern Fens. Second, the outfalls of the tidal rivers were still not secured against tidal influxes and surges and silt accumulation, and so they still caused flooding inland. Third, as in the Netherlands, subsidence through oxidization, compaction and wastage occurred at a rate of about 0.3 m/100 yrs. Consequently, the main embanked rivers were soon flowing some 1.5–2.0 m above the general level of the peat, a difference which has now increased to 3.5–4.0 m (Darby 1983, pp. 92–110). Only pumping could rectify this problem, but whereas the early seventeenth century onwards was the age of the windmill in Holland it did not make its appearance until the beginning of the eighteenth century in the Fens. Windmills were a financial burden thrown on groups of landowners who were forced to supplement the larger schemes by local district enterprise at their own expense (Darby 1983, pp. 112–14). Even if the landowners did get the water into the high-level channels they still hoped to get it to the sea somehow. It was an age of plans, proposals and conflicting interests; nothing was decided and only minor tinkering with schemes occurred. But all the time the peat surface became lower and lower until drainage by gravity was impossible.

2.4 *The nineteenth century*

By the opening years of the nineteenth century it was becoming clear in both Holland and England that the windmills were not proving adequate to deal with the flooding that resulted from the lowering of the peat and seepage of water through the embankments. They were too dependent on the wind and could not lift water a sufficient height. As one commentator put it, ‘three years ago five quarters of corn an acre; now sedge and rushes, frogs and bitterns!’ (Darby 1983, p. 148).

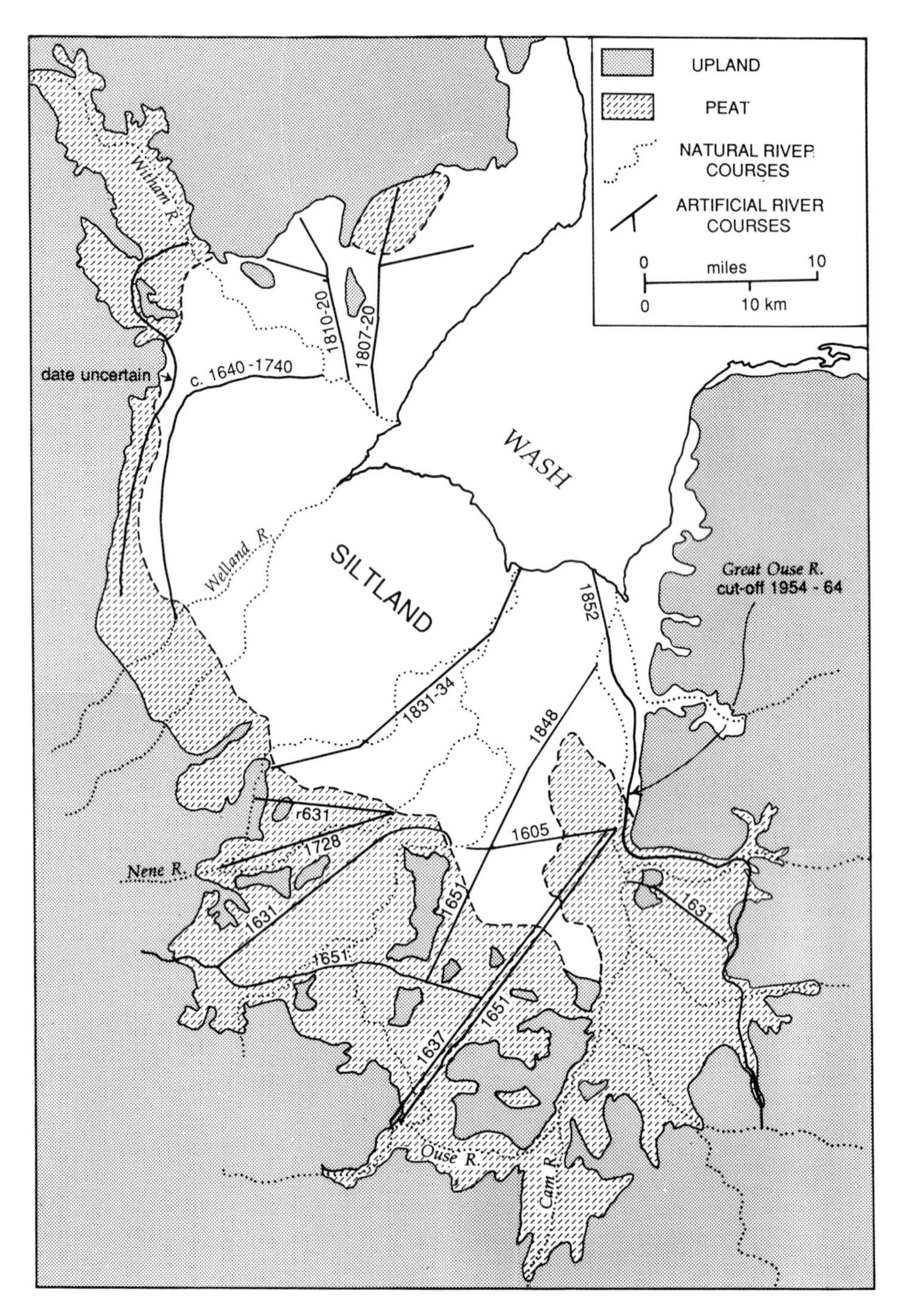

Figure 6.4 The main drains in the Fenland, *c.*1600–1980. Only the main artificial drains are shown here
(after Darby 1983)

Plate 6.2 A view looking southwest for a distance of approximately 30 km into the Fens, approximately from where the Denver sluice meets the Ouse River. The Old Bedford River (right) and the New Bedford or Hundred Foot Drain (left) enclose the area known as the Washes which is used as an overflow to relieve pressure on banks during high water. When dry, much of the Washes is a wildfowl refuge
(Courtesy Committee for Aerial Photography, Cambridge)

Ironically, although the first steam engine installed in the Netherlands in 1787 came from a mining district in Cornwall, steam engines did not appear in the Fens until 30 years later, the lag indicating the crucial nature of draining in the Dutch economy compared with its peripheral and localized nature in England. It was the successful draining of 10 133 ha of Deeping Fen in 1825 and the replacement of 44 windmills by two engines (Darby 1983, p. 176), and the even more spectacular draining of 18 000 ha of Haarlemmermeer by three engines between 1845 and 1852 (Lambert 1985, pp. 233–4) that set the seal on the rapid diffusion of the new technology, the efficiency of which was augmented after 1851 by the application of the centrifugal pump that could lift to great heights many times the 50 tons of water per minute achieved by the old scoop wheels. Windmills disappeared rapidly, over 700 from the Fens by 1852 and possibly thousands in Holland by the end of the century. The changeover was not complete for some time, but soon only a few anachronistic survivors graced the wetland landscape of the twentieth century, structures now lovingly restored and maintained by local preservationist societies.

In addition to the steam engine, the widespread adoption of tile drains in waterlogged soils lowered local water-tables and made the land much more suitable for agriculture in both countries (Darby 1983, Phillips 1989).

A problem that became increasingly clear during these years was that the river and polder banks were porous and/or erodable, so that even though the water was pumped out of the lowlands it usually seeped back. The Dutch had had to face this problem much earlier than the English because of the crucial nature of the sea polders and their susceptibility to wave erosion. By the end of the thirteenth century simple earthen embankments had been replaced by banks faced with turfs of clay, and this construction was improved on again in the fifteenth century by driving wooden piles down parallel to the face of the embankment, filling the gaps between the piles with seaweed and rushes, and facing the whole with stones (Lambert 1985, p. 227). However, the advent of the boring pile worm (*Teredo limmorta* or *Teredo navalis*) in 1731 completely changed construction techniques again. As sea-walls crumbled many experiments were carried out to preserve the timber, but the only alternative was to abandon timber construction. By the end of the eighteenth century the modern Dutch dyke had evolved: a gently sloping outer face of clay faced with stones and brushwood mattresses filled with sand behind (Mazure 1983). In the Fens the problemn was less severe but real enough for all that. All schemes for draining had recommended the rapid evacuation of upland fresh water by new embanked channels reaching the sea by the shortest route possible. This meant that the lowland was traversed by a new high-level drainage that was carried between unstable banks. Increasingly, the original earthen banks had to be replaced by clay-lined or clay-cored banks.

2.5 *The twentieth century*

The twentieth century has seen a trend towards a more comprehensive control of moisture in the former wetlands on each side of the North Sea, the reclamation of more land for agriculture and the creation of what the Dutch call 'standard landscapes'. Central government has taken control of drainage as national goals of self-sufficiency in food production have become dominant (Baldock 1984, pp. 84–157) (chapter 11). In the Fens the emphasis, as during the previous 300 years, has been on improving the evacuation of the upland fresh waters by improving existing channels wherever possible, constructing new cut-offs, relief channels and diversions, particularly the Great Ouse cut-off completed in 1964, and improving the outfalls with new sluices. A few of the major works are shown in figure 6.4. While what might be termed the high-level drainage of the uplands has gone ahead, the low-level drainage of the peatlands has not been neglected: tile draining has rid the soil of excess water, efficient diesel engines have replaced the inefficient steam pumps, and even more efficient and cheaper automated electrical pumping stations achieve a closely controlled hydrological system, with a total of about 150 stations in the Great Ouse Basin controlling the water levels in over 12 000 km^2 of lowland, and nearly 2000 stations in the Netherlands. Agriculture flourishes; the Fens are the most productive arable area in England and, ironically, spray irrigation is increasingly resorted to in order to maximize yields. The danger of flooding is not eliminated, and the great floods of 1947 and associated with the 1953 storm surge in the North Sea that resulted in the loss of 18 000 lives and the flooding of 4000 km^2 show that total control of the elements that made these wetlands in the first place is not always possible.

In Holland, with limited land space, the agricultural motive has reigned supreme. It culminated in 1918 in the grand plan of Dr Cornelius Lely to seal off the Zuider Zee in order to reduce the coastline by 300 km, to add 205 000 ha of new farmland (equivalent to 10 per cent of existing Netherlands farmland), to create a freshwater reservoir of 120 000 ha to supply agriculture and industry, and to check the infiltration of salt water in the subsoil. Work on four of the five polders (Wieringermeer, Noordoost, Oost Flevoland and Zuid Flevoland), which began in 1927, was complete by 1968 and they are flourishing agricultural districts, almost prairie like in their openness and methodical subdivision (plate 6.3). However, the original policy of agricultural dominance has had to be modified. Urban expansion and overspill have already deposited over 250 000 people and extensive industry in Zuid Flevoland and Lelystad has a population of over 100 000 (Lambert 1985, pp. 292–3).

The fate of the fifth polder, Maarkwaard (41 000 ha), is undecided. In a country of only 30 000 km^2, the need to find nearly 100 km^2 annually to provide for housing, industry and recreation makes every hectare valuable. Maarkwaard might become an urban overspill or a second airport. Alternatively, environmentalists would rather it were left alone, so that it may never be reclaimed, or serve as a recreational reserve, a freshwater lake or an energy basin (Van der Veen 1983, pp. 136–40). That such uses are even being contemplated is indicative of how, in an increasingly crowded world, wetland impacts are changing from the time-honoured imperative of more farmland to more urban-oriented uses. In addition, the new sea defences around the Rhine and Scheldt estuaries – the Delta Plan – have added perhaps another

Plate 6.3 The vast area of reclamation in the prairie-like landscapes of the Noordoost Polder in the former Zuider Zee, looking west from Creil to Bant. New farmsteads have been spaced at regular intervals in uniform-sized holdings. They are grouped in pairs in order to minimize the cost of providing services and to maximize social contact
(Courtey KLM Aerocarto-Schipol)

100–150 km^2 of new land to the country, not as much as was planned originally, again as environmental concerns over wildlife habitats have led to modifications and a reduction in original targets (Stuivel 1956).

In total, perhaps as much as 20 000 km^2 of wetland (two-thirds of the present Netherlands) have been reclaimed or drained, 3500 km^2 of land from the sea, 3150 km^2 from former freshwater lakes, and 13 350 km^2 from other low-lying riverine silts and peat areas (Schultz 1983, p. 33). In eastern England the combined total of reclaimed land might be as much as 7000 km^2. It is extremely unlikely that any substantial new areas will be added to this. The concern is more to maintain the existing converted wetland against the increasing possibility of floods from peat shrinkage, structural subsidence, rising sea levels and the freak combinations of tide and cyclonic activity that can produce storm surges in the funnel-shaped North Sea. Over and above all this is the increasing awareness of habitat destruction and preservation.

3.0 THE WETLANDS OF THE UNITED STATES

Wetlands are nowhere more varied than in the vast area of the coterminous United States (Hofstetter 1983, Cowardin et al. 1985). Wetlands are found in every state, but by far the greatest concentration is in the eastern half of the country. A general idea of their location can be derived from figure 6.5 which shows the distribution of 'wetlands in need of drainage' or 'wetlands that are

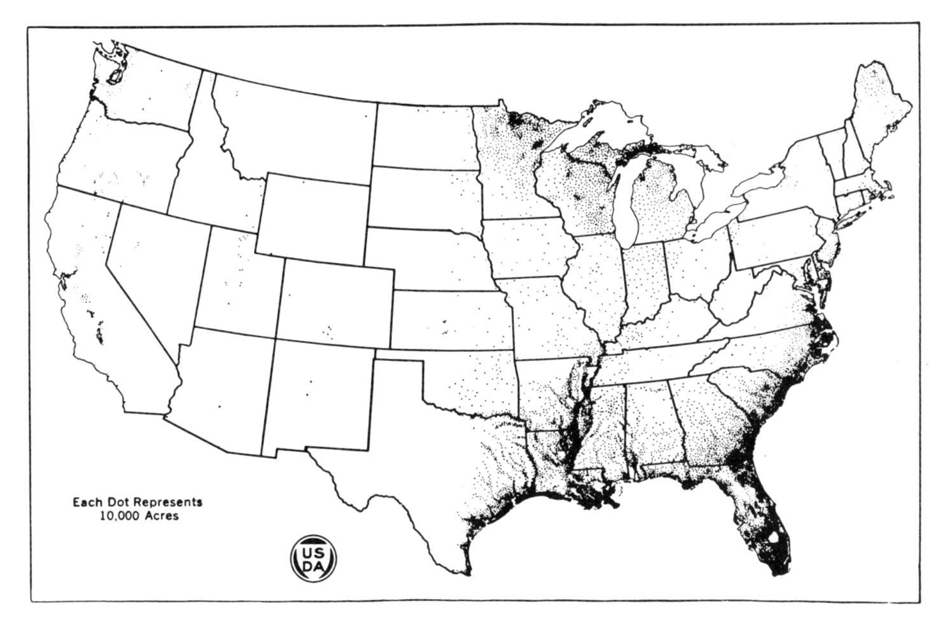

Figure 6.5 'Wetlands in need of drainage' in the United States, 1919 (from US Department of Agriculture 1921)

drainable' as reported in 1919 (US Department of Agriculture 1921) and reproduced in many subsequent works such as Havemeyer (1930), Miller (1939), Land Planning Committee, National Resources Board (1936) and Karnes (1965). They total nearly 37×10^2 ha.

In general, wetlands fall into four main types based on origin and location.

1 Salt marshes on the outer coastal plain of the Atlantic which merge into the mangroves of the Gulf coast. The Everglades of Florida are a special subset of this group.
2 The alluvial riverine bottomlands of the flood plain of the lower Mississippi and its tributaries south of the Ohio, and its delta in Louisiana.
3 The glacially derived lands mainly of heavy clay soils, low relief and immature impeded drainage that stretch across the Midwest from Ohio to Iowa and southern Minnesota, and extend northward with scattered but extensive areas of peat into the three Lake states.
4 Miscellaneous wetlands associated with waterlogged soils and irrigation, mainly in the west.

In addition, there are wet spots on slopes or flat areas where the surface intersects with the general water-table or a perched water-table.

3.1 *Extent and change*

Despite the numerous figures about the wetlands of the United States it is difficult to be precise about their extent and changing area as definitions vary with purpose (e.g. wildlife habitats, reclaimable land, land in drainage enterprises etc.), and with what is meant by 'draining'. Yet, because we know that between 85 and 95 per cent of wetland loss is due to agricuture it is important to understand something of the assessment of wetland magnitude and change, which is summarized in table 6.1.

Table 6.1 Estimates of US wetlands: original, *c.*1975 and intervening losses

	Area (× 10^6 ha)			*Loss (× 10^6 ha)*		
	Original	*c.1955*	*c.1975*	*Original to 1955*	*1955 to 1975*	*Approximate annual loss rate, 1955–75 (ha/yr)*
A Council on Environmental Quality (1978)	51.40	33.18	28.33	18.22	4.85	242 500
B Tiner (1984)	87.01	43.70	40.07	43.31	3.63	181 500
C OTA (1984)	74.87	40.47	36.08	34.40	4.39	219 500

Acres converted to nearest metric equivalent, rounded to two significant figures.
Sources: see text

The original pre-settlement area of wetland has been estimated as being between 87.01×10^6 and 51.40×10^6 ha. The figure of 51.40×10^6 ha long accepted by the US Department of Agriculture Soil Conservation Service has been abandoned as it did not take into account wet soils that contribute such a large part to the extent of former wetland in, for example, the Midwest. The high figure of 87.01 $\times$ 10^6 (Roe and Ayres 1954) is not substantiated. The intermediate figure of 74.87 $\times$ 10^6 ha is now suggested as a reasonable and defensible upper estimate (OTA 1984, pp. 90–1).

Likewise, the rate of wetland loss since the mid 1950s, when concern first began to be expressed about elimination and increasingly accurate inventories were carried out, has similarly been open to debate. The figures in line A of table 6.1 put forward by the Council on Environmental Quality (Council on Environmental Quality 1978, pp. 316–18) suggest a decline of 18.22 $\times$ 10^6 ha for the 300 odd years before 1955, when a figure of 33.18 $\times$ 10^6 ha was established, and a further net decline of 4.85 $\times$ 10^6 ha to 28.33 $\times$ 10^6 ha in the mid 1970s, or a loss of about 242 500 ha/yr. Early in 1984, these estimates were replaced by those of Tiner (line B) in his extensive discussion on *Current Status and Trends in U.S. Wetlands* (Tiner 1984, pp. 28–55). Basing his calculations largely on the work of Frayer et al. (1983), he suggested that the decline from the original wetland to 1955 was possibly 43.31 $\times$ 10^6 ha, and that the net loss between 1955 and 1975 was 3.63 $\times$ 10^6 ha, or 181 500 ha/yr. This rate of decline was less than thought.

In turn these figures have been superseded by those in line C based on the more comprehensive and accurate National Wetlands Trends Study which appeared in the Office of Technology Assessment (OTA) study late in 1984. They show a loss of possibly 34.40 $\times$ 10^6 ha between pre-settlement and 1955, and, more alarmingly, a larger than suspected net loss of 4.39 $\times$ 10^6 ha between 1955 and 1975, or 219 500 ha/yr (see OTA (1984, pp. 87–114) for an extensive discussion). This figure is far higher than the 121 400 ha/yr calculated by the Interagency Task Force (Horwitz 1978) and quoted by President Jimmy Carter in his message to Congress on wetland preservation in 1977, and greater than those put forward by Tiner (line B).

However, calculations on wetland loss are only one strand of evidence in assessing the impact of agriculture on temperate lands. Table 6.2 and figure 6.6 show the growth of the area contained in the administrative areas of drainage – the drainage enterprises, or Special Drainage Districts (SDDs) as they became known later – from 1879 to 1978. The SDDs tend to give an exaggerated view of the areas affected as they include portions of well-drained land within their boundaries and, conversely, do not include lands where considerable drainage had been effected prior to the development of the drainage enterprises (e.g. the Midwest). These administrative organizations grew slowly during the latter part of the nineteenth century, and then gained in popularity between 1910 and 1930 when 22.7 $\times$ 10^6 ha were added. By 1978 they reached their maximum recorded extent at 42.60 $\times$ 10^6 ha, distributed as shown in figure 6.7.

Also shown in figure 6.6 is the area of farmland calculated to be affected by subsurface and surface drainage between 1900 and 1980 (OTA 1984, p. 109). In general it kept up with land in SDDs until 1920, after which it deviated markedly when drought and depression led to the decay and abandonment of many drainage systems (OTA 1982, pp. 38–42). After 1945, however, the area

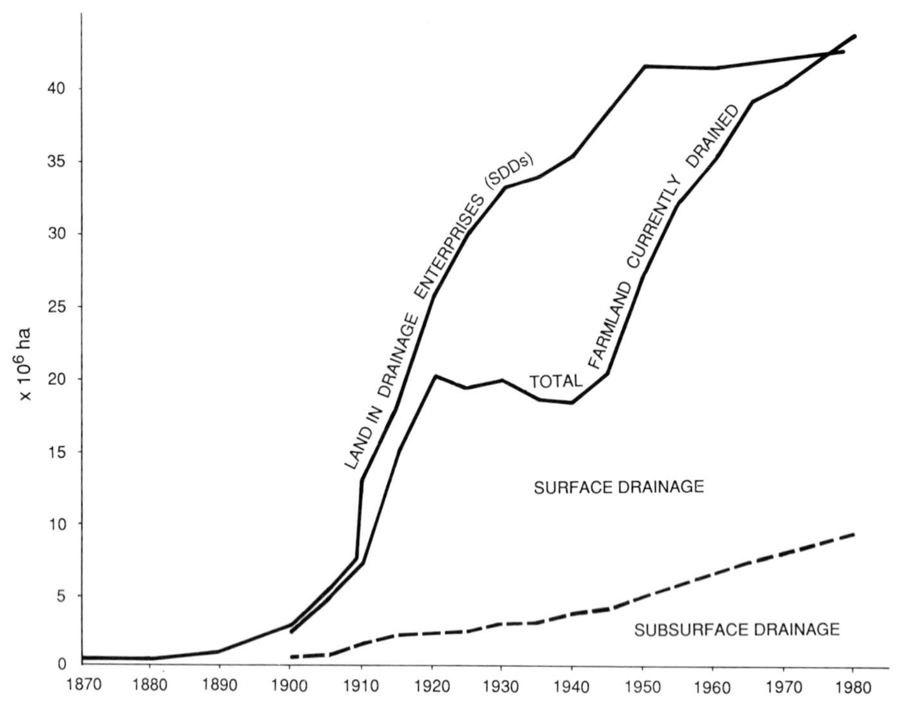

Figure 6.6 Area of land in special drainage districts (1870–1978) and farmland drained by surface and subsurface drains (1900–80)
(data from Wooten and Jones 1955, p. 482; OTA 1984, p. 108; US Bureau of the Census 1978, vol. 5, part 5)

climbed again steadily so that during the 1960s and after 1978 it surpassed the area in SDDs.

Clearly, the area in SDDs (42.60×10^6 ha) and the area of farmland currently drained (43.5×10^6 ha) both exceed the area of wetland considered to have been lost since original settlement (i.e. 38.79×10^6 ha). They are, of course, measuring different things; drained lands (figure 6.7) are not wetlands (figure 6.5). Vast areas of drained wet prairie, for example, do not appear as wetland by any current classification, and vast areas of currently recognized wetlands will never be drained, particularly the peats of the northern states where the growing season is too short for agriculture, and many of the coastal wetlands that are protected under federal and state legislation. Nevertheless, as a crude check on these calculations, if the 42.60×10^6 ha of land in the SDDs is added to the area of wetland not affected by drainage up to 1980, which is calculated to be 33.80×10^6 ha (i.e. 34.9×10^6 ha in 1975, less $5 \times 219\ 500$ ha/yr between 1975 and 1980), then the combined total of 76.40×10^6 ha is not very far removed from the area of 74.9×10^6 ha of original wetland and wet soil areas and gives one some confidence that line C in table 6.1 is reasonably near the truth.

Of the 4.39×10^6 ha lost between 1955 and 1975 only a mere 3 per cent was

Table 6.2 Surface and subsurface drainage of farmland in the United States, 1900–80

Year	*Surface* (× 10^3 *ha*)	*Subsurface* (× 10^3 *ha*)	*Total* (× 10^3 *ha*)
1900	2133	414	2547
1905	3956	770	4726
1910	7557	1470	9027
1915	11875	2307	14182
1920	17585	2425	20010
1925	16762	2486	19248
1930	17271	2706	19977
1935	15624	2932	18556
1940	14800	3604	18404
1945	16499	3867	20366
1950	23464	4836	28300
1955	26303	5532	31835
1960	28646	6403	35049
1965	30809	7216	38025
1970	32276	7823	40099
1975	33421	8425	41846
1980	34284	9214	43498

Source: OTA 1984, p. 109

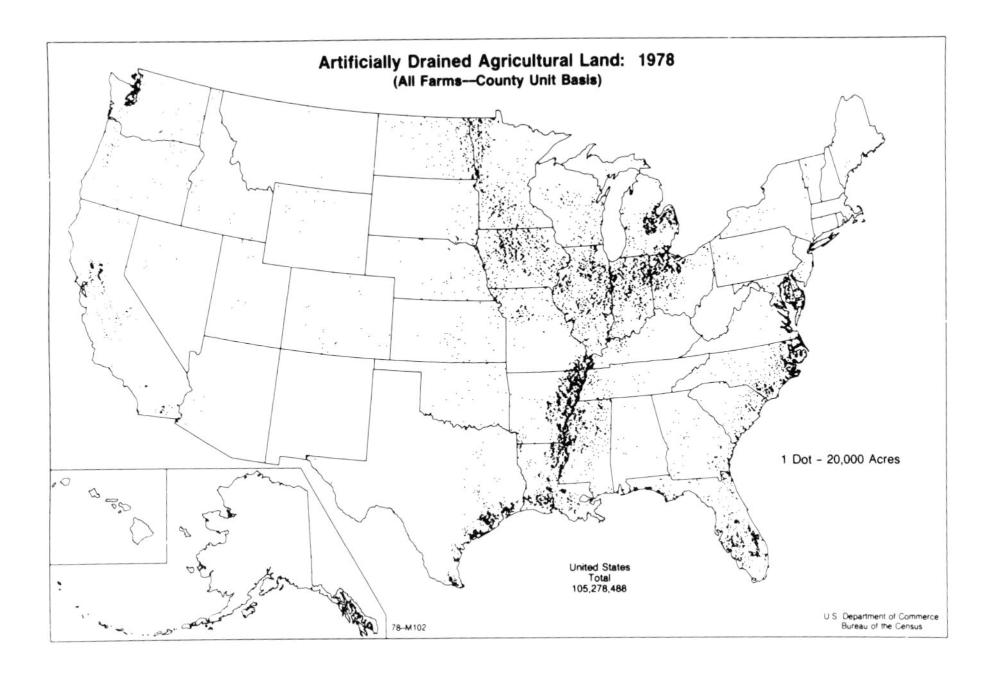

Figure 6.7 Drained farmland in the United States, 1978
(from US Bureau of the Census 1978, vol. 4)

tidal wetland, which had been lost through port, marina and canal construction, and a little urban development (Gosselink and Baumann 1980), in addition to subsidence in Louisiana (Walker et al. 1987) (chapter 11, table 11.5). The overwhelming bulk of the loss had been in the inland freshwater wetlands which are not protected by federal and state legislation and are thus open to agricultural conversion, draining, clearing and land levelling. Two such areas are now considered, the wet prairie of the Midwest which was drained mainly between 1880 and 1930, largely by tile drains, and the river bottomlands of the lower Mississippi and its tributaries which have been drained by open ditches and pumps. From about 1960 onwards the bottomlands have been the main focus of wetland change in the United States, accounting for up to three-quarters of all conversions.

3.2 *The draining of the wet prairie*

From Minnesota south through Iowa, Illinois, Indiana and Ohio, and adjacent areas of the Dakotas, Michigan and Wisconsin, there lies a vast belt of poorly drained land, usually called the wet prairie (Hewes 1951). It is composed largely of glacially derived clays that have an immature drainage system, are generally flat and impermeable, and are covered by a scatter of sloughs, hollows and ponds. The prairie used to be flooded during the winter, and standing water could remain on the surface until June.

The initial reaction to the wet prairie was decidedly negative. Of the many descriptions, one must stand for many. Major Long saw it in 1823 when he travelled the 24 miles from the Indiana-Ohio state border to Fort Wayne. It was a landscape bereft of settlement, not surprisingly as

> the country is so wet that we scarcely saw an acre of land upon which a settlement could be made. We travelled for a couple of miles with our horses wading through water, sometimes to the girth . . . We attempted to stop and pasture our horses, but this was quite impossible on account of the immense swarms of mosquitoes (*Culex*) and horse flies (*Tabanus*), which tormented both horses and riders in a manner that excluded all possibility of rest. (Keating 1825, p. 73)

It was wet, malarial and impossible to farm. Others were more succinct. Quoting a poem, Duis (1874, p. 353) said it was the ‘great western waste of bottom land, flat as a pancake’ but added prophetically, ‘rich as grease’. While the bulk of the wet prairies were merely waterlogged or had seasonal standing water on them, some places such as the Black Swamp of northwest Ohio (Kaatz 1955) and the Kankakee marsh of east central Illinois (Meyer 1935) had more permanent water.

Although the initial assessment was something of an over-reaction (Winsor 1987), the whole area was sufficiently difficult to occupy that only large-scale grazing of cattle and sheep in drier areas was practised during the years before mid-century. The Swampland Acts of 1849, 1850 and 1860 did nothing to alleviate matters, for although 25.8 × 10^6 ha were disposed of to the states by the federal government on condition that they would use sale proceeds to drain the land, improve its value and reduce the risk of malaria, wholesale fraud meant that no drainage works were carried out (Hibbard 1939, pp. 269–88). It was not until the region was penetrated by the railroads between 1850 and 1870, and the pressure of new immigration and settlement became greater, that the economy was transformed, the pastoral economy was intensified and eventually grain crops began to gain in popularity and acreage.

Permanent agriculture could only take place with an alteration in the drainage condition of the land. Initially, a close-spaced system of open ditches was dug by hand. The job was tedious and time consuming; open ditches created access problems and the work required considerable capital. Therefore there was a tendency for larger holdings only to engage in draining. Some attempts at mole draining were undertaken, but this method was soon superseded by tile draining (Bogue 1951, pp. 177–8).

The spread of tile draining after 1870 was the key to the occupation of the wet prairie. While tile drains were not ever-lasting, they were durable, located underground, rarely collapsed and lasted for decades. Above all, they were effective in ridding the heavy clays of surface and subsurface water. It was an expensive operation, costing between $5.00 and $10.00 an acre, and only worthwhile if the expectation of increased yields or rising land values were great enough to warrant it. Clearly, these expectations were upheld; there were nearly 50 000 km of tiled drains in Indiana before 1882 (Wooten and Jones 1955, p. 478) and 61 690 km in Illinois in 1883, and during the next 7 years a further 125 256 km were laid (Destler 1947, p. 109), so that by 1895 there were 19.5 m of subsurface drains for every hectare of improved farmland, to say nothing of many thousands of kilometres of open outlet ditches, levees and pumps. The story was much the same in Indiana and Ohio. In the larger swamp areas, such as Kanakee and the Black Swamp, major drainage works were undertaken.

Tile-making factories, using the easily accessible stiff clays of the prairies, sprung up everywhere to cater for this agricultural need (plate 6.4). They spread rapidly westwards with settlement. There was one in Indiana in 1870 and 143 by 1904 (Perkins 1931, p. 382). Overall, there were over 1140 in operation in the three main prairie wetland states by 1880 (Wooten and Jones 1955, p. 487).

The results of tile draining were dramatic. It allowed a greater density of settlement, a greater intensity of farming and greater yields. Livestock raising and breeding gave way to oats and livestock breeding and feeding, and eventually to an economy of cash grain farming for corn that by the opening years of this century was making the once wet prairie the area of the highest productivity in the country, a position which it has not lost. Land values rose phenomenally; before 1880 undrained portions of the wet prairie could be purchased for $2.00–$3.00 an acre, though $6.00–$7.00 was more common, but after draining values rose by more than 500 per cent by 1920 rendering once crippling mortgages negligible (Hicks 1946, p. 73; Destler 1947; Hewes

Plate 6.4 The factory of the National Drain Tile Company, Terre Haute, Indiana, *c*.1925. This was one of over a thousand such factories in Ohio, Indiana and Illinois at the turn of the century, manufacturing the millions of pipes of various diameters needed to drain the heavy glacially derived soils of the wet prairie lands. In the foreground the abandoned shale pit is being filled with broken tile and drain from the plant
(Courtesy W. L. Perkins)

and Fransdon 1952). Disease was reduced and eventually eliminated. In a study of 16 counties in the Kanakee area of east central Illinois, Winsor (1987) found that mortality from malaria, per 100 000 of the population, declined from 29.7 in 1870 before draining to 28.9 in 1880 as draining got under way, to 10.9 in 1890 when it was completed, and this was not untypical of the new drained areas.

From 1915 to 1922, and particularly during the First World War, draining entered a new expansionist phase when more costly projects were undertaken. Drainage districts were organized and expanded only to be curtailed by falling prices during the Depression (figure 6.6). At present about 16.54×10^6 ha of land in farms is considered drained in the six Midwest and Lake states (US Bureau of the Census 1978), although few people realize that the essential key to productivity in most soils is the pipes that lie buried under the ground.

3.3 *The transformation of the bottomlands*

The area of land that could profit from draining was repeatedly put at about 36.4×10^6 ha throughout the twentieth century (Havemeyer 1930, Miller 1939, Land Planning Committee, Natural Resources Board 1936, Karnes 1965). However, more soberly, Wooten and Jones (1955, p. 488) thought that perhaps no more than 8.1×10^6 ha would repay intensive draining, and suggested that 'roughly 7 million acres (2.8×10^6 ha) of this drainable land is found in the fertile bottom lands of the Mississippi River in Arkansas, Louisiana, and Mississippi'. Their predictions were remarkably correct.

Although the cypress swamps had long been cleared for their timber, since the end of the nineteenth century little thought had been given to draining the land for permanent agriculture. Nevertheless, from the early 1930s clearing had been going on steadily in the bottomland hardwood forests (BHFs) as the levees on the main rivers were heightened and strengthened by the Corps of Engineers in order to contain the massive flood potential of the Mississippi system. Now surplus water in the bottomlands could be simply pumped up and over the levees into the main channel. However, it was after roughly 1960 that the attack began in earnest with millions of hectares (table 6.3) being cleared, ditched, drained and cropped, mainly for soybeans interspersed with cotton, rice and wheat (Sternitzke 1976, p. 76) (see also chapter 10, plate 10.1). In Arkansas, Mississippi and Louisiana alone the BHFs had been reduced from 4.79×10^6 ha in roughly 1932–5 to 2.92×10^6 ha in 1968–74, a decline of at least 1.87×10^6 ha. In another more up-to-date survey of the Mississippi alluvial plain (which included appropriate parts of Kentucky, Tennessee and Missouri, as well as Arkansas, Louisiana and Mississippi) Turner et al. (1981, p. 22) calculated that the BHFs had been reduced from 4.77×10^6 ha in 1937 to 2.10×10^6 ha in 1978, and predicted that they would fall to 1.7×10^6 ha in 1990 if present practices are allowed to continue (based on MacDonald et al. 1978). Taking an even greater area of all the BHFs in the twelve southeasternmost states, the result has been even more startling in recent years with a fall from 15 x 10^6 ha in 1960 to 12.34×10^6 ha in 1975 or an average decline of 175 000 ha/yr with little prospect of it slowing down (chapter 10). Indeed, BHFs throughout the United States have almost uniformly been reduced by agricultural encroachment (Abernethy and Turner 1987).

The reason for this massive attrition is that this is highly productive cropland with a favourable combination of freedom from frost, high temperatures,

Table 6.3 Change in wetland forests, Arkansas, Louisiana and Mississippi, 1932–74

	Wetland forest area (× 10^3 ha)		
Survey	*Arkansas*	*Louisiana*	*Mississippi*
1932	–	–	877.6
1935	1696.1	2215.8	–
1947	–	–	826.8
1950	1415.5	–	–
1954	–	2023.0	–
1957	–	–	777.3
1959	1316.0	–	–
1964	–	1880.1	–
1967	–	–	604.6
1969	799.6	–	–
1974	–	1518.2	–
Difference between first and last survey	896.5	697.6	273.0

Source: Sternitzke 1976, p. 26

equable rainfall during the winter and summer seasons, and even the possibility of irrigation, all in organically rich soils. Soybeans in particular thrive in this environment, and have the added advantage of a short growing season so that they can be planted in areas that are flooded even as late as the end of June and can also be planted in a variety of soil conditions. On better soils they are interplanted with wheat and cotton. It is calculated that if the price received lies between $1.05 and $2.31 per bushel, then conversion and growth are profitable, and as prices have varied between $2.00 in 1950 and $7.00 in 1976 the economic conditions for conversion have been more than met (OTA 1984, p. 111). Some have seen a rapid rise in prices after 1972, which set off the current round of draining as a direct response to the upset pattern of the cold nutrient-rich current off the Peruvian coast, which caused a precipitous decline in the Peruvian anchovy industry and a collapse of protein-rich animal feed/meal supplies (Barber et al. 1979). Whatever the reason, soybean cultivation is one of the fastest growing sectors of the American agricultural economy, with production having risen over 700 per cent in the last three decades, so that now soybeans account for more cropland than the combined acreage of the four traditional Southern crops, cotton, wheat, corn and rice (Kramer and Shabman 1986, pp. 177–9). The wetlands have diminished in proportion as the cultivation has expanded, although the current evidence is of a downward trend in conversion.

4.0 THE SWAMPS OF SOUTH AUSTRALIA

If an area of Australia has a water problem, more often than not it is a problem of water deficiency rather than one of water surplus. However, wetlands exist in a few locations, as in the tropical coasts of the Northern Territory and northern Queensland, the riparian lowlands and estuaries on the tropical Pacific-facing coasts of Queensland and New South Wales, alongside the River Murray, and in a few specific areas like Koo-Wee-Rup swamp in Gippsland, east of Melbourne, Victoria, and the southeast district of South Australia. The later two areas are noteworthy in that unlike the other wetlands which are largely unaffected by purposeful change, they have been the object of deliberate alteration through draining for temperate agriculture.

4.1 *The drainage 'problem'*

In the semi-arid state of South Australia wetlands could mean only one thing – land capable of sustaining agriculture. Consequently, the riverside swamps or bottomlands of the River Murray (plate 6.5) and the vast area of 1.7×10^6 ha in the southeast of the state were the objects of intensive speculation and activity from the very beginning of settlement.

The draining of the wetlands of the southeast was much more difficult than embanking and pumping water out of the Murray swamps. The 'watery waste' resulted from a complex interaction of several natural factors. Impeded natural

Plate 6.5 The Jervois Swamp, beside the lower Murray River, South Australia, looking south towards Tailem Bend. On the opposite bank lies an area of partially reclaimed riparian swamp and some unreclaimed swamp. The characteristic linear arrangement of farmsteads on the sloping land of the old river bank allows each farm to have a narrow strip of reclaimed land in front and upland behind. Irrigated water is let through the riverside embankments to irrigate the pasture strips or 'bays'
(Courtesy Darian Smith)

drainage is compounded by the presence of excessive ground-water flows. The topography of the region consists of a series of parallel low ranges, separated by wide valleys or 'flats', both aligned approximately parallel to the coast (figure 6.8). The ridges are probably former dunes now left stranded as the sea has retreated by successive stages to its present position. Each flat is at a progressively higher level than the one adjoining to the west, the most easterly being about 65–70 m above sea level, and all are tilted slightly towards the northwest. (This and subsequent paragraphs are based on Williams (1974, pp. 178–226).)

Thus the water draining from the flats works its way westwards until one of the ranges is encountered, and if it cannot find a gap to the next lower flat to the west, it is deflected northwest along the side of the ridge. Consequently, sluggish and ill-defined watercourses gravitate slowly to the natural outlet at Salt Creek on the Coorong. Unlike the surface drainage which is so imperfect, the underground drainage is continuous and efficient, and large quantities of water from the neighbouring state of Victoria and the high ground in the east of South Australia gravitate west through the underlying limestone and other porous strata, lying 1–2 m below the surface during the summer months, but rising above the surface in winter and early spring, creating vast lakes which cover up to three-quarters of the land and waterlog all other parts of the flats.

4.2 *Draining activity*

Initially, experiments in draining consisted of government engineers cutting through the narrowest ranges near the coast in 1864, mainly to improve communications between the capital, Adelaide, and the surrounding core settlement, and this remote corner of the province which was threatening to secede to Victoria. However, the agricultural potential of the flats was soon realized, and some 72 km^2 were made fit for agriculture around the little town of Millicent in the southwestern corner of the region (figure 6.8).

Individual settlers, however, were not prepared – or perhaps were unable – to contemplate the outlay necessary either to make more cuts through the ranges which were 40 m high and 5 km wide in places, or to improve the natural channels that flowed some 60 km towards the northwest. The survey and settlement of the most promising soil areas of the flats, often carried out during the dry summer and autumn months, resulted only in farms where settlers had to reap their first year's wheat from boats! Many abandoned their selections, which were bought up by large-scale pastoralists (squatters) who ran flocks of sheep, running in tens of thousands on vast properties (runs) large enough to allow grazing on the flats in the dry months and moving them up on to the ranges during the wet months.

As was so often the case in the states of Australia, settlers in distress looked to the state government to bail them out. By a series of halting steps and widely spaced experiments between 1881 and 1940, the state government improved the northwest flowing channels so that excess water would flow to soak away on the edges of the barren Ninety Mile Desert. It also commissioned many surveys and schemes for draining, but baulked at cross-range cuts with two exceptions, the Drain K-L (69 km) and the Drain M (50 km), both constructed between 1914 and 1916 with massive cuts through the ranges (plate 6.6) in order to achieve the shortest route with the greatest gradient to the coast for the more rapid evacuation of the surplus water (figure 6.8).

Plate 6.6 The Drain L cutting where it slices through the Woakwine Range, about 7 km from the coast, at Robe in the southeast of South Australia. The cutting is about 45 m deep but has been widened considerably on one side since this photograph was taken in the 1940s (Courtesy South-East Drainage Board)

The outcome of these works was a localized extension of the grazing season. However, little subsidiary drainage was carried out by private owners (often now the large-scale pastoralists) as they feared that any further improvement in the quality of the land would encourage the state government to step in, compulsorily purchase their properties and subdivide them into smaller holdings in order to promote 'Closer Settlement', particularly for ex-servicemen from the First World War as happened in many cases here and elsewhere in the state during the 1920s (Williams 1975, pp. 92–4).

After the hiatus of the Depression and the Second World War the state government took the lead in land improvement and settlement schemes in the southeast, which it regarded as the most promising region for settlement intensification in the semi-arid state. Backed by Commonwealth (Federal) funds it embarked on an ambitious programme to settle ex-servicemen on thousands of small intensively farmed and mainly pastoral holdings (plate 6.7). Detailed soil and hydrological surveys were carried out, and the advances in pasture improvement with new strains of medics and subterranean clovers, and

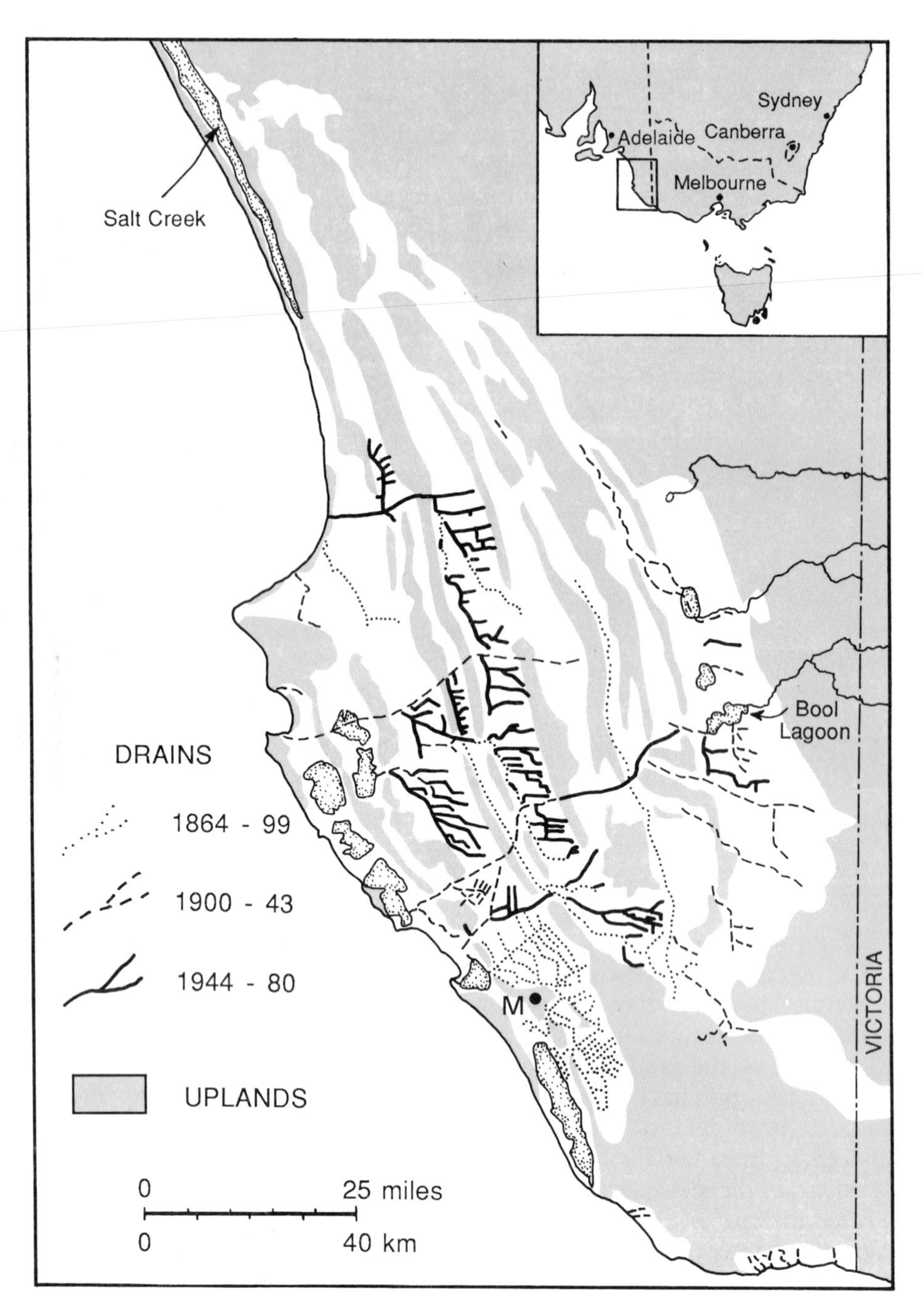

Figure 6.8 Stages in the draining of the swamps of the southeast district of South Australia, 1864–1975
(after Williams 1974)

Plate 6.7 Pasture and stock intensification on the once-flooded flats in the Hundred of Symon, southeast of South Australia
(Courtesy South-East Drainage Board)

the rectification of trace element deficiencies in the poorer soils, especially those on the wind-sorted deposits of the ranges, were integral parts of a comprehensive plan of drainage and transformation. Over 500 km of new drains were excavated, together with new cuts through the ranges between 1948 and 1972 (figure 6.8).

At present the 'watery waste' is all but eliminated and it is difficult to find much standing water on the flats, except in a few lowland swamp areas that are preserved as wildlife habitats :(e.g. Bool Lagoon). The wide but shallow drains are designed to lead off the surface water but preserve a moderately high water-table so that water will be retained in the ditches for stock in summer (plate 6.8). Nevertheless, the aquifer has fallen more than planned, and deep bores have been sunk in the underlying porous structure in order to bring up water for stock and now irrigation, which, in itself, is putting pressure on the underground supplies and leading to 'over-draining' and some subsidence of organic soils. Everything points to the fact that, like many other wetland areas converted by draining, the transformation has gone about as far as it can or should.

Plate 6.8 A typical drain in the flats of the southeast of South Australia; it is wide and shallow so as not to lower the water-table too much, and the concrete weirs control the level of the water-table at various stages along the length of the drain
(Courtesy South-East Drainage Board)

5.0 CONCLUSION

Human activity to transform wetlands has mainly been powered by the desire or need to increase agricultural production. The pace and scale of change has accelerated since the late nineteenth century when new commodity demands and rising prices and the encounter of new immigrant groups with wetlands stimulated change. In addition, the advent of machinery for mass movement of earth (dredges and draglines) has certainly helped, but has not been crucial, in the development of drainage, as most the major schemes in the world were initiated using animal and human power, as the example of the North Sea fringes shows clearly. Nevertheless, draining work has been vastly speeded up and tasks undertaken that would not have been contemplated before (plate 6.9). Perhaps of more importance has been the development of steam- and

Plate 6.9 Aids to modern draining: the dragline. This photograph, taken in 1939, shows the widening of the previously hand-dug King's Sedgemoor Drain that runs for about 23 km through King's Sedgemoor in the Somerset Levels. What possibly several hundred 'navvies' accomplished in just over six years between 1791 and 1798 was more than doubled in width by just over two dozen men in about a year in 1939–40. Today, drainage machinery is far larger and more efficient still
(Courtesy Somerset River Authority)

diesel-powered pumps (plate 6.10), but again note the impact of the windmill, and the simple expedient of cheap clay tile (now plastic) piping for draining waterlogged soils. Everywhere, the involvement of the state at various levels from the district to the region to the nation has been crucial to the carrying out of large-scale schemes.

Most draining falls into two broad categories: those that facilitate natural hydrological and sedimentation processes, and those that mitigate or circumvent natural hazardous situations. The former requires the more rapid flow and greater scouring power of straightened and regraded channels, flood containment within embankments, sediment build-up with groynes and soil-water evacuation with open ditches or buried pipes. The latter category requires all these, and, in addition, the building of polders in order to create totally artificial drainage basins and pumps and sluices to negotiate disjunctions in natural drainage flows and periodic differences in water levels.

Either way, however, these works require a remarkable degree of cooperative action in a society in order to create and, more importantly, to maintain the works, and a clear vision and commitment to the benefits to be gained. Without this constant vigilance, the carefully controlled agricultural landscape could soon become wetland again.

Plate 6.10 Aids to modern draining: the pumping station. Pumping stations allow the rectification of disjuncturions in drainage flows which are often the cause of wetness. Pumps have progressed from simple human- and animal-powered scoops to windmills, the steam engine, the diesel engine and totally automated electrical engines. There are two generations of pumps at Westonzoyland main rhyne (drain) in the Somerset Levels. The steam pump house on the right was erected in 1830; the new diesel-driven pumps are in the the small building located in the rhyne
(Courtesy Somerset River Authority)

7

Agricultural Impacts in Tropical Wetlands: Rice Paddies for Mangroves in South and Southeast Asia

John F. Richards

1.0 INTRODUCTION: THE DOMESTICATION OF WETLANDS

During the last two to three hundred years humans have substantially depleted the wetlands of South and Southeast Asia. Most of these wild areas have become domesticated or managed wetlands under rice cultivation. Inland, innumerable smaller freshwater marshes and swamps have been filled, drained or reduced in size as peasant farmers have expanded their operations. Along the coastlines of the region thousands of square kilometres of wetlands have been cleared and embanked to protect them against tidal inflow or river flooding. Thousands of square kilometres of rice paddies now define the modern landscape. Aggressive private and public efforts at water management have made possible this major transformation which is still under way. This chapter is concerned with the more easily measured fate of coastal wetlands, rather than with the problem of surveying the changes occurring in the multitude of smaller freshwater wetlands of the region's interior. Decades of human effort have brought about large gains in agricultural productivity. At the same time the ecological effects of these changes have been large and, to date, are imperfectly known.

Coastal wetland clearance, drainage and embankment processes betray remarkable similarities across the region. These similarities imply that linked causal forces and common human responses to these forces have been at work. Despite innumerable variations in local ecology and agricultural practices, each local landscape bears a striking resemblance to others throughout this general region.

The rich alluvial soils of the river deltas have been a focal point for agricultural expansion. Beginning in the early nineteenth century, rapidly moving frontiers of settlement emerged at the mouths of the Ganges-Brahmaputra, Irrawaddy, Chao Phraya, Mekong, Mahanadi, Godavari, Krishna and Penner rivers, among others. Peasant pioneer settlers cleared and transformed the wetlands forests of these tracts into rice paddies. The colonial states of the region and their independent national successor states vigorously encouraged expansion of wet rice production. With few exceptions officials and the general populace viewed mangrove swamps and other coastal wetlands as mere wastelands lying dormant until they could be reclaimed. Each regime made available vast stretches of deltaic wetlands for land reclamation at little or no cost to pioneers. The end result has been an unrelenting assault on river deltas over the past century. Subsequent land reclamation has expanded laterally along the coasts from the deltas to include virtually all tidal wetlands. Only the recent willingness of each government to protect tidal forests from clearing by legislation has preserved current wetlands from reclamation.

Agricultural expansion coupled with timber felling and other forms of resource extraction have pressed strongly and steadily from the interior towards the sea in each river delta in the past century. So strong has been this pressure that, for the most part, the inland reaches of each delta have largely been reclaimed and transformed. The interior wetlands ecosystems are now a domesticated landscape under intensive management and control. The evergreen *Heritiera fomes* of the Ganges-Brahmaputra delta or the Irrawaddy delta have virtually disappeared. The process of land reclamation by millions of pioneer settlers has stripped away the protective buffer between dryland settlement and the mangrove formations on the coast. Sharply rising timber and fuel-wood needs have also put additional pressure upon these limited resources. Even when protected by law under some form of forest or natural reserve area, current human activities continue to deplete the remnant fringe of tidal mangrove formations. In South and Southeast Asia the 64 230 km^2 of mangrove formations, 35.3 per cent of the world total, form a much reduced area compared with that which flourished in 1700 or 1800 (World Resources Institute 1986, p. 314).

Human pressures on the remaining tidal wetlands continue. Supposedly 'undeveloped' tracts have been subject to woodcutting, hunting, fishing and other forms of exploitation at levels rising in intensity in recent years. Those coastal areas left in unreclaimed wetlands in South and Southeast Asia are probably less luxuriant and less diverse than they were in an earlier time. Although some definitive evidence remains for future research efforts, both qualitative and anecdotal material strongly suggest that reductions in biomass and species diversity have already occurred. If nothing else the effects of encroaching agriculture and expanding settlement on the moving frontier have contributed to these impacts. More recently, diversion of upstream river waters for irrigation and power has threatened the viability of these downstream wetlands.

Growing state power, burgeoning regional and world markets, and swelling populations joined to propel frontier settlers into the fertile lands of each major river delta. In most of these cases, directly exercised colonial power began the process of opening each deltaic region to reclamation. New rules first claimed public ownership of these 'waste' lands, and then made them available for reclamation and settlement under favourable terms. Tax incentives, transport systems, peace and order, all newly provided, as well as the guarantee of tenure on the land created a settlement frontier in each delta. Generally, before the Second World War, the opening of each frontier was the signal for the establishment of strong linkages to the world commodity market for rice. Between the 1860s and 1950 the terms of trade were favourable to rice farmers and other commodity producers in the region (Bairoch 1975, p. 93). In addition, rising land prices, commodity prices and profits stimulated frontier dynamism.

After 1950, under newly independent regimes, internal markets were capable of absorbing rice production as each nation in the region fought for food self-sufficiency. Nevertheless, in reviewing the current plight of the tidal wetlands in South and Southeast Asia, it is essential to understand the power, longevity and extent of the social forces encouraging land reclamation. Development policies such as that of the Indonesian government which seek to settle millions of peasant rice farmers on tidal wetlands in Kalimantan emerge from a long tradition of such settlement (chapter 11). While the emergence of export-rice-oriented economies in Burma, Thailand and Vietnam is a common theme noted in the history of that region, similar developments in the river deltas of the Indian subcontinent have not been so readily acknowledged. In part, this oversight stems from the absorption of rice in India's internal urban markets rather than on the world market, and in part from the regional boundaries of scholarship. In any event the Ganges-Brahmaputra, Mahanadi and other Indian river deltas share in this common process of wetlands transformation (Sinha 1981, p. 156).

In the bulk of this chapter we describe in detail the evolution of three of the most important deltaic zones in South and Southeast Asia: the earliest, and in some ways the most obscure, the Ganges-Brahmaputra in India and Bangladesh; the largest and most dramatic example of reclamation, the Irrawaddy in Burma; finally, the Chao Phraya in Thailand. Detailed estimates of land use change over the past century are now possible for the Ganges-Brahmaputra and Irrawaddy deltas. These data have been compiled as part of a larger effort to reconstruct the history of land use changes in South and Southeast Asia. Only a less ambitious descriptive, rather than quantitative, account is possible for the Chao Phraya.

2.0 GANGES-BRAHMAPUTRA DELTA

In the latter years of the eighteenth century the lower reaches of the Ganges-Brahmaputra delta formed a distinctive wetlands swamp and forest area known as the Sundarbans (plate 7.1). This broad flat low-lying area – rarely more than a metre above sea level – extended over 18 000–20 000 km^2 in the lower delta. The rivers flowing into the delta drained much of eastern India. In the spring

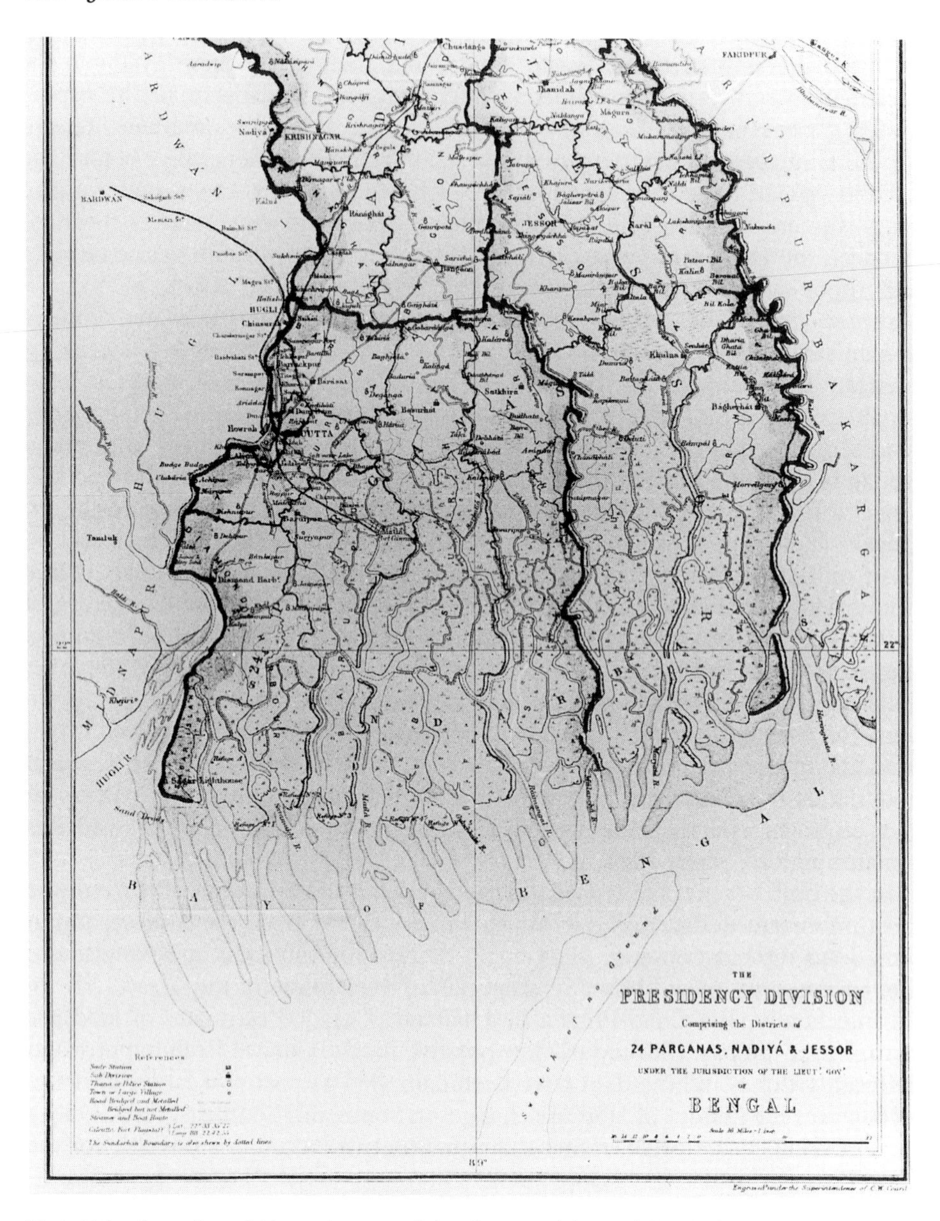

Plate 7.1 A portion of Hunter's map of the Ganges delta and Sundarbans, 1875

in particular the annual Himalayan snowmelt and monsoon rains brought enormous quantities of water into the system. Silt carried in the rivers was deposited along the river channels and at the mouths of the delta. At a conservative estimate 10 km^2 or more of new land is created each year by deposition.

Inland, the Sundarbans were dominated by the tropical evergreen species

Heriteria Fomes known in Bengali as *sundri*. The coastal half of the region displayed salt-tolerant mangrove forests. Throughout the Sundarbans several hundred other plant and animal species were linked in a dense productive wetlands ecosystem. An intricate series of water channels stretching outward from the main river courses braided throughout the Sundarbans. As much as a quarter of the land area was under water in the rainy season. Recurrent small depressions or basins collected and retained water through much of the year. Bengal tigers, monkeys and crocodiles were among the large animals found in the Sundarbans forests and swamps. The human population was limited to a few fishermen, salt-makers, smugglers and pirates living on the islands of the coastal mangroves. Parties of woodcutters and hunters made regular forays into the interior forest by boat, but rarely, if ever, made permanent homes in the wetlands. Hunter's (1875, vol. 1, pp. 285–350) account of the Sundarbans during the 1870s is rich in detail.

In 1793 Cornwallis, the British Governor-General of Bengal for the East India Company, imposed a new rule of landed property for Bengal under the terms of the 'Permanent Settlement'. The Sundarbans, along with other lands lying outside the area of cultivation and settlement, fell under state ownership. It was not until 1816, however, that the Bengal Government appointed a civil officer as Commissioner of the Sundarbans. This officer was charged with demarcating and managing the water-logged forests and swamps of the lower delta. He was to regulate and encourage extraction of timber and fuel wood for the growing needs of Calcutta and other towns and cities in Bengal. However, the Commissioner was above all to ensure that private landowners cleared, settled and reclaimed Sundarbans forests and swamps for rice cultivation. Large tracts of land were made available without charge to individuals or groups on long-term renewable leases, which were inheritable and transferable. The grantees needed capital sufficient to finance pioneer settlers who could bring a quarter of the leased lands under rice culture within 5 years. At the end of 20 years three-quarters of the land taken up by each grantee became liable for the land tax assessment at normal rates. Upon payment of the land tax each grantee was free to charge market rate land rents to his tenant farmers. A protracted survey operation completed in 1830 demarcated boundaries and offered security of tenure to improving landowners in this difficult terrain (Hunter 1875; Pargiter 1934).

The British colonial government saw the Sundarbans as a resource to be developed in order to increase the productivity of the Bengal countryside. It was a resource that required only peace and security and the framework of guaranteed property rights, together with predictable modest revenue demands, to unleash private entrepreneurial energies. The Bengal government slowly but steadily invested in canals, levees and embankments for water control. The river system offered a long-standing efficient transport network for country boats and, increasingly, steamers. Modest investments in piloting aids and port facilities were deemed sufficient to meet the needs of growing river traffic between the delta and the larger cities.

Land reclamation and settlement in the Sundarbans progressed each year as the wetlands proved to be generally fertile and productive. Nevertheless, land clearing was time consuming, arduous and expensive. The *sundri* trees, largely undisturbed by human activity, had grown to great size and were surrounded by thick underbrush. Hundreds of settlers were injured or killed each year by tigers, crocodiles and poisonous snakes. The ubiquitous depressions had to be embanked, and channels dug and maintained to control the inflow of water from riverine flooding.

By the early 1870s British officials, in what was probably a serious underestimate, believed that Bengali settlers had cleared and brought under rice cultivation 2790 km^2 of wetlands in the 80 years since the Permanent Settlement of 1793. This was nearly a fifth of the officially surveyed land area of 14 627 km^2 (and 4881 km^2 in waterways) for the Sundarbans at that time. However, to complicate matters somewhat, silt deposition had probably added 800 km^2 or more of new lands to the Sundarbans over the same period. Despite this increment, land reclamation far exceeded formation of new alluvial lands (Jack 1915, p. 10).

Affronted by the sight of so much 'culturable waste' land lying unused, Bengal officials adjusted their land policy to encourage smaller peasant farmers to engage in land reclamation on their own behalf (Ascoli 1921, p. 121). The new concessions, in tandem with rising rice and land prices, brought a new round of land clearing and settlement. By the early years of the twentieth century over 5000 km^2 of the Sundarbans was under cultivation, and, in the course of the twentieth century, clearance and cultivation continued to cut into the Sundarbans forest as pioneer settlers approached the coastal tidal islands.

An intensive reconstruction of land-use changes in Bengal for the past century confirms this picture of wetlands depletion. Within the districts of Twenty-four Parganas (India), and Bakanganj and Khulna (Bangladesh), which include the Sundarbans in their boundaries, total wetlands declined by 2750 km^2 in the 60 years between 1880 and 1940 (table 7.1). Between 1940 and

Table 7.1 Land-use changes in the Sundarbans, 1880–1980

Land-use type	*1880*	*1900*	*1920*	*1940*	*1960*	*1980*
Total arable and settled (km^2)	14570	16140	15830	16710	20820	21860
Wet rice[a] (km^2)	11240	11560	12620	12120	15490	16050
Forest-woodlands (km^2)	680	630	640	600	440	400
Grass-shrub (km^2)	800	500	820	1500	1430	1790
Barren (km^2)	500	500	500	500	500	500
Total wetlands (km^2)	15160	13960	13940	12410	8530	7180
Mangrove-tidal[a] (km^2)	6149	5574	5402	5301	4231	3909
Surface water (km^2)	5740	5740	5740	5740	5740	5740
Total population (million)	5.5	6.8	8.0	11.5	15.9	25.1

Sundarbans as here defined consists of twenty-four Parganas (India) and the districts of Bakanganj and Khulna (Bangladesh), and has a total area of 37 460 km^2.
Source: see appendix (page 233)

1980 the pace of reclamation quickened. The wetlands area dwindled by 5230 km^2 as subsistence demands for population and crowding in the countryside pressed against every available scrap of land. *Heritiera fomes* and mangrove formations were left intact only by virtue of competing state priorities.

Early on, the colonial government established a countervailing policy that succeeded in preserving about 10 000 km^2 of wetland forest from reclamation. In 1878 the government turned over administration of much of its unclaimed public lands to the newly formed Forest Department. Concerned for water control and for the supply of wood for energy and building materials, the state now acted to constrain the forces of development. Sundarbans lands were classified and bounded as either 'protected' or 'reserved' forest lands (Stebbing, 1923–6, vol. 2, pp. 470–81). Those under the protected classification were eligible for eventual leasing and clearance by settlers. Those denoted reserved forest were kept intact for exploitation for timber, but not for conversion to agriculture. By 1947 some 10 000 km^2 of Sundarbans lands fell under government forest status. After independence, 60 per cent went to East Pakistan (later Bangladesh) and 40 per cent to India.

By mid-century Bengali cultivators had either arrived at the sea-face, or they had reached the boundaries of government forest lands in their quest for new lands. After 1950 the assault on *sundri* and mangroves turned inward as cultivators cleared and reclaimed interstitial lands not consumed in the initial movement to the sea. In the three decades after independence from colonial rule another 1570 km^2 of wetlands was reclaimed (table 7.1). By this estimate 7180 km^2 of wetlands and an additional 5740 km^2 of watercourses remained. Of these some 10 000 km^2 lay in the Sundarbans reserve forests lying partially in India and partially in Bangladesh. Thus, since the late eighteenth century as much as 12 000 km^2 of deltaic wetlands have been transformed to the present-day landscape of peasant homesteads and rice paddies. Most of the *sundri* forests have disappeared, as have their wild denizens.

The protected coastal mangrove formations along the delta in India and Bangladesh have been subjected to growing pressures, and since Independence there have been many potential threats. Despite exemplary management and explicit policies the needs of the larger societies have intruded into these wetlands reserves. Bangladesh, for example, depends heavily for its fuel wood and timber on harvesting the Sundarbans. Although controlled, continued timber harvesting and fuel-wood cutting in the Sundarbans forest divisions has diminished forest density and biomass. New industrial needs in newsprint and matches have caused exploitation of the *gewa* tree (*Excoecaria appallocha*). Illegal poaching has sharply reduced the numbers of tigers, monkeys and other animals as well as reptile and bird species. Fish populations have been reduced (Seidensticker and Hai 1983). Over all hangs the threat of a water scarcity caused by diversion of the Ganges waters upstream by the Farraka barrage.

Land reclamation in the Sundarbans has created a new wet rice landscape in the Ganges-Brahmaputra delta. Domesticated wetlands – rice paddies – have met the food needs of a soaring population in West Bengal and Bangladesh.

Bakarganj long-grain rice, carried on country river boats, has now entered the intricate market system focused on Calcutta's hungry markets. During the last century, the population in the three districts of the delta, including Calcutta, grew fivefold, from 5 to 25 million. Because delta settler farmers supplied rice to Calcutta, their compatriots up river were able to grow the world's supply of jute to meet the world's needs for burlap bagging and sacking, turned out in Calcutta's mills. At the same time the Sundarbans forests fed the fuel and timber needs of Calcutta. The price for this success, however, has been high. The undomesticated wetlands and their animal populations have been reduced and depleted (plate 7.2). Recently, the limitations and fragility of this immensely fruitful domesticated landscape have become more apparent.

Plate 7.2 Satellite photograph of the western portion of the Ganges delta. The darker shading of the mangrove and swamp forest of the Sundarbans is clearly visible,and it extends for between 50 and 60 km inland. It has been reduced considerably during recent decades. The view encompasses an area south and east of Calcutta, and it stretches approximately 150 km from the mouth of the Malta River on the extreme west of the photograph to the channel of the Harlinghat River, a major distributary of the Ganges, on the extreme east (Courtesy NASA, Space Shuttle S15 50–63, 1988)

3.0 THE IRRAWADDY

In 1852 the British defeated the Konbaung regime in Burma and annexed 98 000 km^2 comprising the lower half of the kingdom. Several decades later, in the third Anglo-Burman war of 1885, Britain added the remaining lands of the kingdom to its colonial regime. British conquest immediately opened the Irrawaddy delta to a new intensive form of capitalist economic development. Under the old regime the deltaic tracts of lower Burma were relatively sparsely populated with between 1 and 1.25 million people at mid-century (Adas 1974, p. 21). The majority of the population were rice farmers engaged in subsistence farming. Like the Sundarbans the delta also supported communities of fishermen, salt-makers, smugglers and bandits. Communities who gathered the *dhani* palm for thatching made a living in this area.

The Burmese delta consists of approximately 31 000 km^2 of well-watered fertile gently sloping lands stretching from Henzada to the sea. The vegetation and ecological regime strongly resembles that of the Sundarbans. Most of the lower delta areas are subject to some form of inundation and bear tree formations of evergreen *Heritiera fomes* known in Burma as the *kanazo*. The latter often grew to heights of 45 m. Along the nine main branches of the Irrawaddy and their creeks fringes of *Rhizopora* grew luxuriantly from 12 to 25 m. Palms (*Nypa fruticans*) also grew profusely in these tidal forests. Interspersed throughout these main deltaic forests were large areas covered by *kaing* grasses (*Saccharum spontaneum*) growing up to 3 m in height. In the upper delta the great *kanazo* forests shaded off into mixed scrub delta forests (Stamp 1924, Davis 1964). Wildlife was abundant. Tigers, wild buffalo, elephants and other large mammals coexisted with many species of land and water birds, reptiles and fish.

Despite abundant fertile land, prior to 1852 there were few incentives for Burmese cultivators to brave the dangers and difficulties of land clearing and reclamation in the delta. Other natural impediments also existed. In many sections of the delta annual flooding left lands inundated for several months of the year. The threat of tigers, poisonous snakes and elephants was as immediate here as in the Sundarbans. In the immediate aftermath of jungle clearing the *Anopheles hyrcanus* mosquito, the principal vector for malaria, became extremely active, resulting in heavy mortality. Little capital and virtually no hired labour were available to support pioneer ventures. The forced labour demands of the Burmese state with its annual corvée levies discouraged population movements. Land was abundant and difficult to mortgage for loans because of ill-defined property rights. Smallholders 'owned' land as long as they occupied and tilled it. Unoccupied land reverted to common property status. The Konbaung monarchs prohibited exports of rice outside the kingdom and depressed the domestic market by holding vast quantities in government reserves. Some limited expansion of rice cultivation had occurred in Lower Burma, but overall only 3200 km^2 was under wet rice cultivation at mid-century (Adas 1987, p. 100).

After the conquest the new colonial regime took rapid measures to draw the Burmese into a commercially oriented imperial economy by providing markets for Burmese produce and consumer goods for their consumption. Almost immediately the ban on the export of rice was lifted as were other internal restrictions on trade imposed by the defeated regime. Simultaneously, European demand for rice soared. Over the next two decades Burma began to overtake the Carolinas and India as a supplier to the European rice milling market. By the early 1870s nearly 500 000 tons of rice left Rangoon each year (Adas 1974, p. 3).

The new regime next turned its attention to the agrarian order. The new rules abolished the corvée system which had largely immobilized the peasantry. The new rulers adopted a revenue and tenure system which recognized the property rights of peasant smallholders and, to a lesser extent, those tracts held by monasteries. Lands formerly held by the Burmese crown came under the direct control of the new administration. But the conquerors went even further by asserting state ownership of all other 'unoccupied' lands – even those inhabited by tribal groups engaged in shifting cultivation (Nisbet 1901, vol. 1, p. 276). With few exceptions, all unoccupied lands in lower Burma were thrown open for clearing, reclamation and settlement by peasant farmers after the conquest.

The Burma Land and Revenue Act of 1876 codified the new system (Nisbet 1901, vol. 1, pp. 271–7). Unoccupied 'jungle' lands in the delta were free to all comers. Cultivators could readily obtain a written authorization for occupancy of a tract of land from district officials. After the lands had been surveyed by revenue officials the holders were eligible for exemption from normal land tax payments for periods of up to 7 years. Squatter-settlers were given full rights of ownership if they had cultivated and paid revenues to the state on their holdings for 12 years. Both procedures conveyed permanent alienable heritable rights to the smallholder. He could thereby sell, mortgage or transfer it (Adas 1974, pp. 33–4).

Over the first three decades of colonial administration expansion in rice production occurred primarily in the upper delta and, to a much smaller extent, in the area adjacent to Rangoon. During this period 470 000 ha of new lands were placed under paddy rice (Adas 1974, pp. 59–60). A network of immigrant Indian rice millers, brokers and moneylenders as well as British export agents and firms had grown up. The river system served to bring paddy or milled rice to the port facilities at Rangoon and to carry seasonal labourers and brokers into the hinterland. By 1868 the newly founded Irrawaddy Flotilla Company had begun to operate a fleet of government-subsidized steamboats on the rivers of the delta (Adas 1974, p. 35). The state repaired existing embankments and began constructing new embankments which, by the turn of the century, would protect 400 000 ha of rice lands from the Irrawaddy's annual flooding. At the same time the state began to build canals between various tributaries which greatly facilitated transport of paddy, labourers and consumer goods.

By the 1880s the upper delta and increasingly the lower reaches of the

Irrawaddy emerged as a new frontier for Burma. This was a new land of opportunity. When the Third Anglo-Burman war ended, all restrictions on migration formerly imposed by the Knobaung monarchs ended. Streams of migrants began pouring in to grow rice in the delta. At this juncture all elements of the system were in place: capital, land tenures, peace and security, markets, transport, credit and, if needed, additional seasonal labour from Indian labourers. Over the next half century, until the depression, rice cultivation in lower Burma expanded from 1.3×10^6 ha in 1880 to $4.0 \times$ 106 ha in 1930 (Siok-Hwa Cheng 1968, pp. 241–2). Thereafter, the area under wet rice contracted under the double impact of the depression and the disruption of the Second World War, and only slowly climbed back to its pre-war level by 1980.

This explosive trend in wet rice agriculture had a devastating effect on the forests and wetlands of the lower delta. Only the decision of the government to set aside several hundred thousand hectares of swamp forest as government reserved forest in the 1890s permitted the remaining tracts of delta wetlands to survive.

A recent reconstruction of land-use change in Burma permits a more precise estimate of these changes. The 35 138 km^2 Irrawaddy division included within its boundaries the majority of lower delta wetlands (table 7.2). In 1880, 3979 km^2 of wet rice (95 per cent of all seasonal crops) was under cultivation; wetlands comprised 9059 km^2 (4941 km^2 of mangrove/tidal forests). In 40 years the area of wet rice had grown to 12 059 km^2 and reached a peak of 14 390 km^2 as the world depression broke in 1930. Wetlands dropped precipitously in area as a result. During the post-1930 period, although rice cultivation declined sharply before recovery, abandoned land did not mean regrowth of *kanazo* evergreen growths or mangroves. Instead land abandonment produced various grass-shrub formations shown by the rise of grass-shrub and interrupted woods categories. Overall, the secular trend moved remorselessly downward. In a

Table 7.2 Land-use changes in the Irrawaddy division of Burma, 1880–1980

Land-use type	*1880*	*1900*	*1920*	*1940*	*1960*	*1980*
Total arable and settled	4664	10263	14273	17535	17633	18439
Wet rice[a]	3979	8626	12059	13774	11485	13440
Forest-woodlands	15372	12091	9754	7873	7723	7049
Grass-shrub	2745	2986	3093	3062	3572	4028
Barren	275	291	297	292	338	365
Total wetlands	9059	6483	4698	3353	2848	2234
Mangrove-tidal[a]	4941	3496	2498	1749	1448	1094
Surface water	3024	3024	3024	3024	3024	3024
Total population (million)	1.0	1.7	2.0	2.7	3.5	5.0

[a] Subtotal.
Source: see appendix (page 233)

hundred years all types of wetlands decreased by 6825 km^2 or 75 per cent. Mangroves alone suffered losses of 3847 km^2. Government reserved forests in the delta, comprising 7071 km^2, sheltered the remaining wetlands as well as other forest types in the Irrawaddy division (Government of Burma 1961).

In Burma the combined forces of economic development – state, market and peasant farmer – have combined in a long-standing powerful force for reclamation of wetlands. Only state power directed to other goals has been able to slow or halt the process of wetlands transformation when forest lands have been demarcated for other productive uses. The modern landscape of the Burma delta, like that of the Bengal delta, is one of domesticated wetlands.

4.0 THE CHAO PHRAYA

Imposition of British imperial hegemony over Thailand was expressed in the Bowring Treaty of 1855. This agreement opened wide a controlled regional economy to world economic forces. The 1855 treaty provided for extraterritorial rights for British subjects, unhindered free trade, the abolition of royal monopolies of trade and fixed modest rates for import and export duties (Ingram 1971, pp. 33–4). Thailand may not have undergone defeat and conquest, but it lost considerable sovereignty and in effect came under informal imperial rule. Under this external impetus successive Thai rulers fostered the export of rice, sugar cane and other agricultural commodities. In the latter half of the nineteenth century and on into the twentieth century, the market for rice in Europe boomed. Asian rice was useful as a cheap dietary staple, as a brewing ingredient, as starch for sizing textiles and for numerous other uses. Thai rice took an increasing share of this market.

The Thai rulers quickly adapted their policies to the new market-oriented economy to which they were now linked. Adult males between the ages of 18 and 60 were no longer subject to annual and extraordinary corvée labour which exacted as much as 3 months of effort every year. Instead, the government substituted an annual capitation tax to be paid in money. Further, the government abolished slavery – especially debt bondage which, although not hereditary, immobilized 10–20 per cent of the rural population and hindered settler migration (Johnston 1975, pp. 21–3). As a result of the new economic climate, expanded cultivation occurred in the central plain around the old capital at Ayutthya in the 1850s and 1860s.

Bangkok rapidly became a bustling metropolis filled with rice mills, warehouses, docks and all the confusion of a major trading centre on the river. The export warehouses at Bangkok were fed by a growing body of Chinese traders who operated small fleets of river boats up and down the waterways of the delta. Simultaneously other Chinese capitalists invested in powered rice mills in Bangkok and the provinces to process the crop. The entrepreneurial division between Thai peasants investing in expanding rice cultivation and the Chinese intermediaries became more and more noticeable (Johnston 1975, pp. 247–62).

The export boom stimulated interest in new land. The largest and most accessible frontier lay between Bangkok and Ayutthaya. In the mid-nineteenth century the Chao Phraya river delta below the old capital at Ayutthaya was a largely uninhabited and undeveloped resource (Takaya 1987, pp. 179–81). The triangular area, nearly 100 km wide at its base on the coastline, comprised 12 700 km^2 of grassland and patches of swamp forest. Nipa palm and mangroves followed the tidal reaches of brackish water inlets at the mouth. The plain of the delta, less than 2.5 m above sea level, had a gentle slope to the sea with only minimal relief. During the 6 months of the rainy season river flooding placed the delta under water up to a metre in depth. Despite this temporary excess, the region was not abundantly watered since rainfall was between 1000 and 1500 mm/yr, less than that required for rice production. As the dry season proceeded the flood water disappeared and the surface of the delta became desiccated. This hydrological regime discouraged most forms of human settlement. Only scattered colonies of fishermen, charcoal burners and salt-makers inhabited the coastal fringe of the delta.

To develop potential rice lands in the delta required investment in transport. Roads were almost non-existent and the river system was inadequate for either migration or for shipping produce to markets. Further, the grasslands of the Chao Phraya, more than those of the Ganges-Brahmaputra or Irrawaddy, required systematic water management and capital investment by the Thai state. A complex of planned large-scale interventions were necessary to transform the water regime of the delta. Without this investment profitable rice cultivation was impossible. The Thai monarchy had to address three interlocking problems of water management: provision of water for cultivation in the young delta during the dry season, limiting the tidal inflow of saline water in the coastal zone, and flood control and reservoir management for the inflow of river water in the wet season. The state responded by planning and developing a proliferating network of canals and embankments. These works were the primary means for attracting pioneers and reclaiming lands in the delta.

Drawing upon long experience in canal building for transport purposes, in the 1860s the Thai government began to construct canals to bring settlers into the delta grasslands and to provide a means of carrying their produce to Bangkok's markets (Takaya 1987, pp. 188–97). In the 1870s the colonial state dug canals expressly to open portions of the delta's grasslands to rice cultivation. The new canals provided a means for settlers to reach new lands provided by the state and, for the first time, were seen as a source of irrigation water for the dry season. The king granted lands to aristocrats or other landlords who were exempt from payment of the land tax on newly reclaimed lands.

The most impressive of these projects was the development of the Rangsit area east of the river in the interior of the young delta. This was a 2000 km^2 wilderness area known as the Royal Meadow in which herds of wild elephants still flourished. Under contract to the king the Siam Canals, Land and Irrigation Company undertook to dig three primary east-west canals and 40 or more north-south intermediary channels. The 890 km of canals provided transportation and irrigation water for the new settlers. Initially some 560 km^2 of rice land were brought into cultivation by this project. Six other individual canals brought other lands under rice cultivation (Takaya 1987, pp. 196–7). By 1900, 800 km^2 were under cultivation in the Rangsit area. Poor canal design meant that water shortages still occurred, despite access to the Chao Phraya waters. If the rivers were low these early canals could not ensure an adequate water supply. One difficulty lay in the fact that the ungated canals acted to draw accumulated rainwater off the rice-growing areas in the rainy season (Takaya 1987, p. 213). Nevertheless, new settlers continued to pour into the delta.

Early in the century, a Dutch engineer, Homan van der Heide, was named head of the new Canal Department and proposed a regional irrigation plan for the entire delta. Van der Heide's master plan aimed at the construction of a large dam at Chainat on the Chao Phraya at the apex of the delta. Waters impounded there would be directed into the delta lands by three major canalized rivers, controlled by water gates, and fed by gravity flow through a series of canals to the fields. About 600 km of existing canals could be used and another 600 km of canals would have to be dug. Van der Heide also called for a tidal embankment to stretch across the base of the delta to create an immense polder. This barrier would prevent loss of fresh water to incoming tides in the rainy season and convert the land behind it to a freshwater rather than a brackish regime. The advantages of this scheme, according to its architect, included reliable access to adequate fresh water for rice and for animal and human consumption, distribution of silt throughout the delta, thus raising soil fertility, and better regulation of the cropping season for better varieties of rice. Only a portion of van der Heide's expensive proposals were adopted by the Thai government. Nevertheless, his scheme strongly influenced all subsequent development in the delta (Takaya 1987, pp. 220–3).

From 1915 until the Second World War the Thai government sponsored a series of planned irrigation works designed to encourage expansion of rice production. Under Thomas Ward, formerly employed in India as a canal engineer, the Canal Department completed the South Pasak project between 1915 and 1924. The Rama VI dam on the Pasak diverted river water into the Raphiphat canal which bore irrigation water into the Rangsit tract canals which acted as feeder canals leading to the irrigation ditches of the cultivators. Provision of an assured water supply in this region meshed with the boom in prices and demand for rice after the First World War. Thousands of cultivators rushed to acquire land to expand cultivation in the delta (Takaya 1987, pp. 232–3).

Bang Hia, a 10 year project completed in 1931, brought 220 km^2 under cultivation. A newly built road running along the east coast of the delta served as a tidal embankment. This was designed to link with a strengthened tidal lock begun by van der Heide. The borrow pit beside the road became a navigable canal. The Bang Hia project permitted cultivators to occupy potentially fertile lands south of Rangsit and the sea. Formerly saline, these lands were cleansed by fresh water carried by the irrigation canals leading south from Rangsit. Several other projects of similar scope were begun in the period between the wars. Some were completed; work on others continued after the Second World War.

After the war, the Food and Agriculture Organization (FAO) of the United Nations sent a mission to Thailand which strongly urged complete development of the Chao Phraya delta. In its essential recommendations for water management, the FAO plan was very similar to that of van der Heide, conceived a half century earlier. Funded by the World Bank, the Thai government began the Greater Chao Phraya project in 1952 and it was completed in 1957. The centre-piece of this plan was the Chainat dam located at the apex of the delta on Chao Phraya. Above the dam were the headworks of five main canals and canalized rivers which led irrigation water to secondary channels throughout the delta. When supplemented by a network of irrigation ditches dug at field level by the government in the 1960s the Chao Phraya project truly transformed the delta.

In the 1960s the government, worried about flood-water threats to Bangkok, decided to use the relatively undeveloped west bank region of the delta as a reservoir for flood control. To this end several canals diverted river water into what became a large flooded polder. So extreme were the conditions that those farmers in the region were forced to shift to wet rice farming in the dry season. Other measures for the gradual improvement of water control and agricultural production have continued in the Chao Phraya delta.

Throughout this hundred year period the Thai government, landlords and cultivators have worked unceasingly to extend and improve management of the delta's lands. Little, if any, cultivable wasteland is left. Reliable water supplies have made it possible to grow sugar cane along with rice in the delta. Yields of rice have risen steadily; so also have land prices. The swamp and swamp forest are gone. On the coast within the line of tidal inundation a thin fringe of mangrove forests still survives, although it is intensively exploited for fuel wood. Interspersed among the mangrove are ponds for prawn farming and salt fields. Inland from the mangrove are nipa palm tracts and also coconut tree plantations. Older modes of exploiting the coastal mangrove formations have been brought to a new intensive level. No forest reserves or protective classification for these remaining coastal wetlands has been adopted by the state.

5.0 CONCLUSION

State direction and investment and the entrepreneurial drive of millions of peasant settlers have transformed the wetlands in these three deltas. They are only the most visible examples of a much greater process at work along the entire coastline of South and Southeast Asia. Frontier expansion has marked the histories of these regions and, characteristically, has caused a massive transformation of the land. Few areas of alluvial soil, few stretches of coastline, however remote, have been spared. For example, in Burma as a whole, wetlands reclamation has quietly proceeded along the Arakan coast to the west of the Irrawaddy and in Tenasserim to the east. Overall we estimate that coastal wetlands in Burma have declined by 12 300 km^2 since 1880. Of that total mangrove losses have reached 8140 km^2. Total wetlands in the country cover 9650 km^2, of which 5780 km^2 are mangrove-tidal formations (Richards et al. 1987, p. 927). The losses have been profound. Although estimates are currently not possible, it is likely that similar depletion can be assumed for the other countries of the region.

Over the same century wet rice lands in Burma have grown by an estimated 29 860 km^2 to a 1980 total of 52 660 km^2. This is an enormous new form of freshwater wetlands which remain directly under human management and control. It is this model which has driven the recent Indonesian transmigration schemes aimed at settlement of the coastal wetlands of Kalimantan (chapter 11). Currently, the Indonesian government assumes that more than 22 000 km^2 of tidal wetlands in the Outer Islands have potential for conversion to wet rice production (Ruddle 1987, p. 178). Despite the reservations of many informed observers and scientists regarding the differences between the river-deposited sediments and the tropical peatlands, the experience of the past century in other coastal areas offers a persuasive example to inspire development planners.

From one perspective these are immensely productive wetlands which feed great numbers of human beings every year. For the small farmer, wet rice is a rewarding crop. It has a high ratio of seed to yield; it is possible to harvest two or even three crops a year on the same plot. Wet rice cultivation in alluvial regions does not deplete the soil as rapidly as other crops. Risk in wet rice farming is minimized by comparison with other crops and other agricultural regimes. The water supply for rice supplies nutrients naturally. Wet rice will absorb continuing inputs of labour and land improvements and return increased yields. As a result rice supports high population densities because it rewards intensive labour inputs more than virtually any other foodgrain (Bray 1985).

If rice farmers adopt more sophisticated aboriculture and aquaculture – as in the example of the intricately organized wetlands of the Pearl River delta in Canton – rice culture is sustainable in the long term (Ruddle 1987, pp. 186–8). The 12 000 km^2 Zhuziang delta region boasts a sophisticated dike-pond system that produces rice, mulberry for silkworms, carp, pigs, sugar cane, soybeans, peanuts and fruits in a complex interlocking system. In the long run some version of this model may be the necessary end-point for sustainability. Those domesticated wetlands given over to rice monoculture in the process of frontier settlement described above (now adding prawn culture and other adaptations) may become less vulnerable. In the end, it may be necessary to turn inward, to invest in intensive management of those domesticated wetlands already created in South and Southeast Asia. Ultimately, even those remaining wild wetlands may not survive.

APPENDIX: SOURCES FOR TABLES 7.1 AND 7.2

Table 7.1

Land use data for West Bengal at the district level were drawn from various volumes of the *Agricultural Statistics of India* series covering the period from 1884–5 to 1980. This series also covers the districts now in Bangladesh for the period before Partition. Other sources consulted include the following: West Bengal Bureau of Applied Economics and Statistics, *Key Statistics of the District of 24-Parganas for 1979 and 1980 (Combined)*, Government Printing, Calcutta, 1981; West Bengal, 'Land utilisation statistics of West Bengal (excluding Calcutta) for the year 1980–81', personal communication from the Director of the Bureau of Applied Economics and Statistics, West Bengal, 3 December 1985; *Abstract of Agricultural Statistics of East Pakistan 1966*, No. 2, East Pakistan Bureau of Statistics, Dacca, 1971; *Bangladesh Agriculture in Statistics*, Bangladesh Ministry of Agriculture, Agro-Economic Research Section, Dacca, 1974; Bangladesh Bureau of Statistics, Statistics Division, Ministry of Planning, *Agricultural Production Levels in Bangladesh (1947–1972)*, Bangladesh Government Press, Dacca, 1976; Bangladesh Bureau of Statistics, 'Land utilization statistics by districts', *Monthly Statistical Bulletin of Bangladesh*, 11, 17–18, January 1982.

Table 7.2

Information has been drawn from the series *Agricultural Statistics of India* for the period 1880–1930. Other quantitative and descriptive data have been obtained from the gazetteer series for the Bassein, Henzada, Maubin, Myaungmya and Pyapon districts published between 1912 and 1924. The land revenue 'settlement' reports for these districts completed between 1880 and 1910 have also been consulted. More recent statistics were available in the Union of Burma, *Agricultural Statistics*, various years. The Ministry of Planning and Finance, *Report to the People* 1971–73–74, 1978, 1980, contains useful information. *Season and Crop Reports* issued by the Commissioner of Settlements and Land Records also reproduce land-use data.

Additional information on sources is contained in Flint and Richards (1990).

8

Port Industrialization, Urbanization and Wetland Loss

David A. Pinder and Michael E. Witherick

1.0 INTRODUCTION

Port expansion, industrialization and urbanization rank among the strongest forces placing pressure on wetland environments. Their impact has been felt for centuries as city ports have grown and extended their harbour areas. Although these pressures have been long established, it is in the twentieth century – and most particularly in the post-1950 era – that their significance has increased dramatically. For much of this period, gigantism has dominated thinking in shipping, port development and industrial circles, and many port cities have expanded so rapidly that their early-twentieth-century development has been dwarfed. Therefore it is appropriate that this chapter should focus on recent rather than historical pressures.

At the outset we explore the nature and consequences of large-scale port development and coastal industrialization, together with the forces underpinning the era of economic expansion and wetland decline. Subsequently it is argued that the long-standing industrial pressures on remaining wetlands in industrialized countries have been eased by the onset of an uncertain economic climate and the rise of environmentalism. Notwithstanding this respite, however, wetland colonization for industrial purposes continues in a muted form, and new types of demand have also arisen. Pressure caused by urbanization remains significant, and is now particularly important in the Far East. Here, quite apart from industrial momentum and associated seaport expansion, rapid population growth and polarization towards major cities have combined to make urbanization a seemingly insatiable consumer of wetland environments. This, above all, is the case when population pressure is accompanied by an acute shortage of developable land.

Three further introductory points are necessary. First, the impacts of port growth and industrialization are considered largely in the Western European context, while impacts of urbanization are analysed through case studies of three dynamic Pacific rim countries: Japan, Hong Kong and Singapore. These different regions illustrate forces and outcomes very effectively, yet it should be recognized that most of the processes observed are of global significance. Secondly, this chapter does not adopt the standpoint that all wetland reclamation has been unnecessary or undesirable. Without the development that has normally followed it, standards of living – particularly in advanced countries – would be far lower than they are today. Benefits, as well as costs, must not be overlooked. Thirdly, the aim is not to itemize the precise ecological losses resulting from wetland conversions but to bring into focus the processes and forces that have been detrimental to wetland environments. This approach has been chosen partly to deepen understanding of why wetlands have proved extremely vulnerable, but also to contribute to current debates concerning their protection. Strategies which aim to achieve more effective preservation can only benefit from an appreciation of the nature of the threat and its underlying causes.

2.0 POST-WAR PORT GROWTH AND WETLAND DECLINE

Port expansion and associated industrialization have provided the most readily identifiable process of wetland encroachment. Growth has affected innumerable ports of all sizes, and the nature of encroachment has naturally varied from port to port. At one end of the scale ports may possess simply a modest group of container berths on newly reclaimed land; at the other end are the large-scale maritime industrial development areas (MIDAs). Their acronym neatly summarizes the priority given to the goal of economic development rather than ecological conservation. Despite this diversity, however, it is possible to identify a general process of port expansion and wetland decline. This process is closely related to Bird's Anyport model of port development, although this model does not emphasize environmental degradation (Bird 1971, pp. 66–74). In western countries the process was particularly powerful during the twentieth century up to the early 1970s when, as is demonstrated later, industrial crisis and the rise of environmentalism brought about a significant shift in the balance of power between port industrialization and environmental interests.

The essence of the process is phased physical expansion. Each phase is designed to match port facilities with the anticipated demands of the shipping industry and the industrial sector, each normally extends the port one step further downstream and each may well pose a threat to undisturbed wetlands. This threat may be to the tidal margins of either the mainland or islands, but it may also entail the reclamation of many square kilometres of wetland. From the viewpoint of environmental impact, a key feature is the increasing scale with each successive phase; harbour basins become deeper, larger and simpler in outline than those in earlier port areas, and more and more extensive land areas are created for industrial, trans-shipment and storage purposes.

2.1 *Setting the pace: physical growth in post-war Rotterdam*

Wetland encroachment brought about by the process described above is admirably exemplified by the post-war history of Rotterdam, the dynamism of which has encouraged many ports around the world to expand in a similar, if less spectacular, fashion (Vigarié 1981, p. 25). During the late 1940s the western extremity of the port was the Pernis oil complex, only 12 km downstream from the earliest harbour areas. Between 1950 and 1970 growth extended the port an additional 23 km to the northwest, with almost no consideration being attached to the rapidly increasing loss of wetland (plate 8.1).

Three phases in this post-war expansion era were significant (figure 8.1). In the immediate post-war period plans were devised for a new port area of approximately 11 km^2, known as Botlek. This was to cater for the oil and associated industries and was to be accessible to ships that were then considered exceptionally large – up to 80 000 dead weight tonnes (dwt). Construction began in 1954 and was completed in 1960. In environmental terms this scheme entailed first damming the southwest outlet of a river arm – the eponymous Botlek – to form the main channel of the new port area. Secondly, shallows separating the Botlek and the Scheur were dredged to provide access from the main shipping lane. Thirdly, and most seriously in terms of wetland loss, the eastern tip of the agricultural island of Rozenburg, and a former island known as the Welplaat, were totally remodelled to provide industrial land surrounding the new Botlek harbour. This remodelling entailed reclamation of the extensive tidal flats, as well as the loss of wetland environments on the islands which supported a rich flora and associated animal and bird populations.

In 1957, while the Botlek project was still under construction, the ambitious port authority obtained approval for its second major post-war project, the construction of Europoort. Although this scheme was far larger than its predecessor Botlek (it was to extend 12 km downstream and cover more than 30 km^2), the concepts involved were very similar (Pinder 1981, pp. 184–5). The fundamental assumption was that agricultural land – in this case all the remainder of Rozenburg Island which stretched westwards to join the original Hook of Holland – and adjoining waterways and wetlands could readily be sacrificed to ensure the continued momentum of the oil-based economy. Construction took place throughout the 1960s. Over the entire island, wetland elements surviving in the agricultural landscape were obliterated to create industrial sites even larger than those in Botlek (plate 8.2) plus the access channels and harbours necessary for supertankers that were expected to exceed 200 000 dwt. While this loss was significant, there was also a major impact on surrounding waterways, particularly south of Rozenburg Island. Here the Brielse Maas had previously flowed through and among estuarine wetlands, but the creation of an easily navigable inland waterway, the Hartel Canal, erased this environment. Although an attempt at compensation was made by the construction of a recreation zone along the line of the Brielse Maas, this did nothing to restore the undisturbed character of the earlier environment.

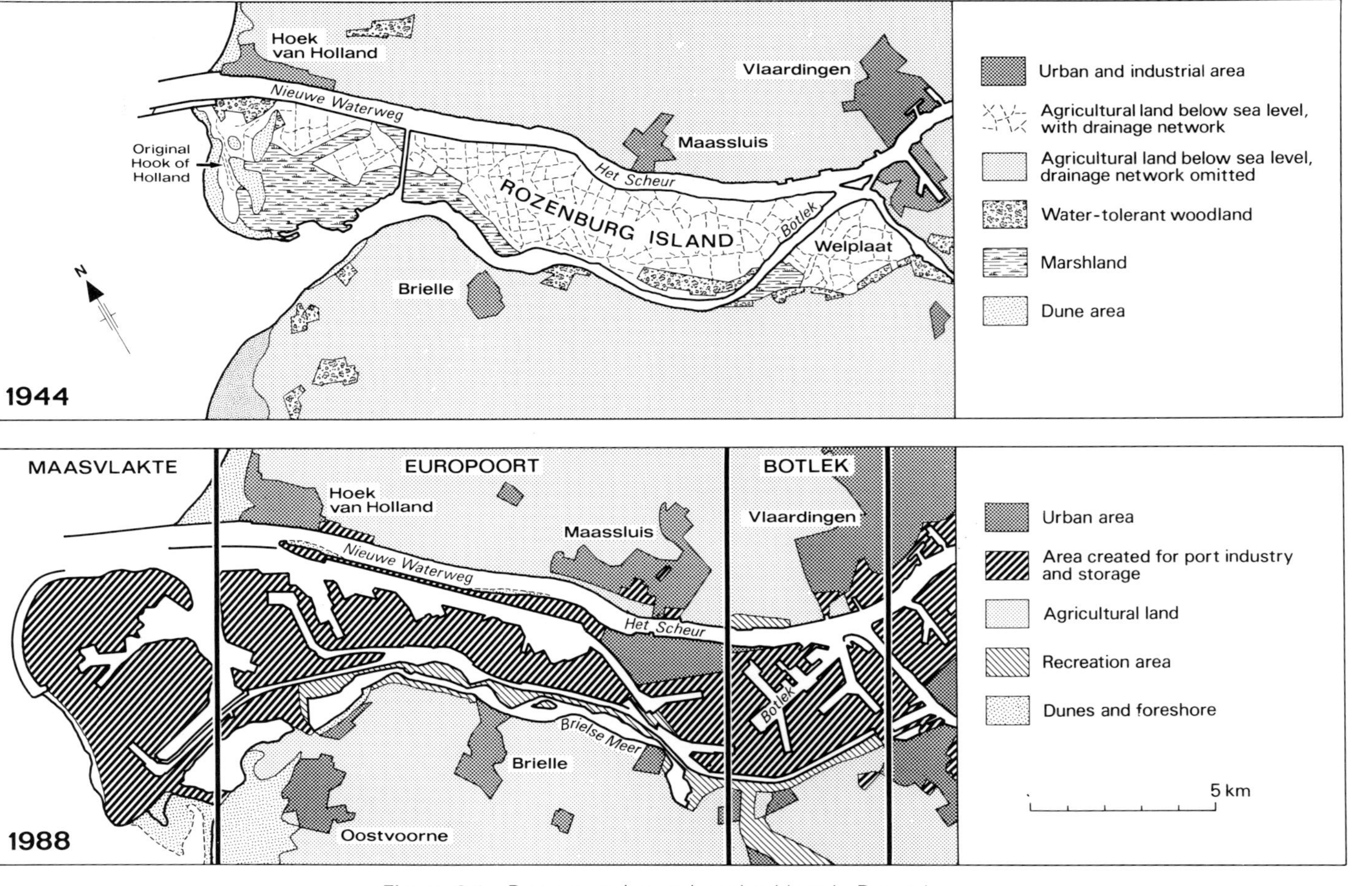

Figure 8.1 Port expansion and wetland loss in Rotterdam

Plate 8.1 Reclamation in the port of Rotterdam looking east from the North Sea for about 16 km and across the newly reclaimed land of Maasvlakte (former Hook of Holland). The oil refineries and storage facilities of Europoort are in the middle distance and in the far distance is Botlek, all created out of former estuarine wetlands. The Nieuwe Waterweg is on the extreme left of the channel
(Courtesy KLM Aerocarto-Schipol)

Moreover, in 1966 all tidal influences were lost when the Brielse Maas was dammed during implementation of the Netherlands' major flood protection scheme, the Delta Plan (chapter 6) (Dutt and Heal 1985).

Work began on the third and final post-war expansion scheme, the Maasvlakte, in 1965, well before the Europoort project was complete. By the early 1970s this scheme had added a further 30 km^2 to the port area, land that was once more designated for heavy industry, although in this case steel and not oil was to be the propulsive activity. The Maasvlakte scheme had as its centre-piece a steelworks with a capacity that would eventually reach 10 million tonnes. This plant was to be entirely dependent on imports for its raw material supplies, and would therefore require extensive storage areas for iron ore and coal. However, space demands were also substantial because the steelworks was planned as the heart of a maritime industrial complex. Other

Plate 8.2 Low-lying agricultural landscape and drainage network of the type lost to the Botlek and Europoort expansion schemes, Rotterdam
(Courtesy D. A. Pinder)

major components of this complex were to be a power station generating electricity for the steelworks by using gas produced in the coking process, and a shipyard capable of building the world's largest supertankers, thus consuming locally produced steel plate. Apart from increased pollution, the environmental price to be paid for the economic benefits of the Maasvlakte scheme was first, the loss of the De Beer nature reserve. Situated at the western extremity of Europoort, this was the original Hook of Holland sandspit, an environment that had been inadvertently protected when the sandspit was severed by the opening in 1871 of Rotterdam's ship canal, the New Waterway (de Graaf et al. 1982, pp. 142–5). Secondly, the eponymous Maasvlakte – extensive tidal flats beyond the De Beer reserve – were to be reclaimed, resulting in the loss of an important staging post for wading birds on their migratory route along the European coastline.

2.2 *Causal factors*

While it is important to analyse the process of physical expansion, it is also necessary to identify the forces underlying the process and therefore generating the environmental threat. Economic imperatives have, of course, been of central significance, and to a great extent have sprung from the perceptions of the port authorities of the need to respond to technological change. This economic-technological relationship is graphically demonstrated by the well-known development of crude-oil tankers in the post-1950 era. By the 1960s and 1970s, significant operating economies could be obtained by employing vessels of more than 100 000 dwt on journeys of 4000 km or more. On a 16 000 km journey transport costs for a 200 000 dwt ship were almost 30 per cent lower per tonne than for a 100 000 dwt vessel. With a 300 000 dwt supertanker the differential was often as high as 40 or 45 per cent (van den Bremen 1982, pp. 66–7).

To enable oil importers to exploit these economies, it was essential that ports should develop harbour areas and approach channels that were not simply of adequate depth. Extensive water areas were also required to enable larger ships, carrying dangerous cargoes with a high pollution potential, to manoeuvre safely. Moreover, the lessons learned in oil-tanker construction were quickly applied to other forms of maritime transportation, such as chemical tankers, natural gas carriers and ore, coal and grain carriers. Similarly, container ships, roll-on-roll-off vessels and, somewhat later, car transporters achieved major economies of scale through the application of innovations which would enable diverse cargoes to be handled in bulk. In terms of harbour construction, the direct consequence of this technological dissemination was the creation of new space demands, and therefore threats to wetlands, in almost all ports (Hilling 1987).

Improved shipping technologies were also fundamental to escalating demand for land in port areas, not least because new and highly efficient plant could be created adjacent to the modern habour basins which enabled low-cost raw materials to be imported. This factor undoubtedly encouraged activities such as steel production, aluminium smelting, chemical production and oil refining to flourish around the coastlines of industrial nations. In most ports, however, increased land demand was at least as heavily dependent on the scale and nature of cargoes carried by the new generations of ships (Takel 1974). Imports arriving as large-scale individual shipments could not be consumed immediately, either by port-based industry or by industries in the wider market area. Increasingly, therefore, it became necessary to expand port areas in such a way that shortage of space for commodity storage was not likely to impose economic penalties. Tank farms for crude oil and refined products thus became major elements in the port landscape, port zones were expanded to stockpile ores and coal, and container terminals were surrounded by the familiar aprons which now optimize the loading, discharge and temporary storage of general cargoes. In Rotterdam, for example, more than 80 per cent of the land made available to industry following the construction of Eurtpoort was ultimately used for commodity trans-shipment and storage, rather than processing (plate 8.3).

While it is important to relate wetland consumption to revolutions in maritime technology, it is equally necessary to recognize that quite different factors have also stimulated the impressive physical expansion of ports. In many developed countries after 1950, port growth was a necessary adjunct to

Plate 8.3 The Botlek and Pernis areas in the port of Rotterdam. Relatively little space is occupied by the refineries of Esso (foreground) and Shell and Texaco (background). Far more land has been consumed by storage tanks and, to the right of the installations, by the road and rail infrastructures
(Courtesy Esso Netherlands BV)

national and industrial development; without greater capacity for imports and exports, national economic development would have been impeded. Strategic considerations also played a part; port areas became the base for activities considered vital for national economic security. In Western Europe this was particularly true of oil refining, the coastal capacity of which rose from less than 50 million t in 1950 to more than 600 million t in the mid-1970s. One factor contributing to this impressive development was increasing political instability in the Middle East after the Second World War, which prompted governments to encourage oil companies to shun refining in the main production region and invest instead in the politically stable market areas of Western Europe. Most companies were very amenable to this strategy, the popularity of which was boosted by the economies to be gained by shipping crude oil to the European market (Odell 1986, pp. 116–7).

Governmental support for port expansion was also founded on the belief that port industrialization could make a major contribution to the modernization of the national industrial base. This belief was closely related to the rapid acceptance of growth-pole theory in the late 1950s and 1960s. Many ports were viewed as emergent industrial complexes destined to become major nuclei of interrelated activities that would impart significant impetus to the industrial sector as a whole (Stornebrink 1960). This was the basis for the French national planners' decision to permit the extension of the Marseilles port area at Fos, a project which led to the loss between 1965 and 1975 of some 70 km^2 of lagoons and wetland in the western half of the Grand Rhone delta (figure 8.2). However, the Fos project also highlights an additional force that has strongly encouraged port expansion: the use of port industrialization as a regional planning instrument leading to rapid regional industrialization (Tuppen 1984). Many other ports in problem areas, as well as localities with no history of port development, have been earmarked for port-based growth-pole development intended to force sluggish regional economies into upward transition. At Cagliari, the Machlareddu MIDA was planned as the largest employment centre on Sardinia, with a target labour force of 28 000 in petrochemicals, manufacturing and service facilities (King 1977, p. 91). Described as an ideal site for major industrial expansion, its creation – like that of Fos and the Frontignan refinery – entailed the loss of 15 km^2 of coastal lagoons and salt pans.

In the early post-war decades, therefore, wetlands were threatened by a potent combination of forces, making successful protection difficult. It could have been worse. In Western Europe the consumpton of estuarine and coastal land would have been even greater if transportation technologies, and particularly pipelines, had not facilitated inland production. By the early 1970s a third of all refineries had inland locations, with the large majority being dependent on pipelines from Bremerhaven, Rotterdam, Marseilles, Genoa and Trieste. Although most of these refineries were relatively small, if they had been built in coastal locations they would have increased land demand by at least 100 km^2. Similarly, rail and waterway improvements, particularly to the Federal Republic of Germany, helped retard the coastal migration of industries such as steel.

Conversely, organizational forces greatly facilitated the demise of wetlands, primarily because the post-war era witnessed the rapid development of physical planning systems in Western countries, not least with respect to industrialization and port development. Much has been written on planning processes (Healey et al. 1982), and one widely recognized approach is the incremental method. This approach is based on phased developments and it has proved particularly appropriate for port authorities seeking to sustain long-term growth by periodic strategy modifications to exploit shifting economic opportunities and a rapidly evolving technological environment (e.g. Rotterdam). However, an important feature of incremental planning is that phased

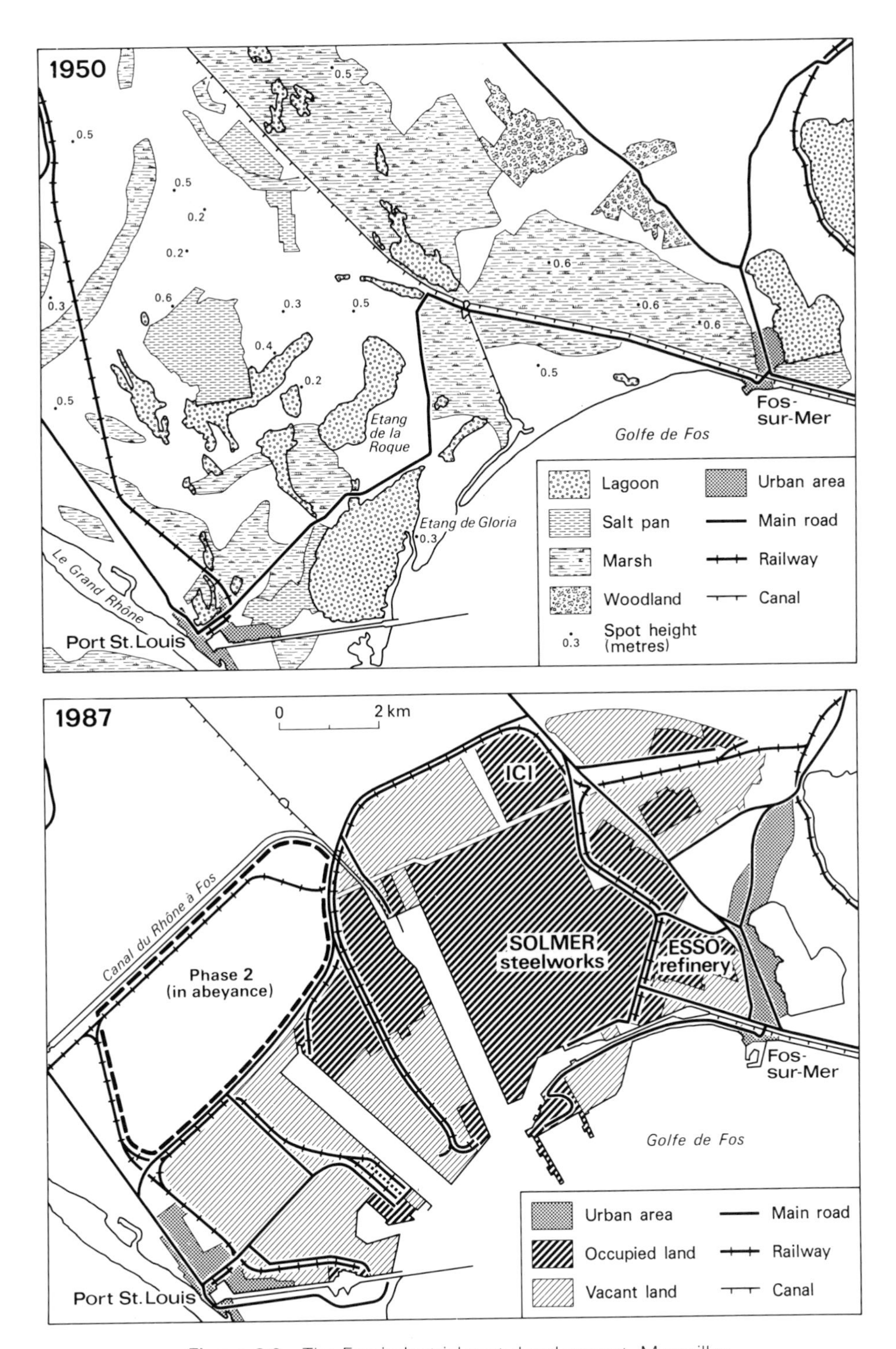

Figure 8.2 The Fos industrial port development, Marseilles

policy reviews are likely to produce adjusted versions of past practice rather than radical revisions. Thus, in the context of post-war port development, the trend was for physical expansion to be more adeptly implemented, with little chance that port planners would voluntarily re-assess expansionist intentions in the light of their environmental consequences. For many planners, as Vigarié (1981, p. 25) has also noted with respect to Japanese port development, wetlands remained merely 'sandy or swampy zones that would [in the absence of development] remain underutilized'. They were particularly vulnerable because, given the expansionary ethos of the time, organizations dedicated to preservation either failed to develop or found it impossible to generate sufficient influence to deflect firmly established incremental planning strategies. This imbalance of power does much to explain the ease with which 600 km^2 of coastal land between the Seine and the Elbe, and no less than 1000 km^2 in western continental Europe as a whole, became available to industry by the late 1970s (Vigarié 1981, p. 25).

2.3 *Coastal industrialization outside port areas*

While it is essential to recognize the part played by planned port development in the demise of wetlands, variations on the theme must not be overlooked. Some industries have taken advantage of land made available by port expansion, but have also developed impressively at coastal sites outside port areas. Once again, the oil-refining and petrochemical industries, together with energy production (plate 8.4) have been to the fore. Despite the impetus they have given to port development, when port location patterns, site attributes or expansion policies have not matched company requirements the response has frequently been to eliminate the mismatch by developing free-standing sites (Pinder and Husain 1988, pp. 239–41). Moreover, locations developed in this way have in many instances been large projects. In the United Kingdom, for example, the Baglan Bay petrochemical complex, at the mouth of the Neath estuary, extends over 4 km^2. Similarly, the BP refinery site on the Isle of Grain in the Medway estuary occupies over 5 km^2 of Grain Marsh. Developments of this type may not be built entirely on wetlands, not least because land above the high-water mark may have the greater load-bearing capacity. Yet it has been common for reclamation to be undertaken in the adjacent tidal zone. Thus the Baglan Bay site is built partly on coastal dunes but also spreads onto reclaimed tidal flats in the bay itself. Similarly, the Esso refinery at Fawley on Southampton Water extends over almost 5 km^2, more than a quarter of which has been gained by salt marsh reclamation. In addition, pressure on the local environment has frequently been caused by jetty construction, while unreclaimed wetlands in the vicinity have come under the intermittent threat of fuel and product spillages from visiting vessels (see section 4.0).

Growth on free-standing sites also illustrates a further problem that has increased the difficulties of protecting wetlands: early encroachment has in some instances been on a modest and apparently innocuous scale, yet has set a precedent making later expansion proposals difficult to resist. Thus the Fawley

Plate 8.4 Energy production, just like the provision of port storage and handling facilities, is a voracious consumer of wetlands. This view shows the construction during the early 1970s of the Torrens Island gas-fired power station at Port Adelaide, South Australia, in the unique mangrove assemblages of Spencer Gulf. In the background are solar evaporation pans (Courtesy Darian Smith)

site, owned originally by the Anglo-Gulf West Indies company, began operations in 1921. During the 1920s the annual capacity of the refinery was less than 100 000 t/yr, and the installations made very marginal demands on adjacent wetlands. However, this proto-refinery was ideal for Esso to purchase and expand from 1949 onwards. Similarly, the annual capacity of the Frontignan refinery in southern France was expanded by Mobil from 1.0 million to 5.9 million tonnes, and the site for this growth was one of the numerous lagoons which fringe the Languedoc-Roussillon coast. In the case of BP's Isle of Grain plant, the initial development did not involve the oil industry but, instead, construction of a now forgotten harbour, Port Victoria. This venture led to almost no growth on the Medway shore, yet it left an important legacy – a railway which provided the future refinery site with a ready-made link to its markets.

3.0 WETLANDS REPRIEVED? ENVIRONMENTALISM AND ECONOMIC TRENDS POST-1970

Since the mid-1970s there has been a marked relaxation of industrially induced pressure on wetlands in western countries and, indeed, in the leading eastern industrial nation, Japan. The scramble to construct MIDAs has long since ceased, and the general reversal is as impressive as the earlier post-war colonization process. This new situation clearly offers the prospect of reprieve from further wetland loss, and is attributable to a variety of factors.

One is the rise of the environmental movement as an effective force. Viewed broadly, this has depended heavily on improved educational levels and on the role of the media – particularly television – in publicizing the importance of ecological issues. However, it has also required a weakening of the belief that the continued growth of heavy industry is central to Western prosperity, assisted by the emergence in society of groups and generations willing to question these firmly held assumptions. The Green movement in the Federal Republic of Germany, for example, is a minority force, yet it has been responsible for many successful challenges on physical planning issues.

While these are important general factors, however, it is arguable that the environmental movement has found particularly fertile ground in major port regions because of the concentration of heavy industries in them. Substantial populations have been subject to the impact of these industries, and willingness to accept that impact has decreased as the activities have become increasingly automated, significantly altering the balance between environmental costs and local economic benefits. As early as 1973, Stigter and Andreae were arguing that this balance had become so uneven that future growth should take place on man-made islands at sea, well away from cityport populations and estuarine and coastal environments. By 1979, many participants in a cityport industrialization conference were reporting significant environmental opposition to port development plans (Pinder and Hoyle 1981, p. 330). Subsequently Bird (1984, p. 31) has confirmed the importance of this trend by highlighting the recognition by port authorities of the power of the environmental movement. Naturally, environmental opposition is not simply geared to the protection of wetlands. In the case of Rotterdam, much of the effort centred on halting the Maasvlakte steelworks project because of a feared increase in air pollution (Pinder 1981, pp. 192–3). However, wetland protection may be a direct goal: the other dimension of resistance in Rotterdam concerned large-scale port expansion plans, including a proposal for even more extensive marine reclamation than that undertaken for the Maasvlakte. Moreover, whatever the focus of protest, wetland conservation is likely to benefit indirectly from any successful environmental movement which curtails the expansionist ambitions of a port.

Pressure on wetlands has also been alleviated by market forces. In some instances growth-pole development – the spatial concentration of linked activities – has been reasonably successful, as King (1977, p. 96) has documented in the case of Porto Torres. However, more frequently the impetus of planned growth poles, the heart of the MIDA concept, has proved far weaker than anticipated. This reflects over-estimation by port planners of the need, in the late twentieth century, for linked activities to agglomerate (Pinder and Hoyle 1981, pp. 331–2). Land created by port expansion programmes has therefore been consumed less rapidly than expected, so that the pressure for new expansion schemes, with almost inevitable wetland encroachment, has been reduced.

In addition to the relative failure of growth-pole projects, the major change in the world economic climate since the early 1970s has led to widespread reductions in the pace of industrial land consumption in ports. This partly reflects the global spread of manufacturing capacity, as in the shipbuilding and steel industries. However, it is also a consequence of recession initiated by the oil crisis of 1973–4 and intensified by the second crisis of 1979–80 (plate 8.5). In Europe the consequences of recession in terms of falling demand for additional, and largely coastal, industrial land were most evident in oil refining,

Plate 8.5 Part of the Sloehaven, Vlissingen, the Netherlands. Growth in this new port area, impressive in the late 1960s and early 1970s, ceased abruptly after the first oil crisis. Between the Total refinery (foreground) and the road around the port are large areas created for industry but never developed
(Courtesy Total Raffinaderij NV)

the industry that had previously underpinned port expansion. Between 1973 and 1976, Western European refining capacity rose by 16 per cent as companies completed installations that were under construction before the first oil crisis. Thereafter, expansion ceased abruptly and has subsequently shown no sign of recovery (Pinder and Husain 1987, p. 300; 1988, p. 233). Similarly, new refinery construction has ceased in both North America and Japan.

3.1 *From wetland to redundant space*

While this reversal has greatly reduced pressure on remaining wetlands, it has also meant that many Western countries now have stocks of former wetland that were converted into industrial zones in the late 1960s and early 1970s, but have subsequently stood idle. This was largely the fate of the Rotterdam Maasvlakte where environmental opposition led to complete cancellation of the steelworks project, except for the first phase of the power station. Part of the northern Maasvlakte became an oil storage site, while a terminal for dry-bulk cargoes was developed in the south. However, until the mid-1980s more than half the Maasvlakte lay totally unused. Wetland had given way to a sand desert and, despite current expansion of containerization in this part of the port, full usage of the site remains a distant prospect. Moreover, even in Rotterdam's Europoort zone, several square kilometres of land remain idle because companies have not fully developed their sites. At Fos, meanwhile, a third of the 70 km^2 site that was originally prepared lies unused (figure 8.2). Here the environments lost range from salt marshes through inland lagoons to a substantial coastal lagoon (the Etang de Gloria) and finally the coast itself. The one redeeming feature is that demand growth has been so slow that the second phase of the Fos project has not been undertaken. This has preserved almost 20 km^2 of marshes and salt pans lying inland from the first phase. Le Havre provides a similar less well recognized example. To support this port's designation as a development pole in northern France, a 20 km zone on the north shore of the Seine estuary was earmarked for industry (figure 8.3). A state-owned refinery, petrochemical plants, a cement works and a Renault factory have been attracted, yet these activities account for less than half the 60 km^2 of reclaimed wetland. Virtually all the undeveloped areas are those that, before construction of the zone, were well protected by their distance from Le Havre.

Two further examples demonstrate that the stock of unused industrial land that was formerly wetland may be boosted, at least locally, by other factors. First, de-industrialization is now leading to the release of land colonized in the post-war expansion era. Above all, this release is associated with the restructuring of oil refining and, to a lesser extent, the petrochemical industry (Pinder and Husain 1988). Part of the oil industry's strategy to deal with the crisis created in Western Europe by the second oil price shock was the closure of 24 coastal refineries (a fifth of the total) between 1979 and 1987. Most disinvestment affected at least some former wetland, and in a few instances this was true of the entire site. As was indicated earlier, BP's Isle of Grain refinery

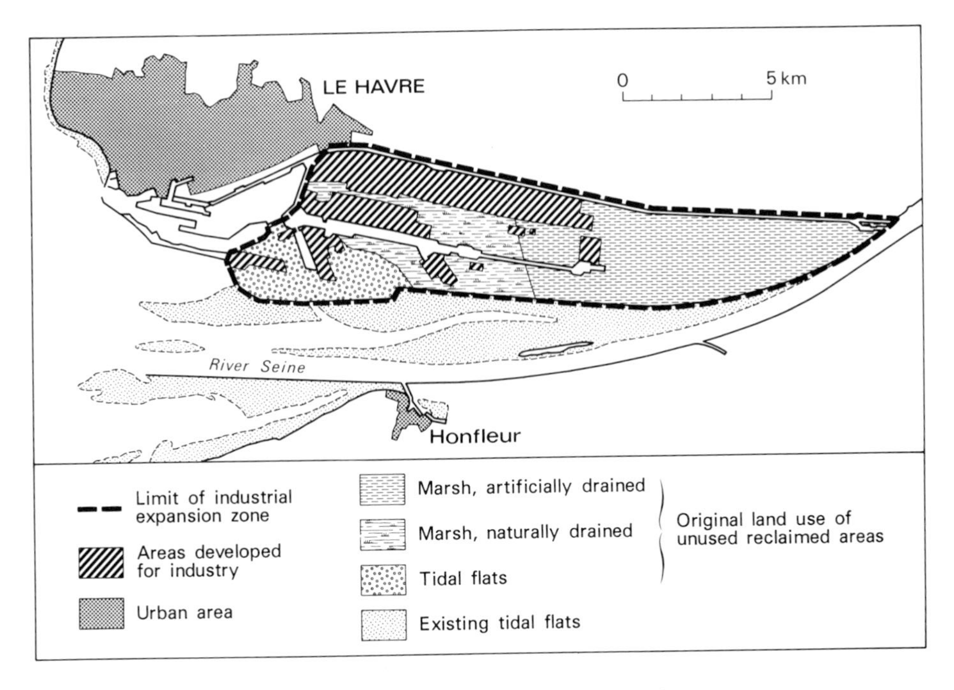

Figure 8.3 Redundant space in Le Havre's reclaimed industrial zone

was entirely developed on Grain Marsh. This is one of the largest closures made to date. At Frontignan the site extended over only 1 km^2 but was carved entirely from the Etang d'Ingril, immediately inland from the coast.

Secondly, wetlands have in some instances been regarded so poorly that they have been reclaimed as a matter of convenience, with no clear economic land use in mind. One such example is to be found in Southampton, where frequent dredging of the upper estuary, producing up to 500 000 m^3 of spoil a year, is necessary to maintain access for cruise liners and container ships. Dredged material is now dumped at sea, but between the early 1930s and the late 1970s it was used to fill salt marshes on the southwest side of the estuary (Coughlan 1979, p. 110). Although this occurred in connection with the construction of two power stations and expansion of the Fawley refinery, no specific plans existed for the largest site, Dibden Bay. Instead, for decades this area – larger than Southampton's central business district (CBD) and nineteenth-century docks combined – functioned as a low-cost disposal site, accounting for more than two-thirds of all salt marsh loss along the western side of the estuary. The implication that this zone was a convenient disposal facility, rather than a serious contender for port development, was greatly strengthened during the 1960s, when construction of a container terminal became necessary. This was built on the opposite side of the estuary, where all port expansion had previously taken place and where further reclamation almost on the scale of Dibden Bay was required. In the 1980s, one leisure-related development has at last been undertaken on the Dibden Bay site. Yet, more than half a century after this wetland's fate was sealed – quite literally – by the construction of an enclosing dam for the first phase of reclamation, no plans exist for more than 90 per cent of the area.

4.0 PRESSURE SUSTAINED

Despite the remarkable decrease in demand, with its associated accumulation of unused space, there are several reasons to think that the reprieve of wetlands should not be over-emphasized. Even without further reclamation, surviving wetlands are vulnerable to pollution from industrial effluents, and from fuel and cargo spillages from vessels. Data relating to these threats are very sparse, and there is a tendency to assume that the problem is largely confined to economically backward localities where the legislative regime is likely to be lax. For example, King (1977, p. 91) has highlighted the existence of such a situation in the vicinity of Cagliari where, even before a major expansion programme was implemented, lagoon-based fishing was banned because of the accumulation of noxious residues in catches. Yet recent investigations in the Netherlands, a country which now projects an image of strict environmental control, provide evidence that the pollution problem remains extensive. It has been estimated that 100 000 t of oil-contaminated residues and 275 000 t of chemical waste disappear in Rotterdam each year, much of it into local waters. Here is a clear threat to the environment of the tidal zone (Anon. 1986), a threat that is now becoming much more widely recognized. In 1989 Hamburg hosted a major international conference on the ecological impact of port pollution.

Pressure has also been maintained because pollution hazards in estuarine and coastal wetlands do not emanate simply from local industrial ports. Inland industrial areas, particularly the major concentrations of heavy industry, also impact on wetlands through riverine pollution. During the 1980s the severity of this problem has become more widely appreciated as analyses have been made of silt dredged from port access channels. Heavy metal deposits are commonly found, sometimes in concentrations far exceeding levels that would be permitted on land (Anon, 1985, de Ruiter 1985, van Horssen 1987). Clearly, pollution of this type has affected adjacent wetlands, and not simply the navigable channels. During the late 1980s, in fact, the suspicion has rapidly grown that general industrial and urban pollution has been responsible for a major decline in the largest mammals of the European marine wetlands, the grey and common seals. Mechanisms underlying this decline are still under investigation, but death is caused by viruses which the animals' immune systems cannot combat. It is known that persistent pollution lowers resistance and, since seals occupy the top of the marine food chain, it may well be that the problem is caused by the concentration of pollutants through that chain (Osterhaus and Vedder 1988).

Other pressures resulting from developments in locations remote from the affected wetlands can also be identified. Walker et al. (1987) in their study of coastal Louisiana have shown that, while natural pressures – including sea-level changes, compaction and catastrophic events – all contribute to wetland erosion, human activity inland in the Mississippi Basin has greatly reduced the volume of sediment available for wetland development in the delta. Channel 'improvement' projects, such as river diversion schemes and dam construction, are largely responsible for this decline. In the Atchafalaya Basin, through which 30 per cent of the Mississippi's water flows, the sediment load has fallen from over 400 million t per year in the early 1960s to little more than 250 million t per year in the late 1980s (chapter 10). Wetland loss in Louisiana is also the product of subsidence induced by human activity – water abstraction from aquifers to meet the needs of urban Louisiana – but in addition it is the consequence of long-term hydrocarbon extraction to satisfy national energy requirements. Wetland loss caused by hydrocarbon extraction is particularly associated with shallow reservoirs and has been recognized in the United States for several decades (Gilluly and Grant 1949).

Lastly, although Western countries have now ceased the pursuit of major port expansion schemes, less spectacular reclamation projects continue. Some are generated by the needs of industries that have long been responsible for wetland encroachment. Zeebrugge, for example, has recently completed reclamation on its North Sea foreshore, with one major purpose of this project being the construction of a terminal to import a highly dangerous source of energy, liquefied natural gas (Charlier 1984, pp. 432–4, 1987, p. 244). In other instances demand has come from less traditional sources, with the most significant port-based activity in this category being containerization. More and more small and medium-sized ports now feel the need for a container terminal, and even modest developments are likely to require at least some reclamation. The success of the UK port of Felixstowe in following this strategy highlights the attractions from the port authority's viewpoint. Also, its current scheme to sustain expansion by colonizing 45 ha of intertidal flats that are an important feeding ground for wintering wading birds and wildfowl, typifies the steady erosion of wetlands that is still occurring. Both these examples illustrate a major problem relating to the redundant-space issue. The outstanding concentrations of unused land are in large ports which in the growth era had the resources, or sufficient government backing, to undertake substantial reclamation projects, whereas much of the current demand comes from smaller ports. Thus the existence of port land available for development in one locality is no guarantee that wetlands elsewhere will not be threatened. This is particularly true when planning processes are made subservient to market forces, as increasingly happened during the 1980s.

5.0 URBANIZATION PRESSURES

Although port expansion and industrialization have exerted severe pressure on wetlands during much of the post-war period, they are but two of a range of developmental processes falling under the broad heading of urbanization which can affect wetlands. This also embraces major space consumers such as residential development, the urban infrastructure, commercial development and educational and health services. It has been estimated that some two-thirds of the world's population lives within 160 km of the sea (Clarke 1972, p. 16). The majority of the world's cities with populations exceeding 0.5 million are located along the coast, and 10 of the world's 15 largest cities occupy coastal, estuarine or lacustrine sites.

As with port development, wetland loss caused by urbanization has a long history. However, the pace of change has accelerated rapidly during the industrial era, and by the middle of this century cityports around the world were extensively regularizing adjacent shorelines to create urgently needed land. Creeks and tidal flats were prime targets in this expansionary process, as the case of New York graphically demonstrates (figure 8.4). This example also underlines the fact that, in contrast to port expansion and industrialization, the purposes for which new land was required were very varied. Strategically, this made the defence of wetlands particularly difficult since, to satisfy a range of demands, encroachment might simultaneously be proposed at several different locations, perhaps by several organizations or powerful branches of the city administration. Moreover, the types of activity for which land was required were, and still are, less sensitive than industry to changes in the economic climate. Thus pressure has, in most instances, been sustained in the economic crisis era as city authorities have sought to maintain the functional viability of the urban area.

Today the demands made by urbanization are particularly intense around the western rim of the Pacific basin where countries are confronted by complex pressures which force authorities towards solutions based on wetland reclamation. Therefore it is now appropriate to focus on this region, comparing the pressures and their consequences as experienced by three countries: Hong Kong, Japan and Singapore. Although there are basic differences between these countries, particularly between Japan and the other two as regards stage of development and size, they also have much in common. In all three, a potent mix of remarkable economic dynamism, considerable population growth and, above all else, an acute shortage of land suitable for large-scale development has fuelled a high rate of urbanization, generating an intense demand for the artificial creation of land.

5.1 *Post-war economic dynamism*

The economic miracle of Japan's recovery, from comprehensive defeat at the end of the Second World War to her ranking today as the free world's second most affluent economy, is well documented (e.g. Allen 1981, Uchino 1983). During the 'high-growth' phase from the early 1960s up to the 1973 oil shock, economic growth took place at a mean rate of 10 per cent per annum. Even in the subsequent 'low-growth' phase, Japan has maintained a growth rate of between 3 and 5 per cent per annum – a performance superior to that of most countries. Accommodating this rapid economic expansion has required

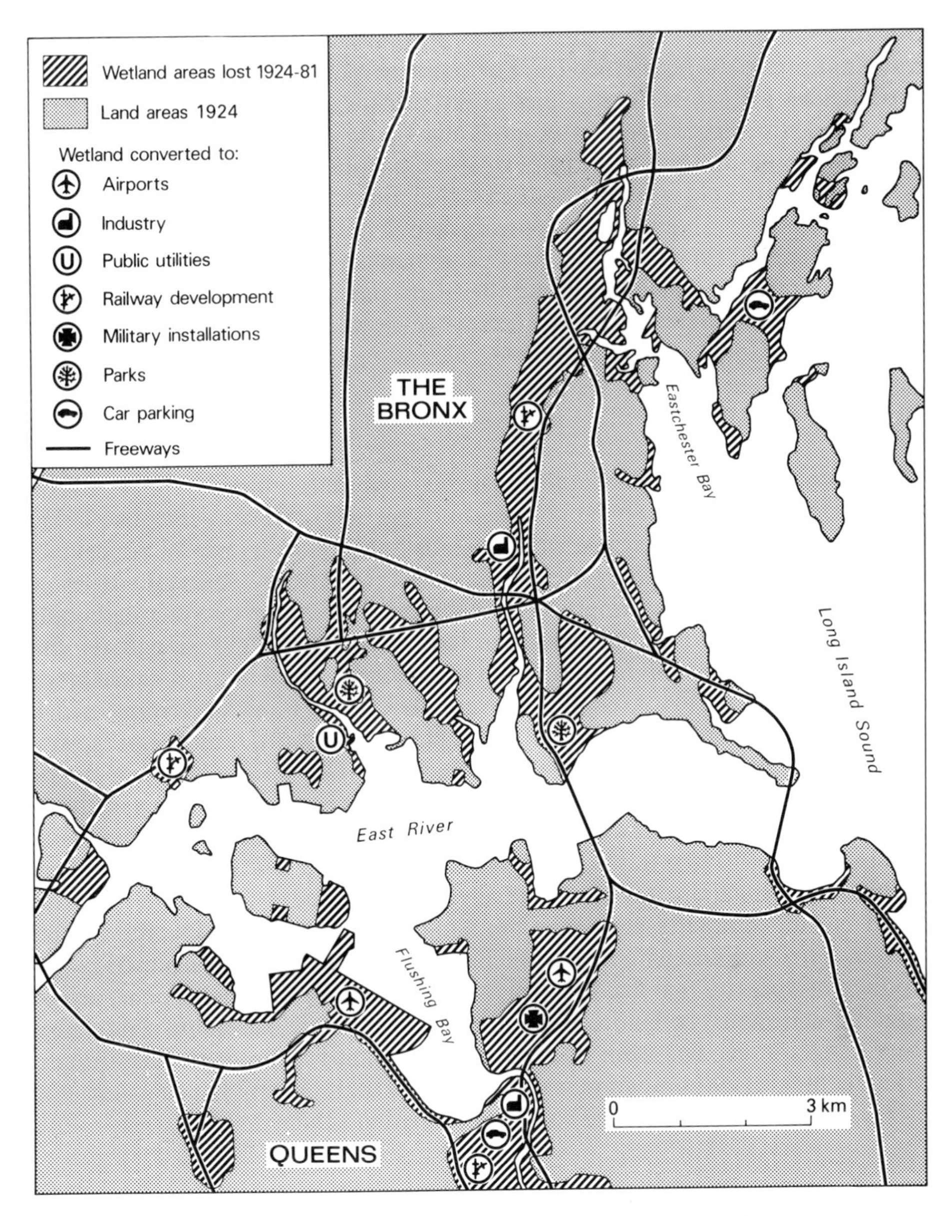

Figure 8.4 Urbanization pressure and wetland loss: New York, 1924–81

immense amounts of space but, as elsewhere, economic prosperity has also generated considerable personal affluence. This, in its turn, has raised consumer spending and aspirations, especially with regard to housing. This, too, has contributed significantly to the aggregate demand for urban space.

Hong Kong and Singapore, like Japan, can both claim to be devoid of natural resources, yet they too have enjoyed dramatic post-war economic growth. Since achieving independence in 1965, Singapore has maintained growth at a rate averaging about 10 per cent per annum, and now enjoys the third highest per capita income in Asia, after Brunei and Japan. Several indices similarly confirm the degree of Hong Kong's post-war economic success. For example, between 1970 and 1985 gross domestic product (GDP) increased more than twelvefold. In both countries, this has been accomplished largely by government-led strategies to encourage manufacturing and promote tourism and international financial services. This dynamism has, of course, had major space implications, as evidenced by the many prestigious office blocks, high-rise hotels and vast shopping complexes that now characterize the downtown areas of both Hong Kong and Singapore.

5.2 *Population growth and land resources*

Population growth has also made a major contribution to the overall need for space. In Japan's case, population has grown by nearly 50 per cent since 1951, to 121 million in 1985. Because mountainous terrain makes only 28 per cent of the land area suitable for settlement and development, population densities of 1000/km^2 and in places approach 10 000/km^2 are characteristic. Although absolute numbers are much smaller in both Hong Kong and Singapore, the rate of population growth has been even greater. Here total numbers have more than doubled since 1950, from 2 to 5.5 million in Hong Kong and from 1 to 2.5 million in Singapore. The average population density in Hong Kong is now 5175/km^2 compared with 4160/km^2 in Singapore; Hong Kong's higher figure reflects the more serious shortage of flat land. Hong Kong is almost exclusively upland, with about 80 per cent of the territory classified as 'undevelopable' (Bristow 1988, p. 170). In places, therefore, population densities are as high as 16 000/km^2. Singapore appears relatively well endowed, in the sense that the island is almost totally lowland. Yet Singaporians frequently refer to the existence of 'land hunger', which Buchanan (1972, p. 131) has claimed is the product of institutional factors, such as property speculation, poor urban planning and laxity in land-tax and land-development legislation. For many years, land hunger has been used as a justification for, among other things, reducing the rate of population growth, bulding high-density housing and, not least, embarking on expensive coastal reclamation schemes.

5.3 *Urbanization*

Since the Second World War Japan has experienced massive rural-urban migration, triggered by the parlous state of its agriculture, rapid industrialization and the changing perception of urban opportunities. This migration, combined with natural population increase, has greatly accelerated the rate and degree of urbanization. Today over 60 per cent of the Japanese live in cities with populations of over 100 000. Clearly, this urbanization has served to concentrate population and economic activity in the larger and more favoured lowlands. The result has been a ravenous demand for land in the coastal zone, and particularly in the vicinities of all the major cities. The impact of this growth on land prices in those cities has been immense. In 1986 alone, for example, land prices in Tokyo soared by just over 75 per cent. In this situation, land reclamation is not only a strategic necessity but also a financially attractive proposition. The pressures of urbanization have been no less acute in Hong Kong and Singapore. Today, both are essentially urban societies, possibly more so than even Japan. For example, just under 10 per cent of the Japanese labour force is still engaged in agriculture and fishing, compared with 2 per cent in Hong Kong and less than 1 per cent in Singapore.

6.0 WETLAND RECLAMATION: POTENTIAL AND TRENDS

Rapid wetland loss in Japan is not simply a reflection of the length of the coastline and the littoral location of development. The coastline is also highly indented, and most of the sheltered inlets and embayments contain lowland with a potentially vulnerable wetland fringe. Wetlands came under pressure as early as the feudal period (beginning in the ninth century), and there are few lowlands which have not been touched by reclamation. Traditionally, reclamation was undertaken mainly to extend the cultivated area, particularly for rice production. Usually it involved the drainage of marshes, ponds and lakes (Pezeu-Massabuau 1978, pp. 19–21), and the colonization of coastal lagoons such as Kojima Bay (Inland Sea) and Nakanoumi on the Japan Sea coast (Ohtake 1984). However, since 1945, urban pressures have fundamentally changed both the causes and the scale of wetland loss, especially in the megalopolitan corridor which stretches along the Pacific coastlands of Honshu, westwards from Tokyo, and spills over into northern Kyushu. Within this corridor, which now accommodates over 65 per cent of Japan's urban population, there has been a wholesale resort to wetland reclamation to meet the space requirements of late-twentieth-century society.

Nowhere is this more true than around the shores of Tokyo Bay. The need here has been to provide additional space for the capital itself and for the other sizeable cities that together make up the Tokyo metropolitan area, a complex of some 20 million people (Witherick 1981). These include Yokohama (the second-largest city in Japan), Kawasaki and Chiba. Figure 8.5 indicates the degree to which the original shoreline has been altered and the amount of land that has been created. Although what is represented here is the accumulation of centuries of land reclamation work, early reclamation, including that stimulated by the Meiji Restoration of 1868 which initiated industrialization and reaffirmed Tokyo as the capital, has been dwarfed by post-war schemes (plate 8.6). Initially, port-based industrialization of the type discussed in the European context was fundamental to post-war wetland encroachment. Reclamation for heavy industry occurred close to Tokyo, Kawasaki and Yokohama, but also extended along a new urban limb reaching round the eastern shores of Tokyo Bay from Narashino to Chiba and on towards Kisarazu. As the New York example and the discussion of pressures have implied, however, the purposes

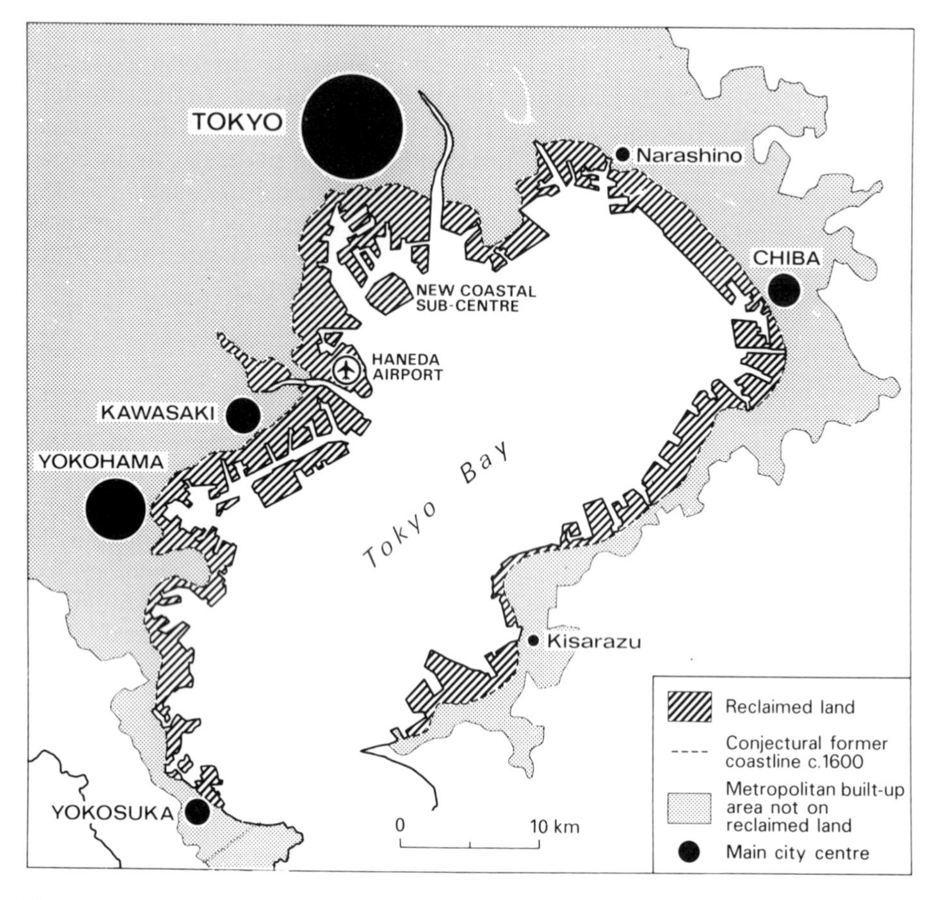

Figure 8.5 Coastal reclamation around Tokyo Bay

for which wetlands were consumed inexorably became more diverse. We shall return to this point later.

The Hong Kong coastline, like that of Japan, is indented but there is a virtual absence of coastal lowlands of any extent. Consequently, the need to reclaim land from the limited intertidal zone and from the sea was recognized from the very beginning of British settlement in 1841 (Hudson 1979). Reclamation has concentrated around the shores of Victoria Harbour (figure 8.6), and tended initially to involve the infilling of small inlets. Since 1945, however, it has extended to more exposed sections of the intertidal zone and more than 25 per cent of the land now in urban use around the Harbour has been won from the sea. Here it may be noted that even more reclamation would have been necessary, but for the extensive quarrying of hills to create terraces for urban growth, with the quarried material being used as landfill for marine reclamation.

In Singapore the range of wetlands exposed to development in the twentieth century has been particularly great. The coastline was broken by a number of

Plate 8.6 Harumi-futo (pier), one of the six islands reclaimed for port and office construction from the western shores of Tokyo Bay, about 3 km north of Haneda airport, under the Takehiba, Hinode and Shibaura and Okawataba redevelopment projects. Nearly all the land visible in this photograph is reclaimed from the Bay
(Courtesy Japanese Information Centre, London)

Plate 8.7 New urban development on reclaimed land in Singapore City: the Marina Bay Project
(Courtesy Singapore Tourist Bureau)

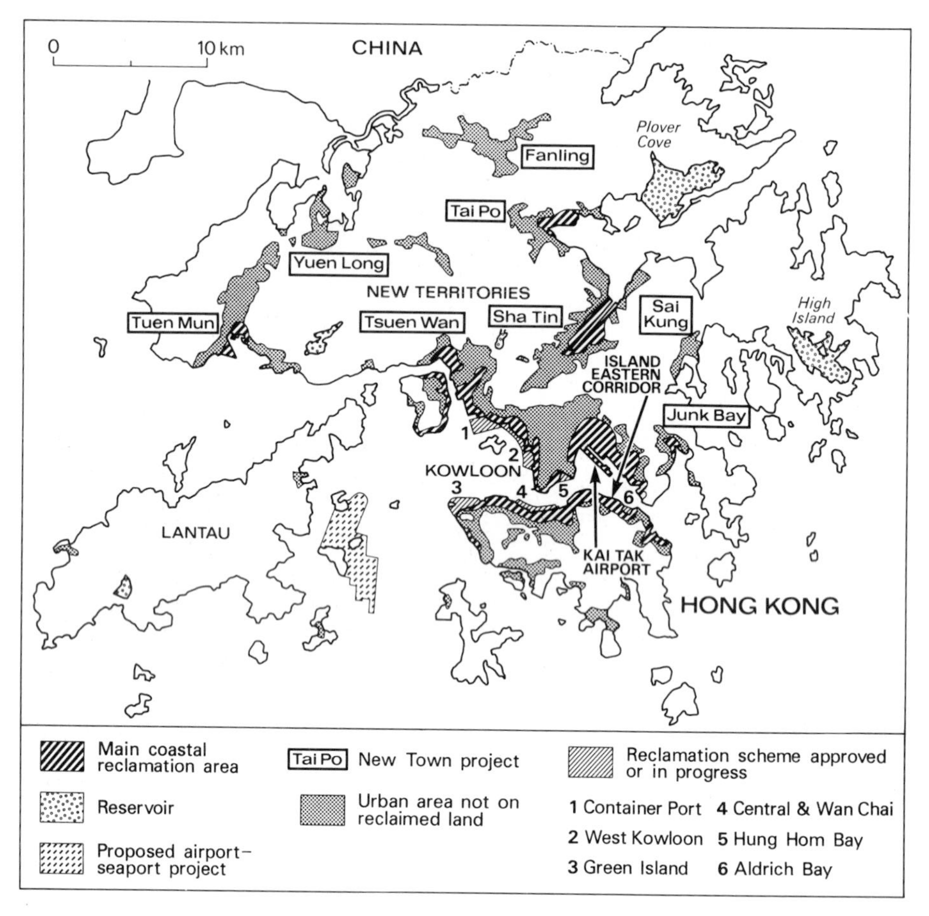

Figure 8.6 Hong Kong: urbanization pressures and wetland loss

estuaries (notably those of the Singapore, Kallang, Jurong and Kranji rivers) which, particularly in the northeast and the northwest, offered large sheltered intertidal zones and fostered the growth of mangrove swamps. Mangroves were also prominent along the broad concave sweeps of the southeastern and southwestern coastlines, where the intertidal margins and coastal shallows were also extensive. As in Hong Kong, wetland encroachment focused initially in the vicinity of the main urban area of Singapore City (plates 8.7 and 8.8). Prior to Independence in 1965, reclamation here was primarily aimed at displacing the port's shoreline towards deeper water, providing new docks, and draining and infilling swampy areas both for health reasons and for construction purposes (Vreeland 1977). Since Independence, economic impetus and institutional factors have brought about an abrupt shift to large-scale wetland reclamation projects. Over 50 km^2 of land has been reclaimed from the sea, most of it from the intertidal zone (figure 8.7), spreading the impact of encroachment from Singapore City around much of the island's coastal zone.

Plate 8.8 Changi International Airport in the course of construction on land reclaimed from mangrove swamps on the northeast shore of Singapore Island
(Courtesy Department of Civil Aviation and Public Works Department, Singapore)

One final background observation is necessary concerning the institutional arrangements that exist in these countries for the planning, commissioning and implementation of land reclamation. All three countries are frequently held to be leading examples of free-market non-interventionist economies, yet analysis of the land-reclamation process in Hong Kong and Japan reveals an interesting blend of public and private enterprise. What is equally clear is that the partnership is uneven, with the public sector rather more prominent. In Japan the responsibility is dominantly at the prefectural level, but the Ministry of Construction maintains a national overview. In Hong Kong control is centralized in the Lands and Works Branch and, in both countries and in varying degrees, construction is mainly left to the private sector. However, land reclamation in Singapore is now entirely a public sector matter, with the Housing and Development Board involved at all stages from planning through to completion (Yeung 1973). In practice, the emphasis given in these countries to assisting market forces, and the facilitating role adopted by the public sector,

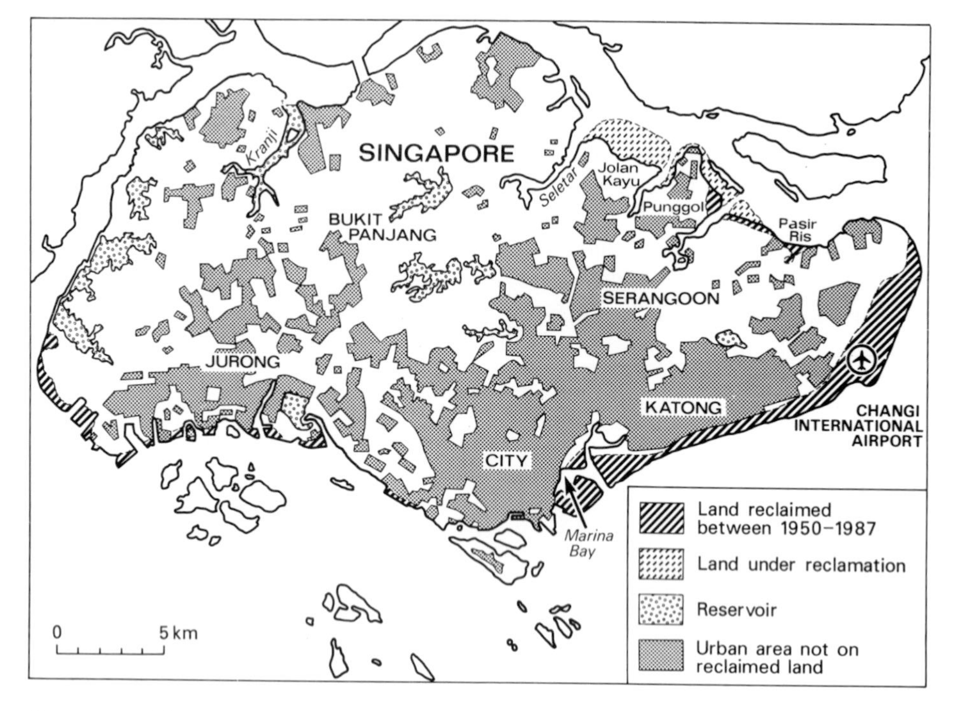

Figure 8.7 Singapore: urbanization pressures and wetland loss

have combined with the pressures outlined earlier to keep wetland protection well down the political agenda.

7.0 OUTCOMES

Quite apart from Western-style port expansion and industrialization schemes, wetlands in the Asian world region have been converted to an impressive range of uses. A major long-term reclamation project currently being undertaken within the Port of Tokyo, close to the commercial centre of the capital, demonstrates well the multifaceted nature of urbanization pressures. Launched in 1961, it has not lost momentum during the 'low-growth' phase, and so far it has involved the reclamation of some 2440 ha of land. The planned allocation of this land is particularly noteworthy, with 29 per cent set aside for terminal, port-related and distribution facilities, 24 per cent for the improvement of urban transport systems, 25 per cent for residential development and related urban facilities, and 22 per cent for commercial and cultural facilities and public open space (*Tokyo Municipal News* 1982).

The economics of civil engineering, which often make it cheaper to build upwards then encroach on wetlands, and the compatibility of central businesses and vertical development have generally served to protect wetlands from CBD expansion. None the less, commerce around Tokyo Bay has recently begun to motivate reclamation, and in both Hong Kong and Singapore the process is more deeply rooted. Here, medium-scale reclamations have occurred at various times in the post-war period to increase CBD capacity and facilitate the construction of luxury international hotels. Perhaps the most impressive development resulting from CBD pressure is the concentration of shopping complexes and hotels on the reclaimed fringe of the Tsim Sha Tsui district of Kowloon. Less striking, but equally noteworthy from the viewpoint of wetland loss, are Hong Kong's large wholesale markets located along the waterfront on both sides of the Harbour (figure 8.6).

Much wetland reclamation has also been undertaken because of the basic need to provide residential space to accommodate the population pressures noted earlier. This is certainly true of Hong Kong, where residential development has been a major occupier of reclaimed land. Most of the so-called new towns – notably Tsuen Wan, Sha Tin, Tuen Mun, Junk Bay and Sai Kung – have been, or will be, constructed largely on reclaimed land (figure 8.6). These are part of the government's policy of providing affordable and adequate housing, in this case for some 2.7 million people. Recently, five new reclamation areas (Aldrich Bay, Hung Hom Bay, West Kowloon, Central and Wan Chai, and Green Island) have been identified to supply some 630 ha of land for urban growth in the 1990s. It is intended to provide housing for nearly half a million more people, thereby maintaining residential development as a major outcome of wetland reclamation.

Whilst individual housing projects have involved encroachment on relatively small areas of foreshore around Tokyo Bay, collectively their numbers have made housing a conspicuous land use around the modified shoreline. Despite the ecological loss, these projects have played a major part in helping to improve the housing situation in metropolitan Tokyo. The Japan Housing Corporation has been particularly active in this regard (Witherick 1972). With schemes launched during the 1960s, such as that at Sodegaura (built on 112 ha of reclaimed land and housing some 15 000 people), the Corporation has pioneered the way to better housing and a better residential environment for millions of suburbanites throughout Japan (Witherick 1981). Ecological loss has therefore run parallel with social gain. But whilst there is much to be said in favour of these housing projects built on reclaimed land, costs and hazards have been incurred that are additional to ecological loss. For example, because land reclamation is expensive, there has been no significant reduction of the site-cost element in house construction. Secondly, Tokyo Bay is located on an active part of the earth's crust, and during more vigorous earthquakes the load-bearing capacities of reclaimed sands, clays and silts are significantly reduced. This is a worrying hazard, especially when blocks of flats have been built on such land. To make the situation worse, there is the additional hazard associated with the vulnerabiity of these low-lying areas to the 'tsunamis' generated by earthquakes and to the tidal waves whipped up by summer typhoons. Yet another cost, but of a rather different character, arises from the fact that wetlands must be reclaimed where they are available, and their coastal location pattern has not brought about a rational juxtaposition of new residential areas and employment centres. Most of the workers living in these schemes are forced to suffer the physical rigours of commuting into central city areas and, if anything, the schemes around Tokyo Bay have merely accentuated the spatial dislocation of workplace and residence.

This last indictment also holds true for many of the renowned housing estates and new town projects undertaken by the Singapore Housing and Development Board. Here, however, only two of the major schemes have involved encroachment on the intertidal zone. The remainder are located away from the coast, and wetland reclamation as such has been confined to the draining of small swampy areas.

Infrastructure is also a widespread consumer of wetland in rapidly expanding cityports. To a degree, infrastructure investment requires the construction of facilities such as sewage treatment plants, and shoreline locations are frequently convenient for these. However, investment of this type is only one aspect of the urban infrastructure likely to affect the wetland zone. Transport is an even more conspicuous user. Quite apart from seaport development, new expressways commonly exploit the open passages provided by fringes of reclaimed land, as Hong Kong Island's impressive Eastern Corridor, running to the east of downtown Victoria, and Singapore's East Coast Parkway both well exemplify. Here, as elsewhere, roads parallel to the present waterfront represent former shorelines, to which have been added successive stages of reclamation.

Airports may consume even larger extents of wetland. Both Hong Kong and Singapore have modern international airports which have involved major wetland reclamations. Hong Kong's busy Kai Tak Airport (annual throughput of over a million passengers and 520 000 t of general cargo) has its main runway built on a finger of reclaimed land extending some 3 km into the Harbour (figure 8.6). Singapore's Changi International Airport, opened in 1981, involved a huge coastal reclamation of some 12 km^2 at the eastern end of the island (figure 8.7 and plate 8.8). In the case of Tokyo Bay, Tokyo's first airport at Haneda has become the hub of domestic air traffic (Kikuta 1985). Over the last 10 years, the growth of this traffic has been such as to require extension of the airport onto 870 ha of newly created land. Here, the official view is that an important advantage to be set against the ecological loss is that the project will allow the operational area of the airport to be shifted to the west and away from adjoining residential development. Two of the three new runways will also allow aircraft to take off and land over water, improving both safety and noise pollution. A final advantage quoted is that reclamation has provided a useful outlet for Tokyo's solid waste. In this connection, however, it is pertinent to question whether seepage pollution has been effectively prevented (Sivalingham 1984).

Another major dimension of urban infrastructure is water supply. Although as yet this is not a conspicuous wetland consumer in Tokyo Bay, it has been critical in Singapore. Here the demands of a growing population and the need to remove the strategic vulnerability of being almost wholly dependent upon

Malaysia for water have prompted schemes of central interest in the present context. Wetland encroachment began with reservoirs created on the island itself in low-lying areas formerly occupied by swamps (figure 8.7). However, these have been unable to cope with demand and, because the topography offers very few opportunitues to create further inland reservoirs, attention has focused firmly on former tidal and mangrove-filled inlets. Along the northwest coast, coastal dykes have sealed off four freshwater reservoirs covering a total area of approximately 10 km^2. Similarly in the north, the Kranji River has been dammed at its mouth, drowning an extensive area of fluvial wetland. Recently, work has started on reclaiming 276 ha of swampland and foreshore on the northeast coast, near Pasir Ris and Punggol. This will be extended towards Jalan Kayu by another 685 ha and may well lead to closure of the deep inlet at Seletar to form another freshwater reservoir.

In Hong Kong, the uplands of the New Territories have permitted the construction of several valley reservoirs (of which High Island is by far the largest), yet here also the wetlands have not escaped attention, particularly at Plover Cove (figure 8.6). Here a barrier running from the mainland to Harbour Island has sealed a large area of Tolo Harbour; seawater has given way to freshwater and the tidal margin has been lost. Clearly, the provision of this type of infrastructure constitutes an unusual form of wetland encroachment in that it has not involved reclamation *per se*, yet the ecological impact is none the less far-reaching.

Lastly with respect to infrastructure, growing leisure-oriented demand is now consuming wetland, even though in all three countries the work ethic remains strong. Rising levels of personal affluence and the impact of Western mass media have no doubt contributed to this trend. The economics of formal recreation are such that reclamation undertaken solely for this purpose has been limited to date, but recent developments in Singapore suggest that this may be changing. Land has been reclaimed on either side of the entrance to the Singapore River to create Marina Bay, and the marina's infrastructure is currently under construction on the larger reclamation (approximately 2 km^2) on the south side (figure 8.7 and plate 8.7). A little further east, the National Stadium and a complex of leisure and amusement facilities have been built on reclaimed land. With the emergence of this trend, it is interesting to speculate how long it will be before the golf-addicted Japanese construct golf-courses on former wetland areas. Certainly, it is easy to see the potential conflict in wetland environments between formal and informal recreation, with the former cast in the role of a force for encroachment and the latter (walking, birdwatching etc.) favouring conservation.

7.1 *From shore to offshore*

Since 1973 approximately 24 km^2 of wetland have been reclaimed in Hong Kong and 33 km^2 in Singapore, while both countries have large projects in progress. In Japan momentum has been similarly maintained as urban demand has replaced industrial pressure since the early 1970s. Linked with this trend, there has emerged a shift towards schemes that do not simply involve seaward displacement of the shoreline. In Japan, in particular, offshore islands have been built, not on tidal mud flats, but in the shallow waters of Tokyo Bay (plate 8.6).

A good example of this new generation of reclamation activity is provided by a scheme launched in 1987 by the Tokyo Metropolitan Government. The intention is to build a new subcentre for Tokyo (one of seven) on a 440 ha man-made island (*Tokyo Municipal News* 1987). This proposal is part of Tokyo's Second Long-term Plan, the principal objective of which is to restructure Tokyo from a 'single-core' to a 'multi-core' city and to achieve a proper locational balance between workplaces and housing. It is planned that 115 000 people will work there and that there will be housing for 44 000 people. The plans include the provision of business facilities (such as a Teleport, a convention centre and an international exhibition hall) and cultural and recreational facilities, as well as housing. This plan illustrates very effectively the varied demands placed on wetlands by urbanization pressures. The Teleport project is also interesting in that it is intended to enhance Tokyo's attractiveness as a financial centre, and this may generate further land-use pressures. It will have a total floor area of 340 ha and will be equipped to handle the latest telecommunications systems, including a satellite communications base. A conspicuous cost element in the first phase of the island's development will be the construction of a bridge to carry road and rail links, and it is interesting to speculate how long it will be before further reclamation welds this project to downtown Tokyo by reclamation of the intervening shallows. What may also be noted is that the concept of 'island' reclamations is now spreading from Japan to other countries. Outstanding in this respect is the recent private-sector proposal in Hong Kong to build a vast new airport-seaport complex off Peng Chau on some 10 km^2 of reclaimed land (figure 8.6). This proposal has been precipitated by the increasing recognition that Kai Tak Airport's days are numbered because of its lack of capacity to cope with continually rising air traffic, but also because of its high environmental costs and questionable safety.

7.2 *Outcomes in retrospect*

Because wetland reclamation generated by urbanization has been impressively dynamic and diverse in terms of outcomes, it is helpful to conclude this section with a synthesis. A threefold classification scheme, based on the general relationship of the new land uses to the established uses of the old land, can be proposed. This scheme cuts across the conventional land-use categories. *Expansion* reclamations are those where the established land uses have need of more space and simply extend onto the new land, maintaining their dominance of zones from which colonization occurs. Although they are by no means exclusively of this type, many of the reclamation projects around Tokyo Bay fall into this category. In contrast, *clean-break* reclamations are those where developments on the new land constitute a complete departure from surrounding established land uses, as happens when a new through route, power station or reservoir is constructed along a hitherto undeveloped stretch of shoreline. As a type, they are well exemplified in Singapore where, because of the prevalence of lowland, substantial sections of the coastal fringe remained available for development in the post-war period. Thirdly, there are *remedial* reclamations, where wetlands are consumed to provide detached overspill space for the amelioration of particularly severe problems, such as slum housing or a congested obtrusive airport. *Remedial* reclamations may be variations on the *expansion* and *clean-break* themes, but pressure may well mean that they are physically separate from the mainland. In Japan and Hong Kong, certainly, they are closely associated with offshore reclamations developed in response to the immense difficulties of extending the existing built-up area to provide *in situ* solutions for congestion problems.

8.0 CONCLUSIONS

In this survey we have explored the nature of the industrialization and urbanization pressures that have led to recent wetland loss, and we have also sought to demonstrate the power of these pressures. It is evident that, in some instances, this power has not been consistent through time. Coastal industrialization and major port development have both waned since the early 1970s under the combined influence of economic crisis and the rise of the environmental movement. Yet the cancellation of spectacular port-industrialization projects cannot be interpreted as the dawn of a new era in which industrial and urban threats to wetlands have sunk to minimal levels. Urbanization forces have not weakened in harmony with the industrial downturn, and wetland loss caused by these forces in countries such as Japan, Hong Kong and Singapore is commonly replicated, sometimes less intensively, around the world (e.g. Bombay, Boston, San Francisco, Sydney, Tunis). Redundant space resulting from the over-optimistic expansion of major port areas will eventually be consumed, resulting in further demands for physical growth. In the meantime, numerous relatively unspectacular development schemes are extending the pattern of wetland decline by eroding wetlands around many small and medium-sized ports. Such schemes may generate local environmental opposition, but controversy surrounding them is often insufficient to provide an effective platform for wetland defence. Moreover, it is arguable that, in the recent economic crisis era, the environmental movement has found it increasingly difficult to protect wetlands affected by relatively modest port, industrial and urban development proposals. Unless large areas are involved, it is all too easy for developers to present wetland loss as a minor penalty to be paid for economic and socio-economic gain. In countries where economic, social and physical pressures are particularly severe, even major wetlands are difficult to defend in the light of the socio-economic gain argument.

Today, therefore, the issue to be faced is that of how wetland protection can be made more effective in the face of continuing societal pressures. Far less imbalance in the struggle between protection and economic development is essential if this goal is to be achieved. Three avenues leading towards a reduction of this imbalance can be proposed. Much can be gained from the systematic analysis of past defensive battles. How have successful protection campaigns been mounted? What have been the characteristic features of failed campaigns? Is there evidence that the ingredients for success have changed with time? It is also necessary to promote considerably greater awareness of the ecological value of wetlands. In most economically advanced countries, public opinion may now be environmentally aware in a general sense, yet it cannot be claimed that wetlands are typically perceived to be high-value habitats. Without this perception, achieving influence over the political decision-makers who control development will inevitably remain an uphill task. Lastly, the protection movement requires much more evidence relating to the ecological value of threatened wetlands and to the nature and extent of wetland decline. Much is known about causes and processes but, as Walker et al. (1987, p. 199) have stressed in the context of coastal Louisiana, the systematic quantification of the effects of industrial and urban development is in its infancy. So, too, is comprehensive evaluation, which could do much to concentrate protection efforts on areas of particular ecological significance. Although the scale of the quantification and evaluation that is required is immense, in the era of remote sensing it is increasingly within our grasp, and such scientifically generated evidence has the potential to add great strength to the protectionist cause.

9

Recreation and Wetlands: Impacts, Conflict and Policy Issues

David C. Mercer

1.0 INTRODUCTION: THREE CASE STUDIES

In this chapter we explore a number of themes concerning the relationship between wetlands and recreation and tourism. In view of the fact that the pressures for physical change being addressed here are merely representative of the more general 'preservation-development' conflict over wetland 'futures', at the outset the problems and complexities surrounding the precise definition of 'recreation' will be sidestepped. Instead, by way of introduction to the discussion which follows, three brief case studies are presented for initial consideration.

1.1 *The Amberley Wildbrooks, United Kingdom*

Between the two small towns of Arundel and Pulborough in Sussex, in the south of England, lies 400 ha of low-lying pasture land known as the Amberley Wildbrooks. Formerly a lake, the region is now principally used as grazing land for dairy cattle in the summer months, but is usually waterlogged in the winter (figure 9.1). An intricate arrangement of drainage channels and brooks intersects the meadows. As elsewhere in Britain, these serve as an important haven for a rich variety of birds, butterflies, flowers and grasses with which this area is especially well endowed. One of the last remaining natural peat bogs in southeast England is located within the Wildbrooks and there are also some particularly important remnant swamp woodlands in the district. This small area, and others like it, is of special significance given that about 5×10^6 ha of wetlands had been drained in England and Wales by 1939, a far higher rate of

The author wishes to acknowledge the assistance of the following people in drawing his attention to relevant literature during the preparation of this chapter: C. L. and D. E. Mercer of Prestbury, Gloucestershire, Professor G. Wall, Department of Geography, University of Waterloo, Ontario, Canada.

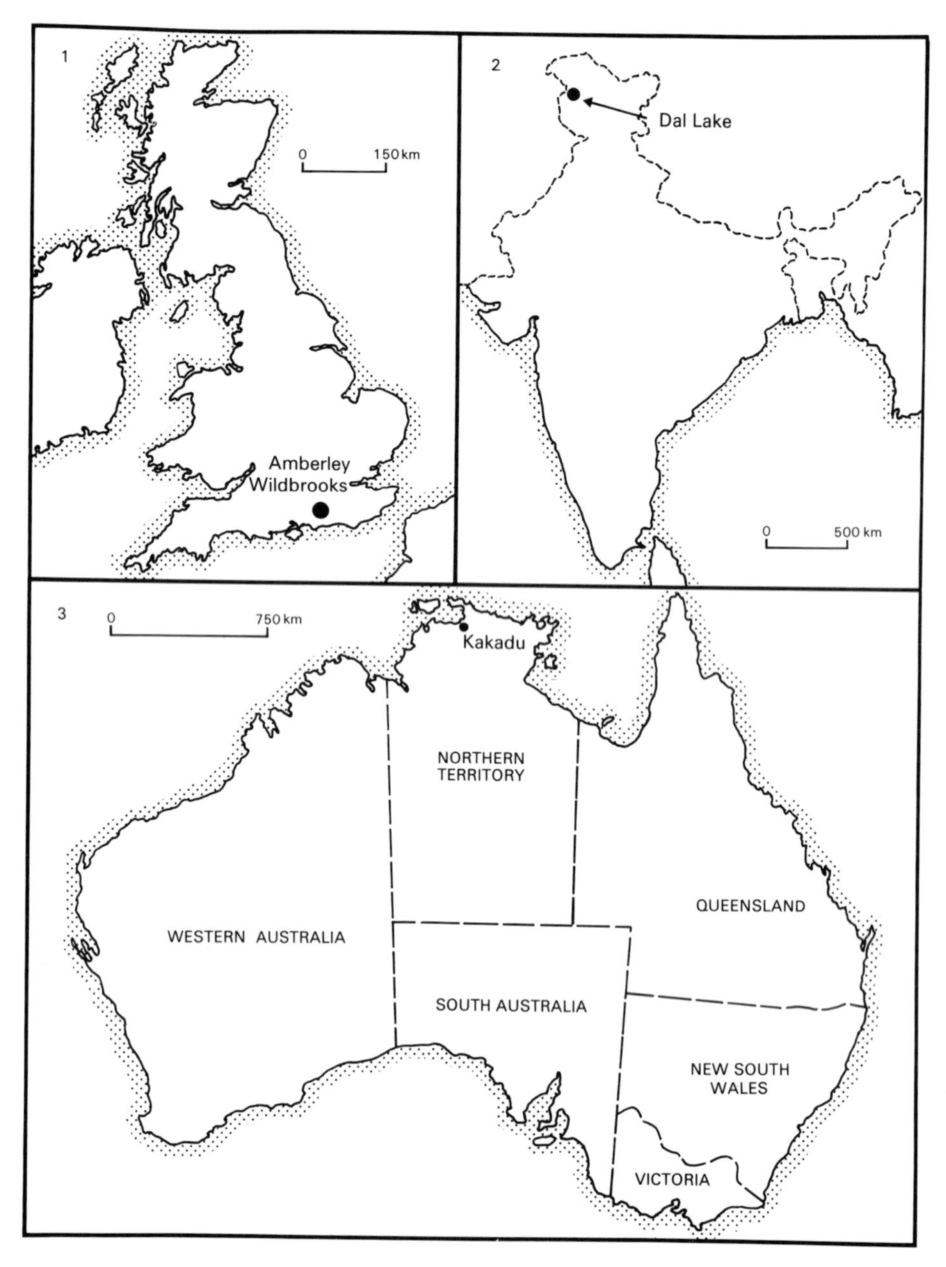

Figure 9.1 Location of the three case studies: 1, Amberley Wildbrooks, United Kingdom; 2, Dal Lake, Kashmir; 3, Kakadu National Park, Northern Territory, Australia

depletion of the original wetlands than has occurred in North America, for example (Nelson 1986, Parcells 1988).

In 1978 the Wildbrooks were the focus of a bitter dispute which centred around conflicting uses and values of the meadowlands. On the one hand a small group of farmers wished to install powerful electric pumps to reduce the water level further, extend the seasonal use of their operations and thereby raise agricultural productivity. To this end, through the Southern Water Authority, they petitioned the Ministry of Agriculture, Fisheries and Food (MAFF) for a £340 000 grant. However, this plan was vigorously opposed by the local Amberley residents, supported and encouraged by the Council for the Protection of Rural England, the Royal Society for the Protection of Birds and the Nature Conservancy Council, backed by financial assistance from all over Britain as well as from as far afield as New Zealand, Central America and Hong Kong. The opposition group argued vigorously in favour of the amenity values of the Wildbrooks, asserting that these would be irrevocably destroyed if the proposed pumping scheme were allowed to proceed. Shoard (1980, p. 94) notes that

> The villagers . . . no longer depend on the Wildbrooks as they once did for reeds to make baskets and to thatch roofs, for cranberries for food and peat for fuel. But local people still use the Wildbrooks for a host of activities that matter to them: birdwatching, tadpoling, or an evening stroll, for example.

The Amberley residents eventually succeeded in forcing a public enquiry to resolve the issue. Evidence was heard in March 1978, and in July of that year, upon a recommendation from the inspector, the then Minister of Agriculture – John Silkin – ordered that the grant should not be offered. Amenity considerations were a major factor in the inspector's final recommendation, which in the final analysis drew heavily on the evidence presented by an expert economic witness, Mr John Bowers. Bowers calculated that the scheme would not be cost effective. He also pointed out that while the benefits would accrue to a mere handful of individuals, the costs ultimately would have to be borne by a much larger group.

From the environmentalist standpoint the outcome of this particular controversy was fairly satisfactory. Yet in many ways the Amberley Wildbrooks decision went well against the tide of post-war wetland destruction in Britain (chapter 11). A 1983 report of the Nature Conservancy Council, for example, documented what Rose (1986, p. 73) uncompromisingly called '36 years of failure' in terms of habitat preservation in Britain. This included the loss of an estimated 50 per cent of lowland fens, valley and basin mires, 60 per cent of lowland 'raised mires' and 30 per cent of upland grasslands, heaths and blanket bogs. Much of the blame for this sad environmental record clearly has to be apportioned to the peculiar legislative and administrative separation of agriculture, wildlife and landscape protection in the United Kingdom.

1.2 *Kakadu National Park, Northern Territory, Australia*

Kakadu National Park lies 250 km east of Darwin in northern Australia. The first stage of this park – an area of 6144 km^2 – was proclaimed in 1979. An additional 7000 km^2 was added in 1984 and the park now has an area of about 20 000 km^2. Internationally, the reserve is of outstanding ecological significance (Braithwaite and Werner 1987). Loss and disturbance of native species have been minimal and there are very few alien plants and animals. Nearly 250 bird species – or one-third of Australia's total – have been recorded at Kakadu, as well as 1000 plant species, 5000 insects, 75 reptiles and 50 mammals. The area is the first point of arrival in Australia for many migrating birds from the north, and it also forms a dry season refuge for several important bird species (plate 9.1). The dry seasons of 1983 and 1984, for example, saw over 2 million magpie geese at Kakadu (Skeat 1986). A large proportion of the park consists of an extensive wetland ecosystem centred on the flood plains of the South and West Alligator Rivers. Three main wetland landscapes can be identified: tidal flats, flood plains and coastal swamps. Together, they total almost 3000 km^2 of seasonally or permanently inundated lowlands which, *inter alia*, contain all but eight of Australia's 29 mangrove species. In 1980 these vast coastal wetlands were listed formally according to the conditions of the Convention on Wetlands of International Importance. In the following year the entire park became the first Australian site to be accepted for listing as a World Heritage Property under the terms of the World Heritage Convention.

Plate 9.1 Yellow Water, Kakadu National Park, Northern Territory, Australia (Courtesy D. Mercer)

Kakadu National Park is also unique in another respect. It has been totally owned by Aborigines since its proclamation in 1979. However, the area is jointly managed by the Australian National Parks and Wildlife Service to whom the park has been leased for a century. It is of immeasurable spiritual significance to the Aborigines who have had associations with the region for at least 25 000 years. Indigenous Australians are now returning to Kakadu in growing numbers, and are increasingly asserting their rights to live traditional life styles based around subsistence hunting, fishing and foraging. However, this is happening at the same time as a major tourist explosion is occurring at Kakadu.

The park currently attracts about 200 000 domestic and international tourists a year, the majority of whom visit in the 6 month dry season, between May and October. Visitor numbers are growing at the rate of around 50 per cent annually. Inevitably, such a spectacular growth rate is creating pressing management problems. The natural environment is under pressure from a growing army of campers, caravanners, coach parties and four-wheel drive vehicle enthusiasts, and local hunters from Darwin and Jabiru are increasingly competing with traditional Aborigines for fish and wildlife resources. Skeat (1986) reports that amateur fishing can be extremely intense, with five Kakadu rivers yielding a reported 80–85 t of barramundi in one year. Yet, whereas hunting and fishing for white Territorian residents are patently 'sporting activities', for Aborigines these pursuits have a quite different function and are approached very differently (Meehan 1988). Over thousands of generations, in common with other native peoples living in harsh environments, the Aborigines have learned to 'manage' their environment in a highly sophisticated caring manner. They embrace a spiritual concept of 'stewardship' toward their land, water and wildlife resources which is often totally at variance with the exploitative attitudes of European tourists. Kesteven (1986, p. 2) recently summarized the general Aboriginal reaction to tourists at Kakadu as follows:

> . . . bad news. 'Tourists' wandered aimlessly, got lost and had to be rescued; they got themselves into trouble by tempting crocodiles; they transgressed on sacred sites or burial areas; even worse, they sometimes stole relics or vandalised sites. They over-fished, they couldn't be trusted with rifles . . . Tourists have no commitment to the people of Kakadu or to the land.

As yet, the tensions between Aborigines and tourists have not reached what might be termed 'crisis' proportions, but if visitor numbers continue to escalate at their present rate, the ecology of the unique tropical wetlands, so important to Kakadu's traditional owners, could become seriously overtaxed. In the meantime some badly stressed areas have already been closed to recreational fishing, a wetland margin road has been constructed, and three major campgrounds and associated facilities have been positioned in such a way as to minimize damage to the fragile wetland ecosystems. The danger period will begin soon when Darwin airport becomes upgraded to accept large inter-continental passenger aircraft that will disgorge thousands of tourists.

1.3 *Dal Lake, Kashmir*

Dal Lake is situated in the centre of Srinagar, high in the heart of the celebrated Vale of Kashmir. Its peaceful waters, backed by hills clothed with orchards, willows and poplars, have made the site one of the most popular and highly publicized tourist venues in India ever since the Moghul period. Like Kakadu, Dal Lake is now under extreme tourist pressure and ecologically it is in a sorry state. Visitor numbers in the town of Srinagar have risen by over 2000 per cent in the last 40 years. This growth has both encouraged and been supported by an enormous expansion of lakeside tourist infrastructure construction in the form of new hotels, boating facilities and restaurants. Raza and Bano (1985, p. 17) noted that 'In the last five years more construction has taken place around the lake than in the past two decades.'

Houseboats have always been a unique and popular form of tourist accommodation in Srinagar; indeed, they are synonymous with the vacation experience there. These elaborate brightly painted floating apartments are usually about 30 m long and have up to five bedrooms. In the mid-1970s Dal Lake had 369 of these structures; there are now around 1000. Notwithstanding this substantial increase, the last few years have seen a declining annual houseboat occupancy rate as the lake has become steadily more polluted and degraded, notably in the vicinity of the heavily used Dal Gate region in the western part of the lake. Raw sewage and other effluents are routinely discharged directly into the lake waters from both the houseboats and on-shore residences, and this had led to extremely high water pollution in parts of the lake as well as the expansion of thick beds of aquatic weeds such as macrophytes. The Dal Gate area used to be a popular venue for a wide range of water sports such as swimming and angling, but these activities are now largely confined to the relatively cleaner eastern Gagribal basin.

Dal Lake is generally shallow. Nowhere is it more than 4 m deep and for much of its area it has a depth of less than 0.5 m. This compounds the pollution problem created by the annual addition of 50 000 t of refuse and sullage. At 1.11–1.93 mg/l, ammonia concentration is particularly high in the lake waters in the main tourist season from August to October. Eutrophication can occur if phosphorus levels exceed 0.1 mg/l. With average readings of 1.31 mg/l Dal Lake is clearly well above this limit. Eutrophication is occurring, as is serious choking by numerous weeds. Dissolved oxygen levels are also lower than widely accepted standards. Perhaps more serious are the readings relating to the concentration of coliform and faecal streptoccoci. The former are common in the vicinity of the houseboats; the latter occur widely throughout the lake system and are generally in proportions '. . . in excess of the commonly used reference level for public water supply and primary contact recreation' (Raza and Bano 1985, p. 19). The prognosis for Dal Lake is not good. Unplanned construction activities and the attendant pollution inputs are gathering pace and the predictions are that, on the basis of current trends, eutrophication will be complete well within a century.

2.0 THE THEMES

2.1 *Diversity of character*

Four key themes are suggested by these case studies. The first, and perhaps most obvious, concerns the diverse character of wetlands. A small sample of some of the many terms used to describe wetland environments in different parts of the world provides one indication of this richness and variety: sloughs, bottomlands, bayous, ox-bows, billabongs, sinks, fens, estuaries, bogs, swamps, ponds, kettles, bays, sounds, meadows etc. Apart from size and cultural setting, wetlands were initially defined scientifically in the United States in the 1920s according to their hydrological and vegetation characteristics. Thus, hydrologically, wetlands can be either essentially freshwater or tidally influenced coastal marshes. As a general rule freshwater wetlands around the world have been most seriously affected to date by agricultural drainage practices, while the impact of recreation has been evidenced most strongly in coastal regions. In addition to the water characteristic, wetlands can take the form either of transitional zones on sloping land through which water flows from a terrestrial to an aquatic environment (e.g. riverine flood plains, riparian wetlands) or they can be located in relatively self-contained isolated basins, such as the millions dotted throughout the 500 000 km^2 prairie pothole region in North America. The type and depth of water and the periodicity of inundation affect the composition of the vegetation, and it is this factor that has been most commonly used to differentiate various wetland types.

Recently soil characteristics have been added to the vegetation and hydrological criteria to refine further the important definitional aspects of wetland ecosystems. On this basis the comprehensive US Fish and Wildlife Service (FWL) classification (Cowardin et al. 1979) now recognizes five main wetland *systems* (marine, estuarine, riverine, lacustrine and palustrine), ten *subsystems* and no less than 55 wetland *classes*, the latter being assessed largely on the physical characteristics of the bed and shore (for an amended version see table 2.1). Gradually, a much better understanding of the diversity within the broad category of 'wetlands' has been arrived at. Some wetlands, for example, are much more productive as habitat or nursery areas than others, and such information is clearly important from the management perspective. In addition, there is now a growing recognition of the radical view that many European and even tropical and subtropical wetlands are ecosystems that have been shaped by human actions over a very long period (Gordon and Duncan 1988). The continued 'health' of areas such as the Camargue, it now appears, may well depend on the acceptance or reinstatement of traditional grazing practices.

Enightened environmental management involves a clear understanding of the important differences between the various categories of wetland, both large and small, and a sensitivity to their enormous biological and amenity value. To this end, representative examples of the recreational use of wetlands will be drawn from many different kinds of wetland environments. An additional concern here is that, given the rapid decline in the area of undisturbed wetland resources and the progressive fall in the quality of recreational experiences everywhere (Dustin and McAvoy 1982), environmental policies on all scales should be predicated on the maintenance of wetland diversity. With this in mind, reference will be made later in the chapter to the concept of the Recreation Opportunity Spectrum (Clark and Stankey 1979).

2.2 *Conflicting value positions*

A second important issue concerns the question of conflicting value positions over wetland resources (see chapter 1 for an extensive discussion of values, functions and benefits). Table 9.1 itemizes the familiar three main groups and 23 subcategories of wetland values identified by the US Fish and Wildlife Service (1984). Of necessity, the items listed in the table are highly generalized, and a considerable refinement of the process of wetland values assessment has been seen in recent years, particularly in the United States (Clairain 1985). A wetland values data base has been established and significant steps have been taken towards the development of a unified assessment technique for all

Table 9.1 Major wetland values

Environmental quality values
Water quality maintenance
Pollution filter
Sediment removal
Oxygen production
Nutrient recycling
Chemical nutrient absorption
Aquatic productivity
Microclimate regulator
World climate (ozone layer)
Fish and wildlife values
Fish and shellfish habitat
Waterfowl and other bird habitat
Furbearer and other wildlife habitat
Socio-economic values
Flood control
Wave damage protection
Erosion control
Ground-water recharge and water supply
Timber and other natural products
Energy source (peat)
Livestock grazing
Fishing and shellfishing
Hunting and trapping
Recreation
Aesthetics
Education and scientific research

Source: US Fish and Wildlife Service 1984

wetlands in the United States. As we shall see in the case of recreation, there are numerous conflicts operating within what appears initially to be a fairly homogeneous category. At the risk of stating the obvious, there are also multiple interconnections between all the values listed. Thus, overfishing or peat extraction, for example, would inevitably have an adverse effect on recreational values as would the influx of pollutants or sediments on a scale beyond the capacity of the wetland to process them. Various kinds of recreational impact can also exacerbate problems in what might already be a stressed environment from other pressures. In the Norfolk Broads O'Riordan (1985a) has described the adverse effect of water pollution from sewage treatment plants and fertilized fields on the ecologically significant fringing reed banks. These are becoming lopsided in growth and unstable, and are frequently subsequently dislodged from the banks through either the action of mobile or moored boats or the trampling actions of pedestrians on the shore.

A basic value conflict in capitalist societies frequently surrounds the issue of whether wetlands should be seen principally as private or public goods. Shoard (1987, pp. 266–7) emphsizes that in the British context private ownership has traditionally bestowed more exclusive rights to land and water than in many other countries and that, moreover, 'the private pursuit of game has been the primary leisure activity which the land of Britain has sustained since the time of William the Conqueror'. In practice, many coastal wetlands, in Britain and the United States in particular, are privately owned. Indeed the figure is as high as 70 per cent in the latter country. However, given that in their natural state such wetlands more often than not provide an important habitat for fish – which are, of course, a common property resource – the line between 'private' and 'collective' interests is often indistinct. In short, we are dealing with a biological system where one part is not infrequently in private ownership while another part lies in the public domain. Inevitably this raises the issue of the rights and responsibilities of private landowners when contemplating actions such as dredging or landfilling which may have adverse consequences for recreational or commercial fishing.

Odum (1981) argues that there are three main 'levels' of wetland values: population, ecosystem and global (see chapter 1, table 1.11). Recognition of the different values has evolved historically so that we are now belatedly at the stage where the all-important global values are gradually being accorded their true status. Fish and wildlife resources at the population level were recognized first and their value was largely determined through the workings of the market system. Much more recently the global 'work of nature' values of wetlands have been widely publicized. Odum (1981, p. 153) has calculated that 'for tidal wetlands . . . the total value is 20 times the dollar value of the seafood byproducts'. Later in this chapter several examples of major tourist-oriented wetland destruction projects will be mentioned. Odum would argue that, with hindsight, such schemes almost certainly should never have been allowed to proceed, for, generally, he notes '. . . the alternative management decision of leaving land in its natural state is not adequately defended nor seriously considered' (Odum 1981, p. 150). In what has since become something of a classic study of the economic and ecological value of the San Francisco Bay wetlands, Luken (1976) presented a persuasive argument for his conclusion that about 90 per cent of San Francisco Bay's 174 000 ha of wetlands would have greater value if they were preserved to sustain natural system functions than if they were 'developed' for residential or other purposes.

A characteristic, and not unsurprising feature of most discussions of wetland values is that the values are identified by, and ultimately on behalf of, human beings. This is what Sylvan (1986, p. 3) and others have referred to as the 'shallow' approach to the natural environment: 'Humans come first, and . . . they are all that matter.' In contrast, the 'deep' ecological perspective totally rejects the assumption that humans are a superior species endowed with the exclusive right to manipulate ecosystems as they see fit. As Sylvan (1986, p. 3) puts it, 'wetlands are valuable in and of themselves, they have a right to continued existence'.

2.3 *Impact*

A third theme suggested by the case studies concerns the notion of impact. All three examples discussed are currently experiencing a range of direct and indirect impacts, some of which are the result of recreational pressures. However, the pressures being experienced are quite different. An obvious differentiating characteristic is proximity to population. Clearly, wetlands in densely populated southern England, the northeastern United States (Barlow 1971) or Hong Kong (chapter 8) are under constant concentrated pressure from numerous external forces. The problems of somewhere like Kakadu or Muddus National Park in remote Swedish Lapland are rather less immediate. However, as in the case of Alaska, geographical isolation does not necessarily result in minimal recreational pressures. In these days of high mobility, aircraft of all sizes have brought formerly inaccessible wetlands into the tourist's orbit. High-speed power-boats and specialist air-cushioned wetland vehicles (Pinto-Silva 1987) have had a similar impact on the mobility patterns of recreationists. The present health of the environments mentioned is, of course, a function of historical patterns of human interference and their future state will, in turn, be determined by decisions that are now being made. To take a further example, it is currently fashionable for old run-down urban waterfront areas in many affluent western countries to be revitalized in order to attract greater numbers of tourists (e.g. Richardson 1986). Wetlands are frequently routinely dredged or filled as a part of such developments. The current fashion actually represents an engineering and architectural fad that was 'rediscovered' and transported from Europe to the United States in the early part of this century. When, in 1904, the American real estate developer Albert Kinney carved up Ballona Creek's bayside marshes in Los Angeles to form an exclusive residential canal-based development, he appropriately named it 'The Venice of America'. The idea spread rapidly and has subsequently become a major cause of wetland destruction.

Human actions can have both short- and long-term environmental consequences, and the source of any one identifiable impact can be both local or geographically distant. Sediments or pollutants, for example, can be carried considerable distances by rivers to affect wetlands many miles away. For example, Tuttle (1985) in her research in Humboldt County, California, measured the precise impact of residential subdivisional activities in a small 44 km^2 watershed on sedimentation rates in a coastal wetland downstream at the creek mouth. She was able to demonstrate that the creek mouth delta had grown by some 7 ha in a period of about 50 years and that at least five of the 13 sub-watersheds were overcommitted to residential development.

2.4 *Ecological interdependence*

A final, related theme of some relevance is that of ecological interdependence. Whether we are talking about the extensive tropical wetlands of the Alligator River systems of Northern Australia, those of the 166 000 km^2 Chesapeake Bay watershed in the United States or much smaller examples such as the Amberley Wildbrooks in the United Kingdom, it has to be recognized that these wetlands represent just one somewhat artificially delineated part of much larger ecological systems with which they are interconnected. Coastal land loss in Louisiana is another case in point. The Louisiana coastal region wetlands are among the most significant in the world. As well as sustaining the largest fur harvest in North America they provide the winter habitat for over 400 000 geese and numerous other migratory birds. They also generate the largest catches of estuarine-dependent fish and shellfish in the United States and well in excess of 5 million man-days of recreational salt-water fishing and 700 000 man-days of waterfowl hunting (Fruge 1982). Davis (1983) has reported that marsh losses in the Louisiana coastal zone have been averaging 10 000 ha/yr during the 1980s as a result of the changed sedimentation balance caused by human engineering activities upstream along the Mississippi River (chapter 10). This rate of wetland loss has more than doubled since 1956. The effects on recreational and commercial activities in this important wetland environment have been devastating. A final example of ecological interdependence is provided by the Everglades National Park in Florida. The park itself – which currently attracts in excess of 600 000 visitors each year – encompasses only a small portion (6 per cent) of the much larger Everglades swamp, by far the largest of its kind in North America. The water entering the park is of course regulated externally, and the recent pattern has been for the periodic release of unseasonably high water volumes during the annual dry season and early summer which have wrought severe and largely irreversible biological changes to the park's ecosystem (Kushlan 1987).

One of the central arguments here is that environmental impact research – not least where wetlands are concerned – is still at an extremely rudimentary stage (Nelson 1983). The wide use of the word 'impact', for example, is telling for it conjures up simple mechanistic images of a meteorite striking an unyielding surface and having fairly localized effects. In reality, organic ecosystems behave in highly complex, often unpredictable and little understood ways. Wilden (1983, p. 76) underscores the profound uncertainty characterizing much of the contemporary research on open systems such as wetlands when he comments:

> . . . an ecologist will deal in detail with one part of a complex cycle, or with one aspect of the ecological damage occurring in it. But he is unable, for practical and theoretical reasons, to deal adequately with a whole set of other interdependent and interrelated factors – some of which he hasn't heard of yet anyway.

For many of the world's threatened wetlands the iconoclastic 'meteorite' metaphor is inappropriate because the main changes taking place are relatively slow, long term, cumulative and synergistic rather than dramatic in their effects (Odum 1970).

3.0 RECREATION

3.1 *Definition and perception*

Before proceeding to a detailed appraisal of the association between recreation and wetlands one further introductory task remains – to discuss some of the complexity implied by the term 'recreation'. The important point to recognize here is that behaviour patterns and the resultant environmental outcomes are representations of underlying attitudes and perceptions. Thus different recreational activities are characterized by varied 'attitude clusters' with respect to the natural environment. The early research on perception in outdoor recreation (Hendee et al. 1971) distinguished two main kinds of recreational activity: 'appreciative' (e.g. viewing scenery, hiking, photography) and 'consumptive' (e.g. fishing, hunting). These were then further subdivided to yield four categories in terms of their primary motivations: appreciative-symbolic, sociable learning, extractive-symbolic and passive-freeplay.

More recently, Eagles (1980) has expanded this typology considerably to include the ten finely differentiated attitude dimensions and manifestations listed in table 9.2. A close reading of this table reveals a wide spectrum of recreational attitudes and associated activities ranging from 'negativism' at one extreme to 'moralism' at the other. It can be seen, for example, that according to Eagles' schema the 'dominionistic' and 'utilitarian' attitudes tend to be associated with such pursuits as sport fishing, while painting and bird-watching are more closely aligned with the'aesthetic' and 'naturalistic' attitude dimensions. The relationship between the polar attitude clusters listed in table 9.2 and the shallow-deep ecological value split alluded to earlier should be obvious. Conflict between different recreational user groups or between recreation and other uses is essentially conflict between markedly varied attitude-behaviour groupings. The 1970s provided some evidence from a number of affluent Western societies of a fairly pronounced contemporary

Table 9.2 Recreational behaviour, attitudes and manifestations – ten dimensions

Attitude	*Key indicators*	*Common manifestations associated with attitude*	*Examples of activities and associated institutions*
1 Negativistic	Common feature is the desire to avoid the natural environment (nature) Typical feelings are fear, dislike, superstition, separated and alienated from nature	Includes a number of actions ranging from avoidance to the destruction of nature Nature perceived as evil, supernatural beyond the control of man Very anthropocentric view No sense of empathy for or kinship with wildlife	Killing of wildlife Killing to protect own life, crop or livestock Forest clearance Wildlife bounties, wetland drainage
2 Dominionistic	Featured by a sense of superiority and a desire to master nature Nature regarded from the perspective of providing opportunities for dominance and control A quest of challenge, prestige, skill, superiority	Actions which display desire to control, dominate and compete with nature Expressions of prowess and skill in competition Considerable attachment to outdoors may be present	Rodeos Trophy hunting Trophy fishing Obedience training such as in circuses White water canoeing
3 Utilitarian	Nature perceived in terms of its practical or profitable qualities Nature is regarded largely for its material benefits to humans Indifference to issues of natural area protection which do not affect the performance or practical value Profitable qualities are emphasized	Natural environment often perceived as an inexhaustible resource	Wildlife management, harvesting, and conservation activities Hunting Fishing Commercial fish Trapping Game laws Conservation (not preservation) Wildlife management area

Table 9.2 Cont.

Attitude	*Key indicators*	*Common manifestations associated with attitude*	*Examples of activities and associated institutions*
4 Scientific	Objective, intellectualized, somewhat circumscribed perspective Nature regarded more as an object for study and as means for acquiring specific knowledge Emotional detachment Curiosity often constitutes the primary motivation for interest	Experimentation applied to acquire physiological, biological and taxonomical knowledge Opportunities for problem solving Accepts experimentations on and killing of animals for laboratory purposes	Experimentation on animals for curiosity or knowledge Scientific study Typical biological researcher
5 Neutralistic	Associated with indifference towards nature Detachment No strong positive or negative feelings	Little interaction with natural environment Nature outside normal, daily concerns	Lack of membership in organizations dealing with natural environment Unconcern
6 Aesthetic	Associated with emotional detachment Central interest is the beauty or symbolic properties of nature	Interest towards nature almost exclusively on the artistic appeal Remains aloof from physical elements, especially if beauty not present	Photography Painting/sculpture Movies Viewing Animal showmanship Nature books
7 Naturalistic	Profound attraction to wildlife and outdoors Pets seen as inferior to wildlife Wildlife is valued particularly for opportunities it provides for activity in the natural environment Represents the 'romantic' idea of the wild Knowledge of nature is usually present	General interest in outdoors, specifically wildlife and wilderness Satisfaction from direct personal contact with wilderness Atavistic reward derived from experiencing wilderness as an escape from the perceived pressures and deficiencies of modern industrial life	Bird-watching Wildlifers, outdoor groups Naturalists Wilderness areas Nature reserves

	Knowledge of nature is usually present		
8 Ecologistic	Primarily orientated toward wildlife and natural settings Major emphasis and affection is for species of animals and plants in their natural setting and habitats Tends to concentrate on a systems approach including the behavioural, physical and biological components	Marked by considerable knowledge of animals Perceives man and animals as equals in a system Futuristic outlook Emphasis on preservation	Study natural habitats and wildlife in wilderness Protect wildlife Future oriented Environmental planning
9 Humanistic	Strong personal affection for individual animals, typically pets rather than wildlife Love felt for animals can often be compared with that felt for human beings No deep philosophical or ethical principles behind the empathy or general concern for nature	General concern for the well-being of all animals Animals viewed as friends Identification with St Francis Nature is friendly	Humane society Protects animals Birds fed in winter Cruelty to animals opposed More interest in animals than plants
10 Moralistic	Strong nature ethic Great concern for the welfare of animals, both wild and domesticated Has consideration for all nature and is typically more philosophical, sense of equality between humans and animals	Opposed to the exploitation and infliction of any harm, suffering or death of animals Moral basis for actions emphasized	Associations for animal rights Protects and preserves nature

Soure: based on Eagles 1980

'value shift' away from a predominantly dominionistic/utilitarian view of the natural environment towards a much stronger emphasis on 'moralistic' attitudes. The 1971 RAMSAR Convention on Wetlands of International Importance and the 1982 Bern Convention on the Conservation of European Wildlife and Natural Habitats can both be seen as indicators of this trend (chapter 11). Key judicial decisions also provide important clues to changing values. In this context mention should be made of the landmark decision handed down by the US Supreme Court in 1985 in the case of *United States v Riverside Bayview Homes Inc.* This particular interpretation of the Army Corps of Engineers' jurisdiction under Section 404 of the Clean Water Act served to broaden considerably the definition of 'wetlands' under that legislation and to provide enhanced legislative support for preservation in the United States (DeVoe 1986).

If this attitudinal transformation continues, the future is likely to witness greatly increased demands for environmental management strategies directed much more towards the naturalistic-ecologistic end of Eagles' spectrum. However, the situation in less affluent nations or in poorer regions of rich countries is less clear. For example, in energy-poor countries such as Jamaica there are continuing economic pressures to mine coastal peat deposits as a substitute for escalating oil imports (Rubino 1984). These concerns clearly conflict with conservation and recreational values. More recently, Winkler and DeWitt (1985) have analysed the economics of potential peat mining projects in parts of the United States and, interestingly, have concluded that peatland ecosystems are far more valuable to society when left in an undisturbed state.

In large measure the wetland recreational 'profile' that is demonstrated by a particular country at a given time is a function of where that nation can be located along Eagles' spectrum in terms of its habitat protection policies. Thus a country like Denmark, for example, with some of the strictest wetland preservation statutes of any country in the world, exhibits a much more 'naturalistic' and less exploitative national recreational profile by comparison with a country like Italy where the level of legislated habitat protection is low and the uncontrolled shooting of birds is commonplace (Robertson 1987).

The relationship between the first three attitude dimensions listed in table 9.2 and the status of wetlands is by no means unambiguous. For instance, while the total destruction of a wetland for the purposes of marine construction could clearly be seen as a 'utilitarian' or 'dominionistic' action, it is important to emphasize that in many countries supporters of the 'negativistic' sport of wildfowl hunting have frequently been at the forefront of battles to preserve threatened wetland environments. This is particularly the case in the United States (chapter 1). Another obvious point that needs to be made is that the distinction between 'recreational' and other impacts on wetland resources is often an irrelevance. If extensive dredging or filling activities are taking place, for example, wetlands are affected in an equally adverse fashion whether the ultimate purpose is for a marine or resort development on the one hand, or an industrial plant or commercial harbour on the other. Additionally, from the point of view of the ecological 'health' of a particular wetland ecosystem it scarcely matters whether pollutants are escaping from commercial or pleasure craft. The end result is the same biological damage.

3.2 *Recreational activities*

Table 9.3 lists the more common recreational activities associated with both coastal and inland wetland environments. Clearly the most serious disturbances to the natural environment are the result of disruptive fixed-accommodation construction activities such as resort towns, camping grounds and hotels or infrastructure provision in the form of major highways, aircraft landing facilities or marinas. These engineering facilities are often an essential adjunct to many of the activities listed in the table; they provide the means of access to the wetland attractions themselves. The pursuits listed in the table can be seen to represent the complete spectrum (outlined in table 9.2) ranging from 'negativism' at one extreme to 'moralism' at the other. Thus such activities as nature study, painting and photography obviously characterize a quite different response to the natural environment on the part of recreationists by comparison with power-boating, game shooting or the driving of off-road vehicles. Yet it has to be said that even within the latter categories there are considerable internal preference and experience variations that are now being recognized as significant from a management and social science perspective. Increasingly, recreation researchers are highlighting the heterogeneity of recreational pursuits through a focus on the concept of specialization within such broad categories as boating, fishing or hunting (e.g. Donnelly and Vaske 1986).

Table 9.3 Wetlands and recreation – the main activities

Aquatic Activities	*Intertidal activities*
Swimming	Bait collecting
Wind surfing	Shell food collection
Scuba diving	Reef-fossicking
Angling	Nature study/bird watching
Sailing	Photography
Power boating	Shooting (wild fowl)
Canoeing/kayaking	
Water skiing	
Hover crafting	
Land activities	
Painting	
Walking/jogging	
Sightseeing	
Motoring	
Off-road vehicle driving	
Picnicking	
Horse riding	
Game shooting	
Fixed accommodation (hotels, camps etc.)	

Inevitably, in view of the enormous value of fisheries and wildlife resources to many of the recreational pursuits – both active and contemplative – listed in table 9.3, much of the remainder of the present discussion will also focus on wildlife management issues. Such overlap is inescapable given that the principal management aim in many national parks and equivalent reserves around the world, for instance, is to attempt to maximize both recreation and wildlife habitat values. Writing of the national wildlife refuge system in the United States 30 years ago Clawson (1958, p. 49) commented that '. . . the refuges are heavily used for recreation . . . this use is increasing'. He noted that at that time 6 per cent of total recreational use was for hunting, 37 per cent for fishing and 57 per cent for a wide range of 'other pursuits'. Earlier, mention was made of the important influence of proximity to population where recreational pressures are concerned. In this context it is also important to recognize that many people actually live in, or immediately adjacent to, national parks or equivalent reserves containing valuable wetland assets. In such instances the wetlands are simply a part of the local 'neighbourhood' amenity setting rather than representing some exotic reserve 'out there'. Areas fitting this description range from Kakadu through many of the English and European national parks such as Prespa in Greece (Pyrovetsi 1984) and resort towns along the Gulf of Mexico littoral in the United States, to coastal swamplands in south Sumatra currently being settled as a result of the Indonesian government's transmigration programme (chapter 11).

4.0 THE VALUE OF WETLANDS FOR RECREATION

4.1 *Factors in spatial recreational patterns*

Spatial recreational patterns and participation trends are influenced by numerous factors. These include changing supply – in terms of both quantity and quality – in various regions over time, variations in population growth, distribution and demographic change, technological developments in equipment and transport media (Hummel and Foster 1986), and leisure time fads and fashions. The latter two elements are notoriously difficult to predict, yet they can be responsible for some of the most dramatic changes in recreation in a very short time. Wind surfing, for example, has only become popular on a mass scale in recent years, yet is is a technological leisure innovation of some relevance to wetland environments in that it 'encourages the use of shallow waters over soft substrates that previously had not been accessible to recreationists' (Edwards 1987, p. 87). Clawson (1985) reminds us that snowmobiling, hang gliding and dune buggies were virtually unknown 25 years ago. He also comments that in the 1950s the 'fitness' revolution of the 1980s and the contemporary interest in wilderness areas were both vastly underestimated, especially the interest that is now being demonstrated by people who never actually visit such areas.

Population growth is a particularly important variable and southeastern Florida, adjacent to the vast Everglades hyperseasonal savanna, provides a spectacular example. Kushlan (1987, p. 110) comments that up until the late 1890s Miami was only a small village but that 2 million people now live along the southeastern coast. He adds 'Nowhere in the USA does such a large population reside on the doorstep of such a vast wetland.' A current tendency in affluent countries, in particular, is for population growth to be attracted to amenity coastal environments, thereby placing added pressures on already stressed wetlands. Australia is an obvious exemplar and the United States provides another. Platt (1987) notes that by 1980 over 118 million people (53 per cent of the US population) lived within 80 km of the coast. In 1940 the comparable figures were 60 million and 46 per cent respectively. Population growth has been particularly high in the 'sunbelt' states, and it is no surprise that southern California has the dubious distinction of having lost a higher proportion of its original wetlands than any other region in the country. The figure is put at between 75 and 90 per cent (Lockhart 1986).

That wetlands in different parts of the world have enormous 'value' for a wide range of often conflicting recreational activities is beyond dispute. The visitor statistics at particular sites and participant numbers in specific activities provide abundant evidence to support this claim. Moreover, as wetlands around the world progressively diminish in area the plants and animals that survive in remnant wetland pockets will become even more highly valued as tourist attractions. Crocodiles are already a major drawcard in northern Australia and Brazil and will become more so in the future. The same can be said for the Bengal tiger in India, flamingos in southern France and grizzly bears, bald eagles and whooping cranes in North America. Indeed, in the United States, many court cases in recent years have established precise monetary values for such things as individual species of fish, game birds, mangrove swamps and river frontages in the course of settling damage claims of various kinds (Yang et al. 1984). The seven reserves controlled by the Wildfowl Trust in Britain attracted over 600 000 day tourists in 1986, and almost a third of this total visited only one site – Slimbridge, on the Severn Estuary. Moreover, visitor numbers at these wild refuges grew by 57 000 in the 12 month period between 1985 and 1986. Additional British data demonstrate an equally high level of public interest in wetland-oriented recreational pursuits. The Anglian Water Authority reported a 21 per cent increase in boat licence registrations on the River Great Ouse between 1973 and 1980. British angling experienced a similar percentage increase nationwide over the same period, and the Royal Society for the Protection of Birds now has over 300 000 members (Patmore 1983).

Between 1951 and 1956 the recreational use of national wildlife refuges in the United States more than doubled in comparison with a 48 per cent increase for the national park system in the same period (Clawson 1958). In 1965 the Department of the Interior estimated that 11 million people in the United States were actively engaged in nature study (Kusler 1983). By 1973 the US Fish and Wildlife Service sites alone registered over 5 million visitor days. Seven years later the figure had risen to over 6 million (Westphal 1984). Interestingly, by far the highest visitor statistics at the overall state level were recorded for Alaska, a relatively isolated state with only a small population. Wisconsin, Illinois and Florida registered the next most heavily visited refuges. Similarly, Patterson (1987) reports that Ontario's wetlands generate over 53 million user-days per year. European and African wetlands are no less popular. Maltby (1986) writes that, with 250 000 yearly visitors, the 40 ha island of Texel in the Wadden Sea is testimony to the enormous tourist-drawing power of large concentrations of birds. Wildlife safaris to such areas as the Okovango delta in Botswana are also becoming an increasingly important source of foreign earnings for many poorer countries.

The most comprehensive national outdoor recreation participation study ever undertaken formed part of the massive 26 volume Outdoor Recreation Resources Review Commission investigation which presented its final report to the United States President and Congress in 1962 (ORRRC 1962). On the basis of that exhaustive enquiry forward projections for participation rates in various outdoor activities were made up to 1976. In 1976 a further survey was carried out in the United States to assess the reliability of the earlier projections (Brown and Hustin 1978). Table 9.4 presents a comparison of these two sets of data for 16 key activities. It can be seen that projected participation rates were consistently under-estimated for all activities. In the context of the present discussion particular note should be taken of the contrast between the projected and reported 1976 participation rates for the wetland-associated pursuits of fishing, boating, hunting, hiking and – most spectacularly – nature walks. Between 1933 and 1980, for example, the number of fishing licence

Table 9.4 Recreational participation in the United States as projected by the ORRRC and reported in the 1976 participation survey

Activity	*Participation rate projected by ORRRC for 1976 (% of US population)*	*Participation reported in 1976 survey (% of survey respondents)*
Driving for pleasure	56	69
Swimming	55	70
Walking for pleasure	37	68
Sightseeing	47	62
Picnicking	57	73
Fishing	32	55
Bicycling	11	47
Attending outdoor sports events	27	61
Boating (excluding canoeing and sailing)	28	35
Nature walks	16	49
Hunting	14	20
Camping	11	37
Horseback riding	8	15
Water skiing	9	17
Hiking	8	28
Attending outdoor concerts, plays etc.	12	40

Source: Outdoor Recreation Policy Review Group 1983

holders in the United States increased by almost 500 per cent and the proportion of the population holding a licence grew by 216 per cent (Hummel and Foster 1986). Ashe (1986) has presented additional data from the United States which demonstrate that annual expenditures on fish and wildlife recreation increased tenfold (from $2.8 billion to $27 billion) between 1955 and 1980. With 20 million sport fishermen, fishing is now second only to swimming as the most popular water-based recreational activity in the United States. Moreover, many argue that a fish caught as 'recreation' has far greater economic value than one caught commercially. One indication of this is that several US states have now designated certain fish as 'recreation-only' species (Simon 1984). Other activities also grew in popularity throughout the 1970s but not as rapidly as they had done in the past. Expenditure on outboard motors in the United States, for example, stopped rising sharply from about the early 1960s onwards. Nevertheless, participation in boating doubled in the United States between 1962 and 1983.

The consensus among recreation researchers in the United States now is that over the next few years recreational participation will increase, though not as sharply as in the exceptional 1960s and 1970s. Further marked increases are anticipated in such activities as backpacking, camping, bicycling and canoeing. A levelling-off in participation is projected for boating, fishing (except on private land), swimming and driving for pleasure, and hunting and nature study activities are expected to decline in popularity (McLellan 1986). From the vantage point of the early 1990s it is now apparent that some of the site visitation predictions made for the United States in the 1960s represented rather extravagant over-estimates. For example, we have already noted that there were 6 million visits to national wildlife refuge areas in 1980. Clawson and Knetsch (1966) had earlier estimated that 30–50 million could be expected by this date. A probable explanation of the discrepancy is that many more alternative attractions of a similar type became available to the American public in the intervening period. Thus, from a base of 71 million visitors in 1956, the US Corps of Engineers' reservoirs attracted almost 400 million more tourists by 1980 (Clawson 1985). Yet, notwithstanding the addition of many new recreational sites, it is also important to keep in mind the parallel reduction in wetland resources that has occurred in countries such as the United States in recent years. Less than 50 per cent of America's original wetlands survived to 1970, and between 1950 and 1970 alone some 4×10^6 ha were destroyed for agriculture or other purposes (Ashe 1986).

4.2 *Multiple values*

Earlier in the chapter mention was made of the multiple 'values' of wetland resources, including the all-important global 'life support' values. Larson (1985, p. 119) has argued that 'a significant change in our approach to wetland assessment is now underway'. In particular, the use of alternative measurement techniques to include amenity and life support values is beginning to cast serious doubt on the viability of many large-scale wetland conversion schemes.

Several studies of the economic significance of wetlands as an amenity resource have been carried out. One of the most widely cited is Kreutzwiser's (1981) evaluation of the Long Point and Point Pelée National Park marshes on the northern shore of Lake Erie. Eight provincial parks and one national park on the Canadian side of Lake Erie all have significant wetland resources and in 1978 attracted over 2 million visitors. Long Point is one of these sites. Kreutzwiser used the Clawson travel cost method to compute the economic value of the marsh for the 17 000 visitors in 1978. This was calculated to exceed $213 000 but did not include the estimated $225 000 generated in local business activity. At that time the Long Point marsh site was poorly provided with facilities for visitors, certainly in contrast with the nearby Point Pelée National Park where a boardwalk, interpretive displays and an observation tower had been constructed. Visitor numbers (143 000) and resultant benefits ($1.6 million) were consequently much higher at Point Pelée.

Kreutzwiser's reseach was concerned with only one aspect of economic value, namely that which derived from the actual travel behaviour of visitors to the Lake Erie sites. This particular approach has nothing to say about important 'existence benefits' or 'the utility that people receive from simply knowing that something exists' (Bishop 1978). Existence benefits are certainly more difficult to measure, but this has not prevented researchers such as Helliwell (1969, 1973) and Bennett (1982) from attempting to develop techniques for their assessment. Helliwell (1969) used measures such as genetic scarcity and research and educational value to develop a workable equation for assessing the value of areas such as wetlands. In his more recent research, based on questionnaire surveys of nature conservationists, town planners and landscape architects, Helliwell (1973, p. 89) estimated that 'the capitalized "value" of wildlife in Britain would average about £100 per acre and the visual amenity value about £200'. He concluded that 'such a value is equal to current market prices for agricultural land'. Comparable US calculations for the Charles River, Massachusetts, wetlands in their natural state have produced a conservative value of $150 000 per acre, over six times greater than the average real estate value of farmland in that country. 'Local amenity' and 'recreation' represented significant components of the final figure, though they were not as important as either the water supply or flood prevention elements (Thibodeau and Ostro 1981). Bennett's (1982) Australian work was concerned with a specific natural area, the Nadgee Nature Reserve in southern New South Wales. This important site is one of the few remaining coastal sites in southeastern Australia that is still in its natural state and it contains several significant habitats, including wetland environments. Few people visit this little-known and deliberately poorly publicized site, and it is managed by the New South Wales National Parks and Wildlife Service primarily as a wildlife refuge. Bennett found that the residents of Canberra – the nearest large city – would be prepared to pay at least $20 per adult for the continued preservation of the Reserve's existence benefits regardless of whether or not they would ever visit the site. Finally, Patterson (1987, p. 16) has calculated that whereas Ontario's wetlands have an annual worth of around $300 million for such products as timber and fish, the much larger sum of $800 million is 'generated as a direct result of tourism and recreational opportunities.

In some parts of the world it has long been recognized by governments and regional planning agencies that a large injection of funds into recreation and wildlife management projects in certain backward rural areas can do much to revive depressed rural economies and improve environmental conditions. One of the most widely publicized examples of such an approach is the so-called Land Between the Lakes experiment in western Kentucky and Tennessee. Since the 1960s this formerly run-down 68 000 ha area of lakes, forests, marshes and rivers has been managed successfully for a wide range of compatible multiple uses including forestry, wildlife and both consumptive and non-consumptive outdoor recreation. Currently the area attracts some 250 000 annual visits for hunting purposes (especially for turkey and deer) and approximately 200 000 non-consumptive wildlife-oriented recreational visits. Turkey hunting alone increased thirteenfold over a 20 year period (Thach et al. 1986).

5.0 RECREATIONAL IMPACTS

5.1 *Physical impacts*

Physical impacts on wetlands can be classified along several different dimensions, for example direct-indirect, trivial-serious, innocent-malicious, transitory-non-transitory, avoidable-non-avoidable. Two major international overviews of the environmental impact of recreation and tourism in general have so far been published (Wall and Wright 1977, Edington and Edington 1986). Wetlands do not figure prominently in either text although the more recent review does address the issue of wildlife disturbance in various settings. Wall and Wright (1977), in particular, highlight the enormous difficulties involved in measuring the precise effect of the recreation component on a given site or region in comparison with the range of other environmental impacts on that same area. They also emphasize another complicating factor, namely that the environment is of course not a static entity but is always changing, whether or not man is present. For example, of crucial importance to the future of wetlands is the issue of global atmospheric warming as a result of the build-up of carbon dioxide and other gases in the atmosphere. The work of Wall et al. (1986) on Point Pelée National Park and Presqu'ile Provincial Park in Ontario has suggested that the recreational and habitat values of the closed marsh of Point Pelée are likely to be seriously affected in the future by a projected temperature rise and declining water levels. However, because of its quite different physiography, the open marsh of Presqu'ile is likely to respond quite differently.

Wetlands are extraordinarily dynamic ecological systems and, together with other external forces, recreational activities may sometimes have the effect of deflecting or halting primary successional processes such as those in salt marsh communities. Subject to the qualifications just mentioned, table 9.5 presents a selective summary of some of the effects of recreational activities of various kinds on wetland environments. The table is for illustrative purposes only and makes no pretence at being exhaustive. Care needs to be taken in interpreting the table because the degree and seriousness of impact vary considerably depending upon such parameters as the size and setting of the wetland resource, the visitor numbers, their behaviour, the timing and intensity of visitation and – most significantly – the management techniques that are (or are

Table 9.5 Selected recreational impacts on wetland environments

Activity	*Environmental impact*	*Sample studies*
Wildfowl hunting	May alter population structure in certain areas if unchecked (e.g. may endanger rare species); lead contamination from spent bullets; impact of associated facilities such as campgrounds, pollution from boats, noise etc.	Rogers et al. 1979 Boyd and Lynch 1984 Van de Zande and Voss 1984 Cairns and Elliot 1987
Resorts/marinas	Dredging and filling; land drainage; habitat loss on large scale; alteration of circulation and sedimentation patterns; added problems of access roads, ancillary facilities, water pollution, sewerage, rubbish and waste-water disposal; eutrophication; aesthetic effects	Giannio and Wang 1974 Chmura and Ross 1978 Ris 1982 Heliotis 1985 Meyer-Arendt 1987 Platt et al. 1987
Fishing	Alterations to population structure through overfishing, bait collection or introduction of exotic species; can also impact on associated bird populations; pollution from boats; effects of ancillary facilities; problems with discarded fishing lines and angling weights	Soltz and Naiman 1978 Regier 1979 Scowan 1984 Davies 1984–5 Cryer et al. 1987
Nature study	Minimal impact if carefully managed; otherwise, physical trampling and damage to vegetation, soils etc; habitat disturbance as a result of noise, trampling and consruction of ancillary facilities such as boardwalks, viewing platforms	Usher et al. 1974 Burger 1986 Liddle and Kay 1987
Skiing	Construction of pistes and wide range of ski resort facilities (including buildings, roads, water supply, sewrage disposal and energy infrastructure) can disturb and fragment wildlife habitat, destroy endangered species and result in dredging and filling of fragile mountain wetlands; increased incidence of rock and mudslides can also occur as a result of the destruction of the water-retention function of highland wetlands	Ricciuti 1976 Cooper and Lee 1987 Simons 1988

not) in place. It is also necessary to consider 'packages' of impacts. A pursuit such as fishing, on its own, may not be that significant in terms of its physical effects. The more serious impact may well result from the construction and use of a broad range of ancillary facilities such as roads, campgrounds, marinas, launching ramps and the like. Thus the five activities listed in table 9.5 are really key foci for clusters of impacts of various kinds.

What is perhaps surprising about the corpus of literature on recreational impact is that whereas there has now been a considerable amount of research carried out on the effect of trampling or vehicular traffic at the fairly localized microscale (see, for example, Liddle (1975), Liddle and Scorgie (1980), Calais and Kirkpatrick (1986) and many of the sample studies listed in table 9.5), this has not been matched to anything like the same degree by a research interest in altogether larger, and in many ways much more significant, development activities aimed at the commercial tourist market. In the Everglades context Kushlan (1987, p. 111), for example, has concluded that the direct impact of some 400 000 annual visitors 'is slight'. This appears to accord with Edwards' conclusion that 'coastal habitats may be better able to withstand recreational disturbance than other terrestrial systems' (Edwards 1987, p. 84). However, he does make a clear distinction between so-called 'soft' and 'hard' coasts and, in the process of applying Doody's (1984) ecological 'sensitivity index' to recreational pressures along the British coastline, constructed the damage estimates from which table 9.6 is adapted. An interesting point arising from the information in the table is that several stretches of Heritage Coast in England and Wales already show recreational damage. The problem here of course is that the formal designation and subsequent publicity of a site as a Heritage Coast, national park or nature reserve invariably sets in train a veritable flood of tourists which may in turn, accelerate the degradation problem.

Table 9.6 Sensitivity of and ecological damage due to 13 recreation activities on three 'soft' coastal environments

Recreation	*Salt marsh*	*Mud flats*	*Reed beds*
Off-road vehicles	+	+	–
Camping-caravanning	–	–	–
Trampling	+(~)	–	–(~)
Path erosion	+(~)	–	+
Horse riding	+	–	
Diving	–	–	–
Canoeing	+	+*	+*
Power boating	+	+	+*
Sailing	+	+*	+*
Wind surfing	+*	++*(~)	++*
Wild fowling	++*	+++*	–
Fishing and bait digging	++	++(~)	–
Natural history interest	+(~)	–	+*(~)

Sensitivity index: – little or no sensitivity; + slightly sensitive; ++ moderately sensitive; +++ highly sensitive; * effect principally due to disturbance; (~) effect recorded on British Heritage Coasts
Source: adapted from Doody 1984 and Edwards 1987

The discussion here will not even attempt a comprehensive coverage of the many small-scale recreational impact investigations that have now been carried out on many different wetland environments in various parts of the world in recent years, most notably in Britain. For details concerning these and other studies readers should consult Edington and Edington (1986), the sample references listed in table 9.5 and recent issues of such journals as *Biological Conservation* and *Environmental Conservation*. Mention has already been made in this chapter of the often devastating impact of major resort, highway and marina developments on coastal wetlands in particular. Two case studies have been chosen to illustrate these.

5.2 *Languedoc-Roussillon, France*

One of the most spectacular cases of state-sponsored coastal wetland destruction on a grand scale is provided by the Languedoc-Roussillon region in southern France. In the 1950s the French government expressed mounting concern at two aspects of burgeoning tourist demand in affluent post-war France. The first problem was that the traditional Riviera resorts along the Mediterranean coast were starting to show multiple signs of environmental stress as a result of unprecedented levels of tourist demand in the peak summer months. A related concern was that French tourists were beginning to demonstrate a growing predilection for travelling overseas to countries like Spain and Italy for their annual vacations. Accordingly, a bold decision was made by the national government to develop a set of entirely new planned seaside resorts, first in Languedoc on the Mediterranean shore and later in Aquitaine on the Atlantic littoral. Languedoc is the main concern here, since as recently as the early 1960s the extensive and ecologically significant coastal wetlands to the west of the Rhone delta were a sparsely inhabited region that was seen at the time as being little more than an undeveloped wasteland. Today, there exists a string of six major coastal resorts along that particular 200 km long stretch of coast which, in 1974 alone, attracted as many as 1.5 million visitors (Bosselman 1978).

The massive task of transforming the Languedoc marshlands was coordinated by a powerful central government authority known as the Mission Interministerielle pour L'Amenagement Touristique de Littoral Languedoc-Roussillon. This agency was set up in 1963 and was granted enormous legislative, manpower and financial resources to complete its engineering mission in the shortest possible time. Well within a decade – and often in the face of bitter local landowner and environmentalist opposition – thousands of hectares of the flat Mediterranean shoreline had been bulldozed, dredged and filled, and instant 'futuristic' tourist playgrounds such as La Grande Motte and Cap d'Agde had been constructed. Twenty new harbours were also dredged along the coast, providing anchorage for 15 000 boats. At the time the project was heralded as the largest earth-moving scheme in Europe, with the equivalent of $141 million being earmarked by the state for swamp drainage and other engineering works (Strong 1971). Physically, the area has been changed so fundamentally that it is now difficult for newcomers to imagine what the region was like before the bold regional plan was realized. However, Bosselman (1978, p. 63) remarks that

> . . . a vital wetland resource, which provided a breeding area for marine life, a bird habitat, and flood absorption area, has been lost. Arguments have been made that the marshes were filling in anyway, but had this occurred slowly, it might have offered some opportunity for species adaptation . . . The Languedoc experience suggests that, even when there is planning for tourism development . . . it does not ensure a harmonious relationship between development and environment.

More recently, Allen and Hardy (1980) have provided a comprehensive review of the impact of such dredging and filling activities on fish and wildlife populations generally. Invariably the effect is either partial or total habitat destruction leading to a radical change in the kinds of recreational activities being catered for in particular areas. In the recreation research literature such access and environmental transformations are now referred to as 'opportunity shift' (Pitts 1983). In the terminology of the Recreation Opportunity Spectrum concept referred to earlier, the Languedoc-Roussillon experiment involved an enormous expansion of sites at the modern end of the opportunity spectrum at the expense of primitive (or wilderness) settings. The project was conducted with extraordinary speed and an invaluable stretch of Mediterranean wetland was the ultimate victim. We can only speculate whether such an extravagant exercise in wetland destruction would be tolerated in the 1990s.

From the international engineering perspective many valuable lessons were learned in southern France about dredging and construction techniques in wetland environments. Worldwide, the 1970s and 1980s witnessed an enormous expansion in marina construction and the increasingly popular canal resort developments. These proliferated in the US sunbelt states, throughout Europe and the Caribbean and in Australasia. The second example is drawn from Australia.

5.3 *Noosa, Queensland*

When Europeans first surveyed the Noosa River region in southern Queensland 140 years ago, they were presented with the spectacle of a beautiful winding river flowing to the Pacific via a series of large lakes and lagoons fringed by mangroves and providing an abundance of fish and water birds for the local Aboriginal population. However, in the 1970s the estuary at the mouth of the Noosa River, like many other similar areas in Queensland and New South Wales, was transformed by a massive resort development that ultimately completely changed the hydrology, vegetation and sedimentation patterns of the picturesque river.

The physical transformation started in 1972 when a company known as Cambridge Credit was granted permission by the Queensland state government to proceed with an ambitious plan to develop a canal estate of 400 homes on 59 ha of land at Hay's Island, an area of mangroves and mud flats at the mouth of the Noosa River, adjacent to Noosa National Park. No detailed environmental impact or hydrographic studies were carried out. First, Aus $3.5 million were spent pumping sand from the river to raise the island's level by 1 m. Then the existing natural channels through the island were dredged and widened and a connecting bridge was constructed to link the island to the mainland. Large earth-moving equipment was subsequently moved on to the island where the existing vegetation was totally removed. Such rare birds as mangrove honeyeaters and azure kingfishers were displaced. Cato (1979, p. 106) notes that

> The amount of wildlife destroyed in this single operation is inestimable, if you count crabs, prawns, minnows, baby birds, lizards, snakes and insects. The whole life-support system of a complex, interweaving mass of bio-energy was swept away.

The Managing Director of Cambridge Credit saw things quite differently. At the resort's opening ceremony he proudly reported that

> My company believes in conservation . . . We don't apologize for taking this land away from the mosquitoes and sand flies. We have turned an ecological desert into a fine estate. (Quoted by Cato 1979, p. 107)

Prior to the development the estuary was one of the richest fish-breeding areas in southern Queensland, but this is no longer the case. Mangroves are a particularly rich source of nutrients for young fish. Their destruction for the resort development and for other purposes throughout the Noosa River system has now seriously decimated the local fish population and affected both recreational and commercial fisheries. Moreover, deep scouring of the tidal channels and associated severe bank erosion are now continual problems requiring constant engineering attention. Black sand and silt detritus has also been stirred up by the deep sand pumping. This now covers local sandy beaches which were formally white and has resulted in the destruction of valuable seagrass beds. These are familiar effects. Indeed, together with a host of ancillary impacts (Westman 1975), they have been well known since the early 1900s when the Ballona Creek development in Los Angeles mentioned earlier in the chapter, started to deteriorate badly.

6.0 CONCLUSION

This chapter has focused on certain aspects of the recreation-wetlands 'problematic'. Wetlands of various kinds have been found to have considerable economic significance for a wide range of recreational and associated wildlife habitat values. These are increasingly being recognized explicitly in US legal compensation cases, in particular. Several wetland-oriented recreational activities such as fishing, hunting and nature study have shown spectacular growth rates in many countries in recent years. The recreation and wildlife management literature suggests that wetlands can be managed satisfactorily to cope with such pressures provided that sufficient funds and personnel are made available on a continuing basis and provided, of course, that preservation is also guaranteed through adequate legislation. Above all, successful management needs to be grounded firmly in scientific information about wetland functioning and potential impacts. At the present time there is often a serious mismatch between 'science' and 'policy'. In the US context Nelson and Logan (1984), for example, have argued that 'New knowledge of the wide variation from place to place in the physical, chemical, and ecological functions and values of wetlands tends to invalidate a policy that fails to account for this variation.'

Much has been made in the discussion of the adverse effects of recreation and tourism on wetland environments. But it needs to be stressed equally that in many countries, both rich and poor, there is now a growing recognition of the considerable economic and other benefits that can flow from wetland preservation. Thus while a deliberate emphasis was placed here on some of the more blatant examples of wetland destruction in the name of tourism, it is only fair to point out that in many parts of the world recent years have also seen a significant increase in the number of successful campaigns to save wetlands threatened by development activities of various kinds. From the environmentalist standpoint there have been gains as well as losses. The 77 000 ha Coto Doñana in southern Spain is certainly a shining example of a world-class wetland region that has successfully survived a whole series of potentially devastating threats over hundreds of years. The important southern Moreton Bay wetlands between Brisbane and the Gold Coast in southern Queensland provide another example, following a bitter public dispute in the late 1960s. Moreover, the new mitigation initiatives at such places as Ballona in Los Angeles (Metz 1987) and the use of 'down-zoning' elsewhere in the United States to preserve wetlands (Anderson and Edwards 1986) are all indicative of the recent emergence in affluent countries of a considerably heightened level of awareness of wetland values where new residential housing developments are concerned. In common with the parallel problem of tropical deforestation the real question for the future where wetlands are concerned is: can the conservation momentum be maintained? Arguably, as with the forests, it is the tropical wetlands that are currently under the greatest threat.

10

Wetland Losses and Gains

James G. Gosselink and Edward Maltby

1.0 INTRODUCTION: DIVERSITY AND DYNAMICS

The foregoing chapters have shown that wetland is a term applied to ecosystems dominated by water in their formation, development and ecological functions. Nevertheless, despite the significance and importance of hydrology in their genesis and characterization, they are extremely diverse and dynamic ecosystems, all of which has implications for this chapter on wetland gains and losses. The need for accurate definition is not academic (Cowardin et al. 1979; see also chapter 2); it is now assuming legal importance, especially in the United States where federal and state legislation now attempts to regulate wetland changes. This legislation has arisen as a result of increasing awareness of wetland functions in maintaining environmental quality and also constant losses which have occurred.

1.1 *Wetland diversity*

Wetlands occupy about 6 per cent of the world's land surface. They vary according to their origin, geographical location, water regime, chemistry and dominant plants, and they are usually sustained by water sources other than direct rainfall. They include some of the most productive ecosystems in the world. Tidal salt marshes, typical of temperate shorelines, are found over large areas of the eastern seaboard of North America and coastal Europe. Freshwater marshes, dominated by grasses and sedges, occur in all latitudes where groundwater, surface springs or streams cause frequent flooding.

Swamps are flooded throughout most or all of the growing season and develop in still-water areas, around lake margins and in parts of flood plains. Varied terminology means that the term includes both forested systems such as the cypress swamps of the southern United States, the *Melaleuca* swamp forests of New Guinea or the mangrove forests of the tropical coasts, as well as herbaceous systems such as *Phragmites*-dominated reed swamps. It is suggested that there may be more swamp than open water in tropical Africa (Beadle 1974). More than a quarter of Indonesia is swamp; in Sumatra the proportion is 30 per cent. Kalimantan supports nearly 20×10^6 ha of swamp, more than half with peaty soils. Mangrove forests cover at least 14×10^6 ha. The greatest concentration is in the Indian Ocean–West Pacific region with about 20 per cent of the world's total area bordering the Sunda Shelf region enclosed by Vietnam, Thailand, Malaysia, Sumatra, Java and Borneo (chapter 4). The Niger delta extends over 700 000 ha and the Sundarbans forest covers nearly 10^6 ha of the Ganges delta (chapter 7).

Peat produces distinctive wetland landscapes of bog, moor, fen and muskeg, collectively called mires, but also forms in association with marsh and swamp in tropical and subtropical lakes, flood plains and coastal regions. Peatlands were thought to cover 150×10^6 ha in 1969, but this figure was revised by Kivinen and Pakarinen (1981) to 422×10^6 ha. Peatlands probably cover at least 500×10^6 ha from tundra to tropical environments (Bord na Móna 1985). The greatest proportion of peatland occurs in the temperate and boreal zone, with three-quarters of the total in the USSR and Canada alone (chapter 1, figure 1.2). More than 75 per cent of all peat soils in the tropics are found in one area bordering the western, southern and eastern extremities of the South China Sea (chapter 4). Tropical peat resources together with those in higher latitudes are attracting increased attention as a source for fuel (Maltby 1985). Their role as geochemical and particularly carbon sinks is still imperfectly understood and there is growing concern about the global implications of changes in the atmospheric carbon balance associated with their large-scale exploitation (Winkler and De Witt 1985, Maltby 1986).

The periodic flooding of land between river channels and valley sides is a common feature of the lower reaches of rivers throughout the world and produces a complex variety of wetlands. In the United States such periodically flooded bottomlands produce hardwood forests that once covered vast areas of the southeast, east and central regions. The largest contiguous areas occurred in the lower Mississippi River valley. Bottomland hardwood wetlands still cover more than 23.5×10^6 ha in the United States (Frayer et al. 1983; see also chapter 6). However, the wetland complexes once present in the fringing flood plains of Europe and North America have now largely disappeared through the deepening of river channels, levee construction and land development. The world's remaining major seasonal flood plains are now limited to the tropics and subtropics, and they are under ever-increasing pressure from development projects.

Nearly half the total wetland area of Africa consists of forested or savanna flood plain (Drijver and Marchand 1985). In special circumstances deltas form and further diversify the mosaic of wetland types on the African continent. These may be inland, such as the inner Niger and the Okavango, or coastal such as the Nile. In some areas the terrain is so flat that seasonal rainfall alone can produce flooding over large areas. Extensive sheet flooding occurs in the Chari-Lagone river basin in southern Chad (chapter 11). Some of the largest sheet flood regions, however, are in South America. The Pantanal of the Paraguay River comprises shallow interconnected lakes and wetland complexes, which in some years can cover 14×10^6 ha (Alho et al.1988).

Man-made wetlands, which include reservoirs, ponds, lagoons, extraction pits, waterways and, more recently, mimics established as mitigation for wetland losses elsewhere, are an increasing feature of both the developed and developing world. They have become some of the most important wildlife habitats in western Europe. Such has been the loss of wetlands that 'virtually any water body assumes conservation value' (Tydeman 1984). Man's ability to create artificial wetlands has led developers to argue against unnecessary protection of natural wetlands where they can be replaced or recreated. The acid test of the acceptability of mitigation, however, lies in the ability of artificial wetlands to mimic functions as well as appearance. Considerable research is being directed into this line of development (Larson and Neill 1987, Maltby 1987, 1988a, b).

1.2 *Wetland dynamics – processes of change*

Another significant characteristic of wetlands is their dynamic nature. This is recognized in the classical view of plant succession (Pearsall 1920, Wilson 1935), in which wetlands are considered to be transient stages in the hydrarch development of a terrestrial forested climax community from a shallow lake. The early literature on the subject leaned heavily on studies of inland freshwater wetlands, mostly in north temperate regions. Here the typical successional sequence was described as follows: infilling of shallow lakes through run-off and organic production; formation of minerotrophic emergent marshes or fens starting at the lake periphery and moving towards the centre as infilling continued; accumulation of peats to form increasingly ombrotrophic bogs; occasionally transition to mesic forests depending on changes in local hydrology (chapter 3). The pattern emphasizes the importance of biotic, i.e. autogenic, factors in wetland development, and it applies primarily to regions of the north temperate zone where the water-table is at or near the land surface. In these climates peat-building wetlands could develop over thousands of years. Eventually they are dominated by biotic processes that isolate them from their mineral substrates.

Other kinds of wetlands follow different patterns of formation and succession. Riverine forested wetlands, which cover large areas of the globe, are typified in temperate zones by such flood-tolerant species as bald cypress (*Taxodium distichum* (L.) Rich.), tupelo gum (*Nyssa aquatica* L.), alder (*Alnus* species) and oak-dominated bottomland hardwood species. In the tropical areas of the world these species are replaced by trees such as *Melaleuca* species. These wetlands are usually high-energy systems, often characterized by seasonally pulsed flooding and high sedimentation and erosion rates. Riparian ecosystems are particularly expansive on coastal plains where valleys incised into Pleistocene deposits during the last glacial period were filled with sediments as the sea gradually rose to its present level during the past

10 000 years. In these broad flood plains the energy of rivers draining out of uplands is dissipated by lateral translation into meanders. The shifting river channels result in considerable local instability and natural cycles of wetland formation and destruction as some areas dry up, others are inundated, new land is formed and old land erodes. On the scale of the whole river system, however, the net effect of all these changes may be a steady state. The pattern of biotic development in these riverine wetland systems follows the topographic variability, and diversity is often unusually high (Wharton et al. 1982).

Coastal ecosystems are not as extensive as inland wetlands, but because two-thirds of the human population live in one-third of the earth's land area adjacent to its oceans, they are exposed to particularly heavy human pressure. The largest expanses of coastal wetlands are deltas, the seaward edge of riverine systems, dominated by river flow and high sediment levels (chapter 2). Other coastal wetland systems have developed from marine sediment deposition in shallow protected coastal embayments. Typically, both types have formed during the past 5000 years of slowly rising sea level, expanding seaward as sediments were either dropped from river flows or marine currents slowed over shallow flats (Nixon 1982), and landward as rising waters inundated former uplands (Redfield 1972, Ellison and Nichols 1976, Froomer 1980a, b). As emergent marshes expanded on these shallow flats their organic production contributed to peat accumulation and their biomass reduced flow velocities further, enhancing the deposition of mineral sediments.

On coasts the stability of a wetland is determined by the balance between submergence of the land due to eustatic sea-level rise, sediment compaction and crustal down-warping, and vertical accretion due to both mineral and organic deposition. On the east coast of the United States the submergence rate has been about 1 mm/yr for the last 3000 years, and slightly higher (2–3 mm/yr) over the past 35 years (Nixon 1982). East coast marshes have accreted more rapidly than this and have been steadily expanding. In contrast the submergence rate on the US Gulf of Mexico coast exceeds 1 cm/yr (Nummedal 1982), and most marshes are not accreting that rapidly. As a result they are gradually submerging and dying, creating large shallow open lakes.

The Canadian wetlands on the south coast of James Bay are an interesting exception to the general rule of subsidence. Here a gradual uplift of the land as a result of isostatic rebound has resulted in an enormous area of wetlands 'naturally reclaimed' from the bay bottom.

Coastal wetlands provide the clearest examples of the interactions of sediment supply and hydrology determining the fate of wetlands (chapter 2). The same principle applies to other types of wetlands, although the local dynamics may be quite different. In riverine systems the migration of the river bed may change the local flooding regime and sediment supply, leading to modification of a wetland. In peatlands subsidence (compaction and mineralization) or a change in local hydrology can substantially modify the character of the wetland ecosystem, creating new areas of open water, for example.

These examples illustrate the dynamics of natural wetlands. However, many wetlands are affected by human activities which cause modification of hydrology and sediment supply. Often the impact is explicit and expected, as when a wetland is drained and impounded for agricultural production. In other circumstances, however, the impacts are unexpected by-products of human actions taken for other purposes that modify hydrology and/or sediments, and thus indirectly wetlands. These effects can be major, chronic and remote in space and time. For example, an anticipated direct effect of building a dam on a river is the flooding of a reservoir area, which may directly destroy or create wetlands. Unexpected results of the same action may be changed flooding patterns of downstream wetlands. Further, because sediments are trapped behind dams, downstream wetlands may begin to experience sediment deficits. The sediment-depleted river may begin to erode downstream, causing long-term changes in the relationship of the river to the channel and flood plain.

In the following sections we discuss rates and causes of losses and gains of wetlands world-wide, and explore the implications of these changes in the light of the key roles of hydrology and sediment supply in their stability and the way they function.

2.0 NATURE, CAUSES AND RATES OF WETLAND LOSS

Causes of wetland loss are many and often complex, and perhaps owe as much to their natural diversity and dynamics as to purposeful transformation. Wetlands are lost and gained as a result of natural processes of formation, change and degradation, as illustrated by the cycle of growth, abandonment and decay of a typical river delta (figure 10.1). Human kind has accelerated or slowed these processes in a number of ways, sometimes dramatically. Table 10.1 summarizes and lists examples of some of the more common types of wetland alteration. These vary from areal loss to functional loss or change, from direct anticipated effects to indirect, often unintentional, effects, from immediate discrete events to gradual long-term and/or chronic processes and from local to catchment or even regional impact. The permanence of the action also varies from transient to irreversible. Generally, impacts that change substrate or hydrology are more permanent than those that influence biota. For example, Lee and Gosselink (1988) ranked human activities that alter bottomland hardwood forests in the United States by extensiveness, permanence and intensity (figure 10.2).

Mining is the most disruptive because it permanently destroys the substrate, but it affects relatively small areas. Large public works projects have changed hydrology over much of the bottomland area and their impacts are difficult to reverse. Agricultural clearing is potentially reversible on the scale of regrowth of the forest (100 years). Timber harvest and hunting disrupt wetlands least, if the best current management practices are used.

Recent regulatory efforts to control wetland loss in the United States have focused on small-scale activities, which tend to be discrete events with direct local impacts incurred over short periods of time (although the effects may be permanent). Unfortunately the cumulative impact of many such activities

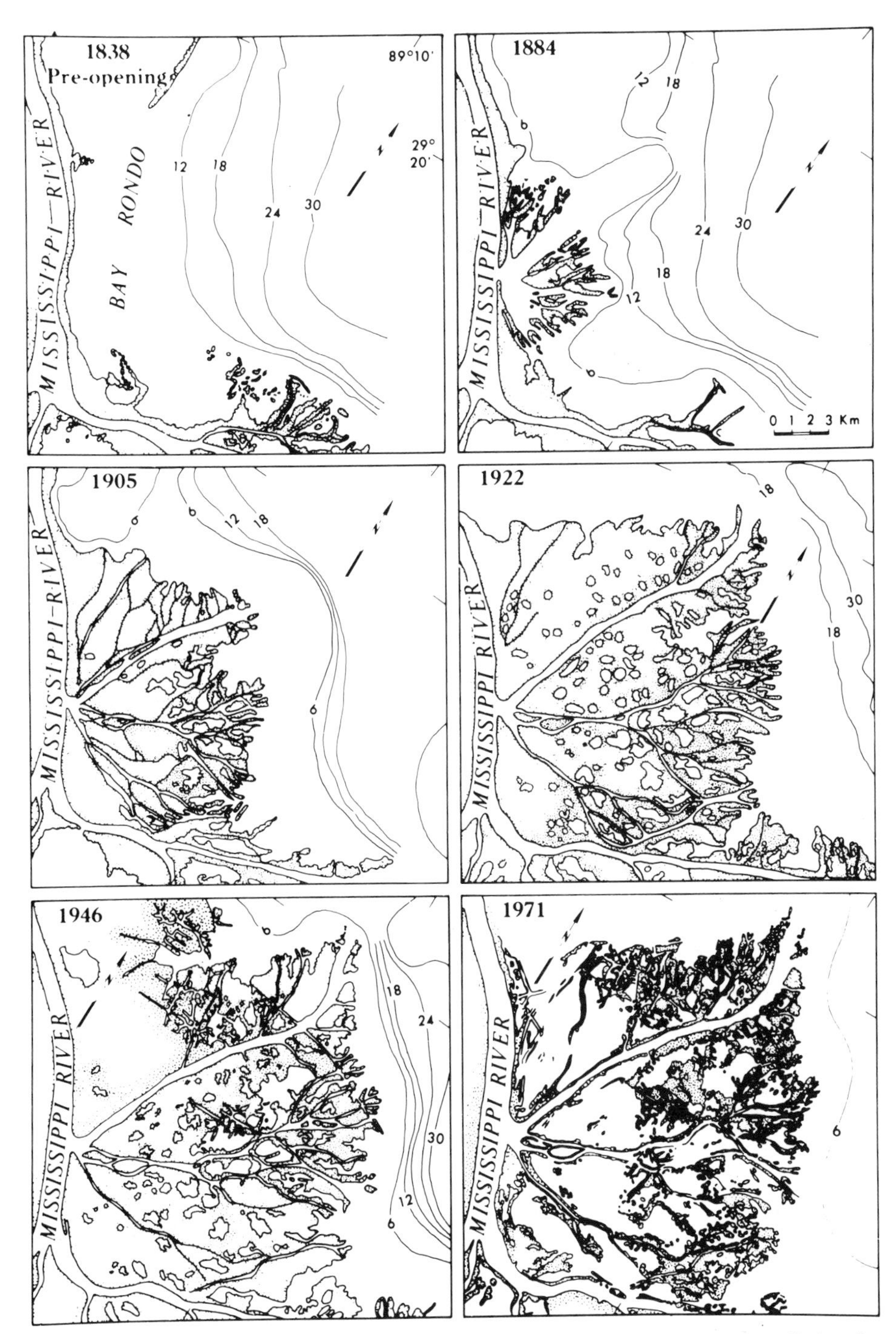

Figure 10.1 The sequential development of Cubits Gap subdelta (Wells et al. 1982). A major delta lobe of the Mississippi is made up of a number of subdeltas such as this in various stages of development. Overall, the sequence of the whole delta lobe is the same as shown, but the time sequence is of the order of 1000–5000 years

Table 10.1 Types and causes of wetland alteration

Type of change	*Discrete events*	*Gradual long-term processes*
Physical		
Changes in topography or elevation	Filling or excavation	Waterborne sediment increase
	Mining, dredge and fill	Denuding watersheds (clearing)
	Natural deposition or erosion	Waterborne sediment decrease
	Floods	Reservoirs, flood-control levees
Changes in local or regional hydrology	Reduction in available water	Reduction in available water
	Draining agricultural land	Increasing upstream withdrawal
	Diverting water	Ground-water overdraft
	Increases in water	Increased water amount or depth
	Flooding from reservoir filling	Watershed clearing
		Coastal submergence
Chemical		
Changes in nutrient levels	Increased loading	Increased loading
	Point-source discharge	Agricultural run-off
		Wetland waste water disposal
	Decreased loading	Decreased loading
		Upland reforestation
Change in toxic substances or contaminants	Increased loading	Increased loading
	Pesticide application	Chronic low-level disposal
	Oil or toxin spill	Pesticide run-off
		Industry waste water discharge
		Deposition from air

Changes in salt levels		Increased levels Reduced freshwater inflow Canal construction Decreased levels Reduced irrigation return flow
Changes in pH		Increased acidity Acid precipitation Acid mine drainage Natural bog succession Decreased acidity Increased irrigation return flow
Change in temperature	Discharge of heated effluents	Climate change
Biological		
Changes in biomass	Biomass decrease Fire, clearing, lumbering Biomass increase Planting	Biomass decrease Grazing, many adverse physical and chemical changes Biomass increase Regrowth, eutrophication
Changes in community composition	Selective harvesting Introduction of exotic species	Natural succession Selective harvesting Habitat loss Change in hydrology, noise
Changes in landscape pattern through clearing, selective forest harvest, modified hydrology		All kinds of cumulative impacts

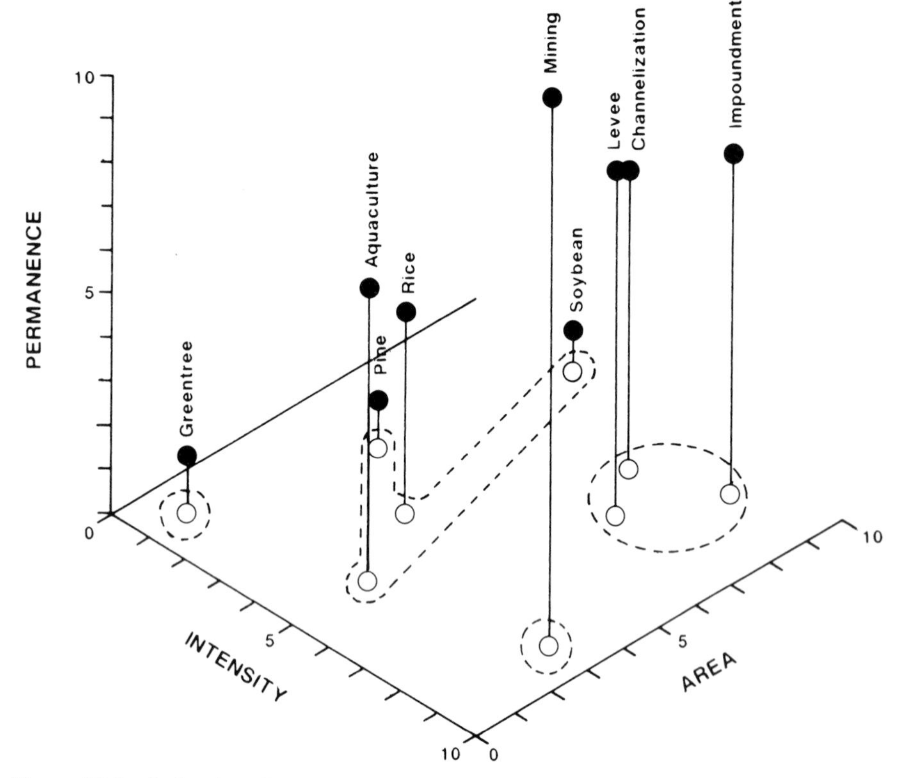

Figure 10.2 A simple ordination of activities by the importance of their cumulative impacts on forested wetlands based on the area impacted, the intensity of the impact and its permanence
(after Lee and Gosselink 1988)

influences large areas (entire drainage basins, or even continents), appear gradually over a long period of time, are chronic and are largely unrecognized and unregulated.

2.1 *Inland freshwater marshes*

Inland freshwater wetlands comprise most of the world's wetlands. In the United States more than 90 per cent of wetlands are interior, about equally distributed between emergent marshes and forested wetlands (Tiner 1984). The largest single cause of loss of these wetlands between the 1950s and 1970s (80 per cent of the total loss) was conversion to agriculture (OTA 1984). In Europe the pattern of conversion began much earlier than in the United States, with impounding and draining being well under way in medieval times (chapter 6). In the United States the Swampland Acts of 1849, 1850 and 1860 were passed to remove the federal government from the reclamation business. Ironically a large portion of the wetlands deeded to the states by these Acts soon found its way into private hands, and the new owners put strong pressure on public agencies to assist in the cost of draining. Some indication of the magnitude of this effort is shown in figure 10.3 which summarizes trends in surface and subsurface drainage of farmland between 1900 and 1980. Probably about 65 per cent of this land was wetland (OTA 1984). The figure shows dramatically the high rate of drainage after the First World War, the effect of the depression years of the late 1920s and 1930s, and the rapid expansion of drained farmland again in the 20 year period following the Second World War.

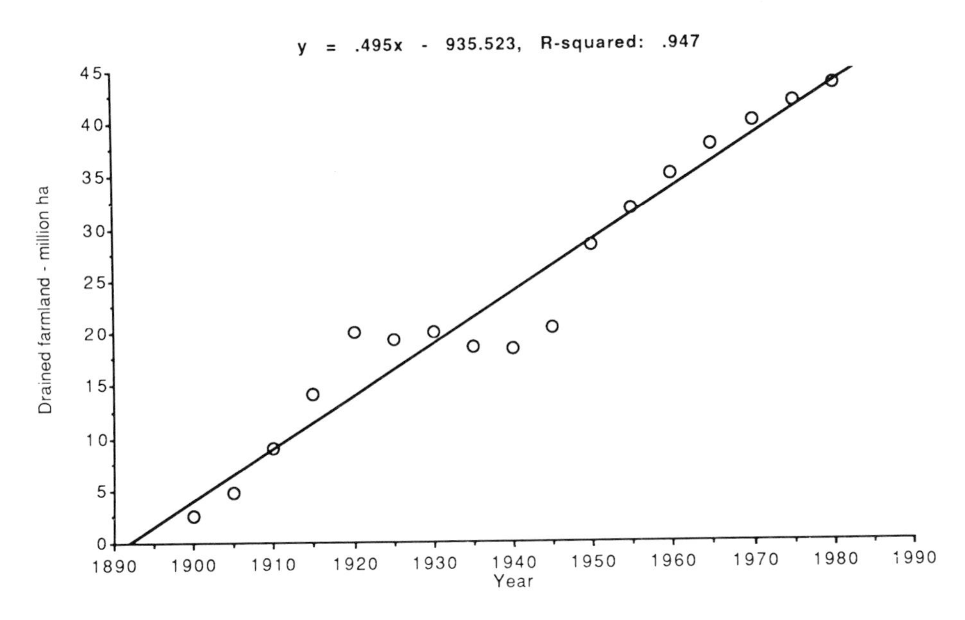

Figure 10.3 Drained farmland in the United States, 1900–80
(data from OTA 1984)

Table 10.2 summarizes changes in US inland wetlands during a 20 year period ending in the mid-1970s (Frayer et al. 1983). Of the 13 405 000 ha of inland marshes in the 1950s, 74 per cent remained in the 1970s. Over 1 800 000 ha (13.7 per cent) was converted to agricultural production.

Conversion of inland marshes to agricultural production reflects two different processes. The first is the purposeful draining of marshes via surface ditches, subsurface tiles, impounding and pumping to make them suitable for cultivation. Tax incentives and drainage improvements associated with new highways are contributing factors (OTA 1984). The second process is more subtle. The expansion of irrigation systems, especially the development of centre-pivot irrigation, had a twofold effect. Small wetland pools became sources of irrigation water, for example in the playa region of the Texas highlands. Further, subsurface pumping, mostly for irrigation, reduced ground-water levels (OTA 1984). This tended to dry out many isolated wetlands in the Midwest, making them easier to convert to agricultural

Table 10.2 Fate of freshwater wetlands in the United States

	Wetland type	*Area (× 10^3 ha)*	*Percentage of 1950s*
1950s	Palustrine emergent	13400	100
1970s	Palustrine emergent	9916	74
	Palustrine scrub/shrub and forest	970	7.2
	Open water and lacustrine	298	2.2
	Agriculture	1843	13.7
	Urban	172	1.3
	Other	207	1.5
1950s	Forested and scrub/shrub	27006	100
1970s	Forested and scrub/shrub	23009	85
	Palustrine emergent	575	2.1
	Open water and lacustrine	187	0.7
	Agriculture	2902	10.7
	Urban	152	0.6
	Other	129	0.5

Source: Frayer et al. 1983

production. A further complication of irrigation practices in arid regions is the fate of return flows. Water flowing across arid fertilized land accumulates various chemicals. In California, loss of wetland habitat for migrating waterfowl has concentrated remaining populations into a few remaining areas such as the Kesterson Wildlife Refuge. Agricultural return flows into this refuge have high selenium concentrations, which cause high egg mortality rates and severely malformed chicks (Willard, et al 1988). The refuge has been closed until some solution to this problem can be found.

2.2 *Riparian wetlands*

In the United States the largest remaining wetland areas are bottomland hardwood forests, especially those that occupy the broad flood plain of the Mississippi. These are also the most vulnerable wetland areas of the nation at present, with a loss rate of between 1960 and 1975 exceeding 1 per cent per year (Abernethy and Turner 1987; see also table 10.2). Nearly all the loss is attributed to clearing for agricultural production, which was supported by large federally financed flood-control projects, farm subsidies in various forms and the high price of soybeans on the world market.

As with wetland impacts elsewhere, a number of interacting factors have contributed to bottomland hardwood forest loss. The severe Mississippi flood of 1927 led directly to federal flood-control financing, which has been one responsibility of the US Army Corps of Engineers since that time. Flood-control levees along the river have dramatically reduced the area of bottomlands receiving back-water flooding and made these areas easier to drain for farming. An additional unanticipated result of confining the river to its channel was to increase stage heights, so that flooding actually increased downstream (Belt 1975). This resulted in a new round of flood protection projects in the affected areas and more forested wetland conversion. Stavins (1987) attributed at least 25 per cent of land clearing since the 1950s to Corps public works projects. In addition to the direct wetland loss from agricultural clearing, flood-control projects changed flooding patterns in remaining forested bottomlands. The mature forests appear much the same as they used to, but there is concern that they may be relict ecosystems in the sense that they will be gradually replaced by more upland plant communities as individual trees die.

The pattern of wetland loss in forested bottomlands is typified by the incremental disappearance of forests in the Tensas River basin in northeast Louisiana (Gosselink et al. 1988; see also chapter 6). This 1 million ha basin, all bottomland, was almost completely forested at the time of first European settlement. In 1937, the first year for which good survey data are available, about 65 per cent of these forests remained. Today 18 per cent remains (plate 10.1). A comparison of land-use maps dating back to 1947 reveals a pattern of progressive conversion of bottomland forest to agricultural production. This conversion was accompanied by deforestation of stream borders and increasing fragmentation of the remaining forest. Presently only about 15 per cent of

Plate 10.1 Bottomland forest in the Tensas River basin, Louisiana, part of a wetland forest that was formerly over 1 million ha in extent. In the foreground trees have been sheared off and felled with a bulldozer blade. Above, a line of standing trees remains along a slight wet depression. Above the standing trees, felled trees have been pushed into a line for burning. In the distance land has been harrowed for planning, probably for soybeans, the most popular crop in the bottomlands
(Courtesy Larry N. Harper)

stream edges are forested. Forest patches are increasing in number and decreasing in size. Although in 1957 the two largest patches covered 316 000 ha, by 1987 only four patches larger than 10 000 ha remained, and these were less than 30 000 ha in size. These structural changes in the landscape were associated with significant cumulative changes in the functional ecology of the Tensas basin. Public flood-control projects have changed the flooding pattern of the wetlands from river back-water flooding in the spring, to flooding dominated by local rainfall. Water quality has declined; streams now seldom meet US Environmental Protection Agency recommended standards for phosphorus concentrations. Several mammal and bird species endemic to the basin are nationally or regionally extirpated. Forest-dependent bird species are decreasing in number at the rate of three to four per decade, and populations of other species are also declining.

2.3 *Coastal wetlands*

World-wide coastal wetlands represent only a small fraction of all wetlands; for example, in the United States they comprise less than 5 per cent. These wetlands have received a disproportionate share of wetlands research interest, and are probably better understood than inland systems. Because the social values of these ecosystems have been well studied and publicized they enjoy greater protection than their inland counterparts in most developed countries. In many US states coastal wetland development is now virtually forbidden. Much of the current loss is either a lingering legacy of past development or related to secondary or indirect effects of current projects. In the country's early years agricultural development took its toll of coastal wetlands, primarily in the fresher parts of estuaries and along coastal rivers. For example, on the south Atlantic coast many thousands of hectares of wetland were impounded for rice production, in South Carolina alone about 60 000 ha (Devoe and Baughman 1987). The rice industry declined in the early 1900s, but many of the impoundments are still in operation to provide waterfowl habitat. In the early 1900s many similar impoundments were constructed in coastal Louisiana, but here frequent hurricanes made the cost of impoundment maintenance prohibitive. The coastal wetlands are chequered by straight-sided shallow lakes that testify to failed agricultural developments (plate 10.2).

In the United States as a whole, the coastal wetland loss rate appears to have been about 0.2 per cent per year between 1922 and 1954, increasing to 0.5 per cent between 1954 and 1974 (Gosselink and Baumann 1980). Data since the mid-1970s are poor, but the rate from direct wetland conversion has probably decreased dramatically as a result of wetland protection regulations enacted in 1977. Very little coastal wetland loss between 1954 and 1974 was agriculturally induced (chapter 11). Along the Atlantic coast most of it was associated with post-war urban development. For example, several large airports have been constructed on filled wetlands. Marinas and finger-fill housing developments also occupy large expanses of former wetland.

On the central Gulf of Mexico coast, which has 40 per cent of the nation's

Plate 10.2 This infrared vertical air photograph taken at about 65 000 ft from a U-2 plane shows a portion of the freshwater wetland along an abandoned distributary of the Mississippi River, Bayou Lafourche. Residential and agricultural development has occurred on the high levees of the Bayou. The large black rectangular lake (1) was part of an agricultural development in the early part of the century. The levees were breached by a severe storm and the bayou was abandoned. Below it (2) is a similar development, still in sugar cane production. The soil surface inside the levees is now about 2 m below the surrounding water level as a result of compaction and oxidation of the organic soils. Man-made canals (3) are straight and deep; natural channels (4) are tortuous and shallow
(Courtesy NASA, Ames Research Center, Flight 78–143, October 1978)

coastal wetlands, the picture is quite different and very complex. Here the rate of wetland loss found between the 1950s and 1970s has continued, and perhaps even accelerated to the present. Little loss is ascribed to urban development. Rather, it is related to management of the Mississippi, navigation projects, and intensive oil and gas exploration and extraction, all acting on a geomorphically active sedimentary environment. Various estimates have been given for the influence of natural delta subsidence, as distinct from human impacts (Boesch 1982, Scaife et al. 1983, Turner and Cahoon 1988). Turner and Cahoon (1988) estimated that 29 per cent of the total net wetland loss in the Louisiana coast between 1955 and 1978 was due to direct conversion by agricultural and urban expansion (10 per cent), canals and spoil banks (16 per cent), and other (3 per cent). The other 71 per cent was due to indirect impacts of human activities interacting with natural processes. The coastal zone is submerging at a rate of about 1 cm/yr. Historically the Mississippi delivered enough sediment to offset submergence by accretion during spring floods. Now, however, dams on the upper reaches of its tributaries trap almost half the sediment load (Keown et al. 1980). Furthermore, flood management has confined the river to its channel so that it seldom floods the fringing marshes. Hence they experience a sediment deficit and do not accrete fast enough to keep up with submergence. Finally, the combined effects of navigation canals and channels dredged for oil and gas extraction change water flow patterns, and their spoil banks prevent sheet flow across the marsh (plate 10.3). The resulting decreased sediment supply, increased flooding duration and salt-water intrusion stress the marsh vegetation (Swenson and Wiseman 1987). Turner and Cahoon (1988) estimated that the indirect impacts associated with canals and associated spoil banks account for 20–60 per cent of wetland loss. This figure emphasizes the magnitude of the indirect effects attributed to canals, but the range of the estimate also highlights the uncertainty surrounding their precise impacts. Nevertheless, the case is not an isolated instance. Recent estimates indicate that the Nile delta is receding at up to 16–30 m/yr. Most of the sediment yield of the river, which previously counterbalanced the natural rate of delta subsidence, is now retained behind the Aswan dams, resulting in progressive coastal land loss (Stanley, 1988).

2.4 *Peatlands*

Peat normally accumulates relatively slowly with rates of accretion usually less than 2 mm/yr. Some areas of high-latitude deep blanket bog and tropical coastal peats have been developing for up to 10 000 years. However, in many areas surface elevations are currently decreasing at rates often several orders of magnitude faster than the normal accretion rate, primarily as a result of agricutural drainage and conversion to alternative land uses. Fen peat in eastern England has been lost at the rate of 3 cm/yr since 1848 (chapter 6). South of Lake Okeechobee, Florida, surface lowering of more than 3 m of peat has occurred, a rate of loss estimated as 2.5 cm/yr (Stephens 1974). In North Carolina, Dolman and Buol (1967) found that drainage alone reduced peat

Plate 10.3 A marsh scene in coastal Louisiana. The road on the bridge crosses an abandoned natural distributary of the Mississippi and then follows the slightly elevated natural levees of the channel bank to the small fishing settlement. The large canal entering the picture on the lower right was dredged for navigation about 40 years ago. In the background is an extensive network of oil-well access canals. Each short spur contains one or more well-heads. The high banks of dredged material along these canals isolate portions of the marsh, which then deteriorate rapidly into shallow ponds, such as that in the centre of the photograph
(Courtesy Charles E. Sasser)

thickness by 58 cm in 50 years but that the combined effects of compaction, fire and oxidation could increase that rate by a factor of three. Levin and Shoham (1983) cited surface losses of 10 cm/yr between 1958 and 1965 and of 7.5 cm/yr between 1970 and 1980 in the Hula Valley, northern Israel, where drainage was completed in 1958. In the case of some tropical lowland peats, however, subsidence of more than 50 cm can occur in the first year of drainage (Andriesse 1988). Drainage, as well as other forms of human disturbance, increases the fire hazard in organic soils and has considerably accelerated the rate of surface lowering in diverse systems which include blanket peat, papyrus swamp and swamp forest (Maltby 1980).

In Ireland, 80 000 ha of bog have been drained since 1946 and 50 per cent of Irish peatlands have been lost as natural ecosystems (Van Eck et al. 1984). A 1983 European Parliamentary report warned that the unique ecosystems of the Irish bogs would vanish completely in the succeeding 5 years unless effective preventive measures were taken (Baldock 1984). Without action that has included purchases of bogs with money raised largely from abroad (especially the Netherlands), these ecosystems would certainly have an extremely uncertain future.

Between the middle of the nineteenth century and 1978 about 84 per cent of lowland raised bog in Britain was lost through afforestation, agricultural reclamation and commercial peat cutting. Much of the remainder has been severely damaged by burning and draining, leaving only 6 per cent of the original 13 000 ha ecologically intact. Thirty per cent of the blanket peat on the Kintyre peninsula has been lost to forestry since 1945 (Nature Conservancy Council 1986). One of the largest single expanses of blanket bog in the world, located in Caithness and Sutherland, northern Scotland, has not been able to avoid development pressures. Despite the increasing global scarcity of this peatland type, and the primeval ecosystem it represents in northwest Europe with a particularly rich birdlife, the blanket bog has been lost progressively to coniferous afforestation, deep ploughing and drainage. Over the last 20 years, but mainly within the present decade, an original 401 375 ha area of blanket bog was reduced by 16 per cent. Only eight of the 41 river catchments in the region have no new plantations within them (Stroud et al. 1987).

2.5 *Wetland loss in the Third World*

Until the second half of the present century major wetland loss has been a feature mainly of the developed countries. Recently, more attention has focused on Third World countries and the tropics in particular, where increasing pressures exist for their conversion to alternative land uses. Precise data on rates and causes of loss are generally lacking because of the absence of the necessary administrative frameworks. However, several examples provide an indication of the scale of wetland loss. Areas of natural mangrove have been and are being converted, particularly to rice paddy and aquaculture, at an unprecedented rate (de la Cruz 1980). Only 25 per cent of the original mangrove areas of 24 000 ha remains in Puerto Rico. Thailand has lost up to 20 per cent of its mangroves in recent decades (McIntosh 1983). Data from the Natural Resources Management Centre (Jara 1984) show that the 448 310 ha of mangroves present in the Philippines in 1968 had been halved by 1981 (213 350 ha). The trend is mirrored by a progressive increase in the area of fishponds, which increased from 88 681 ha in 1952 to 195 831 ha in 1981 (Jara 1984) (figure 10.4). More recent estimates put fishpond creation as high as 242 000 ha (Naamin 1986).

McVey (1988) has recently surveyed the loss of mangroves to aquaculture throughout southeast Asia. Using data from his table 34.1, the estimated areas of loss to aquaculture as a percentage of total mangrove area are 6 per cent for Indonesia, 9 per cent for Malaysia and 12 per cent for Thailand. Potentially enormous losses threaten the flood plains of Africa. Large areas of natural flood-plain grazing have already been lost as a result of regulated river flow and large-scale irrigation projects throughout Africa. Dams for irrigation upstream led to the recession by 40 km of Lake Chad in Nigeria between April 1984 and January 1985. In the Senegal River delta, 2400 ha of flood plain were recently

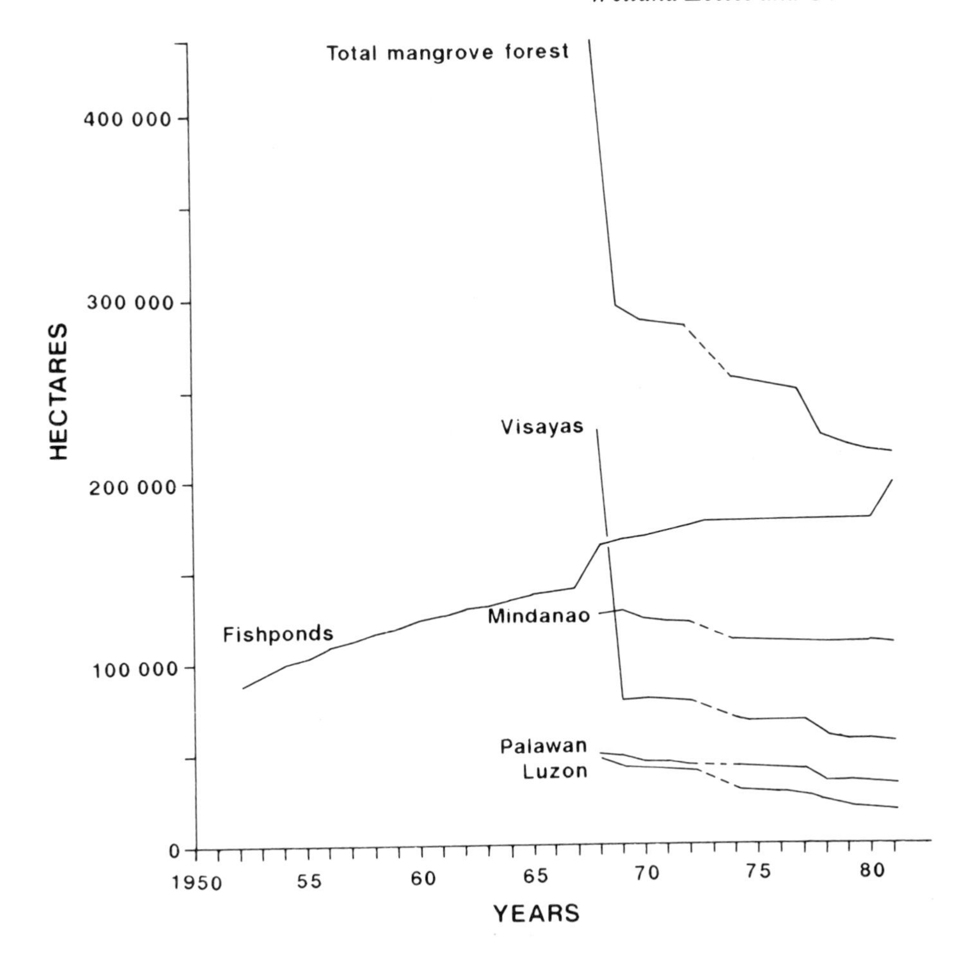

Figure 10.4 Trends in areas of mangrove forest (by region and total) and fishponds in the Philippines (Bureau of Forest Development and Fisheries Statistics of the Philippines) (after Jara 1984)

lost through dike construction in an irrigation scheme which not only failed but also impaired other ecological and environmental functions (Braakhekke and Marchand 1987). A recent study of a range of African flood-plain ecosystems concluded that the traditional multi-functional use of these wetland complexes actually had a higher financial margin of profit than that of agricultural conversion projects (Drijver and Marchand 1985; see also chapter 11).

In Central and South America nearly a fifth of the wetlands identified as internationally important are threatened by direct drainage for farming or ranching (Scott and Carbonell 1985). A large proportion of the rest are liable to a wide range of other deleterious impacts. More than 900 million ha world-wide may eventually be lost if drainage and water-control projects continue unabated (table 10.3).

Table 10.3 Potential for impounding (poldering) wetlands

Country	*Area (× 10^6 ha)*
North America	40.0
Mexico and Central America	20.7
South America	155.5
Europe	87.8
Africa	191.8
South Asia	104.9
North and Central Asia	219.4
Southeast Asia	53.0
Australia	43.5
Total	917.1

Source: *Polders of the World* (1982) after Braakhekke and Marchand (1987)

3.0 WETLAND GAINS

Man-made wetlands are not new. Ponds for farming fish have a long tradition in Asia and Europe. Man-made ponds in Guangdong province, China, are commonly stocked with five or six species of fish, each exploiting slightly different ecological niches in the pond. The ponds form part of a comprehensive land-use strategy. Duck waste, human excreta and bank vegetation are commonly the basis for fish feed. Organic-rich bottom detritus is exposed by periodic drainage and is used to fertilize the surrounding vegetated banks. The eutrophic water from the pond is often used to fertilize paddy fields at lower elevations. Up to 10 000 ducks/ha/yr and 1.5–5 t/ha/yr of fish can be harvested in addition to horticulture and other crops grown on the man-made 'stacked soils' of the banks (South China Agricultural University unpublished data). The state fisheries in the Trebon Biosphere Reserve, Czechoslovakia, originated in the Middle Ages and today produce about 2000 t of fish, 1000 t of duck and 100 t of geese. There are now some 4600 ha of fishponds in this part of Bohemia, giving an average fish production of 500 kg/ha.

The financial returns from aquaculture are particularly attractive in the Third World. Indirect benefits may also be generated. Artificial coastal inlet lagoons (*gei wais*) were excavated in Hong Kong to raise shrimp harvests and now contribute significantly to the wildlife value of the Mai Po wetland complex. A survey in Bangladesh found that more than 95 per cent of its 628 780 ha of mangroves were suitable for aquaculture (de la Cruz 1980). However, the ecological and environmental costs of conversion are increasingly being realized, including loss of important support functions for natural fisheries. The true overall profit-loss equation may not be favourable. Removal of the valuable nursery habitat for seed fish needed to stock the fishponds themselves, reduction in natural fishery harvests and increase in erosion and flood hazard all detract from any gains due to aquaculture production.

Possibilities for creation and/or enhancement of wetlands are currently receiving considerable attention, particularly in the developed world (Wolf et al. 1986, Larson and Neill 1987, Strickland 1986). Probably the largest single impetus has been generated in the United States in support of the duck-hunting lobby. Since 1937 a private organization, Ducks Unlimited, has raised over $400 million for waterfowl habitat development. More than 100 projects, including 53 dam and water-control programmes, have been completed by the Great Plains Regional Office alone. These have created or enhanced over 28 350 ha of wetlands on public wildlife management areas exceeding 60 750 ha (Hoffman 1988).

It has been estimated (OTA 1984) that 740 000 ha of freshwater wetlands were created around the peripheries of small farm ponds, which were built at the rate of about 50 000 per year from the 1950s to the 1970s (see chapter 11, table 11.5). These ponds serve as sources of water for cattle and for irrigation, and also make excellent habitats for waterfowl and other birds and small mammals. In many ways they mimic natural prairie pothole marshes, which go through a natural 5–20 year cycle of emergent marsh and open lake related to periodic droughts (Weller 1981). However, they hardly replace the 4 750 000 ha of inland wetland lost to agriculture during the same period.

Wetlands have actually been physically transplanted to avoid destruction by engineering projects. Highway construction in the Canton of Zurich in 1968 threatened an area of fen. The fen basin was enlarged and tussocks of the sedge *Caricetum paniculatae* (rare in middle Europe) were transplanted to the new site. Pumps were installed to mimic the continuous movement of ground-water and ensure survival of the wetland in a new environment. This project was the precursor of one of the more imaginative wetland transplantation operations. Runway extensions at Zurich airport proposed in 1971 threatened rare wetland plant communities. The planning authorities, engineers and scientists collaborated to move the threatened ecosystem physically. Special techniques were developed to handle soil-vegetation blocks of the wetlands. They were moved the shortest distance possible and old and new sites were matched in terms of water and nutrient regimes. Resetting of the blocks required elevators and draglines. Fissures and cracks had to be minimized because of the possible problems of aeration, accelerated organic matter breakdown, nutrient release and weed establishment. The work was carried out in winter when biological activity was at a minimum and the frozen ground facilitated handling.

Subsequent management of the transplants has involved selective cutting for weed control and detailed water regulation. Nevertheless the system suffered 'transplantation shock' – some species spread, some disappeared and others appeared. *Orchidaceae*, *Apiaceae* and *Equisetum* species were the most vulnerable to loss or dieback. Despite these problems plant communities have been maintained that are directly comparable with the originals. Monitoring has also provided important information on the impact tolerated by different wetlands and component species. However, the cost is staggering, amounting in this case to more than $1.5 million per hectare (Klötzli and Maltby 1983).

Experience with scientific and engineering aspects of wetland creation demonstrates that if proper attention is given to the hydrological requirements of wetlands, vigorous production of plants and animals is possible. However, how well these wetlands approximate the functional properties of natural ecosystems is not at all certain, and creation of wetlands for certain functions is probably not feasible. There is considerable expertise and experience in management of wetlands for waterfowl, which usually involves impoundment and water level control structures. It is also possible to design and engineer wetland systems for flood mitigation and sediment trapping (Ogawa and Male 1986). However, creation of the complex sediment profile of a mature marsh is not feasible; hence the nutrient cycling and retention functions of these marshes are difficult, if not impossible, to create instantaneously. In addition, a growing literature from the field of conservation ecology suggests that we need to pay much more attention to the context of the wetland created, i.e. its role in the landscape, than has been the case up until now (Soulé and Wilcox 1980).

Less controlled kinds of coastal wetland creation possibilities that capitalize on the natural sediment supply and the energy of rivers are the 'freshwater diversion projects' on the northern Gulf of Mexico. These projects divert fresh river water and its associated suspended sediments out of the river channel into shallow estuaries to build new marshes. Louisiana has a number of these projects, in either planning or early stages of implementation, to take advantage of the enormous sediment load of the Mississippi, but few data are available to indicate their success. White (Loyola University, New Orleans, LA, personal communication) has documented the emergence and growth of sedimentary islands resulting from intentional breaching of the natural levee on one of the Mississippi's distributaries near its mouth. Subaerial land appeared rapidly and invasion by willows and emergent herbs soon followed. Within a season after emergence the islands were used extensively by deer, nutria, ducks and geese. The best documented similar example is the growth of a natural delta in Atchafalaya Bay, at the mouth of the Atchafalaya River, a distributary of the Mississippi that now carries about a third of its flow. Following subsurface deposition in the first half of the century, islands began to appear after the severe spring flood of 1973 (Roberts and Van Heerden 1982). The delta has continued to expand each spring to its present area of over 20 km^2 (figure 10.5). As with the previous example the islands vegetated rapidly, and are used extensively by wildlife. The growth of the Atchafalaya delta wetlands results from the natural process of diversion of the Mississippi that has occurred about every 700–1000 years since the last glaciation. However, its potential is curtailed by management of the river, which limits the diversion to one-third of its flow. Small diversion projects at the mouth of the Mississippi will build wetlands, but their potential is small compared with the losses occurring on this coast. Louisiana currently loses about 130 km^2 of coastal wetland per year. Day and Craig (1982) estimated that 30–40 km^2/yr could be saved by strict regulatory control of new canal construction, compared with about 1 km^2/yr created through freshwater diversions and a maximum of 18 km^2/yr by the land-building processes of the Atchafalaya River. This analysis emphasizes the importance, in this instance, of conservation of existing resources compared with creation of new wetlands.

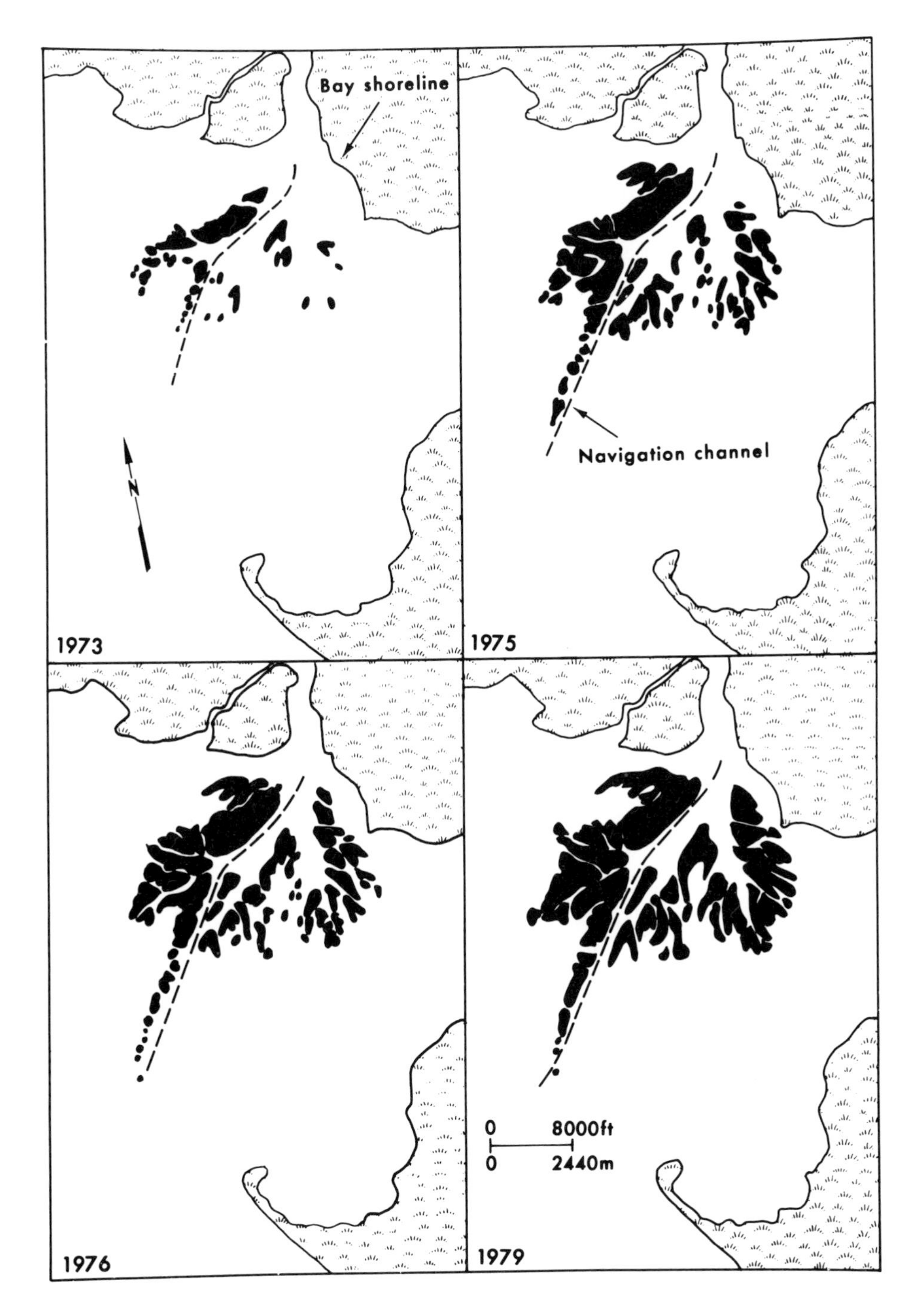

Figure 10.5 Areas of subaerial exposure obtained from LANDSAT images and aerial photographs depicting progressive evolution of the Atchafalaya delta
(from Roberts and Van Heerden 1982)

4.0 CUMULATIVE AND GLOBAL IMPLICATIONS OF WETLAND LOSS

The values of wetlands to society are well documented (Maltby 1986, Mitsch and Gosselink 1986; see also chapter 1). However, the implications of cumulative losses on the regional, continental or even global scale are less clearly understood. Several examples are discussed below to indicate the kinds of impacts that could occur and the scale on which they occur.

4.1 *Regional flooding*

River channels and flood plains tend to be in equilibrium with their discharge, so that width and depth are (within broad limits) predictable from a knowledge of discharge (Leopold et al. 1964). When extensive areas of flood plains are leveed, confining adjacent rivers to their channels, this equilibrium is altered and rivers become unstable. Belt (1975) described how confining and shortening the Mississippi (by removing meanders) has changed its historic stage-to-discharge ratio. Prior to the construction of major flood-control projects in 1927 the ratio was virtually constant from year to year (figure 10.6). Since that time it has become increasingly unstable. In the 1973 flood the river stage at peak flood was 3 m above the stage for the same discharge in 1927.

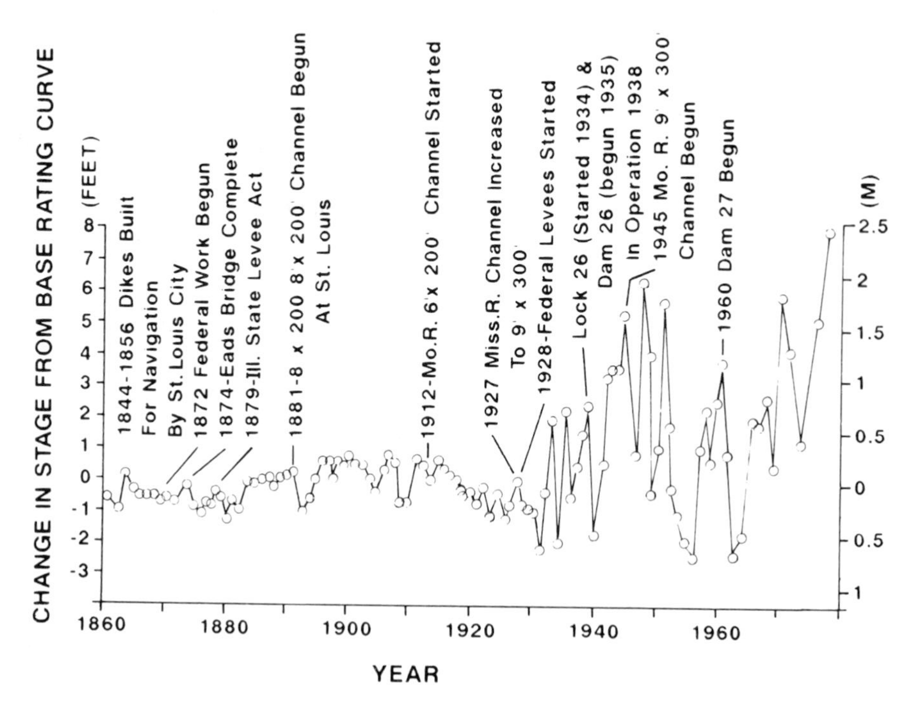

Figure 10.6 Change in stage from base rating curve of the Mississippi at St Louis (after Belt 1975)

During the low flow years, such as 1988, the channel tends to silt up and navigation is impeded by shallow water. The cost of dredging to maintain navigation and of building higher levees is enormous. Much of this increased cost is related to the conversion and 'flood-proofing' of flood-plain wetlands that formerly stored flood waters so that peak flows were smaller and minimum flows larger.

4.2 *Food supply*

Wetlands provide food chain support, protective cover and essential feeding, breeding or maturation areas for a wide range of species. Many wetland-dependent plants and animals are important for subsistence communities and some make a significant contribution to local, regional and even natural economies. Considerable debate has surrounded the effects of incremental loss or change of the wetland habitat on its capability to provide living resources. Turner and Boesch (1988) summarized the increasing evidence of linkage with particular reference to stocks of penaeid shrimp. Positive relationships have been established between shrimp harvest and coastal wetland areas in locations which include Australia, Malaysia, Philippines and the Gulf of Mexico. The corollary of progressive wetland loss or modification is that the yield of shrimp declines (Doi et al. 1973, Trent et al. 1976). Turner and Boesch (1988) concluded that shrimp and many other fisheries were directly limited by the quantity and quality of wetland habitat. However, the precise mechanisms of linkage – for example, the relative importance of food chain support, protection from predators or water quality maintenance – are still imperfectly understood (chapter 1). Because individual development projects are usually small in relation to the total wetland resource, their impact on dependent aquatic species is generally not measurable. However, the cumulative effects of many individual projects lead to predictable consequences.

4.3 *Genetic diversity and wildlife reserves*

Wetlands offer a diverse range of habitats for wildlife because of their temporal as well as their spatial variability. They are rich in endemic, rare and endangered species. The Great Lakes of Africa are particularly rich in endemic fish, especially cichlids. Eighty per cent of identified species in Lake Tanganyika are endemic. The Sundarbans coastal forest of India and Bangladesh is the largest remaining habitat of the Royal Bengal tiger and the last refuge for a large number of endangered mammals, reptiles and amphibians (Seidensticker and Hai 1983). More than half of Europe's most endangered birds depends on wetlands (Braakhekke and Marchand 1987). In Belgium 97 of the 306 plants classified as rare, vulnerable, endangered or already extinct are wetland species. The figures for Britain are 61 out of 303, and for the Netherlands 124 out of 440. Only a fraction of the rich genetic resources has been studied and a still smaller fraction tapped for human use. Yet the economic value of rice, sago, oil palm, mangroves, shrimp, crayfish, oysters, waterfowl, fish and fur-bearing animals is indisputable. It is a reasonable assumption that at least as important genetic material for human utilization awaits discovery.

Some of the most endangered animal species require the largest continguous areas of protected habitat. The pattern of wetland loss may be at least as significant as its magnitude in threatening the survival of these species. The Florida panther (*Felix concolor coryi*) is one of the most endangered animals in the world. It has suffered significantly, not only because of habitat reduction but also because of fragmentation and isolation (Noss 1987). Highway mortality is the largest single cause of death; only 20–50 individuals remain (US Fish and Wildlife Service 1986). One way in which a viable population of this species might be supported is by establishment of protected forested riparian corridors to enable safer movement between more exensive wetland refuges or reserves across otherwise hostile open habitats (Belden 1983, cited by Noss 1987).

4.4 *Anthropogenic sulphate and nitrate production and deposition*

Wetlands are important elements in the global cycles of nitrogen and sulphur. Completion of their cycles depends on chemical reduction, which occurs by microbial activity in a reducing environment (Deevey 1970). Although the earth's atmosphere is 80 per cent nitrogen, only a small fraction is fixed in biologically active forms (ammonia, nitrate, organic nitrogen). During the present century world atmospheric nitrogen fixation in fertilizer production has doubled the amount fixed by natural microbial activity (Delwiche 1970). Some of this reduced nitrogen is accumulating in the slowly increasing biomass on the earth's surface, as shown by increasingly eutrophic water bodies, but apparently the global biosphere has compensated for increased nitrogen reduction to some extent by increased denitrification to volatile nitrogen. Because this microbial process requires the close proximity of oxidized and reduced zones, wetlands are particularly important in maintaining the global balance of biologically active nitrogen.

The sulphur cycle is somewhat different, in that coastal wetlands receive oxidized sulphate primarily from sea water, in addition to that washed out of the atmosphere by rain (one cause of acid rain). This sulphate is reduced in anaerobic muds to volatile hydrogen sulphide, which can be recycled to the atmosphere or accumulate in the sediment as pyrites and other insoluble reduced sulphur compounds (Meyer 1979). The atmospheric sulphur burden is about equally split between anthropogenic sources (104×10^{12} g/yr, chiefly fossil fuel combustion (Cullis and Hirschler 1980)) and natural biogenic sources (103×10^{12} g/yr (Andreae and Raembonck 1983)). Coastal wetlands appear to be responsible for about 25 per cent of the flux of natural reduced sulphur to the atmosphere (calculated from Adams et al. 1981 and Andreae and Raembonck 1983), despite the fact that they cover only about 6 per cent of the land area of the continents. These figures emphasize the importance of wetlands in global cycles of both nitrogen and sulphur. Inevitably the continuing loss of wetlands through drainage must have signifiant impacts on these cycles, impacts whose repercussions we do not at present clearly understand.

4.5 *Carbon cycle*

The scale of human impact in altering the role of wetlands as carbon sinks has been examined recently by Armentano and Menges (1986). Before recent human disturbance of wetlands, global storage of carbon in organic soils and peats was (57–83) × 10^6 t/yr with two-thirds of this in boreal peatlands. The balance of carbon movement between wetlands and the atmosphere has shifted, primarily as a result of agricultural conversion. The shift has wide regional variations, with some areas of the world acting as carbon sinks and others actually converted to net sources of carbon. Although by 1900 there had been no significant change in boreal Canada and Alaska, the net carbon sink in Finland and the USSR had been reduced by 21–33 per cent, that in western European wetlands by almost half and that in central Europe had been lost completely through drainage. By 1980 the total annual shift in carbon balance due to agricultural drainage was estimated as (63–85) × 10^6 t, with a further (32–39) × 10^6 t/yr released from peat combustion. The loss of pre-disturbance carbon sinks and the accelerated oxidation of previously accumulated organic matter has undoubtedly resulted in a shift of carbon balance. However, its full significance in terms of global climate, sea-level change and biogeochemical cycling is a matter of considerable current debate and high research priority.

5.0 CONCLUSIONS

Realization of the values of wetlands to human society has led to measures to control losses in some developed countries, but wetland conversion continues and in many Third World countries appears to be accelerating. Present losses are a result of many processes, natural and human, direct and indirect. Many are a lingering legacy of past actions taken out of ignorance of the environmental consequences.

The ecological sensitivity of wetlands, and many of their values to society, derive from three properties. First, wetlands are ecotones between open water and upland ecosystems. As with any ecotone, biotic diversity and many ecological processes are enhanced and concentrated in this shared transition area. Second, in many wetlands productivity is naturally subsidized by hydrological energy that supplies nutrients to the biota. This is particularly true of coastal and riparian wetlands, which are among the most productive areas on earth. Third, wetlands are generally open systems strongly influenced by nutrients, sediments and water from upstream and upslope; they modify these inputs and release them again to influence organisms, including man, downstream.

The same characteristics of wetlands that make them valuable, their ecotonal nature and their ecological openness, especially their critical hydrology, make them difficult to engineer and to replace. As a result wetland losses are not easily reversible. This fact puts a premium on conservation of the remaining resource. However, strong demographic and economic factors combine to promote conversion in the face of the need for conservation. The high rate of population growth in Third World countries, the extremely strong water-related development pressure in such areas as coastal zones and river corridors, and the high crop yields to be had from draining fertile organic wetland soils are all economic incentives for alternative uses of wetlands. This pressure is particularly difficult to manage because of the disparity between private wetland ownership and public benefits. A private owner, who carries the cost of wetland ownership, reaps small direct economic benefit from natural wetlands. Most of the benefits accrue to the public at large – the community downstream that enjoys good water quality, the hunter at the other end of the continent who shoots duck, the offshore fisherman who harvests wetland-grown shrimp. Wetland development is in the economic interest of the owner. Conservation is in the interest of the public. The solution to this discrepancy is not easy, but its recognition is a first step in wetland conservation efforts. Actions to make costs and benefits congruent are possible, and are being implemented in many areas. Such actions include the development of incentives such as tax concessions and conservation easements to encourage owners to maintain their wetlands in natural conditions, better research and local education to enhance the owner's economic return from the natural (or near natural) wetland through controlled harvest of timber and leasing for hunting and trapping, removal of incentives for development that have been common in many areas, such as accelerated depreciation and government drainage projects, public acquisition or purchase of development rights to key wetlands and a strong regulatory programme to protect areas that will otherwise be lost. Such options, however, are largely unavailable to Third World countries whose gross national product is generally inadequate to support wetland conservation programmes. Here the effort must be directed towards developing land-use regimes in and around wetlands which do not impair the resource and which optimize the natural benefits that can be derived from the ecosystem (chapter 11). The concept of sustainable utilization of wetlands underpins the current initiatives of the International Wetlands Programme of the World Conservation Union (ICUN), but in order to be successful it requires the cooperation not only of the underdeveloped nations but also of those countries and international development or aid agencies which traditionally have paid scant attention to the functional importance of natural wetland ecosystems in serving the needs of local populations. Thus worldwide, much improved research and public education are needed to manage wetlands so that the landowners' economic incentives reinforce the wise use of the wetlands to conserve the public benefits of this resource.

11

Protection and Retrospection

Michael Williams

1.0 INTRODUCTION

It is fitting that in a book about a threatened landscape consideration should be given in the final chapter to protection against and understanding of those threats. This is perhaps best done by looking at a spectrum of actual experiences, first for the United States, the country with the most elaborate and complex legislation in place for the longest time, then Western Europe where the first stirrings of awareness about wetland loss are becoming evident, and finally to the Third World countries where there are few restrictions but great pressures for transformation. Efforts at international cooperation in protection are also considered. In conclusion, a retrospective look is taken at the preceding chapters to see what light they throw on general principles that might be borne in mind in the pursuit of wetland protection.

2.0 PROTECTION

2.1 *American efforts*

No country has come anywhere near the United States in its effort to protect its wetlands (Kusler 1983). The legislation of both federal and state bodies is voluminous and complex, and its interpretation is labyrinthine. Nevertheless it is worth looking at it broadly as it illustrates well the problems of implementation, responsibility and interpretation that bedevil wetland protection measures, particularly in societies in the developed world.

The main measures that both encourage and also discourage conservation are summarized in table 11.1, together with the main implementing agency and the likely effect of the legislation.

Other than the wetland acquisition programmes of the 1930s (e.g. Migratory Bird Hunting and Conservation Stamps (1934) and Federal Aid to Wildlife

Table 11.1 Federal legislation affecting wetlands

Programme or act	*Primary implementing agency*	*Effect on wetlands*
Discouraging or preventing wetland conversions		
Regulation		
Section 404 of the Federal Water Pollution Control Act (1972) amended as the Clean Water Act (1977)	US Army Corps of Engineers Department of Defense	Regulates activities that involve disposal of dredged or fill material
Acquisition		
Migratory Bird Hunting and Conservation Stamps (1934)	FWS	Acquires or purchases easements from revenue from fees paid by hunters for Duck Stamps
Federal Aid to Wildlife Restoration Act (1937)	FWS	Provides grants to states for acquisition, restoration and maintenance of wildlife areas
Wetlands Loan Act (1961)	FWS	Provides interest-free federal loans for acquisitions and easements
Land and Water Conservation Fund	Forest Service, Bureau of Land Management FWS, National Park Service (DOI)	Acquires wildlife areas
Water Bank Programme (1970)	Agriculture Stabilization and Conservation Service (USDA)	Leases wetlands and adjacent upland habitat from farmers for waterfowl habitat over 10 year period

US Tax Code	Internal Revenue Service	Provides deductions for donors of wetlands
Other general policies or programmes		
Executive Order 11988 Floodplain Management (1977)	All agencies	Minimizes activity from federal activities
Executive Order 11990 Protection of Wetlands (1977)	All agencies	Minimizes impacts from federal activities
Coastal Zone Management Act (1972)	Office of Coastal Management	Provides funding (up to 80%) for state wetland initiatives
Food Security Act (1985)	USDA	Witholds subsidies for agricultural improvements involving wetland conversion
Encouraging wetlands conversion		
US Tax Code	IRS	Encourages farmers to drain and clear wetlands by providing tax deductions and credits for all types of general development activities
Payment-in-kind (PIK) Programme	USDA	Indirectly encourages farmers to place previously unfarmed areas, including wetlands, into production

FWS, Fish and Wildlife Service; USDA, US Department of Agriculture; IRS, Internal Revenue Service; DOI, Department of the Interior.
Source: based on OTA 1984, with additions from Kusler 1983 and Mitsch and Gosselink 1986

Restoration Act (1937)) that were the result of the combined pressures of the duck-hunting lobby and a public consensus that migratory birds were an integral part of the wild heritage of America, most legislation has occurred since the early 1970s when there was a major shift in public attitudes to wetlands, and an increase in scientific knowledge about their functions and hence their values. The reasons for this shift were threefold.

First, there was the realization that the US Army Corps of Engineers was making massive modifications to wetlands as it dredged about 300×10^6 m^3 of sediment annually out of the shallow channels and navigable waterways and then deposited the material as fill in other wetlands to make suitable land for urban/residential development, often as marinas. This activity was first questioned seriously in 1966 after the Corps refused to consider the ecological implications of its activities, so that eventually it was put under pressure to scrutinize carefully all permits for change (Wood and Hill 1978).

Secondly, there was a rising public awareness during the late 1960s and early 1970s that wetlands were scenically attractive and had positive natural functions that were valuable. Several polls during the 1970s revealed a high degree of public support for conservation measures (Hays 1986, p. 149). By 1972 seven coastal states from Massachusetts and Georgia had enacted legislation to protect their coastal wetlands. Activity thereafter was encouraged by the passing of the Coastal Zone Management Act of 1972 which applied to all states bordering the ocean and the Great Lakes. To qualify for federal grants-in-aid a state had to adopt and regulate use or establish standards for local regulation. By 1983, all states except Texas, South Carolina, Florida and Oregon had set up coastal zone management plans, which generally speaking prohibited coastal developments (e.g. Delaware) or allowed them only by special permit as in San Francisco Bay (Odell 1972), although there seem to be many legal loopholes for reclamation to continue (Hedgpeth 1978). In addition, many states compiled detailed and comprehensive inventories of their wetlands as a prelude to their legislative programmes, for example Delaware (Tiner 1985a) and New Jersey (Tiner 1985b).

Thirdly, the concern for the coastal wetlands expanded to the interior freshwater wetlands as part of a general concern over the loss of open space near urban areas (plus the added perturbation over the dumping of toxic wastes in swamps) and concern by hunters and bird-watchers at the draining and infilling of the wildlife habitats by agriculturalists (Hays 1986, p. 158). Only Arizona, Delaware, Georgia, Idaho, New Mexico and Utah had no laws or interest regulations concerning inland waters, or were considering them as of 1983 (Mitsch and Gosselink 1986, p. 448).

However, little could be done to control inland wetland loss as opposed to water quality as there was no restrictive legislation. It was different on the coast. Originally the Corps had been given authority to regulate all activity on navigable rivers and coastal waters used in interstate commerce under the River and Harbor Act of 1899. In 1972, Congress gave the Corps the added responsibility of regulating the discharge of dredged and fill material under section 404 of the Federal Water Pollution Control Act. Environmentalists argued that this implied total wetland protection, an interpretation which the Corps resisted, arguing that its responsibility did not extend to the headwaters of rivers where many wetlands were situated. Nevertheless, after legal action by environmental groups, the responsibility had to be admitted, and the Act was strengthened in 1977 (and now called the Clean Water Act). From now on 'all the waters of the United States' were included, which was legal and not a scientific concept. In addition, the Corps could now embark on coastal and river alteration only after schemes had been reviewed by the Environmental Protection Agency (EPA), the Fish and Wildlife Service (FWS) and the National Marine Fisheries Service (NMFS). If the impact of any proposed change was considered significant by any of these bodies, the permit for change can be denied or the project altered in order to minimize the impact. In addition the EPA can have an absolute veto over the use of any sites to be used for the dumping of dredged material (Council on Environmental Quality 1977, pp. 77–9, Horwitz 1978).

Over and above all this, Executive Order 11990 of 1977 (42 Fed. Reg. 26961: 1977) made wetlands protection a matter of national policy. The many positive virtues of wetlands were stressed, and each federal agency was required to 'provide leadership' and 'take action to minimize the destruction, loss, or degradation of wetlands' by avoiding 'direct or indirect support of new construction in wetlands where there is a practical alternative'. Funds were provided to further these aims (Horwitz 1978).

Yet, despite all this complex legislation and the vigilance of zealous bureaux, agencies and environmental groups, wetland conversion still continues at an average rate of about 250 000 ha/yr, 95 per cent of which is due to human alteration. Briefly two major reasons for this can be put forward. First, there is a lack of coordination between the several agencies with different areas of responsibility. Secondly, wetland protection has been approached through either the medium of land-use legislation or water quality legislation, which is a legacy of the land or water mentality that has bedevilled all comprehensive legislation. Wetlands are uniquely both, but are rarely treated as such.

In the case of the Corps of Engineers, action has foundered on a number of points (OTA 1984, pp. 10–11, 177–82); Mitsch and Gosselink 1986, pp. 433–6).

1 The responsibility of the Corps lies only in those waters that are affected by interstate commerce, which excludes much of the coastal and nearly all inland waters.
2 In those wetlands affected by interestate commerce Section 404 fully regulates the discharge of dredged material onto adjacent wetlands, but not the draining, clearing or flooding of those wetlands. This explains the massive reclamation now going on in the Mississippi bottomlands, under the impetus of high crop prices, which accounts for the bulk of current wetland transformations.
3 The interpretation of Section 404 is still open to lively debate. The Corps views its responsibility as primarily one of protecting water quality only in

the water it affects. The FWS, EPA and NMFS believe that the Clean Water Act requires the Corps to protect the total integrity of wetlands, including habitats.

4 The Corps is overstretched and does not have the resources to maintain and regulate all activities in its districts. Therefore it tends to resort to general permits rather than to permits for specific schemes, and accordingly many smaller schemes which are individually insignificant, but cumulatively important, slip by unnoticed.

5 Finally, there are variations in the implementation from district to district which impair the effectiveness of section 404 legislation.

Despite these difficulties, it is thought that perhaps only half the post-1975 wetland conversions along the coastline are approved, which together with state regulatory programmes reduce the applications approved to between 70 and 85 per cent. Thus only abut 20 200 ha are currently still being converted on the coastlands, but over 100 000 ha are being converted in the unregulated inland wetlands, primarily for agriculture.

It is also clear that federal policies do not always deal consistently with wetlands. In fact some legislation dealing with tax credits and deductions has encouraged conversions, and the policies of the Soil Conservation Service and Bureau of Reclamation have actually encouraged wetland destruction (Kusler 1983). Since 1985, however, the Food Security Act, under what are commonly called the 'Swampbuster' provisions, linked eligibility to farm subsidy benefits directly with what farmers did with their wetlands. If they were left alone subsidies were paid; if drained land surplus to present needs producing surplus output was being created subsidies were not paid (Dunkle and Misso 1988). In addition, a scheme to exchange farm debts for conversion of land back to wetland was put into operation. The measures began to bite early in 1988 when North Dakota farmers who were energetically draining potholes in order to use larger farm machinery protested, but it was pointed out that they were already receiving $700 million in federal subsidies and that the loss over wetlands was a fraction of that (*Washington Post* 27 January 1988). Under the same bill the Agricultural Stabilization and Conservation Service (ASCS) can authorize cost sharing for re-establishing bottomland hardwood forests in land cleared during the period of high soybean prices in the 1970s but since abandoned.

Increasingly the link between the financial encouragement of agriculture and the destruction of wetlands is being realized. In addition, all federal agencies have had to revise their guidelines with respect to wetlands after Executive Orders 11990 and 11988. Thus, greater awareness of wetland protection is coming about, but at the same time losses are still occurring. The battle is far from won.

2.2 *European awakening*

The same degree of awareness and concern about wetland loss, and hence protection, has not characterized the countries of Europe. As outlined in chapter 1, unlike the United States there has never been a politically powerful or numerous hunting lobby, and generally environmental matters were much slower in taking a hold on public opinion, and when they did they were rarely related to matters essentially rural. Food production and self-sufficiency have been the overwhelming goals of rural policy.

Even more important, the history of Europe has never been the history of virgin land, its disposal, settlement and use or misuse (except, perhaps, briefly during the late twelfth and early thirteenth centuries). The fact that there is no wilderness 'ethic' in Europe is because there is little wilderness left. The history of European land use has been largely one of transforming difficult environments into productive land. The landscape is not natural; it is an artefact, the creation of man and not of God, the product of many centuries of altering, shaping and manicuring the visual scene to the cosy, well-settled, picturesque and polished landscape of today (Darby 1951, Hoskins 1959, Glacken 1967). Even wetlands are not excluded from this. For example, there are many artificial 'wet' meadows that have been created and managed for winter hay and summer pasture for centuries. They have acquired a characteristic assemblage of fauna and flora and have become an integral part of the traditional aesthetically valued landscape.

Nevertheless, there are some stirrings on the wetlands front and Europe is awakening slowly to the fact that the last remaining pieces of wetland need protecting. Increasingly, the positive natural functions of wetlands and their susceptibility to damage from industrial, urban and agricultural pollution, water supply schemes, waste disposal and tourism are being appreciated, although agriculture is far and away the greatest threat.

This is not the place to go into the details of the amounts and rates of wetland conversion by agriculture, even if we had the figures which are difficult to obtain for so many differing national units operating under so many conflicting authorities and pieces of legislation. Nevertheless, table 11.2 summarizes some of the salient figures for four countries (Baldock 1984). Rates of draining in these countries now exceed 330 000 ha/yr not all of it necessarily environmentally damaging. Most of it is tile draining that is nibbling away at the edges of the few remaining freshwater wetlands, the filling-in of farm ponds that are no longer perceived as being useful and the draining of small areas of coastal salt

Table 11.2 Agricultural draining in four West European countries

	Area of agricultural land ($\times 10^6$ ha)	*Drained (%)*	*Current annual rate of draining (ha)*
France	19.0	10	140 000
UK	7.0	60.9	120 000
Ireland	0.77	20–30	30 000
Netherlands	0.90	65.2	25 000
			315 000

Source: Baldock 1984

marshes (Green 1979). Most large-scale conversions as in the Fens and Holland are in the past now, although the fate of Markewaard Polder in the Zuider Zee (40 000 ha) is undecided, as is the fate of the so far untouched coastal marshes of France, particularly those around Brittany and adjacent coasts that total over 500 000 ha (Mermet and Mustin 1983), and the Camargue and Etangs de Languedoc-Roussillon (170 000 ha) on the Mediterranean, of which the latter are already radically altered in places by tourist development and marinas. Another unknown is the fate of the great Shannon estuary in Eire where large-scale industrial developments are proposed (Baldock 1984, pp. 39–45, 69–70; see also chapter 9).

In the bulk of the cases, the object is to intensify agriculture and raise production, which as far as wetlands are concerned can mean many other things in addition to draining *per se*. For example, surface ditches that act as habitats are eliminated and increased inputs of fertilizer cause pollution, as does the application of herbicides and pesticides. Heavier machinery compacts the soil and eliminates fauna and flora, water-tables are reduced, and regular dredging to maintain main river flow and use of aquatic herbicides to control weed growth in ditches can be fatally damaging to wetland species of all kinds. In addition to these agricultural impacts there are others. In Ireland, peat bogs have been drained and water-tables lowered as a prelude to peat extraction; over 80 000 ha have been affected since 1946, and the lowland raised bogs of Ireland and western Scotland have been severely reduced by afforesation schemes (Baldock 1984, pp. 75, 143; Bowler 1985, p. 135).

Actual losses are difficult to quantify in the same way as in the United States. In total perhaps as much as 615 135 ha has been drained in France (5.2 per cent of the country) between 1970 and 1982 alone, and probably as much as 1 418 000 ha of Ireland (24.3 per cent of the country) between 1945 and 1980, of which nearly four-fifths was field drainage and the rest arterial or main river drainage. In total, perhaps as much as half of the lowland fens and mires in France and the United Kingdom have been destroyed or damaged. Another measure of change is the number of species endangered or threatened. For example, 47 per cent of all European bird species, all 111 of European Economic Community (EEC) breeding species of reptiles and amphibians, and 2000 plant species are in decline (Baldock 1984, pp. 158–60).

As the overwhelming amount of wetland conversion is undertaken for agricultural purposes, any preservationist measures must be directed at agriculture and its support. Therefore the need is to examine the nature of the financial arrangements that fuel the change, boost drainage activity and generate high price levels that set off a circular cause-and-effect process that encourages further investment.

Broadly, financial encouragement comes in the form of national public funds that subsidize draining by anything between 25 and 100 per cent, depending on the country, with the subsidy usually being greater for arterial drainage schemes than for field drainage and for group schemes than for individual schemes. The new element in the early 1970s was the infusion of large capital inputs via the EEC's Agricultural Guidance and Guarantee Fund (FEOGA).

The aims are both social and economic: to upgrade farm incomes, enlarge farms, slow the migration to towns and generally to boost farm production. Funds are generous, especially where draining is a part of land consolidation and/or farm rationalization schemes (Directive 72/159) or part of policies to boost production in the Less Favoured Areas (Directive 75/268) which include, for example, western Ireland, the Highlands and Islands of Scotland and parts of Mediterranean France and Italy. Typically, 5–15 per cent of the cost of draining is covered. In addition, a number of special regional aid programmes have been initiated, particularly in western Ireland (e.g. directive 78/628), which meet up to half the cost of draining (Baldock 1984, Bowler 1985, pp. 55–6, 206–11).

Support for farm improvement is accompanied by support for prices. Broadly speaking, there is now a free market for food products amongst all countries of the EEC, which increases the competition and therefore development pressures, particularly in the more marginal Less Favoured Areas. Prices for products are kept high with subsidies and guarantees which encourage more investment in conversions. Therefore there are strong incentives to increase production in all aspects of farming, transforming pasture into cultivated land and previously 'unused' or under-used land, such as wetland, into both. With high prices a farmer knows that drainage expenditure can be recouped in a year or two.

Against this background, the protection of wetlands is having a hard time. There is no presumption not to drain as the virtue of increased production and farm income is assumed, and the EEC grant mechanism tends to favour long-term infrastructural projects, especially in the Less Favoured Areas. Paradoxically, however, in the very success of the community policies lies the seed of hope for change. Gross over-production, high storage costs of surpluses, adverse public opinion and the drain that the Common Agricultural Policy (CAP) is having on the EEC's finances has caused re-evaluation in some cases. The imposition of milk quotas on member countries and the consequent slaughter of hundreds of thousands of dairy cattle took some of the pressure off the draining of wetlands after the mid-1980s. More recently new initiatives to encourage set-aside schemes, usually thought of as forestry and/or some sort of recreational use on drylands, could be applied to wetlands causing the cessation of draining and even ultimately the possibility of re-flooding to re-create wetlands, if the benefits of such an alternative use through fees from bird-watchers, hunters etc. can be marketed effectively.

2.3 *The British experience*

Within the general European context, the United Kingdom affords an example of complexities of legislation which probably rival those of the United States. It is also an example of how limited success in the protection process is being achieved in the last remaining wetlands.

In England and Wales, specifically under the 1973 Water Act there are nine Local Water Authorities (LWAs) which control all aspects of water management in their catchment areas. The evacuation of drainage water falls to them, as they have the responsibility for the main (arterial) channels and sea defences. However, the administrative situation is complicated by the fact that the land drainage within a catchment is controlled by a regional land drainage committee, the chairman of which is appointed by the Ministry of Agriculture, Fisheries and Food (MAFF) and which will often have a majority of members with agricultural interests. Consequently it may be at odds with the larger LWA. In addition, there are, at the local level, some 270 Independent Drainage Boards (IDBs) located in the 1.2×10^6 ha of the lowest-lying land in the country (figure 11.1). They carry out the smaller draining works in the most environmentally sensitive areas. The IDBs are composed almost entirely of farmers, whose voting power is proportional to the amount of land they own. Financed out of local rates (taxes), but also eligible for general MAFF and EEC grants and encouraged by high agricultural prices, the IDBs want drainage and conversion. Thus, although fragmented, evacuation of surplus water is usually a shared objective at all levels of the drainage administration but, conversely, because they are fragmented there can be neither a check on the desirability of draining nor any enquiry as to the environmental or ecological effects of the process (Cole 1976; Hollis 1980; Parker and Penning-Rowsell 1980, pp. 203–12; Penning-Rowsell 1983).

The forces of conservation and protection are equally fragmented. There are over 4000 Sites of Special Scientific Interest (SSSIs) in existence, many of them in wetland areas; these are administered by the Nature Conservancy Council (NCC), a subagency of the Department of the Environment (DoE). Before 1981, SSSIs were being lost at a rate of 12 per cent per annum because the NCC had no means of stopping their destruction by high farming. Protracted battles, often engaged by the Royal Society for the Protection of Birds (RSPB) which was in the forefront of the opposition to habitat destruction, aroused the attention of a nascently environmentally conscious public. Nevertheless, the loss and attrition of large areas of ecologically rich wildfowl habitats in the north Kent marshes, alongside the lower Thames estuary (Williams 1983), in the small but significant Amberley Wildbrooks in Sussex (chapter 9) and in the more extensive washland of the rivers Idle and Misson that drain into the Trent in north Nottinghamshire (Purseglove 1987, p. 238) could not be prevented as there was no legislation to protect them.

In 1981 there was a significant change with the passing of the Wildlife and Countryside Act which, amongst other things, empowered the NCC to pay farmers compensation for *not* draining their land, at, of course, the current high incentive rates encouraged by the CAP, and required the LWAs and IDBs to further conservation and the enhancement of natural beauty. This was the first official justification for an environmental standard for preservation, but it did replace goodwill with a formal legalistic exercise determined by cash and not conscience (Pye-Smith and Rose 1984).

The battles which followed between the NCC and agricultural interests were intense and sometimes bitter. They had varying success. The case of Welland Marsh, the last 75 ha vestige of the once great Romney Marsh, ended with the

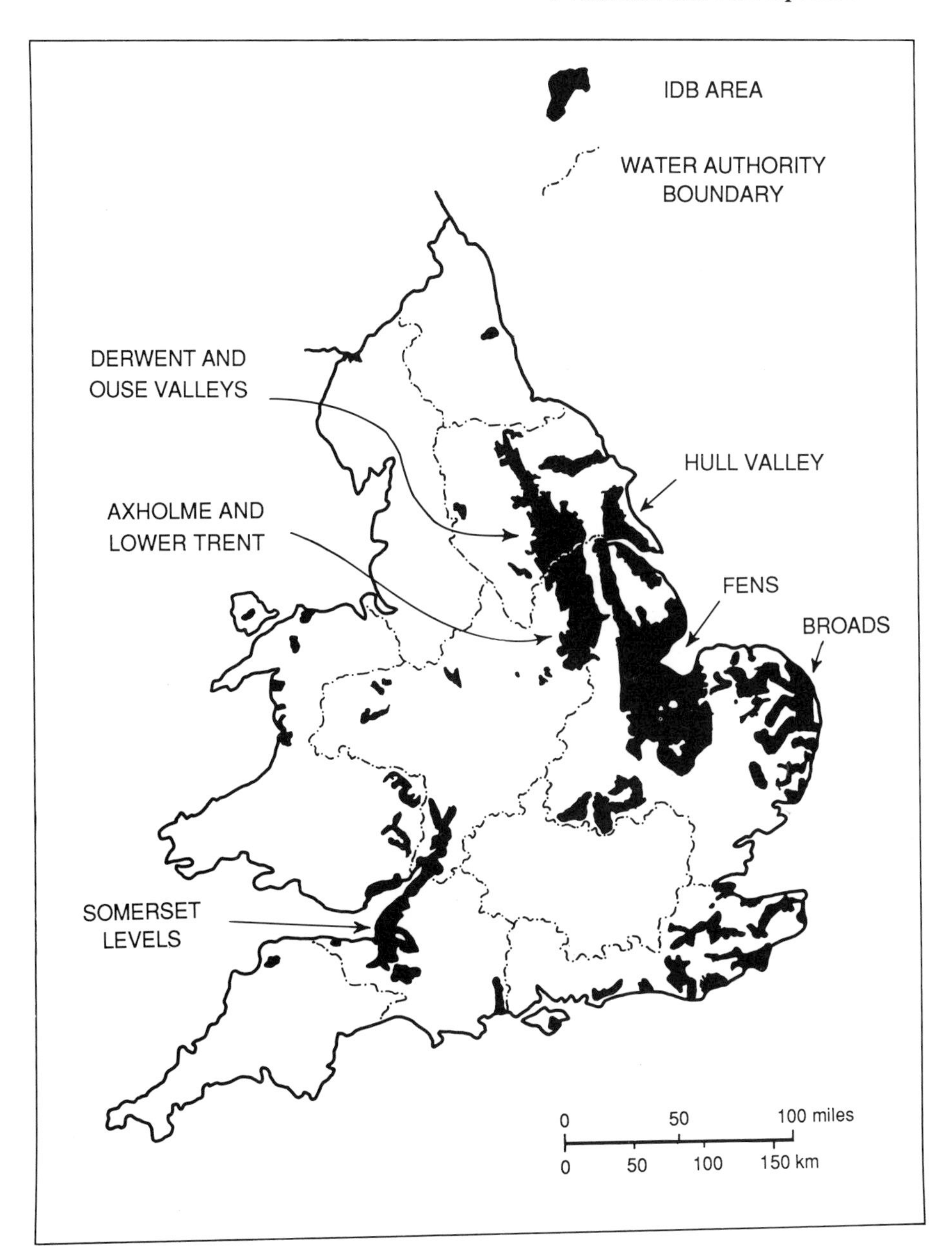

Figure 11.1 Major wetland areas and internal drainage boards in England and Wales

NCC not being prepared to allocate the money to protect it and then declaring it a site not worth protecting, thus effectively washing its hands of the affair. The official equivocation only strengthened the resolve of those concerned to win the next case, which became a *cause célèbre* in the battle for conservation. The wetland was West Sedgemoor in the Somerset Levels in the west of

England, a 1000 ha basin almost totally enclosed by surrounding hills and containing a unique assemblage of plants, insects and birds on wet pastures that were periodically flooded. Initially there were many farmers who did not want a change in the traditional summer grazing way of life and they were opposed by those who wanted to lower the water-table and increase the grass yield and stock densities for dairying (Ajax-Lewis 1982). The peremptory and somewhat inept designation by the NCC of the whole of the Moor as an SSSI under the new act united all farmers against conservation groups, which achieved notoriety in the British press and elsewhere with photographs of local farmers burning effigies of environmentalists strung up on gallows over bonfires (Purseglove 1987, pp. 250–8) (plate 11.1). Eventually, however, a management agreement was negotiated and compensation agreed, an outcome undoubtedly aided by the growing over-production of milk and the threat of the imposition of quotas by the EEC in 1984, which soon came about.

In a sense, the protracted and bitter West Sedgemoor dispute was the turning point in attitudes to protection, although it did not stop all subsequent conversions. The draining of the Soar Valley lowlands was lost because conservationists did not coordinate their lobbying of Parliament, whereas in the 500 ha of low-lying ground at Otmoor, near Oxford, the case was won

Plate 11.1 The conflicts between reclamation and conservation are neatly summarized in this photograph taken in West Sedgemoor, Somerset, in 1983, when local farmers burned effigies of conservationists to publicize their disapproval of the declaration of the Moor as a Site of Special Scientific Interest and wildlife reserve when they wanted improved drainage (Courtesy Anthony Gibson)

through the well-organized and effective opposition of articulate local residents, many in the University. It all pointed to the fact that conservation and protection were as much a matter of politics as of science or anything else.

Two other successes followed, the non-draining of the periodically flooded lowlands or Ings on each side of the Derwent River, a tributary of the Ouse in Yorkshire, and the preservation of some 7500 ha of seasonal grazing in the Halvergate marshes at the junction of the Brue and Yare valleys at the eastern extremity of the Norfolk Broads. The latter was particularly noteworthy from a number of points of view. It was the scenic and not scientific values of the marshes that were at stake, and the issue raised such strong controversy that it provoked Prime Ministerial action in the extraordinary use of a Planning Directive to stop draining, a measure usually reserved for urgent urban conservation such as the imminent demolition of a listed historical building. In addition, with government prompting, the MAFF changed its attitude from intensification at all costs to support for no change and cashing in on EEC approval to aid traditional agricultural practices in order to maintain the wetland and to manipulate water-tables so as to attract wildfowl, thus setting a new precedent for protection (O'Riordan 1984, 1985a, b).

The future of British wetlands is clouded by some uncertainty. The new Water Bill, which will privatize the water industry, has just gone through Parliament and is now law. A new National Water Authority will oversee and administer water conservation and resource planning, fisheries, pollution control, navigation, and flood protection and land drainage. The new private water companies will administer water supply, sewerage, and sewage treatment and disposal. The strength and power of the National Water Authority to consolidate draining and even to take over some of the functions of the IDBs, which all parties agree are anachronistic, is not clear, but the opportunity exists to create an efficient, comprehensive and environmentally aware body that will serve wetlands well. In another move the EEC, long the villain of the piece, might come to the protection of some wetlands such as the Somerset Levels and the Norfolk Broads in the guise of declaring them Environmentally Sensitive Areas (ESAs), susceptible to unnecessary intensification and change, at the same time as it looks at the efficiency of agricultural structures and the problems of surpluses (Directive 85/797). The UK government has taken a leading role in this initiative.

2.4 *Third World pressures*

The complex infrastructure of legislation, the establishment of legal precedent and the emergence of appropriate scientific knowledge and active conservation groups has little counterpart in the less developed world. Here the urgent need is to expand food production to cope with rising population and dwindling resources which makes the vast wetland areas seem like potential sources of unlimited agricultural production, particularly of rice. It is commonly thought that all that is needed is the input of appropriate amounts of technology and capital and that the food will flow. The past has shown many successes such as, for example, the massive reclamation of the Irrawaddy delta in the later nineteenth century (chapter 7). Nevertheless, there have also been many failures of schemes to attain the planned levels of productivity.

Fundamental to the problem is ignorance of the physical capabilities and properties of the wetlands to be reclaimed, and also ignorance of the pre-existing systems of exploitation, which may be unconventional to western and western-trained minds. Indigenous systems may be rich in their use of a considerable range of renewable resources, highly sustainable and low energy-using, and may offer better returns than can conversion to agricultural land. Thus, given the fragility of the natural system and the potential of the economic system, tropical wetlands need protection against outside initiated schemes, particularly if, as so often is the case, they are characterized by little planning, large-scale works and heavy capital investment, for example large multi-purpose dams, barrages, canals, polderization etc. Until the virtues of traditional polycultural systems of agriculture-livestock-aquaculture are proved to be inferior to monoculture, these wetlands need protection.

The list of threatened wetland landscapes in tropical freshwater locations in tropical Africa and South America is large, as is the area of threatened coastal tidal peats and mangroves in south and southeast Asia. In South America, the interconnected swamps, lakes and waterways in the upper reaches of the Rio Paraquai that make up the Gran Panatal can be as large as 100 000 km^2 in a wet year, and the combined flood plains of the Apure-Aranca tributaries of the Orinoco in Venezuela may be as extensive as 70 000 km^2 (Maltby 1985, pp. 108–10; see also chapter 4). The wetlands of the Amazon are incalculable. In Africa, there are at least 224 000 km^2 of wetlands, most of it papyrus marsh except in Zaire (see chapter 3), that seasonal flooding expands to nearly double that size to 395 000 km^2 (Burgis and Symoens 1987). Some of the main flood-plain wetlands are listed in table 11.3; those of East Africa, North Africa, most of the Sahara and south of the Zambezi are not considered. Nearly all these support prolific fish life, seasonal grazing for migratory herds of cattle and some agriculture during the dry season. All are major habitats for millions of waterfowl and hundreds of thousands of the larger African vertebrates (e.g. lechwe, wildebeest, elephant, water buffalo, orihi, zebra, steenbok) as they move in synchronization with hydrobiological events.

The example of the inner Niger delta must stand for others. It supports approximately half a million people, about 175 000 of whom are the Peulh who engage in semi-nomadic grazing with 'le cycle de l'herbe' with about 1.2 million cattle and 1.5 million sheep and goats. Through October and November they move across the rangelands and mass on the edge of the delta, moving in as the floods recede in February and March, congregating around the more permanent waterholes and streams by the end of the season in April through to July, finally to move out again to graze on the rain-fed rangelands when the delta floods again in August (figure 11.2). Within the delta, about 150 000 Bambana and Marka tribesmen make use of the saturated soil as the flood recedes, growing a variety of garden crops and vegetables, more staple foods such as millet, maize and sorghum, and even some floating rice in the

Table 11.3 Some major wetlands of Africa and their products

	Flooded area (× 10^3 km^2		*Products*	
	Minimum	*Maximum*	*Fish (x 10^3 t)*	*Stock*
Nile delta Egypt)	8	8.2	?	?
Interior drainage delta and flood plains				
Niger (Mali)	15	17	*c.*100	1.2 million cattle 1.3 million sheep/goats
Lake Chad (Chad)	20	25	60–228	?
Logone Plains (Chad, Nigeria)	5	8	?	?
Other plains draining in/out Chad (Niger, Chad, Central African Republic) Sudd (Sudan)	3	16	*c.*100–200	400 000 people dependent on stock
Zaire Basin (Zaire)				
Upper basin wetlands	9.2	33.5	36–53	?
Swamp and periodically flooded forest Central section	132	220	Incalculable	Few
Okavango Basin (Botswana)	10	18	Low density	250 000 cattle
Zambesi Basin (Zambia)				
Barotse Flats	5(?)	7.7	Bulk of protein for 200 000 people	*c.*300 000 cattle
Kafue Flats	2.1	5.6	2.5–10.2	200 000–300 000 cattle
Other flats	3.7	4.6	15+	?
Total	223.8	394.7		

Maximum area of wetland will depend on annual severity of flood and interpolation from maps and comments.
Sources: Burgis and Symoens 1987, Gallais 1984

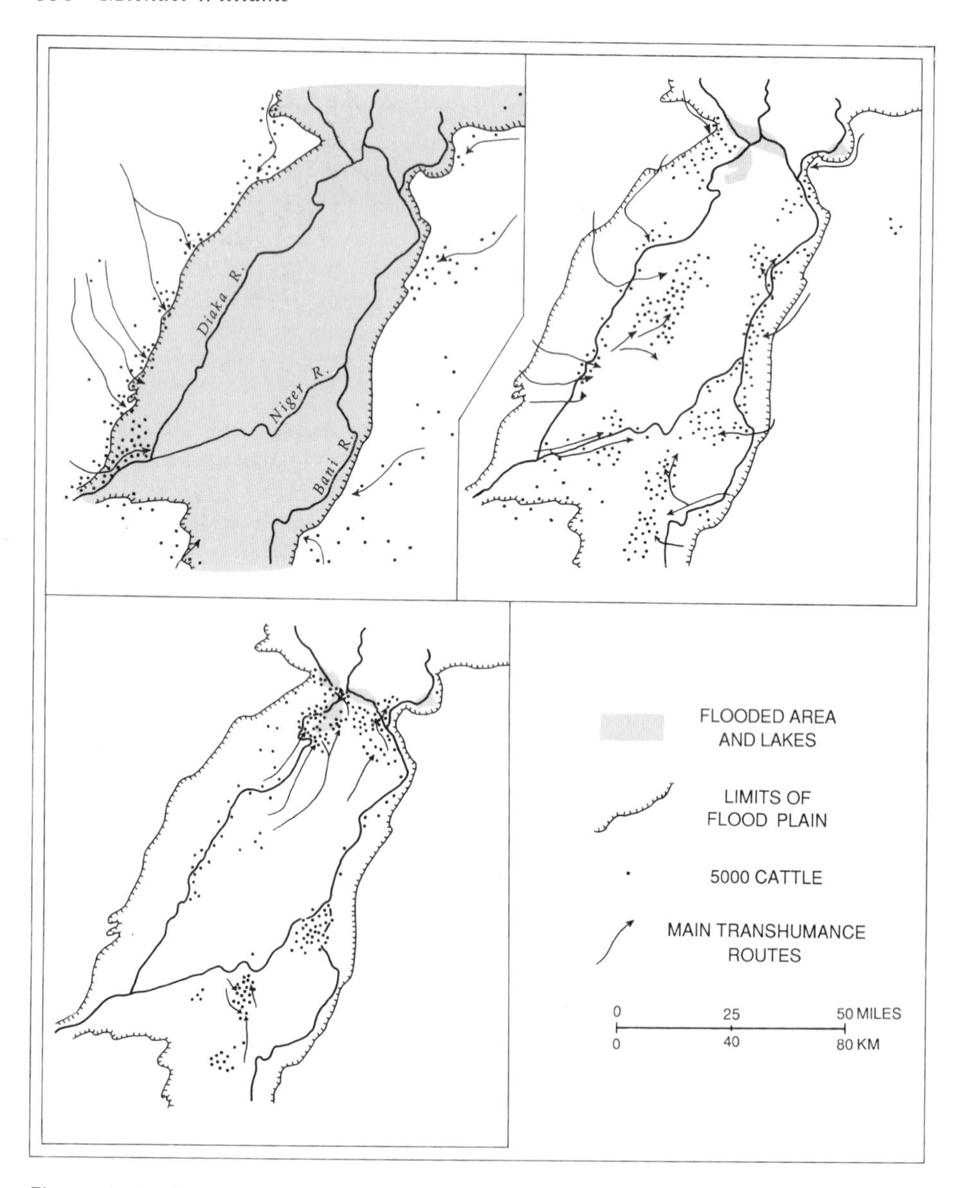

Figure 11.2 The cycle of pastoral migration in the inner Niger delta: top left, October-November, waiting; top right, February-March, dispersal; bottom left, April-June, reassembling (after Gallais 1984, pp. 81, 87, 91)

wetter season. In addition, some 100 000 Bozo and Somono fishermen, who live in thousands of small villages near the edge of the delta, harvest approximately 100 000 t of fish during April-July, supplying much-needed protein for all inhabitants (Gallais 1984).

The interweaving of pursuits with the seasonal biological rhythms of the onset and recession of the annual flood waters, is repeated in all other flood plains in wetlands in the Sahel and southern Africa (Drijver and Marchand 1985, Dugan 1988). Nevertheless, the intimate adaptation to the terrestrial and aquatic components of the environment, and its undoubted productivity, low energy requirements and sustainability, have received little consideration in foreign aid schemes which have sought to develop such areas. Large dams, barrages, canals and associated irrigation works (as happened in the Kafue Flats with the damming of the Kafue Gorge in 1972, and the suggested barrages on the Niger) disrupt the age-old rhythms by reducing the flood regimes, disrupting wildlife and domestic migratory routes, and destroying their sustenance. They may even tend to spread water-borne parasitic diseases such as bilharzia and schistosomiasis in cattle and humans (Sheppe 1985, Burgis and Symoens 1987, pp. 518, 523).

Controversy is highlighted in the case of the proposed construction of the 350 km long Jonglei canal that cuts off the land in the bend of the white Nile between Bor and Malakal, and so bypasses the Sudd wetlands. When completed it will extract $(20–25) \times 10^6\ m^3$ of water daily from the river above the swamp area for irrigation, much of which will eventually re-enter the Nile downstream, but it is thought that this might lead to the shrinkage of the flood plain of the Sudd by 15–17 per cent, and of the flood plain by 21–25 per cent, although others think that it could be double that (Maltby 1985, pp. 123–5). The implications of such a shrinkage on the traditional pastoral migratory way of life of up to 400 000 people, to say nothing of the seasonal movement of wildlife, would be immense. It is even being suggested that irrigation would put the land into the hands of a few with access to the cash economy and deprive the majority of access to land and sustenance, so that the Sudd might end up having to import food (Charnock 1983). Those nearer to the event take a more sanguine view, and while conceding that the canal will undoubtedly bring a new way of life it can only be 'a more satisfactory one than that which exists at present' (El Moghraby and El Sammani 1985).

Undoubtedly, the need is for donor and adviser countries to recognize that the dependence of the indigenous population on the natural wetland system may be great and would affect large numbers, and that therefore the need is to modify existing systems that are sustainable to produce more food, rather than superimposing 'outside' systems. Consequently, the protection and conservation of the economic system must accompany the protection of the ecosystem.

The need for sensitivity to the realities and subtleties of the wetland environment is displayed in the vast reclamation schemes currently being undertaken in Indonesia. Of the approximately 200 000 km^2 of peat swamps on the Malesian coastal plains, about 50 000–70 000 km^2 are tidally influenced coastal non-mangrove plains in Sumatra and Kalimantan (chapter 4, figure 4.3) that are probably only marginally useful for agriculture. Nevertheless, the pressure of 178 million people in Indonesia, growing at a rate of 1.72 per cent per year which means an increment of just over 3 000 000 persons annually, and population densities of over 3000/km^2 in Java and Bali make these 'unused' wetlands seem attractive. Thus, since the late nineteenth century there have been a variety of reclamation schemes, with those since the late 1960s being linked to the government-sponsored transmigration schemes to move surplus population from Java to the outer islands, which can be divided into six major phases (table 11.5). It is hoped that eventually between 100 000 and 250 000 families will be moved annually (although this has never been achieved) and that a surplus rice production of 750 000–1 000 000 t will be available from the new lands (Hanson 1981, p. 225).

The success of the late nineteenth and early twentieth century migrations of the Banjarese natives from the uplands to the wetlands in the south of Kalimantan, and of the Buganese of Sulawesi to the wetlands of southern Sumatra (Phase I), has been a constant lure to those involved in the larger schemes. However, there were important differences. The gradual folk experiment of the indigenous groups adapted carefully to the subtleties of the wetland environment. The clearing of the wetland forest and canal digging were gradual and enough for immediate needs only. The use of digging sticks and local rice varieties meant that the organic layers of the wetland were barely disturbed and remained moist. Monoculture rice was abandoned after 4 or 5 years when weed infestation and declining yields became too pressing, and the rice was interplanted with coconuts which, in turn, were interplanted with coffee, bananas and vegetables. Rice was eventually confined to shallow ditches between for a further 3 years until yields declined so much that it was no longer worth cultivating. In this system, rice was planted for subsistence only until

Table 11.4 Summary of draining attempts in the wetlands of Sumatra and Kalimantan, 1880–1989

Phase I 1880–1948	Small-scale, spontaneous migrations to Kalimantan and Sumatra; simple canal systems; relatively successful
Phase II 1949–52	Dutch-initiated Kalimantan polder and pumping scheme; 8400 km^2 over 15 years; probably no more than 400 km^2 completed
Phase III 1952–66	Plans to reclaim 150 000 km^2 over 15 years; shift to simple gravitational schemes and no pumping; canal 700 km long planned for northern Sumatra wetlands; little accomplished
Phase IV 1967–73	Plans for tidal irrigation of 625 000 km^2; FAO and foreign consultants employed; Reduced to 50 000 km^2 in First 5 Year Plan (Repelita I, 1969–74); 32 000 ha actually reclaimed; some transmigration
Phase V 1974–7	Expansion of Repelita I project to 100 000 km^2 under Repelita II (1974–7); machinery imported and canals dug; 1976 downward revision to 2500 km^2; World Bank design, survey and financial support, and Netherlands training and hydrological studies
Phase VI 1977–89	Repelita III, 4000 km^2 planned – outcome unknown; Repelita IV (1984–9) focuses reclamation on 5000 ha and the annual movement of 140 000 families

FAO, Food and Agriculture Organization.
Source: Hanson 1981, Donner 1987, Ruddle 1987

the coconuts and other crops came to maturity. They produced a good return. In addition, the gradual clearing and draining process allowed different soil types to be selected for rice and deeper peats for more acid-tolerant tree crops. New areas were gradually opened up in order to repeat the process (Hanson and Koesoebiono 1979, Collier 1980, Ruddle 1987).

The migration schemes, in contrast, are aimed at the rapid resettlement of large numbers of people and the production of surplus rice for the whole country, hopefully through double cropping. To achieve this wetland reclamation schemes with massive infrastructural investment are being promoted, often with the backing of foreign aid (Hardjono 1977, Hanson 1981). Phase II was a grandiose imported solution and was a failure, but the subsequent schemes are little better. Typically, under Phases III and IV the land is first cleared by government contractors for the timber, and then drained by giant canals, often 5 m deep, 30 m wide and up to a 100 km long, excavated by heavy machinery. Consequently the peat dries out rapidly and is compacted, and brackish water can seep backwards inland. It is intended that rice is to be irrigated by tidal water, which often does not happen because drainage levels are not accurate and pumping is avoided because of costs. Therefore, the rice relies on rain-fed growth and double cropping is an impossibility.

However, the soil problems are the most intractable and threaten to undermine the schemes and render the wetlands useless for any purpose. The best of the riverine eutrophic peats that are chemical and nutrient rich have already been selected by the spontaneous migrant groups whose polycultural systems seem well adapted to them. The transmigration schemes, however, have had to utilize the remaining peats, the bulk of which (95 per cent) are nutrient-poor oligotrophic raised bog peats that lie in the interfluvial areas. These are often underlain by acid sulphate clays which, when the peat subsides, oxidizes or otherwise dries out after a few years, eventually render the surface useless (chapter 4, figure 4.4). It is estimated that between 200 000 and 300 000 ha have already been abandoned. Even where the acid sulphate soils are absent, drainage levels need careful manipulation to avoid the drying out, subsidence and other changes that stem from decreasing the soil moisture content. High pH levels and even toxic concentrations of iron and aluminium, as well as low nutrient levels, also hinder cultivation, so that only acid-tolerant tree crops like oil palm, coffee, pineapples and coconuts can be grown successfully, and these are not normally encouraged in the drive for monoculture rice (Donner 1987, pp. 204–15; Ruddle 1987). The deep peats (over 2 m) are so lacking in nutrients as to be useless unless large amounts of fertilizer are applied, which is costly. Perhaps, in reality, only about 10 000 km^2, at most, of the peat swamps may be suitable for rice cultivation in Kalimantan and Sumatra, although possibly four times that amount may be available in the untouched swamps of Irian Jaya.

In Third World situation of growing populations and the pressure to produce ever more food, protection might best be considered as the gradual and sensitive modification of the existing economic system and ecosystem, rather than no transformation at all (Dugan 1988). New values have entered into the equation of transformation; large scale must give way to small scale, 'outside' planning to 'inside' experiments, the hurried for the gradual, and the monocultural system aimed at producing short-term high yields for a polycultural system that produces long-term sustainable moderate yields. In almost every way, local systems are superior to imported systems, and in their protection and adoption might lie the opportunity to preserve some of the last remaining great wetlands of the world.

2.5 *International cooperation*

The efforts of individual countries to conserve their wetlands are parallelled by a growing number of international efforts by governments and non-government organizations such as the Audubon Society and the World Conservation Union (recently created from the World Wide Fund for Nature (WWF) and International Union for the Conservation of Nature (IUCN)) (Maltby 1988b, Munro 1988). The oldest of these efforts, and perhaps the main one, is the 'Convention on Wetlands of International Importance, especially as Waterfowl Habitats', more commonly known as the Ramsar Convention from the Caspian Sea resort in Iran where it was first adopted in 1971.

Rising out of earlier deliberations of the International Waterfowl Research Bureau (IWRB), the convention came fully into force in 1975 with the aim of stemming the 'progressive encroachment or loss of wetlands now or in the future'. By 1987 it had 45 signatories, mainly, but not exclusively from the countries of the developed world. Signatories to the convention are required to include wetland conservation issues in their national planning initiatives, establish protected wetlands, train wardens and designate wetlands that can be included in the List of Wetlands of International Importance (figure 11.3) maintained by the IUCN at the International Conservation Monitoring Centre in Switzerland (Navid 1988).

The criteria for identifying Wetlands of International Importance was finally agreed at the Cagliari Convention in Italy in 1980, and wetlands were to be included if they regularly supported 10 000 ducks, geese, swans or coots or 20 000 waders or 1 per cent of species of waterfowl or 1 per cent of the breeding pairs of a species.

In addition, a wetland is considered important if it supports an appreciable number of vulnerable or endangered plant or animal species, or is considered to be a particularly good example of a specific type of wetland which is characteristic of a region. By June 1986 a list of 335 sites totalling nearly 20×10^6 ha was completed for the neotropical and western Palearctic world, and volumes for Afro-tropical and Australasian realms are in preparation. The list is now tending to become extended to include wetlands of botanical and limnological importance as well as waterfowl importance (Maltby 1988a). Clearly, there are vast areas of significance to the Ramsar Convention (figure 11.3), particularly in Central and South America, and presumably the same

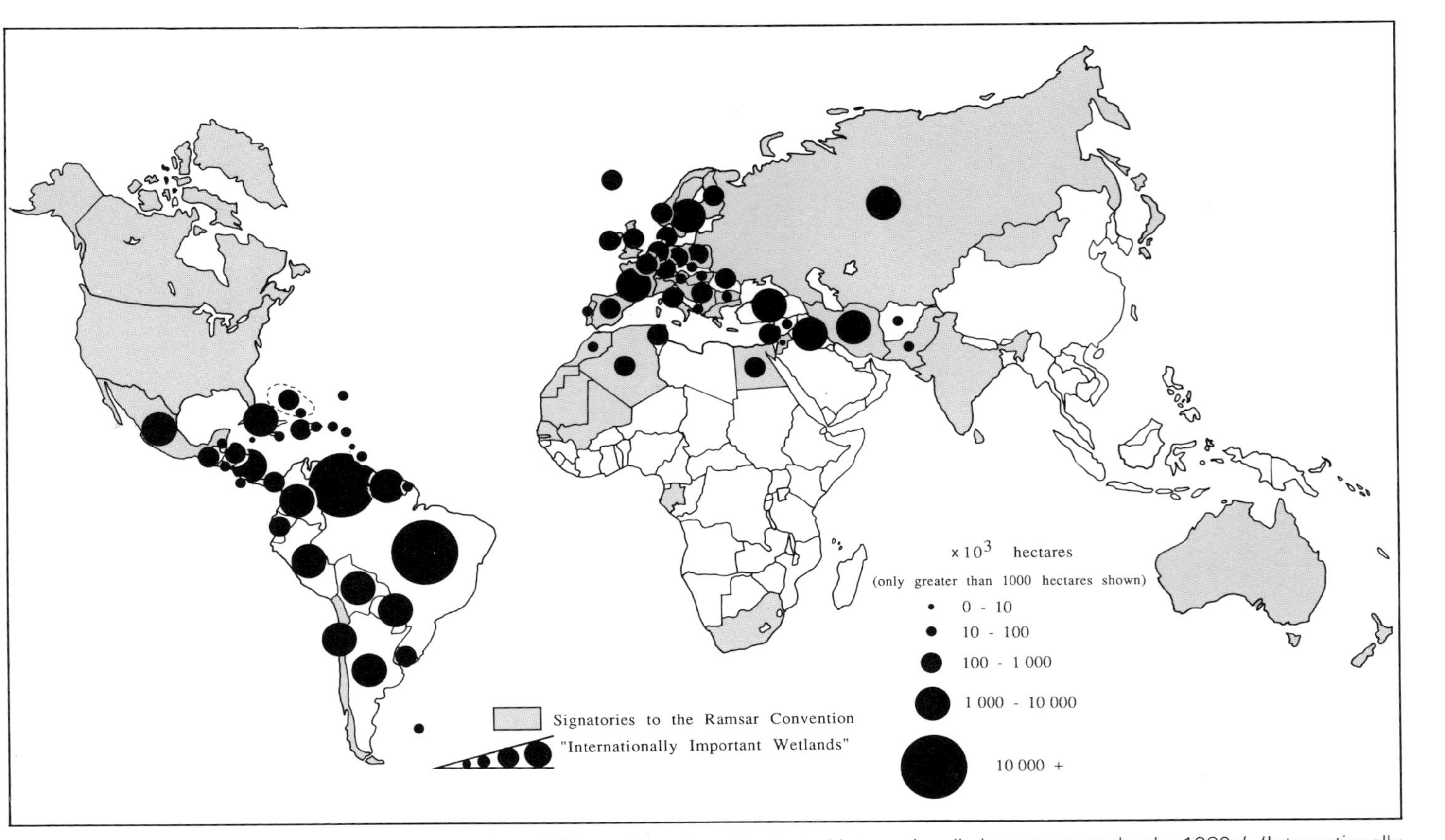

Figure 11.3 Signatories to the Ramsar Convention, 1987, and location of 'selected internationally important wetlands, 1980s'. 'Internationally important wetlands' in the Afro-tropical and Australasian realms have not yet been fully identified
(date from World Resources Institute 1987, pp. 180, 270–1)

will be shown to be true in Africa and Southeast Asia when the data become available.

Interestingly enough this international cooperative effort has the same mainsprings of concern as had the initial protectionist efforts in the United States, namely preservation of waterfowl habitat, perhaps the one positive function that all parties can perceive, appreciate and agree upon. None of the obligations are too specific or onerous that countries cannot agree. Although the Convention has no strict legal powers, it relies on moral persuasion and has been useful as a tool in preventing detrimental changes in already designated wetlands as many countries would attest. For example, the draining of the Colfiorito Marshes in Italy has been stopped, commercial fishing in Lake Haleje in Pakistan has ceased and the harbour extensions in the Wadden Sea between the Netherlands and the Federal Republic of Germany which would have adversely affected breeding grounds are no longer being built. Its great disadvantage up to the present has been that its one official language is English, which has been a barrier to countries from Spanish- and French-speaking parts of the world joining in (Navid 1988), but equivalence of languages is now agreed.

However, the limitations of the Convention are considerable and must be recognized. It is not driven by much urgency or force and does not go far beyond the wildfowl remit, while clearly other considerations are looming larger all the time. Also many countries do not belong to it, and many of those that do are reluctant to list wetland which by any criteria are internationally important.

Other international efforts are more recent and perhaps more comprehensive in their aims. In 1985 the WWF and IUCN launched a major campaign to increase public awareness of wetland issues. A wetland data base has been established at the IUCN Conservation Monitoring Centre (CMC) in Cambridge and in addition, the WWF has backed the Centre for Environmental Studies at Leiden University in the Netherlands which is involved in a project called EDWIN, an information base compatible with that at Cambridge. It has three aims, to create an information base on the various developmental schemes in wetlands, to evaluate the ecological soundness of projects and to develop recommendations to improve the design of drainage works, polders and dams, all with particular emphasis on the developing countries of the tropical world where the greatest wetland changes are yet to come (World Resources Institute 1987, p. 140). These are small but significant beginnings in a long process of heightening global awareness about wetland functions and values. How successful they are in stemming the flow of transformations is yet to be seen.

3.0 RETROSPECTION

In conclusion, it would seem appropriate to look back at the preceding chapters to see if they contain insights into general principles that might be wetlands has divorced them from the larger ecological and hydrological system borne in mind in the pursuit of wetland protection. To that end we shall look at wetland values, processes and impacts.

3.1 *Values*

The emphasis of wetland studies has shifted in line with, and sometimes in advance of, public opinion. Three phases can be detected in the Western developed world. Before the mid-1960s, the assumption was simply that drained wetland was superior to undrained wetland. No positive values could be seen in a bog or marsh which in its natural state was 'wasted'; it did not fit in with Western landscape ethics or economics. This view probably still prevails in the newly industrializing countries of the world such as Japan, Singapore and Hong Kong (chapter 8).

After the mid-1960s, however, there was a change. The positive functional and ecological values of wetlands, such as the maintenance and improvement of water quality or the mitigation of flood peaks etc., were used as counter-arguments to drainage or infill and halted or held up many schemes for transformation. After the mid-1980s, yet another shift in attitude has occurred, that of attempting to assess and order the relative social merits/values of different and competing positive functions with a view to allocating choices.

The 1960s and 1970s phase saw the creation of a massive 'wetlands industry', particularly amongst biological scientists, largely as a response to environmental legislation in the United States (chapter 1). It has extended and refined our knowledge of wetland functions immensely. Obviously, the positive ecological values need to be kept in mind when assessing the potentialities and implications of wetland change, especially in the less developed world, where the natural wetland ecosystems and traditional forms of exploitation may well provide as great a yield as the projected converted ecosystem (Dugan 1988). Nevertheless, in the developed world this phase has probably gone about as far as it can in policy terms. Moreover, some arguments contain a central paradox, even contradiction, while others have a note of special pleading and exaggeration embedded within them which can cause confusion and lessen their impact.

As an example of the contradictions, the emphasis on the value of the consumptive socio-economic functions of food, fibre, fuel, fish, fowl and fauna almost inevitably implies the destruction of the wetland, the very thing one wishes to save. Peat extraction, in particular, strips the land of its surface layers and completely destroys the ecosystem, although ultimately, perhaps, even more wetland is created. All agriculture leads to wetland elimination. These are not persuasive arguments for preservation. In addition, other positive functions of wetlands that are used as arguments for retaining them can be amplified by human action, and therefore can cause unintended modification. For example, the natural primary productivity of wetland, while great, can be augmented significantly by rudimentary draining and the growth of, say, corn or sugar cane; the aquatic yield of natural mangals can be at least doubled with artificial fish ponds and the timber yield increased fivefold or sixfold with careful management. There are other examples. Another contradiction is that many ecological and social functions are in opposition to each other, and therefore the argument is not one of development/change versus non-development/stability, but which non-development to emphasize. For example, the natural tertiary treatment of sewage and recreation are not wholly compatible, and in the United States it is ironic that one of the most potent reasons for wetland preservation, namely the beauty and wonder of the sight of migratory birds, can be accompanied in the same breath with their wholesale slaughter that runs into millions.

It is also possible that the claims for the expenditure on wetland-related recreation may well be exaggerated in order to justify preservation, as Odum (1979) has suggested.

All these contradictions point to the fact that those concerned with wetland preservation will have to become more interdisciplinary. The emphasis during the 1960s and 1970s on the functional/ecological values and interactions will have to be augmented by contributions in the social, humanistic and economic fields if the work is to have any practical significance and be transferred to policy-makers.

Somehow, each function will have to be assigned a value. The problem is, of course, how anyone can assign an imprecise ecological value (Krutilla and Fisher 1975, pp. 219–32), let alone an intangible socio-cultural value such as an archaeological or scenic value, to functions and then allocate relative priorities to one function *vis-à-vis* another? The whole exercise is highly subjective. Economic assessments also suffer problems, for while they appear on the surface to be more precise and definitive all are valued in terms of their ultimate effects on humanity, which is a subjective assessment. Also the economic assessments are often poorly applied. Leitch and Shabman (1988) review a number of economic costing strategies, including the travel cost method (TCM), contingent values (CV), the least-cost alternative approach (Gosselink et al. 1974) and replacement, option and existence values (Randall 1981), and conclude that all have conceptual and practical difficulties that will have to be resolved before wetland science can have its full impact on wetland politics. The problems associated with valuing a zero-priced environment when it serves economic functions that have positive values is clearly indicated by Pearce et al. (1989).

One of the greatest difficulties of all methods of allocation is that the unit of analysis for any given function or value is usually small. If taken in isolation, this results in an incomplete view of the wetland value and an estimate of the value of the function at the economic margin which is too low, i.e. the value of all wetlands may be great, but a single isolated wetland may be of little value. For example, an individual pothole in the middle of the North Dakota prairie may not be of great value, but collectively all potholes are of immense value to migratory wildfowl. If, however, the thousands of individual case studies are used as a basis for generalization, one is in danger of running counter to the widely held belief that wetlands are individually unique, which has been a potent reason for preservation in Europe where few wetlands are left. It may be that the effort in recent years to highlight the importance and utility of wetlands has divorced them from the larger ecological and hydrological system of which they are an integral part, and not until wetlands are seen again in relation to, for example, the rivers that flood them, run through them or as part of whole watersheds will their true importance be capable of evaluation. In this respect the more holistic view of the total geographical and historical milieu needs to be undertaken, as has been done in some of the chapters in this book.

The task for the 1990s, therefore, is the difficult one of converting technical assessments into regulatory or legislative procedures. One thing is certain: whatever happens, any regulation, zoning or conservation decision involves the 'redistributing of rights to use the environment' (Leitch and Shabman 1988, p. 100) and by implication an allocation of wealth. Consequently these allocations will be part of the political acrimony and legal wrangling between interested parties for years to come. From the examples of the United States and Britain it is clear that in that process protectionists will have to become well organized and politically active. The battle has barely been engaged in the newly industrializing countries bent on achieving higher per capita growth at all costs (chapter 8).

In the less developed world, with its pressing problems of food and resources, these nice arguments about wetland values have a ring of unreality. Nevertheless, values are not a dead issue. The greatest need is to be aware that Western and Western-influenced schemes are often steeped in ethnocentric cultural values about 'development', 'improvement', and 'productivity'. We need to shed these preconceived and assumed value systems and see the wetland through the eyes of the traditional user, whose economic system may well be vastly superior to anything the developed world can offer in its subtle integration of the territorial and aquatic worlds. We have swept away most of our own traditional wetland systems, but must not aid the process elsewhere without being fully aware of their values.

3.2 *Natural processes*

The rationale for wetland studies has largely been that, despite their varied location throughout the world, they occupy a similar niche between the aquatic and terrestrial ecosystems, and thereby exhibit commonalities in their natural processes and characteristics. The effort to find commonalities of process has largely been an ecological effort. Many thousands of intensive case studies have revealed their characteristics. In addition, some workers have begun to attempt to synthesize a higher order of commonalities and have examined the importance of water-flow in the maintenance of the productivity of the ecosystem, the energy flows and the anoxic biochemical processes, even between temperate and tropical wetlands (Gosselink and Turner 1978, Brown and Lugo 1982, Odum 1984).

Some of these ideas have been reiterated, emphasized and elaborated in chapters 3 and 4 by P. D. Moore and T. V. Armentano on temperate and tropical soils and ecology, and they provide a basis for generalizing about the structure and functions of wetlands in these environments. Consequently, we are better able to appreciate the success or failure of reclamation schemes that alter the nutrient status, hydrological regime or soil composition, the effect of pesticides from surrounding farms and even the trampling of vegetation by recreationalists. In brief, knowledge of the natural processes ultimately becomes a model for the protection and management of wetlands anywhere in the world (Good et al. 1978, Kusler and Montanari 1978) and certainly for their mitigation and re-creation (Zelazny and Feieraband 1988).

However, there is one aspect of natural processes that needs further comment and attention. The emphasis on the commonalities of the ecological processes has tended to lead to the relegation and even neglect of their morphological commonalities and hydrodynamic/sedimentational processes. Chapter 2 by A. R. Orme is a timely correction in this respect in that it lengthens the time-frame (usually through the Quaternary) of understanding of wetland formation and emphasizes the dynamics of wetland accretion and erosion that may well be just as important as the ecological factor in wetland maintenance. Indeed, if left alone, the probability is that wetlands everywhere would become more extensive. The hydrodynamics are crucial in that wetlands are not only half water and half land but are also shallow-water environments. Themes such as sedimentation, salinity, tidal range and gradient, erosion and depositional rates, bioturbation, tectonic uplift and isostatic rebound add a range of commonality of processes that have very largely been ignored in the management of existing wetlands. Of all these, perhaps only the sedimentation and subsidence at the mouth of the Mississippi have entered the wetland literature to date (Walker et al. 1987). Even broader global physical processes, such as global climatic change, biogeochemical cycles of nutrients, the distribution of nitrogen in air, soil and water and global sea-water levels, are relevant. The simple point is that wetlands are not in a static equilibrium, and because they are shallow-water bodies they are unstable and easily affected by atmospheric/hydrological changes. In addition, like every other resource, they are subject to extreme events and therefore have social impacts or hazards, particularly in coastal areas (White 1978).

One further point needs to be made. Long-run physical processes can be changed dramatically into short-term processes when alterations to the environment, such as forest clearing, over-grazing, canalization of streams and embankment of rivers occur in the upstream regions of wetlands and then affect the downstream open-water systems and associated wetlands (Goudie 1986). Chapters 6 and 7 by M. Williams and J. F. Richards on agricultural impacts touch upon these themes, but only tangentially, and they have not dealt specifically with accelerated natural processes, as has Trimble (1970, 1974), for example, in a number of significant studies of the effect of agricultural exploitation on sediment yield in the Piedmont of the United States from 1700 to 1970. In comparison, the human activities that affect the ecological processes, e.g. pollution, nutrient enrichment etc., have had a greater exposure.

Thus the history of the settlement and human use of a wetland region is an essential element in any attempt to calibrate physical change, to understand natural processes better and to manage the wetland. Just as a holistic cross-disciplinary input was advocated as necessary in allocating values, so it must be in order to understand the human-physical interface that results in processes. What is needed is a whole range of what might be termed individual wetland 'biographies'.

3.3 *Impacts*

The greater part of this book has been about the impacts that make wetlands the threatened landscape of the title, either through alteration or extinction. However, little has been said about the generic nature of these impacts. As the chapters in this book show, the impacts could be categorized as follows:

1 modification for agriculture through draining, flood control, sea exclusion and pumping (chapters 6 and 7);
2 conversion of land through landfill (or even excavation) for commercial, industrial, transport and residential purposes (chapter 8);
3 pressurizing of the natural ecosystem by recreation and leisure through increased numbers, increased mobility, increased leisure and the greater sophistication of leisure equipment, from speed boats to dune buggies (chapter 9);
4 direct exploitation of some wetland resources such as peat, water, timber and fauna.

Ideally, another chapter devoted to pollution impacts, particularly on coasts, would have been timely (the *Exxon Valdez* oil spill in Prince William Sound, Alaska, is fresh in one's mind). The pressure of increasing urbanization and industrialization, and the transport and use of harmful and toxic chemicals suggest that impacts of this nature will become increasingly prevalent and harmful (chapter 9). On a different level, agricultural pollution from the over-use of nitrates, phosphates, pesticides and herbicides is becoming a major issue in the high-technology farming of Western Europe, geared by the price support policies of the Common Market, and has led to new regulations in the United Kingdom (*The Times*, 11 May 1989). Suggestions that wetland reserves rich in nutrient-absorbing macrophytes be established alongside rivers in order to act as buffers to protect water quality are being hotly debated (Klötzli 1982), but they can act as a positive safeguard to drinking-water supplies only if agricultural chemical over-applications are reduced so that the wetlands themselves are not rendered inoperative.

Indeed, it would be difficult to think of any human activity that could not either actually or potentially have an effect on wetlands, and hence constitute an impact. In the upland portions of watersheds vegetation change, the surfacing of roads and soil compaction all accelerate run-off and possibly reduce the recharge of ground water. Agricultural draining works enhance and accelerate these processes. Mineral extraction, building and construction of all kinds and cultivation increase the rate of erosion and the transport of sediment downstream. A variety of chemical and thermal discharges, such as acid run-off from old coal-mining areas or heated cooling water from power stations, to mention but a few, come from industry, agriculture and sewage.

Downstream in the wetlands themselves, a variety of direct activities have immediate and often lasting impact, e.g. dredging, filling, the construction of dams and pipelines, road embankments, coastal protection works, piers and quays, and the excavation of canals and ditches. Less directly, offshore drilling and gas, water and mineral extraction might have wider regional effects, as might offshore 'island' creation.

As so often in matters relating to wetlands, the only place for which we have a reasonably complete record of different types of impacts is in the United States. There the net 4.625×10^6 ha lost between 1955 and 1975 was attributed to the following causes (table 11.5).

Of overwhelming importance in freshwater wetland loss is agricultural conversion (79.8 per cent), followed by urban infilling (6.3 per cent) and, perhaps surprisingly, impounding for reservoirs and lakes (4.2 per cent). In the salt-water wetlands, dredging for canals, ports and marinas still accounted for 109 000 ha or 55.6 per cent of the total, followed by fill for urban development (22.2 per cent). What table 11.5 also illustrates is that not all impacts are losses – some may be gains – and that salt-water wetlands may beome freshwater wetlands and vice versa. By far the greatest gain in freshwater wetlands was that which occurred by succession on the edges of new farm ponds, a staggering 740 000 ha or just over half of all gains, which when the 182 000 ha of succession from the margins of existing ponds and 123 000 ha from the margins of larger deep-water bodies is added accounts for over 70 per cent of all gains. Lack of drainage maintenance accounts for 22.3 per cent of gains. Salt-water wetlands are almost exclusively the result of natural processes of accretion and vegetation colonization in shallow water environments. How much the relative proportions of these impacts can be transferred to other areas of the world is open to question, but it would not be too far-fetched to suggest that agricultural conversion will still be the overwhelming (over four-fifths) agent of change, with urban and transport impacts accounting for a good tenth, depending on the degree of economic activity and population density of the area, as there is a positive relationship between density and conversions (Gosselink and Baumann 1980).

In an attempt to simplify the complexity of wetland modifications, Maltby and Gosselink (chapter 10) suggest a categorization of impacts not based on cause but on process – whether they are physical, chemical or biological (table 10.1). This has obvious utility as it parallels the discussion in chapter 1 on the positive natural functions of wetlands. In addition, an attempt is made in table 10.1 to assess the severity and permanence of impacts by looking at the immediate, discrete and long-term processes, which adds another dimension to the impacts.

Simply, what wetlands do well naturally is lost first with increasing impacts, and the maintenance of any or all of these functions can be looked at as being a desirable management aim (Stearns 1978).

However, none of this gives us a generalized working framework for

Table 11.5 Impacts on wetlands, United States, *c.*1955–75

Losses (× 10^3 ha)		*Gains (× 10^3 ha)*	
Freshwater Wetlands		*Freshwater Wetlands*	
Agricultural draining, conversion	4743	Succession on margins of new farm ponds	740
Fill, urban development	374	Lack of drainage maintenance	364
Impoundments for deep water	251	Succession on margins of existing farm ponds	182
Draining etc., forest management, mining	250	Succession on margins of larger water bodies	123
Impoundments, draining/flooding, excavation climatic change to produce open water	234	Vegetation establishment on unconsolidated share	26
		Drainage and open space management in urban areas	15
Impoundments, grazing, ploughing, climatic change to produce unconsolidated shore	76	Increased freshwater flow in saltwater wetlands	10
Miscellaneous	11	Miscellaneous	5
Freshwater losses	5939	Freshwater gains	1465
Salt-water wetlands		*Salt-water wetlands*	
Dredging, canals, marinas, ports	109	Natural marsh creation in deep water	22
Fill, urban development	43	Natural marsh creation of mud flats	18
Loss to unconsolidated shore by dredged material disposal, death or removal of vegetation etc.	20	Natural marsh creation of other areas	3
Loss to freshwater wetland by increased freshwater flow	10	Destruction of dykes on agricultural land and miscellaneous	1
Dyking for agriculture	4	Saltwater gains	44
Filling for port development	4		
Miscellaneous	5		
Saltwater losses	195		
Total losses	6134	Total gains 1509	Net change −4625

Source: OTA 1984, pp. 92, 94

assessing impacts in wetlands, which is essential in any effort to protect/manage them. The nearest we come is in the work of Darnell (1978) who has suggested that impacts can be broken down into twelve generalizations, or 'principles of environmental impact'. These could be regarded as a set of working rules in wetland impact minimization which would be the first step in their protection, and go some way towards impact prediction. Some of these generalizations are self-evident, but they are none the less important for that. They are paraphrased as follows.

A *Natural values and the nature of the impact*

1 Natural ecosystems are of great value to society and should not be modified without good cause.
2 Most human intrusions into natural ecosystems are likely to be deleterious to that ecosystem.
3 Ecological impacts always come in groups, i.e. natural phenomena are interrelated.

B *Impact as a function of construction type and location*

4 Each general type of intrusion results in a characteristic suite of environmental effects.
5 Each specific type of intrusion induces a specific set of environmental impacts.
6 There is a regional dimension to all impacts, i.e. mangroves are not salt marshes.
7 Each specific location exhibits site-related values and site-related response characteristics which need checking, i.e. field inspection.

C *Impact predictability and environmental response*

8 Effects of intrusion are in part predictable, but in part unpredictable.
9 Different types of intrusion often produce the same type of response in a system.
10 Severe or prolonged intrusion into a natural system produces systemic stress, i.e. total breakdown.
11 Ecosystem responses to severe intrusion take two forms: a generalized stress response somewhat unrelated to the nature of the stress agent, and a specific response which is particular to the nature of the stress agent.
12 Ecosystem responses to stress agents of various types are not well understood, and therefore further study is needed if we are to increase our predictive capability and eventually to minimize the ecological effects of intrusion.

However, such a procedural progression of considerations still begs a number of important questions in wetland management, such as the following. What techniques are available for minimizing the intrusion/development effects? How far is society prepared to go in ameliorating the impacts or creating new wetlands? Is society prepared to forgo immediate monetary gains for future benefits? What institutional mechanisms, which, of course, are different in every country and even transcend national boundaries, are required to achieve the protection desired? The difficult and vexing questions of scenic, heritage and historical issues are still sidestepped.

Ultimately, then, the argument goes full circle. The field of science is not equipped to answer these questions, and wetland protection enters a broad arena of local and national policies (some of which are suggested in chapter 10), hopefully via the medium of a common agreed set of values. Until these tasks are accomplished and values agreed the wetlands of the world will remain a threatened landscape.

One thing is certain: whereas changes in the past were relatively slow and to a certain extent self-adjusting, since the late nineteenth century when the mechanization of earth moving began, and particularly since 1945, when chemicals entered the scene in a big way and population numbers began to grow more rapidly, environmental change has accelerated and spread. Society is now changing wetlands on a scale of years or decades whereas before it required centuries or even millennia. As stressed before, the need is to assess the impacts before irrevocable change takes place. Consequently, if there is one message that arises through all these case histories and examples it is simply this – the transformation and modification of wetlands in the future should not be undertaken without much thought and good cause.

The Contributors

THOMAS V. ARMENTANO Director, Biotic Resources Program, Holcomb Research Institute, Butler University, Indiana. Author and co-author of over 50 articles, papers and book chapters on wetlands, forests and environmental stress effects on natural ecosystems. A recent research interest has been on projecting the significance of rising sea levels on coastal areas. He has been a consultant to US federal agencies, and served on panels of the United Nations Man and Biosphere Programme.

BRYONY COLES Senior Lecturer in Prehistoric Archaeology, University of Exeter. Began work in the Somerset Levels in the early 1970s, and in 1986 set up the Wetland Archaeology Research Project (WARP), to further international communication on the subject. She is the co-author, with Professor J. M. Coles, of *Sweet Track to Glastonbury* (1986) and *People of the Wetlands* (1989), and author (as Bryony Orme) of *Anthropology for Archaeologists* (1981).

JAMES G. GOSSELINK Professor of Marine Sciences at Louisiana State University, Baton Rouge, and twice Director of the Coastal Ecology Laboratory of the Center for Wetland Resources. He is co-author with Professor W. J. Mitsch of *Wetlands* (1986), and has served as consultant to the Sierra Club, The Environmental Defense Fund and the US Environmental Protection Agency. In 1987–8 he was a member of the National Wetland Policy Forum.

EDWARD MALTBY Senior Lecturer in the Geography Department at the University of Exeter. His research has focused on the changes in peat and waterlogged soils which result from human activities. From 1983 to 1985 he worked on problems associated with minefield clearance in the Falkland Island peats. A wide interest in wetland management has led to extensive world-wide research including Europe, Canada, United States, Australia, New Zealand, Fiji, Jamaica, India and Malaysia. He is an adjunct Professor in the Center for Wetland Resources, Louisiana State University and a member of the European Commission's Technical Advisory Group on Integrated Management of Coastal Wetlands of Mediterranean Type and is on the IUCN Wetland Programme Advisory Committee.

DAVID C. MERCER Senior Lecturer, Monash University, Melbourne. His main research interests are in the fields of environmental policy, recreational planning and land-use conflict. He is presently writing a book on *Conservation and Development in Australia*.

PETER D. MOORE Reader in Ecology, Department of Biology, King's College, London University. His main research interests are in wetland ecology and use of pollen analysis in tracing the history of vegetation, particularly in peatlands. He has made major contributions to elucidating the history of British blanket mires and their initiation in relation to the fire and clearance impacts of prehistoric cultures. He is the co-author with David Bellamy of *Peatlands* (1973), with Judy Webb of *An Illustrated Guide to Pollen Analysis* (1978) and with Barry Cox of *Biogeography* (1985). He is a regular contributor to *Nature* as an ecology correspondent, and to BBC science and natural history programmes.

ANTONY R. ORME Professor of Geography, University of California, Los Angeles. His research has focused on coastal and watershed geomorphology and Quaternary studies, including sea-level change, near-shore morphodynamics, coastal dunes, wetlands and mass movement, and in applying these findings to management plans. He has worked extensively in Africa, North America, the West Indies and the British Isles, is author of over 100 scientific papers and a book on *Ireland* (1970) and is Editor-in-Chief of *Physical Geography*.

DAVID A. PINDER Senior Lecturer in Geography, Southampton University. His research has focused on economic geography and planning, and during a previous appointment at the Economic Geography Institute, Erasmus University, Rotterdam, he developed a major interest in conflicts arising in port-city relationships due to environmental pressures.

JOHN F. RICHARDS Professor of History, Duke University, Durham, North Carolina. He has published numerous books and articles on the early-modern and modern history of South Asia. He is currently engaged in an extensive study of land-use changes in South and Southeast Asia, under the auspices of the US Department of Energy Carbon Dioxide Research Program. With Richard Tucker he has edited *Global Deforestation and the Nineteenth Century World Economy* (1983) and *World Deforestation in the Twentieth Century* (1988).

MICHAEL WILLIAMS Reader in Geography and Fellow of Oriel College, Oxford. He has had a long-standing interest in initial settlement and landscape evolution in Britain, Australia and the United States, particularly the processes of wetland draining and forest clearing. He is the author of over 70 articles and book chapters on these themes, and of *The Draining of the Somerset Levels* (1970), *The Making of South Australian Landscape* (1974), *Australian Space, Australian Time* (1975), with J. M. Powell, *The Changing Rural Landscape of South Australia* (1977) and *Americans and their Forests* (1989). He was editor of the *Transactions of the Institute of British Geographers* from 1983 to 1987 and was elected Fellow of the British Academy in 1989.

MICHAEL E. WITHERICK Lecturer in Geography, Southampton University. His interests are in the field of urban geography and planning, latterly with a major regional interest in Japan, its economic evolution and its relationships with other countries in the western Pacific region.

Bibliography

Aaby, B. and Tauber, H. 1974: Rates of peat formation in relation to degree of humification and local environment, as shown by studies of a raised bog in Denmark. *Boreas*, 4, 1–17.

Abernethy, Y. and Turner, R. E. 1987: U.S. Forested wetlands: 1940–1980. *Bioscience*, 37, 721–7.

Adams, D. F., Farwell, S. O., Robinson, E., Pack, M. R. and Bamesberger, W. L. 1981: Biogenic sulfur source strengths. *Environmental Science and Technology*, 15, 1493–8.

Adamus, P. R. 1983: A method for wetland functional assessment. *Critical Review and Evaluation Concepts* and *FHWA Assessment Method*, Vols 1 and 2. Washington, DC: Department of Transportation, Federal Highway Administration Reports, FHWA–18–82–23, FHWA–1P–82–24.

Adamus, P. R. 1988: The FWHA/Adamus (WET) method for wetland functional assessment. In D. D. Hook et al. (eds) *The Ecology and Management of Wetlands*, vol. 2. London: Croom Helm, 128–36.

Adas, M. 1974: *The Burma Delta*. Madison, Wi: University of Wisconsin Press.

Adas, M. 1987: Colonization, commercial agriculture and the destruction of the Deltaic rainforests of British Burma in the late nineteenth century. In R. P. Tucker and J. F. Richards (eds), *Global Deforestation and the Nineteenth Century World Economy*. Durham, NC: Duke University Press, 95–110.

Aiton, W. 1811: *Treatise on the Origin, Qualities and Cultivation of Moss-earth, with Directions for Converting it into Manure*. Ayr.

Ajax-Lewis, N. 1982: West Sedgemoor: An old battle. *Ecos*, 3(4), 4–9.

Al-Bakri, D. 1986: Provenance of the sediments in the Humber estuary and the adjacent coasts, eastern England. *Marine Geology*, 72, 171–86.

Alho, C. J. R., Lacher, T. E., Jr., and Goncalves, H. C. 1988: Environmental degradation in the Pantanal ecosystem. *Bioscience*, 38, 164–71.

Allen, G. C. 1981: *A Short Economic History of Modern Japan*. New York: St Martin's Press.

Allen, G. P., Salomon, J. C., Bassoullet, P., du Penhoat, Y. and de Grandpré, C. 1980: Effects of tides on mixing and suspended sediment transport in macrotidal estuaries. *Sedimentary Geology*, 26, 69–90.

Allen, K. O. and Hardy, J. W. 1980: Impacts of navigational dredging on fish and wildlife: a literature review. Washington, DC: US Fish and Wildlife Service, Biological Services Program, FWS/OBS-80/07.

Andersen, S. H. 1987: Tybrind Vig: a submerged Ertebolle settlement in Denmark. In J. M. Coles and A. J. Lawson (eds), *European Wetlands in Prehistory*. Oxford: Clarendon Press, 253–80.
Anderson, G. D. and Edwards, S. F. 1986: Protecting Rhode Island's coastal salt ponds: an economic assessment of downzoning. *Coastal Zone Management Journal*, 14, 67—91.
Anderson, J. A. R. 1964a: The structure and development of the peat swamps of Sarawak and Brunei. *Journal of Tropical Geography*, 18, 7–16.
Anderson, J. A. R. 1964b: Observations on climatic damage in peat swamp forest in Sarawak. *Commonwealth Forestry Review*, 43, 145–58.
Anderson, J. A. R. 1983: The tropical peat swamps of western Malesia. In A. J. P. Gore (ed.), *Mires: Swamp, Bog, Fen and Moor, Regional Studies. Ecosystems of the World 4B*. Amsterdam: Elsevier, 181–99.
Andreae, M. O. and Raembonck, H. 1983: Dimethyl sulfide in the surface ocean and the marine atmosphere: a global view. *Science*, 221, 744–7.
Andriesse, J. P. 1988: *Nature and Management of Tropical Peat Soils*. FAO: Bulletin 59, Rome.
Anon. 1985: Much has been done to purify waste water. *Rotterdam-Europort-Delta*, 85 (5), 26–7.
Anon. 1986: Port of Rotterdam given new weapons in the battle against illegal dumping. *Rotterdam-Europort-Delta*, 86 (2), 8–9.
Armentano, T. V. and Menges, E. S. 1990: Patterns of change in the carbon balance of organic soil wetlands of the temperate zone. *Journal of Ecology*, 74, 755–74.
Armentano, T. V. and Verhoeven, J. T. A. 1989: The contribution of freshwater wetlands to the global biogeochemical cycles of carbon, nitrogen, and sulfur. In B. Patten (ed.), *Wetlands and Shallow Continental Water Bodies*. The Hague: SPB Academic Publishers.
Arnold, B. 1986: *Cortaillod-Est, un village du Bronze finale, I. Fouille subaquatique et photographie aérienne*. Saint-Blaise: Editions du Ruau (Archéologie neuchâteloise I).
Ascoli, F. D. (1921): *A Revenue History of the Sundarbans from 1870 to 1920*. Calcutta: Bengal Secretariat.
Ashe, V. H. 1986: Needs and opportunities for outdoor recreation. *Transactions, 51st North American Wildlife and Natural Resources Conference*. Washington, DC: Wildlife Management Institute, 11–16.
Atkinson-Willes, G. L. 1976: The numerical distribution of ducks, swans and coots as a guide in assessing the importance of wetlands in midwinter. In M. Smart (ed.), *Proceedings: International Conference on the Conservation of Wetlands and Wildfowl, Heiligenhafen FRG*. Slimbridge: International Wildfowl Research Bureau, 199–254.
Atwater, B. F., Hedel, C. W. and Helley, E. J. 1977: Late Quaternary depositional history, Holocene sea-level changes, and vertical crustal movement, southern San Francisco Bay, California, United States Geological Survey, Professional Paper 1014. Reston, VA: US Geological Survey.
Avoine, J., Allen, G. P., Nichols, M., Salomon, J. C. and Larsonneur, C. 1981: Suspended-sediment transport in the Seine estuary, France: effect of man-made modifications on estuary-shelf sedimentology. *Marine Geology*, 40, 119–37.
Bairoch, P. 1975: *The Economic Development of the Third World Since 1900*. Berkeley and Los Angeles, CA: University of California Press.
Baldock, D. 1984: *Wetland Drainage in Europe: The Effects of Agricultural Policy in Four EEC Countries*. London: Institute for European Environmental Policy/International Institute for Environment and Development.
Balek, J. 1977: *Hydrology and Water Resources in Tropical Africa*. Amsterdam: Elsevier.
Barber, K. E. 1981: *Peat Stratigraphy and Climatic Change*. Rotterdam: Balkema.
Barber, R. T., Kirby-Smith, W. W. and Parsley, P. E. 1979: Wetland alterations from agriculture. In P. E. Greeson, J. R. Clark and J. B. Clark (eds), *Wetland Functions*

and Values: The State of Our Understanding. Minneapolis, MN: Water Resources Association Technical Publication, 642–51.
Barlow, E. 1971: *The Forests and Wetlands of New York City*. Boston, MA: Little, Brown.
Barusseau, J. P., Diop, E. H. S. and Saos, J. L. 1985: Evidence of dynamic reversal in tropical estuaries: Geomorphological and sedimentological consequences (Salum and Casamance Rivers, Senegal). *Sedimentology*, 32, 543–52.
Bastian, R. K. and Benforado, J. 1988: Water quality functions and wetlands: natural and managed systems. In D. D. Hook et al. (eds), *The Ecology and Management of Wetlands*, vol. 1. London: Croom Helm, 87–97.
Beadle, L. C. 1974: *The Inland Waters of Tropical Africa*. London: Longmans.
Beek, K. J. and Bramao, D. L. 1968: Nature and Geography of South American soils. In E. J. Fittkau, J. Illies, H. Klinge, G. H. Schwabe and H. Sioli (eds), *Biogeography and Ecology in South America*. The Hague: W. Junk, 82–112.
Belknap, D. F. and Kraft, J. C. 1977: Holocene relative sea level changes and coastal stratigraphic units on the northwest flank of the Baltimore Canyon trough geosyncline. *Journal of Sedimentary Petrology*, 47, 610–29.
Bellamy, D. J. and Bellamy, S. R. 1967: An ecological approach to the classification of the lowland mires of Ireland. *Proceedings of the Royal Irish Academy*, B65, 237–251.
Bellrose, F. C. and Trudeau, N. M. 1988: Wetlands and their relationship to migrating and winter populations of waterfowl. In D. D. Hook et al. (eds), *The Ecology and Management of Wetlands*, vol. 1. London: Croom Helm, 183–94.
Bellwood, P. 1971: Fortifications and economy in prehistoric New Zealand. *Proceedings of the Prehistoric Society*, 37(i), 56–95.
Bellwood, P. 1978: *Archaeological Research at Lake Mangakaware, Waikato, 1968–70*. Otago: University of Otago.
Belt, C. B. 1975: The 1973 flood and man's constriction of the Mississippi River. *Science*, 189, 681–4.
Bennett, J. W. 1982: Valuing the existence of a natural ecosystem. *Search*, 13, 232–5.
Berquist, J. R. 1978: Depositional history and fault-related studies, Bolinas Lagoon, California, United States Geological Survey Open-File Report 78–802. Reston, VA: US Geological Survey.
Berthois, L. 1960: Étude dynamique de la sédimentation dans la Loire. *Cahiers Océanographiques*, 12, 631–57.
Besteman, J. C. 1988: The history of medieval settlement in north Holland and the reclamation of the peat areas in archaeological perspective. In P. Murphy and C.French (eds), *The Exploitation of Wetlands. Symposia of the Association for Environmental Archaeology, no. 7, BAR British Series 186*. Oxford: BAR, 327–568.
Biggs, R. B. 1970: Sources and distribution of suspended sediment in northern Chesapeake Bay. *Marine Geology*, 9, 187–201.
Billamboz, A. 1985: Premières investigations archéodendrologiques dans le champ de pieux de la station de Hornstaad-Hörnle 1 sur les bords du lac de Constance. *Berichte zu Ufer-und Moorsiedlungen Sudwestdeutschlands*, 2, 124–47.
Bird, E. C. F. 1986: Mangroves and intertidal morphology in Westernport Bay, Victoria, Australia. *Marine Geology*, 69, 251–71.
Bird, E. C. F. and Ranwell, D. S. 1964: *Spartina* marshes in southern England, IV. The physiography of Poole Harbour, Dorset. *Journal of Ecology*, 52, 355–66.
Bird, E. C. F. and Soegiarto, A. (eds) 1980: *Proceedings of the Jakarta Workshop on Coastal Resources Management, 11–15 September 1979*. Jakarta: The Indonesian Institute of Sciences (LIPI) and The United Nations University.
Bird, J. H. 1971: *Seaports and Seaport Terminals*. London: Hutchinson.
Bird, J. H. 1984: Seaport development: some questions of scale. In B. S. Hoyle and D. Hilling (eds), *Seaport Systems and Spatial Change*. Chichester: Wiley, 21–41.
Bishop, R. C. 1978: Endangered species and uncertainty: the economics of a safe minimum standard. *American Journal of Agricultural Economics*, 60, 11–18.

Bjork, S. and Graneli, B. 1978: Energy needs and the environment. *Ambio*, 7, 150–6.
Bloom, A. L. 1964: Peat accumulation and compaction in a Connecticut coastal marsh. *Journal of Sedimentary Petrology*, 34, 599–603.
Blytt, A. 1876: *Essay on the Immigration of Norwegian Flora during Alternating Rainy and Dry Periods*. Christiana: Cammermeye.
Boate, G. 1652: *Ireland's Naturall History*. London: John Wright.
Boesch, D. F. (ed.) 1982: *Proceedings of the Conference of Coastal Erosion and Wetland Modification in Louisiana: Causes, Consequences, and Options*. Washington, DC: US Fish and Wildlife Service, Biological Services Program, FWS/OBS-82/59.
Bogue, M. B. 1951: The swamp land act and wetland utilization in Illinois, 1850–1890. *Agricultural History*, 25, 169–80.
Bond, G. 1974: Root-nodule symbioses with actinomycete-like organisms. In A. Quispel (ed.), *The Biology of Nitrogen Fixation*. Amsterdam: North-Holland, 324–78.
Bord na Móna (Irish Peat Development Authority) 1985: Fuel peat in developing countries, World Bank Technical Paper No. 41. Washington, DC: World Bank.
Bosselman, F. P. 1978: *In the Wake of the Tourist*. Washington, DC: Conservation Foundation.
Botch, M. S. and Masing, V. V. 1983: Mire ecosystems in the USSR. In A. J. P. Gore (ed.), *Mires: Swamp, Bog, Fen and Moor, Regional Studies*. Amsterdam: Elsevier, 95–152.
Boto, K. G., Bunt, J. S. and Wellington, J. T. 1984: Variations in mangrove forest productivity in northern Australia and Papua New Guinea. *Estuarine, Coastal and Shelf Science*, 19, 321–9.
Boto, K. G. and Patrick, W. H., Jr. 1979: Role of wetlands in the removal of suspended sediments. In P. E. Greeson, J. R. Clark and J. B. Clark (eds), *Wetland Functions and Values: The State of Our Understanding*. Minneapolis, MN: Water Resources Association Technical Publication, 479–88.
Boto, K. G. and Wellington, J. T. 1984: Soil characteristics and nutrient status in a northern Australian mangrove forest. *Estuaries*, 7(1), 61–9.
Bowler, I. R. 1985: *Agriculture under the Common Agriculture Policy*. Manchester: Manchester University Press.
Boyd, H. and Lynch, J. L. 1984: Escape from mediocrity: a new approach to American waterfowl hunting regulations. *Wildfowl*, 35, 5–13.
Braakhekke, W. G. and Marchand, M. 1987: *Wetlands in the Community's Wealth*. Brussels: European Environmental Bureau.
Bradbury, I. K. and Grace, J. 1983: Primary production in wetlands. In A. J. P. Gore (ed.), *Mires: Swamp, Bog, Fen and Moor, General Studies. Ecosystems of the World, 4A*. Amsterdam: Elsevier, 285–310.
Bragg, O. M. 1982: The acrotelm of Dun Moss: plants, water and their relationships, Ph.D. thesis, University of Dundee.
Braithwaite, R. W. and Werner, P. A. 1987: The biological value of Kakadu National Park. *Search*, 18, 296–301.
Bray, F. 1985: *The Rice Economies*. Oxford: Basil Blackwell.
Bristow, R. 1988: Market forces ascendant: dynamics of change on the Hong Kong waterfront. In B. S. Hoyle, D. A. Pinder and M. S. Husain (eds), *Revitalizing the Waterfront: International Dimensions of Dockland Redevelopment*. New York: Belhaven Press, 167–82.
Brown, S. L. and Lugo, A. E. 1982: A comparison of structural and functional characteristics of saltwater and freshwater forested wetlands. In B. Gopal, R. E. Turner, R. G. Wetzel and D. F. Wigham (eds), *Wetlands: Ecology and Management*. Jaipur: National Institute of Ecology, 109–30.
Brown, T. L. and Hustin D. L. 1978: Evaluation of the 1976 ORRRC projections. Survey Technical Report 4, Appendix II, The Third Nationwide Outdoor

Recreation Plan. Washington, DC: US Department of the Interior, Heritage Conservation and Recreation Service.
Bruenig, E. F. 1987: The forest ecosystem: tropical and boreal. *Ambio*, 11 (2–3), 68–79.
Bubberman, F. C. and Vink, A. T. 1965: Ditch blasting – opening up tropical swamps in Surinam. *Unasylva*, 19(4), 184–91.
Buchanan, I. 1972: *Singapore in South-east Asia*. London: Bell.
Bunt, J. S. and Williams, W. T. 1980: Studies in the analysis of data from Australian tidal forests (mangroves). In Vegetational sequences and their graphical representation, *Australian Journal of Ecology*, 5, 385–90.
Burger, J. 1986: The effect of human activity on shorebirds in two coastal bays in northeastern United States. *Environmental Conservation*, 13, 123–30.
Burgis, M. J. and Symoens, J. S. (eds) 1987: *African Wetlands and Shallow Water Bodies: Directory. Collection Traveaux et Documents, 211*. Paris: Editions de l'Ornstom; Institut Français de Recherche Scientifique pour le Développement en Coopération.
Burke, W. 1975: Aspects of the hydrology of blanket peat in Ireland. In *Proceedings of the Minsk Symposium, 1972, Hydrology of Marsh-Ridden Areas*. Paris: UNESCO Press, 171–82.
Cairns, D. K. and Elliot, R. D. 1987: Oil spill impact assessment for seabirds: the role of refugia and growth centers. *Biological Conservation*, 40, 1–9.
Calais, S. S. and Kirkpatrick, J. B. 1986: Impact of trampling on natural ecosystems in the Cradle Mountain-Lake St Clair National Park. *Australian Geographer*, 17, 6–15.
Carter, V., Bedinger, M. S., Novitzki, R. P. and Wilen, W. O. 1979: Water resources and wetlands. In P. E. Greeson, J. R. Clark and J. E. Clark (eds), *Wetland Functions and Values: The State of Our Understanding*. Minneapolis, MN: Water Resources Association Technical Publication, 344–76.
Carter, V. and Novitzki, R. P. 1988: Some comments on the relationship between ground water and wetlands. In D. D. Hook et al. (eds), *The Ecology and Management of Wetlands*, vol. 1. London: Croom Helm, 68–86.
Caseldine, A. E. 1984: Palaeobotanical investigations at the Sweet Track. *Somerset Levels Papers*, 10, 65–78.
Casparie, W. A. 1982: The Neolithic wood trackway XXI (Bou) in the raised bog at Nieuw-Dordrecht (The Netherlands). *Palaeohistoria*, 24, 115–64.
Casparie, W. A. 1984: The three Bronze Age footpaths XVI (Bou), XVII (Bou) and XVIII (Bou) in the raised bog of Southeast Drenthe (The Netherlands). *Palaeohistoria*, 26, 41–94.
Casparie, W. A. 1986: The two Iron Age wooden trackways XIV (Bou) and XV (Bou) in the raised bog of southeast Drenthe (The Netherlands). *Palaeohistoria*, 28, 169–210.
Cato, N. 1979: *The Noosa Story*. South Melbourne: Jacaranda.
Chabreck, R. H. 1979: Wildlife harvest in wetlands of the United States. In P. E. Greeson, J. R. Clark and J. E. Clark (eds), *Wetland Functions and Values: The state of our Understanding*. Minneapolis, MN: Water Resources Association Technical Publication, 618–31.
Chambers, M. J. 1980: The environment and geomorphology of deltaic sedimentation: some examples from Indonesia. In J. I. Furtado (ed.), *Tropical Ecology and Development: Proceedings of the 5th International Symposium of Tropical Ecology*. Kuala Lumpur: University of Malaysia Press, 1091–5.
Chan, Y. H. 1982: Storage and release of organic carbon in peninsular Malaysia. *International Journal of Environmental Studies*, 18, 211–22.
Chapman, S. B. 1967: Nutrient budgets for a dry heath ecosystem in the south of England. *Journal of Ecology*, 55, 677–89.

Chapman, V. J. 1938: Studies in salt marsh ecology, I–III. *Journal of Ecology*, 26, 144–221.
Chapman, V. J. 1940: Studies in salt marsh ecology, VI–VII. *Journal of Ecology*, 28, 118–79.
Chapman, V. J. (ed.) 1977: *Wet Coastal Ecosystems. Ecosystems of the World I.* Amsterdam: Elsevier.
Charlier, J. J. 1984: Is medium-size beautiful? L'example du port de Zeebrugge. *Transports*, 298, 423–35.
Charlier, J. J. 1987: Les problèmes d'aménagement suscités par la croissance du port de Zeebrugge. *Norois*, 34, 239–51.
Charnock, A. 1983: A new course for the Nile. *New Scientist*, 27 October, 287.
Childe, V. G. 1956: *Piecing Together the Past.* London: Routledge & Kegan Paul.
Chmura, G. L. and Ross, N. W. 1978: The environmental impacts of marinas and their boats: a literature review with management considerations, *Marine Memorandum 45.* Providence, RI: University of Rhode Island.
Christensen, B. 1983: Mangroves – what are they worth? *Unasylva*, 35, 139, 2–15.
Clairain, E. J. 1985: National wetlands functions and values study plan. *Transactions, 50th North American Wildlife and Natural Resources Conference.* Washington, DC: Wildlife Management Institute, 485–94.
Clark, J. 1979: Fresh water wetlands: habitats for aquatic invertebrates, amphibians, reptiles and fish. In P. E. Greeson, J. R. Clark and J. E. Clark (eds), *Wetland Values and Functions: The State of Our Understanding.* Minneapolis, MN: Water Resources Association Technical Publication, 330–43.
Clark, J. G. D. 1954: *Excavations at Star Carr.* Cambridge: Cambridge University Press.
Clark, J. G. D. 1972: Star Carr: a case study in bioarchaeology. *Addison Wesley Module in Anthropology*, 10, 1–42.
Clark, J.R. and Benforado, J. (eds) 1981: *Wetlands of Bottomland Hardwood Forests. Proceedings of a Workshop on Bottomland Hardwood Forest Wetlands of the Southeastern United States, Lake Larnier, GA, 1–5 June 1980.* Amsterdam: Elsevier.
Clark, R. N. and Stankey, G. H. 1979: The recreation opportunity spectrum: a framework for planning, management and research, USDA Forest Service, General Technical Report PNW–98. Seattle, WA: Pacific Northwest Forest and Range Experiment Station.
Clarke, J. I. 1972: *Population Geography.* New York: Pergamon.
Clawson, M. 1958: *Statistics on Outdoor Recreation.* Washington, DC: Resources for the Future Inc.
Clawson, M. 1985: Outdoor recreation: twenty-five years of history, twenty-five years of projection. *Leisure Sciences*, 7, 73–99.
Clawson, M. and Knetsch, J. L. 1966: *Economics of Outdoor Recreation.* Baltimore, MD: Johns Hopkins University Press.
Clements, F. E. 1916: *Plant Succession: An Analysis of the Development of Vegetation.* Washington, DC: Carnegie Institution, Publication 242, 1–512.
Clymo, R. S. 1965: Experiments on breakdown of *Sphagnum* in two bogs. *Journal of Ecology*, 53, 747–58.
Clymo, R. S. 1983: Peat. in A. J. P. Gore (ed.), *Mires: Swamp, Bog, Fen, and Moor, General Studies. Ecosystems of the World 4A.* Amsterdam: Elsevier, 159–224.
Cole, G. 1976: Land drainage in England and Wales. *Journal of the Institution of Water Engineers and Scientists*, 30, 345–67.
Coleman, J. M. and Wright, L. D. 1975: Modern river deltas: variability of processes and sand bodies. In M. L. Broussard (ed.), *Deltas, Models for Exploration.* Houston, TX: Houston Geological Society, 99–149.
Coles, B. and Coles, J. 1986: *Sweet Track to Glastonbury.* London: Thames and Hudson.

Coles, J. 1986: Precision, purpose and priorities in Wetland Archaeology. *Antiquaries Journal*, 66, 227–47.
Coles, J. 1987: The preservation of archaeological sites by environmental intervention. In H. W. M. Hodges (ed.), *In Situ Archaeological Conservation*. Century City, CA: Getty Conservation Institute, 32–55.
Coles, B. and Coles, J. 1989: *People of the Wetlands*. London: Thames and Hudson.
Coles, J. M. and Lawson, A. J. (eds) 1987: *European Wetlands in Prehistory*. Oxford: Clarendon Press.
Coles, J. M. and Orme, B. J. 1983: *Homo sapiens* or *Castor fiber? Antiquity*, 57, 95–102.
Collier, W. L. 1980: Resource use in the tidal swamps of Central Kalimantan: a case study of Banjanese and Javanese rice and coconut producers. In J. I. Furtado (ed.), *Tropical Ecology and Development*, vol. 2. Kuala Lumpur: University of Malaysia Press, 1047–64.
Conway, V. M. 1936: Studies in the autecology of *Cladium mariscus* R.Br. I. Structure and development. *New Phytologist*, 35, 177.
Conway, V. M. 1949: The bogs of central Minnesota. *Ecological Monographs*, 19, 173–206.
Cooper, D. J. and Lee, L. C. 1987: Rocky Mountain wetlands: ecosystems in transition. *National Wetlands Newsletter*, 9, 2–6.
Coughlan, J. 1979: Aspects of reclamation in Southampton Water. In B. Knights and A. J. Phillips (eds), *Estuarine and Coastal Reclamation and Water Storage*. Farnborough: Saxon House, 99–124.
Council on Environmental Quality 1977: *Seventh Annual Report, 1976, Executive Office of the President*. Washington, DC: US Government Printing Office.
Council on Environmental Quality, 1978: *Environmental Quality – 1978: Ninth Annual Report of the Council on Environmental Quality*. Washington, DC: US Government Printing Office.
Cowardin, L. M., Carter, V., Golet, F. C. and La Roe, E. T. 1979: *Classification of Wetlands and Deepwater Habitats in the United States*. Washington, DC: US Department of the Interior, Fish and Wildlife Service, FWS/OBS-79/31.
Cowardin, L. M., Carter, V., Golet, F. C. and La Roe, E. T. 1985: *Classification of Wetlands and Deepwater Habitats of the United States*. 2nd edn. Washington, DC: US Department of the Interior.
Croes, D. R. (ed.) 1976: The excavation of water-saturated archaeological sites (wet sites) on the northwest coast of North America. *Archaeological Survey of Canada, No. 50*. Ottawa: National Museum of Man Mercury Series.
Croes, D. R. 1988: The significance of the 3000 B.P. Hoko River waterlogged fishing camp. In B. Purdy (ed.), *Wet Site Archaeology*, 131–52.
Crow, J. H. and MacDonald, K. B. 1979: Wetland values: secondary production. In P. E. Greeson, J. R. Clark and J. E. Clarke (eds), *Wetland Functions and Values: The State of Our Understanding*. Minneapolis, MN: Water Resources Association Technical Publication, 146–61.
Cryer, M. Whittle, G. N. and Williams, R. 1987: The impact of bait collection by anglers on marine intertidal vertebrates. *Biological Conservation*, 42, 83–93.
Cullis, C. F. and Hirschler, M. M. (1980): *Atmospheric Environment*, 14, 1263.
Dachnowski-Stokes, A. P. 1935: Peat land as a conserver of rainfall and water supplies. *Ecology*, 16, 173–7.
Darby, H. C. 1940a: *The Medieval Fenland*. Cambridge: Cambridge University Press.
Darby, H. C. 1940b: *The Draining of the Fens*. Cambridge: Cambridge University Press.
Darby, H. C. 1951: The changing English landscape. *Geography Journal*, 117, 377–98.
Darby, H. C. 1983: *The Changing Fenland*. Cambridge: Cambridge University Press.
Darby, H. C., Glasscock, R. E., Sheail, J. and Versey, G. R. 1979: The geographical distribution of wealth in England, 1334–1535. *Journal of Historical Geography*, 6, 315–20.

Darnell, R. M. 1978: Overview of major development impacts on wetlands. In J. A. Kusler and J. Montanari (eds), *Proceedings, National Wetland Protection Symposium*. Washington, DC: Government Printing Office, 19–28.

Daugherty, R. 1988: Problems and responsibilities in the excavation of wet sites. In B. Purdy (ed.), *Wet-site Archaeology*. New Jersey: Telford Press, 15–29.

Davidson, J. 1979: Status and methods of forest land classification in Papua New Guinea. In R. A. Carpenter (ed.), *Assessing Tropical Forest Lands: Their Suitability for Sustainable Uses*. Dublin: Tycooly, 247–76.

Davies, G. H. 1984–5: Tackling the weight problem. *Natural World*, 12, 11.

Davis, D. W. 1983: Economic and cultural consequences of land loss in Louisiana. *Shore and Beach*, 51, 30–9.

Davis, J. H., Jr. 1942: The natural features of south Florida, especially the vegetation and the Everglades. *Florida Geological Survey Bulletin*, 25, 1–333.

Davis, J. H., Jr. 1964: The forests of Burma. *Sarracenia*, No. 8, November (New York Botanical Gardens).

Day, J. W., Jr. and Craig, N. J. 1982: Comparison of effectiveness of management options for wetland loss in the coastal zone of Louisiana. In D. F. Boesch (ed.), *Proceedings of the Conference on Coastal Erosion and Wetland Modification in Louisiana: Causes, Consequences, and Options*. Washington, DC: US Fish and Wildlife Service, Biological Services Program, FWS/OBS-82/59.

Day, J. W. Jr, Conner, W. H., Ley-Lou, F., Day, R. H. and Navarro, A. M. 1987: The productivity and composition of mangrove forests, Laguna de Terminos, Mexico. *Aquatic Botany*, 27, 267–84.

Dean, R. G. 1979: Effects of vegetation on shoreline erosional processes. In P. E. Greeson, J. R. Clark and J. E. Clark (eds), *Wetland Functions and Values: The State of Our Understanding*. Minneapolis, MN: Water Resources Association Technical Publication, 403–15.

Deevey, E. S., Jr. 1970: In defense of mud. *Bulletin of Ecological Society in America*, 51, 5–8.

de Graaf, J., Nijenhuis, W. and van Dansik, D. 1982: Een Schoone stad: Rotterdam maakt de sprong naar Zuid. In Rotterdamse Kunststichting, *De Kop van Zuid*. Rotterdamse Kunststichting Uitgeverij, 85–184.

de Jong, J. and Wiggens, A. J. 1983: Polders and their environment in the Netherlands. In *Polders of the World An International Symposium: Final Report*. Wageningen: International Institute for Land Reclamation and Improvement, 221–41.

de la Cruz, A. A. 1979: Production and transport of detritus in wetlands. In P. E. Greeson, J. R. Clark and J. E. Clark (eds), *Wetland Functions and Values: The State of Our Understanding*. Minneapolis, MN: Water Resources Association Technical Publication, 162–74.

de la Cruz, A. A. 1980: Economic evaluations and ecological implications of alternative uses of mangrove swamps in S.E. Asia, *Proceedings of the Asian Symposium on Mangrove Evaluation: Research and Management, Kuala Lumpur, 25–29 August 1980*.

de la Cruz, A. A. 1984: A realistic approach to the use and management of mangrove areas in Southeast Asia. In H. J. Teas (ed.), *Physiology and Management of Mangroves*. The Hague: W. Junk, 65–8.

de la Cruz, A. A. 1985: The importance of detrital resources in tropical estuaries. In K. C. Misra (ed.), *Ecology and Resource Management in Tropics*, vol. I, *Forest, Grassland, Cropland and Detrital Systems*. Chowk, Varanasi, India: Bhargava Book Depot, 271–88.

DeLaune, R. D., Patrick, W. H. and Buresh, R. J. 1978: Sedimentation rates determined by Cs^{137} dating in a rapidly accreting salt marsh. *Nature, London*, 275, 532–3.

Delwiche, C. C. 1970: The nitrogen cycle. *Scientific American*, 223, 137–46.

Denny, P. 1984: Permanent swamp vegetation of the Upper Nile. *Hydrobiologia*, 110, 79–90.

de Ruiter, F. G. (1985): Vuil slib in rivieren: een onbetaalde rekening. *NRC Handelsblad Weekeditie*, 3 December 1985, 13.

Destler, C. M. 1947: Agricultural re-adjustment and agrarian unrest in Illinois, 1880–1896. *Agricultural History*, 21, 104–16.

DeVoe, C. 1986: Army Corps of Engineers' jurisdiction over wetlands under Section 404 of the Clean Water Act; United States v. Riverside Bayview Homes Inc. *Ecology Law Quarterly*, 13, 579–91.

DeVoe, M. R. and Baughman, D. S. (eds) 1987: *Coastal Wetland Impoundments: Ecological Characterization, Management, Status and Use*, vol. 1, *Executive Summary*. Charleston, SC: South Carolina Sea Grant Consortium, Publication No. SC-SG-TR-86-1.

Dickinson, C. H. 1983: Micro-organisms in peatlands. In A. J. P. Gore (ed.) *Mires: swamp, bog, fen and moor, General studies. Ecosystems of the World 4A*. Amsterdam: Elsevier, 225–45.

Dideriksen, R. I., Holebaugh, A. R. and Schmude, K. O. 1979: Wetland soils for crop production in the United States. In P. E. Greeson, J. R. Clark and J. E. Clark (eds), *Wetland Values and Functions: The State of Our Understanding*. Minneapolis, MN: American Water Resources Association Technical Publication, 632–43.

Dillehay, T. 1987: Monte Verde: a late Pleistocene wetland site in southern Chile. *NewsWARP*, 2, 6–7.

Dillehay, T. 1988: Early rainforest archaeology in southwestern South America. In B. Purdy (ed.), *Wet-site Archaeology*. New Jersey: Telford Press, 117–206.

Dillehay, T. D. 1989: *Monte Verde: A Late Pleistocene Settlement in Chile* Washington and London: Smithsonian Institution Press.

Dingman, S. L. 1973: Effects of permafrost on stream flow characteristics in the discontinuous permafrost zone of central Alaska. *Proceedings, North American Contribution to the Second International Conference on Permafrost*. Washington, DC: National Academy of Sciences, 447–53.

Dionne, J. C. 1969: Tidal flat erosion by ice at La Pocatière, St Lawrence Estuary. *Journal of Sedimentary Petrology*, 39, 1174–81.

Dionne, J. C. 1984: An estimate of ice-drifted sediments based on mud content of the ice cover at Montmagny, Middle St Lawrence Estuary. *Marine Geology*, 57, 149–66.

Doi, T., Okada, K. and Isibashi, K. 1973: Environmental assessment on survival of Juruma prawn, *Penaeus japonicus* in tideland. I. Environmental conditions in Saizya tideland and selection of essential characteristics. *Bulletin of Tokai Regional Fishing and Research Laboratories*, 76, 37–52.

Dolman, J. D. and Buol, S. W. 1967: A study of organic soils (histosols) in the tidewater region of North Carolina. Technical Bulletin No. 181, North Carolina Agricultural Experiment Station, Raleigh, NC.

Donnelly, M. P. and Vaske, J. J. 1986: Degree and range of recreation specialization: toward a typology of boating related activities. *Journal of Leisure Research*, 18, 81–95.

Donner, W. 1987: *Land Use and Environmentalism in Indonesia*. Honolulu, HI: University of Hawaii Press.

Doody, P. 1984: Nature conservation and Heritage Coasts. The role of the Nature Conservancy Council. In J. R. Edwards (ed.), *Heritage Coasts, Recreation Ecology Research Group, Report No. 10*. Ashford, Kent: Wye College, University of London, 7–10.

Doran, G. H. and Dickel, D. N. 1988: Multidisciplinary investigations at the Windover site. In B. Purdy (ed.) *Wet Site Archaeology*. New Jersey: Telford Press, 263–89.

Driessen, P. M. 1978: Peat Soils. in *Soils and Rice*. Laguna, Philippines: International Rice Research Institute, 763–79.

Driessen, P. M. and Rochimah, L. 1976: The physical properties of lowland peats from

Kalimantan, *Peat and Podzolic Soils and their Potential for Agriculture in Indonesia*. Bogor: Soil Research Institute.

Drijver, C. A. and Marchand, M. 1985: *Taming the Floods: Environmental Aspects of Floodplain Development in Africa*. Leiden: State University of Leiden Centre for Environmental Studies.

Duboul-Rasavet, C. 1956: Contribution à l'étude géologique et sédimentologique du delta du Rhône. *Mémoires de la Société Géologique de France*, 76.

Dugan, P. J. 1988: The importance of rural communities in wetlands conservation and development. In D. D. Hook et al. (eds), *The Ecology and Management of Wetlands*, vol. 2. London: Croom Helm, 3–11.

Dugdale, W. 1662: *History of Imbanking and Drayning of Rivers, Fennes and Marshes*. London.

Duis, E. 1874: *The Good Old Times in McLean County, Illinois*. Bloomington, IL: Lender Publishing and Printing House.

Dunkle, F. and Misso, B. 1988. Farm Bill related wetland protection and restoration opportunities. In J. Zelazny and J. S. Feieraband (eds), *Increasing Our Wetland Resources*. Washington, DC: National Wildlife Federation, 244–6.

Dustin, D. L. and McAvoy, L. H. 1982: The decline and fall of quality recreation opportunities and environments? *Environmental Ethics*, 4, 49–56.

Dutt, A. K. and Heal, S. 1985: The delta works: a Dutch experience in project planning. In A. K. Dutt and F. J. Costa (eds), *Public Planning in the Netherlands*. Oxford: Oxford University Press, 184–202.

Dyer, K. R. 1973: *Estuaries: A Physical Introduction*. London: Wiley.

Eagles, P. 1980: An approach to describing recreation in the natural environment. *Recreation Research Review*, 8, 28–36.

Edington, J. M. and Edington, M. A. 1986: *Ecology, Recreation and Tourism*. Cambridge: Cambridge University Press.

Edwards, J. M. and Frey, R. W. 1977: Substrate characteristics within a Holocene salt marsh, Sapelo Island, Georgia. *Senckenbergiana Maritima*, 9, 215–59.

Edwards, J. R. 1987: The U.K. Heritage Coasts. An assessment of the ecological impacts of tourism. *Annals of Tourism Research*, 14, 71–87.

Ellison, R. L. and Nichols, M. M. 1976: Modern and Holocene foraminifera in the Chesapeake Bay region. *Marine Sediment Specialist Publications*, 1, 131–51.

El Moghrabhy, A. I. and El Sammani, M. O. 1985: On environmental and socio-economic impact of the Jonglei Canal Project, Southern Sudan. *Environmental Conservation*, 12, 41–8.

Eurola, S., Hicks, S. and Kaakinen, E. 1984: Key to Finnish mire types. In P. D. Moore (ed.), *European Mires*. London: Academic Press, 11–117.

Evans, G. 1965: Intertidal flat sediments and their environments of deposition in The Wash. *Quarterly Journal of the Geological Society of London*, 121, 209–41.

Evans, G. 1970: Coastal and nearshore sedimentation, a comparison of clastic and carbonate deposition. *Proceedings of the Geologists' Association*, 81, 493–508.

Ewel, K. C. and Odum, H. T. (eds) 1978: *Cypress Swamps*. Gainesville, FL: University Press of Florida.

FAO (Food and Agriculture Organization) 1981a: Proyecto de evaluacion de dos recursos forestales tropicales. In *Los Recursor Forestales de la America Tropical*. Rome: United Nations.

FAO (Food and Agriculture Organization) 1981b: Tropical forest resources assessment project. In *Forest Resources of Tropical Asia*. Rome: United Nations.

Farnham, R. S. 1979: Wetlands as energy sources. In P. E. Greeson, J. R. Clarke and J. E. CLark (eds), *Wetland Functions and Values: The State of Our Understanding*. Minneapolis, MN: American Water Resources Association Technical Publication, 661–72.

Faverjee, J. Ch. L. 1951: The origin of the Wadden mud. *Mededelingen Landbouwhogesch Wageningen*, 51, 113–41.

Fisk, H. N. 1944: *Geological Investigation of the Alluvial Valley of the Lower Mississippi River*. Vicksburg, MS: Mississippi River Commission.
Fisk, H. N. and McFarlan, E. 1955: Late Quaternary deltaic deposits of the Mississippi River. In A. Poldevaart (ed.), *The Crust of the Earth*. Geological Society of America, Special Paper 62, 279–302.
Flake, L. D. 1979: Wetland Diversity and Waterfowl. In P. E. Greeson, J. R. Clark and J. E. Clark (eds), *Wetland Values and Functions: The State of Our Understanding*. Minneapolis, MN: American Water Resources Association Technical Publication, 312–19.
Flint, E. P. and Richards, J. F. 1990: Historical analysis in landuse and carbon stock of vegetation in South and Southeast Asia. *Canadian Journal of Forest Research* (Forthcoming).
Folkerts, 1982: The pitcher plant bogs. *American Scientist*, 70, 260–6.
Fong, F. 1985: Nypa swamps in Peninsular Malaysia. In K. C. Misra (ed.), *Ecology Resource Management in the Tropics*, vol. II. Chowk, Varanusi, India: Bhargava Book Depot, 31–8.
Forrest, G. I. and Smith, R. A. H. 1975: The productivity of a range of blanket bog vegetation types in the Northern Pennines. *Journal of Ecology*, 63, 173–202.
Foster, D. R., King, G. A., Glaser, P. H. and Wright, H. E. 1983: Origin of string patterns in boreal peatlands. *Nature, London*, 306, 256–8.
Foster, J. H. 1979: Measuring the social value of wetland benefits. In P. E. Greeson, J. R. Clark and J. E. Clark (eds), *Wetland Values and Functions: The State of Our Understanding*. Minneapolis, MN: American Water Resources Association Technical Publication, 84–92.
Franken, N. A. P. and Roos, M. C. 1983: *Studies in Lowland Equatorial Forest in Jambi Province, Central Sumatra*. Biotrop., Special Publication No. 14.
Frayer, W. E., Monahan, T. J., Bowden, D. C. and Graybill, F. A. 1983: *Status and Trends of Wetlands and Deepwater Habitat in the Coterminous United States, 1950s to 1970s*. Fort Collins, CO: Department of Forest and Wood Sciences, Colorado State University.
French, C. N. and Moore, P. D. 1986: Deforestation, *Cannabis* cultivation and schwingmoor formation at Cors Llyn (Llyn Mire), central Wales. *New Phytologist*, 102, 469–82.
French, R. A. 1959: Drainage and economic development of Poles'ye, USSR. *Economic Geography*, 35, 173–80.
Frey, R. W. and Basan, P. B. 1978: Coastal salt marshes. In R. A. Davis (ed.), *Coastal Sedimentary Environments*. New York: Springer Verlag, 101–69.
Fritzell, P. A. 1979: American wetlands as a cultural symbol: place of wetlands in American culture. In P. E. Greeson, J. R. Clark and J. E. Clark (eds), *Wetland Functions and Values: The State of Our Understanding*. Minneapolis, MN: American Water Resources Association Technical Publication, 523–34.
Froomer, N. L. 1980a: Sea level changes in the Chesapeake Bay during historic times. *Marine Geology*, 36, 289–305.
Froomer, N. L. 1980b: Morphologic changes in some Chesapeake Bay tidal marshes resulting from accelerated soil erosion. *Zoological Geomorphology NF*, 34, 242–54.
Fruge, D. W. 1982: Effect of wetland deterioration on the fish and wildlife resources of coastal Louisiana. In D. F. Boesch (ed.), *Proceedings of the Conference on Coastal Erosion and Wetland Modification in Louisiana: Causes, Consequences and Options*. Baton Rouge, LA: US Fish and Wildlife Service, FWS/OBS-82-59, 99–107.
Furedy, C. 1983: Calcutta wetland for sewage management and re-use. *Environmental Conservation*, 10, 32–43.
Furtado, J. I. and Mori, S. (eds), 1982: *Tasek Bera: The Ecology of a Freshwater Swamp*. London: W. Junk.
Gallais, J. 1984: *Les hommes du Sahel*. Paris: Flammarion.

Ganong, W. F. 1897: Upon raised bogs in the Province of New Brunswick. *Proceedings and Transactions of the Royal Society of Canada, Second series*, vol. 4, 131–9.
Garofalo, D. 1980: The influence of wetland vegetation on tidal stream channel migration and morphology. *Estuaries*, 3, 258–70.
Gaudet, J. J. 1975: Mineral concentrations in papyrus in various African swamps. *Journal of Ecology*, 63, 483–91.
Gaudet, J. J. 1979: Seasonal changes in nutrients in a tropical swamp: North Swamp, Lake Naivasha, Kenya. *Journal of Ecology*, 67, 953–81.
Gaudet, J. J. 1980: Papyrus and ecology of Lake Naivasha. *National Geographic Society Research Reports*, 12, 267–72.
Geyh, H. R., Kudrass, H. R. and Steif, H. 1979: Sea level changes during the late Pleistocene and Holocene in the Straits of Malacca. *Nature, London*, 278, 441–3.
Ghosh, D. and Sen, S. 1987: Ecological history of Calcutta's wetland conversion. *Environmental Conservation*, 14, 219–26.
Giannio, S. P. and Wang, H. 1974: *Engineering Considerations for Marinas in Tidal Marshes*. Newark, DE: College of Marine Studies, University of Delaware.
Gierloff-Emden, H. C. 1961: Nehrungen und Lagunen. *Petermanns Geographische Mittelung*, 105, 81–92, 161–76.
Gilbert, G. K. 1908: Tomales Bay to Bolinas Lagoon. In A. C. Lawson (ed.), *The California Earthquake of April 18, 1906 – Report of the State Earthquake Investigation Commission*. Washington, DC: Carnegie Institute, 87.
Gilbert, G. K. 1917: Hydraulic-mining debris in the Sierra Nevada. *US Geological Survey, Professional Paper 105*. Reston, VA: US Geological Survey.
Gilliam, J. W., Chescheir, R. W., Skaggs, R. W. and Broadhead, R. G. 1988: Effects of pumped agricultural drainage water on wetland water quality. In D. D. Hook et al. (eds), *The Ecology and Management of Wetlands*, vol. 1. London: Croom Helm, 275–83.
Gillieson, D., Gorecki, P. and Hope, G. 1985: Prehistoric agricultural systems in a lowland swamp, Papua New Guinea. *Archaeologia Oceania*, 20, 32–7.
Gilliland, M. S. 1975: *The Material Culture of Key Marco*. Gainesville, FL: University Press of Florida.
Gilluly, J. and Grant, U. S. 1949: Subsidence in Long Beach Harbor area, California. *Geological Society of America Bulletin*, 60, 461–530.
Girling, M. 1984: Investigations of a second insect assemblage from the Sweet Track. *Somerset Level Papers*, 10, 79–91.
Glacken, G. 1967: *Traces on the Rhodian Shore: nature and culture in western thought from ancient times to the end of the eighteenth century*. Berkeley, CA: University of California Press.
Glangeaud, L. 1939: Le mouvement des sédiments et la formation des bancs, seuils et mouilles dans la Garonne et l'estuaire de la Gironde. *International Association of Scientific Hydrology, Proceedings*, 1, Report 6.
Gleason, H. A. and Cronquist, A. 1964: *The Natural Geography of Plants*. New York: Columbia University Press.
Glooschenko, J. H. Archboco, J. H. and Herman, D. 1988: The Ontario wetland evaluation system: replicability and bird habitat selection. In D. D. Hook et al. (eds), *The Ecology and Management of Wetlands*, vol. 2. London: Croom Helm, 103–27.
Godshalk, G. L. and Wetzel, R. G. 1978: Decomposition in the littoral zone of lakes. In R. E. Good, D. F. Whigham and R. L. Simpson (eds), *Freshwater Wetlands: Ecological Processes and Management Potential*. New York: Academic Press, 131–43.
Godwin, H. 1940: Studies of the post-glacial history of British vegetation. III, Fenland pollen diagrams. IV, Post-glacial changes of relative land and sea-level in the English Fenland. *Philosophical Transactions of the Royal Society, B*, 230, 239–303.
Godwin, H. 1956: *The History of British Flora: A Factual Basis for Phytogeography*. Cambridge: Cambridge University Press.

Godwin, H. 1978: *Fenland: Its Ancient Past and Uncertain Future.* Cambridge: Cambridge University Press.
Godwin, H. 1981: *The Archives of the Peat Bogs.* Cambridge: Cambridge University Press.
Good, R. E., Whigham, D. F. and Simpson, R. L. (eds) 1978: *Freshwater Wetlands: Ecological Processes and Management Potential.* New York: Academic Press.
Goodwin, R. H. and Niering, W. A. 1975: *Inland Wetlands of the United States Evaluated as Potential Registered National Landmarks.* Washington, DC: US Department of the Interior, National Park Service.
Gopal, B., Turner, R. E., Wetzel, R. G. and Wigham, D. F. (eds) 1982: *Wetlands: Ecology and Management.* Jaipur, India: National Institute of Ecology and International Scientific Publications.
Gordon, I. and Duncan, P. 1988: Pastures new for conservation. *New Scientist*, 17 March, 54–9.
Gore, A. J. P. (ed.) 1983a: *Mires: Swamp, Bog, Fen and Moor. General Studies. Ecosystems of the World 4A.* Amsterdam: Elsevier.
Gore, A. J. P. (ed.) 1983b: *Mires: Swamp, Bog, Fen and Moor. Regional Studies. Ecosystems of the World 4B.* Amsterdam: Elsevier.
Gorecki, P. P. and Gillieson, D. S. 1985: The highland fringes as a key zone for prehistoric developments in Papua New Guinea. *Bulletin of Indo-Pacific Prehistory Association*, 5, 93–103.
Gornitz, V., Lebedeff, S. and Hansen, J. 1982: Global sea level trend in the past century. *Science*, 215, 1611–14.
Gosselink, J. G. and Baumann, R. H. 1980: Wetland inventories: wetland loss along the United States coast. *Zeitschrifte für Geomorphologie, N.E. Suppl.*, 34, 173–87.
Gosselink, J. G. and Turner, R. E. 1978: The role of hydrology in freshwater wetland ecosystems. In R. E. Good, D. F. Whigham and R. L. Simpson (eds), *Freshwater Wetlands: Ecological Processes and Management Potential.* New York: Academic Press, 63–78.
Gosselink, J. G., Odum, E. P. and Pope, R. M. 1974: *The Value of the Tidal Marsh.* Baton Rouge, LA: Louisiana State University, Center for Wetland Resources, LSU–SG–74–03.
Gosselink, J. G., Burdick, D., Childers, D., Taylor, N., Shaffer, G. P., Hamilton, S., Burmans, R., Chushman, D., Koch, M., Visser, J. and Field, S. 1988: *Cumulative Impact Assessment and Management in the Tensas River Basin – A Pilot Study.* Baton Rouge, LA: Louisiana State University, Center for Wetland Resources LSU–CEI–89–02.
Goudie, A. S. 1986: *The Human Impact.* Oxford: Basil Blackwell.
Government of Burma 1961: Season and crop report for the year ending June 30, 1960. Rangoon Appendices, Statement IIB.
Gower, S. T., Lea, R., Fredrick, D. J., Clark, A. and Philips, D. R. 1985: Above ground energy production and distribution of southeastern hardwood swamp forests. *Biomass*, 7, 185–97.
Gramsch, B. 1987: Ausgrabungen auf dem mesolithischen Moorfundplatz bei Freisack, Besirk Potsdam. *Veröffentlichungen des museums für Ur-und Frühgeschichte Potsdam*, 21, 75–100.
Granhall, U. and Sernander, H. 1973: Nitrogen fixation in a subarctic mire. *Oikos*, 24, 8–15.
Grant, R. R. Jr. and Patrick, R. 1970: Tinicum Marsh as a water purifier, *two studies of Tinicum Marsh.* Washington, DC: Conservation Foundation, 105–23.
Green, F. H. W. 1979: *Field Drainage in Europe: A Quantitative Survey.* Wallingford: Institute of Hydrology.
Greeson, P. E., Clark, J. R. and Clark, J. E. (eds) 1979: *Wetland Functions and Values: The State of Our Understanding.* Minneapolis, MN: Water Resources Association Technical Publication.

Grove, R. 1981: Cressey Dymock and the draining of the fens: an early agricultural model. *Geographical Journal*, 147, 26–37.

Guilcher, A. 1981: Shoreline changes in coastal salt marshes and mangrove swamps (mangals) within the past century. In E. C. F. Bird and K. Koike (eds), *Coastal Dynamics and Scientific Sites*. Tokyo: Komazawa University, 31–53.

Guilcher, A. and Berthois, L. 1957: Cinq années d'observations sédimentologiques dans quatre estuaires – témoins de l'ouest de la Brétagne. *Revue de Géomorphologie Dynamique*, 8, 67–86.

Haas, L. W. 1977: The effect of the spring-neap tidal cycle on the vertical salinity structure of the James, York and Rappahannock Rivers, Virginia, USA. *Estuarine, Coastal and Marine Science*, 5, 485–96.

Hafsten, U. 1983: Biostratigraphical evidence for late Weichselian and Holocene sea-level changes in southern Norway. In D. E. Smith and A. G. Dawson (eds), *Shorelines and Isostasy*. London: Academic Press, 161–81.

Hagen, G. 1863: *Handbuch der Wasserbaukunst, 3: Das Meer*. Berlin.

Hale, P. B. and McCann, S. B. 1982: Rhythmic topography in a mesotidal low wave-energy environment. *Journal of Sedimentary Petrology*, 52, 415–30.

Hallam, H. E. 1965: *Settlement and Society: A study of the early agrarian history of South Lincolnshire*. Cambridge: Cambridge University Press.

Hallam, S. J. 1970: Settlement around the Wash. In C. W. Phillips (ed.), *The Fenland in Roman Times*. London: Royal Geographical Society Research Series, 22–112.

Hanson, A. J. 1981: Transmigration and marginal land development. In G. E. Hansen (ed.), *Agriculture and Rural Development in Indonesia*. Boulder, CO: Westview Press, 219–35.

Hanson, A. J. and Koesoebiono, J. 1979: Settling coastal swampland in Sumatra: a study for integrated resource management. In C. MacAndrews and L. S. Chia (eds), *Developing Economies and the Environment*. Singapore: McGraw-Hill, 121–75.

Hardjono, J. M. 1977: *Transmigration in Indonesia*. Kuala Lumpur: Oxford University Press.

Haslam, S. M. 1973: The management of British wetlands: I. Economic and amenity use. *Journal of Environmental Management*, 1, 303–20.

Havemeyer, L. (ed.) 1930: *Conservation of our Natural Resources Based on Van Hise's 'The Conservation of Natural Resources in the United States'*. New York: Macmillan.

Hayen, H. 1987: Peat bog archaeology in Lower Saxony, West Germany. In J. M. Coles and A. J. Lawson (eds), *European Wetlands in Prehistory*. Oxford: Clarendon Press, 117–36.

Hays, S. P. 1986: *Beauty, Health and Permanence: Environmental Politics in the United States, 1955–1985*. Cambridge: Cambridge University Press.

Healey, P., McDougall, G. and Thomas, M. J. 1982: Theoretical debates in planning: towards a coherent dialogue. In P. Healey, G. McDougall and M. J. Thomas (eds), *Planning Theory: Prospects for the 1980s*. New York: Pergamon Press, 5–22.

Hedgpeth, J. W. 1978: San Francisco Bay: the wetlands besieged. In J. A. Kusler and J. Montanari (eds), *Proceedings: National Wetland Protection Symposium*. Washington, DC: US Fish and Wildlife Service, FWS/OBS/78/97, 143–52.

Heliotis, F. D. 1985: A wetland impacted by wastewater: ecosystem analysis and evaluation, Ph.D. Thesis, University of Wisconsin, Madison, WI.

Helliwell, D. R. 1969: Valuation of wildlife resources. *Regional Studies*, 3, 41–7.

Helliwell, D. R. 1973: Priorities and values in nature conservation. *Journal of Environmental Management*, 1, 85–127.

Hendee, J. C., Gale, R. P. and Catton, W. R., Jr. 1971: A typology of outdoor recreation activity preferences. *Journal of Environmental Education*, 3, 28–34.

Hewes, L. 1951: The Northern wet prairie of the United States: nature, sources of information and extent. *Annals, Association of American Geographers*, 41, 307–23.

Hewes, L. and Frandson, P. E. 1952: Occupying the wet prairie: the role of artificial drainage in Story County, Iowa. *Annals, Association of American Geographers*, 42, 24–50.

Hibbard, B. H. 1939: *A History of the Public Land Policies*. New York: Macmillan.

Hicks, J. D. 1946: The western Middle West, 1900–1914. *Agricultural History*, 20, 65–77.

Hill, A. R. 1976: The environmental impact of agricultural land drainage. *Journal of Environmental Management*, 4, 251–74.

Hilling, D. 1987: Cargo handling technology and changing waterfront land use. *Journal of Shoreline Management*, 3, 23–37.

Hoffman, J. S., Keys, D. and Titus, J. G. 1983: *Projecting Future sea-level Rise: Methodology, Estimates to the year 2100, and Research Needs*. Washington, DC: Environmental Protection Agency, EPA 230–09–007.

Hoffman, R. D. 1988: Ducks Unlimited's United States construction program for enhancing waterfowl production. In J. Zelazny and J. S. Feierabend (eds), *Increasing our Wetland Resources*. Washington, DC: National Wildlife Federation, 109–13.

Hofstetter, R. H. 1983: Wetlands in the United States. In A. J. P. Gore (ed.), *Mires: Swamp, Bog, Fen and Moor. Regional Studies. Ecosystems of the World 4B*. Amsterdam: Elsevier, 201–44.

Hollis, A. R. 1976: The environmental impact of agricultural land drainage. *Journal of Environmental Management*, 4, 251–74.

Hollis, E. 1980: Land drainage and nature conservation: is there a way ahead? *Ecos*, 1.

Hook, D. D., McKee, W. H. Jr., Smith, H. K., Gregory, J., Burrell, V. G. Jr., DeVoe, M. R., Sojka, R. E., Gilbert, S., Banks, R., Stolzy, L. H., Brooks, C., Matthews, T. D. and Shear, T. H. (eds) 1988: *The Ecology and Management of Wetlands*, vols 1 and 2. London: Croom Helm.

Horwitz, E. L. 1978: *Our Nation's Wetlands: An Interagency Task Force Report co-ordinated by the Council on Environmental Quality*. Washington, DC: US Government Printing Office.

Hoskins, W. G. 1959: *The Making of the English Landscape*. London: Hodder and Stoughton.

Hudson, B. J. 1979: Coastal land reclamation, with special reference to Hong Kong. *Reclamation Review*, 2, 3–16.

Hummel, R. L. and Foster, G. S. 1986: A sporting chance: relationships between technological change and concepts of fair play in fishing. *Journal of Leisure Research*, 18, 40–52.

Humphreys, A. A. and Abbot, H. L. 1861: *Report on the Physics and Hydraulics of the Mississippi River*. Philadelphia, PA: Corps of Topographical Engineers, Professional Papers.

Hunt, C. B. 1966: Plant ecology of Death Valley, California. *US Geological Survey, Professional Paper 509*. Reston, VA: US Geological Society.

Hunter, W. W. 1875: *A Statistical Account of Bengal*, 2 vols. London: Trubner.

Hurr, R. T. 1983: Ground-water hydrology of the Morman Island Crane Meadows, Wildlife Area near Grand Island, Hall County, Nebraska. *US Geological Survey, Professional Paper 1277H*. Reston, VA: US Geological Survey.

Inglis, C. C. and Allen F. H. 1957: The regimen of the Thames estuary as affected by currents, salinities and river flow. *Proceedings of the Institute of Civil Engineers*, 7, 827–78.

Ingram, H. A. P. 1967: Problems of hydrology and plant distribution in mires. *Journal of Ecology*, 55, 711–25.

Ingram, H. A. P. 1978: Soil layers in mires: function and terminology. *Journal of Soil Science*, 29, 224–7.

Ingram, H. A. P. 1983: Hydrology, in A. J. P. Gore (ed.), *Mires: Swamp, Bog, Fen and Moor, General Studies. Ecosystems of the World 4A*. Amsterdam: Elsevier, 67–158.

Ingram, J. C. 1971: *Economic Change in Thailand, 1850–1970*. Stanford, CA: Stanford University Press.

International Institute for Land Reclamation and Improvement (ILRI) 1982: *International Symposium: Polders of the World*, 3 vols. Wageningen: ILRI.
Irmler, U. 1979: Considerations on structure and function of the Central-Amazonian inundation forest ecosystem with particular emphasis on selected soil animals. *Oecologia (Berlin)*, 43, 1–18.
Jack, J. C. 1915: *Final Report on the Survey and Settlement Operations in the Bakarganj District, 1900–1908*. Calcutta: Bengal Secretariat.
Jara, R. S. 1984: Aquaculture and mangroves in the Philippines. In *Productivity of the Mangrove Ecosystem: Management Implications*. Penang Malaysia: Universiti Sains Malaysia, Unit Pencetakan Pusat, 97–107.
Jelgersma, S. 1979: Sea-level changes in the North Sea basin. In E. Oele, R. T. E. Schüttenhelm and A. J. Wiggers (eds), *The Quaternary history of the North Sea*. Uppsala: Almquist and Wiksell, 233–48.
Jervis, R. A. 1969: Primary production in the freshwater marsh ecosystem of Troy meadows, New Jersey. *Bulletin of the Torrey Botanical Club*, 96, 209–31.
Jessen, K. 1949: Studies in late Quaternary deposits and flora-history of Ireland. *Proceedings of the Royal Irish Academy*, 52B, 85–290.
Johnson, R. L. 1979: Timber harvest from wetlands. In P. E. Greeson, J. R. Clark and J. E. Clark (eds), *Wetland Functions and Values: The State of Our Understanding*. Minneapolis, MN: American Water Resources Association Technical Publication, pp. 598–605.
Johnson, R. L. and McCormick, J. F. 1979: *Strategies for the Protection and Management of Floodplain Wetlands and other Riparian Ecosystems. Proceedings of the Symposium, Callaway Gardens, GA, 11–13 December 1978*. Washington, DC: US Forest Service, General Technical Report WO–12.
Johnston, D. B. 1975: Rural society and the rice economy in Thailand, 1880–1930, Ph.D. Dissertation, Yale University. Ann Arbor, MI: University Microfilms.
Johnston, W. A. 1921: Sedimentation of the Fraser River delta. *Memoirs of the Canadian Geological Survey*, 125.
Jones, M. B. and Muthuri, F. M. 1985: The canopy structure and microclimate of papyrus (*Cyperus papyrus*) swamps. *Journal of Ecology*, 73, 481–91.
Jordan, C. F. 1982: The nutrient balance of an Amazonian rain forest. *Ecology*, 63, 647–54.
Jordan, C. F. and Herrera, R. 1981: Tropical rain forests: are nutrients really critical? *American Naturalist*, 117, 167–80.
Junk, W. J. 1970: Investigations on the ecology and production-biology of the floating meadows (*Paspalo-Echinochloetum*) on the Middle Amazon. *Amazoniana*, 2 (4), 449–95.
Junk, W. J. 1983: Ecology of swamps on the Middle Amazon. In A. J. P. Gore (ed.) *Mires: Swamp Bog, Fen and Moor*. Regional Studies. Ecosystems of the World 4B. Amsterdam: Elsevier.
Kaatz, M. 1955: The Black Swamp: a study in historical geography. *Annals, Association of American Geographers*, 45, 1–35.
Kadlec, R. H. 1979: Wetlands for tertiary treatment, in P. E. Greeson, J. R. Clark and J. E. Clark (eds), *Wetland Functions and Values: The State of Our Understanding*. Minneapolis, MN: American Water Resources Association Technical Publication, 490–504.
Kadlec, R. H. and Kadlec, J. A. 1979: Wetlands and water quality. In P. E. Greeson, J. R. Clark and J. E. Clark (eds), *Wetland Functions and Values: The State of Our Understanding*. Minneapolis, MN: American Water Resources Association Technical Publication, 436–56.
Kainuma, K. 1982: Utilization of sago palms in Sarawak, South Kalimantan and Papua New Guinea. *Japanese Journal of Tropical Agriculture*, 26(3), 177–86.
Karnes, L. B. 1965: Reclamation of wet and overflow lands. In G. H. Smith, *Conservation of Natural Resources*, 3rd edn. New York: Wiley, 133–44.

Keating, W. H. 1823: *Narrative of an Expedition to the Source of the St Peter's River (Minnesota River), Under the Command of Stephen H. Long, Major U.S. Topographical Engineers*. London: George Whittaker.

Keeley, L. H. 1980. *Experimental Determination of Stone Tool Uses: A Microwear Analysis*. Chicago, IL: University of Chicago Press.

Keller, F. 1878: *The Lake Dwellings of Switzerland and Other Parts of Europe*, 2nd edn. London: Longman.

Keown, M. P., Dardeau, E. A. and Causey, E. M. 1980: Characterization of the suspended-sediment regime and bed-material gradation of the Mississippi River basin, US Army Engineers District, New Orleans, Louisiana, Potamology Investigations Report No. 221. Vicksburg, MS: Environmental Laboratory, US Army Engineers Waterways Experimental Station.

Kesel, R. H. and Smith, J. S. 1978: Tidal creek and pan formation in intertidal salt marshes. *Scottish Geographical Magazine*, 94, 159–68.

Kesteven, S. 1986: Aborigines in the tourist industry, East Kimberley Working Paper, No. 14, East Kimberley Impact Assessment Project. Canberra: Australian National University, Center for Resource and Environmental Studies.

Kikuta, M. 1985: Outline of Tokyo International Airport offshore development project. *Civil Engineering in Japan*, 24, 92–104.

Kindle, E. M. 1917: Recent and fossil ripple marks. *Museum Bulletin, Geological Survey of Canada*, 25.

King, C. J. H. 1980. A small cliff-bound estuarine environment: Sandyhaven Pill in South Wales. *Sedimentology*, 27, 93–105.

King, R. 1977: Recent industrialization in Sardinia: rebirth or neo-colonialism? *Erdkunde*, 31, 87–102.

Kirby-Smith, W. W. and Barber, R. T. 1979: The water quality ramifications in estuaries of converting forest to intensive agriculture, Water Resources Research Institute Report No. 148. University of North Carolina, Water Resources Research Institute, 7–70.

Kivinen, E. and Pakarinen, P. 1981: Geographical distribution of peat resources and major peatland complex types in the world. *Annals, Academy Sciencia Fennicae, Series A, Geology-Geography*, 132, 1–28.

Klopatek, J. M. and Stearns, F. W. 1978: Primary productivity of emergent macrophytes in a Wisconsin freshwater marsh ecosystem. *American Midland Naturalist*, 100, 320–32.

Klötzli, F. 1982: Some aspects of conservation in over-cultivated areas of the Swiss Midlands. In B. Gopal, R. E. Turner, R. G. Wetzel and D. F. Whigham (eds), *Wetlands: Ecology and Management*, Part II. Jaipur: International Scientific Publications and National Institute of Ecology, 15–20.

Klötlzi, F. and Maltby, E. 1983: Mires on the move in Europe. *Geographical Magazine*, 55(7), 346–51.

Knight, R. J. and Dalrymple, R. W. 1975: Intertidal sediments from the south shore of Cobequid Bay, Bay of Fundy, Novia Scotia, Canada. In R. N. Ginsburg (ed.), *Tidal Deposits*. New York: Springer-Verlag, 47–55.

Knutson, P. L. 1978: Role of coastal marshes in energy dissipation and shore protection. In D. D. Hook et al. (eds), *The Ecology and Management of Wetlands*, vol. 1. London: Croom Helm, 161–75.

Kokabi, M. 1985: Vorlaufiger Bericht über die Untersuchungenn Tierknochenfunden aus Hornstaad-Hörnle I am Westlichen Bodensee. *Berichte zu Ufer-und Moorsiedlungen Sudwestdeutschlands*, 2, 148–63.

Komiyama, A., Ogino, K., Aksornkoae, S. and Sabhasri, S. 1987: Root Biomass of a mangrove forest in southern Thailand: estimation by the trench method and the zonal structure of root biomass. *Journal of Tropical Ecology*, 3, 97–108.

Kraft, J. C., Biggs, R. B. and Halsey, S. D. 1973: Morphology and vertical sedimentary sequence models in Holocene transgressive barrier systems. In

D. R. Coates (ed.), *Coastal Geomorphology*. Binghamton: State University of New York, 321–54.

Kramer, R. A. and Shabman, L. A. 1986: Incentives for agricultural development of U.S. wetlands: a case study of the bottomland hardwoods of the lower Mississippi Valley. In T. T. Phipps, P. R. Crosson and K. A. Price (eds), *Agriculture and Environment*. Washington, DC: Resources for the Future, National Center for Food and Agricultural Policy, 175–204.

Kreutzwiser, R. 1981: The economic significance of the Long Point Marsh, Lake Erie, as a recreational resource. *Journal of Great Lakes Research*, 7, 105–10.

Kroodsma, D. E. 1979: Habitat values for nongame wetland birds. In P. E. Greeson, J. R. Clark and J. E. Clark (eds), *Wetland Values and Functions: The State of Our Understanding*. Minneapolis, MN: American Water Resources Association Technical Publication, 320–9.

Krutilla, J. V. and Fisher, A. C. 1975: *The Economics of Natural Environments: Studies in the Valuation of Commodity and Amenity Resources*. Baltimore, MD: Johns Hopkins University Press.

Kushlan, J. A. 1987: External threats and internal management: the hydrologic regulation of the Everglades, Florida, USA. *Environmental Management*, 11, 109–19.

Kusler, J. A. 1983: *Our National Wetland Heritage: A Protection Guidebook*. Washington, DC: Environmental Law Institute.

Kusler, J. A. and Montanari, J. 1978: *Proceedings of the National Wetland Protection Symposium, Reston, VA, 1977*. Washington, DC: Fish and Wildlife Service, FWS/OBS/78/97.

Kvet, J. 1971: Growth analysis approach to the production ecology of reedswamp communities. *Hidrobiologia*, 12, 15–40.

Lamb, H. H. 1982: *Climate, History and the Modern World*. London: Methuen.

Lambert, A. M. 1985: *The Making of the Dutch Landscape: An Historical Geography of the Netherlands*, 2nd edn. London: Academic Press.

Lambert, A. M., Jennings, J. N., Smith, E. T., Green, C. and Hutchinson, J. N. 1960: *The Making of the Broads*. London: Royal Geographical Society.

Land Planning Committee: National Resources Board 1936: *Supplementary Report of the Land Planning Committee to the National Resources Board*, Part IV, *Land Available for Agriculture through Reclamation*. Washington, DC: US Government Printing Office.

Larson, J. S. 1982: Wetland value assessment – state of the art. In B. Gopal, R. E. Turner, R. G. Wetzel and D. F. Whigham (eds), *Wetlands: Ecology and Management*. Jaipur: National Institute of Ecology and International Scientific Publications, 417–24.

Larson, J. S. 1985: Valuing liquid assets. *IUCN Bulletin*, 16, 119.

Larson, J. S. and Neill, C. (eds) 1987: *Mitigating Freshwater Alteration in the Glaciated Northeastern United States: An Assessment of the Science Base*. Amherst: University of Massachusetts Environmental Institute, Publ. 87–1.

Lassoudiere, A. 1976: Banana cultivation on hydromorphic soils of the Agneby Marsh in the Ivory Coast. *Proceedings of the Fifth International Peat Congress*, vol. III. Poznan: International Peat Society, 104–10.

Leakey, M. 1971: *Olduvai Gorge*, vol. III. Cambridge: Cambridge University Press.

Leatherman, S. P. 1983: Barrier dynamics and landward migration with Holocene sea-level rise. *Nature, London*, 301, 415–18.

Lee, L. C. and Gosselink, J. G. 1988: Cumulative impacts on wetlands: linking, scientific assessments and regulatory alternatives. *Environmental Management*, 12 (5), 591–602.

Le Fournier, J. and Friedman, G. M. 1974: Rate of lateral migration of adjoining sea-marginal sedimentary environments shown by historical records, Authie Bay, France. *Geology*, 2, 497–8.

Legge, A. J. and Rowley-Conwy, P. A. 1988: *Starr Carr Revisited*. London: Birkbeck College, University of London.

Leitch, J. A. 1981: Wetland hydrology: state of the art and annotated bibliography, Agricultural Experimental Station, Research Report No. 82. Fargo, ND: North Dakota State University.

Leitch, J. A. and Scott, D. F. 1977: *A Selected Annotated Bibliography of Economic Values of Fish and Wildlife and their Habitats*. Fargo, ND: Department of Agricultural Economics, North Dakota State University.

Leitch, J. A. and Shabman, L. A. 1988: Overview of economic assessment methods relevant to wetland evaluation. In D. D. Hook et al. (eds), *The Ecology and Management of Wetlands*, vol. 2. London: Croom Helm, 95–102.

Leith, H. 1975: Primary Productivity of the Major Vegetation Units of the Woreld. In H. Leith and R. H. Whittaker (eds), *Primary Productivity of the Biosphere*. Berlin: Springer-Verlag, 203–16.

Leopold, L. B., Wolman, M. G. and Miller, J. P. 1964: *Fluvial Processes in Geomorphology*. San Francisco, CA: W. H. Freeman.

Letzsch, W. S. and Frey, R. W. 1980: Erosion of salt-marsh tidal creek banks, Sapelo Islands, Georgia. *Senckenbergiana Maritima*, 12, 201–12.

Levin, I. and Shoham, D. 1983: Ground-surface elevation loss in the reclaimed Hula swamp in Israel during the period from 1958 to 1980. In K. M. Schallinges (ed.), *Proceedings from the Second International Symposium on Peat in Agriculture and Horticulture*. Jerusalem: The Hebrew University.

Lewis, F. J. and Dowding, E. S. 1926: The vegetation and retrogressive changes of peat areas (muskegs) in central Alberta. *Journal of Ecology*, 14, 317–41.

Librero, A. R. 1984: Mangrove management in the Philippines. In H. J. Teas (ed.), *Physiology and Management of Mangroves*. The Hague: W. Junk, 79–87.

Liddle, M. J. 1975: A selective review of the ecological effects of trampling on natural ecosystems. *Biological Conservation*, 7, 17–35.

Liddle, M. J. and Kay, A. M. 1987: Resistance, survival and recovery of trampled corals on the Great Barrier Reef. *Biological Conservation*, 42, 1–18.

Liddle, M. J. and Scorgie, H. R. A. 1980: The effects of recreation on freshwater plants and animals: a review. *Biological Conservation*, 7, 17–35.

Lockhart, S. H. 1986: Management considerations related to the physical alterations of estuaries. In *Papers from the Estuarine Management Practices Symposium, 1985*. Baton Rouge, LA: Louisiana State University, Center for Wetland Resources, 17–30.

Lucas, G. L. I. and Walters, S. M. 1971: *List of Rare, Threatened and Endemic Plants for the Countries of Europe. Nature and Environment Series 14*. Strasbourg: Council of Europe.

Ludden, A. P., Frink, D. L. and Johnson, D. H. 1983: Water storage capacity of natural depressions in the Devil's Lake Basin of North Dakota. *Journal of Soil and Water Conservation*, 38(1), 45–8.

Luebbers, R. A. 1975: Ancient boomerangs discovered in South Australia. *Nature, London*, 253, 39.

Lugo, A. and Snedaker, S. 1974: The ecology of mangroves. *Annual Review of Ecology and Systematics*, 5, 39–64.

Luken, R. A. 1976: *Preservation Versus Development*. New York: Praeger.

L'Vovich, M. I. and White, G. F. 1990: Water. In B. L. Turner III, W. C. Clark, R. W. Kates, J. Matthews, W. Meyer and J. R. Richards (eds), *The Earth as Transformed by Human Action*. New York: Cambridge University Press.

MacDonald, P. O., Frayer, W. G. and Clauser, J. K. 1978: *Documentation, Chronology and Future Projections of Bottomland Hardwood Habitat Loss in the Lower Mississippi Alluvial Plain*, 2 vols. Vicksburg, MS: Fish and Wildlife Service Division, Ecological Services.

Malmer, N. 1975: Development of bog mires. In A. D. Hasler (ed.), *Coupling of Land and Water Systems*. New York: Springer-Verlag, 85–92.

Maltby, E. 1980: The impact of severe fire on Calluna moorland in the North York moors. *Bulletin D'Ecologie*, 11(3), 683–708.

Maltby, E. 1985: Peat mining for energy, Report SIEP-2. Gland, Switzerland: International Union for the Conservation of Nature.

Maltby, E. 1986: *Waterlogged Wealth: Why Waste the World's Wet Places?* London: International Institute for Environment and Development.

Maltby, E. 1987: Soil science base for freshwater wetland utilization in the northeastern United States. In J. S. Larsen and C. Neill (eds), *Mitigating Freshwater Alteration in the Glaciated Northeastern United States: An Assessment of the Science Base*. Amherst, MA: Environmental Institute, University of Massachusetts, Publ. 87–1.

Maltby, E. 1988a: Wetland resources and future prospects – an international perspective. In J. Zelazny and J. S. Feierabend (eds), *Increasing our Wetland Resources*. Washington, DC: National Wildlife Federation, 3–13.

Maltby, E. 1988b: Global wetlands: history, current status and future. In D. D. Hook et al. (eds), *The Ecology and Management of Wetlands*, vol. 1. London: Croom Helm, 3–14.

Maltby, E. 1989: Peatlands – dilemmas of use and conservation. In J. C. Lefeuvre (ed.), *Conservation and Development: the Sustainable Use of Wetland Resources. Proceedings of the 3rd International Wetlands Conference, Rennes, 19–23 September 1988*. Paris: Laboratory of Evolution and Natural Systems.

Manheim, F. T., Meade, R. H. and Bond, G. C. 1970: Suspended matter in surface waters from Cape Cod to the Florida Keys. *Science*, 167, 371–6.

Mason, C. F. and Bryant, R. J. 1975: Production, nutrient content and decomposition of *Phragmites communis* Trin. and *Typha angustifolia L. Journal of Ecology*, 63, 71–95.

Mazure, P. K. 1983: The development of the Dutch polder dikes. *Proceedings in International Symposium Polders of the World: Final Report*. Wageningen: International Institute for Land Reclamation and Improvement, 64–81.

McCann, S. B. and Dale, J. E. 1986: Sea ice breakup and tidal flat processes, Frobisher Bay, Baffin Island. *Physical Geography*, 7, 168–80.

McHugh, J. L. 1976: Estuarine fisheries: are they doomed? In M. Wiley (ed.), *Estuarine Processes*, vol. 1, *Uses, Stresses and Adaptations to the Estuary*. New York: Academic Press, 15–27.

McIntosh, D. J.1983: Riches lie in tropical swamps. *Geographical Magazine*, 55(4), 184–8.

McLellan, G. 1986: The future of outdoor recreation: what the trends tell us. *Parks and Recreation*, 21, 44–8, 63.

McNae, W. 1968: A general account of the fauna and flora of mangrove swamps and forests of the Indo-West-Pacific region. *Advances in Marine Biology*, 6,73–269.

McVey, J. P. 1988: Aquaculture in mangrove wetlands: a perspective from southeast Asia. In D. D. Hook et al. (eds), *The Ecology and Management of Wetlands*, vol. 2. London: Croom Helm, 303–16.

Meade, R. H. 1972: Transportation and deposition of sediments in estuaries. *Geological Society of America, Memoir* 133, 91–120.

Meehan, B. 1988: Wetland hunters: some reflections. In C. D. Haynes, M. G. Ridpath and M. A. J. Williams (eds), *Monsoonal Australia: Landscape, Ecology and Man in the Northern Lowlands*. Rotterdam: Balkema.

Merefield, J. R. 1981: Caesium in the up-estuary transport of sediments. *Marine Geology*, 39, 45–55.

Mermet, L. and Mustin, M. 1983: *Assainissement Agricole et Regression des Zones Humides en France*. Institute for European Environmental Policy.

Metz, E. D. 1987: The Ballona wetland project: habitat restoration and environmental education. *National Wetlands Newsletter*, 9, 16–18.

Meyer, A. H. 1935: The Kankakee 'marsh' of Northern Indiana and Illinois. *Papers of the Michigan Academy of Science, Arts and Letters*, 21, 359–96.

Meyer, B. 1979: *Sulfur, Energy, and Environment*. Amsterdam: Elsevier.

Meyer-Arendt, K. J. 1987: Resort evolution along the Gulf of Mexico littoral: historical, morphological and environmental aspects, Ph.D. Thesis, Louisiana State Unviersity, Baton Rouge, LA.

Middleton, G. V. (ed.) 1965: *Primary Sedimentary Structures and Their Hydrodynamic Interpretation*. Tulsa, OK: Society for Economic Paleontologists and Mineralogists, Special Publication 12.

Miller, G. M. 1939: Reclamation of wet and overflow lands. In A. E. Parkins and J. R. Whitaker (eds), *Our Natural Resources and Their Conservation*. New York: Wiley, 152–68.

Milliman, J. D. Shen, H.-T., Yang, Z.-X. and Meade, R. H. 1985: Transport and deposition of river sediment in the Changjiang estuary and adjacent continental shelf. *Continental Shelf Research*, 4, 37–45.

Mitchell, G. F. 1965: Littleton Bog, Tipperary: an Irish vegetational record. *Geological Society of America, Special Paper 84*, 1–16.

Mitchell, G. F. 1976: *The Irish Landscape*. London: Collins.

Mitsch, W. J. and Gosselink, J. G. 1986: *Wetlands*. New York: Van Nostrand Reinhold.

Moore, P. D. 1982: How to reproduce in bogs and fens. *New Scientist*, 95, 369–71.

Moore, P. D. 1984: The classification of mires: an introduction. In P. D. Moore (ed.), *European Mires*. London: Academic Press, 1–10.

Moore, P. D. 1987a: Ecological and hydrological aspects of peat formation. In A. C. Scott (ed.), *Coal and Coal-bearing Strata: Recent Advances*. London: Geological Society, Special Publication No. 32, 7–15.

Moore, P. D. 1987b: Man and mire, a long and wet relationship. *Transactions of the Botanical Society of Edinburgh*, 45, 77–95.

Moore, P. D. and Bellamy, D. J. 1973: *Peatlands*. London: Paul Elek.

Morgan, R. A. 1988: *Tree-ring Studies in the Somerset Levels*. Oxford: BAR.

Morley, R. J. 1981: Development and vegetation dynamics of a lowland ombrogenous peat swamp in Kalimantan Tengah, Indonesia. *Journal of Biogeography*, 8, 383–404.

Morner, N.-A. 1973: Eustatic changes in the last 300 years. *Palaeogeography, Palaeoclimatology and Palaeoecology*, 13, 1–14.

Morris, J. T. 1988: Pathways and controls of the carbon cycle in salt marshes. In. D. D. Hook et al. (eds), *The Ecology and Management of Wetlands*, vol. 1. London: Croom Helm, 497–510.

Morrison, I. 1985: *Landscape with Lake Dwellings*. Edinburgh: Edinburgh University Press.

Munro, D. A. 1988: Wetlands conservation world wide. In J. Zelazny and J. S. Feierabend (eds), *Increasing our Wetland Resources*. Washington, DC: National Wildlife Federation, 20–3.

Murkin, H. R. and Wrubleski, D. A. 1988: Aquatic invertebrates of freshwater wetlands: function and ecology. In D. D. Hook et al. (eds), *The Ecology and Management of Wetlands*, vol. 1. London: Croom Helm, 239–49.

Murray, J. W. and Hawkins, A. B. 1976: Sediment transport in the Severn Estuary during the past 8000–9000 years. *Journal of the Geological Society*, 132, 385–98.

Myers, J. G. 1935: Zonation of vegetation along river courses. *Journal of Ecology*, 23, 356–60.

Naamin, N. 1986: Conversion of mangrove areas to tambak aquaculture in Indonesia, *Workshop on the Conversion of Mangrove Areas to Aquaculture, 24–6 April, 1986, Iloilo, Philippines*. Sponsored by UNDP/UNESCO Research and Training Pilot Program on Mangrove Ecosystems in Asia and the Pacific, University of the Philippines in the Visayas, and the Natural Resources Management Center of the Ministry of Natural Resources, Philippines.

Nash, R. 1973: *Wilderness and the American Mind*. New Haven, CT: Yale University Press.

Nature Conservancy Council 1986: *Nature Conservation and Afforestation in Britain*. Peterborough: Nature Conservancy Council.

Navid, D. 1988: Developments under the Ramsar Convention. In D. D. Hook et al (eds), *The Ecology and Management of Wetlands*, vol. 2. London: Croom Helm, 21–7.

Nelson, R. W. 1983: Wetland impact assessment: problems under the Clean Water Act (USA). *Environmental Impact Assessment Review*, 4, 25–40.

Nelson, R. W. 1986: Wetlands policy crisis: United States and United Kingdom. *Agriculture, Ecosystems and Environment*, 18, 95–121.

Nelson, R.W. and Logan, W. J. 1984: Policy on wetland impact mitigation. *Environment International*, 10, 9–19.

Nickerson, N. H. and Thibodeau, F. R. 1985: Association between pore water sulfide concentrations and the distribution of mangroves. *Biogeochemistry*, 1, 183–92.

Niering, W. A. 1979: Our wetland heritage: historic, artistic, and future perspectives. In P. E. Greeson, J. R. Clark and J. E. Clark (eds), *Wetland Functions and Values: The State of Our Understanding*. Minneapolis, MN: American Water Resources Association Technical Publication, 505–22.

Niering, W. A. and Palmisano, A. W. 1979: Use values: harvest and heritage. In J. R. Clark and J. E. Clark (eds), *Scientist Report: The National Symposium on Wetlands*. Washington, DC: National Wetlands Technical Council, 100–13.

Nisbet, J. 1901: *Burma Under British Rule – and Before*, 2 vols. Westminster: Archbold Constable.

Nixon, S. W. 1982: *The Ecology of New England High Salt Marshes. A Community Profile*. Washington, DC: Fish and Wildlife Services, FWS/OBS-81/55.

Noss, R. F. 1987: Protecting natural areas in fragmented landscapes. *Natural Areas Journal*, 7, 2–13.

Novitzki, R. P. 1979: Hydrologic characteristics of Wisconsin's wetlands and their influence on floods, stream flow and sediment. In P. E. Greeson, J. R. Clark and J. E. Clark (eds), *Wetland Functions and Values: The State of Our Understanding*. Minneapolis, MN: American Water Resources Association Technical Application, 377–88.

Nummedal, D. 1982: Future sea level changes along the Louisiana coast. In D. F. Boesch (ed.), *Proceedings of the Conference on Coastal Erosion and Wetland Modification in Louisiana: Causes, Consequences, and Options*. Washington, DC: Fish and Wildlife Service, FWS/OBS-82/59.

Odell, P. 1986: *Oil and World Power*, 8th edn. Harmondsworth: Penguin.

Odell, R. 1972: *The Saving of San Francisco Bay: A Report on Citizen Action and Regional Planning*. Washington, DC: Conservation Foundation.

Odum, E. P. 1969: The strategy of ecosystem development. *Science*, 164, 262–70.

Odum, E. P. 1979: The value of wetlands: a hierarchical approach. In P. E. Greeson, J. R. Clark and J. E. Clark (eds), *Wetland Functions and Values: The State of Our Understanding*. Minneapolis, MN: American Water Resources Association Technical Publication, 16—25.

Odum, E. P. 1981: A new ecology for the coast. In T. C. Jackson and D. Reische (eds), *Coast Alert*. San Francisco, CA: Coast Alliance/Friends of the Earth, 145–65.

Odum, H. T. 1984: Summary: cypress swamps and their regional role. In K.C. Ewel and H. T. Odum (eds), *Cypress Swamps*. Gainesville, FL: University of Florida Press, 416–43.

Odum, W. E. 1970: Insidious alteration of the estuarine environment. *Trans-American Fisheries Society*, 99, 836–47.

Odum, W. E., McIvor, C. C. and Smith, T. J. III 1982: *The Ecology of the Mangroves of South Florida: A Community Profile*. Washington, DC: Fish and Wildlife Service, FWS/OBS/81–24.

Ogawa, H. and Male, J. W. 1986: Simulating the flood mitigation role of wetlands. *Journal of Water Resource Planning and Management*, 112(1), 114–28.

Ohtake, H. 1984: Nakanoumi land reclamation and freshening project. *Water Science and Technology*, 16, 151–70.

Ong, J.-E. and Gong, W.-K. (eds) 1984: *Proceedings of the Workshop on Productivity of the Mangrove System: Management Implications, 4–6 October, 1983*. Penang: University of Malaysia, UNESCO/UNDP Regional Project, RAS-79-002-G-01-13.

Oomkens, E. 1974: Lithofacies relations in the late Quaternary Niger delta complex. *Sedimentology*, 21, 195–222.

O'Riordan, T. 1984: Halvergate Marshes: the story so far. *Ecos*, 6, 24–31.

O'Riordan, T. 1985a: Managing broadland. *Natural World*, 14, 11–3.

O'Riordan, T. 1985b: Environmental issues. *Progress in Human Geography*, 9, 407–9.

Orme, A. R. 1970: *Ireland*. London: Longman.

Orme, A. R. 1973: *Coastal Salt Marshes of Northwest Baja California, Mexico*. US Navy Office of Naval Research, Report 0–73–2, p. 33.

Orme, A. R. 1975: Ecological stress in a subtropical coastal lagoon: Lake St. Lucia, Zululand. *Geoscience and Man*, 12, 9–22.

Orme, A. R. 1990: The instability of Holocene coastal dunes: the case of the Morro dunes, California. In K. F. Nordstrom, N. P. Psuty and R. W. G. Carter (eds), *Coastal Dunes: Process and Morphology*. Chichester: Wiley.

ORRRC (Outdoor Recreation Resources Review Commission) 1962: *Outdoor Recreation for America*. Washington, DC: US Government Printing Office.

Oshibkina, S. V. 1982: Wooden artifacts from the Mesolithic site of Nizhneye Veretye. *Archaeologicke Rozheldy*, 34, 414–29.

Osterhaus, A. D. M. E. and Vedder, E. J. 1988: Identification of virus causing recent seal deaths. *Nature, London*, 335, 20.

OTA (Office of Technology Assessment) 1982: *Impacts of Technology on U.S. Cropland and Rangeland Productivity*. Washington, DC: US Government Printing Office, OTA-F-166.

OTA (Office of Technology Assessment) 1984: *Wetlands: Their Use and Regulation*. Washington, DC: US Government Printing Office, OTA-0-206.

Outdoor Recreation Policy Review Group 1983: *Outdoor Recreation for America – 1983*. Washington, DC: Resources for the Future.

Paijmans, K. (ed.) 1976: *New Guinea Vegetation*. Oxford: Elsevier.

Palmisano, A. W. 1979: Harvest from wetlands. In P. E. Greeson, J. R. Clark and J. E. Clark (eds), *Wetland Values and Functions: The State of Our Understanding*. Minneapolis, MN: American Water Resources Association Technical Application, 589–97.

Pannier, F. 1979: Mangroves impacted by human-induced disturbances: a case study of the Orinoco Delta mangrove ecosystem. *Environmental Management*, 3(3), 205–16.

Parcells, S. 1988: Tropical wetlands and the development assistance agencies. *National Wetlands Newsletter*, 10, 6–8.

Pargiter, F. E. 1934: *A Revenue History of the Sundarbans from 1765 to 1870*. Allipore, Bengal: Bengal Government Press.

Parker, D. J. and Penning-Rowsell, E. C. 1980: *Water Planning in Britain*. London: George Allen and Unwin.

Parker, G. R. and Schneider, G. 1975: Biomass and productivity of an alder swamp in northern Michigan. *Canadian Journal of Forest Research*, 5, 403–9.

Parsons, K. A. and de la Cruz, A. A. 1980: Energy flow and grazing behavior of conocephaline grasshoppers in a *Juncus roemerianus* marsh. *Ecology*, 61, 1045–50.

Patmore, J. A. 1983: *Recreation and Resources*. Oxford: Basil Blackwell.

Patten, B. C., Gopal, B., Jorgensen, S. E., Koryavov, P. P., Kvet, J., Loffler, H., Svirezhev, Y. and Tundisi, J. 1984: *Ecosystem Dynamics in Freshwater Wetland and Shallow Water Bodies. Proceedings of Meeting in Tallinn, USSR, August 1983*. New York: Wiley.

Patterson, N. 1987: Towards a wetland protection strategy for Ontario. *National Wetlands Newsletter*, 9, 16–17.
Pearce, D., Barbier, E. A. and Markandya, A. 1988: *Sustainable Development and Cost-Benefit Analysis* London: London Environmental Economics Centre, University College, Paper 88–01.
Pearce, D., Markandya, A. and Barbier, E. A. 1989: *Blueprint for a Green Economy*. London: Earthscan Publictions Ltd.
Pearsall, W. H. 1920: The aquatic vegetation of the English Lakes. *Journal of Ecology*, 8, 163–201.
Penning-Rowsell, E. C. 1983: An evaluation of wetland policy in England and Wales. In. R. C. Smardon (ed.), *The Future of Wetlands*. Totowa, NJ: Allanheld, Osmun, 25–44.
Perini, R. 1984: *Scavi archeologici nella zona Palafitticola di Fiavé-Carera. Parte I*. Provincia Autonoma di Trento: Servizio Beni Culturali.
Perini, R. 1987a: The typology of the structures on Bronze Age wetland settlements at Fiavé and Lavagnone in the Italian Alpine foothills. In J. M. Coles and A. J. Lawson (eds), *European Wetlands in Prehistory*. Oxford: Clarendon Press.
Perini, R. 1987b: *Scavi Archeologici nella Zona Palafitticola di Fiavé-Carera. Parte II*. Provincia Autonoma di Trento: Servizio Beni Culturali.
Perkins, W. L. 1931: The significance of drain tile in Indiana. *Economic Geography*, 7, 381–9.
Pestrong, R. 1972: San Francisco Bay tidelands. *California Geology*, 25, 27–40.
Peters, D. S., Ahrenholz, D. W. and Rice, T. R. 1979: Harvest and value of wetland associated fish and shellfish. In P. E. Greeson, J. R. Clark and J. E. Clark (eds), *Wetland Functions and Values: The State of Our Understanding*. Minneapolis, MN: American Water Resources Association Technical Publication, 506–17.
Peterson, C., Scheidegger, K. and Komar, P. 1982: Sand dispersal patterns in an active-margin estuary of the northwestern United States as indicated by sand composition, texture and bedforms. *Marine Geology*, 50, 77–96.
Pethick, J. 1981: Long-term accretion rates on tidal salt marshes. *Journal of Sedimentary Petrology*, 51, 571–7.
Pétrequin, P.1984: *Gens de l'Eau, Gens de la Terre*. Paris: Hachette.
Pezeu-Massabuau, J. 1978: *The Japanese Islands: A Physical and Social Geography*. Rutland, VT: C. E. Tuttle.
Phillips, A. M. 1989: *The Underdraining of Farmland in England during the Nineteenth Century*. Cambridge: Cambridge University Press.
Pinder, D. A. 1981: Community attitude as a limiting factor in port growth: the case of Rotterdam. In B. S. Hoyle and D. A. Pinder (eds), *Cityport Industrialisation and Regional Development*. New York: Pergamon Press, 181–99.
Pinder, D.A. and Hoyle, B. S. 1981: Cityports, technologies and development strategies. In B. S. Hoyle and D. A. Pinder (eds), *Cityport Industrialization and Regional Development*. New York: Pergamon Press, 323–38.
Pinder, D. A. and Husain, M. S. 1987: Oil industry restructuring in the Netherlands and its European context. *Geography*, 72, 300–8.
Pinder, D. A. and Husain, M. S. 1988: Deindustrialisation and forgotten fallow: lessons from Western European oil refining. In B. S. Hoyle, D. A. Pinder and M. S. Husain (eds), *Revitalising the Waterfront: International Dimensions of Dockland Redevelopment*. New York: Belhaven Press, 232–46.
Pinto-Silva, J. 1987: Non-conventional land transport systems. *Journal of Terramechanics*, 24, 153–8.
Pitts, D. J. 1983: Opportunity shift, Ph.D. Thesis, Griffith University, Nathan, Queensland.
Platt, R. H. 1987: Overview of developed coastal barriers. In R. H. Platt, S. G. Pelczarski and K. R. Burbank (eds), *Cities on the Beach. Management Issues of*

Developed Coastal Barriers. Chicago, IL: University of Chicago, Department of Geography, Research Paper No. 224.

Platt, R. H., Pelczarski, S. G. and Burbank, K. R. (eds) 1987: *Cities on the Beach. Management Issues of Developed Coastal Barriers*. Chicago, IL: University of Chicago, Department of Geography, Research Paper No.224.

Prance, G. T. 1979: Notes on the vegetation of Amazonia III; the terminology of Amazonian forest types subject to inundation. *Brittonia*, 31(1), 26–38.

Prater, A. J. 1976: The distribution of coastal waders in Europe and North Africa. In M. Smart (ed.), *Proceedings; International Conference on the Conservation of Wetlands and Wildfowl, Heiligenhafen, FDR*. Slimbridge: International Wildfowl Research Bureau, 255–71.

Pratt, D. C. and Andrews, N. J. 1981: Research in Biomass and Special Energy Crops in Wetlands. In B. Richardson (ed.), *Proceedings of Midwest Conference on Wetland Values and Management*. Navarre, MN: The Fresh Water Society.

Pritchard, D. W. 1955: Estuarine circulation patterns. *Proceedings of the American Society of Civil Engineers*, 81, 717–1 to 717–11.

Pritchard, D. W. 1967: Observations of circulation in coastal plain estuaries. In G. H. Lauff (ed.), *Estuaries*. Washington, DC: American Association for the Advancement of Science, Special Publication 83, 37–44.

Purdy, B. (ed.) 1988: *Wet-Site Archaeology*. New Jersey: Telford Press.

Purseglove, J. 1987: *Taming the Flood: Rivers and Wetlands in Britain*. Oxford: Oxford University Press.

Putz, F. E. and Chan, H. T. 1986: Tree growth, dynamics, and productivity in a mature mangrove forest in Malaysia. *Forest Ecology and Management*, 17, 211–30.

Pye-Smith, C. and Rose, C. 1984: *Crisis and Conservation: Conflict in the British Countryside*. Harmondsworth: Pelican.

Pyrovetsi, M. D. 1984: Ecodevelopment in Prespa National Park, Greece, Ph.D. Thesis, Michigan State University.

Queen, W. H. 1977: Human uses of salt marshes. In V. J. Chapman (ed.), *Wet Coastal Ecosystems. Ecosystems of the World, 1*. Amsterdam: Elsevier, 363–9.

Rabinowitz, D. 1978: Early growth of mangrove seedlings in Panama and an hypothesis concerning the relationship of dispersal and zonation. *Journal of Biogeography*, 5, 113–33.

Rai, H. and Hill, G. 1980: Classification of central Amazon lakes on the basis of their microbiological and physio-chemical characteristics. *Hydrobiologica*, 72, 85–99.

Rajewski, Z. 1970: *Biskupin. A fortified settlement dating from 500 B.C.* Poznan: Wydawnictwo Poznanskie.

Randall, A. 1981: *Resource Economics: An Economic Approach to Natural Resource and Environmental Policy*. Columbus, OH: Grid Publishing.

Raza, M. and Bano, H. 1985: Ecological burden of tourism: a case study. *Geographer*, 32, 13–20.

Reader, R. J. 1978: Primary production in northern bog marshes. In R. E. Good, D. F. Whigham, and R. L. Simpson (eds), *Freshwater Wetlands: Ecological Processes and Management Potential*. New York: Academic Press, 53–62.

Reader, R. J. and Stewart, J. M. 1972: The relationship between net primary production and accumulation for a peatland in south-eastern Manitoba. *Ecology*, 53, 1024–37.

Redfield, A. C. 1972: Development of a New England salt marsh. *Ecological Monograph*, 42, 201–37.

Regier, H. A. 1979: Changes in species composition of Great Lakes' fish communities caused by man. In *Transactions, 44th North American Wildlife and Natural Resources Conference*. Washington, DC: Wildlife Management Institute, 558–66.

Reimold, R. J., Gallager, J. L., Linthurst, R. A. and Pfeiffer, W. J. 1975: Detritus production in coastal Georgia salt marshes. In L. E. Cronin (ed.), *Estuarine Research*, 1, 217–28.

Reimold, R. J. and Hardinsky, M. A. 1979: Non-consumptive use values of wetlands. In P. E. Greeson, J. R. Clark and J. E. Clark (eds), *Wetland Functions and Values: The State of Our Understanding*. Minneapolis, MN: American Water Resources Association Technical Publication, 558–64.

Reineck, H. E. 1960: Über Zeitlücken in rezenten Flachseesedimenten. *Geologische Rundschau*, 49, 149–61.

Reineck, H. E. 1967: Layered sediments of tidal flats, beaches and shelf bottoms of the North Sea. In G. H. Lauff (ed.), *Estuaries*. Washington, DC: American Association for the Advancement of Science, Special Publication 83, 191–206.

Reiners, W. A. 1972: Structure and energetics of three Minnesota forests. *Ecological Monographs*, 42, 71–94.

Rennie, R. 1807–10: *Essays on the Natural History and Origin of Peat Moss*, Parts I-IX. Edinburgh: Constable.

Reppert, R. T., Sigleo, W., Stakhiv, E., Messman, L. and Meyers, C. 1979: *Wetland Values: Concepts and Methods for Wetlands Evaluation*. Fort Belvoir, VA: US Army Corps of Engineers, Institute for Water Resources, IWR Research Report 79-R-1.

Ricciuti, E. R. 1976: Mountains besieged. *International Wildlife*, 6, 24–35.

Richards, P. W. 1953: *The Tropical Rain Forest*. Cambridge: Cambridge University Press.

Richardson, C. J. 1979: Primary productivity values in freshwater wetlands. In P. E. Greeson, J. R. Clark and J. E. Clark (eds), *Wetland Functions and Values: The State of Our Understanding*, 131–45.

Richardson, S. L. 1986: A product life cycle approach to urban waterfronts: the revitalization of Galveston. *Coastal Zone Management Journal*, 14, 21–46.

Richmond, B. M., Nelson, C. S. and Healy, T. R. 1984: Sedimentology and evolution of Ohiwa Harbour, a barrier-impounded estuarine lagoon in the Bay of Plenty. *New Zealand Journal of Marine and Freshwater Research*, 18, 461–78.

Ris, H. 1982: Integrating visual management into the coastal zone planning process: the Massachusetts experience. *Coastal Zone Management Journal*, 9, 299–312.

Ritter, J. R. 1970: *A Summary of Preliminary Studies of Sedimentation and Hydrology in Bolinas Lagoon, Marin County, California*. Reston, VA: US Geological Survey, Circular 627.

Roberts, H. H. and Van Heerden, I. 1982: Reversal of coastal erosion by rapid sedimentation: the Atchafalaya delta (South-central Louisiana). In D. F. Boesch (ed.), *Proceedings of the Conference on Coastal Erosion and Wetland Modification in Louisiana: causes, consequences and options*. Washington, DC: Fish and Wildlife Service, FWS/OBS–82/59.

Robertson, T. 1987: Wildlife protection: a European view. *Natural World*, 20, 20–1.

Rodelli, M. R., Gearing, J. N., Marshall, N. and Sasekumar, A. 1984: Stable isotope ratio as a tracer of mangrove carbon in Malaysian ecosystems. *Oecologia (Berlin)*, 61, 326–33.

Rodin, L. E., Bazilevich, N. I. and Rozov, N. N. 1975: Productivity of the world's main ecosystems. In D. E. Reichle, J. F. Franklin and D. W. Goodall (eds), *Productivity of the World's Main Ecosystems*. Washington, DC: National Academy of Science.

Roe, H. B. and Ayres, Q. C. 1954: *Engineering for Agricultural Drainage*. New York: McGraw-Hill.

Rogers, J. P., Nichols, J. D., Martin, F. W., Kimball, C. F. and Pospahala, R. S. 1979: An examination of harvest and survival rates of ducks in relation to hunting, *Transactions, 44th North American Wildlife and Natural Resources Conference*. Washington, DC: Wildlife Management Institute, 114–26.

Rohde, H. 1978: The history of the German coastal area. *Kuste*, 32, 6–29.

Romanov, V. V. 1968: *Hydrophysics of Bogs*. Jerusalem: Israel Programme for Scientific Translations.

Rösch, M. 1985: Die Pflanzenreste der neolithischen Ufersiedlung von Hornstaad-

Hörnle I am westlichen Bodensee. *Berichte zu Ufer-und Moorsiedlungen Sudwestdeutschlands*, 2, 164–99.

Rose, C. 1986: The destruction of the countryside. In E. Goldsmith and N. Hildyard (eds), *Green Britain or Industrial Wasteland?* Cambridge: Polity Press, 66–78.

Rose, F. 1953: A survey of the ecology of the British lowland bogs. *Proceedings of the Linnaean Society of London*, 164, 184–211.

Roulet, N. T. and Woo, M.-K. 1986: Hydrology of a wetland in the continuous permafrost region. *Journal of Hydrology*, 89, 73–91.

Rubino, M. C. 1984: Evaluating development alternatives: the Negril and Black River morasses of Jamaica, Ph.D. Thesis, University of Michigan.

Ruddle, K. 1987: The impact of wetland reclamation. In M. G. Wolman and F. G. A. Fournier (eds), *Land Transformation in Agriculture, SCOPE 32, SCOPE/ICSU*. Chichester: Wiley, 171–202.

Russell, R. J. 1936: Physiography of the lower Mississippi River delta. *Louisiana Department of Conservation: Geological Bulletin*, 8, 3–199.

Ryan, J. J. and Goodell, H. G. 1973: Marine geology and estuarine history of Mobile Bay, Alabama. Part 1: Contemporary sediments. In B. W. Nelson (ed.), *Environmental Framework of Coastal Plain Estuaries*. Washington, DC: Geological Society of America, Memoir 133, 517–54.

Rzoska, J. 1974: The upper Nile swamps, a tropical wetland study. *Freshwater Biology*, 4, 1–30.

Sakellaridis, M. 1979: *The Mesolithic and Neolithic of the Swiss Area*. Oxford: BAR.

Salo, J., Kallida, R., Hakkinen, R., Makinen, I., Niemela, Y., Puhakka, P. and Coley, P. 1986: River dynamics and the diversity of Amazon lowland forest. *Nature, London*, 322, 254–6.

Samingan, M. T. 1980: Notes on the vegetation of the tidal area of South Sumatra, Indonesia. In J. I. Furtado (ed.), *Tropical Ecology and Development: Proceedings of the Vth International Symposium of Tropical Ecology, Kuala Lumpur.* Kuala Lumpur: International Society of Tropical Ecology, 1107–12.

Sather, J. M. and Smith, R. D. 1984: *An Overview of Major Wetland Functions and Values*. Washington, DC: Fish and Wildlife Service, FWS/OBS-84/18.

Scaife, W. B., Turner, R. E. and Costanza, R. 1983: Recent land loss and canal impacts in coastal Louisiana. *Environmental Management*, 7, 433–42.

Schlesinger, W. H. 1978: Community structure, dynamics and nutrient cycling in the Okefenokee cypress swamp forest. *Ecological Monographs*, 48, 43–65.

Scholander, P. F., Hammel, H. T., Hemmingsen, E. and Cary, W. 1962: Salt balance in mangroves. *Plant Physiology*, 37, 722–9.

Schubel, J. R. and Meade, R. H. 1977: Man's impact on estuarine sedimentation. In *Estuarine Pollution Control and Assessment*, vol. 1. Washington, DC: Environmental Protection Agency, 193–209.

Schultz, E. 1983: From natural reclaimed land – land and water management in the polders of the Netherlands. *Proceedings of the International Symposium, Polders of the World: Final Report*. Wageningen: International Institute for Land Reclamation and Improvement, 26–51.

Scott, D. A. and Carbonell, M. 1985: *A Directory of Neotropical Wetlands*. Gland, Switzerland: IUCN.

Scowan, A. 1984: Case study of the North Norfolk Heritage Coast. In J. R. Edwards (ed.), *Heritage Coasts; Recreation Ecology Research Group, Report No. 10*. Ashford, Kent: Wye College, University of London, 26–8.

Segeren, W. A. 1983: Keynote address. *Polders of the World. Papers of the International Symposium Lelystad, Netherlands, 1982. Final Report*. Wageningen: Institute for Land Reclamation and Improvement, 15–25.

Seidensticker, J. and Hai, Md. A. 1983: *The Sundarbans Wildlife Management Plan: conservation in the Bangladesh coastal zone*. Gland, Switzerland: IUCN; Dacca: Government of Bangladesh and World Wildlife Fund.

Shabman, L. A. and Batie, S. S. 1980: Estimating the economic value of coastal wetlands: conceptual issues and research needs. In V. S. Kennedy (ed.), *Estuarine Perspectives*. New York: Academic Press, 3–16.
Shaw, H. F. 1973: Clay mineralogy of Quaternary sediments in The Wash embayment, eastern England. *Marine Geology*, 14, 29–45.
Shaw, S. P. and Fredine, C. G. 1956: *Wetlands of the United States: Their Extent and Their Value to Waterfowl and Other Wildlife*. Washington, DC: Fish and Wildlife Service, Circular 39.
Sheail, J. and Wells, T. C. E. 1983: The fenland of Huntingdonshire, England: a case study in catastrophic change. In A. J. P. Gore (ed.), *Mires: Swamp, Bog, Fen and Moor. Regional Studies*. Ecosystems of the World 4B. Amsterdam: Elsevier, 375–94.
Shennan, I. 1983: Flandrian and late Devensian sea-level changes and crustal movements in England and Wales. In D. E. Smith and A. G. Dawson (eds), *Shorelines and Isostasy*. London: Academic Press, 255—83.
Shepard, F. P. 1956: Late Pleistocene and Recent history of the central Texas coast. *Journal of Geology*, 64, 56–69.
Sheppard, J. A. 1958: *The Draining of the Hull Valley*. York: East Yorkshire Local History Series.
Sheppe, W. A. 1985: Effects of human activities in Zambia's Kafue Flats ecosystems. *Environmental Conservation*, 12, 49–54.
Shinn, E. A., Lloyd, R. M. and Ginsburg, R. N. 1969: Anatomy of a modern carbonate tidal-flat, Andros Island, Bahamas. *Journal of Sedimentary Petrology*, 39, 1202–28.
Shoard, M. 1980: *The Theft of the Countryside*. London: Temple Smith.
Shoard, M. 1987: *This Land is Our Land*. London: Paladin.
Siegel, D. I. 1988: A review of the recharge-discharge function of wetlands. In D. D. Hook et al. (eds), *The Ecology and Management of Wetlands*, vol. 1. London: Croom Helm, 59–67.
Simon, A. W. 1984: *Neptune's Revenge: The Ocean of Tomorrow*. New York: F. Watts.
Simons, D. B. and Richardson, E. V. 1966: *Resistance to Flow in Alluvial Channels*. Reston, VA: US Geological Survey, Professional Paper 422J.
Simons, P. 1988: Après ski le deluge. *New Scientist*, 14 January 1988, 49–52.
Sinha, B. N. 1981: *Geography of Orissa*, 2nd edn. New Delhi: National Book Trust.
Siok-Hwa Cheng 1968: *The Rice Industry of Burma, 1852–1940*. Kuala Lumpur: University of Malaya Press.
Sissons, J. B. 1983: Shorelines and isostasy in Scotland. In D. E. Smith and A. G. Dawson (eds), *Shorelines and Isostasy*. London: Academic Press, 209–25.
Sivalingham, P. M. 1984: Ocean disposal and land reclamation problems of Penang, Malaysia. *Conservation and Recycling*, 7, 85–98.
Skeat, A. J. 1986: Wetland management – Kakadu National Park. *Australian Journal of Environmental Education*, 2, 17–20.
Skiba, U., Cresser, M. S., Derwent, R. G. and Futty, D. W. 1989: Peat acidification in Scotland. *Nature, London*, 337, 68–9.
Skoropanov, S. G. 1961: *Reclamation and Cultivation of Peat-Bog Soils*. Jerusalem: Israel Programme for Scientific Translations; Springfield, VA: US Department of Commerce, Clearinghouse for Federal Scientific and Technological Information.
Slater, F. M. and Agnew, A. D. Q. 1977: Observations on a peat bog's ability to withstand increasing public pressure. *Biological Conservation*, 11, 21–7.
Sloey, W. E., Spangler, F. L. and Fetter, C. W. 1978: Management of freshwater wetlands for nutrient assimilation. In R. E. Good, D. F. Whigham and R. L. Simpson (eds), *Freshwater Wetlands: Ecological Processes and Management Potential*. New York: Academic Press, 321–40.
Smardon, R. C. (ed.) 1983: *The Future of Wetlands: Assessing Visual-Cultural Values*. Totowa, NJ: Allanheld, Osmun.

Smardon, R. C. 1988: Visual-cultural assessment and wetland evaluation. In D. D. Hook et al. (eds), *The Ecology and Management of Wetlands*, vol. 2. London: Croom Helm, 103–14.

Smith, R. A. L. 1943: *Canterbury Cathedral Priory*. Cambridge: Cambridge University Press.

Snyder, B. D. and Snyder, J. L. 1982: *Feasibility of Using Oil Shale Wastewater for Waterfowl Wetlands*. Washington, DC: Fish and Wildlife Service, FWS/OBS-84/01.

Soltz, D. L. and Naiman, R. J.1978: The natural history of native fishes in the Death Valley system. *Natural History Museum of Los Angeles Centenary Science Series*, 30, 1–76.

Somerset Levels Project 1975–1989: *Somerset Levels Papers 1–15*.

Soulé, M. E. and Wilcox, B. A. (eds) 1980: *Conservation Biology*. Sunderland, MA: Sinauer Press.

Spence, D. H. N. 1982: The zonation of plants in freshwater lakes. *Advances in Ecological Research*, 12, 37–125.

Spencerley, A. P. 1977: The role of pneumatophores in sedimentary processes. *Marine Geology*, 24, 31–7.

Stamp, L. D. 1924: *The Vegetation of Burma*. Rangoon: University of Rangoon.

Stanley, D. J. 1988: Subsidence in the northeastern Nile Delta: rapid rates, possible causes, and consequences. *Science*, 240, 497–500.

Stavins, R. 1987: *Conversion of Forested Wetlands to Agricultural Uses: executive summary*. New York: Environmental Defense Fund.

Stearns, 1978: Management potential: summary and recommendations. In R. E. Good et al. (eds), *Freshwater Wetlands: Ecological Processes and Management Potential*. New York: Academic Press, 357–63.

Stebbing, E. P. 1923–6: *The Forests of India*, 3 vols. London: Bodley Head.

Steers, J. A. 1960: *Scolt Head Island*. Cambridge: Heffer.

Steers, J. A. 1964: *The Coastline of England and Wales*. Cambridge: Cambridge University Press.

Steers, J. A. 1973: *The Coastline of Scotland*. Cambridge: Cambridge University Press.

Stephens, J. C. 1974: *Subsidence of Organic Soils in the Florida Everglades Region of Florida*. Washington, DC: US Department of Agriclture Soil Conservation Service, Division of Drainage and Water Control.

Stepniewski, W. and Glinski, J. 1988: Gas exchange and atmospheric properties of flooded soils. In D. D. Hook et al. (eds), *The Ecology and Management of Wetlands*, vol. 1. London: Croom Helm, 269–78.

Sternitzke, H. S. 1976: Impact of changing land use on delta hardwood forests. *Journal of Forestry*, 74(1), 25–7.

Stevenson, A. C. and Moore, P. D. 1988: Studies in the vegetational history of Huelva, Spain. IV Palynological investigations of a valley mire at El Acebron. *Journal of Biogeography*, 15, 339–61.

Stevenson, J. C. Kearney, M. S. and Pendleton, E. C. 1985: Sedimentation and erosion in a Chesapeake Bay brackish marsh system. *Marine Geology*, 67, 213–35.

Stigter, C. and Andreae, J. F. R. 1973: Offshore land reclamation provides solution to environmental problems. *World Dredging and Marine Construction*, 9/10, 14–17.

Stornebrink, D. P. I. O. 1960: Location tendencies in the new Rotterdam waterway port area. *Tijdschrift van het Koninklijk Nederlandsch Aardrijkskundig Genootschap*, 77, 332–40.

Stout, J. P. 1988. Irregularly flooded salt marshes of the Gulf and Atlantic coasts of the United States. In D. D. Hook et al. (eds), *The Ecology and Management of Wetlands*, vol. 1. London: Croom Helm, 511–25.

Strickland, R. (ed.) 1986: *Wetland Functions, Rehabilitation, and Creation in the Pacific Northwest: The State of Our Understanding*. Olympia, WA: Washington State Department of Ecology, Publication 86–14.

Strong, A. L. 1971: *Planned Urban Environments*. Baltimore, MD: Johns Hopkins Press.
Stroud, D. A., Reed, T. M., Pienkowski, M. W. and Lindsay, R. A. 1987: *Birds, Bogs and Forestry: the Peatlands of Caithness and Sutherland*. Peterborough: Nature Conservancy Council.
Stuivel, H. J. 1956: *Het Delta Plan*. Amsterdam: Scheltma and Holkema.
Sukachev, V. V. 1914: *Bolota, ikh Obrazovanie, Razvitie i Svoistva*. St Petersburg.
Swenson, E. and Wiseman, W. 1987: Movement of salt water through a marsh substrate: a preliminary analysis. In K. Mutz and L. C. Lee (Technical Coordinators), *Proceedings of the Society of Wetland Scientists 8th Annual Meeting, Seattle, WA, 26–29 May 1987*. Denver, CO: Planning Information Corporation.
Sylvan, R. 1986: A deep ecological approach to wetlands. *Australian Journal of Environmental Education*, 2, 3–5.
Symington, C. F. 1943: Foresters' manual of dipterocarps. In *Malayan Forest Records, No. 16*. Kuala Lumpur: Penerbit Universiti Malaya (reprinted 1974).
Takaya, Y. 1987: *Agricultural Development of a Tropical Delta. Honolulu*, HI: University of Hawaii Press.
Takel, R. E. 1974: *Industrial Port Development with Case Studies from South Wales and Elsewhere*. Bristol: Scientechnica.
Tallis, J. H. 1973: The terrestrialization of lake basins in north Cheshire, with special reference to the development of a Schwingmoor structure. *Journal of Ecology*, 61, 537–67.
Tallis, J. H. 1983: Changes in wetland communities. In A. J. P. Gore (ed.), *Mires: Swamp, Bog, Fen and Moor, General Studies. Ecosystems of the World 4A*. Amsterdam: Elsevier, 311–47.
Tan, K. 1980: Logging the swamp for food. In W. R. Stanton and M. Flach (eds), *SAGO, the Equatorial Swamp as a Natural Resource: Proceedings from the Second International Sago Symposium. Kuala Lumpur, Malaysia, 15–17 September 1979*. London: Martinus Nijhoff, 13–34.
Teal, J. M. 1962: Energy flow in the salt marsh ecosystem of Georgia. *Ecology*, 43, 614–24.
Teas, H. J. (ed.) 1984: *Physiology and Management of Mangroves*. The Hague: W. Junk
Tebrake, W. H. 1985: *Medieval Frontier: Culture and Ecology in Rijnland*. College Station, TX: Texas A & M University Press.
Terwindt, J. H. J. 1977: Mud in the Dutch delta area. *Geologie en Mijnbouw*, 56, 203–10.
Thach, E. E., Doyle, L. M., Mechler, J. L. and Lowe, R. L. 1986: Wildlife management, an integral part of intensive multiple use: Land Between the Lakes, a case history, *Transactions, 51st North American Wildlife and Natural Resources Conference*. Washington, DC: Wildlife Management Institute, 141–50.
Thibodeau, F. R. and Ostro, B. D. 1981: An economic analysis of wetland protection. *Journal of Environmental Management*, 12, 19–30.
Thirsk, J. 1953: The Isle of Axholme before Vermuyden. *Agricultural History Review*, 1, 16–28.
Thom, B. G. 1967: Mangrove ecology and deltaic geomorphology: Tabasco, Mexico. *Journal of Ecology*, 55, 301–43.
Thompson, K. 1976: Swamp development in the head waters of the White Nile. In J. Rzoska (ed.), *The Nile, Biology of an Ancient River*. The Hague: W. Junk, 177–214.
Thompson, K. and Hamilton, A. C. 1983: Peatlands and swamps of the African continent. In A. J. P. Gore (ed.), *Mires: Swamp, Bog, Fen and Moor. Regional Studies. Ecosystems of the World 4B*. Amsterdam: Elsevier, 331–73.
Thompson, K., Shewry, P. R. and Woolhouse, H. W. 1979: Papyrus swamp development in the Upemba Basin, Zaire: studies of population structure in Cyperus papyrus stands. *Botanical Journal of the Linnean Society*, 78, 299–316.

The Times 11 May 1989.

Tiner, R. W. 1984: *Wetlands of the United States: Current Status and recent Trends*, Washington, DC: Fish and Wildlife Service.

Tiner, R. W. 1985a. *Wetlands of Delaware*. Dover, DE: Department of Natural Resources and Environmental Control.

Tiner, R. W. 1985b: *The Wetlands of New Jersey*. Newton Corner, MA: Fish and Wildlife Service.

Tokyo Municipal News 1982: 32/1, 1–4.

Tokyo Municipal News 1987: 37/3, 1–3.

Tooley, M. J. 1978: *Sea-level Changes in Northwest England During the Flandrian Stage*. Oxford: Clarendon Press.

Transeau, E. N. 1903: On the geographic distribution and ecological relations of the bog plant societies of northern North America. *Botanical Gazette*, 36,401–20.

Trent, L., Pullan, E. J. and Proctor, R. 1976: Abundance of macrocrustaceans in a natural marsh and a marsh altered by dredging, bulkheading and filling. *Fishing Bulletin*, 74, 195–200.

Trimble, S. W. 1970: The Alcovy River Swamps: the result of culturally accelerated erosion. *Georgia Academy of Science Bulletin*, 28, 131–41.

Trimble, S. W. 1974: *Man-Induced Soil Erosion on the Southern Piedmont, 1700–1970*. Soil Conservation Society of America.

Trowbridge, A. C. 1930: Building of the Mississippi delta. *Bulletin of the American Association of Petroleum Geologists*, 14, 867–901.

Tuppen, J. N. 1984: The port-industrial complex at Fos: a regional growth center? In B. S. Hoyle and D. Hilling (eds), *Seaport Systems and Spatial Change*. Chichester: Wiley, 303–41.

Turner, R. E. and Boesch, D. F. 1988: Aquatic animal production and wetland relationships: insights gleaned following wetland loss or gain. In D. D. Hook et al. (eds), *The Ecology and Management of Wetlands*, vol. 1. London: Croom Helm, 25–39.

Turner, R. E. and Cahoon, D. R. (eds) 1988: *Causes of Wetland Loss in the Coastal Central Gulf of Mexico*, 3 vols. New Orleans, LA: Minerals Management Service, OCS Study/MMS 87–0120.

Turner, R. E., Forsythe, S. W. and Craig, N. S. 1981: Bottomland and hardwood forestland resources of the Southeastern United States. In J. R. Clark and J. Benforado (eds), *Wetlands of Bottomland Hardwood Forests*. New York: Elsevier, 13–28.

Tuttle, A. E. 1985: Cumulative Impact Assessment in Coastal Wetland Watersheds: Jacoby Creek, Humboldt County, California, Ph.D. Thesis, University of California, Berkeley.

Twilley, R. R., Lugo, A. E. and Paterson-Zucca, C. 1986: Litter production and turnover in basin mangrove forests in Southwest Florida. *Ecology*, 67(3), 670–83.

Tydeman, C. 1984: General value of man-made wetlands for wildlife in Europe, *World Wildlife Fund Wetlands Pack 1*. Gland, Switzerland: World Wildlife Fund-IUCN.

Uchino, T. 1983: *Japan's Postwar Economy*. Tokyo: Kodansha.

US Bureau of the Census 1978: Drainage. *Census of Agriculture, 1978*. Washington, DC: Census Bureau.

US Corps of Engineers 1972: *Charles River Watershed, Massachusetts*. Waltham, MA: US Corps of Engineers, New England Division.

US Department of Agriculture 1921: *Yearbook on Agriculture, 1921*. Washington, DC: US Government Printing Office.

US Environmental Protection Agency 1983: *Freshwater Wetlands for Wastewater Management: Environmental Impact Statement – Phase 1 Report*. Atlanta, GA: US Environmental Protection Agency Region IV, EPA 904/9–83–107.

US Fish and Wildlife Service 1982: *The 1980 National Survey of Hunting and Wildlife Associated Recreation*. Portland, OR: Fish and Wildlife Service.

US Fish and Wildlife Service 1984: *Wetlands of the United States: Current Status and Recent Trends*. Washington, DC: Fish and Wildlife Service.

US Fish and Wildlife Service 1986: *Florida Panther (Felix concolor coryi) Recovery Plan*. Atlant, GA: Fish and Wildlife Service, Florida Panther Interagency Committee.

Usher, M. B., Pitt, M. and de Boer, G. 1974: Recreational pressures in the summer months on a nature reserve on the Yorkshire coast, England. *Environmental Conservation*, 1, 43–9.

Valiela, L., Vinee, S. and Teal, J. M. 1976: Assimilation of sewage in wetlands. In M. Wiley (ed.), *Estuarine Processes*, vol. 1, *Uses, Stresses and Adaptations to the Estuary*. New York: Academic Press, 234–53.

Van Andel, Tj. H. 1967: The Orinoco delta. *Journal of Sedimentary Petrology*, 37, 297–310.

van den Bremen, W. J. 1982: Aspects of maritime transport and port development under the influence of changes in the energy supply in the next decades: Western Europe as a case study. In C. Muscara, M. Soricillo and A. Vallega (eds), *Changing Maritime Transport*. Naples: Istituto Universitario Navale Napoli, 40–73.

Van der Valk, A. G., Davis, C. B., Baker, J. L. and Beer, C. E. 1979: Natural freshwater wetlands as nitrogen and phosphorus traps for land runoff. In P. E. Greeson, J. R. Clark and J. E. Clark (eds), *Wetland Functions and Values: The State of Our Understanding*. Minneapolis, MN: American Water Resources Association Technical Bulletin, 457–67.

Van der Veen, J. 1983: Agricultural aspects in polder areas in the Netherlands. In *Proceedings, International Symposium on Polders of the World: Final Report*. Wageningen: International Institute for Land Reclamation and Improvement, 126–40.

Van de Zande, A. and Voss, P. 1984: Impact of a semi-experimental increase in recreation intensity on the densities of birds in groves and hedges on a lake shore in the Netherlands. *Biological Conservation*, 30, 237–59.

Van Eck, H., Gowers, A., Lemaire, A. and Schanee, J. 1984: *Irish Bogs, a Case for Planning*. Nijmegen: Catholic University.

van Horssen, W. 1987: Slufterdam depot for polluted harbour silt opened. *Rotterdam-Europort-Delta*, 87(5), 38–40.

Van Straaten, L. M. J. U. and Kuenen, Ph. H. 1957: Accumulation of fine-grained sediments in the Dutch Wadden See. *Geologie en Mijnbouw*, 19, 329–54.

Van Veen, J. 1950: Eb- en vloedschoarsystemen in de Nederlandse Getijwateren. *Tijdschrift Koninkl. Nederlandse, Aardrijkskundig Genoot*, 67, 43–65.

Vann, J. H. 1959: Landform and vegetation relationship in the Atrato Delta. *Annals of the American Association of Geography*, 49, 345–60.

Vigarié, A. 1981: Maritime industrial development areas: structural evolution and implications for regional development. In B. S. Hoyle and D. A. Pinder (eds), *Cityport Industrialisation and Regional Development*. New York: Pergamon, 23–36.

Viner, A. B. 1975: The supply of minerals to tropical rivers and lakes (Uganda). In A. D. Hasler (ed.), *The Coupling of Land and Water Systems*. New York: Springer-Verlag, Ecological Studies No. 10, 227–62.

Vreeland, N. 1977: *Area Handbook for Singapore*. Washington, DC: American University.

Wagret, P. 1969: *Polderlands*. London: Methuen.

Waksman, S. A. 1942: *The Peats of New Jersey and their Utilization. Part A. Nature and Origin of Peat Composition and Utilization*. Trenton, NJ: New Jersey Department of Conservation and Development and Rutgers University, Agricultural Experimental Station Bulletin No. 55.

Walker, D. 1970: Direction and rate in some British post-glacial hydroseries. In D. Walker and R. G. West (eds), *Studies in the Vegetational History of the British Isles*. Cambridge: Cambridge University Press, 117–39.

Walker, J. H., Coleman, J. M., Roberts, H. H. and Tye, R. S. 1987: Wetland loss in Louisiana. *Geografiska Annaler, Series A*, 69, 189–200.
Wall, G. and Wright, C. 1977: *The Environmental Impact of Outdoor Recreation*. Waterloo, Ontario: Unviersity of Waterloo, Department of Geography, Publication Series No. 11.
Wall, G., Harrison, R., Kinnaird, V., McBoyle, G. and Quinlan, C. 1986: Climatic change and recreation resources: the future of Ontario wetlands? In J. W. Frazier, B. J. Epstein and J. F. Langowski (eds), *Papers and Proceedings of Applied Geography Conferences, 9*. Department of Geography at State University of New York at Binghampton, Department of Geography at Kent State University, and US Military Academy, West Point, NY, 124–31.
Walsh, G. E. 1977: Exploitation of mangal. In V. J. Chapman (ed.), *Wet Coastal Ecosystems*. Amsterdam: Elsevier, 347–62.
Wapora Inc. 1983: *The Effects of Wastewater Treatment Facilities on Wetlands in the Midwest*. Chicago, IL: US Environmental Protection Agency Region V, EPA-905/3-83—002.
Washington Post 27 January 1988, A4, Swampbuster penalties irk farmers.
Wass, M. L. and Wright, T. D. 1969: *Coastal Wetlands of Virginia: Interim Report*. Gloucester Point, VA: Virginia Institute of Marine Science, Special Report No. 10.
Wauer, R. H. 1977: Significance of Rio Grande riparian system uses upon the avifauna. In R. R. Johnson and D. A. Jones (eds), *Importance of Preservation and Management of Riparian Habitat: A Symposium*. Washington, DC: Department of Agriculture, Forestry Service, General Technical Report RM-43, 165–74.
Weber, C. A. 1900: Über die Moore, mit besondere Berucksichtigung der zwischen Unterweser und Unterelbeliegenden. *Jahresbericht der Manner von Morgenstern*, 3, 3–23.
Weller, M. 1981: *Freshwater Marshes, Ecology and Wildlife Management*. Minneapolis, MN: University of Minnesota Press.
Wells, J. T., Prior, D. B. and Coleman, J. M. 1980: Flowslides in muds on extremely low angle tidal flats, northeastern South America. *Geology*, 8, 272–5.
Wells, J. T., Chinburg, S. J. and Coleman, J.M. 1982: *Development of the Atchafalaya River Deltas: Generic Analysis* (prepared for US Army Engineers Waterways Experiment Station). Baton Rouge, LA: Coastal Studies Institute, Center for Wetland Resources.
Werger, M. J. A. 1978: *Biogeography and Ecology of Southern Africa*. The Hague: W. Junk.
West, R. C. 1956: Mangrove swamps of the Pacific Coast of Columbia. *Annals of the American Association of Geography*, 46, 9–121.
West, R. C. Psuty, N. P. and Thom, B. G. 1969: *The Tabasco Lowlands of Southeastern Mexico*. Baton Rouge, LA: Louisiana State University Press, Coastal Studies Series No.27.
Westenberg, J.1974: *Kennemer Dijkgeschiedenis, First Series*, 27 (2).
Westman, W. E. 1975: Ecology of canal estates. *Search*, 6, 491–7.
Westman, W. E. 1977: How much are nature's services worth? *Science*, 197, 960–4.
Westphal, J. M. 1984: Recreation use of lands adminstered by the U.S. Fish and Wildlife Service. In M. Clawson and C. S. van Doren (eds), *Statistics on Outdoor Recreation*. Washington, DC: Resources for the Future Inc., 202–8.
Wharton, C. H., Kitchens, W. M., Pendleton, E.C. and Sipe, T. W. 1982: *The Ecology of Bottomland Hardwood Swamps of the Southeast: A Community Profile*. Washington, DC: Fish and Wildlife Services, FWS/OBS-81/37.
Wheeler, B. D. 1984: British fens: a review. In P.D. Moore (ed.), *European Mires*. London: Academic Press, 237–81.
Wheeler, B.D. 1988: Species richness, species rarity and conservation evaluation of

rich-fen vegetation in lowland England and Wales. *Journal of Applied Ecology*, 25, 331–52.

Whigham, D. F. 1982: Using freshwater wetlands for wastewater management in North America. In B. Gopal et al. (eds), *Wetland Ecology and Management*. Jaipur: National Institute of Ecology and International Scientific Publications, 507–14.

White, G. F. 1978: The hazards of wetlands use. In J. H. Montanari and J. A. Kusler (eds), *Proceedings. National Wetlands Protection Symposium*. Washington, DC: Fish and Wildlife Service, 3–6.

Whitmore, T. C. 1984: A vegetation map of Malesia at scale 1:5 million. *Journal of Biogeography*, 11, 461–71.

Wijkman, A. and Timberlake, L. 1984: *Natural Disasters – Acts of God or Acts of Man?* London: Earthscan.

Wilcox, D. A., Shedlock, R. J. and Hendrickson, W. H. 1986: Hydrology, water chemistry and ecological relations in the raised mound of Cowles Bog. *Journal of Ecology*, 74, 1103–17.

Wilden, A. 1983: Ecology and ideology. In A. Idris-Soven, E. Idris-Soven and M. K. Vaughan (eds), *The World as a Company Town*. The Hague: Mouton, 73–98.

Willard, D. E., Willis, J. A. and Hillegeist, C. L. 1988: Regional scale impacts from using agricultural wastewater for wildlife refuges. In P. J. Stuber (Coordinator) *Proceedings of the National Symposium on Protection of Wetlands from Agricultural Impacts*. Washington, DC: US Department of the Interior, Fish and Wildlife Service, Biological Report 88(16), 47–54.

Williams, G. M. 1983: The effects on birds of land drainage improvements in the Kent marshes. *Wildfowl*, 34.

Williams, M. 1970: *The Draining of the Somerset Levels*. Cambridge: Cambridge University Press.

Williams, M. 1974: *The Making of the South Australian Landscape*. London: Academic Press.

Williams, M. 1975: More and smaller is better: Australian rural settlement, 1788–1914. In J. M. Powell and M. Williams (eds), *Australian Time, Australian Space*. Melbourne: Oxford University Press.

Williams, M. 1982: Marshland and waste. In L. M. Cantor (ed.), *The English Medieval Landscape*. London: Croom Helm, 86–125.

Wilson, L. R. 1935: Lake development and plant succession in Vilas County, Wisconsin. Part I; The medium hard water lakes. *Ecological Monographs*, 5, 207–47.

Winkler, M. G. and De Witt, C. B. 1985: Environmental impact of peat mining in the United States: documentation for wetland conservation. *Environmental Conservation*, 12, 317–30.

Winsor, R. A. 1987: Environmental imagery of the wet prairie of east central Illinois, 1820–1920. *Journal of Historical Geography*, 13, 375–97.

Winter, T. C. 1983: The interaction of lakes with variably saturated porous media. *Water Resources Research*, 19, 1203–18.

Winter, T.C. and Woo, M.-K. 1988: Lakes and wetlands. In W. G. Wolman (ed.), *Surface Water Hydrology of North America*. Boulder, CO: Geological Society of America.

Witherick, M. E. 1972: The Japan Housing Corporation. *Town and Country Planning*, 40, 521–5.

Witherick, M. E. 1981: Tokyo. In M. Pacione (ed.), *Urban Problems and Planning in the Developed World*. Dover, NH: Croom Helm, 120–56.

Wolf, R. B., Lee, L. C. and Sharitz, R. R. 1986: Wetland creation and resoration in the United States from 1970 to 1985: an annotated bibliography. *Wetlands*, 6(1), 1–88.

Wood, L. D. and Hill, J. R. Jr. 1978: Wetlands protection: the regulatory role of the U.S. Army Corps of Engineers. *Coastal Zone Management Journal*, 4(1978), 378–80.

Woodhouse, W. W., Jr., Seneca, E. D. and Broome, S. W. 1976: *Propagation and Use of Spartina Alterniflora for Shoreline Erosion Abatement.* Fort Belvoir, VA: US Army Corps of Engineers, Coastal Engineering Research Center, TR 76–2.

Wooten, H. H. and Jones, L. A. 1955: The history of our drainage enterprises. In *The Yearbook of Agriculture, 1955, Water.* Washington, DC: US Government Printing Office, 478–91.

World Resources Institute 1986 and annually: *World Resources: An Assessment of the Resource Base that Supports the Global Economy.* New York: Basic Books for World Resources Institute and International Institute for Environment and Development.

Wright, L. D. 1977: Sediment transport and deposition at river mouths: a synthesis. *Geological Society of America Bulletin*, 88, 857–68.

Wyatt-Smith, J. 1959: Peat swamp forest in Malaya. *Malayan Forester*, 23, 5–33.

Wyatt-Smith, J. 1964: A preliminary vegetation map of Malaya with descriptions of the vegetation types. *Journal of Tropical Geography*, 18, 200–13.

Yang, E. J., Dower, R. C. and Menefee, M. 1984: *The Use of Economic Analysis in Valuing Natural Resource Damages.* Washington, DC: Environmental Law Institute.

Yapp, R. H., John, D. and Jones, O. T. 1917: The Dovey Salt Marshes. *Journal of Ecology*, 5, 65–103.

Yeung, Y. 1973: *National Development Policy and Urban Transformation in Singapore.* Chicago, IL: University of Chicago, Department of Geography Research Paper 149.

Zahran, M. A. 1982: Ecology of the halophytic vegetation of Egypt. In D. N. Sen and K. S. Rajpurohit (eds), *Tasks for vegetation science.* The Hague: W. Junk.

Zarillo, G. A. (1985): Tidal dynamics and substrate response in a salt-marsh estuary. *Marine Geology*, 67, 13–35.

Zelazny, J. and Feierabend, J. S. (eds) 1988: *Increasing our Wetland Resources. Proceedings of the Conference, Washington, DC, 4–7 October 1987.* Washington, DC: National Wildlife Federation.

Zinn, J. A. and Copeland, C. 1982: *Wetland Management.* Washington, DC: Environment and Natural Resources Policy Division, Congressional Research Service, Library of Congress, Serial No. 97.

Zoltai, S. C. and Pollett, F. C. 1983: Wetlands in Canada: their classification, distribution and use. In A. J. P. Gore (ed.), *Mires: Swamp, Bog, Fen and Moor. Regional Studies. Ecosystems of the World 4B.* Amsterdam: Elsevier, 245–68.

Zonn, I. S. and Nosenko, P. P. 1982: Modern level of, and prospects for improvement of land reclamation in the world. *ICID Bulletin*, 31(2), 73–8.

Related Titles: List of IBG Special Publications

1. Land Use and Resource: Studies in Applied Geography *(A memorial to Dudley Stamp)*
2. A Geomorphological Study of Post-Glacial Uplift
   John T. Andrews
3. Slopes: Form and Process
   D. Brunsden
4. Polar Geomorphology
   R. J. Price and D. E. Sugden
5. Social Paterns in Cities
   B. D. Clark and M. B. Gleave
6. Fluvial Processes in Instrumented Watersheds: Studies of Small Watersheds in the British Isles
   K. J. Gregory and D. E. Walling
7. Progress in Geomorphology: Papers in Honour of David L. Linton
   Edited by E. H. Brown and R. S. Waters.
8. Inter-regional Migration in Tropical Africa
   I. Masser and W. T. S. Gould with the assistance of A. D. Goddard
9. Agrarian Landscape Terms: A Glossary for Historical Geography
   I. H. Adams
10. Change in the Countryside: Essays on Rural England 1500–1900
    Edited by H. S. A. Fox and R. A. Butlin
11. The Shaping of Southern England
    Edited by David K. C. Jones
12. Social Interaction and Ethnic Segregation
    Edited by Peter Jackson and Susan J. Smith
13. The Urban Landscape: Historical Development and Management *(Papers by M. R. G. Conzen)*
    Edited by J. W. R. Whitehand
14. The Future for the City Centre
    Edited by R. L. Davies and A. G. Champion
15. Redundant Spaces in Cities and Regions? Studies in Industrial Decline and Social Change
    Edited by J. Anderson, S. Duncan and R. Hudson
16. Shorelines and Isostasy
    Edited by D. E. Smith and A. G. Dawson

17 Residential Segregation, the State and Constitutional Conflict in American Urban Areas
R. J. Johnston
18 River Channels: Environment and Process
Edited by Keith Richards
19 Technical Change and Industrial Policy
Edited by Keith Chapman and Graham Humphrys
20 Sea-level Changes
Edited by Michael J. Tooley and Ian Shennan
21 The Changing Face of Cities: A Study of Development Cycles and Urban Form
J. W. R. Whitheand
22 Population and Disaster
Edited by John I. Clarke, Peter Curson, S. L. Kayastha and Prithvish Nag
23 Rural Change in Tropical Africa: From Colonies to Nation-States
David Siddle and Kenneth Swindell
25 Wetlands: A Threatened Landscape
Edited by Michael Williams

Also published by Basil Blackwell for the IBG:
Atlas of Drought in Britain
Edited by J. C. Doornkamp and K. J. Gregory

Index

Notes: (1) All references are to wetlands, unless otherwise indicated; and (2) illustrations and maps are indicated by *italics*. There are frequently textual references also on these pages.